Commercial Real Estate **Investing**

An Evidence-Based Approach to **Risk Management**, **Strategic Valuation**, and **Enhanced Returns**

Randall Zisler, Ph.D.

WILEY

Copyright © 2026 by John Wiley & Sons, Inc. All rights reserved, including rights for text and data mining and training of artificial intelligence technologies or similar technologies.

Published by John Wiley & Sons, Inc., Hoboken, New Jersey.

Published simultaneously in Canada.

No part of this publication may be reproduced, stored in a retrieval system, or transmitted in any form or by any means, electronic, mechanical, photocopying, recording, scanning, or otherwise, except as permitted under Section 107 or 108 of the 1976 United States Copyright Act, without either the prior written permission of the Publisher, or authorization through payment of the appropriate per-copy fee to the Copyright Clearance Center, Inc., 222 Rosewood Drive, Danvers, MA 01923, (978) 750-8400, fax (978) 750-4470, or on the web at www.copyright.com. Requests to the Publisher for permission should be addressed to the Permissions Department, John Wiley & Sons, Inc., 111 River Street, Hoboken, NJ 07030, (201) 748-6011, fax (201) 748-6008, or online at http://www.wiley.com/go/permission.

The manufacturer's authorized representative according to the EU General Product Safety Regulation is Wiley-VCH GmbH, Boschstr. 12,69469 Weinheim, Germany, e-mail: Product_Safety@wiley.com.

Trademarks: Wiley and the Wiley logo are trademarks or registered trademarks of John Wiley & Sons, Inc. and/or its affiliates in the United States and other countries and may not be used without written permission. All other trademarks are the property of their respective owners. John Wiley & Sons, Inc. is not associated with any product or vendor mentioned in this book.

Limit of Liability/Disclaimer of Warranty: While the publisher and author have used their best efforts in preparing this book, they make no representations or warranties with respect to the accuracy or completeness of the contents of this book and specifically disclaim any implied warranties of merchantability or fitness for a particular purpose. No warranty may be created or extended by sales representatives or written sales materials. The advice and strategies contained herein may not be suitable for your situation. You should consult with a professional where appropriate. Further, readers should be aware that websites listed in this work may have changed or disappeared between when this work was written and when it is read. Neither the publisher nor authors shall be liable for any loss of profit or any other commercial damages, including but not limited to special, incidental, consequential, or other damages.

For general information on our other products and services or for technical support, please contact our Customer Care Department within the United States at (800) 762-2974, outside the United States at (317) 572-3993 or fax (317) 572-4002.

Wiley also publishes its books in a variety of electronic formats. Some content that appears in print may not be available in electronic formats. For more information about Wiley products, visit our web site at www.wiley.com.

Library of Congress Cataloging-in-Publication Data is Available:

ISBN: 9781394326372 (Cloth)
ISBN: 9781394326389 (ePub)
ISBN: 9781394326396 (ePDF)

Cover Design: Wiley
Cover Image: © Zidan/stock.adobe.com
Author Photo: Courtesy of the Author

Printed and bound by CPI Group (UK) Ltd, Croydon, CR0 4YY

Contents

ACKNOWLEDGMENTS **vii**
ABOUT THE AUTHOR **xiii**
PREFACE **xvii**

Part I Introduction to Real Estate and Risk 1

1. Who Should Read This Book, and Why? **3**
   Q&A: Interview with Danel Neidich, CEO and Founder, Dune Capital Management and former Goldman Sachs Partner **10**

2. Statistics, Monte Carlo, Bayes Rule, Stochastic Arithmetic, and Uncertain Attributes **13**
   Q&A: Interview with Professor Joseph L. Pagliari, Jr., John Mazarakis and Chicago Atlantic Clinical Professor of Real Estate, The University of Chicago **47**

Part II The Building Blocks: Public, Private, Equity, and Debt 51

3. What Is Real Estate? Leases, Buildings, and Cities **53**
   Q&A: Interview with Michael Fascitelli, Chairman, MDF Capital **62**

4. The Capital Stack, Optimal Leverage, WACC, and Mortgage Default **65**
   Q&A: Interview with Michael Giliberto, Co-Creator of the Giliberto-Levy Indexes; formerly senior portfolio manager at J. P. Morgan; and currently serving on corporate and pension fund boards **79**

5. The Lease: An Options Approach and Upward-Only Adjusting Leases **81**
   Q&A: Interview with Doug Lyons, Managing Principal, Pearlmark **99**

6. The Real Estate Quadrants: Interdependent and Predictive **101**
   Q&A: Interview with Ethan Penner, Chairman, MOSAIC **139**

7. Property: The Macroeconomics of Performance and Risk **141**
   Q&A: Interview with Owen Thomas, Chairman and CEO, BXP, Inc. **152**

8. Office Property: COVID-19, Obsolescence, Work From Home (WFH), and Conversions **155**
   Q&A: Interview with John Sischo, Managing Principal, Coretrust Capital Partners, LLC **185**

iv   Contents

9   Risk Analysis in Practice: Retail, Self-Storage, and Housing   **187**
       Q&A: Interview with Benjamin Shibe Macfarland III, CEO, SROACapital.com, LLC   **199**

Part III   Performance Analysis, Risk, and Popular Myths   **201**

10   Asset Allocation, with and without Liabilities, and Shortfall Constraints   **203**
       Q&A: Interview with Sonny Kalsi, Co-CEO, BGO   **250**

11   Optimal Development: Linkage, the Internal Cost of Capital, and Risk   **253**
       Q&A: Interview with Steve Wechsler, President and CEO of National Association of Real Estate Investment Trusts   **276**

12   Cap Rates and Hidden Information: Avoiding Traps with Caps   **279**
       Q&A: Interview with Steve Rosenberg, Founder and CEO, Greystone   **313**

13   Liquidity: Turnover, MSA Liquidity, and Investment Horizon   **315**
       Q&A: Interview with Ron Havner, Chairman of Public Storage and Chairman Emeritus of Shurgard   **340**

14   Is Real Estate an Effective Inflation Hedge? Only in the Long Run   **343**
       Q&A: Interview with Jason Benderly, President, Benderly Economics and former Chief Economist of Goldman Sachs   **371**

15   A Monte Carlo Model of GP and LP Interests in a Structured Joint Venture   **373**
       Q&A: Interview with Ralph Rosenberg, Chairman of Real Assets, KKR   **391**

Part IV   The Public Sector and Collective Risk   **393**

16   Public-Sector Risk: Introduction to Sprawl and Rent Control   **395**
       Q&A: Interview with Matthew Zisler, Senior Managing Director, Greystone   **401**

17   Sprawl: An Options Perspective   **403**
       Q&A: Interview with Daniel Cummings, Managing Director, Bain Capital   **410**

18   Rent Control Redux: Prediction, Assessment, and Opportunity   **413**
       Q&A: Interview with Aly Worthington, Head of Capital Markets, Summit Development   **425**

Part V   Behavioral Bias, Investment Risk, and an Investor's Guide   **427**

19   Cognitive Errors, Picking Winners, and the Risk of Overpaying   **429**
       Q&A: Interview with Susan Stupin, Managing Director, Prescott Holdings, LLC; The Prescott Group, LLC   **446**

20 Underfunded Public Pension Funds, Risk, and Alternatives **449**
   Q&A: Interview with Richard F. Burns, Senior Advisor & Trustee, The NHP Foundation **460**

21 Investor's Checklist and Conclusions **463**
   Q&A: Interview with Russell Platt, Co-Founder and CEO of Forum Partners **469**

NOTES 471
INDEX 477

Acknowledgments

This book has something for everyone, whether appetites are insatiable or Spartan, or their interests are practical or theoretical. Whatever the appetite, what comes to mind is the Dagwood, a multi-layered sandwich packed with fillings that promote excess, stun the imagination, and satisfy the hunger. The Dagwood, which originated in the comic strip, "Blondie," during the Great Depression, is a super-sized meal; so is this book.

I have written an unorthodox book for frustrated CIOs, investment committees, conflicted managers, ill-informed consultants, and confused investors who hunger for new ideas.

This evidence-based book is a rich layering of ingredients that shine a bright light on the received wisdom, offer practical, performance-enhancing advice, and, I hope, challenge the established practices and investment myths. Interviews with twenty-one experts leaven this confection.

There are no prerequisites. The insatiably curious and astute readers, amateurs as well as experts, should consume its contents in leisurely, thoughtful bites while sitting in a comfortable chair, maybe with a glass of wine or, even better still, a fine Port.

My tone is evidence-based and polemical; I aim to persuade. This book is not Real Estate 101, but it is an excellent supplement for students and an urgently needed industry challenge.

My career seems more like a random walk than the result of a comprehensive plan hatched when I was a ninth grader. My goal then was to be an MIT physics professor. I attended Princeton where I studied math, physics, and architecture; I was surrounded by the world's brightest scholars. Perhaps most importantly, I was blessed with loving parents, great friends, legendary mentors, including Nobel Prize Laureates, and a wonderful, supportive family.

This is my first book, an all-consuming project. After having written more than 100 articles, my wife, Joan, said that now was the time to write THE BOOK. The talented and focused team at John Wiley & Sons, including Zachary Schisgal, was patient and supportive. They restrained my worse instincts, namely writing too much. Mark Twain once advised that, had he more time, he would have written less. Joan reminded me what Mies Van Der Rohe, the architect, once said: Less is more!

I have had outstanding mentors throughout this long odyssey. I thank my late PhD dissertation advisors, Professor Edwin S. Mills of the Princeton Economics Department and Professor Chester Rapkin of Princeton's School of Architecture and Urban Planning, for supporting my economics odyssey as a student and later as a Princeton University professor and colleague.

Goldman Sachs hired me to launch Wall Street's first real estate research group; at Goldman truly talented professionals in and out of real estate mentored me. Many are still my friends; some even agreed to participate as interviewees. I thank them for their fellowship and wisdom.

Many scholars, too numerous to mention, have influenced my thinking. I express my special gratitude to Emeritus Professor Burton Malkiel of Princeton and honor the memory of the late Stephen A. Ross, former MIT Professor and consultant to Goldman Sachs' Real Estate Research Group.

In the 1990s, Ethan Penner hired me to join his path-breaking real estate finance business, which was funded by Nomura Securities International, and to run real estate research. Ethan is a legendary figure in both real estate and finance circles, renowned for launching CMBS and rescuing the commercial real estate industry in the 1990s, no small feat. A brilliant author in his own right, he introduced me to John Wiley & Sons and the rest is history. I learned a great deal from Ethan regarding structured finance and securitization.

Joan, my wife, our children, Matt and Kimberly, their spouses, Taja and John, and their children have been unstinting in their love and encouragement. I could not have written this book without their support.

I have had three superb partners since leaving Nomura. Bart Steinfeld and I launched Apogee Associates in 1996, where we advised many institutional investors and developers from the 50th floor of New York's Chrysler Building. He was a dedicated and trusted partner.

Matt and I launched ZCA, a research and investment banking firm, in 2006 and advised some of the largest and most sophisticated pension funds, investment banks, and money managers in the world. As senior managing director at Greystone, he continues to inspire by his example.

Matt and I were delighted when Richard Burns, one of the original partners at AEW and former managing director at Morgan Stanley, joined us as partner just before the Great Financial Crisis (GFC). Then and now, Dick brings great wisdom.

Kimberly has been a dedicated and inspiring sounding board for new ideas over the years. She is multi-talented and wise.

Kristen Woolley Mehne is a world-class, Emmy award winning producer and editor of video and graphics for various platforms. She has guided the final production of the book's exhibits and worked closely with the entire Wiley team.

The interviews are candid recollections by experts who have made a difference and whom I deeply admire. They represent the very best in commercial real estate investing and economics. These interview sidebars should resonate with the rest of the book:

- Jason Benderly, President, Benderly Economics and former Chief Economist of Goldman Sachs
- Richard Burns, Senior Advisor & Trustee, The NHP Foundation
- Dan Cummings, Managing Director, Bain Capital, LP
- Michael Fascitelli, Chairman, MDF Capital; former CEO of Vornado and former Partner of Goldman Sachs & Co.
- Michael Giliberto, co-creator of the Giliberto-Levy Indexes; formerly senior portfolio manager at J. P. Morgan; and currently serving on corporate and pension fund boards
- Ronald Havner, Chairman of Public Storage and Chairman Emeritus of Shurgard
- Sonny Kalsi, Co-Chief Executive Officer, BGO; former Global Head of Morgan Stanley Real Estate Investing
- Doug Lyons, Managing Principal, Pearlmark
- Benjamin Shibe Macfarland III, CEO, SROACapital.com, LLC
- Daniel Neidich, CEO and Founder, Dune Capital Management; former Goldman Sachs Partner
- Joseph L. Pagliari, Jr., Ph.D., John Mazarakis and Chicago Atlantic Clinical Professor of Real Estate, Chicago Booth School of Business
- Ethan Penner, Chairman, Founder & CEO, Mosaic Real Estate Investors; former Managing Director and head of CMBS Group, Nomura Securities International
- Russell C. Platt, Co-Founder and CEO, Forum Partners, former Managing Director of Morgan Stanley
- Ralph Rosenberg, Chairman of Real Assets, KKR; formerly of Golman Sachs
- Steve Rosenberg, Founder and CEO, Greystone
- John Sischo, Managing Principal of Coretrust Capital Partners, LLC
- Susan Stupin, Managing Director, Prescott Holdings, LLC and The Prescott Group, LLC
- Owen Thomas, Chairman and CEO, BXP, Inc.
- Steven Wechsler, President and CEO, National Association of Real Estate Investment Trusts

- Aly Worthington, Head of Capital Markets, Summit Development
- Matthew Zisler, Senior Managing director, Head of Greystone Equity Services, Greystone

Susan Stupin, my esteemed former Goldman colleague and now Managing Director of the Prescott Holdings, LLC, and Professor Joseph Pagliari of the University of Chicago, who continues to write seminal papers on real estate finance and investments, have been generous, thoughtful, inspiring advisors.

I thank CoStar for its support and cooperation. CoStar maintains a unique data base. This book, the focus of which is the macroeconomics of commercial real estate risk, demonstrates new, creative ways in which investors can and should use this valuable capability.

NCREIF, an important supporter of my research over the years, is a powerful resource created and maintained by very talented professionals, in particular, Daniel Dierking, its president. Early in its history I had the honor to serve on its advisory board. This book demonstrates innovative ways to apply these critically important indexes to practical problems involving risk management.

I owe much to the Pension Real Estate Association and, in particular, to Gail Haynes, President, and to Greg MacKinnon, Director of Research, whose research continues to inspire.

I benefited from and deeply appreciate my discussions with my former client, CBRE Econometric Advisors, and its talented team led by Richard Barkham, Ph.D., CBRE Global Chief Economist and Dennis Schoenmaker, Ph.D., Executive Director and Principal Economist, CBRE Econometric Advisors. I admire their research contribution.

A friend recently opined that I am the only person who could write this book. Maybe so, but more than $6 billion of transactions and solid research credentials, both necessary conditions, are not enough by themselves to justify this generous compliment. My lack of conflicts, a necessary condition, is responsible for this book's acerbic tone and unusual blend of economics, finance, and experience. This work would be impossible were I still an executive at any of the largest brokerage firms, prestigious investment banks, or global institutional investors. I am beholden neither to any investor nor to any money manager; I have no hidden agenda, so I am free to speak as the evidence dictates. Not all money managers (or even institutional investors and consultants) will appreciate a bright light directed at their practices.

I am not a journalist seeking the Pulitzer. Instead, I want to promote sensible institutional investing with fewer self-serving stories, more science, better analytics, and more effective risk assessment. Greater transparency, better interest alignment, and intellectual honesty are essential.

I assume full responsibility for any remaining errors and oversights. My opinions are mine alone and not necessarily those of my 21 brilliant interviewees.

These are challenging, unsettling times, so I must speak truth to power. I am reminded of a quote from Professor Timothy Snyder of Yale University:

To abandon facts is to abandon freedom. If nothing is true, then no one can criticize power, because there is no basis upon which to do so. If nothing is true, then all is spectacle.[1]

Professor Timothy D. Snyder on Tyranny—Twenty Lessons from the Twentieth Century

Voters should demand no less.

Public servants must uphold and protect the constitution, and investment managers should embrace the highest fiduciary standards and speak truth even when doing so is inconvenient. Consultants should do more than facilitate the investment process. They should advocate evidence-based inquiry, challenge the received wisdom, educate, and inspire. Investment committees have an even higher duty: to protect investors and always speak truth to capital.

Randall Zisler, Ph.D. Zisler Capital Associates, LLC

Investors should demand no less.

About the Author

Randall Zisler, PhD, is Chairman of Zisler Capital Associates (ZCA), a research and investment banking firm that serves global institutional investors. Clients have included CALPERS, AT&T, IBM, Deutsche Bank, Morgan Stanley, Guggenheim, Rockefeller Development, various sovereign funds, and the US Department of Labor.

Randy's career has spanned two worlds, that of ideas at Princeton University, where as a professor he taught economics and planning, and the world of capital and applied research at Goldman Sachs & Co., Nomura Securities International, Jones Lang LaSalle, and Pension Consulting Alliance. At Goldman, he launched Wall Street's first real estate research group. He was a partner at Jones Lang Wootton and helped launch Jones Lang Wootton Realty Advisors, which is now called Clarion Partners.

Randy has consummated in excess of $6 billion of transactions, written well over 100 papers, and has advised many institutional investors on matters pertaining to capital placement, strategy, risk mitigation, deal and portfolio structuring, and underwriting.

He has appeared on NBC, CNN, FOX, and PBS and has lectured at Harvard, Yale, University of Southern California, and other universities.

Randy received his undergraduate degree, two master's degrees and a PhD from Princeton University, as well as a master's degree in civil engineering and systems analysis from The Catholic University of America while working full time as a physicist at the US Naval Ship Research and Development Center.

I dedicate this book to Joan, my loving wife and very best friend of over 50 years. She has been unstinting in her love and support for me and our close-knit family.

Preface

Real estate research is the preserve of too many stories and insufficient science.

Nassim Taleb wrote in *The Bed of Procrustes* that "To understand how something works, figure out how to break it."[1] The title is especially apt. Real estate research is the preserve of too many stories and too little science; some breakage is long overdue.

What is a procrustean bed? King Procrustes was the sadistic son of Poseidon, God of the Sea, who forced travelers to conform to his bed by stretching their bodies or amputating their legs.

The problem with research. Real estate research people are compelled to conform to the party line or jam their research into the procrustean bed of whoever is paying their salaries. Upton Sinclair once wrote, "It is difficult to get a man to understand something, when his salary depends on his not understanding it."[2] Manager research, as a result, is less evidence-based than it should be. It often fails to focus on what it should, especially risk, and when it does, it does so superficially with flawed econometrics. Can it be trusted?

The pursuit of assets under management. Money managers emphasize the growth of assets under management (AUM), focus on capital placement, and carefully manage messaging. Research is often the captive of the marketing department. Firms sometimes bend or ignore the truth with the tacit approval of the research group.

Raising capital in the midst of a downturn is not meant for the timid or the faint hearted. Launching two capital raises at once, while managing legacy problems, usually sidelines good research when investors need it the most. Pulling punches is common to real estate research. If you doubt me, consider some quotes during the early months of the GFC. Money manager research during the Great Financial Crisis (GFC) either ignored or minimized the likely effects of the gathering storm even though the evidence was in plain view. Some pension consultants and widely respected CEOs even remarked that caution was a sign of weakness. One well-known money manager in 2008 said at a large gathering of managers and fawning investors that "careful underwriting is for sissies." Another advised, "Anyone with a wallet can make money." Following the crash both left the business or reemerged with new corporate billboards.[3]

Diogenes and the search for truth. Diogenes the Cynic was a Greek philosopher known for his acerbic wit, rejection of materialism, and his relentless search for the truth. Unlike Diogenes, I do not reject materialism but I do seek to critique zealously the received wisdom.

Not everyone likes math, but I do. I truly believe, to the chagrin of some, that if I cannot express something mathematically, then I do not understand it. Math at least promotes clarity, perhaps at the risk of oversimplification.

I passionately love art, music, architecture, biological physics, and economic theory. Alas, I have failed to replicate mathematically my transcendental experience listening to Mahler's *Second Symphony* and the *Verdi Requiem*, or studying Le Corbusier's sublime architectural masterpiece, Villa Savoye.

A sample of thirteen findings
- Prevailing risk analytical methods in commercial real estate are flawed and misguided.
- I show using plausible assumptions that the chance of recommending a seemingly skilled, but truly incompetent, manager to the investment committee, is 81.8%, even though 75% of all the managers may lack sufficient skill.
- Even after assuming no long-term rental growth, as long as markets fluctuate, the option to escalate rents still has value. Most practitioners miscalculate embedded option values.
- Real estate is not a short- to intermediate-term inflation hedge.
- An increase in interest rates will not necessarily increase cap rates.
- Property, which is opaque and relatively illiquid, is just as risky as publicly traded REITs once we econometrically remove return smoothing.
- Property looks too good to be true without de-smoothing using the proper statistical techniques; without this correction, asset allocation models overestimate property's appropriate allocation.
- Opportunistic funds have generally delivered negative 300 bps alpha, roughly equal to fees. (Alpha is the average excess return relative to a market-adjusted portfolio.)
- Office obsolescence and the repricing of the inventory are real long-run challenges. Office-to-apartment conversions are attractive strategies.
- Leverage does not increase risk-adjusted returns; doubling leverage from 30% to 60% quadruples risk.
- At high leverage levels, the probability of loss increases even though expected returns increase.

- Diversification and liquidity are not free, and the benefits are absent when needed the most.
- The promote interacts with leverage to increase gross, not risk-adjusted returns, much of which is beta and not alpha. Why should investors reward managers for incremental returns due to leverage and not alpha?

I embrace the scientific method. Some math seems unavoidable, so I beg readers' patience.

A friend said my formulas are intimidating. For her, I devised the following prescription—three special formulas—which she found helpful. I assure even abstemious readers that they will as well:

1.

2.

3. $$\text{Maximize } \varphi = \sum_{j=1}^{n} P_j Q_j$$

Subject to: $\sum_{j=1}^{n} a_{ij} Q_j \leq U_i$ (i = 1,...,m)

How to read this book. This book has something for everyone. Anyone who owns, rents, or has an interest in real estate will benefit. The narrative will suit all thoughtful readers, students and practitioners alike. If you do not like math, then ignore the equations; if you like pictures, focus on the exhibits.

While each chapter largely stands alone, there is a logical, linked progression and readers can select chapters depending on their interests. Here are some suggestions for busy readers:

- **The real estate student or novice.** It's never too late to learn. Begin with Chapter 1, "Who Should Read This Book, and Why?" and Chapter 3, "What Is Real Estate?," and skip to Chapter 10, "Asset Allocation" and Chapter 14, "Is Real Estate an Effective Inflation Hedge?," and then proceed to Part IV, "The Public Sector and Collective Risk," ending with Chapter 20, "Underfunded Public Pension Funds" and Chapter 21, "Investor's Checklist and Conclusions."
- **The developer.** Focus on risk and interdependency. Start with Chapter 1 and include Chapters 3 through 7. Then proceed to Chapter 11, "Optimal Development," Chapter 12, "Cap Rates and Hidden Information," Chapter 13, "Liquidity," Chapter 15, "A Monte Carlo Model of GP and LP Interests," Chapter 18, "Rent Control," and Chapter 21, "Investor's Checklist and Conclusions."
- **Office investors.** The office sector has lost its allure, at least for now, but I believe that opportunities abound. Start with Chapter 1 and include Chapters 3 through 5 and Chapter 8, "Office Property: COVID-19, Obsolescence, WFH, and Conversions." Read Chapter 12, "Cap Rates and Hidden Information," Chapter 13, "Liquidity," Chapter 15, "A Monte Carlo Model of GP and LP Interests," and Chapter 21, "Investor's Checklist and Conclusions."
- **Tenant and sales brokers.** A leasing broker once said, "Randy, I don't read no reports and I don't write no reports." An exception is due. Start with Chapter 1 and focus on Chapter 5, "The Lease: An Options Approach and Upward Only Adjusting Leases." Patience is a virtue. The sales broker should read Chapters 1 through 15. Do not neglect Chapter 21.
- **The investment manager.** Read the entire book with possible exception of Chapter 11, "Optimal Development." Review some basic statistical tools in Chapter 2, "Statistics, Monte Carlo, Bayes Rule, Stochastic Arithmetic, and Uncertain Attributes." Study Chapter 20, "Underfunded Public Pension Funds, Risk, and Alternatives" because, I guarantee, your investors will ask you about this chapter. Finish with Chapter 21.
- **Financial institutions and their consultants.** Read the entire book with a possible exception, Chapter 11, "Optimal Development." Review some basic statistical tools in Chapter 2. Before you speak with your investment managers, and you should, carefully read Chapter 19, "Cognitive Errors, Picking Winners, and the Risk of Overpaying" and Chapter 20, "Underfunded Public Pension Funds, Risk, and Alternatives." Complete your study with Chapter 21 and reward yourself with a glass of port to prepare you for your defensive (or even hostile) managers.

PART I
Introduction to Real Estate and Risk

CHAPTER 1

Who Should Read This Book, and Why?

Preliminaries

My approach is pragmatic, evidence-based, quantitative, polemical, and sardonic. I aim to help investors avoid uncompensated risk, achieve superior risk-adjusted returns, and enhance their wealth.

This book is not a how-to-get-rich book; but it should help readers think more deeply about real estate. It should have broad appeal to non-professionals, professionals, and students.

I target truth seekers. There are no prerequisites other than deep curiosity and analytical thinking. Professionals can make egregious mistakes and everyone, especially non-professionals, can learn from these errors.

This book is not a moribund introductory text, although it is packed with financial and statistical concepts. I introduce the links between real estate, which is a financial claim on the cash flows generated by buildings and land, and capital markets, leases, deal structure, cities, and regions. They are all interdependent parts of the same fabric. Different property types, such as single-family homes and self-storage, are linked. The demand for self-storage units, a commercial use, is an extension of the household and reflects ratio of the opportunity cost of space in the home and the price of space in self-storage.

The Golden Age of Institutional Investing: Institutional Is What Institutions Do

The golden age of institutional real estate investing began before the Volker Recession of 1981–1982. The Employment Retirement Income Security Act (ERISA), passed in 1974, was a watershed event. ERISA established minimum standards for private pension plans and influenced other retirement systems.

Institutional investors and their consultants debated what exactly is prudent investing, adequate diversification, and institutional grade property. Lacking decades of performance statistics, investors and their managers sought comfort by aggressively bidding for trophy assets, the physicality of which exuded the patina of prudence. In their search for institutional quality returns, investors, to their dismay, received trophy photographs but lackluster returns. "Institutional grade" was, tautologically, whatever institutions did.

Here is a good example of the trophy myth or edifice complex. The 1980s were a time when institutions shunned apartments for fear of rent control even though some research, specifically my own, demonstrated that incidence of rent control was rare but predictable. Only certain cities and towns adopted rent control. I recommended apartments to investment committees, but to no avail. They had other ideas. There was then, and still is, a gap between real estate practice and research. (See Chapter 18, "Rent Control Redux: Prediction, Assessment, and Opportunity.")

I published in 1988 a widely cited paper on return smoothing in the *Journal of Real Estate Finance and Economics*. My co-author, the late Professor Stephen Ross of MIT, and I showed stock prices impounded news immediately, but that property markets were slower to react and this lag complicated any analysis using property return data. Investors were underestimating the true risk of property, which falsely inflated property's allocation. This finding plays an essential role in this book.

Property markets crawled, they did not leap, in their search for equilibrium. I later discovered that this return process is common to other illiquid assets, such as hedge funds.

Most investors today unintentionally ignore risk, but others do so intentionally. Some institutional real estate managers, wealth managers, and pension funds betray the public trust and engage in "volatility laundering," an attempt to wash risk down the drain. In either case, they do so at someone's peril, seldom their own.

The underfunding of public pension funds is a growing problem. Some investment committees actually believe that the return smoothing is a benefit. Disclosure is also a problem. Some, not all, money managers reject full disclosure and, even worse, creatively warm, if not cook, the books.

This problem is especially evident for some managers who offer opportunistic funds and who simultaneously offer multiple fund products. The manager may not speak truthfully about market weakness if doing so undermines the marketing of new products or the valuation of legacy assets. What then is the value of manager research?

Often when transaction volume is low and redemption queues are long, managers meet liquidity needs by raising fresh capital and by selling only the best assets so as not to create a sales history that could impair the perceived value of unsold legacy assets. Some managers promote investment myths that they suspect, or even know, are false. Why? Because doing so is profitable and investors do not seem to care.

Some managers reject this claim. John Maynard Keynes once wrote that "Worldly wisdom teaches that it is better for reputation to fail conventionally than to succeed unconventionally."[1] The timid, conventional herd is slow to adjust.

This Book Is Urgently Needed

Some managers assume uncompensated and even imprudent risk through the misuse of leverage. Their investors confuse beta, or systematic, returns with alpha returns. An alpha return is a measure of how well a manager performs in relation to expected returns or a benchmark that reflects the investment's volatility. Leveraging a deal does not produce alpha or increase risk-adjusted returns. Beta measures an investment's volatility compared to the market. Investors pay opportunistic managers high fees to produce alpha, not beta, but these managers as a group have failed to deliver. As Warren Buffett famously said, "Only when the tide goes out do you discover who's been swimming naked."[2]

Lest you regard me as gratuitously harsh, I shall provide an example: state-run public pension funds. Taxpayers do not know that most public pension funds are woefully underfunded: Liabilities exceed assets. Their approaches to solving this problem lack economic merit, harm the taxpayer, and in some cases betray fiduciary duty. The managers, the pension consultants, and even some state retirement systems are either asleep at the switch or willful betrayers of the taxpayers' interests. (See Chapter 20, "Underfunded Public Pension Funds, Risks, and Alternatives.")

What choices do the state pension systems have? There are basically three: Raise state taxes to fund the shortfall, cut retiree benefits, or assume greater risk in the hope of balancing the books. Most states, judging from their rejection of the first two choices, have embraced the third choice, which, while politically more palatable in the short run, essentially takes the retirement systems to the casino, hoping for the best. Many fund stewards who have embraced the third choice will likely escape unharmed through retirement or lucrative promotions. While the retirement system suffers, few speak truth to capital. Investment committees blunt individual responsibility; if everyone is responsible, no one is responsible, but who then pays the bill? The answer seems obvious: the taxpayer.

I do not reject opportunistic strategies, just misconceived and ill-structured opportunistic funds. These funds are often opaque, expensive, misaligned, and illiquid; they fail to deliver alpha. Some of these funds issue unreliable performance reports that understate or misrepresent risk. The gap between reported, marked-to-model net asset value (NAV) and current market value is often comically wide, especially in a declining market; this gap often brings forth a cascade of withdrawal requests by disbelieving limited partners (LPs), but the manager closes the gates when the demand for withdrawals is most intense.

I am not opposed to risky strategies *per se*, but the risk should be disclosed and priced appropriately. I reject how imprudent strategies are deceptively packaged, marketed to naïve investors and implemented. Public pension funds and their state governments are not innocent, either. They often lack the political will to act responsibly, fight back, and demand more from their managers. In the past, no one was fired for hiring IBM; this instinct is still with us in real estate. Seemingly safe choices still rule the day.

Have their CIOs been asleep at the switch? Do their contracts incentivize excessive risk-taking? The pension fund establishes a performance benchmark, but does this benchmark provide adequate accountability, and is the benchmark adjusted for risk and investment style? Is the benchmark too easy to beat or inappropriate for the strategy? Paying the piper is never painless, but it is inevitable. Who bears the cost and when?

Excessive reliance on total rather than risk-adjusted returns is a problem. Many real estate managers do not want to discuss, much less acknowledge, risk-adjusted returns. Here is a true story: During the 1990s the senior partner of one of the largest, most prestigious real estate pension advisors debated me before a well-attended pension conference. The performance of this excessively leveraged trophy portfolio cratered during the Resolution Trust Corporation (RTC). At the time, my clients, two public and three of the largest corporate pension funds, investors in this advisor's fund, sought a fighter who was not shy, so they hired me. The sponsor argued that risk-adjusted returns do not exist because we cannot measure risk. I retorted that the absence of evidence is not evidence of absence. Many well-credentialled colleagues in the audience were mute, and some LPs were aghast at my temerity to demand accountability. How could I even question a manager whose exciting and coveted "educational" events were held in exotic locations? In the end, the LP investors, two large corporate plans, lost their capital, but the manager retained his fees and remained in business under a different name. Memories are short, managers come and go, but pension bureaucracies are practically eternal.

The real estate money management sector may suffer from excess asset concentration, which reflects significant potential economies of scale through the growth and acquisition of other managers and their portfolios. Investors often ascribe, rightly or wrongly, greater wisdom to the largest firms, even though actual risk-adjusted performance may not justify this praise. The largest firms have an outsized impact on shaping investors' expectations and building capital placement momentum through the proliferation of multiple products (economies of scope).

According to *Institutional Real Estate, Inc.*'s survey of about 125 real estate money managers, the top manager, Blackstone, accounts for about 12% of all AUM; the top two firms manage 17% of total real estate AUM and the largest ten firms represent 43%.[3]

Poor performance reporting is a real challenge. The reporting either ignores or misconstrues risk. This deception contributes to excessively high fees, especially during downturns. Reported performance lags comparable sales data. Many pension funds, money managers, and consultants clearly understand this point, but laundering, especially during a downturn, enhances their reported performance, fortifies investor retention, maintains current fee levels, and provides political cover to investors and boards until the day of reckoning.

The Balkanized real estate landscape is populated with disciplinary silos, each with their own technical jargon that obscures rather than reveals. This book aims to bridge this linguistic chasm.

Statistics, the *lingua franca* of finance, plays a big role, but fear not. I provide a simple tutorial and omit most jargon in Chapter 2, "Statistics, Monte Carlo, Bayes Rule, Stochastic Arithmetic, and Uncertain Attributes," a review of basic statistics using real estate data. "Stochastic" means uncertain or random.

A Holistic View of Risk

Donald Rumsfeld, former United States Secretary of Defense, in 2002 addressed risk in what is now known as the Rumsfeld risk matrix.[4]

Reports that say that something hasn't happened are always interesting to me, because as we know, there are known knowns; there are things we know we know. We also know there are known unknowns; that is to say we know there are some things we do not know. But there are also unknown unknowns—the ones we don't know we don't know. And if one looks throughout the history of our country and other free countries, it is the latter category that tends to be the difficult one.

COVID-19 was not an unknown unknown in the sense of the 1348 Bubonic plague, which decimated up to 50% of Europe. The concept of disease was not understood in this pre-scientific age. Scientists were able to produce a COVID-19 vaccine relatively quickly due to prior genomics research regarding Lassa, Ebola, and other coronaviruses. An even better example of unknown unknowns is the asteroid that eliminated the dinosaurs 66 million years ago and cleared the evolutionary path for the arrival of money managers.

This book probes the influence of COVID-19 on real estate performance and evaluates the impact of urban size and density on the spread of COVID-19. Two-way causality or simultaneity is a characteristic of all markets. An economic shock affects relative prices and choices, and these changes cascade throughout the economy. Chapter 11, "Optimal Development: Linkage, the Internal Cost of Capital, and Risk," addresses interdependency and risk, while Chapter 14, "Is Real Estate an Effective Inflation Hedge?" evaluates the transmission of inflation through the supply chain and estimates the effect of inflation on real estate performance. Risk due to unintended consequences in the public sector is the subject of Chapter 16, "Public Sector Risk: Introduction to Sprawl and Rent Control"; Chapter 17, "Sprawl: An Options Perspective"; and Chapter 18, "Rent Control Redux: Prediction, Assessment, and Opportunity."

The Mythology of Real Estate: Hubris at Work

Perhaps we ourselves introduce risk by virtue of what our models exclude or miscalculate. Is our confidence in deterministic models misplaced? I believe it is. Hubris surely is one of the leading cognitive errors in all phases of real estate, and modeling is just one example. See Chapter 19, "Cognitive Errors, Picking Winners, and the Risk of Overpaying."

Myths cloud the mind and impair performance. Dogma provides convenient answers, often specious, to universal and reoccurring questions.

The ancient story of Daedalus and Icarus is a myth that remains relevant even today:

> Daedalus was a brilliant architect, sculptor, and inventor. He was credited with building for King Minos of Crete the Labyrinth in which the Minotaur was kept. When the king turned against Daedalus and imprisoned him, Daedalus secretly made wings for himself and his son Icarus, intending to escape to Sicily. Despite his father's warnings, Icarus flew too close to the sun; the wax holding the feathers to his wings melted, and he fell into the sea and drowned.[5]

Hubris blinds investors and their managers. Behavioral science shows that we selectively choose information that supports our prior beliefs and we falsely assume that past performance predicts future performance, despite what the documents warn. Recall the "hot hand" fallacy: A string of good returns does not necessarily augur superior future performance. Beware of hot-handed managers.

Conclusions and Investment Implications

- This book is analytical and empirical, with many graphs and stories. I hope it is fun.
- The common thread is the analysis of risk, investment myths, and pathologies.
- Sidebar interviews with top real estate executives provide personal insights.
- Cash is real, but so is risk, even though it may seem abstract and resistant to analysis; this is why we need good risk analytics.

Q&A: Interview with Danel Neidich, CEO and Founder, Dune Capital Management and former Goldman Sachs Partner

The Rockefeller Center REIT and Office Building Conversions

Dan, discuss your career path before you joined Goldman.
I was a Yale undergraduate in mathematics and science and then I attended the Stanford Business School.

You were a partner at Goldman Sachs. When did the business take off?
Real estate was not important at Goldman when I joined in 1978. We hired Claude Ballard as a partner in 1981 and leveraged his position in the industry, which accelerated our growth.

Tell us about the iconic Rockefeller Center deal.
Initially, we represented Columbia University in selling the land under Rockefeller Center to the Rockefeller family. Surprisingly, the family-owned Rockefeller Center was a leasehold. After the acquisition, the family wanted to monetize its value in Rockefeller Center in a tax efficient manner, so we created a convertible mortgage. We raised the money for the convertible mortgage through a public offering, thereby creating the Rockefeller REIT. This billion dollar plus offering was the largest public REIT at the time. After going public, the REIT borrowed more money, which created a problem in 1993. The Whitehall funds, which I ran, and Goldman provided a participating note and an underlying loan; the participating note had a non-dilution clause. The family sold Rockefeller Center to Mitsubishi, which defaulted. The new investors had to respect Goldman's anti-dilution provision. We created a new group with Tishman Speyer, David Rockefeller, and the Agnelli and the Niarchos families. Our group, which was the only competitive buyer due to the anti-dilution provision,

ran the property successfully for many years and ultimately sold the property to Tishman Speyer.

Why did you leave Goldman?

I left Goldman so I could pursue challenging opportunities rather than manage people.

Tell us about your new initiative converting office buildings to apartment buildings.

At Dune we are creating multifamily assets through the conversion of office buildings. This opportunity is bigger than the RTC opportunities. Many office building owners have nowhere else to turn. Since the buildings are cheaper than new construction today, we create product at a 25% discount.

What advice can you give young people contemplating a career in real estate?

Find a firm with a lot of deal flow and increase your value over 10 years. Seek great mentors.

CHAPTER 2

Statistics, Monte Carlo, Bayes Rule, Stochastic Arithmetic, and Uncertain Attributes

Preliminaries

I promised a book that offers something for everyone, a true multilayered Dagwood sandwich. This chapter, in that spirit, surveys the statistical tools readers will find most useful.

We all live in an uncertain, or stochastic, world, but investors and managers evaluate deals as if the world is deterministic.

Investors have good company in the Marquis de Laplace, the great mathematician who lived from 1749 to 1827. Laplace, inventor of the Laplace transform, was a determinist who believed that, if he knew the exact position and momentum of every particle in the universe, he could forecast the future by solving a set of differential equations. Scientists no longer embrace Laplace's view and neither should you when analyzing real estate.

Laplace, like most geniuses, contradicted himself whenever he pleased: "The most important questions in life are indeed, for the most part, really only problems of probability."[1]

Risk and Uncertainty

Probability distributions are the face of uncertainty; they convey much more than averages. Uncertainty is not a single number; it is a shape. Ignoring this insight is equivalent to committing "the Flaw of Averages."[2]

Risk management is often ignored by senior management.[3] Senior leadership addresses the "bigger" risks, but they do so with soft approaches that lack quantitative rigor, focusing just on averages and, in so doing, neglecting risk.

Risk and uncertainty are different. Uncertainty is objective, whereas risk is subjective. Certainty is not the same as the absence of risk. Real estate promoters often act as if it is. Risk, which is the product of the probability of loss and the extent of loss, may seem elusive but it is very real; it is asymmetric, difficult to measure, and at times counterintuitive, as I shall demonstrate.

The cost of information and the burden of complex calculations encourages the use of rules of thumb, or heuristics, some of which may lack sound empirical foundations. Many eventually assume the status of myths disguised as facts: "Real estate is an inflation hedge." Aside from laziness and lack of training, another reason managers ignore the proper analysis of risk is that in the short run managers receive no credit or fees for deals that they did not do.

Econometric Models and Some Challenges

Models force clarity at the risk of oversimplification; most models are too complex. Good models reveal important relationships and suggest good questions.

Many real estate analysts comb data searching for correlations that often suggest spurious causality. Models should reflect theory, but theory only goes so far. Theory is often mute on the optimal number of lags, the model's functional form, or even the variables to include or exclude.

Simultaneity is another consideration. GDP equals the sum of consumption, investment, government spending, and net exports, but consumption and investment are themselves functions of GDP. Ignoring simultaneity is like misplacing one of the two blades of a scissor. Coefficient estimates are biased and the results are often suspect if not useless.

Some market prices, such as stock prices, react quickly to news. Prompt responses to news lead to prices that appear to fluctuate randomly in a statistical sense although causality is very much at play behind the scenes.

Omitted variables are a real problem. Any time you read an analyst's report that includes a bivariate regression, you should question the functional form and the likelihood that the underlying model, if there is one, excludes essential variables. If you exclude a variable that is correlated with included variables, the coefficient estimates are biased and likely useless.

Uncertainty is compounded by model misspecification and the casual sampling of data. Some analysts believe that if they increase the frequency of the data—using daily instead of quarterly or annual data—results will improve. Higher frequency data often just introduces noise.

Some analysts believe that models can *prove* hypotheses. Such is not the case. Models help us reject the null hypothesis. Another dataset might contradict previous results. We may hope that our models are consistent with our hypothesis, but we should not expect a model to "prove" anything. Good models suggest good questions.

Data Exploration Before Theory: Descriptive Statistics

Investors should know the data, including weaknesses; to avoid spurious correlations, they should not data mine. Instead, they should write a note that includes a back-of-the-envelope model with variables and an estimate of the result. Upon completion of the analysis, reread the note and learn.

Proceed beyond readily available data. Do not focus just on data where the light of discovery shines the brightest. The development of proxies for missing variables suggested by theory is important. Misspecification and the omission of variables introduces bias.

The distribution is the shape of uncertainty. Distributions uncover information lurking behind the averages. Investors focus excessively on averages to the exclusion of volatility and the likelihood of extreme events. This practice introduces bias and leaves value on the table while investors shoulder needless risk. Be clear what you mean by "average." The three measures of central tendency include the mean, the mode (the most frequent value), and the median (50–50 split in the data). Often they differ. The average and the standard deviation are sometimes insufficient, which is why I introduce distributions or histograms, which are the face of risk. Exhibit 2.1 shows two distributions, each with the same mean and standard deviation; otherwise, they are quite different.

EXHIBIT 2.1 Superimposition of the normal and lognormal distributions with identical means and standard deviations.

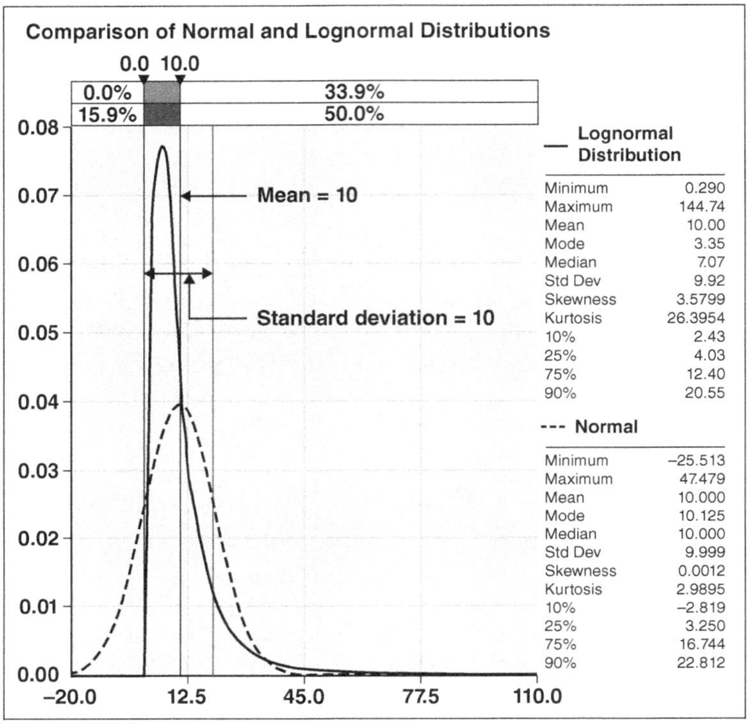
Comparison of Normal and Lognormal Distributions
0.0 10.0
0.0%
33.9%
15.9%
50.0%
Mean = 10
Standard deviation = 10
0.08
0.07
0.06
0.05
0.04
0.03
0.02
0.01
0.00
-20.0
12.5
45.0
77.5
110.0
Lognormal Distribution
Minimum 0.290
Maximum 144.74
Mean 10.00
Mode 3.35
Median 7.07
Std Dev 9.92
Skewness 3.5799
Kurtosis 26.3954
10% 2.43
25% 4.03
75% 12.40
90% 20.55
--- Normal
Minimum -25.513
Maximum 47.479
Mean 10.000
Mode 10.125
Median 10.000
Std Dev 9.999
Skewness 0.0012
Kurtosis 2.9895
10% -2.819
25% 3.250
75% 16.744
90% 22.812

Source: ZCA

The normal distribution is symmetric and all three measures of "average" are equal. By contrast, the lognormal distribution is skewed to the right, which pulls the mean and the median to the right. The median is less variable than the mean or the mode. The lognormal distribution has high kurtosis or thick tails—kurtosis is 26.4, compared with the normal distribution's kurtosis of 3.0. High kurtosis suggests the likelihood of extreme events. The standard deviation and the confidence interval measure variation. The area under any distribution must be 100%. The likelihood of a value greater than 10 is 34%. If skewness, a measure of symmetry, is zero, the distribution is symmetric. The lognormal distribution has a skewness of 3.6, as shown in Exhibit 2.1.

Cross-sectional and time series data. Time series and cross-sectional data raise their own statistical challenges, which I explore.

Data transformation is important. Exhibit 2.2 is a time series plot of office market rental growth and market cap rates. The cap rate, which is the ratio of net operating income to price, does not seem very volatile in this exhibit.

Data Exploration Before Theory: Descriptive Statistics 17

EXHIBIT 2.2 Office market rental growth and cap rates not normalized.

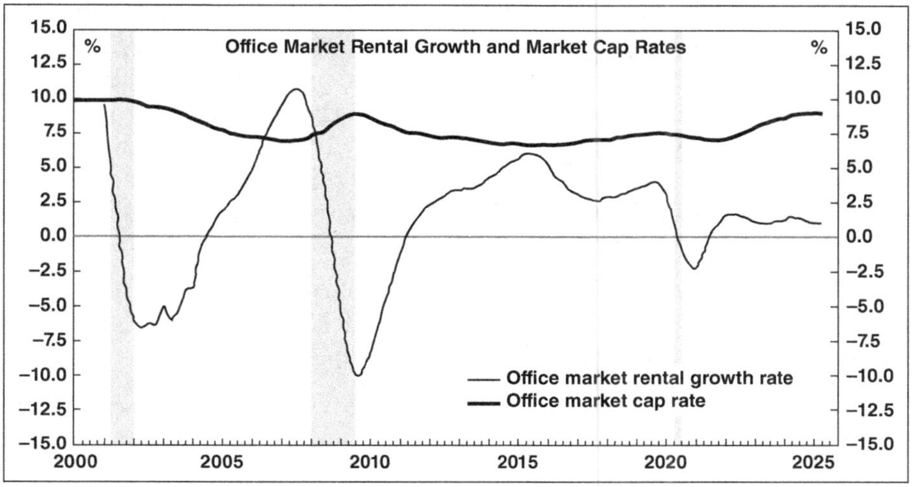

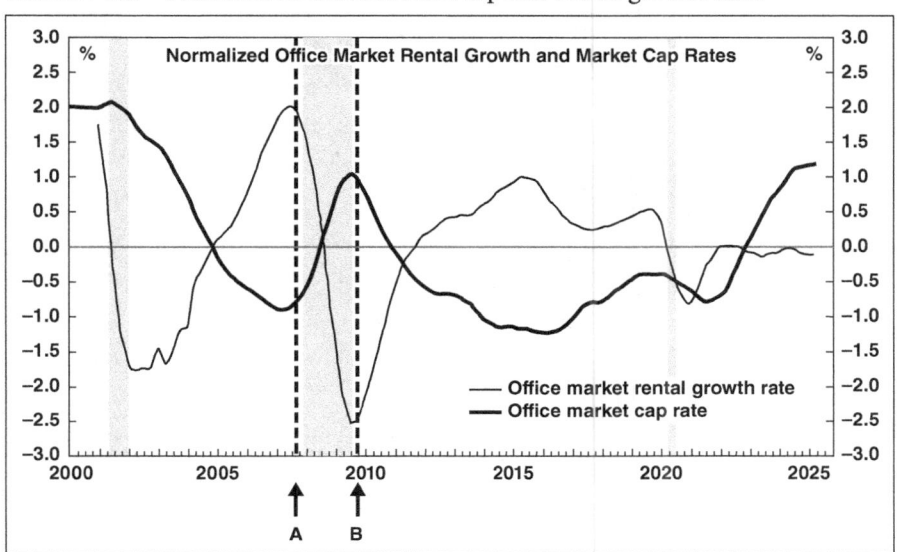

Source: ZCA using CoStar data

Exhibit 2.3 shows a normalized plot of the cap rate depicted in Exhibit 2.2. Normalization entails the subtracting from each data series its mean and dividing by the standard deviation, transforming the time series data into standard deviation units and enhancing the contrast between variables.

EXHIBIT 2.3 Normalized office market cap and rental growth rate.

Source: ZCA using CoStar data

Rental growth and cap rates are maximized and minimized respectively in 2007.IV (A); the reverse occurs one year later (B). The entire cap rate distribution shifts one year later about 214 bps to the right while preserving shape. The variation increases 16.7%, but skewness and kurtosis remain practically unchanged. Most of the increase in the standard deviation derives from the stretching of the right tail in relation to the left tail, a bearish indicator. Exhibits 2.4 and 2.5 show cross-sectional distributions using metropolitan statistical area (MSA) cap rate data. Two years later, the distribution shifts to the left 3.3 percentage points and the volatility increases.

The office rental distribution for the fourth quarter of 2008 is more symmetric but still skewed to the left and the tails remain thick. The logistic distribution is a close approximation of the input data. (See Exhibits 2.6 and 2.7.)

Two years later, the distribution shifts to the left 3.3 percentage points and the standard deviation increases.

EXHIBIT 2.4 Cap rate distribution in the fourth quarter of 2007.

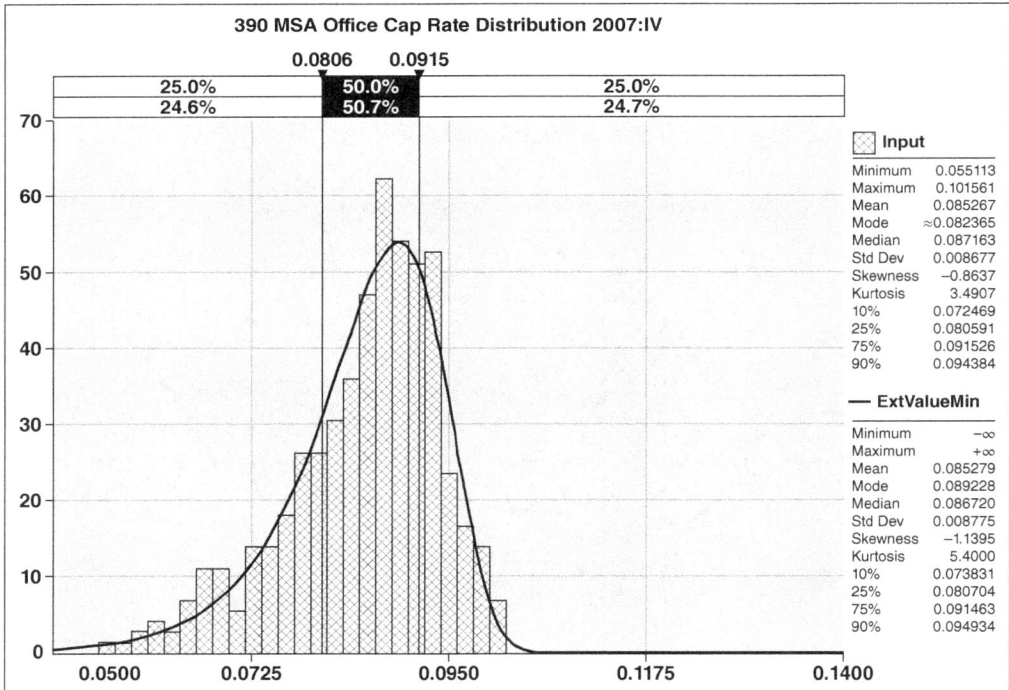

Source: ZCA using CoStar data

EXHIBIT 2.5 In 2009.IV the distribution shifts to the right 214 bps.

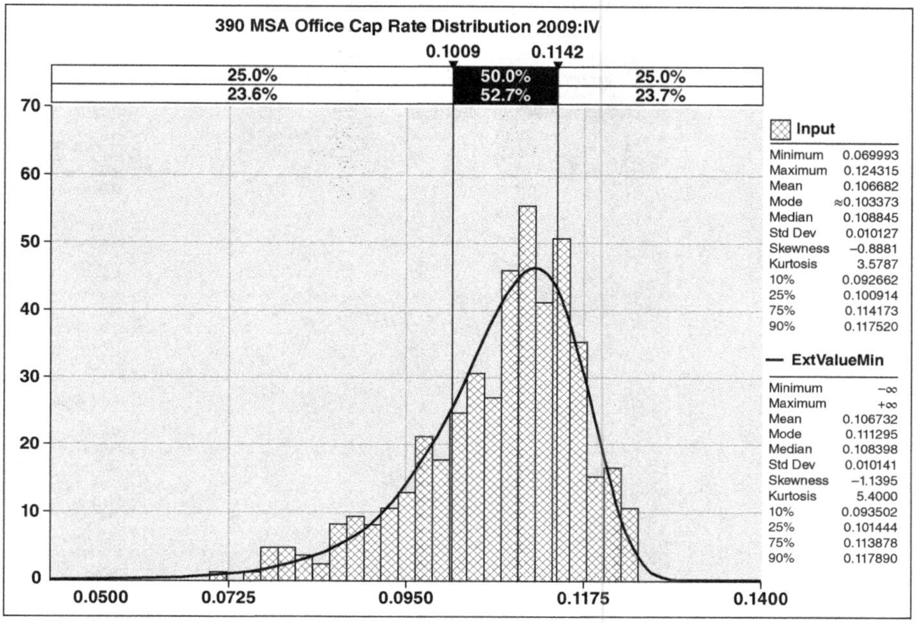

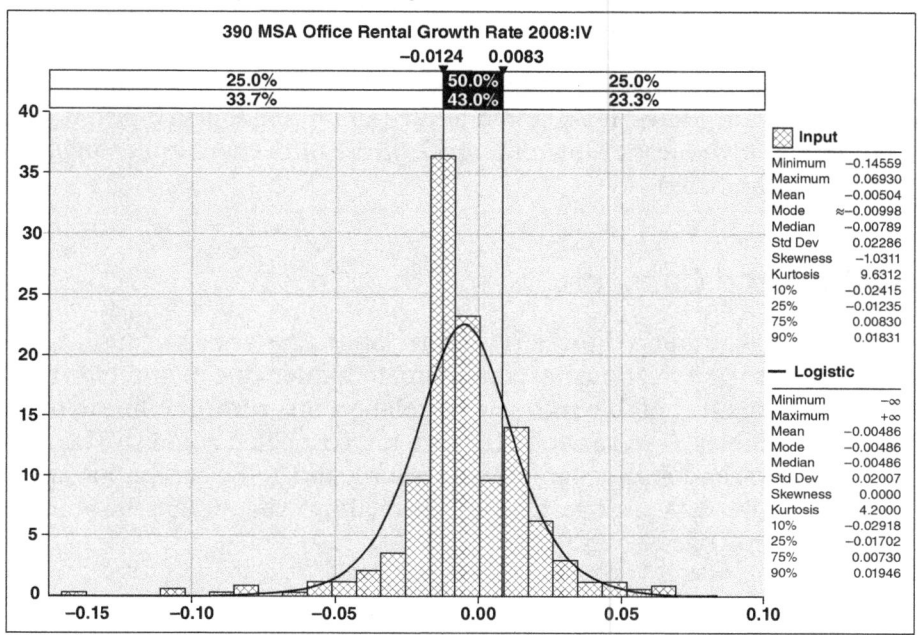

Source: ZCA using CoStar data

EXHIBIT 2.6 Average office rental growth in 2008.IV is −0.5%.

Source: ZCA using CoStar data

EXHIBIT 2.7 Average office rental growth in 2010.IV is −3.8.

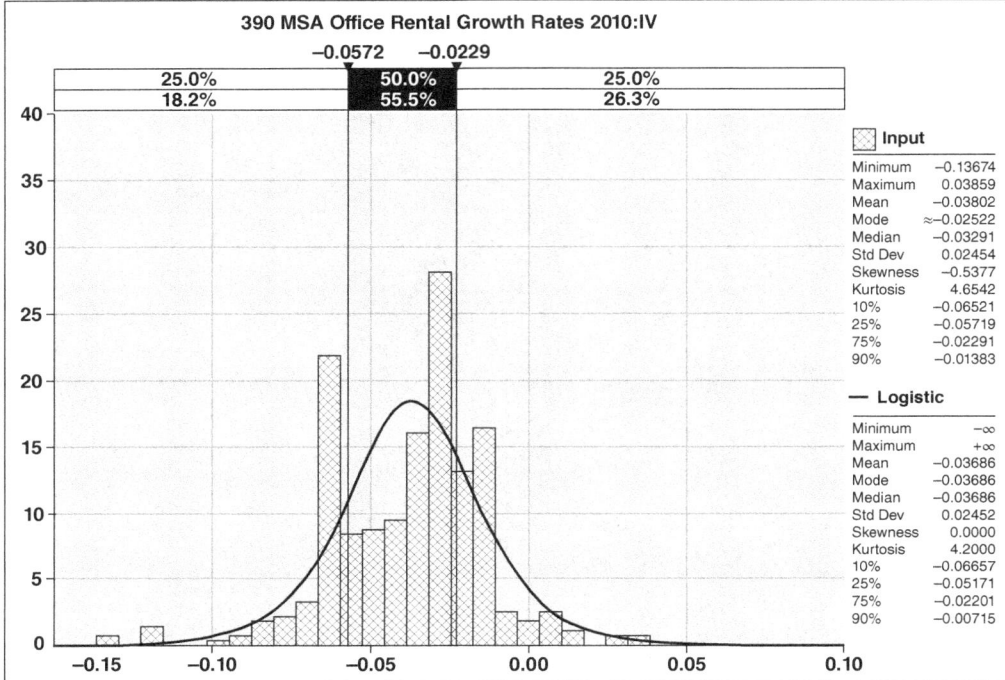

Source: ZCA using CoStar data

The vacancy rate distribution shifts 1.7 percentage points to the right, indicating an increase in vacancy rates; it is skewed to the right in the fourth quarters of 2007 and 2009. The relative vacancy rate difference across MSAs does not change much. (See Exhibits 2.8 and 2.9.)

Correlation and Causality

Correlation is not causality. If there is no correlation, the case for causality weakens, but the true causal relationship could remain hidden due to omitted variables or some other statistical problems.[4] The correlation measures the linear relationship between variables. Two variables that are not correlated could still be related. Exhibit 2.10 shows randomly generated values for X and Y; the correlation is clearly zero whereas Exhibit 2.11, a circle, has zero correlation even though the points conform to the equation of a circle.

EXHIBIT 2.8 Vacancy rates just before the Great Financial Crisis (GFC).

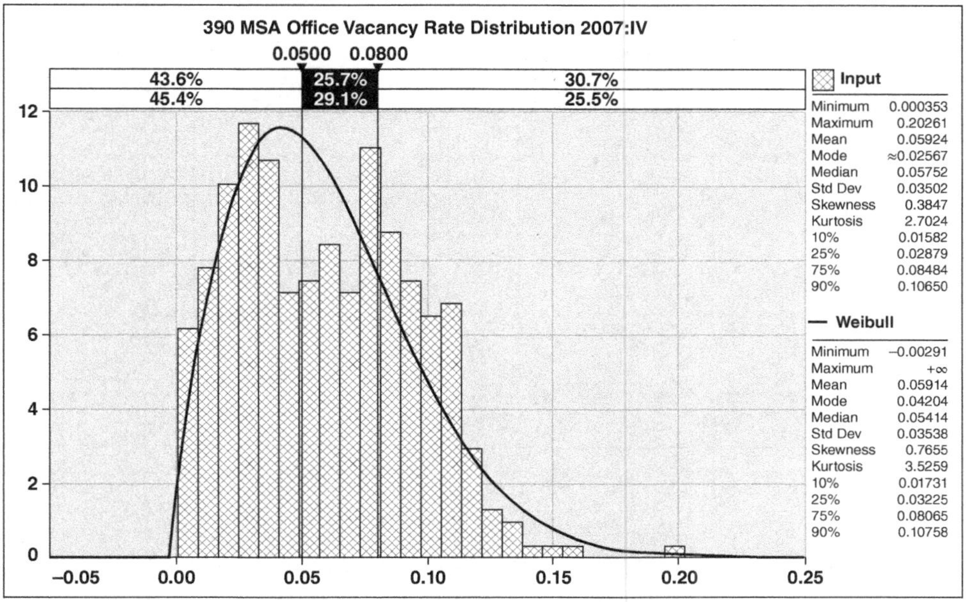

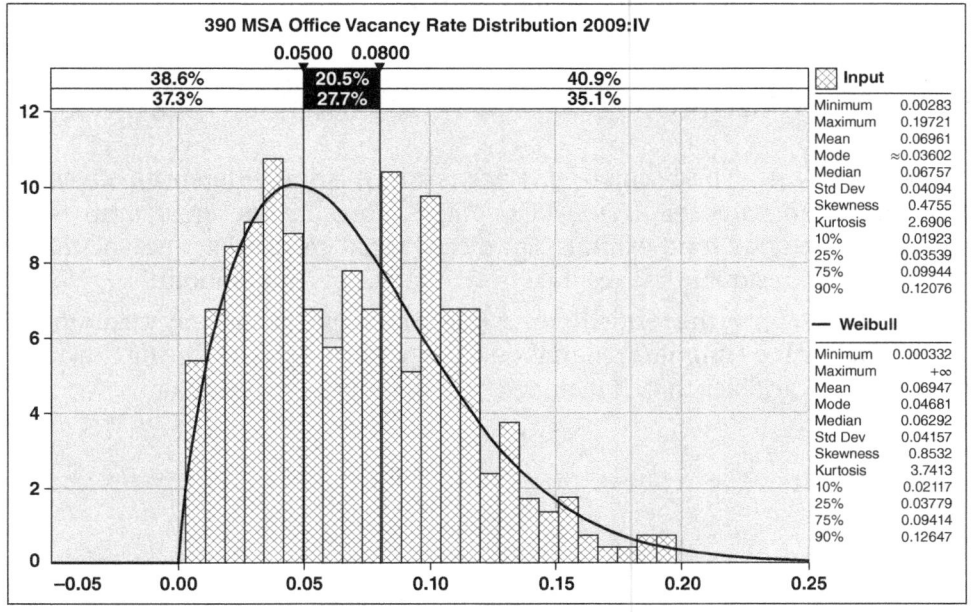

Source: ZCA using CoStar data

EXHIBIT 2.9 Vacancy rates increased as the distribution shifted to the right.

Source: ZCA using CoStar data

EXHIBIT 2.10 Random, no correlation.

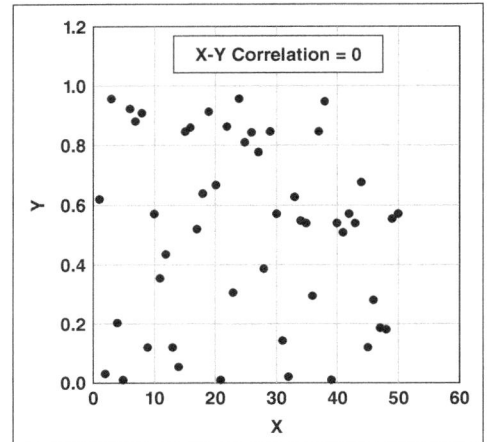

Source: ZCA

EXHIBIT 2.11 Circle, no correlation.

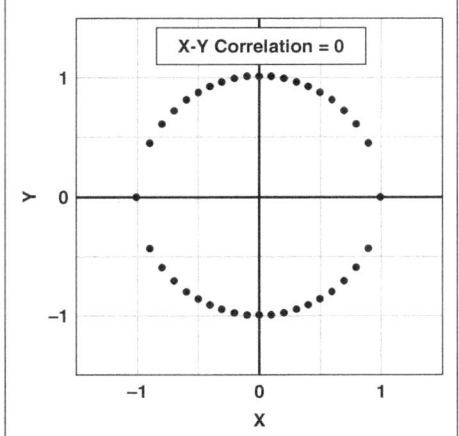

Source: ZCA using CoStar data

Beware of spurious correlations. For example, the importing of Japanese flat screens is correlated with the incidence of neurosis, but most people would likely agree that flat screens do not cause neuroses; they reduce stress.

Another example is the relationship between New York City office vacancy rates and rental growth. The line in Exhibit 2.12 is the following equation's econometric fit:

$$RENTALCHANGE_t = A_0 + A_1 \cdot VAC_t + \varepsilon_t \tag{2.1}$$

The slope is A_1. The residual, or error term, ε_i, is the difference between the actual and fitted value of RENTALCHANGE. Tracking the error term is very instructive. The error term exhibits significant serial correlation and volatility, as indicated by the residual. The residual in Exhibit 2.12 is not random.

Exhibit 2.13 shows the residual (thick line), the actual value (gray medium line), and the fitted value (thin line). Equation (2.1) performs poorly during downturns due to omitted variables that, if included, would reduce the residual.

EXHIBIT 2.12 Simple bivariate time series model of rental change and vacancy rate. The model has serial correlation.

EXHIBIT 2.13 Residual analysis: My simple model performs poorly during the DOT.COM recession, the GFC, and the COVID-19 recession.

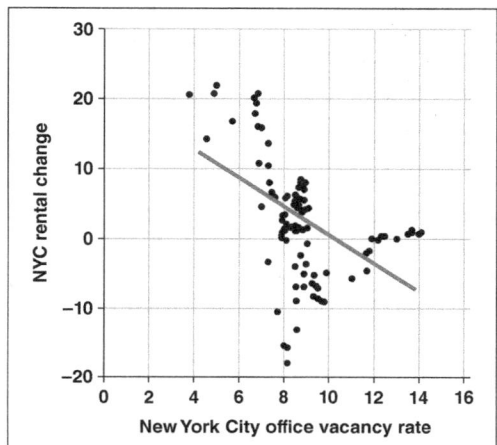

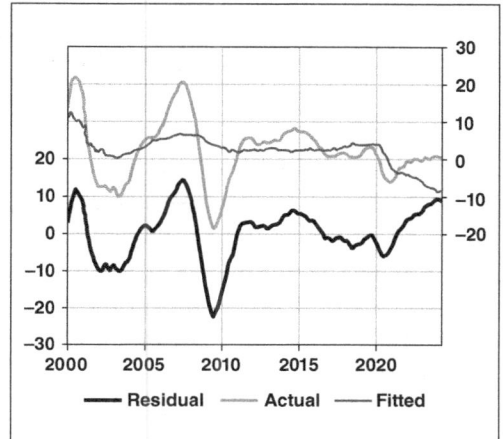

Source: ZCA using CoStar data

Source: ZCA using CoStar data

Serial correlation. Serial correlation of regression residuals biases coefficient estimates. The change in office rents is serially correlated with the previous period's rental change. Serial correlation can signal omitted variables. The coefficient on the lagged dependent variable, 0.938, is highly significant and close to one. The Durbin Watson statistic is low—the ideal is close to two—which confirms serial correlation. (T-statistics are in parentheses.)

$$RENTALCHANGE_i = \underset{(0.075)}{0.021} + \underset{(29.191)}{0.938} \cdot RENTALCHANGE_{t-1} + \varepsilon_i \tag{2.2}$$

Adjusted $R^2 = 0.899$

Mean of dependent variable $= 2.457$

Standard deviation of dependent variable $= 8.128$

Standard error of regression $= 2.588$

Durbin Watson statistic $= 0.408$

Observations $= 97$

Property returns are serially correlated, which causes investors to underestimate risk. See Chapter 10. The coefficient on the VAC in Equation (2.1) is -1.998, without correction, and -2.633, with serial correlation correction, a significant difference.

Serial correlation is not an unalloyed bad; it can indicate the presence of MSA illiquidity when traditional liquidity data, such as bid-ask spreads, are unavailable. I develop this point in Chapter 13.

The best fitting distribution: Letting the data speak. Risk analysis using Monte Carlo simulation requires distributions. Theory, but more often curve fitting, determines the shape of the distribution. Exhibit 2.14 shows a variety of distributions fitted to multifamily sales unit volume. Since sales volume is always positive, I reject the Weibull and normal distributions on theoretical grounds; the uniform distribution's fit is bad, which leaves the lognormal distribution.

The best distributions reflect the lowest Akaike Information Criterion (AIC), a score of the goodness-of-fit. The best fit is the log normal distribution (AIC = 4847), whereas the worst fit is the uniform distribution (AIC = 4997). The normal distribution has a better fit than the uniform distribution, but the normal distribution includes negative numbers. Sales are not negative, so I reject the normal distribution.

EXHIBIT 2.14 Fitting distributions to data.

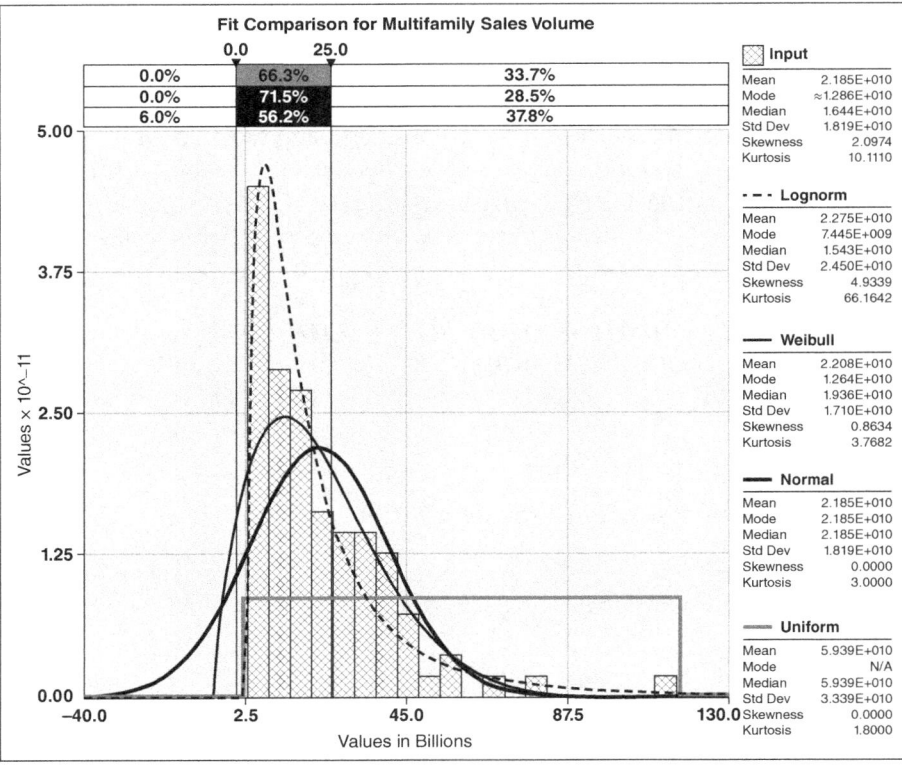

Source: ZCA using CoStar data

AIC is an estimate of prediction error and the relative quality of statistical models for a given data set. AIC provides one way to select the best models. AIC estimates the relative amount of information lost by a given model. The less information a model loses, the higher the quality of that model. In estimating the amount of information lost by a model, AIC makes a trade-off between the goodness of the model's fit and the simplicity of the model. AIC addresses the dual risks of overfitting and underfitting the model. Analysts should not neglect theory by relying just on statistical indicators.

People often reject quantitative analysis because it lacks "perfect" data. When the data are not plentiful, approximations can be useful. I recommend the "lack of knowledge" triangular distribution. Let's say we guess the minimum value (−50), the most likely value or mode (20), and a maximum value (40). The distribution is a triangle, as shown in Exhibit 2.15, which indicates that a value exceeding 20 occurs 22% of the time. Risk simulations are sometimes insensitive to the distribution's shape.

Box-whiskers: Another powerful way to represent data. Exhibit 2.16 is a box-whisker plot, which indicates the extent to which the means and dispersions differ; it includes the interquartile range (IQR), which spans the second and third quartile. Within the IQR are the median and the mean. The mean and the median are identical. In this exhibit, the data are skewed to the right. Beware of skewness.

EXHIBIT 2.15 The "lack of knowledge" distribution.

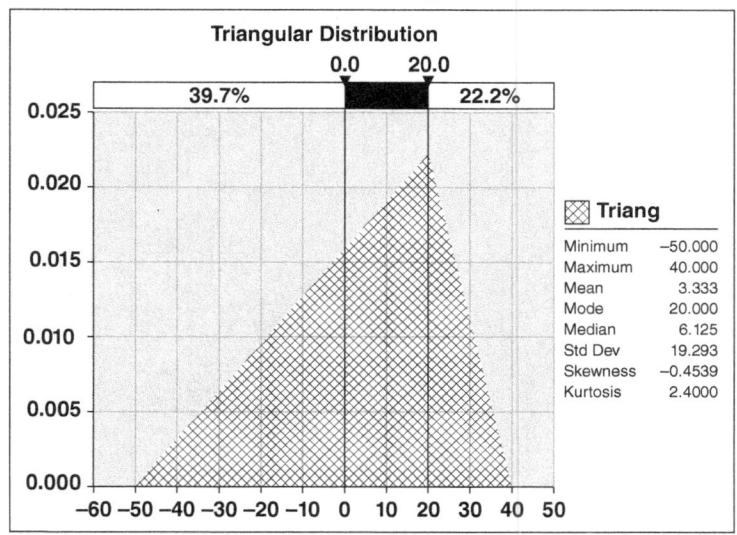

Source: ZCA

EXHIBIT 2.16 Box-whisker plot skewed to right with outliers.

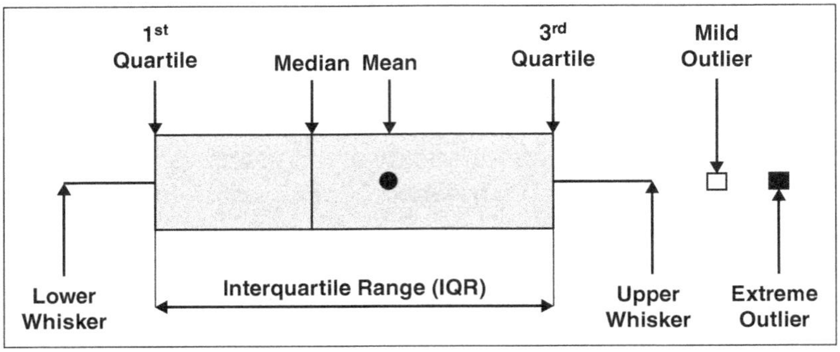

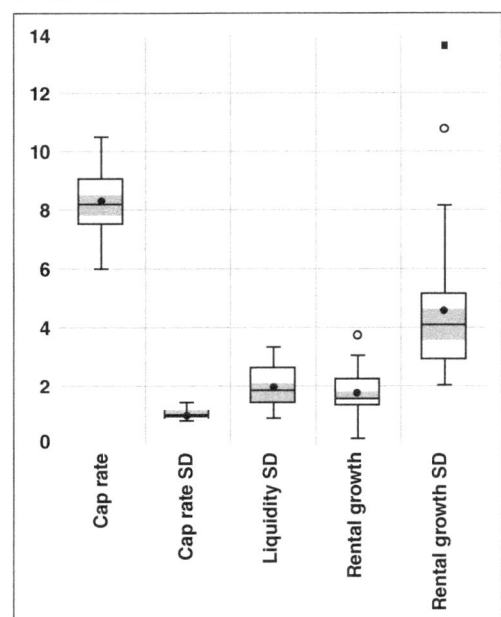

Source: ZCA

Exhibit 2.17 shows box-whisker plots for cross-sectional office variables and Exhibit 2.18 depicts the normal cap rate distribution for 390 Metropolitan Statistical Areas (MSAs). Compare this distribution with the box-whisker representation of cap rates. (Note that the box-whisker plots are rotated 90 degrees.)

EXHIBIT 2.17 Box-whisker plots of variables.

Source: ZCA use of CoStar data for estimation

EXHIBIT 2.18 MSA cap rate distribution.

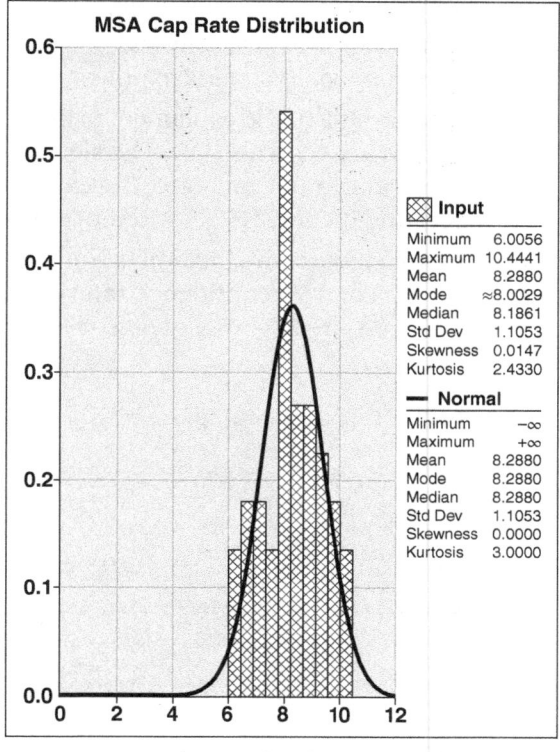

Source: ZCA use of CoStar data for estimation

Outliers that differ significantly from the rest of the dataset are plotted as individual points beyond the whiskers on the box-plot. Rental growth is highly skewed to the right.

Multiple Regression: The Econometric Workhorse

Multiple regression determines the influence of an independent variable on a dependent variable while holding other variables statistically constant. A bivariate regression includes only one independent variable.

Exhibit 2.19 examines office cap rates using multiple regression (Model 1) and bivariate regression (Model 2). Model 1 is a variant of the one discussed in Chapter 12. The bivariate regression includes only the vacancy rate; estimates of the coefficients are biased and the model's statistical power is nil.

The dependent variable, or variable to be explained, is the office capitalization rate (A). The coefficient estimates are shown in (B). The signs of the coefficients in Model 1 agree with theory. If vacancy rates increase, the cap rate should increase; the reverse is true for net operating income (NOI) and rental growth.

The coefficient estimates are significant since the t-statistics at the 95% confidence level are higher than 1.96. The 95% confidence interval (D) for the vacancy rate coefficient is 0.164 to 0.377. At the 99% confidence level, the interval is even

EXHIBIT 2.19 Two models of office cap rates: Multiple regression and bivariate. Which is best?

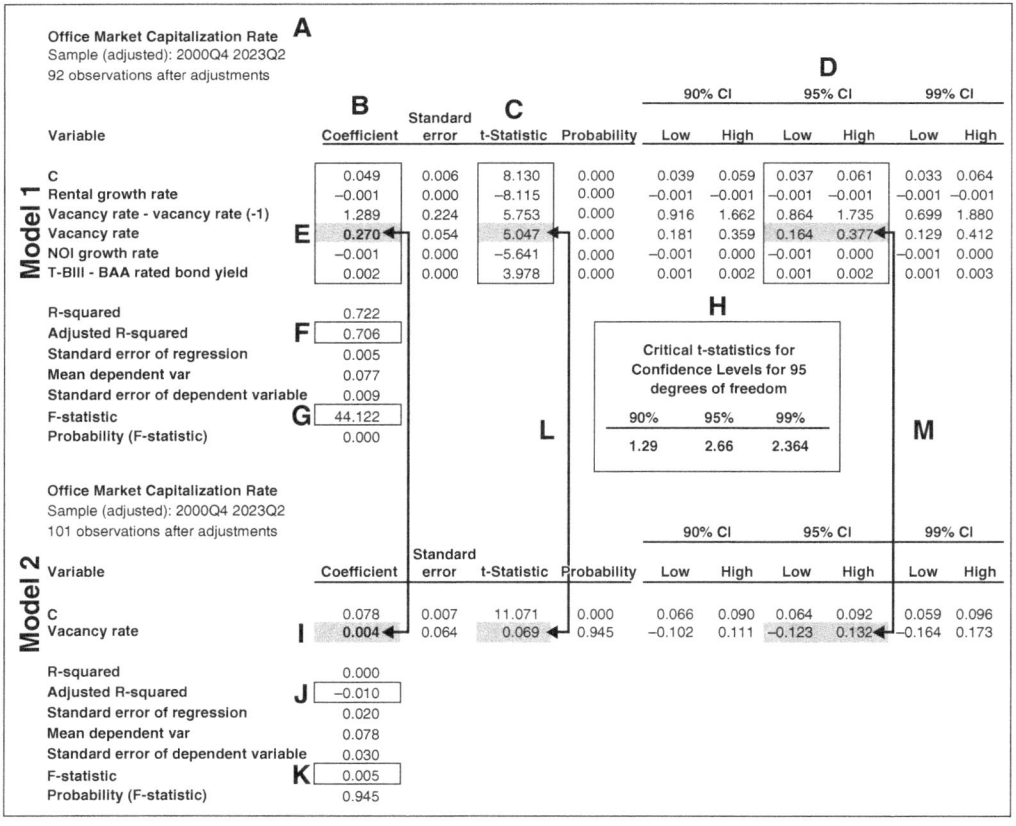

Source: ZCA using CoStar data

wider, 0.129 to 0.412. These intervals do not include zero, so we know that the coefficient is statistically different from zero.

Omitted variables: A common problem.[5] In Model 2, the vacancy coefficient is no longer significant—the t-statistic is low, 0.069, the 95% interval includes zero, and the sign is negative, all of which are inconsistent with theory (E). The cap rate should rise, not decline, when vacancy rates rise. The coefficient's estimate in Model 1, by contrast, is highly significant, but, in Model 2, it is insignificant. This is the effect of omitted variables.

Other statistical pathologies. Multicollinearity, indicated by a high correlation of the independent variables, interferes with our ability to determine the impact of each independent variable on cap rates.

Symptoms of multicollinearity include a high adjusted-R^2 with low t-statistics, and a nearly exact linear relationship among the independent variables.

Simultaneity, or two-way causation, is inherent in all markets. In some situations, where the focus is a small submarket, such as the market for self-storage units, we can safely ignore the impact that self-storage might have on GDP. In some cases, the issue cannot be ignored so an econometrician would likely use two-stage least squares to resolve the problem.

Senior management, which is usually interested in the coefficient estimate and not the confidence interval, essentially ignores risk. This is a mistake. The former gives the illusion of certainty—it is easy to add and subtract. The interval addresses uncertainty and the likelihood that the true value lies within this range.

Contingent Forecasting: Bayes Rule as a Practical Investment Analysis Tool

The good toolbox includes many useful tools. Bayes rule is a tool that every analyst should use.

Bayes Theorem shows how to update probabilities given new information. It addresses the challenge of contingent forecasting and the problem of false positives, which plagues manager selection. Examples include the diagnosis of disease and the search for skilled managers. These examples all deal with rare events.

A medical example illustrates this point. Let's say that breast cancer is relatively rare in the population, occurring about 0.5%. Mammograms are 95% accurate. What is the chance that a patient with a positive mammogram result has cancer? The answer is not 95%. The test is 95% accurate *only if* the patient *definitely* has cancer; the correct answer is 9.1%, which seems counterintuitive, but we are dealing with a rare event, a critical distinction.

Most doctors and money managers do not understand statistics much less accept the relevance of contingent statistical tools, such as Bayes Theorem. As a result, they leave value on the table, incur uncompensated risks, and give bad advice. In real estate, investors can lose money and fire their managers, often for the wrong reasons, but in medicine, people die and mistakes are buried.

The case of recommending good managers to pension fund investment committees. Bayes Theorem, which helps avoid false positives, allows updating the beliefs of an event based on new evidence:

$$P(A:B) = \frac{[P(B:A) \cdot P(A)]}{P(B)}. \tag{2.3}$$

$P(A:B)$ is the probability of event A occurring given that B occurred (posterior probability). $P(B:A)$ is the likelihood of event B occurring, given that A occurred. $P(A)$ is the prior probability of A occurring or your initial belief about A. $P(B)$ is the probability of B's occurring. The manager is unskilled but is perceived as skilled.

Considering all managers, P(NS) is the share of all managers who are definitely unskilled, or, as I estimate, 75%. P(NS) = 1−P(S) implies that skilled managers comprise 25% of the manager population. Let's say that the consultant can identify a skilled manager 20% of the time and an unskilled manager 70% of the time. P(S:NS) is the probability of the manager's being perceived as skilled even though the manager is unskilled; this is a *false positive*. Similarly, P(NS:S) is the probability that a skilled manager is incorrectly identified as unskilled, which is a *false negative*. The chance of recommending a seemingly skilled, but truly incompetent, manager to the investment committee, is 81.8%, even though 75% of all the managers lack skill.

Is the pension consultant incompetent? Maybe so, but she need not be if skilled managers are rare. As a former pension consultant, I know that differentiating skill from luck is very challenging. Can the typical investor do any better? Unlikely.

Application—How to calculate the likelihood of a false positive using Bayes Rule. Let's consider an example close to home: picking a manager. The likelihood of a false positive increases geometrically as skilled managers' share of the manager universe shrinks. Equation (2.4) calculates the probability of a false positive—the manager is incompetent but appears skilled—which is the ratio of the probability of identifying a skilled manager as unskilled divided by the sum of (1) the product of the probability of identifying a skilled manager as unskilled and the share of skilled managers in the universe of all managers, and (2) the product of the probability of correctly identifying an unskilled manager as unskilled and the share of unskilled managers in the universe of all managers. (See Exhibit 2.20.)

$$P(S:NS) = \frac{P(NS:S)}{P(NS:S) \cdot P(S) + P(NS:NS) \cdot P(NS)}$$

$$= \frac{.225}{.225 + .05} = .818 \text{ or } 81.8\% \qquad (2.4)$$

If 50% of the managers are skilled, then the likelihood of a false positive is 60%. However, if a skilled manager is a rare event, say 1 in 50, or 2%, then the probability of a false positive is still high, 98.7%. If we hire the very best consultant, then the likelihood of a false positive is 92.5%.

We should rethink how we interpret performance analytics. Good performance relies on the joint efforts of investment committees, pension consultants, and managers. This raises a question: When we fire managers, exactly whose performance are we measuring? The investment committee's performance? The consultant's performance? Do the data even permit us to make sharp quantitative distinctions? For

EXHIBIT 2.20 The contingent likelihood of picking the wrong manager.

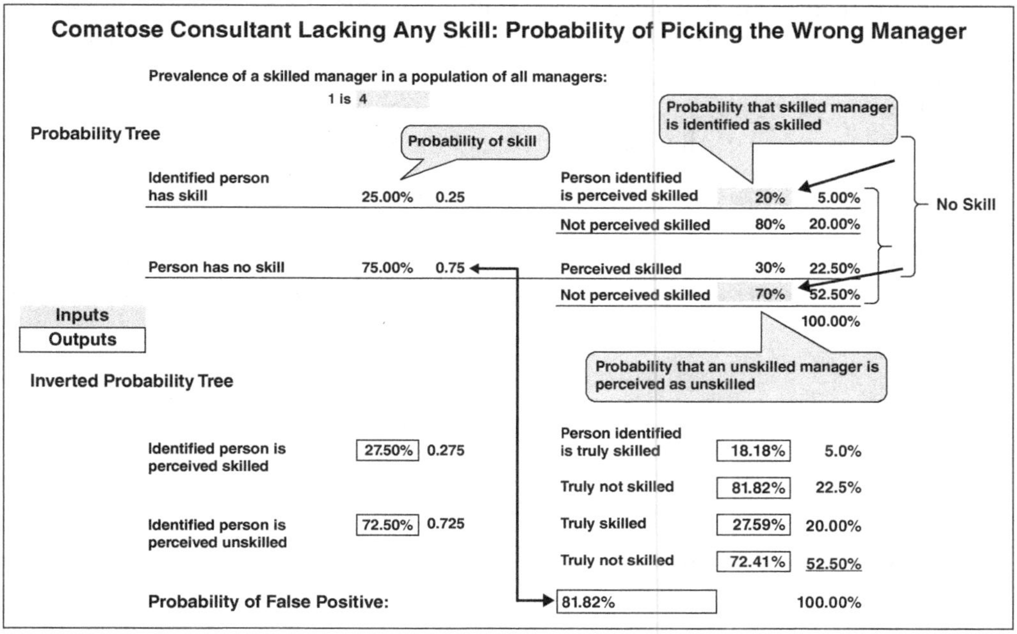

Source: ZCA; Sam L. Savages web site, FlawOfAverages.com

example, is there a statistically meaningful difference between a 10% return and a 12% return? Maybe not.

The likelihoods of accepting unskilled managers (false positive). I array the outcomes as shown in Exhibit 2.21.

When the pension consultant lacks any skill. In picking a skilled manager, what is the likelihood of a false positive? If we set each of the probabilities for which a skilled manager is perceived as skilled and for which an unskilled manager is perceived as unskilled to 100%—the case of the omniscient pension consultant—then the probability of a false positive is zero. Alternatively, setting each to zero—the case of the cognitively impaired consultant—increases the likelihood of a false positive to 100%, as shown in Exhibit 2.22.

What are the attributes of a great consultant and can we measure those attributes with high statistical precision? Some consultants instinctively draw unjustified conclusions that lack statistical support or they simply sidestep quantification entirely and emphasize instead the manager's reputation for probity and her ability to produce useful reports on schedule. Is the bar too low? Can good statistical methods support higher standards?

A graphical analysis. The degree to which a skilled manager is a rare event increases the likelihood of a false positive. Skill in spotting talent is more important if skilled managers are more common, consultants and investors have true selection skills, and manager attributes are easily observable. In practice, such is not the case. The probability of the occurrence of any one assumption may be low, but the likelihood of the presence of all three occurring at the same time is vanishingly small. (See Exhibit 2.23.)

EXHIBIT 2.21 Bayes matrix: False negatives and false positives, two kinds of error.

		Perceived	
		Not Skilled	**Skilled**
Actual	**Not Skilled**	True Negative TN 72.4%	False Positive FP Type I Error 81.8%
	Skilled	False Negative FN Type II Error 27.6%	True Positive TP 18.2%

Source: ZCA

Contingent Forecasting: Bayes Rule as a Practical Investment Analysis Tool   33

EXHIBIT 2.22   If the consultant is totally lacking in skill—I am not making any judgment here—the chance of a false positive is 100%.

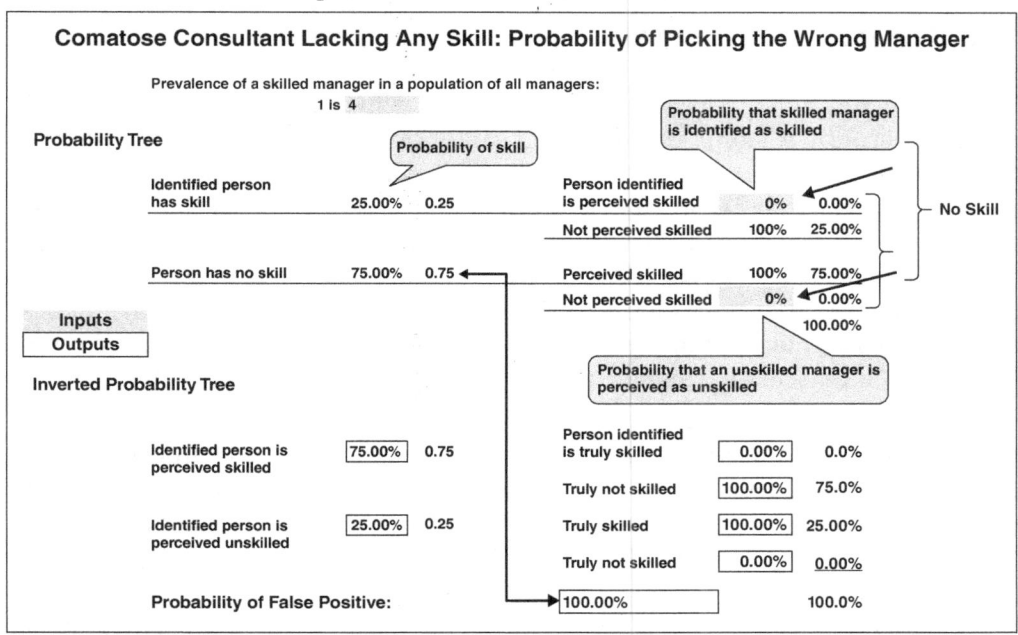

Source: ZCA; these calculations rely on a model found on Sam L. Savage's site, FlawOfAverages.com. Assumptions are my own.

EXHIBIT 2.23   False positive probabilities rise the rarer is a skilled manager.

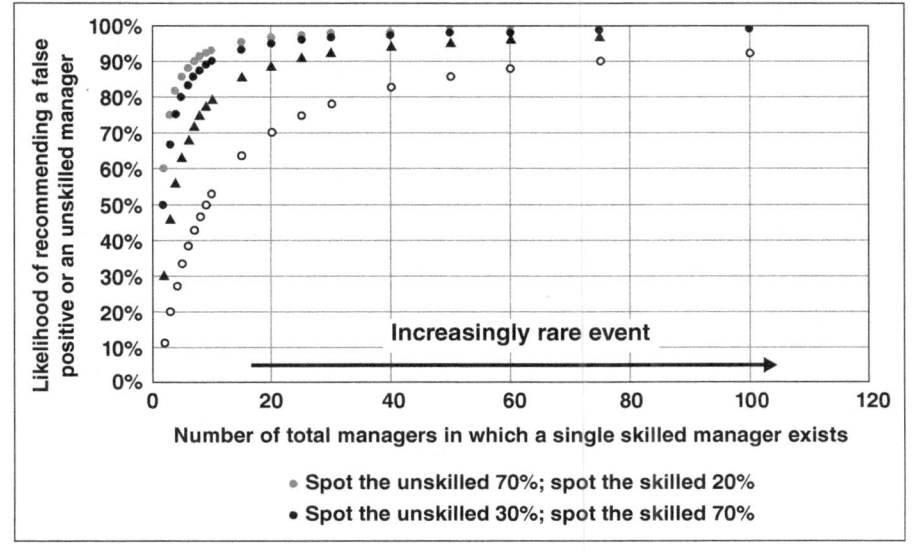

Source: ZCA

Monte Carlo: Not a Charming Town on the Mediterranean

Standard deterministic deal sensitivity analysis, which is flawed, entails tweaking each critical assumption separately and "optimizing" its value within its market-determined acceptable range. Even though each estimate is assumed independent and plausible, the joint probability of all values simultaneously equaling their independent "optimum" is close to zero. Brokers have raised this approach to an art form; they call it, "creating excitement in the marketplace." The assumption is that averages are sufficient, but they are not. Some brokers know that, but are less than forthcoming. This manipulation contributes to the Winner's Curse, which I discuss in Chapter 19.

Monte Carlo analysis is different; it accounts for every possible value that each variable could assume and weights each possible scenario. The computer samples each probability distribution, constrained by a correlation matrix. This constraint eliminates absurd results, such as a building boom when interest rates are high.

Chapter 15 includes a Monte Carlo analysis of a highly structured joint venture with a promote, a limited partner (LP) and general partner (GP), and leverage. The uncertain variables are the rental growth and the exit cap rates. As the holding period increases, uncertainty increases.

Questions include, What is the probability that the LP will receive a return of capital or lose her capital? What is the value of the option to escalate rents in five years or to expand the building in three years on an adjoining lot?

Advocates of softer methods often complain that Monte Carlo analysis gratuitously introduces irrelevant assumptions. No, it makes hidden assumptions explicit when transparency is needed the most.

Stochastic Arithmetic Using Monte Carlo Analysis

Simple arithmetic is not so simple when we introduce uncertainty. Using probability distributions, I demonstrate how correlation and volatility affect the confidence interval and potential downside of the variable, C.

Subtracting two stochastic variables: C = A − B. The difference between A and B is 3, whether we are dealing with uncertainty or not. If the correlation is −1, then 50% of the distribution of C, as shown in Exhibit 2.24, is in the range of −3.7

EXHIBIT 2.24 Subtraction, A − B; correlation = +1.

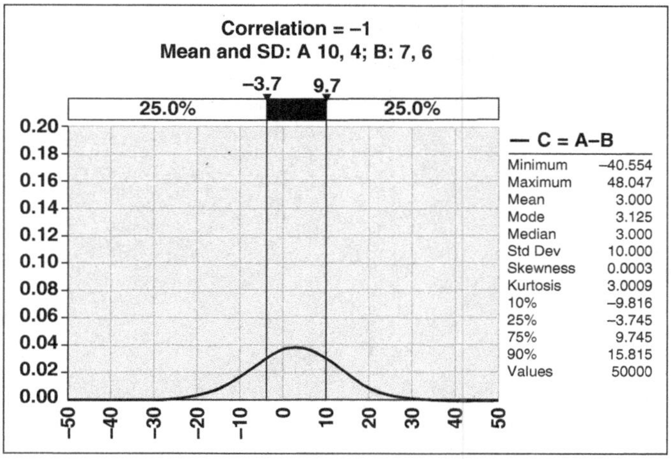

Correlation = −1
Mean and SD: A 10, 4; B: 7, 6

	C = A−B
Minimum	−40.554
Maximum	48.047
Mean	3.000
Mode	3.125
Median	3.000
Std Dev	10.000
Skewness	0.0003
Kurtosis	3.0009
10%	−9.816
25%	−3.745
75%	9.745
90%	15.815
Values	50000

Source: ZCA

to 9.7. If the correlation is +1, then this range becomes 1.7 to 4.3, because A and B move in the same direction, preserving spread, as indicated by the lower standard deviation of the distribution in Exhibit 2.25.

	Mean	Standard Deviation
A	10	4
B	7	6

Source: ZCA

If we increase the standard deviation of A in relation to B, the standard deviations of both distributions increase. The increase is greatest when the correlation is −1.

Adding two stochastic variables: C = A + B. Adding two stochastic variables with the same assumptions presented below produces opposite results. A negative correlation narrows the distribution but a positive correlation widens it. Increasing the standard deviations of A and B simply widens both distributions. (See Exhibits 2.26 and 2.27.)

	Mean	Standard Deviation
A	10	4
B	7	6

Source: ZCA

EXHIBIT 2.25 Subtraction, A − B; correlation = +1.

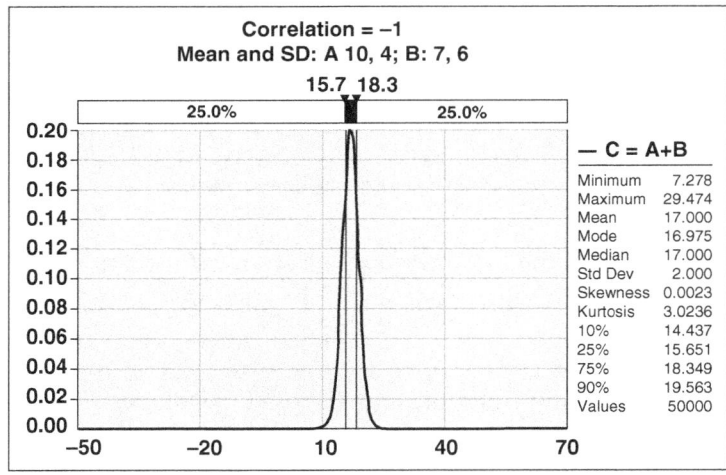

Source: ZCA

EXHIBIT 2.26 Addition, A + B; correlation = −1.

Source: ZCA

EXHIBIT 2.27 Addition, A + B; correlation = +1.

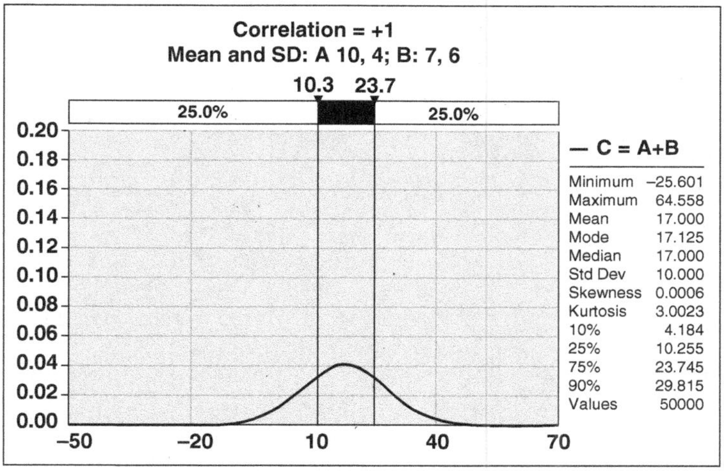
Correlation = +1
Mean and SD: A 10, 4; B: 7, 6
10.3 23.7
25.0%
25.0%
— C = A+B
Minimum –25.601
Maximum 64.558
Mean 17.000
Mode 17.125
Median 17.000
Std Dev 10.000
Skewness 0.0006
Kurtosis 3.0023
10% 4.184
25% 10.255
75% 23.745
90% 29.815
Values 50000
0.20
0.18
0.16
0.14
0.12
0.10
0.08
0.06
0.04
0.02
0.00
–50
–20
10
40
70

Source: ZCA

Dividing two stochastic variables: Cap Rate = NOI/Price. The impact on dividing two stochastic variables depends on the correlation between the numerator and denominator. Cap rates are less volatile than their components, NOI and price. In this example, price is more volatile than NOI, largely due to interest rate and credit shocks.

	Mean	Standard Deviation
NOI	100	20
Price	1,000	75

Source: ZCA

If the correlation is −1, then the spread and cap rate volatility increase, which, in reality, is not the case. The true correlation is positive, which implies that the cap rate is less volatile than its components. (See Exhibits 2.28 and 2.29.)

In Chapter 15, I simulate a joint venture and apply these very principles to modeling the exit cap rate and deriving the distributions of the internal rates of return (IRRs) and the equity multiples for the LPs and the GPs.

EXHIBIT 2.28 The cap rate distribution when the correlation is −1.

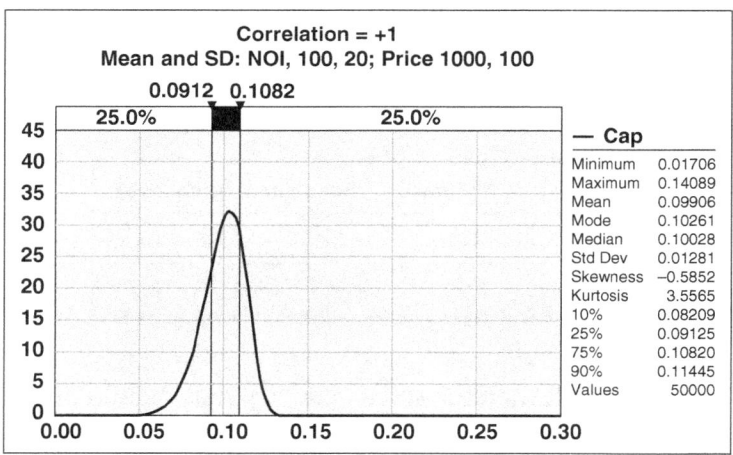

Source: ZCA

EXHIBIT 2.29 The cap rate distribution when the correlation is +1.

Source: ZCA

Attributes: A Trip to Stochastic Grocers

Real estate is an asset consisting of many attributes, none of which the market prices separately. To better understand real estate, we must deconstruct the attributes in order to estimate their value.

Some attributes, such as neighborhood quality, are measured with uncertainty and may require proxy variables, which then introduce additional sources of uncertainty. Hedonic analysis, which I use, is a tool for pricing attributes; it is capable of retrieving hidden information.

Are the implicit attribute prices constant over the business cycle and across property markets and submarkets, property types, owners, and tenants? What is the income elasticity of demand for certain attributes and does this demand increase or decrease during recessions? Which attributes are necessities or luxuries?

An apples-to-apples comparison. I estimate attribute prices and show the impact of omitted variables. Let's say we are visiting Stochastic Grocers to buy fruit. Normally, when we go to the grocery store, we select items reflecting our preferences and each item's price. The cashier scans the prices and computes the total bill.

This grocery is very different. You never see items' prices; you only see the price per bag and a list of items contained within the bag. Let's buy 50 bags of fruit, each containing up to 7 varieties; each bag is labeled with a total price and quantities of each fruit.

If all we know is the total price of each bag and the number of its items, can we recover the prices of each item just with this information alone? Fortunately, the answer is yes and the correct tool is hedonic analysis. What if we only have 1 bag instead of 50 bags? We would not be able to retrieve the prices because we have seven unknowns and only one observation. We lack sufficient degrees of freedom. The greater the number of bags, the more precisely we can estimate fruit prices.

A property is a composite good just like a bag of groceries. Think of each fruit as an attribute. When we buy a bag of groceries, our objective is to consume the contents of the bag. Similarly, when we buy a house, we seek to benefit from its many attributes.

Stochastic grocer. The grocer, not the buyer, knows the prices of each fruit. In fact, our mischievous grocer memorizes, but does not reveal, the following prices in Exhibit 2.30.

Exhibit 2.31 shows 50 bags in which I randomly select between zero and 20 quantities of various fruits. "Price" is the price per bag where prices and quantities are known with full certainty. The cashier's memory is faulty (or stochastic)

EXHIBIT 2.30 Secret fruit prices known only to the stochastic grocer.

Apples	Oranges	Pineapple	Mango	Banana	Kiwi	Lemons
$0.60	$0.79	$2.69	$1.69	$0.20	$0.79	$0.69

Source: ZCA

40 CHAPTER 2 Statistics, Monte Carlo, Bayes Rule, Stochastic Arithmetic

EXHIBIT 2.31 Fifty bags of fruit and known fruit counts: What is the price per item of each fruit?

Bag	Price	Apples	Oranges	Pineapple	Mango	Banana	Kiwi	Lemons	10 X Normal
1	$42.44	11	10	2	4	4	12	8	$36.28
2	$73.90	10	4	10	8	19	12	16	$88.45
3	$98.98	16	12	15	10	19	16	9	$102.65
4	$62.77	6	14	11	3	11	9	6	$56.20
5	$74.61	16	5	14	6	14	8	6	$71.05
6	$61.07	12	13	2	16	10	9	3	$60.56
7	$63.62	13	7	10	7	3	13	1	$58.41
8	$76.91	16	7	10	11	6	6	15	$80.98
9	$72.13	10	8	5	19	18	3	12	$63.99
10	$74.40	15	2	18	1	3	0	19	$65.81
11	$53.21	3	17	5	11	9	0	6	$57.51
12	$51.27	9	7	5	12	0	4	5	$51.10
13	$95.18	3	14	14	18	15	2	14	$96.69
14	$68.88	4	4	18	4	19	2	4	$65.66
15	$43.00	17	8	6	4	10	2	0	$45.36
16	$82.03	8	6	14	14	11	0	13	$91.64
17	$66.71	4	4	10	14	10	10	1	$75.38
18	$80.62	19	13	6	13	10	9	17	$91.94
19	$66.36	2	4	7	11	3	19	13	$70.27
20	$60.84	14	0	9	7	10	6	14	$63.38
21	$107.33	17	4	19	18	4	6	10	$100.38
22	$81.94	12	12	18	5	3	2	9	$87.43
23	$72.95	19	1	11	4	13	18	11	$51.83
24	$73.50	14	3	15	2	17	18	2	$92.09
25	$86.28	18	6	12	13	1	18	3	$83.32
26	$70.82	4	2	13	6	10	11	16	$77.55
27	$61.15	11	5	3	13	13	14	10	$71.32
28	$73.23	6	15	11	6	1	6	19	$94.30
29	$62.25	15	11	8	1	13	15	10	$79.65
30	$68.10	11	10	7	9	6	18	6	$68.07
31	$78.83	7	15	8	15	12	4	15	$71.54
32	$60.33	3	8	6	11	4	15	7	$57.44
33	$41.97	13	5	1	5	16	7	15	$29.92
34	$91.14	2	6	13	14	10	18	15	$86.41
35	$76.14	10	3	8	18	17	7	10	$90.31
36	$63.66	10	1	6	14	4	4	19	$52.86
37	$63.44	18	11	0	16	15	8	11	$64.54
38	$71.17	12	8	10	5	0	16	14	$93.41
39	$57.12	12	7	1	12	4	13	15	$58.35
40	$73.19	1	7	19	5	1	4	6	$67.08
41	$80.82	4	3	15	6	3	15	19	$88.84
42	$87.28	11	11	12	8	17	14	17	$91.00
43	$73.93	4	5	9	19	8	0	14	$78.97
44	$97.85	4	19	13	12	10	18	13	$98.19
45	$77.76	13	11	18	1	4	7	7	$84.59
46	$85.26	14	13	14	1	3	18	18	$94.90
47	$107.99	15	17	19	15	10	2	8	$101.38
48	$76.03	0	11	7	19	5	16	4	$87.18
49	$120.40	8	18	18	18	19	8	18	$129.79
50	$70.19	3	5	4	15	5	18	19	52.48

Source: ZCA

and the prices may be approximate, so we must allow for error. "10× Normal" is the price per bag plus 10 times the standard deviation of a unit normal curve, the mean of which is zero. The price per bag after adding an error term to the calculation of price reflects price uncertainty. "Price" and "10× Normal" tend to diverge more as uncertainty increases.

Using ordinary least squares, I then regress the price of each bag on the quantities of each kind of fruit in each bag and solve for a_i, the implicit price of each kind of fruit, as shown in Equation (2.5).

$$Price_i = C + a_1 APPLES_i + a_2 ORANGES_i + a_3 PINEAPPLE_i + a_4 MANGO_i$$
$$+ a_5 BANANA_i + a_6 KIWI_i + a_7 LEMON_i + \varepsilon_i \qquad (2.5)$$

The term, "ε_i", is an error term. (I do not include the error term in every regression.)

Exhibit 2.32 shows regressions assuming certainty and uncertainty; the latter includes four cases of uncertainty defined by the multiple of the standard normal distribution. The regression for the case of complete certainty provides exact estimates of attribute prices. R^2, which measures the percentage of the total price variance explained, is 100%. I do not report the t-statistics, which are very high.

As long as we know the exact quantity of each fruit, we can recover the prices with complete accuracy as long as the sample size is large When I introduce some random error, the R^2 falls and the estimates' precision declines.

I add five times the variance of the unit normal distribution to the bag price:

$$Price_i = -1.37 + 0.55 * APPLES_i + 0.96 * ORANGES_i$$
$$+ 2.74 * PINEAPPLE_i + 1.60 * + 0.26 * BANANA_i$$
$$+ 0.88 * KIWI_i + 0.73 * LEMON_i + \varepsilon_i \qquad (2.6)$$

The true price of oranges is $0.79, but the regression yields $0.96 with statistical error.

What is the message for real estate investors? Since properties are illiquid and trade infrequently, low transactions volume and quality changes introduce measurement error. Most appraisers' attempts to price these attributes is marred by insufficient data, omitted variables, and poor econometric techniques, all of which cast a shadow on the potential bias of appraisals and other attempts by managers to estimate price.

EXHIBIT 2.32 Implicit fruit prices under complete certainty and varying degrees of uncertainty.

		Certainty	Error term: Multiple of standard normal distribution							
			1		2.5		5		10	
			Coefficient	T-Statistic	Coefficient	T-Statistic	Coefficient	T-Statistic	Coefficient	T-Statistic
APPLE	a_1	0.60	0.59	21.60	0.57	8.41	0.55	4.01	0.49	1.81
ORANGE	a_2	0.79	0.82	28.07	0.88	11.93	0.96	6.55	1.13	3.86
PINEAPPLE	a_3	2.69	2.70	96.59	2.72	38.87	2.74	19.63	2.80	10.01
MANGO	a_4	1.69	1.67	59.17	1.64	23.28	1.60	11.32	1.51	5.33
BANANA	a_5	0.20	0.21	8.54	0.23	3.69	0.26	2.08	0.32	1.27
KIWI	a_6	0.79	0.81	34.15	0.84	14.13	0.88	7.45	0.97	4.12
2.LEMON	a_7	0.69	0.70	27.46	0.71	11.16	0.73	5.73	0.77	3.01
R-squared		1.00	0.996		0.978		0.919		0.745	

Source: ZCA

The problem of omitted variables. What happens if our cashier mislabels the bags? Instead of writing the price of the bag and the quantity of all seven kinds of fruits on the outside of each bag, the cashier carelessly omits pineapples but records the bag price and the quantities of the other six fruits. Can we then, *even in the case of full certainty*, accurately estimate the implicit prices of each kind of fruit? We cannot.

No matter how large the number of bags, our estimates are biased due to omitted variables, a serious problem indicated by Equation (2.7). Compare the t-statistics and R^2 with Exbibit 2.32. The omission of a critical variable introduces not only inefficiency (i.e., lower precision for the overall regression and for the estimate of all six implicit prices) but bias as well; the estimates are inconsistent. It is like shooting arrows at a target; all the arrows may be tightly grouped, which shows good efficiency, but the group is four inches away from the bullseye, an indicator of significant bias.

Due to this omission, the error term is correlated with the right-hand explanatory variables—the quantities of each of the six fruits—which violates one of the basic assumptions of ordinary least squares.

$$PRICE_i = 38.64 + 0.34 * APPLE_i + 0.30 * BANANA_i + 0.35 * KIWI_i + 0.80 * LEMON_i$$
$$(4.08)\ \ (0.86)(0.84)(1.03)(2.15)$$

$$+ 0.87 * MANGO_i + 0.99 * ORANGE_i + \varepsilon_i$$
$$(2.19)(2.30) \tag{2.7}$$

$R^2 = 0.301$

Adjusted $R^2 = 0.203$

Standard error of the regression $= 14.416$

Mean dependent variable $= 73.620$

F-statistic $= 3.087$

Prob (F-statistic) $= 0.013$

The estimated implicit prices bear little resemblance to the actual prices even though the bag prices and the quantities of each of the six fruits are known with complete certainty. The Adjusted R^2 plummets from 100% to 30% and half of the t-statistics are insignificant. See Equation 2.7.

Attention analysts! Beware. A challenge in applying regression analysis to real estate is identifying the relevant characteristics of a property. Omitting a critical attribute biases the estimates of other implicit prices. Worse, we might draw unfounded conclusions from the flawed analysis. No matter how much additional data we collect, the specification problem remains and our estimates are biased and likely useless.

Creating a price index—the problem of sample size. Let's say that we draw two samples of 10 bags each from an unchanging population of 50 bags. We label samples 1 and 2, respectively, "2009" and "2010." The likelihood that each year's sample contains the same number and distribution of fruits is low. Therefore, assuming that prices do not change, chance variation in quantities will lead to differences in average price per bag. The first sample, we label "2009" and the second, "2010." Note that we keep prices of each kind of fruit constant. The average price per "2009" bag could be $73.60 on the first 10 draws and $67.36 on the second set of draws for the "2010" bags. Based on the two samples alone, an observer might conclude that the average price of fruit had declined 8.5% when, in fact, prices had not changed at all. Without taking account of the quantity of fruit in each bag, we might erroneously conclude that prices had declined, when, in fact, they had not.

When constructing price indexes, literally comparing apples with apples is important! Let's say that the prices of fruit change from 2009 to 2010, but that the prices of apples and pineapples, for example, move in opposite directions. The price of apples increases from $0.60 to $0.70, while pineapple prices decline from $2.69 to $2.25. Our sample of bags may or may not suggest a change in prices. However, if we had a standard bag that contained the same amount of each fruit in years 2009 and 2010, we could detect that the standard bag had changed. In our example below, every price, except the price of pineapples, increases. Indeed, fruit prices averaged item-by-item across the seven fruit categories irrespective of quantity weights has increased by 14%. Moreover, in reality, only the price of pineapples has declined. Our standard bag, which holds quantity constant, shows that the price of bags has decreased by $4.49, or 6%, because pineapples constitute a large average share of the items in each bag. (See Exhibit 2.33.)

Performance indexes. This index problem affects real estate performance indexes. Without controlling for changing attribute mix, we cannot be confident that property prices and cap rates have changed and, if so, by how much? The cap rate distribution shifts over time and across markets. Cap rate distributions in overheated markets are typically skewed to the left, as they were in 2009. The median does not change as much as the mean and the extreme tails.

Is the hedonic price of each property's attribute the same over the cycle and are some attribute prices more demand inelastic over time and across markets? Variations in the unadjusted sample characteristics might indicate that cap rates had fallen when in fact they had risen.

EXHIBIT 2.33 The mechanics of quality-adjusted index numbers.

	Apple	Orange	Pineapple	Mango	Banana	Kiwi	Lemons	Bag
				Fruit prices				
2009	$0.60	$0.79	$2.69	$1.69	$0.20	$0.79	$0.69	
2010	$0.70	$0.90	$2.25	$1.75	$0.30	$0.95	$0.75	
			Standard bag (amount of each kind of fruit)					
	4	3	19	2	3	14	8	
				Revenue				
2009	$2.40	$2.37	$51.11	$3.38	$0.60	$11.06	$5.52	$76.44
2010	$2.80	$2.70	$42.75	$3.50	$0.90	$13.30	$6.00	$71.95
			Fruit price increases from 2009 to 2010, $					
	+$0.10	+$0.33	−$0.44	+$0.06	+$0.10	+$0.16	+$0.06	−$4.49
			Individual fruit price increases, %					
	17%	14%	−16%	4%	50%	20%	9%	
	Standard bag change, identical numbers of fruit for 2009 and 2010, −6%							

Source: ZCA

Benchmarks. Benchmark design is another application. Benchmarks often do not fit the manager's style. The benchmark used for LP returns from a mildly leveraged core investment is inappropriate for a highly leveraged unlisted opportunistic fund. Managers purposely recommend and investors accept low-bar benchmarks, which make every manager, no matter how unskilled, look like a winner. Some investment committees and consultants benefit because they themselves "picked a winner."

Conclusions and Investment Implications

- Real estate investors, their managers, and consultants live in an uncertain, or stochastic, world, but act as if the world is deterministic.
- A distribution or histogram is the face of uncertainty.
- Investors should demand that managers provide better risk analytics.
- Averages lull investors into a coma of certainty.
- Too many investors and managers confuse correlation with causation.
- Stochastic arithmetic demonstrates the surprising role of correlations of distributions.
- Standard sensitivity analysis is flawed and misleading.
- Models force clarity, sometimes at the risk of oversimplification.
- Good models reveal knowledge gaps and suggest new questions.
- The omitted variable problem is a major source of bias in econometrics and simple bivariate graphs.
- Model misspecification and poor sampling introduce uncertainty.
- The rarer the event, the greater is the likelihood of false positives, which is why picking a skilled manager is so difficult.
- Quantitatively differentiating skilled from unskilled managers is a statistical challenge that in the end lacks precision.
- Determining the value of property attributes, which do not trade in the market, requires the use of appropriate econometric tools.

Q&A: Interview with Professor Joseph L. Pagliari, Jr., John Mazarakis and Chicago Atlantic Clinical Professor of Real Estate, The University of Chicago

Public Pension Funds and Open-End Real Estate Funds: Pathologies and Misalignments

What seems preferable today: A high- or low-volatility strategy?

At least to-date, the risk-adjusted returns of low-volatility strategies dominate high-volatility strategies, after accounting for fees and leverage. Leverage is poorly understood by most practitioners. Leverage does not improve risk-adjusted returns; it's merely beta, not alpha. Not only does leverage dramatically increase the volatility of your returns (e.g., when leverage goes from zero to 50%, the volatility of returns is doubled), it also increases the expected value of the general partner's promoted interest (which is essentially a call option on the fund's future performance—like any option, its value increases with the volatility of the underlying security); accordingly, limited partners would be better served by computing the promote based on unlevered returns.

These insights are not widely embraced, much less understood. Ironically, investors are reluctant to leverage core beyond 25% but have no problem with 75% leverage on non-core deals. The reverse should hold: Place more leverage on the core and less on the non-core funds.

Why then do public pension funds invest in highly leveraged non-core deals?

Many public-sector (defined-benefit) pension plans are massively underfunded. The political realities often lead to "gambling for redemption" by investing in highly levered value-added and opportunistic real estate funds,

(continued)

(*continued*)
where the higher expected rates of return on these funds enable the pension plans to game the actuarially estimated present value of future benefits. Many politicians are all too eager to kick the financial can down the road.

What about the marks of open-ended funds?

In normal periods, the estimated net asset value (NAV) of the open-ended funds is reasonably close to the "true" market value. However, this comes undone during market downturns. Because market transactions are few during a downturn, some of these funds resort to marking their assets "to model," rather than "to market." The paucity of transaction volume provides cover for slow-moving and inflated marks. This smoothing lowers the reported volatility, thereby making the private-market real estate returns look more compelling than they really are.

These slow-moving marks typically lead to redemption requests (as some investors look to arbitrage the inflated NAV estimates). When the redemption requests become unmanageable, the fund's general partner erects "gates" slowing the exodus of capital. This happens for funds targeting institutional investors as well as those targeting individual investors.

Candidly, I think many investors are unrealistic in their demands for liquidity during a market downturn. It is not sensible to believe that these private-market vehicles can provide full liquidity in such periods. We've seen this movie before (e.g., the late 1980s/early 1990s and the period following the global financial crisis); sophisticated investors should know better.

Is there an incentive for the GP to report inflated marks during a downturn in order to generate higher fees?

There are two aspects to this question: (1) When the investment management fee is computed on the current estimated NAV (as is typically the case for core and core-plus funds), the inflated marks produce higher fees. (2) Regardless of how the investment management fee is computed, all general partners want to show their track record in the best possible light—since, all else equal, a better track record tends to lead to better future fund raising.

Are the benchmarks set too low?

The pension plans' internal benchmarks usually are set too low, are inappropriate for the strategy, and produce style drift in the investment managers. However, just about everyone benefits (except the taxpayer, who ultimately backstops this deception). The lower the benchmark, the greater the likelihood that: (1) the pension plan's senior staff receives their bonuses; (2) the consultant (who helped devise the benchmark and helped set the plan's investment strategy) is rehired; and (3) the plans' trustees (many of whom are political appointees) can tout the remarkable fund performance achieved under their watch (and thereby assuage the trepidation some pension beneficiaries and/or taxpayers feel about the safety of the future retirement benefits).

Why are you a critic of gateway cities?

Most of the so-called gateway cities have significantly underfunded pension plans. These cities have balance sheets which exhibit financial distress; in such instances, state and local officials tend to make sub-optimal decisions. Consequently, services (schools, police, firefighters, infrastructure, etc.) are cut and taxes are increased. Both outcomes are bad for tenants, lenders, and owners. For some time now, taxpayers have voted with their feet, further undermining the viability of some of these cities. The pertinent question is: Are investors being sufficiently paid (via higher going-in capitalization rates) for taking on these risks? My reading of the tea leaves is that they are not.

PART II
The Building Blocks: Public, Private, Equity, and Debt

CHAPTER 3

What Is Real Estate? Leases, Buildings, and Cities

Preliminaries

Real estate, which consists of financial claims on cash flow, is not just about bricks, mortar, space, and location. It is much more.

Real estate is risky and replete with embedded options, the value of which reflects volatility. Investors typically ignore these options.

Buildings are durable but so are airplanes and cruise ships. Unlike planes and ships, however, office buildings are fixed in space. Fixity, the essence of property, confers defining characteristics: Virtually identical buildings with the same tenancy and physical characteristics, but located on different streets in close proximity to each other, generally have different values and rents. By contrast, the value of a cruise ship is the same whether moored at the docks or sailing 300 miles off the coast.

Adam Smith, the Size of the Market, and the Division (Segmentation) of Labor and Property

Adam Smith, the great 18th-century English economist and the author of *The Wealth of Nations*, wrote that the market's size dictates the division of labor.[1] I would add "… and the proliferation of building types." Describing a building as office, retail, residential, industrial, or even hotel is no longer sufficiently specific.

Is the aesthetic essence of the *Venus de Milo* or *Aphrodite of Melos* adequately represented by its shadow? Clearly not, and property is no exception. Property is multidimensional; it consists of many attributes, none of which trades separately. The market implicitly assigns prices to these attributes, but with error. (See Chapter 2.)

The property market today is highly differentiated. Distinct building types have exploded in number. For example, the nature of the office function itself has changed since the advent of simple accounting during the fourth century BCE in Mesopotamia. Office buildings as a building type were not necessary during the agrarian period, but writing was. If office space existed at all, it was combined within a different building type, such as a temple or a palace.

During the Middle Ages, the Church, the nobility, and the crown relied on the work of cloistered monks. Before Luther and the Gutenberg press, access to and control of knowledge was jealously guarded by the Church. The office function, which had not evolved much, awaited the emergence of broad-based literacy, complex organizations, the democratization of knowledge, and the start of the industrial revolution. Out of this cauldron of revolutionary and technological change eventually emerged the office building and many other building types.

Industrialization, the Rise of Capitalism, and the Evolution of the Building Type

Technological innovation and the need for office-related services drove the proliferation of office buildings and the refinement of the office building type. Innovations included the steel frame, electricity, new forms of lighting, air conditioning (cooling as well as ventilating), and the elevator. Floor plate sizes increased with innovations in lighting. Factor substitution, which is the change in the ratio of one input to another, characterized the office building, especially in the downtowns. Higher floor-to-land area ratios—substitution of physical capital for land—and more skilled workers—greater human capital per person—occurred. The demand for office services grew and did so at an accelerating rate as the economies became more knowledge-based. While space per worker increased, the rise in technology per worker was even more dramatic; more devices and gigabytes of information per employee raised worker productivity. The computer and eventually the microchip further reduced space per capita, a substitution effect, but it also made labor much more productive, an income effect. New transportation technologies led to the adoption of the automobile and the orthogonal street grid, the suburbanization of various uses, including office buildings, and the expansion of the urban boundary. Floor-to-land area ratios declined with cheaper land and distance from the CBD. This process accelerated with urbanization.

Urbanization, the percentage of the population living in urban areas, is 56% worldwide and 80% in the US. Suburbanization, which is the dispersion of population from centers to the urban periphery, is the most pervasive and ubiquitous phenomenon of the 20th century.

High floor-to-land ratios support high densities in developed countries. New York's MSA has a population of 21,396,000 (6% of total US population) and a land area of 6,720 square miles. Density is 3,184 people per square mile.

By comparison, Dhaka, Bangladesh, lacks New York's infrastructure and its diversity of building types. Its population is 19,134,000 or 11.2% of its national population; density is 162,152 people per square mile. Without capital-to-land ratios similar to those of wealthy, primate cities, such densities are possible only through extraordinary crowding and poverty.

The densest portion of the New York MSA is 72,129 people per square mile and is dwarfed in density by many cities in the developing world.

Property as a portfolio of leases and unleased space. Property is a hybrid asset with debt- and equity-like features. Leases are debt substitutes with bond characteristics. The joint responses of leases and leveraged equity to shocks—inflation, interest rates, market rental rates, credit spreads, tenant defaults, and credit—determine value.

Exhibit 3.1 is a schematic of a property's lease structure. One firm, Firm 6, signed two separate leases, one for each floor. Each lease includes equity-like embedded options, such as the property owner's option to escalate rents at a specific time. The undulating line in the lower part of the diagram represents fluctuating market rental growth. The building has high vacancy rates during a weak market when rental growth rates are negative. Leasing quickens as the market recovers.

EXHIBIT 3.1 Stylized lease structure and hypothetical market rental growth with forecast showing confidence intervals.

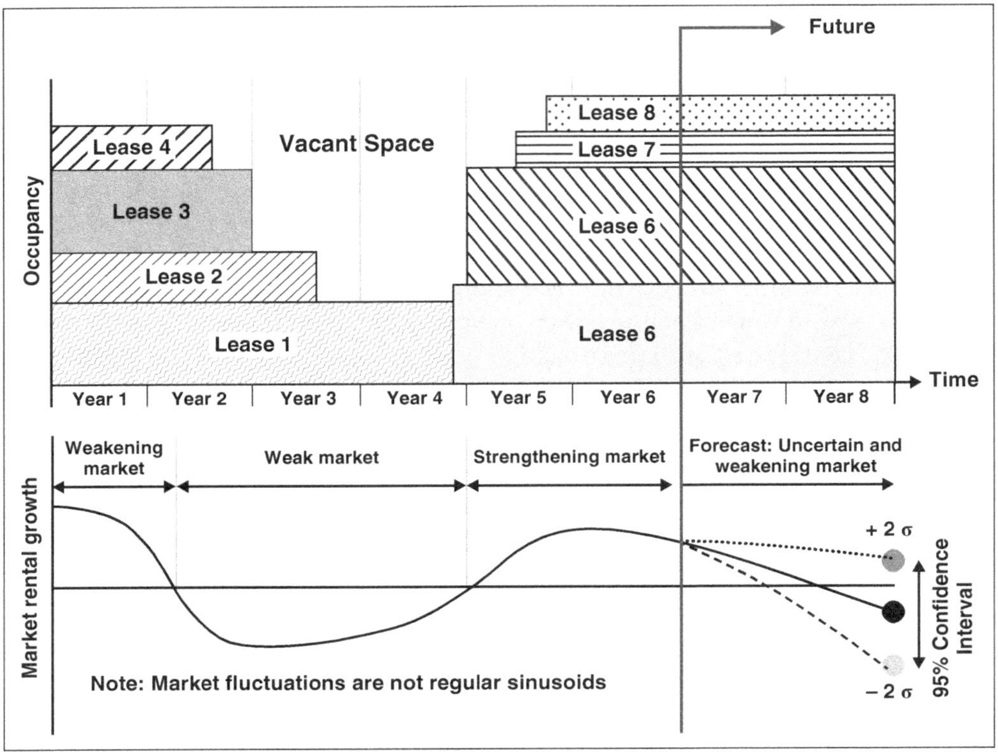

Source: ZCA

The forecast period begins to the right of the vertical line labeled "Future." The dotted bands are 95% forecast confidence intervals. MSA-level excess demand, which affects cash flow, is a source of uncertainty as are the exit cap rate, market rental rate, and expenses. Additional considerations include the term structure of leases, credit spreads, and the likelihood of tenant default and loss.

Capital markets act promptly but the property and the leasing markets take a while to react fully to changes in interest rates and prices. By contrast, total returns across MSAs are less variable than vacancy rates and mask the extreme differences that characterize MSAs operationally, e.g., vacancy and rental rates.

Impact of interest rate volatility. Even though a rise in interest rates hurts the value of in-place leases, many leases specify contract rents that are substantially below prevailing market rates. The rising value of the unleased equity offsets the eroding value of in-place leases.

Similarly, during the 1980s and the early 1990s, as well as during the GFC, interest rates and real estate property returns fell. The gain in the value of the in-place leases was not sufficient to compensate for the steep drop in real estate equity values.

Rising interest rates alone decrease the value of in-place leases, provided that the spread of lease rates over Treasuries does not narrow. If rates rise when leasing fundamentals are improving and asset prices are strengthening, a reduction in the risk premium, expressed by the lease credit spread, could partially offset the price-depressing effect of rising nominal interest rates. Property returns are often, but not always, negatively correlated with interest rates.

Cash flow, value, and the many sources of risk. Property value is the sum of all future cash flows (including any final proceeds of sale, the so-called residual) discounted to the present. (The symbol, $\sum$, is shorthand for summing the numbers to the right from the first year to the terminal year, T.) The discount rate equals the appropriate Treasury rate, R_t plus a risk premium associated with the property, δ, and an inflation risk premium, ρ.

$$VALUE_t = \sum_{t=1}^{T} \frac{CASHFLOW_t}{(1+R_t+\delta+\rho)^t} \tag{3.1}$$

A widely accepted but false assumption is that CASHFLOW increases at a constant growth rate, μ. Trees do not grow to the sky. This makes little sense, especially over an extended period during which supply and demand conditions are highly variable. However, for expository purposes, I incorporate this assumption:

$$CASHFLOW_t = CASHFLOW_0 * (1+\mu)^t \tag{3.2}$$

Thus, unleveraged property value equals the following:

$$VALUE_t = \sum_{t=1}^{T} \frac{CASHFLOW_0 * (1+\mu)^t}{(1+R_t+\delta+\rho)^t} \tag{3.3}$$

Inflation can differ from the cash flow growth rate due to changes in market rental growth rate changes following supply–demand shocks. These shocks need not be highly corrected with inflation. The growth rate, μ, can be less than, equal to, or greater than the sum of the interest rate, the risk premium associated with the property, and the inflation risk premium. If spreads remain constant and cash flows increase faster than inflation, $\mu \geq \rho$, property value increases. Property values rise if the rental growth rate tracks inflation, but lease credit spreads narrow.

If the yield curve shifts upward due to stronger economic growth, then leasing volume and tenant credit quality will likely increase despite rising interest rates. As a result, R_t then increases, δ decreases, and inflation, ρ, rises.

Cash flows are volatile due to changes in rents and expenses. If rents weaken, the operating break-even point declines and δ falls. Thus, δ can fall even if leasing markets do not materially improve. If investor uncertainty declines regarding property or leasing, δ falls even if vacancy rates remain high. If interest rates increase due to inflation, which they need not do, declining discount rates might partially offset the rate rise.

When the economy is weak, business failures are widespread, property markets are fragile, and spreads widen, as they did in the office market beginning in 2023. While interest rates can rise, which itself is negative for real estate, spread narrowing may partially (or even completely) offset the rate increase effects. If office lease spreads return to their long-term equilibrium, then spread narrowing, even without an increase in expected cash flow growth rates, could fully offset even a substantial increase in long-term real interest rates or inflation. See Exhibit 3.2.

The values of the leases and the equity need not move together over time. For example, in a declining real estate market, cash flows decline. Eroding expected cash flow leads to a decline in property value and an increase in property risk, δ. However, interest rates and inflation may either be increasing or decreasing during the period.

Any of the many factors that determine value can offset or overwhelm other factors at any given moment, and these factors are themselves uncertain. The value of the equity in particular may be negatively correlated with the value of the leases, thus suppressing total return volatility. Other relationships in rising and falling real

EXHIBIT 3.2 Valuation for three real estate investment climates.

	Three Real Estate Investment Scenarios		
	Declining NOI	Stable NOI	Growing NOI
Treasury rates, i_T	↓↑	↓↑	↓↑
Tenant risk premium, δ	↑	↓↑	↓
General inflation, ρ	↓↑	↓↑	↓↑
Growth in cash flow, μ	↓	No change	↑

Source: ZCA

EXHIBIT 3.3 Depending upon the directions of rental growth and interest rates, the present value of the leases and the equity may be negatively correlated, thus reducing total return volatility or risk.

Case	Rental Growth	Interest Rates	PV of Leases	PV of Unleased Space	New Effect: PV of property
A	Rising	↑	↓	↑	↓↑
B	Rising	↓	↑	↑	↑
C	Falling	↑	↓	↓	↓
D	Falling	↓	↑	↓	↓↑

Source: ZCA

estate markets are possible depending on the direction of nominal interest rates. Exhibit 3.3 shows that total unleveraged property returns are less volatile in Cases A and D because interest rates, rents (and tenant credit quality) move in the same direction.

Cases B and C are the most volatile and risks are greater: Property prices tend to move rapidly up or down when the leases and the equity are all pulling in the same direction. In Cases A and D, the net effect of changes in the present value of the leases and of the equity depend on the magnitude of each of these changes. Depending on the expected pre-debt, pre-tax cash flows, rising rates may render a property difficult, if not impossible, to finance at current prices. If the owner must transact in a high-rate environment, the owner might face capital rationing that reduces sale proceeds and results in a steep price discount. Some owners may access preferred equity to fill a funding gap, as they did in 2024 and 2024.

Leveraged real estate. Real estate may be financed with equity alone or with equity and debt. The value of unleveraged real estate and its relationship to interest rates is, as mentioned above, determined by the leases. When real estate is leveraged with debt, any change in property value with respect to interest rates will depend on how closely the debt payments match the anticipated lease cash flows. If they roughly match, the leveraged real estate is less sensitive to changes in interest rates. Thus, if property is leveraged, depending on whether the leverage is fixed or floating, leverage can partially hedge the effects of interest rates on lease value. Leverage is a short position. If the borrower's payments roughly match the anticipated lease cash flows, then what remains is just the equity.

Why Do Cities Exist?[2]

MSAs, which include the central city, satellite clusters, and adjoining counties and economically connected towns, exist due to the benefits of centralized exchange and production. Because households and firms are not self-sufficient, they exploit comparative advantage by forming cities. Buildings are not just fixed in space; they are embedded in cities and the cities themselves are part of a broader complex economic, social, and political network of metropolitan areas and regions. If the following were true, there would be no cities: (1) equal productivity of the land; (2) costless transportation; (3) constant returns to scale in exchange—unit costs are constant irrespective of the size of the transaction; and (4) constant returns to scale in production.

Households then would be self-sufficient and there would be no trade; autarky would prevail. Economic activity would be uniform over space, land rents would be equal everywhere, and population would be distributed evenly. None of these conditions exist, so we have cities of various sizes, densities, linkages, and specializations. An evolutionary process is at work. Of all the cities and towns that ever existed, most have not survived and those that have now play a much-diminished role.

The economic benefits that cause firms and households to locate close to each other are called agglomeration economies and the forces that act on firms within a single industry are called localization economies. Agglomeration economies that spill across industry sectors are called urbanization economies.

Scale economies exist if a proportionate change in inputs leads to a greater than proportionate change in output. The reverse is diseconomies. Proximity can often provide scale economies and economies of scope, wherein a firm produces a variety of products. Scale economies are crucial to the existence of cities. In the absence of scale economies, goods and services can be produced at an arbitrarily small scale. Agglomeration economies include the benefits of input sharing, labor pooling, skills matching, knowledge spillovers, and innovations.

Cities are the home of dense economic and social networks, the two operating together to facilitate knowledge transfer and technological change, an essential driver of growth. Concentration and city size enhance worker productivity. As the number of firms increase in a cluster, profits increase, but there is a natural limit regarding the growth of any one sector, its city, the region, or even the nation.

Conclusions and Investment Implications

- The volatility, or risk, of cities, regions, and nations differs.
- Real estate is a claim on cash flow produced by buildings or land.
- The value of physically comparable buildings can vary within a city block.
- The division of the labor market and the proliferation of distinct building types are a function of market size.
- Property, which is a hybrid asset, is a portfolio of debt, equity, embedded options, and debt-like substitutes, called leases.
- Agglomeration is the essence of a city. Economies of scale, heterogeneous land, and costly transportation are necessary conditions.
- Urbanization is the process by which populations increasingly live within urban areas. High ratios of capital-to-land facilitate high densities per square mile. The highest densities are found in the developing world.
- Cities whose inventories adjust slowly to demand shocks have supply curves that are highly inelastic with respect to price and rents. These cities adjust primarily through rental volatility.
- Faster growing cities have a higher transactions demand for vacant space. Each city has its own natural vacancy rate, the rate at which rental change is zero.
- Total return volatility is higher in growing cities. Managers' pursuit of leveraged growth, ignoring risk, often results in misalignment and lower-than-expected risk-adjusted returns.

Q&A: Interview with Michael Fascitelli, Chairman, MDF Capital

My Journey Through Market Crises

Describe your journey.

Having grown up in a lower-middle-class Italian immigrant family, I had come from a different world. I was the first to attend college—the University of Rhode Island. I graduated in 1982 and was accepted at Harvard Business School, which gave me exposure and self-confidence. I was a factory worker before attending Harvard. After Harvard, I worked for McKinsey and then in 1985, I left for Goldman Sachs. I was made partner in 1992 and left Goldman for Vornado in 1997.

Describe life during the S&L crisis and the early 1990s.

Due to the RTC meltdown, Goldman dramatically reduced its workforce. Using many of the skills I learned at McKinsey, I helped restructure the real estate department. The RTC crash, caused by tax law changes, oversupply, and FIRREA, while generally restricted to real estate, was tough for Goldman.

The withdrawal of capital from real estate, a capital-intensive asset, was a disaster. The old players were wounded and could not get out of their own way; the younger ones, lacking legacy problems, pioneered the rise of the UPREIT and CMBS, both of which recapitalized the sector. The traditional sources, such as the life companies, were no longer players. The opportunity fund business grew out of the 1990s and this was a pivotal moment in our careers.

My partner, Dan Neidich, and I launched Whitehall, a series of real estate funds dedicated to buying defaulted loans and distressed properties at a considerable discount to replacement cost. Raising money for the first fund was really hard. This first fund was one of the most successful ever; funds two through four were also very successful.

Real estate was still not quite the institutional investment class in 1983 that it is today. Timing was everything. If you were too early in the 1990s, you got killed. So many firms had no choice but to go public, but there was a public-markets cost such as more covenants, new restrictions, and greater market scrutiny.

When did you leave Goldman?

I left Goldman Sachs in 1996 and joined Vornado in 1997 as its president. At the time it was a relatively small company. Pricing was still favorable. I became CEO in 2009.

We had an incredible run at Vornado. The stock was at a low of $20 when I joined and peaked in 2007 at about $130. The GFC was an existential challenge; the stock price fell from $100 to $20 and we were fearful after the Lehman bankruptcy for the company's survival, but we had a strong balance sheet. The year 2009 was the low point; our stock hit $5. Looking back, we did not take advantage of the low pricing; we should have been more aggressive, because that's how you make money in real estate, but proceeding aggressively would have at the time put the company at risk. Survival was our obsession. Not many people took advantage of the downturn because they were not properly capitalized and fear ruled the day. There was no liquidity.

Discuss your outlook for office.

The dynamics of the office sector are tough to predict. Work from home has permanently changed the office business. During COVID-19, the market differentiated amenity versus non-amenity buildings more closely. Some older inventory will be consigned to a slow death and conversion will be a minor help. There will be less need for marginal quality space. Demolitions will play some role. Generally, investing in suburban buildings has been a bad bet. There was a short-term boost due to COVID-19.

How should we deal with risk?

AI is hard to ignore. I hope the quality of information will improve. There is a generation of people who did not grow up with the new tools, including risk metrics. The new risk-based models are useful, especially if they suggest the right questions to ask. To be successful, you still need a good feel and excellent judgment.

Give us an example of some myths and challenges.

Investors should focus more on the cash flow yield and less on the cap rate, which ignores tenant improvements and capital expenditures. We have a valuation issue. If your required return is a 5% return on cash, instead of a

(continued)

(*continued*)

5% cap rate, the value changes dramatically. Since the older inventory is not trading, we do not know the extent of the damage as yet.

The politics of fiscal finance are not favorable for office, especially given the erosion of urban tax bases. Tenants want to feel safe. They seek amenities and public services.

Another concern is the dependency on 10-year projections and the IRR; typical analyses ignore the many kinds of risk that arise. The exit risk can be huge. I expect that with mathematically more advanced models, such as Monte Carlo, we will adopt shorter projection periods.

Strong balance sheets that can sustain shocks are essential. If there is a break in the capital markets and you lack capital, you have a problem. If you get the timing wrong, you are dead.

What advice would you give young professionals?

Go with the best firm where you will underwrite many deals. Work with the smartest people. During market distress, there are fewer jobs, but during that period, if you can find a job, you will learn a lot. I benefited from world-class deal flow, bright clients, and great colleagues.

CHAPTER 4

The Capital Stack, Optimal Leverage, WACC, and Mortgage Default

Preliminaries

Why study the capital stack? The balance sheet of the firm includes assets and liabilities; the liabilities side of the balance sheet includes debt-like instruments as well as equity. Assets and liabilities must balance, but they need not move together.

The equity holder must pay the creditor the face amount of debt. If the creditor defaults, bankruptcy can result. Creditors during liquidation receive all proceeds up to the amount of their claims. Equity investors are the residual claimants. Recapitalization can occur in which old securities are canceled and new ones issued. Hence, net worth, equity, or the pension surplus are stochastic.

Not all securities trade in liquid public markets. Hence, ascribing value and assessing risk can be difficult. Public securities can be helpful in valuing private securities using spreads and other considerations. In many cases, liabilities are not marked-to-market, so true net worth can be elusive.

What Is the Capital Stack?

Volatility affects the value of components of the capital stack. The capital stack includes senior debt, mezzanine or sub-debt, and equity. (See Exhibit 4.1.) Mezzanine debt includes preferred equity, which is important during times of high interest rates and lower LTVs, during which time a funding gap often emerges. The capital stack includes the equity, which is a call option, the value of which increases with volatility of the underlying asset. The creditors are long the firm and short the call option held by the investors. (This section benefits from the research of Kenneth Garbade.[1])

Exhibit 4.2 shows non-recourse senior debt. The loan is non-recourse due to the presence of a put option, in essence an insurance policy, as shown in Exhibit 4.3. The value of the put option increases as the value of the property declines below F_1. (See Exhibit 4.1 for nomenclature.) In a bankruptcy, the senior lender receives proceeds up to F_1. The equity holders are long an option with a strike price $F_1 + F_2$, while the senior creditor is short an option with a strike price of F_1, so the equity holders are long a different option than the option written by the senior creditors.

Who owns the option written by the senior creditors? Who wrote the option held by the equity holders? The subordinate creditors are long an option with an exercise price of F1, which is the price they would pay to acquire control. The subordinated

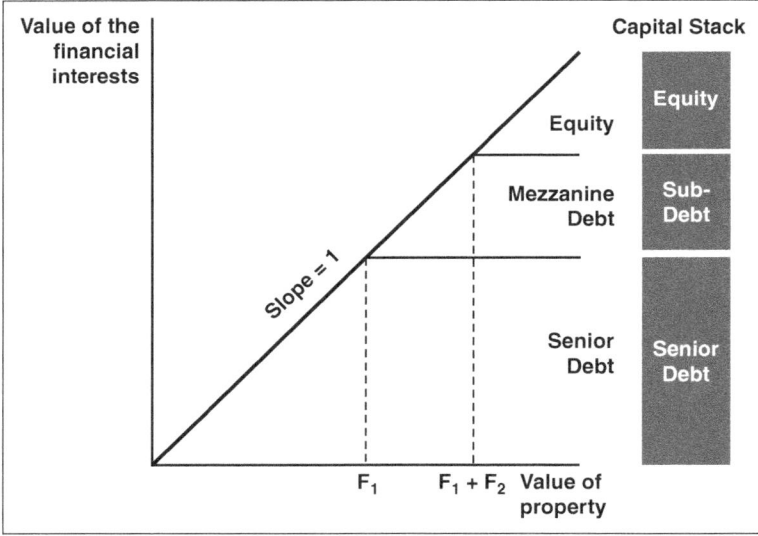

EXHIBIT 4.1 The capital stack.

Source: ZCA and Kenneth Garbade

EXHIBIT 4.2 Non-recourse debt.

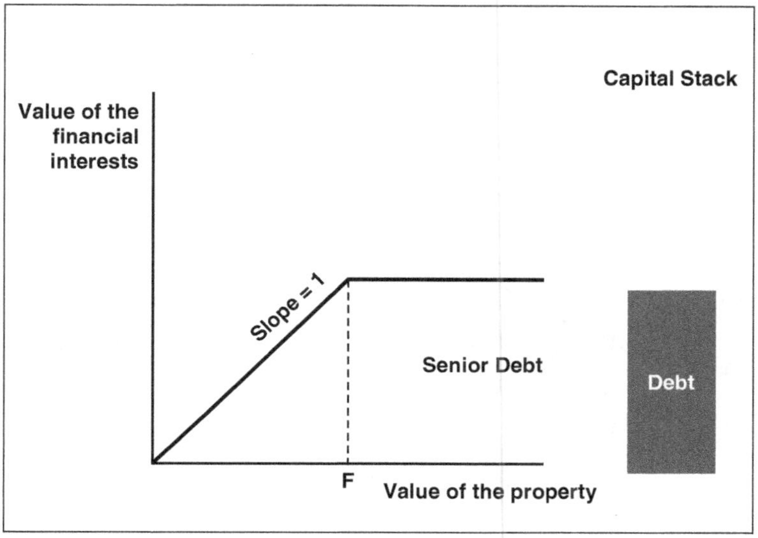

Source: ZCA and Kenneth Garbade

creditors are short a call option with an exercise price $F_1 + F_2$ because the equity holders can acquire control from the subordinated creditors by paying $F_1 + F_2$ and what they paid to senior creditors, F1, or F2, which is the face amount of the debt held by the junior creditors.

The lower priority of the subordinated debt in the event of bankruptcy reduces the contingent value of the debt prior to bankruptcy and enhances the value of the senior debt. Seniority and subordination are concepts that affect debt values before the debt matures. When the value of the firm falls below F_1, the senior creditors in effect own the firm. (See Exhibits 4.1 and 4.2.)

The equity holder owns a put option, which is like an insurance policy and is a feature of non-recourse debt. (See Exhibit 4.3.) The exercise value is the absolute value of the difference, F_1 minus the value of the firm. The mezzanine debt is subordinate to the senior debt. (See Exhibit 4.4.)

Some pension funds invest in property through their managers who, on their behalf, borrow non-recourse. However, these very pension funds refuse in the event of a downturn to exercise the put (or default) option themselves for reasons that include avoiding adverse publicity. The tendency to invest through a commingled fund sometimes cures this hesitancy by shifting the default decision to the fund manager.

EXHIBIT 4.3 The put option that creates non-recourse debt.

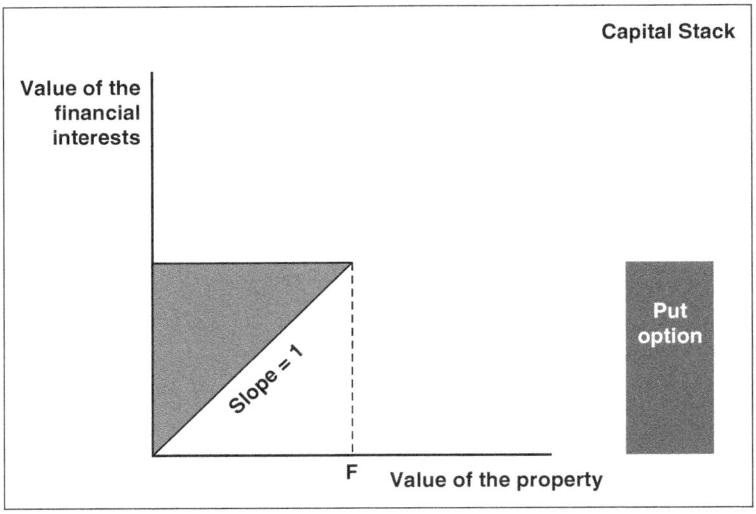

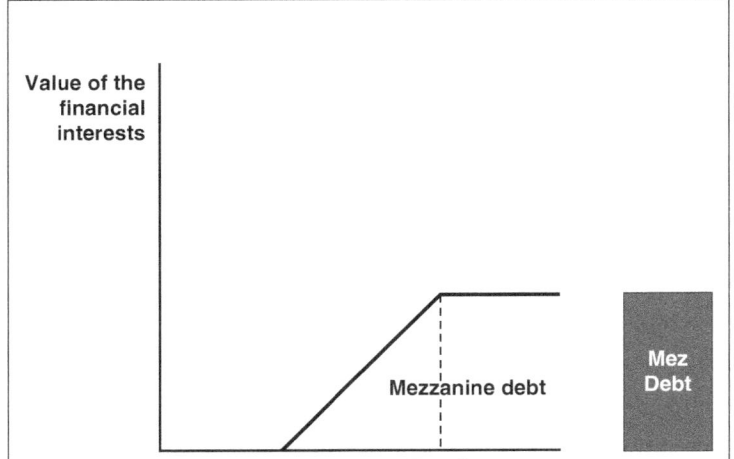

Source: ZCA and Kenneth Garbade

EXHIBIT 4.4 Mezzanine debt is senior to the equity and junior to the senior debt.

Source: ZCA and Kenneth Garbade

EXHIBIT 4.5 The equity is a call option.

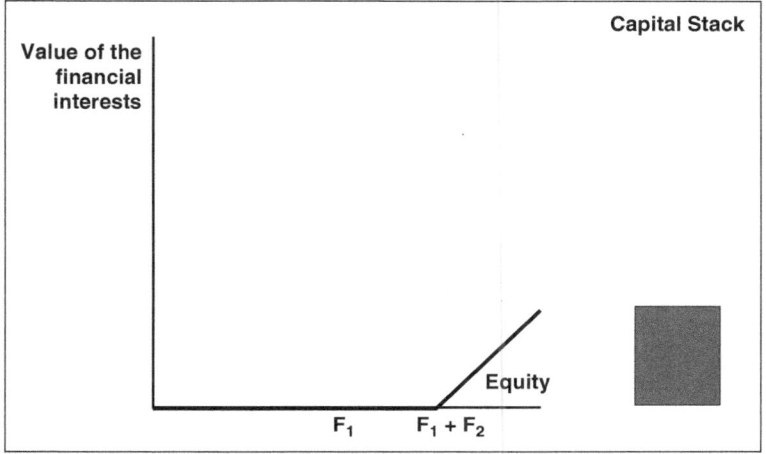

Source: ZCA and Kenneth Garbade

The equity has non-zero value if the value of the entity exceeds $F_1 + F_2$. Creditors receive the full value up to $F_1 + F_2$ if the stockholders fail to exercise their option to redeem the debt, as shown in Exhibit 4.5.

Security values would be different if the absolute priority rule did not apply, such as the equity holders receiving something during bankruptcy even if the value of the firm does not exceed $F_1 + F_2$.

Option value is not a function of the drift or growth rate of the assets. The price already incorporates the drift rate. We will apply this insight in Chapter 5, "The Lease: An Options Approach and Upward-Only Adjusting Leases."

Risk, Contingent Value, and the Capital Stack

Senior debt's contingent value decreases with additional volatility, σ. (See Exhibit 4.6.) The greater the volatility, the more likely that the firm will go bankrupt. As the years to maturity increase, the greater the probability of bankruptcy and loss to the creditors, as shown in Exhibit 4.7.

The value of the equity, which is a call option, increases with greater volatility. This is just the opposite of the reaction of debt to volatility. The fewer the years to maturity, the less likely that the creditors will lose money due to bankruptcy. See also Exhibits 4.8 and 4.9.

EXHIBIT 4.6 The contingent value of the senior debt declines with volatility.

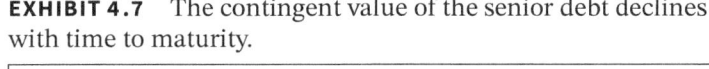

Source: ZCA and Kenneth Garbade

EXHIBIT 4.7 The contingent value of the senior debt declines with time to maturity.

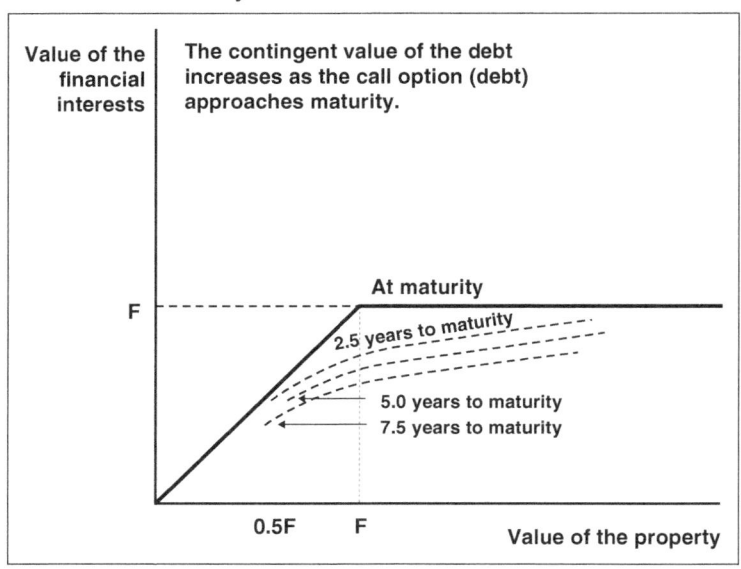

Source: ZCA and Kenneth Garbade

EXHIBIT 4.8 Contingent value of the equity increases with volatility.

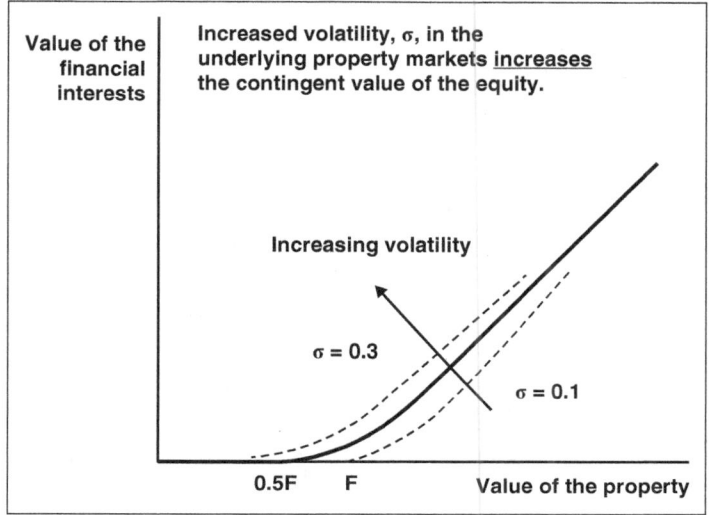

Source: ZCA and Kenneth Garbade

EXHIBIT 4.9 Contingent value of the equity increases with maturity.

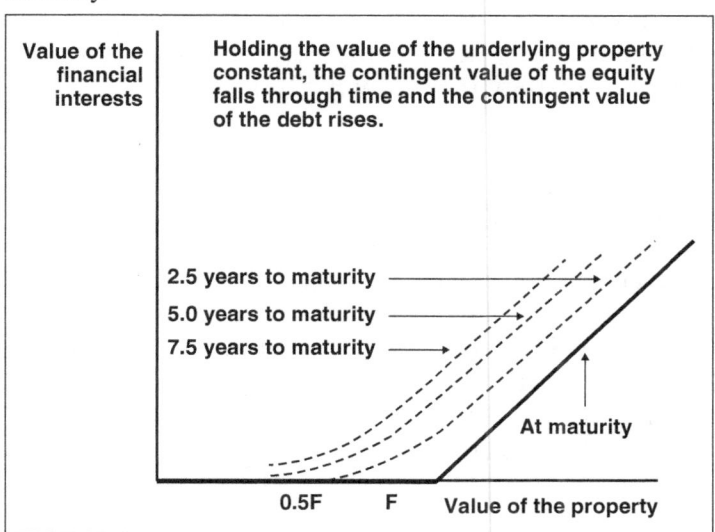

Source: ZCA and Kenneth Garbade

EXHIBIT 4.10 Subordinate debt has the attributes of debt and equity.

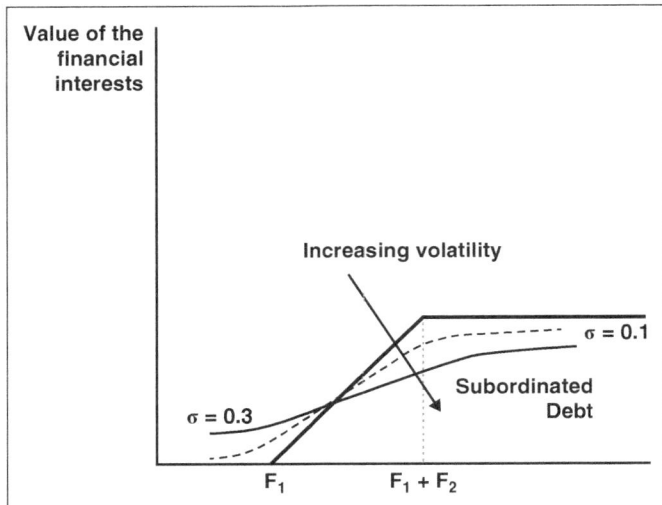

Source: ZCA and Kenneth Garbade

The contingent value of the subordinate debt is not monotonically related to the value of the firm. If the value of the firm is sufficiently greater than F_1, then the value of the debt declines with volatility. Below this level, the value of the debt increases with greater volatility. (See Exhibit 4.10.)

The Impact of Leverage

The return on leveraged equity and the volatility of this equity increases with greater LTV, as shown by Exhibits 4.11 and 4.12. Enhanced volatility with higher LTV increases the likelihood of loss at higher levels of expected return. In Chapter 10, I discuss diversification and how, due to greater risk, the likelihood of shortfall increases at an accelerating rate even though the *expected* return to the right of the efficient frontier is greater.

EXHIBIT 4.11 The return on leveraged equity increases with leverage.

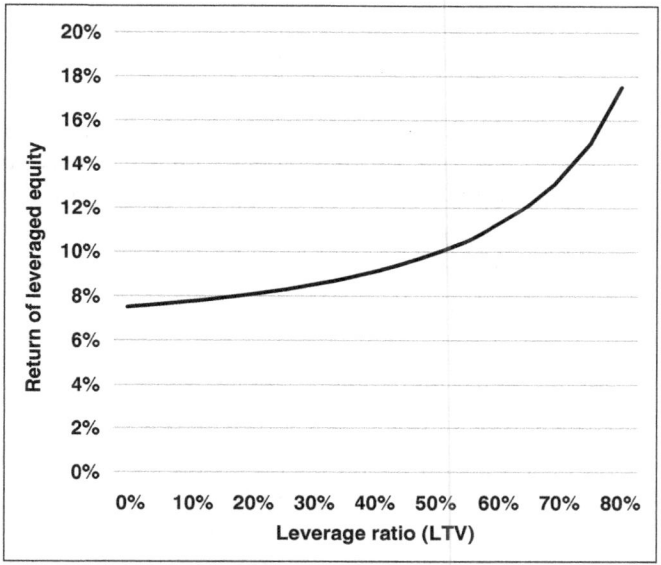

Source: Pagliari, University of Chicago class notes / with permission of Joseph L. Pagliari.

EXHIBIT 4.12 With increased leverage, volatility rises at an increasing rate.

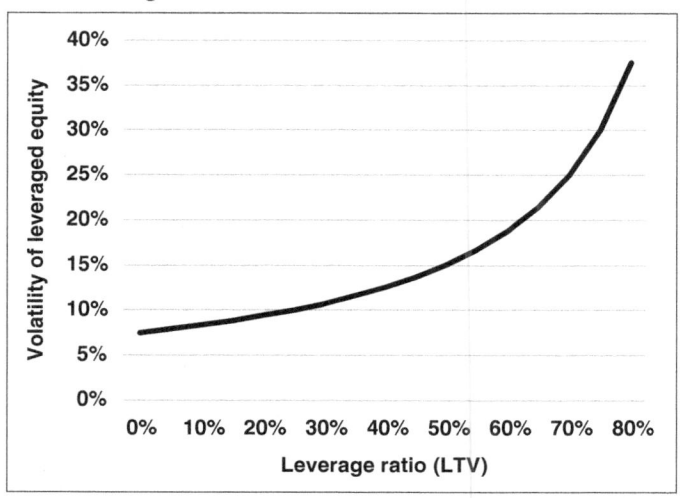

Source: Pagliari, University of Chicago class notes / with permission of Joseph L. Pagliari.

Beta and the Cost of Capital

The security market line (SML) shows the relationship between risk, beta, and expected return, E[r_m]. The SML indicates the minimum return for any level of risk and provides the appropriate discount rate used in calculating the net present value (NPV). A project's beta is equal to the covariance between the project and the market, divided by the variance of the market. The SML guides our calculation of the required return on a risky asset. The risk-free rate is r_f in Exhibit 4.13.[2]

The market risk premium is $E(R_m) - R_f$. Total risk is the sum of systematic (beta) risk and non-systematic risk, which is diversifiable. The expected rate of return on the investment is as follows:

$$E(R_E) = R_f + \beta_E \cdot [E(R_M) - R_f] \tag{4.1}$$

β_E, beta, which is a measure of systematic or undiversifiable risk, is the slope of the SML in Exhibit 4.13. (See also Exhibits 4.14 and 4.15.) The market beta is 1.

The SML, which investors should explicitly adjust for risk, is used in this book to compare and contrast alternative strategies, as shown in Exhibit 4.14. In Exhibit 4.15, I plot a "favorably priced" producer of positive alpha. The SML is convex from above due to the increasing credit risk expressed as a higher cost of debt.

EXHIBIT 4.13 The security market line, SML, beta, and cost of capital.

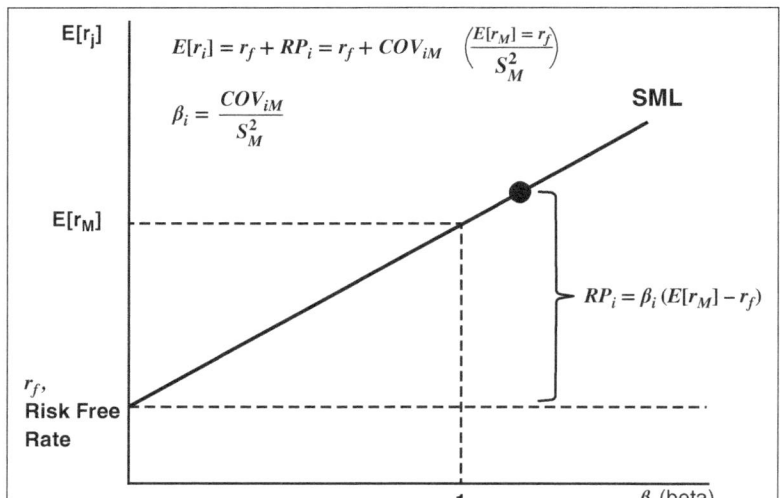

Source: Ross

EXHIBIT 4.14 The SML bends due to the increasing cost of debt.

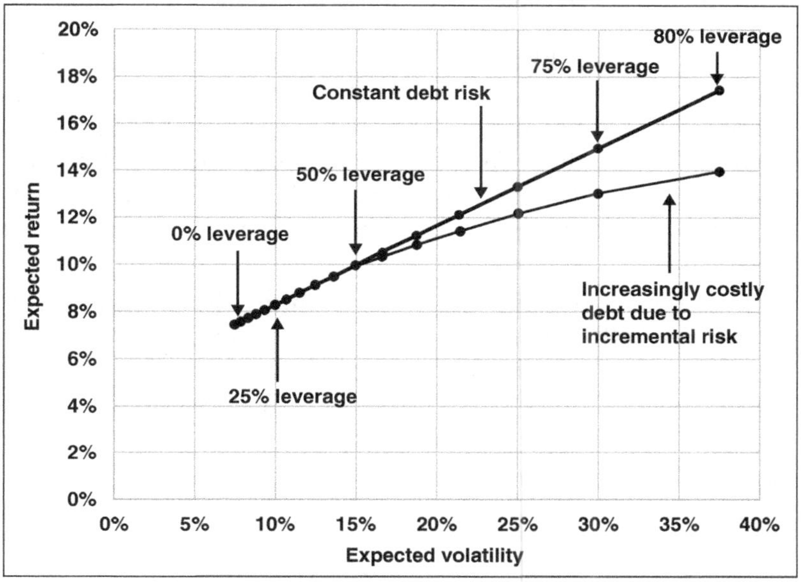

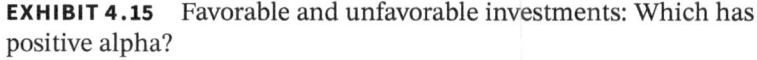

Source: Pagliari

EXHIBIT 4.15 Favorable and unfavorable investments: Which has positive alpha?

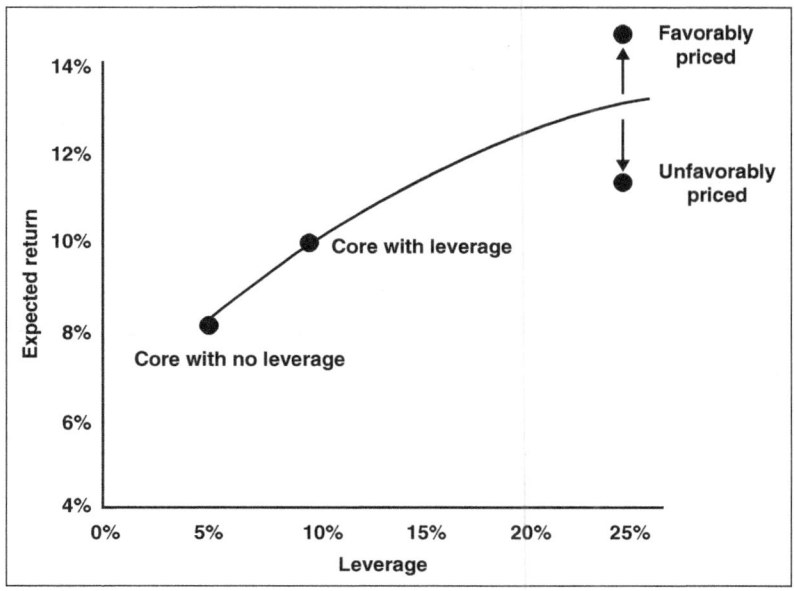

Source: Pagliari

Does Optimal Leverage Exist? Yes!

As the LTV rises, so does the likelihood that the firm will be unable to pay the debt holders, which increases the cost of debt. Bankruptcy results and ownership transfers from the debtors to the creditors, when the value of the liabilities exceeds the value of the assets. (Such is the problem with many state retirement systems that are chronically underfunded.) This transfer is not costless. In bankruptcy, the interests of the agent and the principals diverge and as much as 5% of the firm's asset can dissipate.

The equity holders have strong incentives to control the firm and avoid losing at least the option value of the equity even though, in a deterministic sense, the equity is gone. The creditors want to protect the assets from dissipation by management. At lower levels of leverage, the interests of the equity holders and creditors are better aligned.

These principles apply to any entity where ownership and control are separated. Exhibit 4.16 shows that the firm value initially rises with leverage, assuming that

EXHIBIT 4.16 The value of the firm rises with leverage due to the benefits to a taxable investor of leverage.

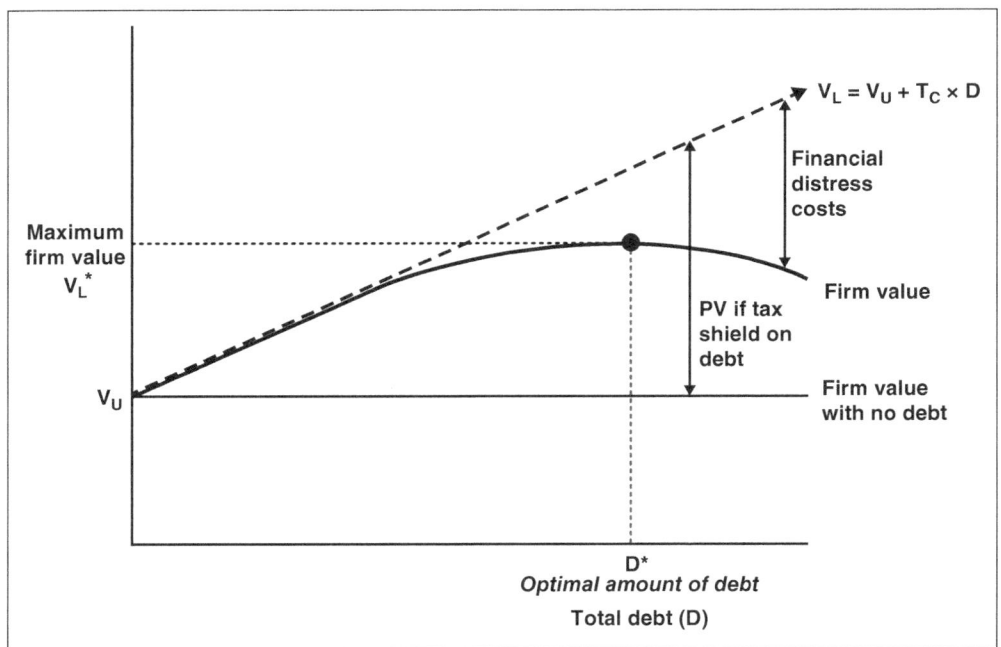

Source: Ross et al.

the owners can use the tax shield—the ability to deduct taxes from income—and then falls as the expected costs of bankruptcy loom larger. The maximum value of the firm is associated with D*, which is the optimal level of debt.

The weighted average cost of capital (WACC) declines at first with additional leverage because the after-tax cost of debt is cheaper than equity, but only up to a point. Beyond the optimal debt level, D*, WACC rises. (See Exhibit 4.17.) This analysis of the optimal debt level applies to a property in isolation. Later in this book, I argue that this conclusion may need modification for a pension fund with a fixed income portfolio. The leverage effectively offsets the intended portfolio contribution of the fixed income assets.

In Chapter 11, using a stochastic constrained optimization model, I show that the internal cost of capital can change in subtle ways depending on constraint interdependencies.

EXHIBIT 4.17 The path of WACC as a function of leverage.

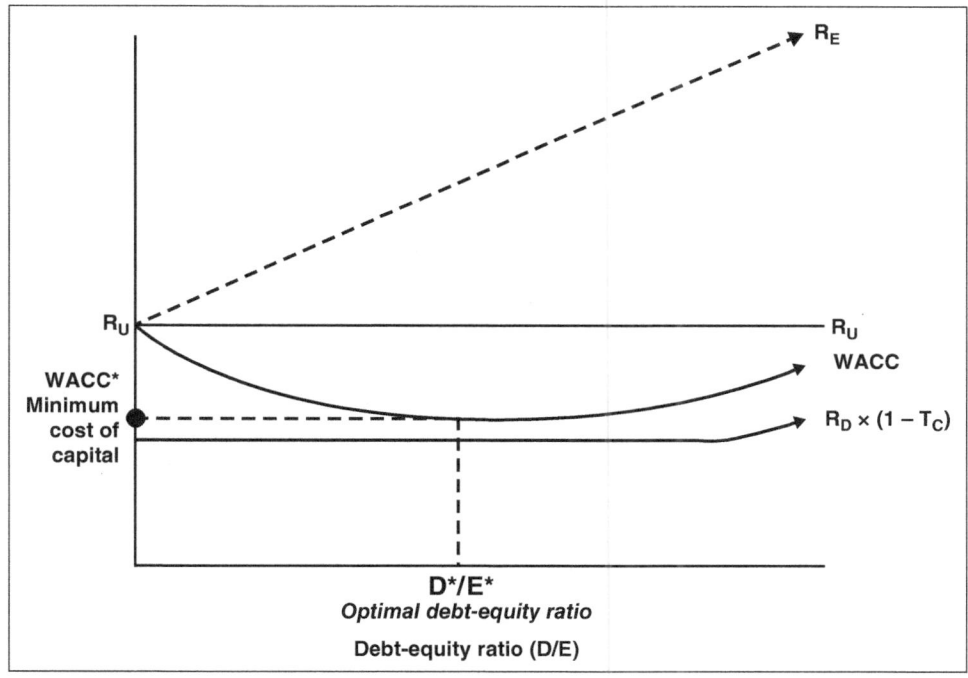

Source: Ross et al.

Conclusions and Investment Implications

- The capital stack includes equity and debt, the values of which are very sensitive to volatility.
- Leverage does not increase risk-adjusted returns.
- The capital stack is a collection of debt and equity claims.
- Volatility affects the value of the capital stack.
- Risk increases at a nonlinear rate with additional leverage. Due to the tax shield and the costs of bankruptcy, there is an optimal leverage and a minimum WACC.
- Mortgage default and prepayment rates are stochastic and respond to volatility.

Q&A: Interview with Michael Giliberto, Co-Creator of the Giliberto-Levy Indexes; formerly senior portfolio manager at J. P. Morgan; and currently serving on corporate and pension fund boards

Tell us about your professional journey.

My real estate career began at Aetna in Hartford. I liked research and decided to earn a Ph.D., which led to a faculty position at SMU. An academic friend had done a stint at Salomon Brothers, and Salomon hired me as his replacement.

Did you like Salomon Brothers?

Salomon was a special place for research. The initial version of what's now the G-L 1 index was created at Salomon in 1992. I left Salomon after the Treasury bid scandal. It was a time when I expected public markets to come to the rescue of real estate.

Seeing this opportunity, I moved to Lehman Brothers in 1993, but I eventually tired of being a talking head. I left in 1996 to join the buy-side at J.P. Morgan, which wanted to build a real estate research function. I retired from the corporate world in 2010 and continued my work on the mortgage indexes, served on boards, consulted, and was an adjunct professor at Columbia.

What is the purpose of the G-L 1 index?

Giliberto-Levy provides two indexes: G-L 1 tracks senior mortgages. The other (G-L 2) covers high yield debt. These indexes help investors make asset allocation decisions and gauge performance for private-market real estate credit.

(continued)

(*continued*)

I noted in the book that the G-L 1 senior mortgage index displays no serial correlation. Why is that the case?

There is little serial correlation because a lot of the mark-to-market price movement is driven by changes in Treasury yields, like most fixed-income investments. Credit spreads can be a bit sticky, however. This is more visible in the G-L 2, in which marks come from managers who participate in the index. In contrast, G-L 1 reflects pricing from consummated transactions, not estimated values, so it is a fully marked-to-market index.

High-yield returns have been higher than senior mortgage returns, even with the COVID-19 challenges. That said, credit impairment in the high-yield space is a multiple of senior mortgage credit losses.

What is your advice to young professionals seeking a career in real estate?

Get an entry job working for an institutional money manager, small or large. Seek out firms with transactions volume, great mentors, and opportunities to work with different teams.

CHAPTER 5

The Lease: An Options Approach and Upward-Only Adjusting Leases

Preliminaries

A lease is a contract between an owner (lessor) and a tenant (lessee). Leases come in a variety of flavors. For example, a ground lease may give the tenant the right to develop or redevelop. A gross or full-service lease is a lease wherein the landlord pays the operating expenses. Hybrid leases require the operating expenses to be shared by tenant and landlord. Expense stops, which are options, require the tenant's paying all operating expenses above a specified annual level.

Embedded lease options can help tenants and landlords write more efficient leases. A tenant's option to purchase the underlying asset can incentivize the tenant to take better care of the asset, which better aligns interests. Options increase flexibility, help hedge risks, control principal–agent problems, mitigate the adverse effects of information asymmetry, and reduce transactions costs. Examples of principal–agent problems, which reduce value, include the conflicts that arise due to the separation of user and ownership rights.

Privately traded property can impose significant transactions costs. Embedded options can mitigate time-consuming bilateral monopoly negotiations and reduce tenants' costs of search and relocation. The landlord benefits by conserving the costs of search, screening prospective tenants, contracting and negotiating a new lease, and managing vacant space. Options can reduce transactions costs associated with continual adjustments to complexity and change. The option to re-lease and to withhold space from the market is a frequently used option that can inhibit the adjustment of aggregate market rental and vacancy rates to demand shocks.

An important option is the landlord's right, but not its obligation, to increase market rent at a pre-specified time and according to a preset formula. Reasons include the need to reflect in the lease terms (upward) changes in market conditions, to share in tenant profitability, and to protect the landlord from increases in expenses that are beyond landlord control, such as unexpected inflation. Lease options are many, varied in kind, and sometimes even path-dependent.

Leases are often regarded as a substitute for debt. For example, leases may conserve a firm's borrowing capacity. Scholars are not in agreement as to whether leases are substitutes for or complements to debt. Leasing to lower-credit tenants can increase the cost of debt and widen lease spreads.

The reverse logic obtains if leases and debt are complements. Investors should be alert to the complex relationship between bonds and leases.

Leases and Options

The lease credit spread is the difference between the equilibrium rent on a lease subject to credit risk (the likelihood of a tenant default) and a similar lease lacking any credit risk. Market volatility increases lease option value. (This chapter benefits from Grenadier's[1] research on lease options.)

Exhibits 5.1 through 5.3 describe three market environments: a hot market that will likely cool as it approaches a long-term equilibrium; a cold market that will improve; and a Goldilocks market, which is neither too hot nor too cold.

Even though lease forward curves are not widely available, forward lease rates exist, at least implicitly. Exhibit 5.4 shows the forward lease rates over time for leases of various maturities. In a hot market, the forward curves are declining in the expectation of declining rents. In a cold market, the reverse is true: Longer-term leases have higher rents. Short-term leases have lower rents but the tenant and the landlord face releasing risk comparable to the refinancing risks inherent in floating debt.

A Goldilocks market is more complex. The forward curves are concave-downward and negatively sloped. The rate at which the forward lease rate falls with respect to time accelerates, which is contrary to the behavior of hot and cold markets.

The office lease is generally long-term, so the spread should be wider; apartment leases should have tighter spreads, and self-storage spreads should be tighter still. (See Exhibits 5.5 and 5.6.)

Leases and Options **83**

EXHIBIT 5.1 The market expects weakness.

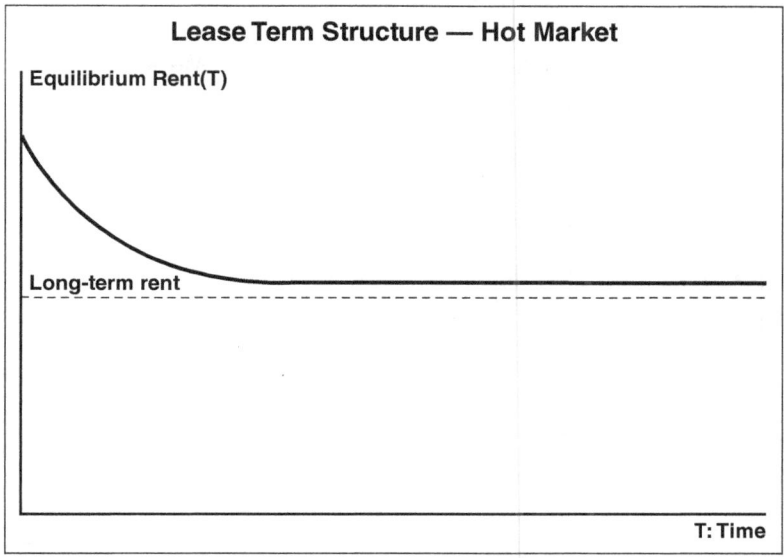

Source: Grenadier

EXHIBIT 5.2 The cold market will improve.

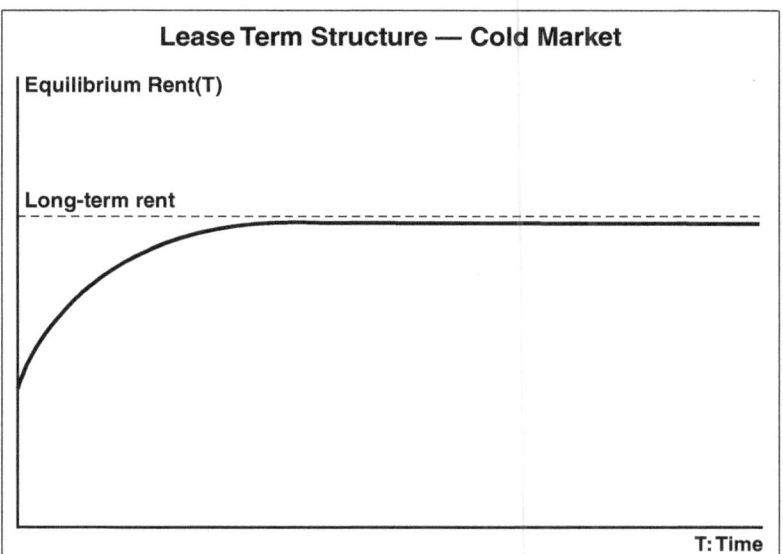

Source: Grenadier

84 CHAPTER 5 The Lease: An Options Approach and Upward-Only Adjusting Leases

EXHIBIT 5.3 The market is warm but just right. The market reverts to a long-run equilibrium.

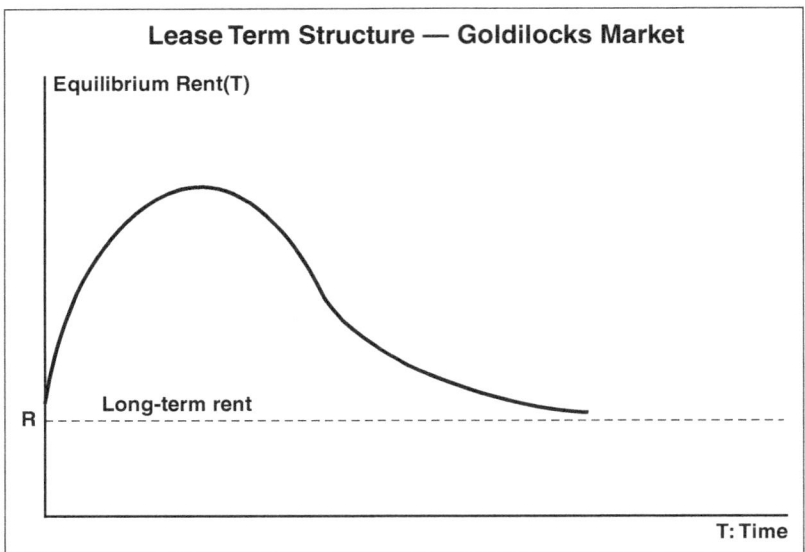

Source: Grenadier

EXHIBIT 5.4 The forward rent declines as the lease term increases.

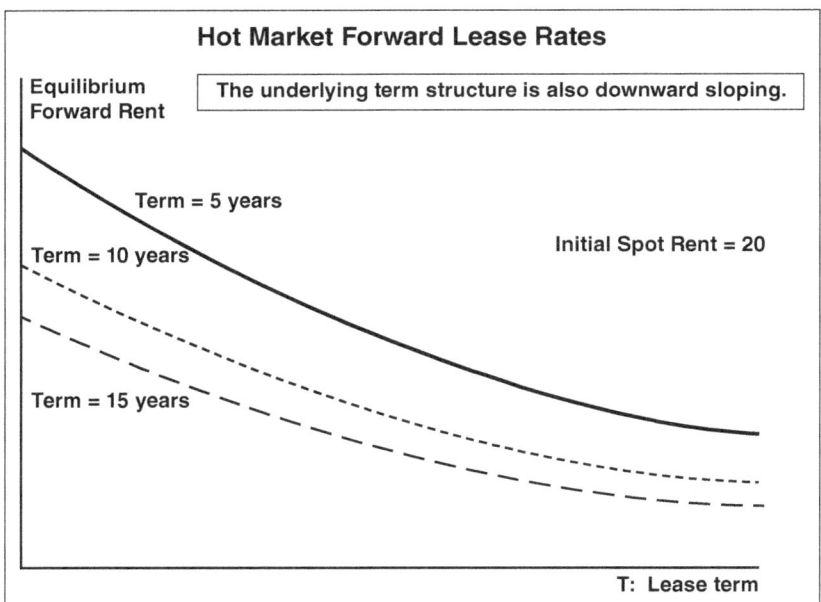

Source: Grenadier

EXHIBIT 5.5 In a Goldilocks market, shorter-term leases may differ from longer-term leases.

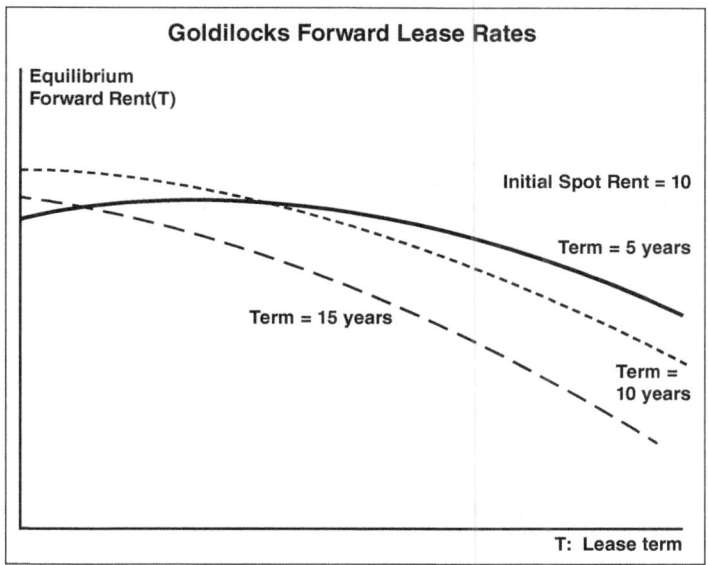

Source: Grenadier

EXHIBIT 5.6 The longer-term leases require a higher forward rent in an improving market.

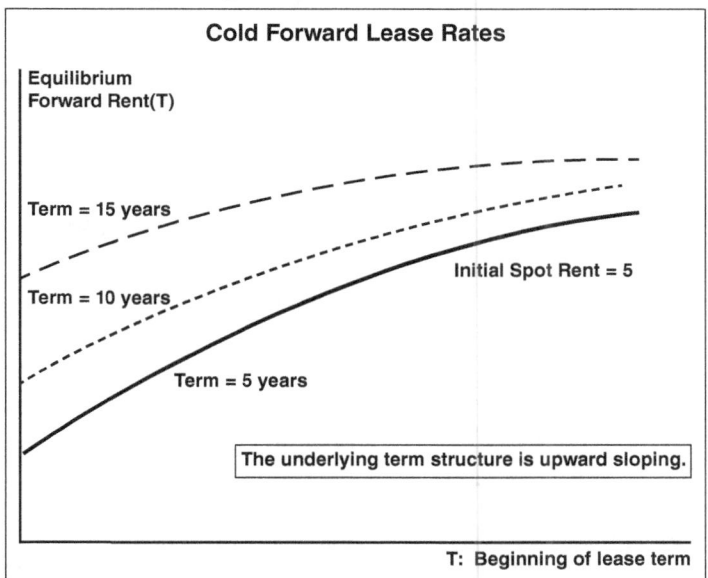

Source: Grenadier

Exhibit 5.7 shows that the lease credit spread increases over time, reflecting the increased cumulative likelihood of a default. Holding credit quality constant, office, apartment, and self-storage leases should have different equilibrium lease terms.

Exhibit 5.8 indicates that the credit spread increases as the ratio of the lease value to the default trigger increases. The impact of default is greater the higher is this ratio, which reflects the number of the lessee's creditors; the more creditors, the greater are transactions costs and the wider is the spread.

If the tenant's business performance is positively correlated with market performance, the spread increases with the volatility of the underlying asset, as shown in Exhibit 5.9. If the correlation is negative, then the spread decreases with volatility.

For example, the demand for cheaper food at a stand-alone fast-food restaurant increases during recessions. The restaurant does well despite weak general business conditions. When the economy is strong, property performance and land values improve but more households eat at upscale restaurants. The correlation between tenant success and overall market conditions is negative. Hence, fast food restaurants might merit a tighter spread than upscale restaurant tenants. When the correlation is positive, default is more likely when the underlying asset is performing poorly.

EXHIBIT 5.7 The term structure of lease spreads is upward sloping. The longer is the term, the greater is the likelihood of tenant default.

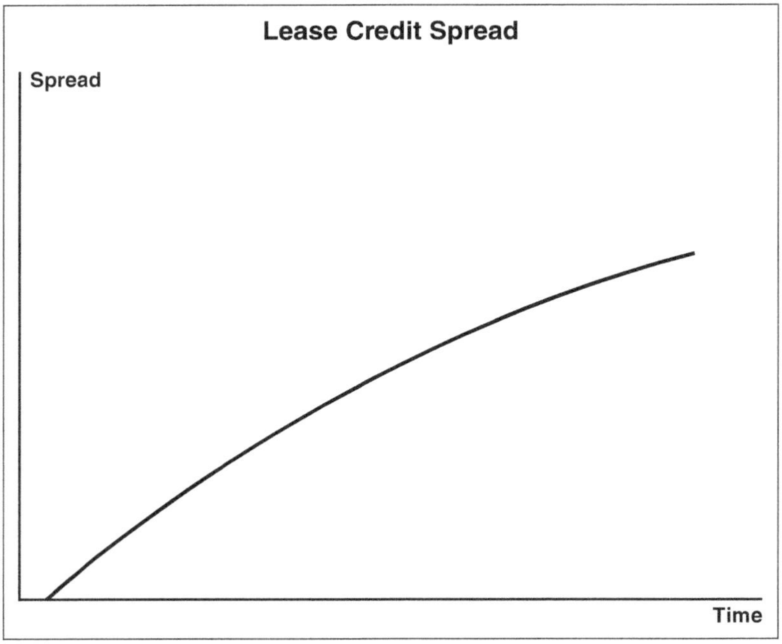

Source: Grenadier

EXHIBIT 5.8 Credit spread increases as the ratio of lease value lost to the default trigger. Larger lessors can charge lower credit spreads.

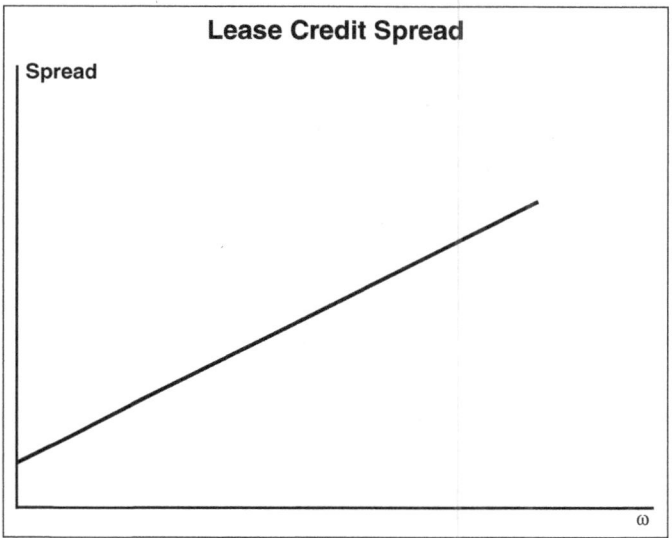

Source: Grenadier

EXHIBIT 5.9 The correlation between the market and the tenant's credit affects the spread as the volatility of the underlying asset value increases.

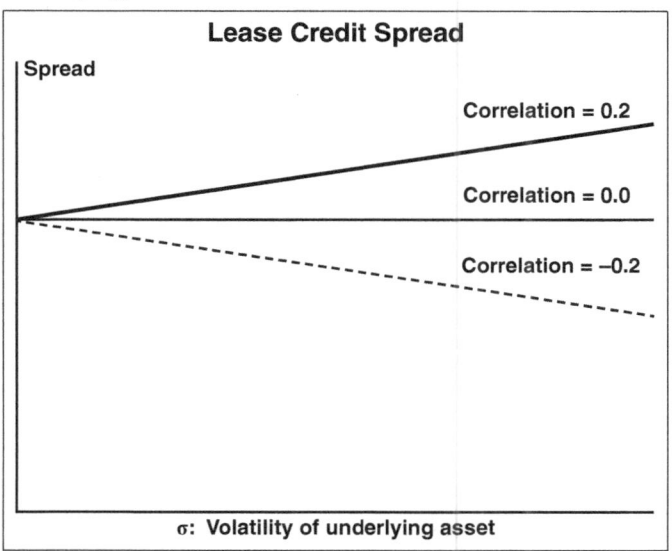

Source: Grenadier

The lessee's firm's volatility increases the spread. Landlords charge lessees a lower spread given lower asset volatility, as shown in Exhibit 5.10.

Often a lessor requires some rent prepayment determined by credit risk. The greater is the ratio of the lease value to the default trigger, lease default becomes less likely and the required prepayment period decreases, holding lessee's volatility constant. The greater is volatility, the less sensitive is the prepayment period to the ratio of value to the trigger. If a tenant is on the knife-edge of default, the landlord demands a significant prepayment. Poor credit leases show greater variation across tenant volatilities, as shown in Exhibit 5.11. As the ratio approaches one, the credit spread rises exponentially, as shown in Exhibit 5.12.

The option to default is valuable, as shown in Exhibit 5.13. The higher the costs of cancelation, the greater is the value of this put option. The greater the time to expiration or the higher is the volatility of the underlying asset, the greater is the time value of this option.

The renewal option increases with time-to-expiration, as shown in Exhibit 5.14.

The value of the option to sublet, a call option, increases with market rent, as shown in Exhibit 5.15, and the value of the option to increase rent is a function of market volatility, which I explore in the next section. See Exhibit 5.16.

EXHIBIT 5.10 The credit spread increases the greater is the volatility of the lessee's business.

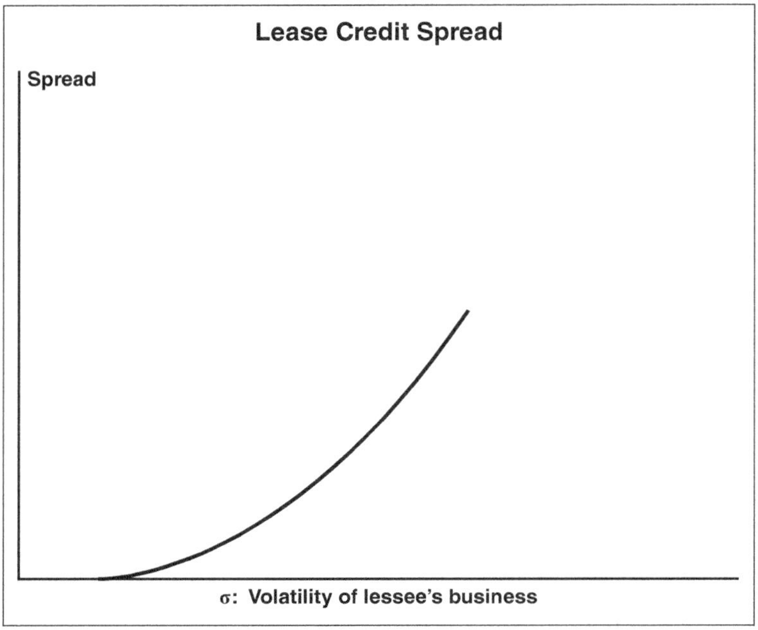

Source: Grenadier

EXHIBIT 5.11 The required rental pre-payment decreases as the ratio of the lessee's asset value increases.

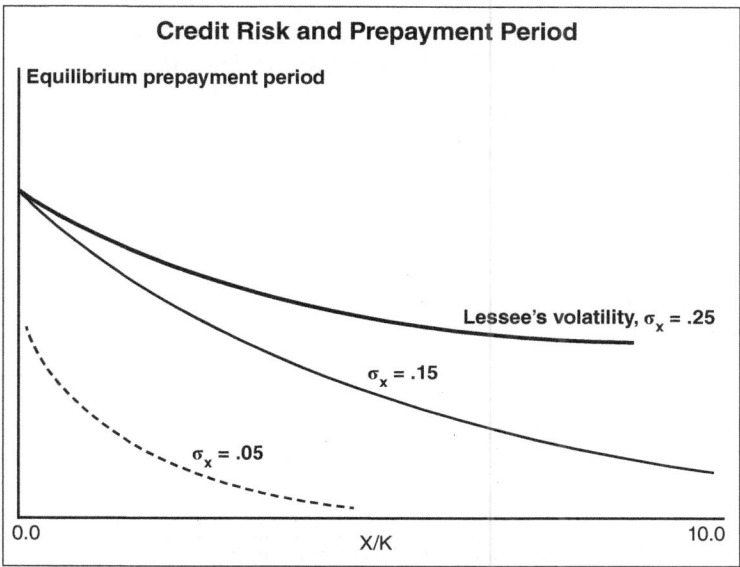

Source: Grenadier

EXHIBIT 5.12 The spread increases rapidly as the ratio of the tenant's asset value to the default trigger approaches one.

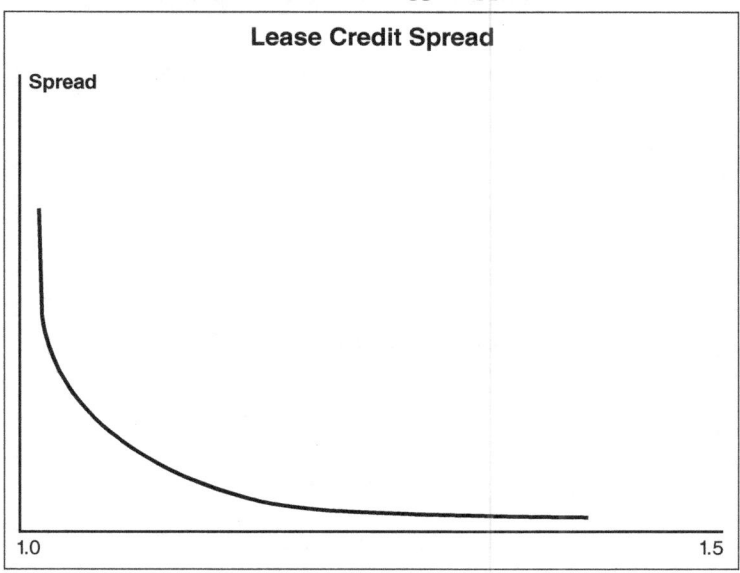

Source: Grenadier

EXHIBIT 5.13 The option to default has value if the tenant's business performance declines. The tenant is long a put option.

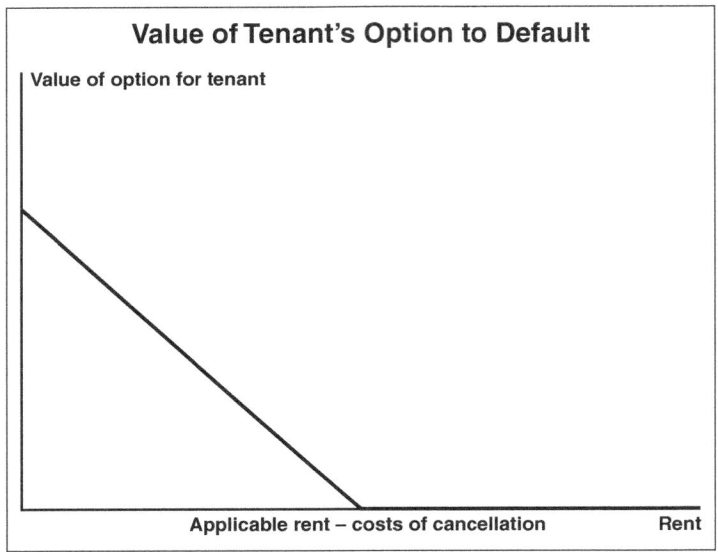

Source: Grenadier

EXHIBIT 5.14 The renewal option premium increases with lease term to expiration even though the equilibrium base rent declines.

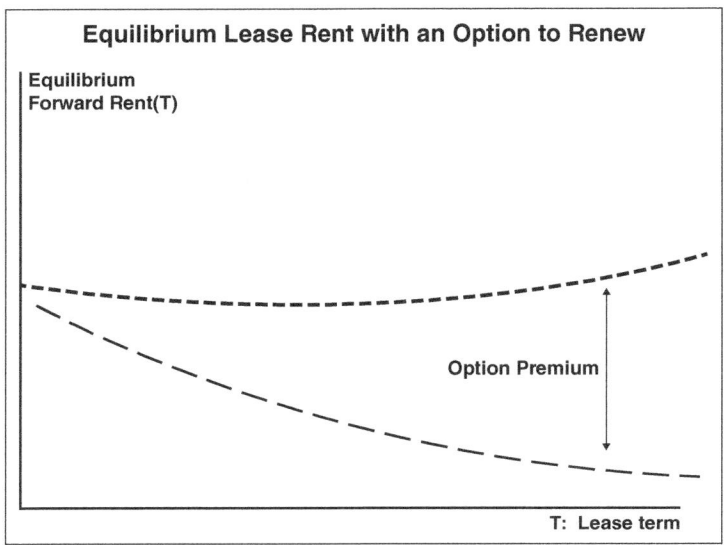

Source: Grenadier

EXHIBIT 5.15 The value of the option to sublet increases with rent.

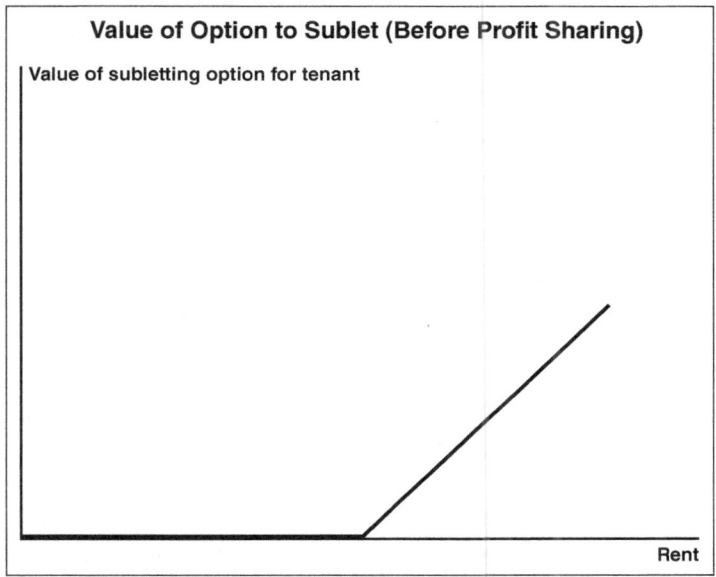

Source: Grenadier

EXHIBIT 5.16 The value of the option to increase rent is a function of rent above the strike rent.

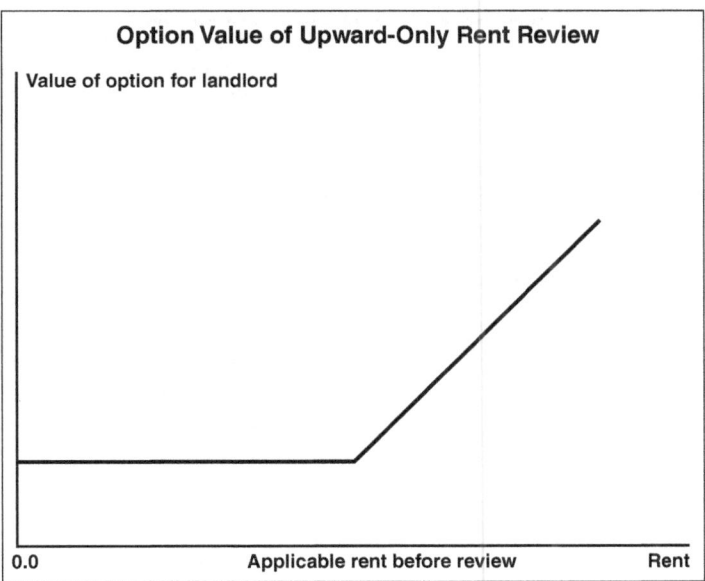

Source: Grenadier

Option to Escalate: A Monte Carlo Analysis

Upward-only adjusting leases. Landlords have the option to compare at a predetermined time during the term of the lease the stated lease rent with the prevailing market rental rate. Assuming that market rents have risen, the landlord has the option to increase the stated lease rent. If market rents fall, the landlord will not lower the prevailing lease rate. The reset rent becomes the new base rent for the next periodic rental review. Lease valuation establishes the value of leases of identical maturities but with different contract terms.

I analyze using Monte Carlo analysis of a specific clause, the upward-only rental rate adjustment provision. The relationship between the initial lease rate and the lease's net present value varies depending on the contract terms and, specifically, upon the embedded options.

The reader should note carefully that even if expected market rental growth is zero, as long as rents are uncertain, the value of the escalation option increases with volatility. Volatility creates landlord value.

Exhibit 5.17 shows the new fifth-year rent, the increase in rent for the adjustable lease, and the NPV of the adjustable lease with the fifth-year reset, as a function of volatility. I include the adjusted flat rental rate required to equate the values of

EXHIBIT 5.17 Simulation results.

Volatility, $	Flat Rent Lease	Adjusted Flat Rent Lease	New Fifth-Year Rent	Increase in Fifth-Year Rent Over Initial Rent	NPV of Lease with Fifth-Year Escalation	NPV of 10-Year $10 Flat Lease
0	$10.00	$10.00	$10.00	$0.00	$73.60	$73.60
1	$10.00	$10.36	$10.69	$0.69	$76.27	$73.60
2	$10.00	$10.73	$11.38	$1.38	$78.98	$73.60
3	$10.00	$11.10	$12.08	$2.08	$81.68	$73.60
4	$10.00	$11.46	$12.75	$2.75	$84.32	$73.60
5	$10.00	$11.83	$13.45	$3.45	$87.03	$73.60
6	$10.00	$12.15	$14.07	$4.07	$89.46	$73.60

Source: ZCA

the two leases and consider a flat coupon lease with term-to-maturity that is identical to the term of an upward-only adjusting lease. To equate the NPVs of the two leases, the flat coupon must rise with market volatility. The volatility increases the value of the escalation option, *even if there is no trend growth assumed in rental payments*.

I simulate two leases using Monte Carlo: a 10-year flat and a 10-year adjusting lease. Volatilities range from no volatility to $6 per year for an adjusting lease whose initial rate is $10. *Note that I assume no trend growth*. The power of this finding seems to elude many otherwise successful leasing brokers.

Even without trend growth, the standard deviation of market rent increases over time because average market rent adjusts stochastically. The probability of rents exceeding the base rent increases. Exhibit 5.18, wherein volatility is slight, shows very little expansion. By contrast, Exhibit 5.19 shows the evolving rental confidence interval over 10 years. Risk expansion increases option value. (Neither simulation has any trend growth.)

These exhibits show that the value of the upward-only adjusting lease increases with volatility. In order to equate the values of the flat lease with the upward-only adjusting lease, the coupon of the flat lease must increase monotonically with market volatility. Exhibits 5.20 and 5.21 show the expected rent adjustment in

EXHIBIT 5.18 The 5%–95% confidence interval does not increase materially over time when the rental growth volatility is low, 1%.

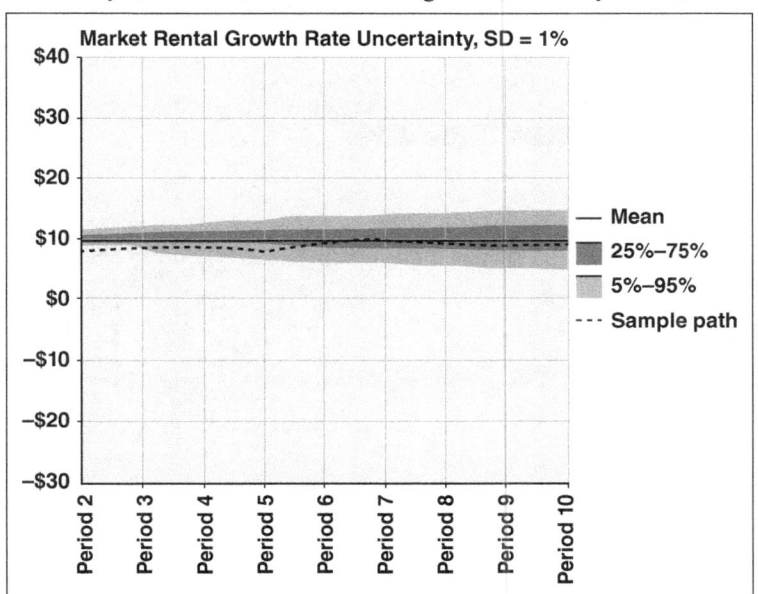

Source: ZCA

EXHIBIT 5.19 The 5%–95% confidence interval expands significantly over time when the volatility is 6%, which increases option value.

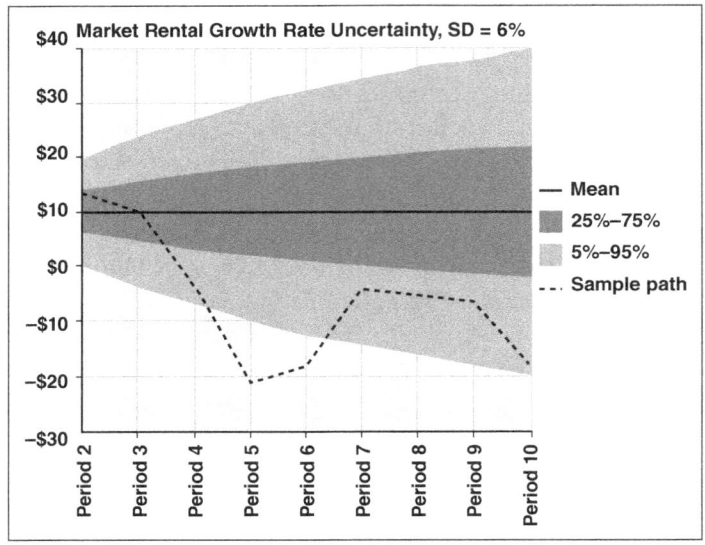

Source: ZCA

EXHIBIT 5.20 Most simulated option values are associated with rents in the $10–$15 range; rental growth standard deviation = 1%.

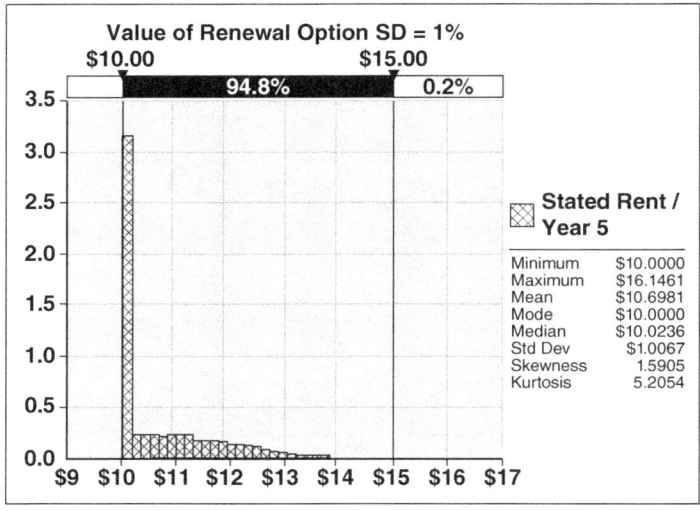

Source: ZCA

EXHIBIT 5.21 32% of the simulated option values are associated with rents exceeding $15; rental growth standard deviation = 6%.

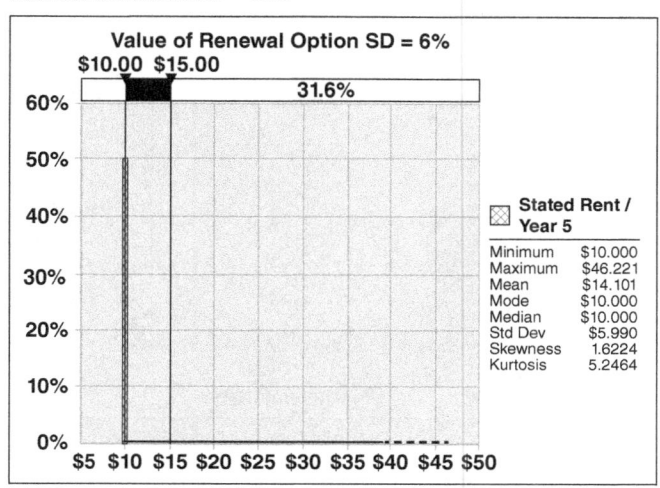

Source: ZCA

the fifth year for 1% and 6% market rental growth volatilities. Rental market volatility increases over time. Exhibit 5.23 shows the increase in equilibrium rent as volatility increases.

The option to escalate has value as long as market rents fluctuate. If everybody in the world was certain that trend growth in rents would be zero, as long as rents fluctuate, despite no trend growth, the value of the option to escalate increases with volatility.

Exhibit 5.22 shows the flat rent equivalent of a lease as a function of volatility and Exhibit 5.23 depicts the new escalated lease with increasing volatility.

Exhibit 5.24 shows that if volatility is low, the likelihood of a rent between $10 and $20 is 50%. If I increase the volatility from 1% to 6%, then the probability of a rent between $10 and $20 is 30%, as shown in Exhibit 5.25.

Investors typically leave value on the table because they improperly analyze the value of embedded options. One of the benefits of Monte Carlo analysis is not only the explicit analysis of risk but the generation of risk measures, specifically probability distributions, that help investors and tenants better understand downside risk (and upside opportunity).

EXHIBIT 5.22 A flat rent equivalent to a lease with a five-year renewal increases with volatility.

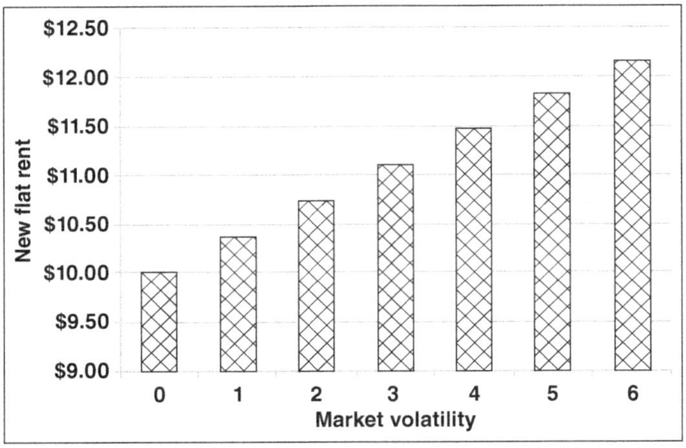

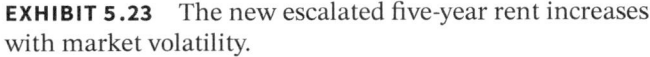

Source: ZCA

EXHIBIT 5.23 The new escalated five-year rent increases with market volatility.

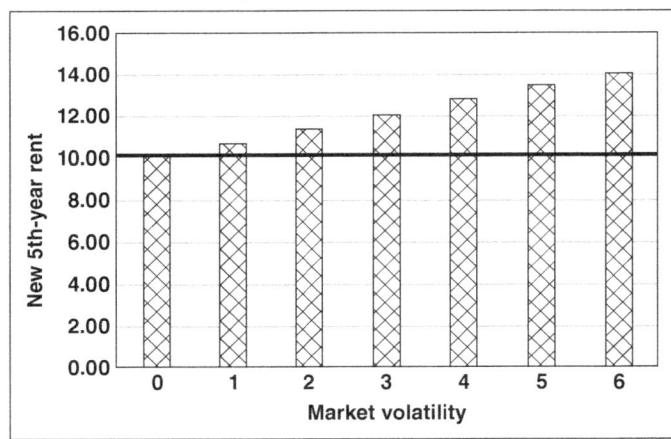

Source: ZCA

EXHIBIT 5.24 For low volatility, standard deviation = 1%, the probability of a rent between $10 and $20 is 50%.

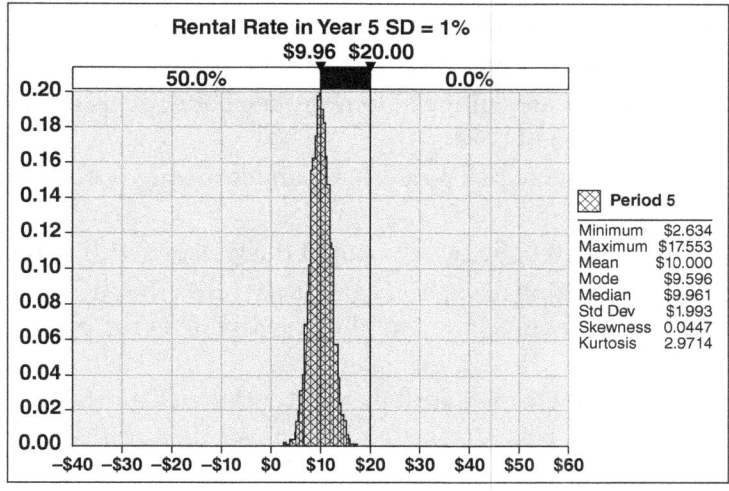

Source: ZCA

EXHIBIT 5.25 For high volatility, standard deviation = 6%, the probability of a rent between $10 and $20 is 30%.

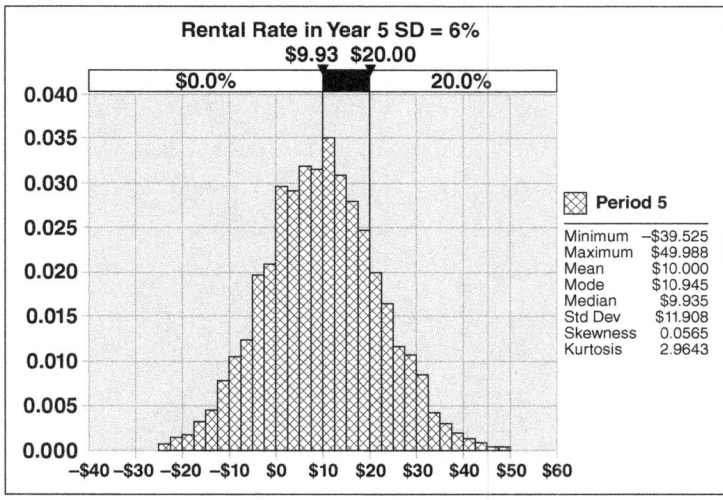

Source: ZCA

Conclusions and Investment Implications

- Tenant credit quality and the probability of default are two sources of volatility. Leverage and overall market volatility are other sources.
- Investors and tenants are equipped to negotiate better deals if they know how to calculate the impact of risk.
- Knowing how to evaluate risk properly separates the high performers from the crowd.
- Leases are replete with options that benefit the lessee as well as the lessor.
- Option value is a function of volatility, the strike price, the current price, time to expiration, and the risk-free rate, not the growth rate of the price of the underlying asset.
- The value of the option to escalate rent, a call option held by the lessor, increases with volatility.
- Even if all market participants assume zero long-term market rental growth, as long as there are market fluctuations, however slight, the option to escalate has value.
- Analysts often incorrectly estimate embedded option value using deterministic methods.

Q&A: Interview with Doug Lyons, Managing Principal, Pearlmark

Looking for Relative Value Across the Capital Stack

Describe your journey into real estate.

In high school and college, I interned for Cushman & Wakefield brokers (where my dad worked). After graduating from Amherst, I went to Wall Street, working for Merrill and Bankers Trust during the 1980s. Then, during the cyclical downturn of the early 1990s, I attended Harvard Business School.

In my second year at HBS and seeking a seat in real estate private equity, I cold-called Sam Zell and invited him to speak at Harvard about entrepreneurship. Steve Quazzo, who worked for Zell, interviewed and hired me. We raised capital for the Zell-Merrill opportunity funds as we prepared to take his companies public. Steve and I became partners when we left Zell and started Pearlmark.

How did you deal with the GFC and COVID-19?

We were better prepared for COVID-19 than for the GFC. We deployed significant capital into the teeth of the GFC with an overweight to leveraged office properties. We had to restructure a lot of debt. Illiquidity and capital requirements in a down market can be devastating. We executed workouts and refocused on multifamily and industrial. Our renewed priority in the middle market and move away from office and retail into multifamily and industrial positioned us well for COVID-19. We also committed to continuing a successful credit strategy through mezzanine debt funds. We have a strong current cycle track record and are playing offense with ample capital. We have attracted super-talented, entrepreneurial colleagues and kept our team together by offering participation in fund and transaction promotes.

(continued)

(*continued*)

What do you do at Pearlmark?

I am a managing principal with primary responsibility for the credit side of our business, including mezzanine lending. We target a 7% cash yield and a 10% IRR net of all fees and expenses to the LPs with an LTV of about 75% (or 25% subordination).

What are views on office? Is it time to be an office mezzanine investor?

We are starting to see distress opportunities at unbelievable discounts. A major Chicago office property that just traded at $50 per square foot has a replacement cost of over $500 per square foot. There is an equity play at these distressed values. That said, it still may be too early.

How would you guide young professionals?

They should seek strong mentors in well-capitalized, entrepreneurial firms with no organizational silos.

CHAPTER 6

The Real Estate Quadrants: Interdependent and Predictive

Preliminaries

The quadrants comprise debt and equity, both private and public, as shown in Exhibit 6.1.

The relationships between quadrants are complex, highly interdependent, and predictable. This chapter shows investors how to extract more information from the quadrants.

What Cap Rate Is Appropriate?

We can predict property performance and volatility using public market data.

Cap rates diverge, as shown in Exhibits 6.2 and 6.3. Which cap rate is appropriate? Managers and especially their investors do not appreciate the differences; too often they pick the cap rate that gives the "right" answer. (See Chapter 12.)

EXHIBIT 6.1 The real estate quadrants: $8.4 trillion total in 2023.

Source: Pension Real Estate Association

EXHIBIT 6.2 CoStar cap rate and NCREIF appraisal value and equity weighted all property cap rates.

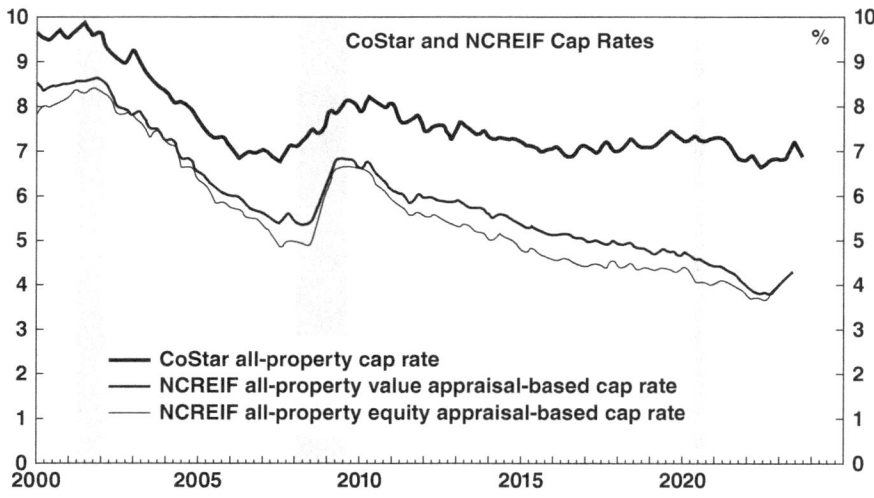

Source: ZCA using NCREIF data

EXHIBIT 6.3 Spread between CoStar cap rate and NPI office appraisal cap rate increased since GFC.

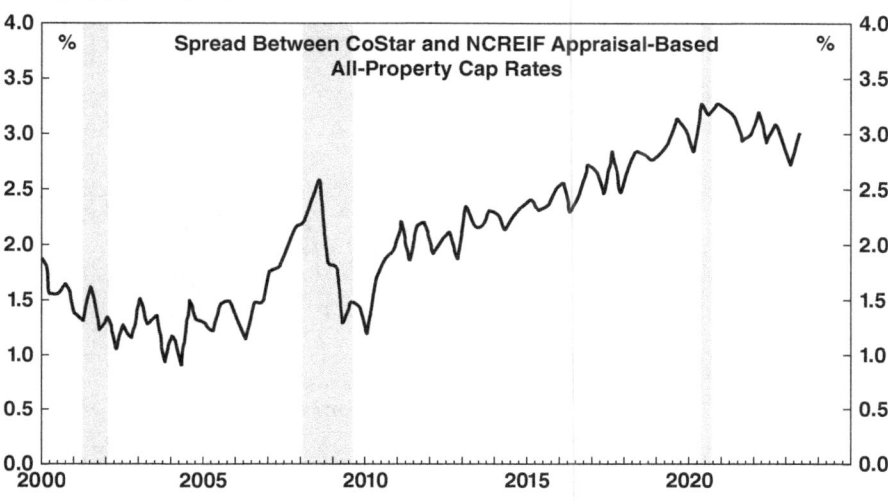

Source: ZCA using NCREIF and COSTAR data

Capital Markets: Equity and Fixed Income

Security spreads, such as AAA- and Baa-rated spreads over Treasuries, affect the pricing of real estate assets, no matter which quadrant. Seemingly unrelated securities, such as small-cap stocks and S&P 500 stocks, are correlated, as shown in Exhibit 6.4 and Exhibit 6.5. REITs perform in ways that resemble small-cap stock performance. Should investors classify REITs as a different form of real estate or as a small-cap stock, or both?

The Challenges of Public and Private Market Data: A Comparative Analysis

Many private market assets do not trade in continuous auction markets. Unlike stocks, property market pricing is backward-looking due to appraisal and other price estimation methodologies, such as mark-to-model. Property markets react to public market shocks with a lag. Hence, public markets are predictive of private market performance.

EXHIBIT 6.4 AAA- and Baa-rated bond returns are important in explaining real estate performance.

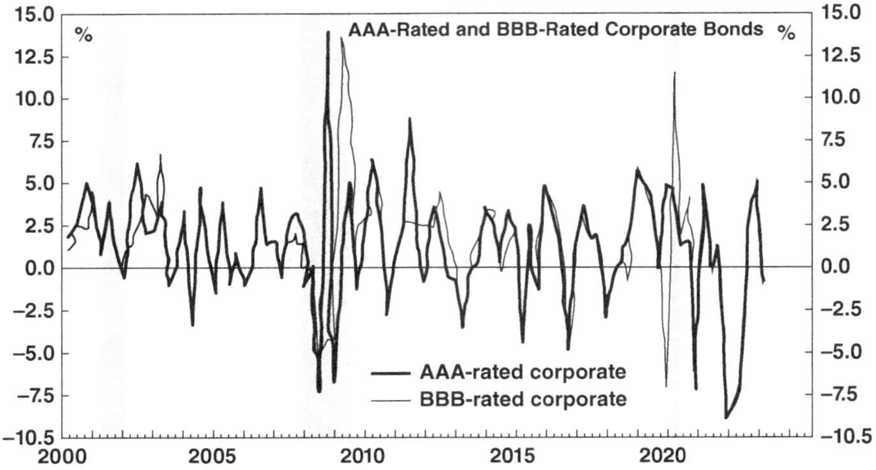

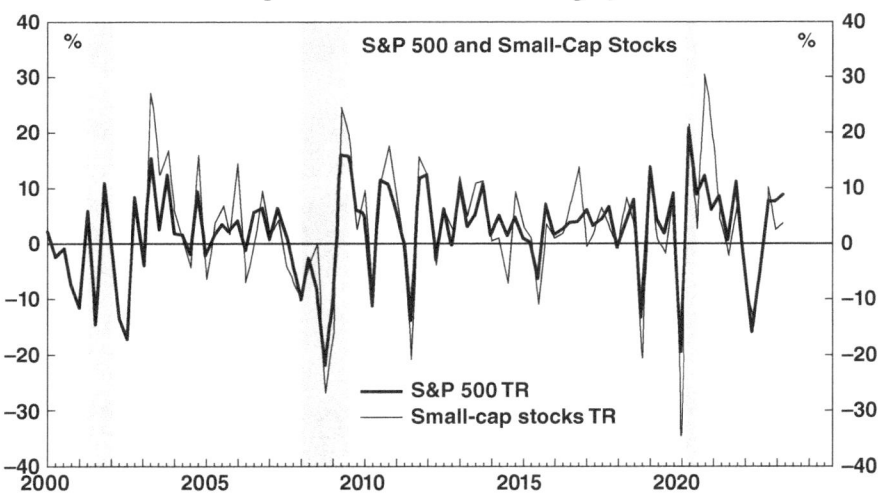

Source: ZCA using Federal Reserve data

EXHIBIT 6.5 Small-cap and S&P 500 stocks are highly correlated.

Source: ZCA using Federal Reserve data

Public markets are more transparent and relatively more liquid than high transactions-cost property markets. Return smoothing makes property performance look too good to be true. As a result, unconstrained portfolio optimizers over-allocate to property.

Past property returns have predictive power; such is not the case with heavily traded stocks like the S&P 500 or even public REITs, which exhibit little, if any, serial correlation.

The lack of serial correlation is consistent with an efficient market in which new information is promptly incorporated in prices. Prices in efficient markets fluctuate randomly so that yesterday's price is not a good predictor of today's performance.

See Equation (6.1), which models a distributed lag of S&P 500 returns. The coefficients are not significantly different from zero, which is in agreement with theory: Past values should not predict the current price.

$$SP_t = 3.218 + 0.021 * SP_{t-1} + 0.003 * SP_{t-2} - 0.051 * SP_{t-3}$$
$$(4.428)\ (0.274) \qquad (0.046) \qquad (-0.676) \tag{6.1}$$

Adjusted $R^2 = -0.014$

DW $= 1.988$

Mean dependent variable $= 3.137$

S.D. dependent variable $= 8.038$

S.E. of regression $= 8.095$

In Chapter 10, I show how to remove serial correlation in property return data. Once corrected, true property return volatility is similar to public equity REIT volatility. In Chapter 13, I demonstrate how investors can use MSA serial correlation as a proxy for liquidity.

I compare past and current total quarterly returns of traded public shares—S&P 500 (SP) and all equity REITs (REIT)—with leveraged property (the NCREIF all-property leveraged index). See Exhibits 6.6 through 6.8. A scatter of the public assets, S&P 500 and equity REITs, indicates that there is no statistically significant relationship between past and current returns, visually confirming the results of Equation (6.3). Exhibit 6.8 shows that past property returns do, in fact, predict current returns.

The past three quarters explain about 64% of the variation in current leveraged property returns.

Current values of the NPI index are functions of previous values. The past three quarters explain about 64% of the variation in current leveraged property returns, as shown in Equation (6.2). I correct for serial correlation in Chapter 10.

EXHIBIT 6.6 Past stock returns do not predict S&P returns.

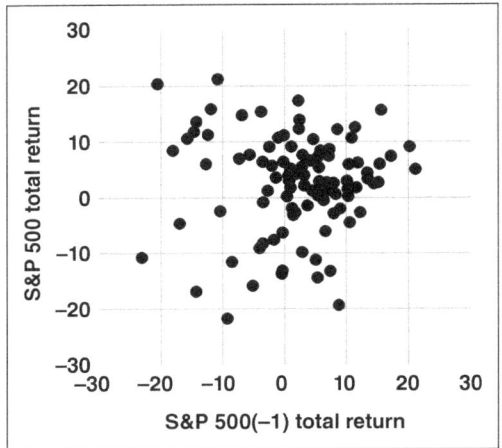

Source: ZCA using NCREIF and COSTAR data

EXHIBIT 6.7 REIT returns do not predict current REIT returns.

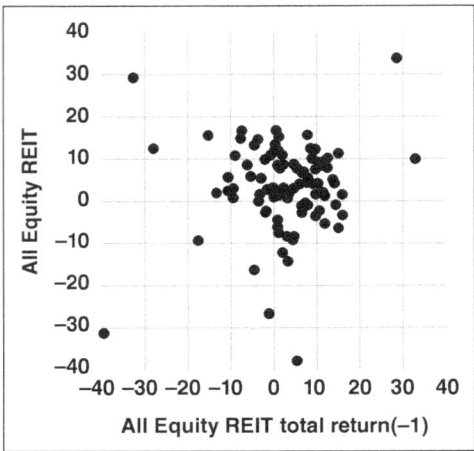

Source: ZCA using NCREIF and COSTAR data

EXHIBIT 6.8 Past property returns predict future returns.

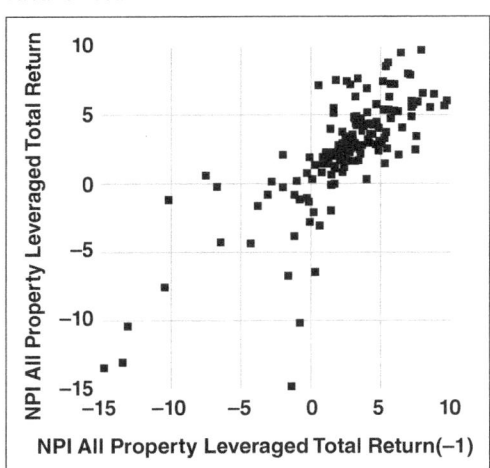

Source: ZCA using NCREIF and COSTAR data

I compare REITs with property. The REIT coefficients for each variable, lagged one quarter, are essentially zero statistically. T-statistics in parentheses and adjusted R^2 are insignificant as well. REITs behave like stocks and follow a random walk.

$$REIT_t = 3.417 + 0.088 * REIT_{t-1} - 0.112 * REIT_{t-2} - 0.058 * REIT_{t-3}$$
$$(4.397)\ (1.174) \qquad\qquad (-1.484) \qquad\qquad (-0.773) \qquad\qquad (6.2)$$

Adjusted $R^2 = 0.008$

DW $= 2.000$

Mean dependent variable $= 3.159$

S.D. dependent variable $= 8.901$

S.E. of regression $= 8.867$

Property is a different matter. The significant coefficients on the lagged leveraged property variables, by contrast, are significant, indicating serial correlation, as shown in Equation (6.3).

$$NPILEV_t = 0.588 + 0.721 * NPILEV_{t-1} + 0.340 * NPILEV_{t-2} - 0.316 NPILEV_{t-3}$$
$$(2.525)\ (9.452) \qquad\qquad (3.697) \qquad\qquad\qquad\qquad (6.3)$$

Adjusted $R^2 = 0.641$

DW $= 1.967$

Mean dependent variable $= 2.387$

S.D. dependent variable $= 4.006$

S.E. of regression $= 2.40$

Turnover and Liquidity

In Chapter 13 I devise a liquidity measure, the turnover or trade ratio, for the US, various property types, and MSAs. Liquidity, which varies across MSAs, affects cap rates.

Due to illiquidity or imperfections in information flow within the property market, property turnover is significantly lower than turnover in the stock market. During recessions, property transaction volume craters and liquidity practically vanishes.

Office property and stock market turnover percentages were 2.7% and 407.6%, respectively, at the onset of the GFC, as shown in Exhibit 6.9. The property turnover rate, which was 3.6% in late 2024, is a small fraction of stock market turnover.

Stock turnover leads property turnover by one year. If stock turnover increases, then office property turnover decreases in the following year, as shown in Equation (6.4). The negative coefficient is statistically significant, albeit small in absolute value. I suspect the reason is that momentum investors increase stock exposure following an upturn and reallocate away from property to stocks.

$$OFFICETURN_t = 6.653 - 0.012 * STOCKTURN_{t-1}$$
$$(9.195) \quad (-3.124) \quad\quad\quad (6.4)$$

Adjusted $R^2 = 0.315$

DW = 0.899

Mean dependent variable = 4.560

S.D. dependent variable = 1.474

S.E. of regression = 1.219

EXHIBIT 6.9 Property turnover is much less than stock market turnover.

Source: ZCA using CoStar and Federal Reserve data

Analysis of the Quadrant Linkages

The quadrant total return models include BBB-rated CMBS (Quadrant 1), mortgages (Quadrant 2), publicly traded equity REITs (Quadrant 3), and leveraged property (Quadrant 4). I include for each quadrant performance graphs and a total return model. BBB-rated CMBS returns lagged by four quarters explain property returns.

Exhibit 6.10 illustrates the data flow between quadrants. Quadrant 4 contributes data to Quadrant 1 (CMBS) and Quadrant 3 (REITs) but receives data from Quadrants 1 and 3. Quadrant 2 just receives data from Quadrants 1 and 3 as well as from the general capital markets, e.g., bond default premium.

EXHIBIT 6.10 Flow of information between quadrant equations.

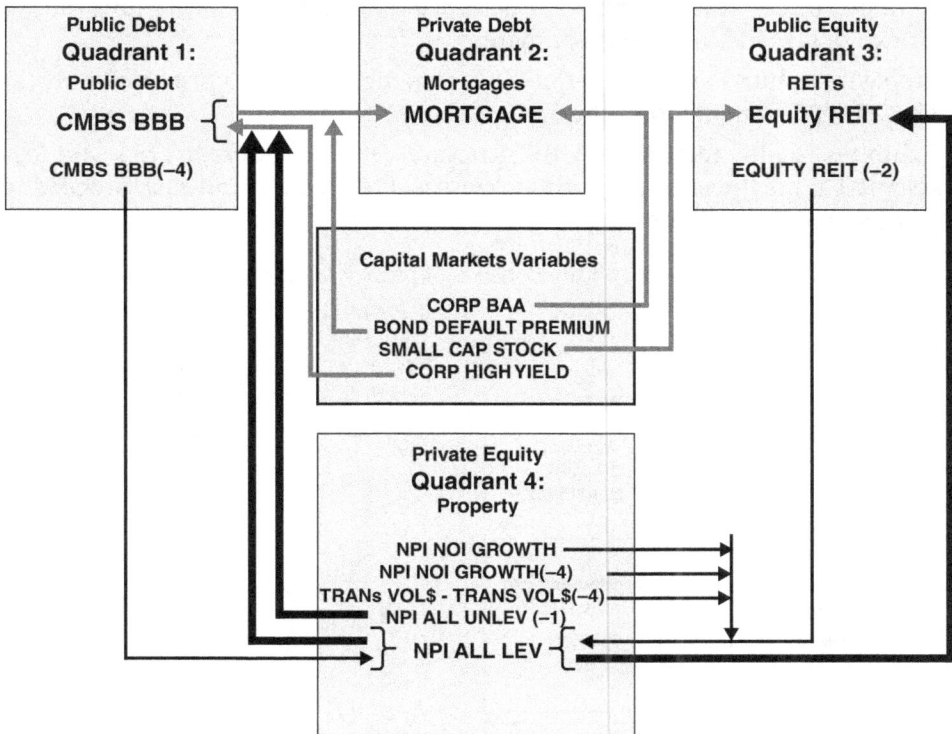

Source: ZCA

Quadrant 1: Public Debt: CMBS

Publicly traded commercial mortgage-backed securities (CMBS) and REITs recapitalized the real estate sector following the Tax Reform Act of 1986 and the RTC crash.

The essence of CMBS is a senior/subordinate structure in which the cash flow from the underlying pool of commercial mortgages is used to create distinct classes of securities or tranches. These classes are assigned priorities with respect to loan retirement—most commercial mortgages have prepayment protection—and credit losses, primarily due to credit risk.

Residential mortgage-backed securities present special problems that include negative convexity and prepayment risk. Prepayment penalties do not apply to residential mortgages. Hence, if rates fall sufficiently, the borrower prepays. By contrast, CMBS offers prepayment protection, such as lockouts, yield maintenance, and prepayment penalties, which makes CMBS attractive to companies with long duration liabilities, such as life insurance companies.

Prepayment hurts an interest-only (IO) tranche but helps a principal-only (PO) tranche. The PO benefits from the early return of capital.

Exhibit 6.11 illustrates the CMBS structure. Default (or credit) risk and losses are assigned to the lower or subordinate classes. Prepayment and cash proceeds are first assigned to the senior classes.

EXHIBIT 6.11 CMBS structure consists of priority assignment.

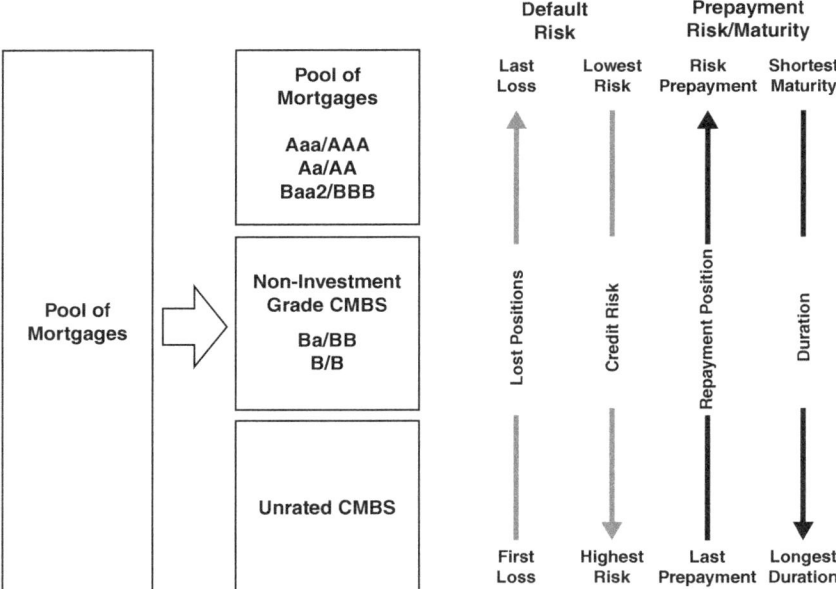

Subordination provides credit support to the higher classes, such as the AAA, AA, A, and BBB, all institutional grade. A larger proportion of the senior securities issued from such a pool typically receives higher credit-ratings, which means lower yields, thereby enabling the overall CMBS issue to obtain a higher average price and to generate greater total proceeds. More credit support means a higher rating.

Different tranches appeal to different types of investors. Conservative institutions favor senior tranches while some real property investors regard subordinate CMBS as a property substitute. The market for the speculative tranches is much thinner. Major buyers and holders of the lower tranches are aggressive investors willing to take on the risk of receiving higher expected returns; these investors typically have specialized knowledge and expertise regarding commercial property risk.

The performance of the lower tranches is more highly correlated with underlying property performance than are the senior classes, which are more interest rate sensitive. The BBB–AAA-rated CMBS bond spread, cyclically wide, is negatively correlated with the leveraged property total return. Exhibits 6.12 and 6.13 show the total returns for the AAA- and BBB-rated tranches.

The coefficients of variation—standard deviation divided by the mean—of AAA- and BBB-rated CMBS are 3.800 and 13.739, respectively. Corporate bonds do not exhibit this disparity, which is consistent with thin trading volume and greater inefficiency in the subordinate CMBS market. (See Exhibits 6.14 and 6.15.)

Subordinate tranches are more sensitive than senior tranches to underlying real estate conditions. They are helpful in forecasting property performance. See Exhibit 6.15.

EXHIBIT 6.12   AAA-rated CMBS returns.

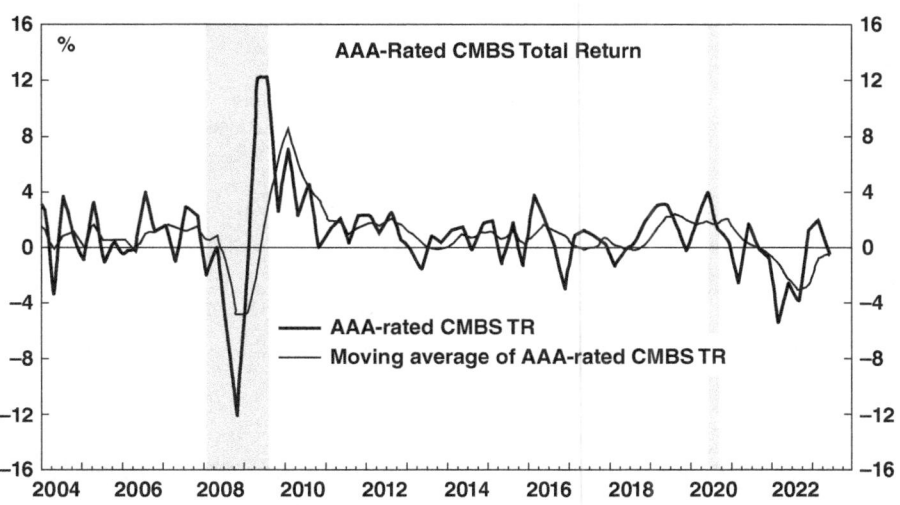

Source: ZCA using Federal Reserve data

EXHIBIT 6.13 BBB-rated CMBS total returns. The correlation with AAA-rated CMBS returns is 0.661.

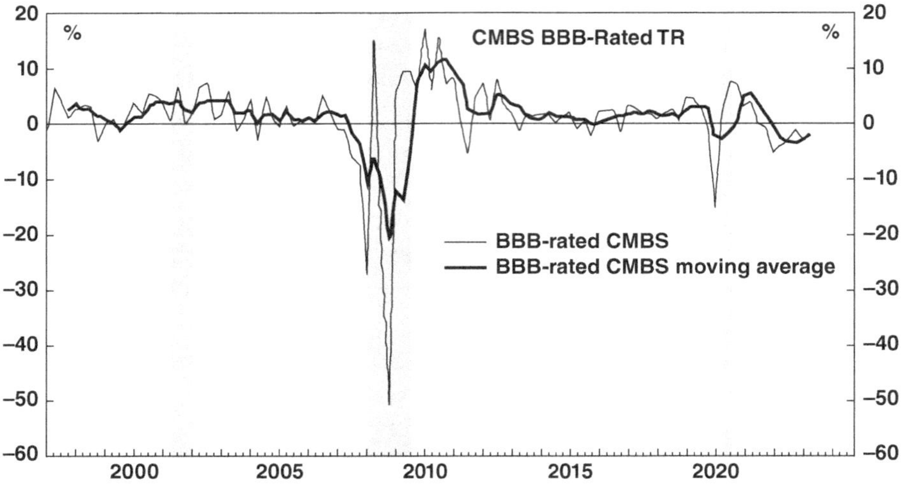

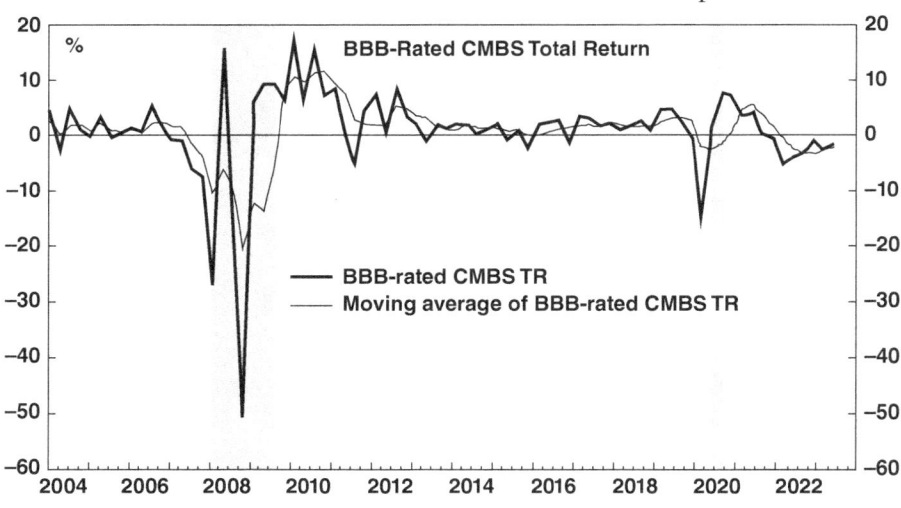

Source: ZCA using Federal Reserve data

EXHIBIT 6.14 BBB-rated CMBS is more volatile than Baa corporate bonds.

Source: ZCA using Federal Reserve data

The CMBS BBB–AAA spread is inversely correlated with the NPI leveraged return, as shown in Exhibit 6.16. The CMBS subordinate and leveraged NPI property return are highly correlated, by contrast. (See Exhibit 6.17.)

Analysis of the Quadrant Linkages   113

EXHIBIT 6.15 CMBS spreads increased after 2021 but are now narrowing a bit.

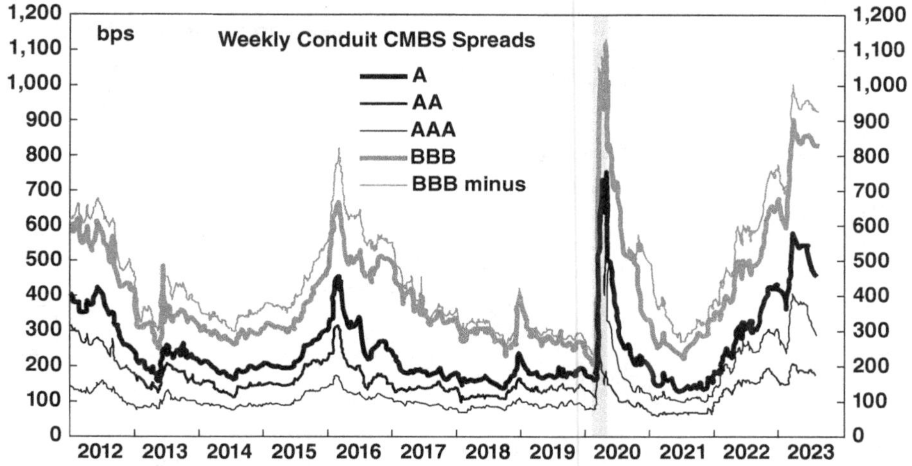

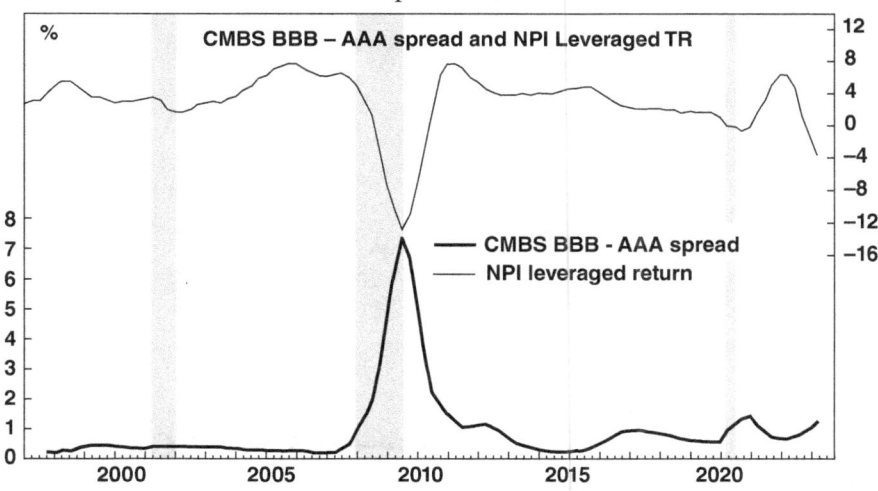

Source: ZCA using Federal Reserve data

EXHIBIT 6.16 CMBS BBB–AAA spread and NPI TR.

Source: ZCA using Federal Reserve data

According to Exhibit 6.18, BBB-rated CMBS and its returns are correlated with the bond default premium, as shown in Exhibit 6.19.

Total CBBS and corporate bond returns. AAA-rated CMBS total returns are most sensitive to the AAA-rated corporate bond total returns and interest rates,

EXHIBIT 6.17 BBB-rated CMBS and NPI TR.

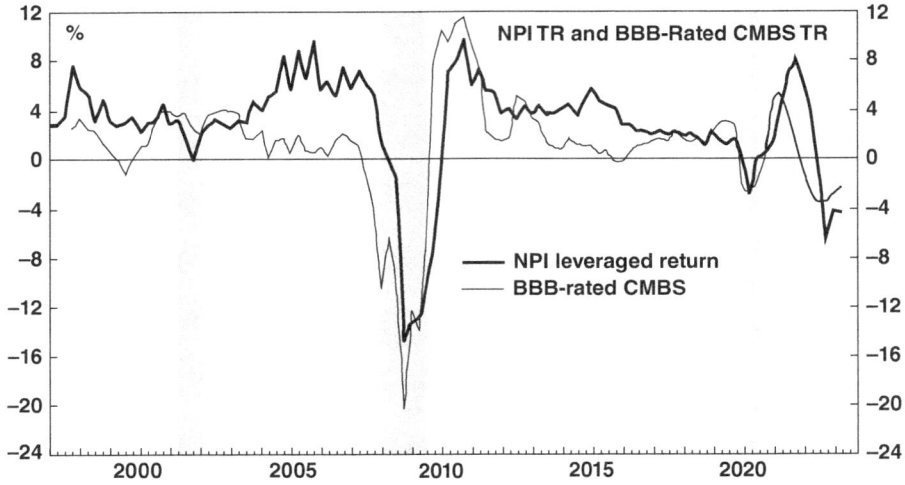

Source: ZCA using Federal Reserve data

EXHIBIT 6.18 CMBS yields rise in weak markets and fall in strong markets.

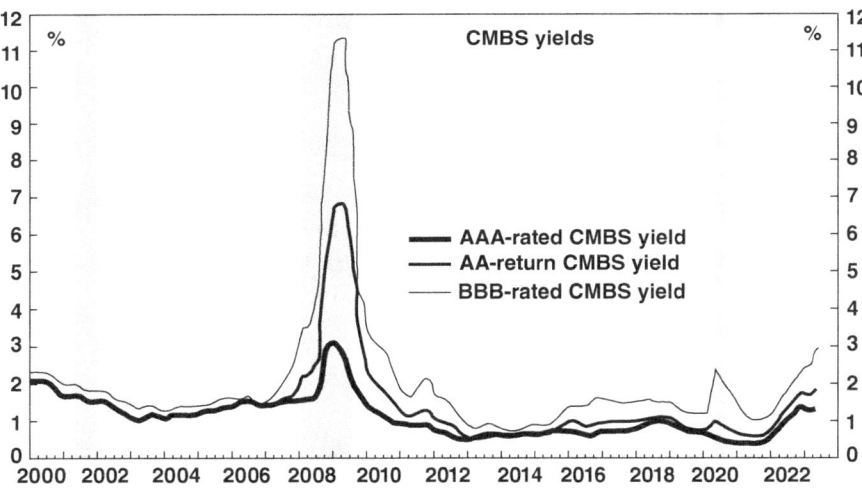

Source: ZCA using Federal Reserve data

whereas the BBB-rated CMBS and Baa-rated corporate bonds are not as strongly correlated, since the BBB-rated CMBS returns are driven more by the usual real estate–specific factors. (See Exhibits 6.20 and 6.21.)

Analysis of the Quadrant Linkages 115

EXHIBIT 6.19 BBB-rated CMBS and default premium.

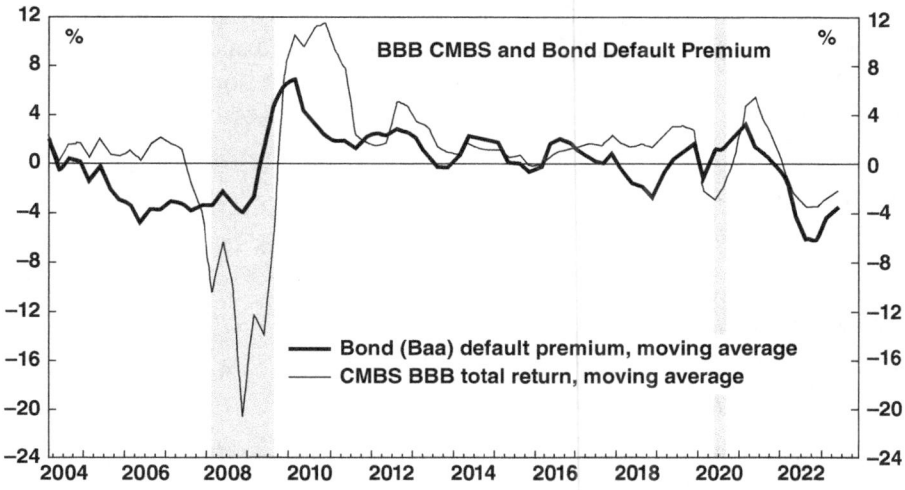

Source: ZCA using Federal Reserve data

EXHIBIT 6.20 AAA-rated CMBS and AAA-rated corporate TR.

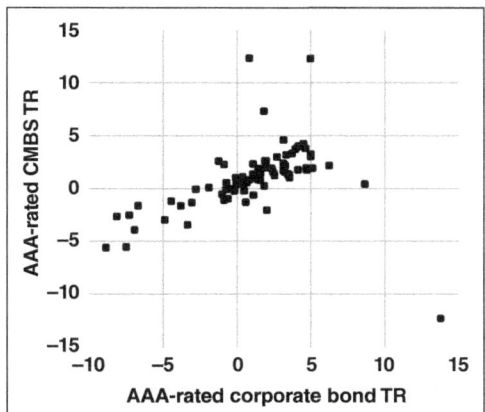

Source: ZCA using Federal Reserve data

EXHIBIT 6.21 BBB-rated CMBS and BBB-rated corporate TR.

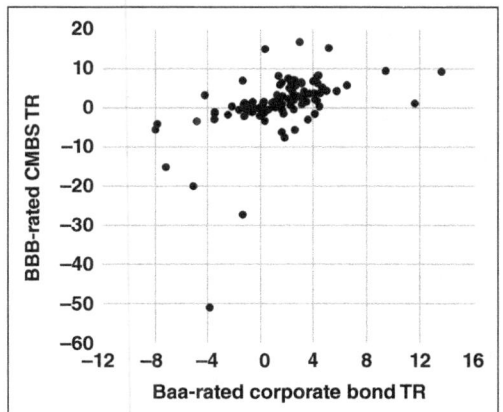

Source: ZCA using Federal Reserve data

Equations (6.5) and (6.6) compare the sensitivities of CMBS bond to corporate bond total returns. AAA-rated CMBS is relatively insensitive as indicated by the coefficient, 0.298, to changes in AAA corporate bond returns. Such is not the case with the BBB-rated CMBS tranche. BBB-rated corporate bond returns are highly corelated with these tranches, as shown in the coefficient of 1.138.

$$CMBSAAA_t = 0.587 + 0.298 * CORPAAA_t$$
$$(\mathbf{1.668})\ \ (\mathbf{3.277}) \tag{6.5}$$

Adjusted $R^2 = 0.112$
DW $= 1.395$
Mean dependent variable $= 0.846$
S.D. dependent variable $= 3.217$
S.E. of regression $= 3.031$

$$CMBSBBB_t = -0.702 + 1.138 * CORPBAA_t$$
$$(\mathbf{-0.767})\ \ \ (\mathbf{4.723}) \tag{6.6}$$

Adjusted $R^2 = 0.217$
DW $= 1.756$
Mean dependent variable $= 0.632$
S.D. dependent variable $= 8.683$
S.E. of regression $= 7.684$

CMBS yields and NOI growth. Bivariate scatter graphs can be misleading, especially when important variables are omitted, as discussed in Chapter 2. For example, the bivariate relationships between NOI growth and either CMBSAAA or CMBSBBB yield—not returns—is insignificant, as shown below. However, high-yield corporate bond yields are significant. See Exhibit 6.22 and Exhibit 6.23.

The coefficient on the moving average of NOI growth, even though it is not statistically significant, is over twice the size of the coefficient in the CMBSAAA equation below. The low t-statistic indicates that the coefficient estimate is not precise. Since the BBB-rate CMBS tranche, which is the subordinate tranche, is the riskiest, I would have expected that the yield for the BBB tranche would be more

EXHIBIT 6.22 NOI growth is not a good *bivariate* predictor of AAA-rated CMBS yield.

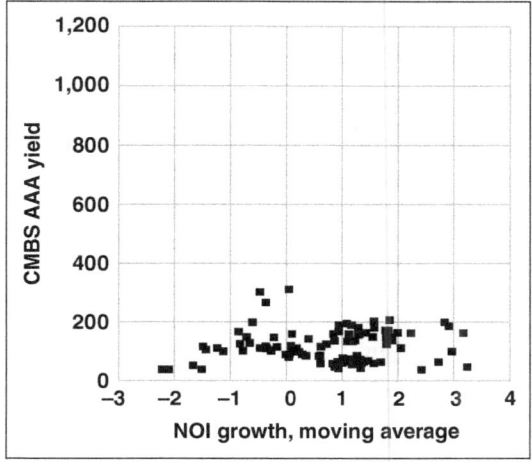

Source: ZCA using CoStar and Federal Reserve data

EXHIBIT 6.23 NOI growth is not a good bivariate predictor of BBB-rated CMBS yield.

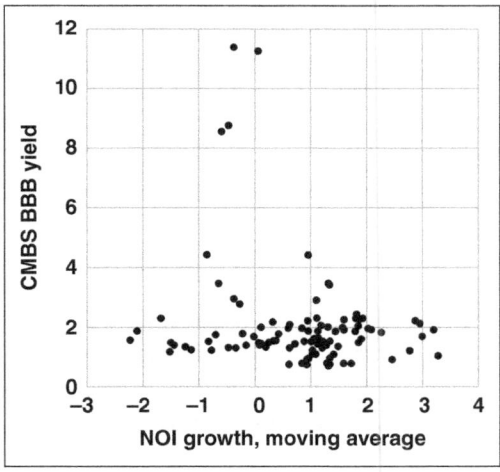

Source: ZCA using CoStar and Federal Reserve data

sensitive to underlying real estate conditions. High-yield bond yields are a significant predictor of subordinate CMBS performance.

$$CMBSBBB_t = -2.973 - 0.080 * MOVAVG(NOIGROWTH_{t-2}) + 1.492 * HYCORPYLD_t *$$
$$(-0.728) \quad (-0.590) \quad\quad\quad\quad\quad (13.349)$$

$$- 0.014 * TREND_t + 0.880 * AR(1) + 0.315 * SIGMASQSIGMASQ$$
$$(0.447) \quad\quad (27.763) \quad\quad (20.980) \quad\quad\quad\quad\quad (6.7)$$

Adjusted R^2 = 0.892

DW = 1.060

Mean dependent variable = 1.989

S.D. dependent variable = 1.757

S.E. of regression = 0.578

$$CMBSAAA_t = 0.843 - 0.004 * MOVAVG(NOIGROWTH_{t-2}) + 0.447 * HYCORPYLD_t$$
$$(1.609)(-0.558) \quad\quad\quad\quad\quad\quad (27.425)$$

$$- 0.005 * TREND_t - 0.920 * AR(1) + 0.012 * SIGMASQ$$
$$(-0.249) \quad\quad (24.791) \quad\quad (9.811) \quad\quad\quad\quad\quad (6.8)$$

Adjusted R^2 = 0.959

DW = 1.303

Mean dependent variable = 1.108

S.D. dependent variable = 0.563

S.E. of regression = 0.114

Current leveraged property returns explain BBB-rated CMBS returns. The negative sign on unleveraged NPI returns lagged one period in Equation 6.9 is a sign of reversion to the mean or negative feedback. The model explains 52% of the variation in the dependent variable and the coefficient values are highly significant. The

Durbin Watson statistic, a measure of serial correlation, indicates no serial correlation in the residuals.

$$CMBSBBB_t = 0.274 + 0.766 * HYCORPRET_t + 1.374 * NPILEV_t - 1.964 * NPIUNLEV_{t-1}$$
$$(0.311) \quad (6.369) \quad\quad\quad\quad (5.746) \quad\quad\quad (-4.026) \quad\quad\quad\quad (6.9)$$

Adjusted $R^2 = 0.523$

DW = 2.076

Mean dependent variable = 1.084

S.D. dependent variable = 7.610

S.E. of regression = 5.258

The yield of the senior or AAA-rated CMBS tranche is highly correlated with the AAA-corporate bond yield, as shown in Exhibit 6.24. By contrast, the relationship between the high-yield corporate bond and the BBB-rated CMBS tranche is much more complicated, as shown in Exhibit 6.25. The returns of BBB-rated CMBS tranches react much faster to exogenous shocks than the property markets.

Real estate–specific risks are more important in pricing subordinate, not the senior, CMBS tranches. Hence, BBB-rated CMBS yields and returns are very useful

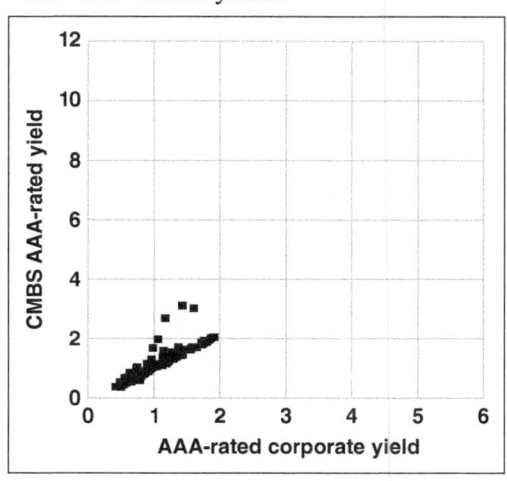

EXHIBIT 6.24 AAA-rated corporate and AAA-rated CMBS yields.

Source: ZCA using Federal Reserve data

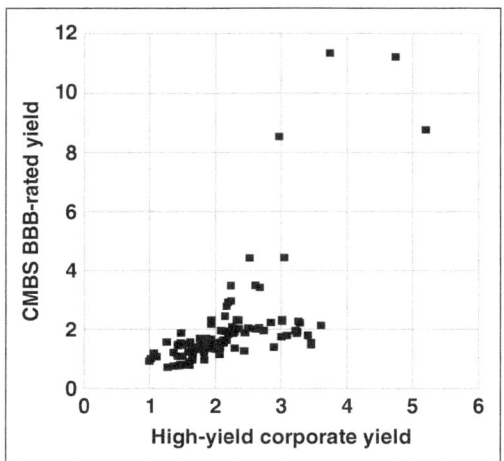

EXHIBIT 6.25 High-yield corporate and BBB-rated CMBS yields.

Source: ZCA using Federal Reserve data

in forecasting property returns, as our leveraged NPI property return forecasting model shows. The relationship between the corporate bond market and the yields of senior and subordinate CMBS tranches is powerful.

Subordinate BBB-rated CMBS total returns increase if returns on high-yield bonds and levered property are higher. The lagged returns for unlevered property and BBB-rated CMBS are inversely correlated.

Quadrant 2: Private Debt: Mortgages

Mortgages, which are collateralized by real estate, are special examples of debt. Commercial mortgages are similar to traditional debt in the sense that the value of the contractual stream of debt payments increases as interest rates decline. This curve has positive convexity. By contrast, a residential mortgage can prepay if interest rates decline sufficiently, which produces negative convexity. See Exhibit 6.26.

Commercial mortgages have better call protection, which includes prepayment penalties and lock-out periods. The borrower defaults when the value of the real estate is less than the value of the loan and the income is less than the debt service. The owner of a commercial mortgage holds a long position in a credit-risk-free, non-callable mortgage, a short call option, and a short put option. The mortgage lender (or investor) has written an option to the borrower (equity holder) to prepay the debt and an option to default or put the real estate to the lender. Lenders receive

EXHIBIT 6.26 Commercial mortgage positive convexity and residential mortgage negative convexity.

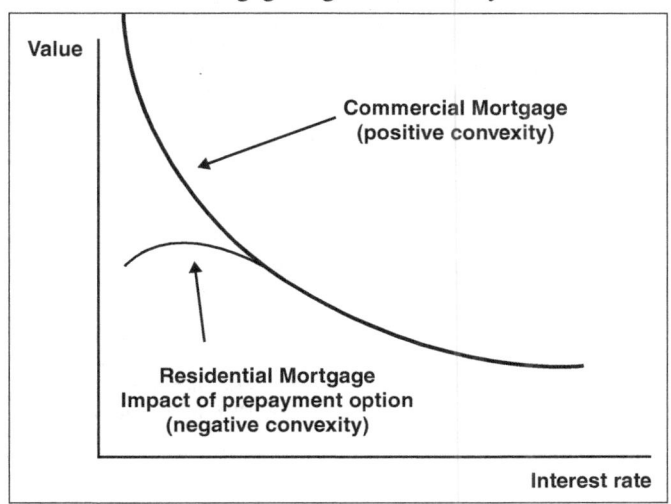

Source: ZCA

compensation in the form of a spread over riskless Treasury bond yields for writing these options in the form of a spread over riskless Treasury bond yields.

Prepayment is triggered if the refinancing is attractive and the owner sells the property but the mortgage is not assumable. Refinancing is also attractive if interest rates drop or if the property value increases, which facilitates refinancing. What are the default triggers? Net operating income (NOI) must be less than the mortgage payment and the market value of the property must be less than the value of the debt. Default can be a method of prepayment so as to avoid a prepayment penalty or the lock-out provision.

There are two conditions that might make this gambit work: The NOI has to be greater than the mortgage payments required when it is time to refinance the loan. In addition, the present value of future payments less the value of the embedded options must be greater than the sum of the face value of the remaining debt plus foreclosure expenses.

The analysis is complicated because factors that cause prepayment also cause default. A lockout or prepayment reduces the value of the call option since the holder will not likely exercise this option. The longer is the term to maturity and the more volatile are interest rates, the more valuable is the prepayment option. The likelihood of default is greater the more volatile is NOI, the higher is the leverage, the lower is the debt service coverage, and the longer is the term to maturity.[1]

EXHIBIT 6.27 Credit and non-credit adjusted mortgage TR do not differ much.

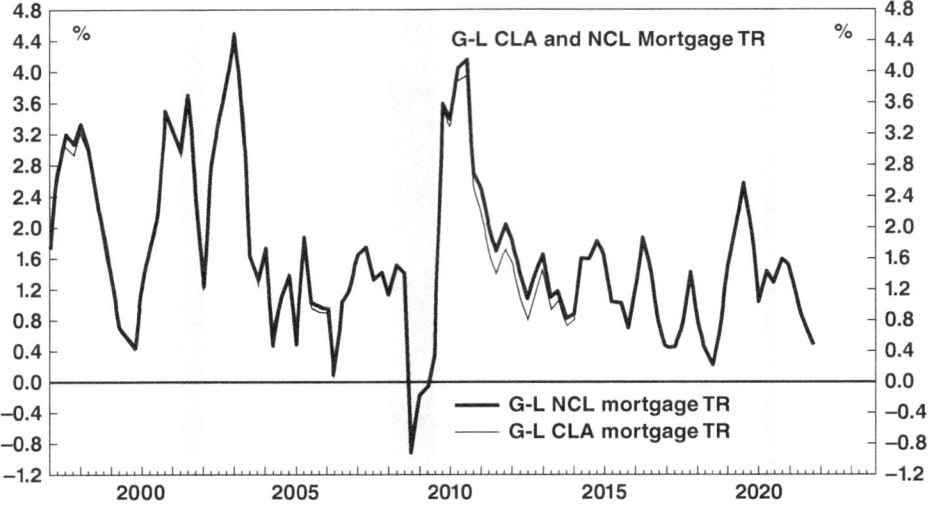

Source: ZCA using G-L data

Mortgage performance index. The Giliberto-Levy Mortgage Index (G-L) is an excellent mortgage performance index. Real estate fundamentals influence senior mortgage returns less than they do equity returns. Exhibit 6.27 shows that the credit and non-credit adjusted mortgage total returns are very similar over time.

Senior mortgage returns across major property types are highly correlated; the average correlation between these returns is 0.963. Exhibit 6.28 shows total mortgage returns over time by property type.

The average correlation of property returns using the NPI property index, by contrast, is only 0.744 as shown in Exhibits 6.29. The lower is the leverage, the likelihood of default (or sensitivities to real estate shocks) is less.

Mortgage losses rose dramatically, albeit with a lag, after the GFC, but since then, they have remained relatively low, as shown in Exhibit 6.30. Exhibit 6.31 shows the positive correlation between the total return for the Baa corporate bond and the CLA G-L mortgage.

Exhibit 6.32 shows the high correlation between the senior mortgage total return and the bond default premium. The leveraged property return and the mortgage total return are inversely correlated with the mortgage total return leading leveraged property performance, as shown in Exhibit 6.33.

EXHIBIT 6.28 Total mortgage returns; average correlation across property types is 0.963.

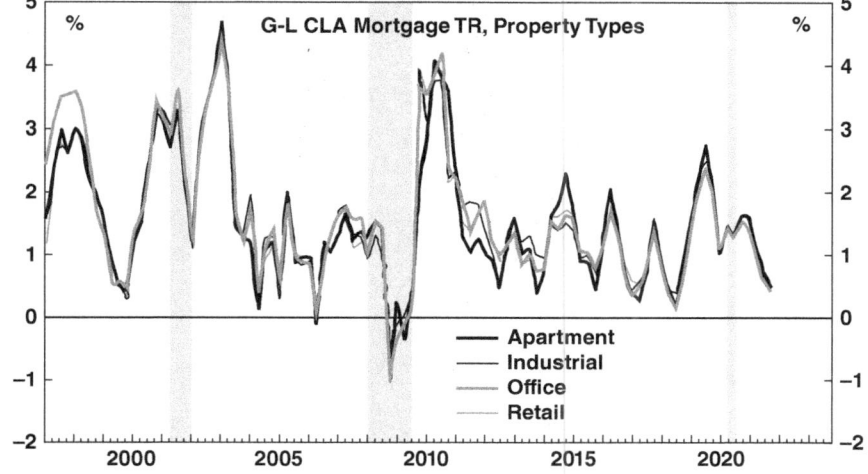

Source: ZCA using G-L data

EXHIBIT 6.29 Total property returns; average correlation across property types is 0.744.

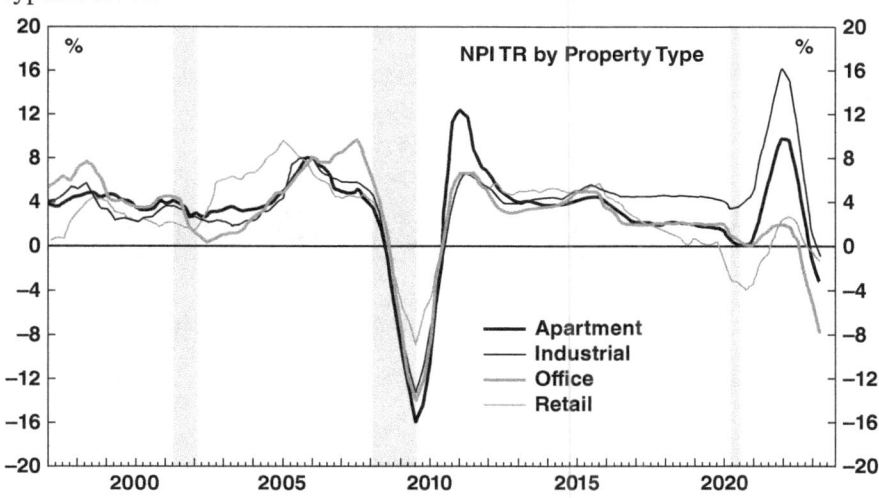

Source: ZCA using G-L data

EXHIBIT 6.30 G-L commercial mortgage loss.

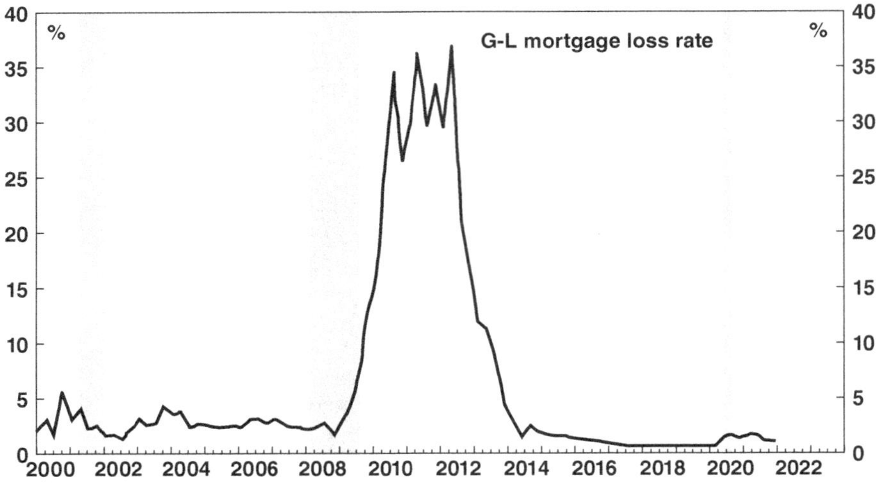

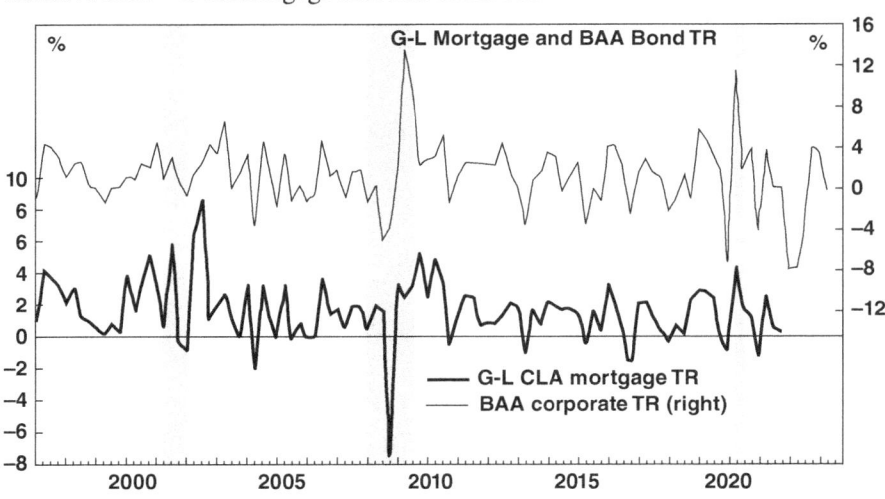

Source: ZCA using G-L data

EXHIBIT 6.31 G-L mortgage and Baa bond TR.

Source: ZCA using G-L data

A regression of the mortgage return on the bond return explains 62% of the variation in the mortgage return. A 10% increase in the corporate bond return results in a 6.4% increase in the G-L mortgage return. The mortgage return is a function of the bond default premium lagged by four quarters.

EXHIBIT 6.32 Mortgage TR and default premium.

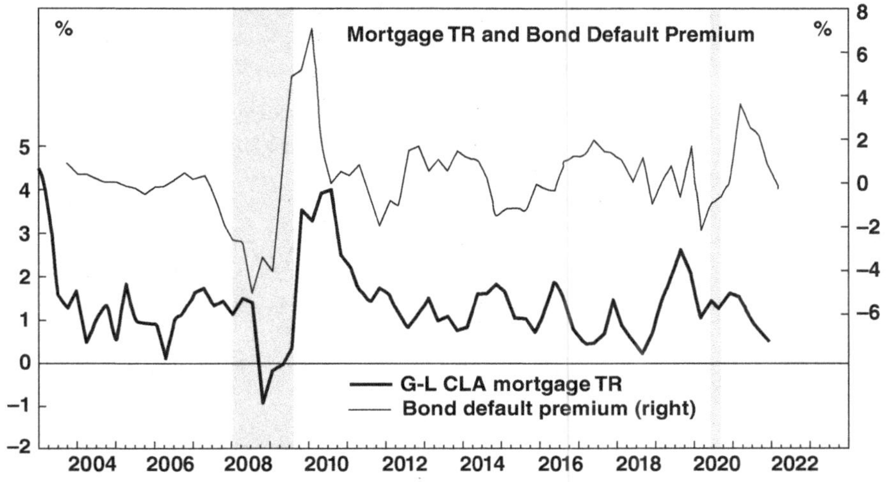

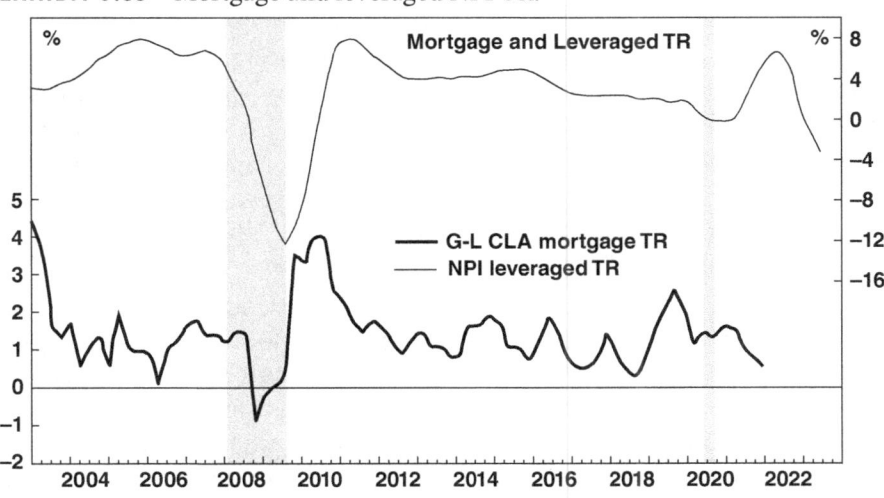

Source: ZCA using G-L data

EXHIBIT 6.33 Mortgage and leveraged NPI TR.

Source: ZCA using G-L data

Exhibit 6.34 graphs the normalized loans and property sales volumes. (In order to scale the variables and provide meaningful comparisons, I normalize each variable by subtracting the mean and dividing by the standard deviation.) The correlations are strong.

EXHIBIT 6.34 Normalized loan and sales volume are correlated: A 10% increase in volume is associated with a 11.6% increase in loans.

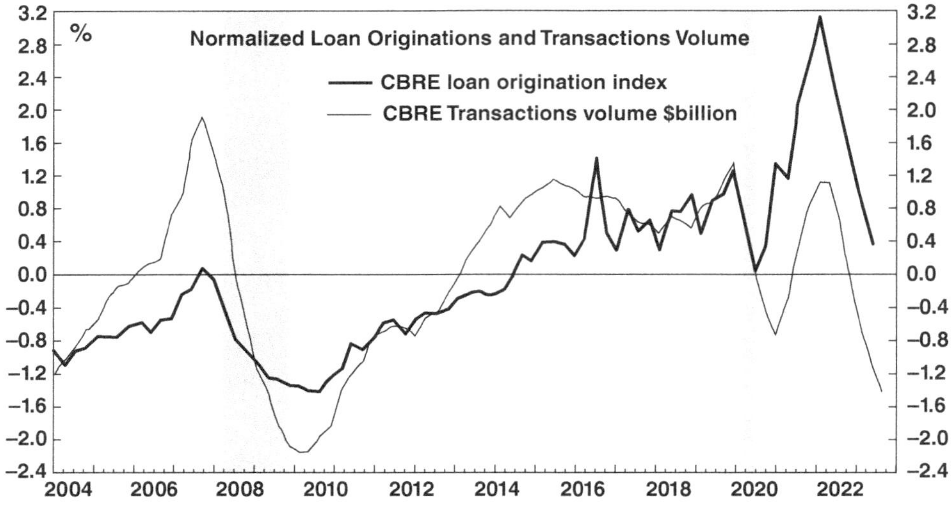

Source: ZCA using G-L data

Equation (6.10) indicates that the total return of the Giliberto-Levy commercial mortgage index increases the higher is BBB-rated CMBS and Baa corporate bonds returns. The greater is the bond default premium—the geometric ratio of long-term Baa corporate bond total returns over long-term government bond returns—the lower is the return for credit-loss-adjusted (CLA) mortgage returns. Bond holders receive a premium for holding bonds with default risk. Callability risk is also incorporated within the bond default premium.

Neither NOI growth nor leveraged property returns, current or lagged, explain senior mortgage total returns directly. This is reasonable since the mortgages comprising the index are relatively safe compared to the equity. Hence, I exclude from the regression both NOI growth and the leveraged property return, but include BBB-rated CMBS total returns because they are a significant fixed income proxy for property risk as a result of myriad other factors that affect total property risk. Importantly, the BBB-rated CMBS returns do not exhibit serial correlation. They are not statistically smooth, so they are a better indicator of property risk than contemporaneous NPI volatility.

The model says that BBB-rated CMBS spreads, BAA-rated bonds, and the bond default premium are important determinants of senior mortgage returns. The model explains 78% of returns and there is no serial correlation.

$$GLMORTCLA_t = \underset{(5.466)}{0.597} + \underset{(6.850)}{0.088 * CMBSBBB_t} + \underset{(11.157)}{0.426 * CORPBAA_t}$$

$$- \underset{(-9.185)}{0.279 * BONDDEFAULT_t} \tag{6.10}$$

Adjusted $R^2 = 0.780$

DW = 2.384

Mean dependent variable = 1.254

S.D. dependent variable = 1.797

S.E. of regression = 0.843

The t-statistics (in parentheses) are highly significant and all variables have the right sign. The Durbin Watson statistic, a measure of serial correlation, is also acceptable. This result is remarkably compelling given that our aim is to explain the total returns of a privately traded, illiquid security.

Subordinate CMBS is useful in explaining property returns. The Baa-rated corporate is more influential than the subordinate CMBS bond returns, however. If the default premium increases by 100 bps, then the total return on mortgages declines by 28 bps. A 1% increase in the BBB-rated CMBS bond return has a smaller effect on senior mortgage returns than does an increase in the Baa-rated corporate bond return. Importantly, a 1% increase in the corporate bond return is associated with a 0.4% increase in the senior mortgage return.

Investors in senior mortgages should monitor the BBB-rated CMBS return, the Baa-rated corporate bond yield, and the bond default premium. These variables explain most of senior mortgage returns! Mezzanine debt total returns, which we do not evaluate in this text, would be much more sensitive subordinate CMBS bond returns.

A 1% increase in the Baa-rated corporate bond yield is associated with a 0.426 increase in senior mortgage returns. Why is the coefficient positive? I believe that substitution plays a role. Investors switch from corporate bonds to senior mortgages. A 1% rise in default expectations, as measured by the bond default premium, leads to a 0.279 decrease in senior mortgage returns.

The message for real estate investors is clear. Look to the capital markets, not to the skies, to which all trees grow without limit.

Quadrant 3: Public Equity: REITs

What is a REIT? REITs do not pay taxes at the entity level. REITs can be either private or publicly traded. Most REITs are equity REITs, but some hold mortgages as assets. REITs must comply with the following rules:

- Minimum of 100 shareholders.
- At least 75% of total assets must be held in real estate, cash, or government securities.
- At least 75% of gross income must derive from property rents, interest on mortgages, gains on sales of property, or dividends from other REITs.
- At least 90% of REITs' taxable income must be distributed to stockholders.

Public REITs played a major role, along with CMBS, in recapitalizing the real estate sector during and following the RTC period. At that time many private real estate companies converted to publicly traded REITs using the Umbrellas Partnership REIT (UPREIT) structure. The UPREIT allows property investors to contribute partnership interests in exchange for operating partnership (OP) units in the UPREIT. The owner could elect to convert OP units into shares. Payment of capital gains taxes would be deferred until the time of conversion. Depreciation, a non-cash expense, and amortization affect taxable income, but do not affect net cash flow. This provision provides the REIT with cash to pay for capital expenditures, among other expenses.

REIT returns. Publicly traded equity REITs have been recognized for three decades as a leading indicator of property returns, but the causality is two-way. REIT performance reflects bond and stock market performance as well as current property performance. Public market pricing incorporates property market information faster than backward-looking private markets that depend on appraisals and discounted cash flow analysis. REIT returns impound real estate news faster than do property returns. Lately, REITs and leveraged property returns have been highly correlated. Exhibit 6.35 shows that REIT returns lead NCREIF property returns by at least one quarter and are good predictors of leveraged and unleveraged property returns.

EXHIBIT 6.35 Equity REIT and NPI property TR.

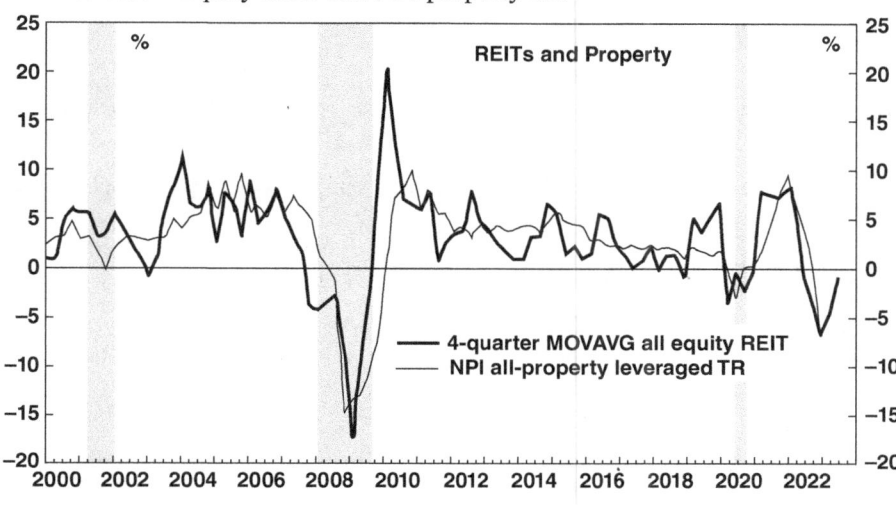

Source: ZCA using Federal Reserve data

Current and lagged NOI growth, BBB-rated CMBS, property returns, and sales transactions have good explanatory powers, as indicated by Equation (6.11).

$$NPILEV_t = \begin{array}{l} 0.174 + 0.148 * CMBSBBB_t + 0.052 * REIT_{t-2} + 0.297 * NOIGROWTH_t \\ (0.658) \ (5.654) \qquad\qquad\quad (2.688) \qquad\quad (2.930) \end{array}$$

$$\begin{array}{l} -0.237 * NOIGROWTH_{t-4} + 0.006 *(TRANSACTIONS_t - TRANSACTIONS_{-4}) \\ (-2.346) \qquad\qquad\qquad\quad (1.964) \end{array}$$

$$\begin{array}{l} +0.763 * NPILEV_{t-1} \\ (11.977) \end{array} \qquad\qquad\qquad\qquad\qquad\qquad\qquad\qquad (6.11)$$

Adjusted $R^2 = 0.861$

DW $= 2.449$

Mean dependent variable $= 2.700$

S.D. dependent var $= 4.818$

S.E. of regression $= 1.796$

The following model explains 86% of the variation in unleveraged NCREIF property returns and the signs are correct.

$$NPIUNLEV_t = 0.307 + 0.082 * CMBSBBB_t + 0.018 * REIT_{t-1} + 0.144 * NOIGROWTH_t$$
$$(1.811)\ (5.779) \qquad\qquad (1.736) \qquad\qquad (2.633)$$

$$- 0.166 * NOIGROWTH_{t-4} + 0.004 * (TRANSACTIONS_t - TRANSACTIONS_{t-4}) +$$
$$(-3.106) \qquad\qquad\qquad (1.952)$$

$$0.752 * NPIUNLEV_{t-1} \qquad\qquad\qquad\qquad\qquad\qquad (6.12)$$

Adjusted $R^2 = 0.859$

DW = 2.381

Mean dependent variable = 2.023

S.D. dependent var = 2.538

S.E. of regression = 0.952

Current, not lagged, property returns explain REIT returns. Why current? REITs impound new information with hardly any lag. Equation (6.13) explains 61% of the variation of total equity REIT returns. Noteworthy is the statistically significant impact of small-cap stock returns on REIT returns. A 1% increase in the small-cap stock return is associated with a 0.65% increase in REIT returns. Unleveraged property returns have a strong contemporaneous impact on REIT returns, but leveraged property returns, lagged one period, have a negative impact. This lagged negative result is an indicator of risks in the property market that affect REIT returns with a one-quarter lag.

$$REIT_t = 0.078 + 0.649 * SMALL_t + 2.094 * NPIUNLEV_t - 1.684 * NPIUNLEV_{t-1}$$
$$(0.078)\ (9.131) \qquad\quad (3.641) \qquad\qquad (-2.877) \qquad\qquad (6.13)$$

Adjusted $R^2 = 0.614$

DW = 2.102

Mean dependent variable = 2.877

S.D. dependent = 10.836

S.E. of regression = 0.614

EXHIBIT 6.36 Small-cap stock returns closely track equity REIT returns.

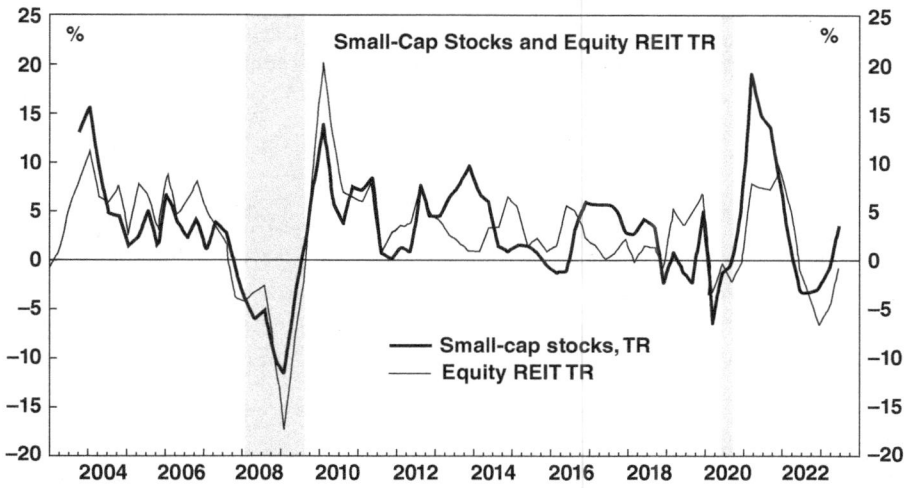

Source: ZCA using Federal Reserve data

The total returns of REITS and small-cap stocks are also highly correlated as shown in Exhibit 6.36. Some investors and especially their wealth managers incorrectly believe that equity REITs are a substitute for property.

Even though REITs are typically collateralized by property, the statistical characteristics of REIT returns do not closely resemble property returns. The return distributions of REITs and property are very different. This important observation is called the REIT paradox.

Are REITs a poor proxy for property? Are they merely small-cap stocks? Whichever real estate quadrants investors prefer, they should still continually monitor the relationship between REIT and property returns because REIT returns lead property returns.

When REIT investors are pessimistic, property transactions volume declines with a lag. REIT returns lagged four quarters are positively correlated with property returns. REITs are the canary in the property coal mine, so real estate investors who do not invest in REITs should still study REIT performance. See Exhibit 6.37.

EXHIBIT 6.37 Total property returns and transactions volume; average correlation = 0.744.

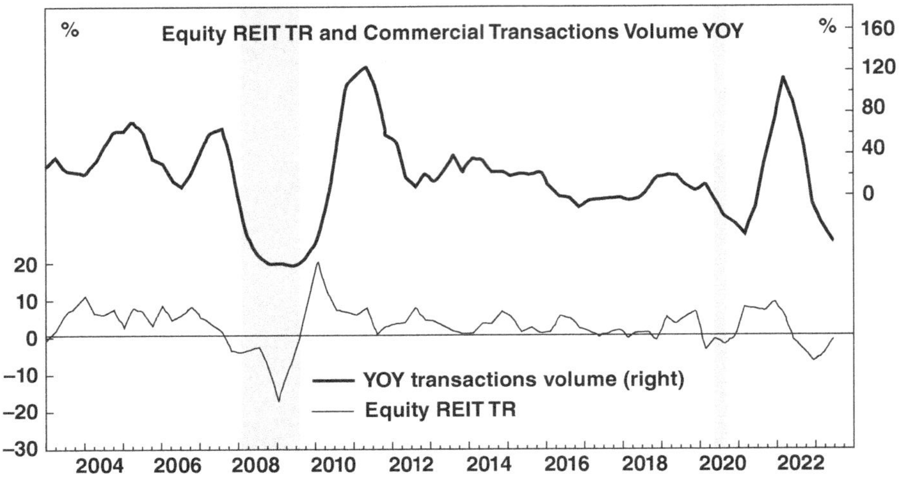

Source: ZCA using Federal Reserve data

Quadrant 4: Private Equity: Property

Chapter 3 discusses the nature of property and Chapter 4 introduces the capital stack and leverage.

From 2023 through 2024, the NOI growth rate declined and transactions volume cratered, which depressed leveraged and unleveraged NPI returns. (See Exhibit 6.38.)

Prices deteriorated after 2023 as the growth rate of effective rents cooled. Total property and BBB-rated CMBS returns were negative.

NCREIF's Open End Diversified Core Equity (NPI-ODCE) is a low-risk investment returns index of the performance of the largest private real estate diversified funds that use low leverage and invest in stable US properties across various regions and property types. The relationship between property returns and NOI growth is statistically significant.

For example, a bivariate regression indicates that NOI growth is a significant factor in explaining unleveraged returns but it explains only about 6.4% of the variation in leveraged returns. Hence, I include in my forecasting model other variables, the omission of which biases the estimated relationship between growth

EXHIBIT 6.38 Leveraged and unleveraged property total returns.

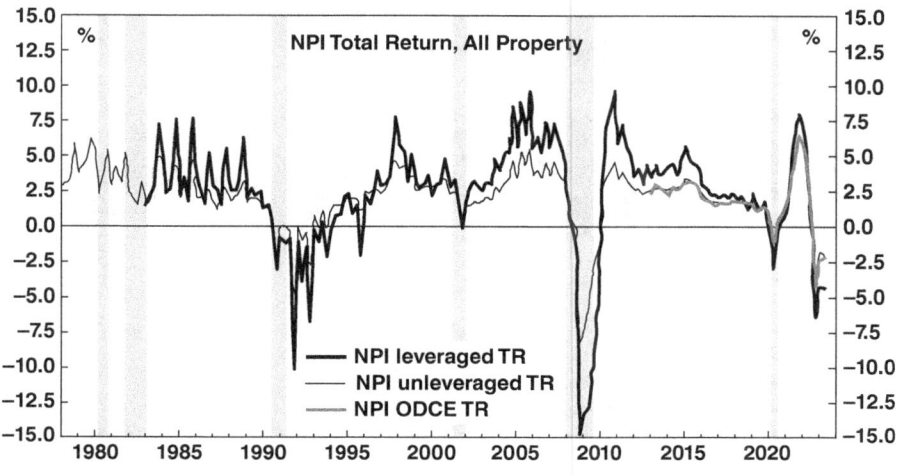

Source: ZCA using NCREIF data

and returns, i.e., the omitted variable problem that I discuss in Chapter 2. Inclusion increases the adjusted R^2 from 6.4% to 85.4%, a substantial improvement. The NOI growth coefficient decreases from 0.330 to 0.263, a reduction in the return's sensitivity to growth.

The 4-quarter moving average of NOI growth leads effective rent by two quarters. A 1% increase in lagged NOI growth is associated with a 1.1% increase in effective rents. See Exhibits 6.39 and 6.40.

Investors should focus on NOI growth because it leads property appreciation by about one quarter, as shown in Exhibit 6.41.

The properties included in the NPI leverage index have loan-to-value (LTV) ratios of 50% to 60%, modest leverage by today's non-institutional standards, as shown in Exhibit 6.42. LTV rises after a property market slowdown due to the fall in property prices, not due to short-term deleveraging. Loans on properties in the NPI leveraged index are not marked-to-market, so most of the change in LTV is due to changes in property value, not book-leverage.

The models of leveraged and unleveraged property performance indicate that lagged REIT returns, as well as current and lagged NOI growth, BBB-rated CMBS,

EXHIBIT 6.39 NOI growth and unleveraged total return.

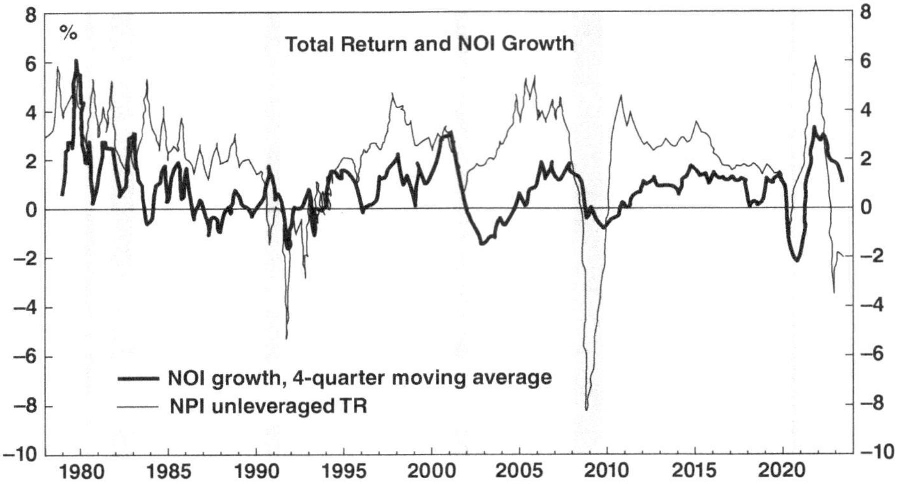

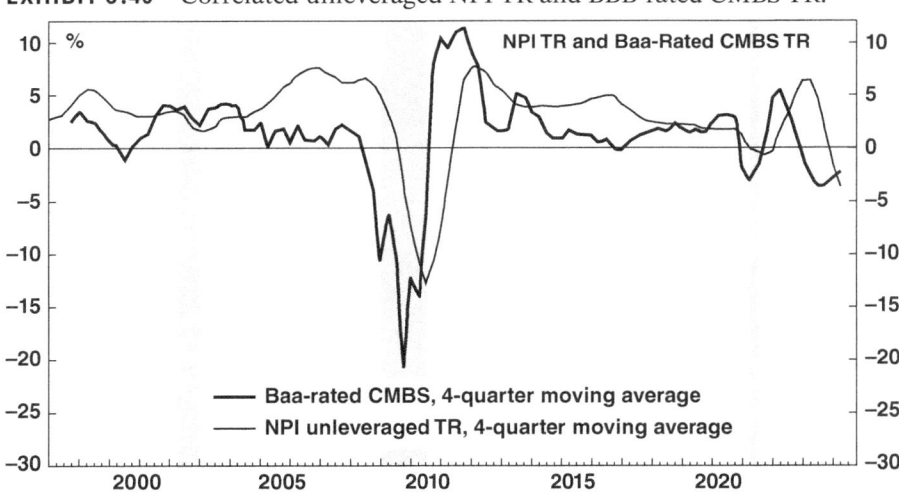

Source: ZCA using NCREIF data

EXHIBIT 6.40 Correlated unleveraged NPI TR and BBB-rated CMBS TR.

Source: ZCA using Federal Reserve data

Analysis of the Quadrant Linkages 135

EXHIBIT 6.41 NOI growth leads appreciation.

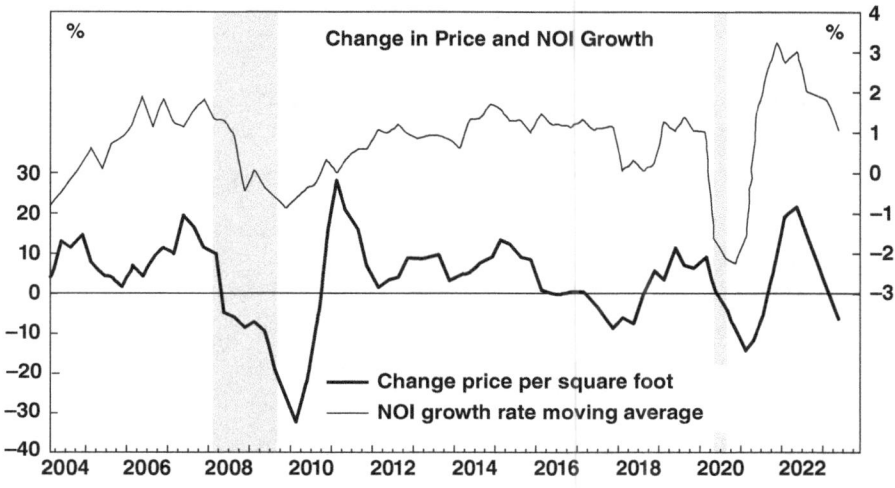

Source: ZCA using CoStar data

EXHIBIT 6.42 NCREIF loan-to-value ratio for leveraged property.

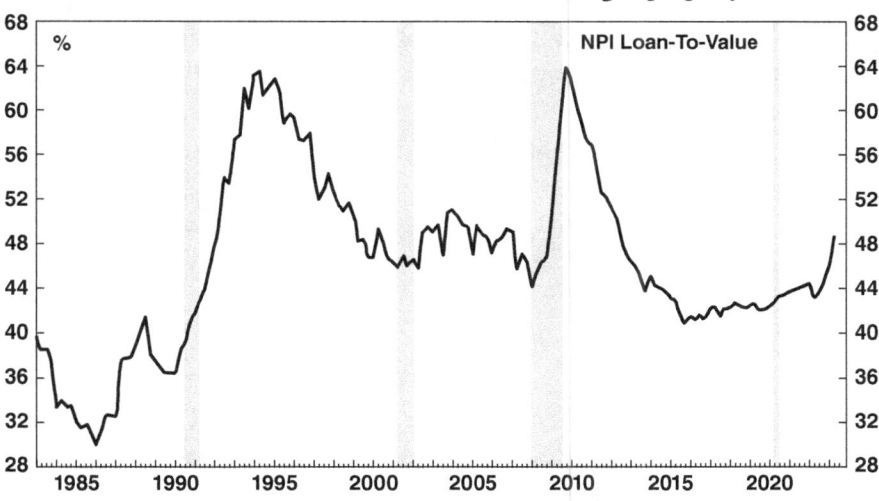

Source: ZCA using NCREIF data

property returns, and sales transactions are good predictors. See Equations (6.14) and (6.15).

$$NPILEV_t = 0.174 + 0.148 * CMBSBBB_t + 0.052 * REIT_{t-2} + 0.297 * NOIGROWTH_t$$
$$(0.658) \quad (5.654) \quad\quad\quad\quad (2.688) \quad\quad\quad (2.930)$$

$$- 0.237 * NOIGROWTH_{t-4} + 0.006 *(TRANSACTIONS_t - TRANSACTIONS_{-4})$$
$$(-2.346) \quad\quad\quad\quad\quad\quad (1.964)$$

$$+ 0.763 * NPILEV_{t-1}$$
$$(11.977) \quad\quad\quad\quad\quad\quad\quad\quad\quad\quad\quad\quad\quad\quad\quad\quad\quad\quad\quad (6.14)$$

Adjusted $R^2 = 0.861$

DW = 2.449

Mean dependent variable = 2.700

S.D. dependent var = 4.818

S.E. of regression = 1.796

Compare this result with that of unleveraged property returns. The REIT coefficient, 0.052, in Equation (6.14) is almost three times as sensitive in explaining leveraged NPI returns in Equation (6.15). Both equations explain about 86% of the variation in returns and are strong predictors of property returns.

$$NPIUNLEV_t = 0.307 + 0.082 * CMBSBBB_t + 0.018 * REIT_{t-1} + 0.144 * NOIGROWTH_t$$
$$(1.811) \quad (5.779) \quad\quad\quad\quad (1.736) \quad\quad\quad (2.633)$$

$$- 0.166 * NOIGROWTH_{t-4} + 0.004 *(TRANSACTIONS_t - TRANSACTIONS_{t-4})$$
$$(-3.106) \quad\quad\quad\quad\quad\quad (1.952)$$

$$+ 0.752 * NPIUNLEV_{t-1}$$
$$(10.712) \quad\quad\quad\quad\quad\quad\quad\quad\quad\quad\quad\quad\quad\quad\quad\quad\quad\quad (6.15)$$

Adjusted $R^2 = 0.859$

DW = 2.381

Mean dependent variable = 2.023

S.D. dependent var = 2.538

S.E. of regression = 0.952

Serial Correlation of Selected Assets

Property is not the only asset that exhibits serial correlation, as indicated by Exhibit 6.43, which includes results from a number of bivariate regressions. Some of them, such as T-bills, sales volume, vacancy rates, and office rental growth have low Durbin Watson statistics, which indicate *serial correlation in the bivariate regression's residuals*. These regressions suffer from omitted variables as discussed in Chapter 2.

A high, statistically significant lagged dependent (right-hand side) variable and a high adjusted R^2 indicates *serial correlation in the variable*. Property, leveraged and unleveraged, T-bills, and to some extent thinly traded corporate high-yield qualify. Hedge fund returns, which I do not include in the table, are also serially correlated.[2]

Conclusions and Investment Implications

- Transactions volume conveys important information that property returns may not capture.
- Subordinate CMBS returns explain property returns.
- Serial correlation facilitates the forecasting of property returns.
- The quadrants, which are more than a framework, are interdependent, complex, and predictive.
- Investors who specialize in any one quadrant should use information from the other quadrants.
- Public and private returns and the markets that generate these returns differ in important ways.
- Quadrant 1. BBB-rated CMBS total returns are a function of the high-yield corporate bond yield, current leveraged, and one-quarter lagged unleveraged property returns.
- Quadrant 2. Mortgage returns reflect BBB CMBS returns, the BBB-rated corporate bond return, the BAA corporate bond return, and the bond default premium.
- Quadrant 3. REITs total returns, which are a function of small-cap stock returns and unleveraged property returns (current and lagged), lead property returns.
- Quadrant 4. Leverage property returns reflect BBB-rated CMBS and equity REIT returns, the NOI growth rate lagged four quarters, the spread between current and four quarter, lagged sales transactions volume, and leveraged property returns lagged a quarter.

EXHIBIT 6.43 Estimates of serial correlation for various assets.

Capital Market Securities	Constant term	Constant term, t-statistic	Lagged dependent variable, coefficient	Lagged dependent variable, t-statistic	Adjusted R²	Durbin-Watson	Mean dependent variable, %
1 S&P 500, TR, %	2.543	2.912	0.002	0.023	−0.010	1.995	2.549
2 T-Bill, %	0.049	0.787	0.977	44.951*	0.951	0.661	2.008
3 Corporate high yield, TR, %	1.217	2.471	0.254	2.685*	0.056	1.900	1.638
4 Corporate, AAA-rated, TR, %	1.153	3.218	−0.002	−0.022	−0.010	1.983	1.151
5 Corporate, BBB-rated, TR, %	1.089	3.198	0.192	2.000	0.028	1.983	1.236
Real Estate Securities, Quadrants 1, 2, 3, and 4							
6 All equity REIT, TR, quarterly, %	0.611	0.385	0.140	1.142	0.005	1.943	0.731
7 AAA-rated CMBS, TR, quarterly, %	0.781	2.588	0.349	3.777*	0.113	1.891	1.198
8 BBB-rated CMBS, TR, %	0.197	1.189	0.197	2.036*	0.029	1.972	1.102
9 Giliberto-Levy Senior Mortgage (CLA), all, %	1.458	5.718	0.047	0.464	−0.008	1.983	1.531
10 Giliberto-Levy Senior Mortgage (CLA), office, %	1.433	5.539	0.080	0.793	−0.004	1.988	1.560
11 NPI unleveraged, all, %	0.424	2.994	0.794	16.977*	0.615	2.151	2.158
12 NPI leveraged, all, %	0.488	2.097	0.783	15.539*	0.600	2.199	2.388
Property Macroeconomic Variables							
11 Office sales volume $ billions	6.259	1.648	0.944	28.622*	0.907	0.483	104.876
12 Office vacancy rate, %	0.660	2.996	0.946	46.681*	0.959	0.746	10.861
13 Office net delivered space, million SQFT	4.063	2.891	0.750	10.951*	0.564	2.394	17.019
14 Change in office inventory, %	0.022	1.352	0.954	64.097*	0.979	1.508	0.891
15 Office inventory, billion SQFT	0.160	10.888	0.982	520.484*	1.000	0.943	7.811
16 Office rental growth, %	0.000	0.002	0.935	28.618*	0.902	0.303	1.403
17 Office net absorption, million SQFT	3.781	2.151	0.553	6.639*	0.319	1.745	9.432
18 Office under construction, million SQFT	4.420	1.387	0.959	40.545*	0.946	1.393	127.478

t-statistic significance, 94 observations
*t-statistic = 2.366 1.0% significance

Source: ZCA using G-L, CoStar, and Federal Reserve data

Q&A: Interview with Ethan Penner, Chairman, MOSAIC

Real estate myths and the birth of CMBS

What are your views on leverage and advisors?

An investment manager should not be compensated for adding leverage.

What do you think about investing in mezzanine debt?

Mostly garbage.

Is real estate an inflation hedge?

Yes, over the long run, but over a shorter horizon, fluctuations in supply and demand mask its hedging ability.

What are some real estate and finance myths?

Lending without a capacity to quickly take over an asset at the point of default is not an attractive business. Structure generally renders a defaulted property difficult to obtain, with the borrower typically able to tie up the property in courts for years during which time performance and value both suffer. So, accepting a lower return might not be so great if a lender's downside protection isn't real.

Liquidity is mostly an illusion. It is there when you don't need it and never there when you do.

Diversification can be of value and must be well thought out. However, it often gives investors a false sense of security. Major market collapses often transcend specific areas such as location or property type and in these instances the return correlation across assets approaches one. Everything becomes correlated.

You are broadly credited with creating CMBS and rescuing the industry in the 1990s when balance sheet lenders all abandoned the business. Share your thoughts on this period.

(continued)

(*continued*)

My career as a part of the pioneering group that developed the structured finance business on Wall Street in the 1980s combined with my attraction to filling great voids led me to establish the CMBS industry. This innovation allowed property owners and acquirers to access financing capital at a time when all portfolio lenders left the industry at once. I was blessed with the support of many other pioneers, including those inside and out of my business.

Do you have some advice for young professionals considering a real estate career?

Real estate is the place where life happens, and its business asks its professionals to solve for optimizing that space to inspire the best life experiences. There is much room for a creative, curious person. Real estate values are affected by everything, so to be a great professional one must be attendant to, if not have expertise in, many areas including finance, economics, sociology, and politics.

CHAPTER 7

Property: The Macroeconomics of Performance and Risk

Preliminaries

This chapter explores the size distribution of space and population across MSAs and serial correlation of returns by property type. It presents a comparative analysis of four property types, and a stylized macroeconomic general equilibrium model of property and asset markets.

The Size Distribution of Space and Population Across MSAs

The size distribution of property types across MSAs is relevant to investors seeking geographic diversification.

Some property types, such as office, are more concentrated in the largest MSAs. The larger cities are more office-intensive, whereas retail is distributed as the general population. Exhibit 7.1 shows that the 20 largest MSAs account for 50% of the US retail inventory; the top 22 MSAs contain 50% of the office stock, whereas 28 cities account for 50% of the industrial inventory. Office scale economies are exhausted in the larger cities where the office inventory draws from a large and diverse labor pool.

EXHIBIT 7.1 Inventory distribution over 390 MSAs: Apartments and office are relatively more concentrated in the larger cities while retail and population are similarly distributed.

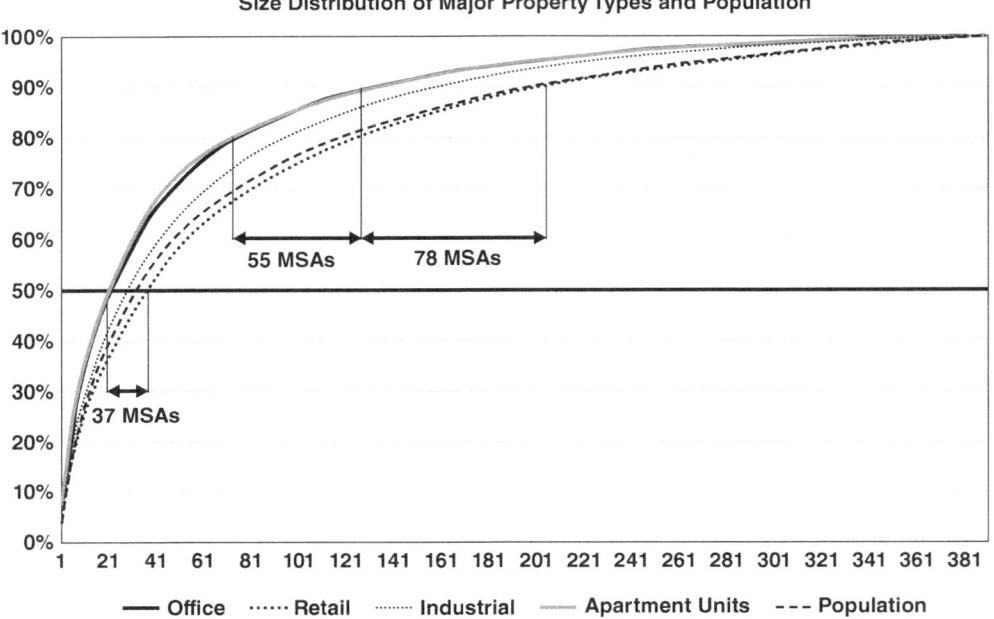

Source: Zisler Capital Associates, LLC using CoStar data

Property Performance Including Return Correlations and Volatilities

The return correlation coefficients for all four property types are very large. Property type diversification may not confer significant or stable overall portfolio benefits. (See Chapter 10, which discusses diversification.)

Exhibit 7.2 shows the correlation between property and other capital asset classes from 1978 to 2024. Property has a low correlation with bonds and stocks. (While smoothing affects standard deviation and average returns, it does not affect correlations.)

Exhibit 7.3 presents property betas calculated with respect to the overall NCREIF Property Index (Box A), serial correlation (Box B), t-statistics for tests of significance, adjusted R^2 (Box C), average return, return volatility, and the coefficient of variation (CV), which is the standard deviation divided by the mean return (Box D).

EXHIBIT 7.2 Correlation matrix for property, bonds, stocks, and REITs, 1978–2024. Property has a low correlation with other capital markets asset classes, which suggests that the benefits of diversification reside between property and other asset classes, not within the property sector itself.

	Property	AAA Corporate	BAA Corporate	High-Yield Corporate	S&P 500	Equity REITs	Mortgage REITs
Property	1.000	−0.130	−0.224	−0.135	0.053	0.197	−0.124
AAA Corporate	−0.130	1.000	0.592	0.067	0.033	0.164	0.211
BAA Corporate	−0.224	0.592	1.000	0.795	0.580	0.614	0.624
High-Yield Corporate	−0.135	0.067	0.795	1.000	0.781	0.710	0.603
S&P 500	0.053	0.033	0.580	0.781	1.000	0.754	0.634
Equity REITs	0.197	0.164	0.614	0.710	0.754	1.000	0.572
Mortgage REITs	−0.124	0.211	0.624	0.603	0.634	0.572	1.000

Source: Zisler Capital Associates, LLC using CoStar data

EXHIBIT 7.3 Risk metrics for four major property types, stocks, and equity REITs, 1978–2024.

	A	B		C			D
	Beta with respect to property	Serial correlation coefficient	t-statistic test of significance	Adjusted R²	Average return	Standard error	Coefficient of variation
Industrial	1.08	0.833	14.611	0.687	2.615	2.977	1.138
Multifamily	1.018	0.838	15.001	0.698	1.916	2.539	1.325
Office	1.083	0.882	17.683	0.763	1.415	2.855	2.018
Retail	0.757	0.785	12.406	0.612	1.922	2.273	1.183
S&P 500		0.036	0.36	−0.009	2.18	8.343	3.827
Equity REITs		0.075	0.733	−0.005	2.919	10.289	3.525

Source: Zisler Capital Associates, LLC using CoStar data

Serial correlation, which is the correlation of the current return with past returns, artificially smooths the return series. However, it is a good proxy for market as well as asset liquidity. Are investors fairly compensated for investing in less liquid MSAs or property types? I suspect not, since MSA liquidity is, as yet, not at the top of investors' concerns.

Stocks and REITS have little serial correlation, but property is highly correlated serially, as shown in Box B in Exhibit 7.3. Stock returns fluctuate as if they follow a random walk. The low t-statistic and adjusted R^2 (Box C) confirm this point.

A statistical random walk does not imply lack of causality. If markets quickly incorporate news in prices, then prices fluctuate *as if* the returns are random. Stock technicians, chart makers and some real estate research professionals who obsess over price or return patterns should not take any comfort in this finding!

While serial correlation means one can predict tomorrow's property return using past values, investors cannot systematically beat the property market after accounting for fees and expenses.

Property returns and their standard deviations are very similar, as shown in Exhibit 7.4. Industrial returns have extreme outliers to the right and left. The distributions are skewed to the left. (I rotated the plots in the exhibit 90 degrees.)

EXHIBIT 7.4 Property and its subcategories have similar means and standard deviations.

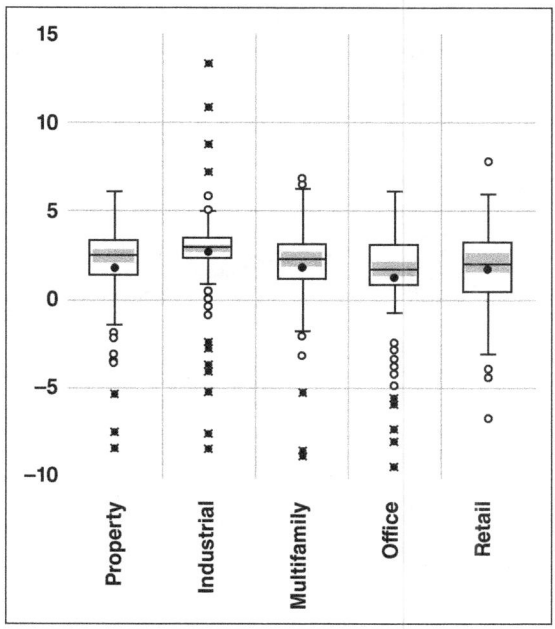

Source: Zisler Capital Associates, LLC using CoStar data

Comparative Analysis of the Fundamentals of Four Property Types

Fluctuations in the underlying fundamentals do not always resemble total returns. Vacancy rates across property types (Exhibit 7.5) are more variable than cap rates (Exhibit 7.6).

MSAs differ in many ways. Their risk characteristics are an important, but poorly understood, factor that affects returns. For example, since the short-run elasticity of supply of property with respect to rents is highly inelastic, demand shifts produce large swings in rents and rental growth rates, especially for the larger, older cities, such as New York and San Francisco, which have extremely low supply elasticities.

Capital flows cause MSA total property returns to converge and, in so doing, the similarities of cap rates, due in part to the positive correlation of NOI and prices, can hide the larger underlying differences in vacancy rates, rental growth rates, and other property fundamentals.

EXHIBIT 7.5 Except for retail, vacancy rates rose after the COVID-19 recession. Office performed the worst.

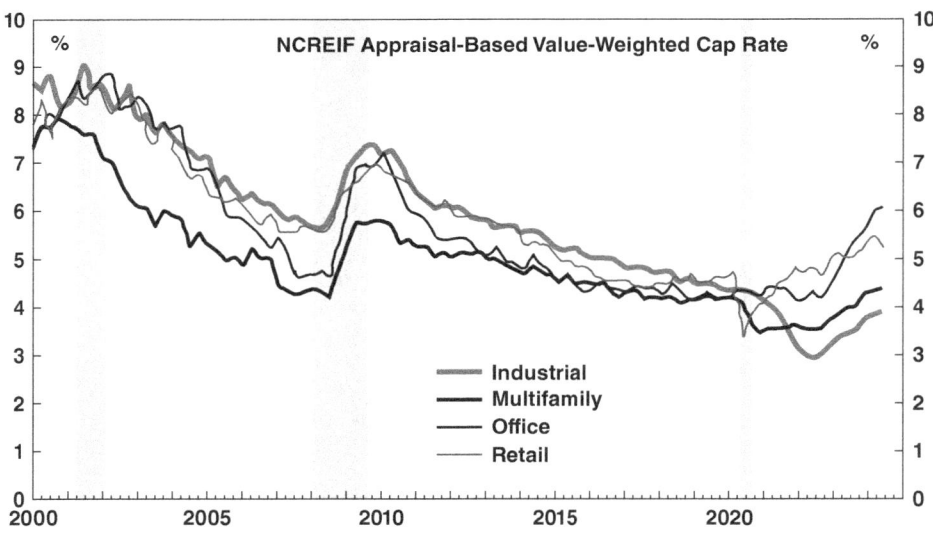

Source: Zisler Capital Associates, LLC using CoStar data

EXHIBIT 7.6 Cap rates are highly correlated across property types. COVID-19 has disturbed this historic relationship.

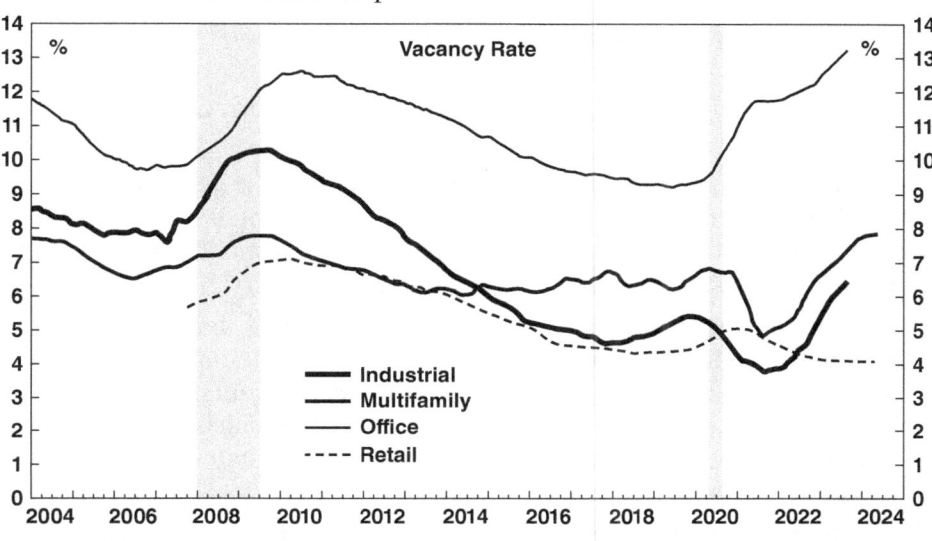

Source: Zisler Capital Associates, LLC using CoStar data

Property Performance by Quality Class Matters

Even though a building might not receive a high-quality CoStar ranking, its investment performance, despite underwhelming photos, could outperform the more highly revered alternatives, such as the most prestigious, high-leveraged property on Park Avenue, New York City. Recently, following a negative shock to the office sector, the C-quality assets generally performed better than the A-quality assets. Is this true for all downturns? We lack a longer, quality-adjusted time series that might help us confirm the general validity of this important observation.

Inventory supply shocks affect the A-class inventory first and then slowly migrate to the rest of the inventory. WFH has had a large and prompt impact on Class-A office. A-quality rental growth cycles are much more volatile than the volatility of the entire office sector. Class-C office rental growth performance increased significantly after COVID-19, but not as much as multifamily, which outperformed Class-A office post-pandemic.

The Macroeconomics of Property and Asset Markets: A Stylized Model

Macroeconomic fluctuations occur within a general equilibrium, and not a partial equilibrium framework. Property markets are no exception.

The demand curve in the northeast corner shows that the demand for space (as represented on the horizontal axis) is inversely related to rent. Were the demand for space a vertical line, the demand would be perfectly inelastic. Demand would not be responsive to rent. Such is not the case. (See Exhibit 7.7.)

Demand is not perfectly elastic (or horizontal). Rental markets and vacancy rates are sluggish, depending on how landlords exercise their options to wait for the next best tenant. Consider the southwest quadrant. A horizontal line extends from the demand curve to the rent-to-price curve, the slope of which is the ratio of rent to interest rates. If interest rates rise, the rent-to-price curve rotates counterclockwise and prices fall.

The southwest quadrant shows the relationship between price and new construction. Price is replacement cost. The greater is construction activity, the greater

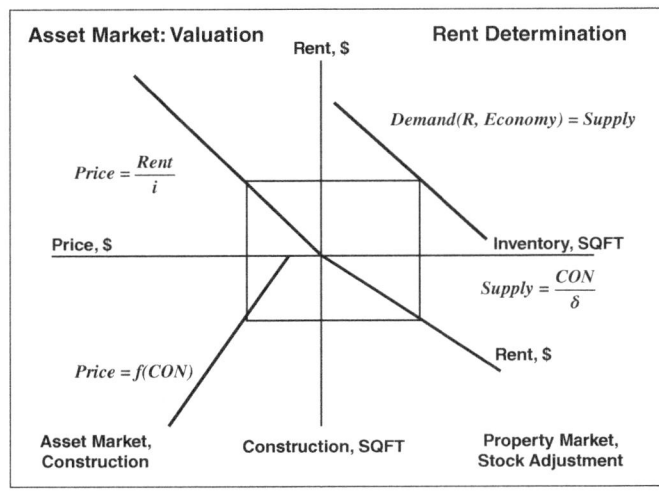

EXHIBIT 7.7 The asset and user markets are linked through the construction and capital markets.

Source: ZCA and DiPasquale and Wheaton

are land prices and replacement cost. The inventory at the end of a period equals the beginning inventory plus additions minus any removals due to demolition or depreciation. We should subtract from the inventory any conversions of office space to apartments or other uses.

The southeast quadrant shows the level of construction and depreciation on the vertical axis. In order that the inventory not decline, the market must deliver enough construction to offset depreciation, which, contrary to the thinking of many accountants, is not all physical nor is it linear over time. The demand for office-to-apartment conversions in 2024 increased due to the unmet demand for urban housing and excess office space, especially in the larger MSAs, such as New York City. The asset market has responded with the issuance of fund vehicles intended expressly to invest in these conversions.

Consider a demand shock due to accelerated economic growth, as shown in Exhibit 7.8. The demand curve shifts outward in response to rising GDP and stable preferences for working in the office. Prices increase, which in turn leads to more construction. The reality, of course, is more complicated. The lines radiating outward from the origin need not be straight lines. The lines could be more vertical or horizontal in order to express less or greater sensitivity to price and interest rate changes. See Exhibit 7.8.

EXHIBIT 7.8 A rightward shift in the demand curve increases rent, new construction, and asset prices.

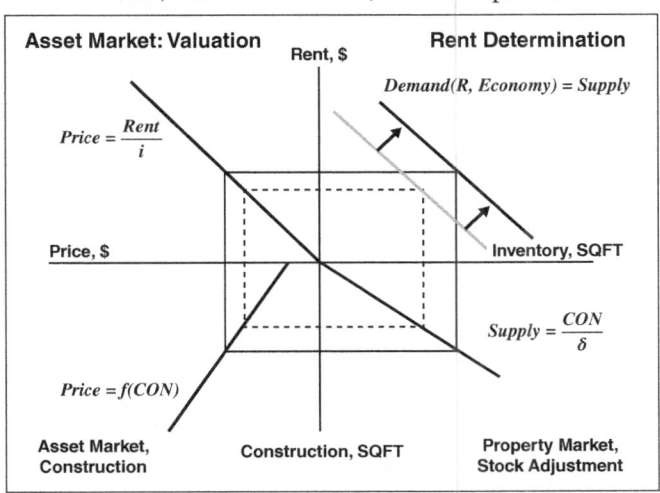

Source: DiPasquale and Wheaton

Tax law changes, such as those that cratered real estate performance in 1986, could lower the after-tax rate of return on equity and depress the demand for property assets.

Prices change. While the acquisition price declines, as shown in Exhibit 7.9, so does the value of property that is owned by taxable and tax-exempt investors. Cap rates could rise if interest rates increase, but the result is ambiguous since cap rates are a function of the risk-free rate plus credit spreads minus expected NOI growth. One factor could swamp the impact of another variable, thus hiding the impact of interest rates. (See Chapter 13.)

In Exhibit 7.9, I assume that the Fed adopts an expansionist monetary policy. In this scenario, interest rates and cap rates drop and prices increase. The price-to-rent curve rotates clockwise. Asset prices increase and the inventory of space expands. The expansion of the inventory, however, depresses rents. Asset prices increase while rents decrease.

When short rates rise, the construction supply curve shifts to the right. Construction loans become costlier, or are heavily non-price rationed for certain classes of borrowers. See Exhibit 7.10.

EXHIBIT 7.9 Expansionary impact of stimulation by the Federal Reserve.

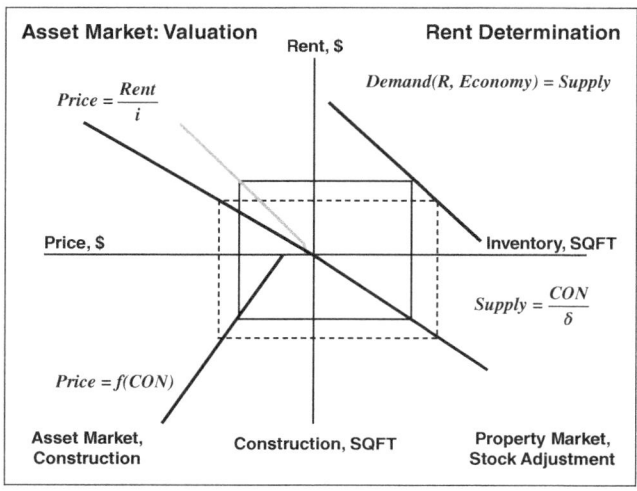

Source: DiPasquale and Wheaton

EXHIBIT 7.10 Impact of a shift in the supply of new construction starts.

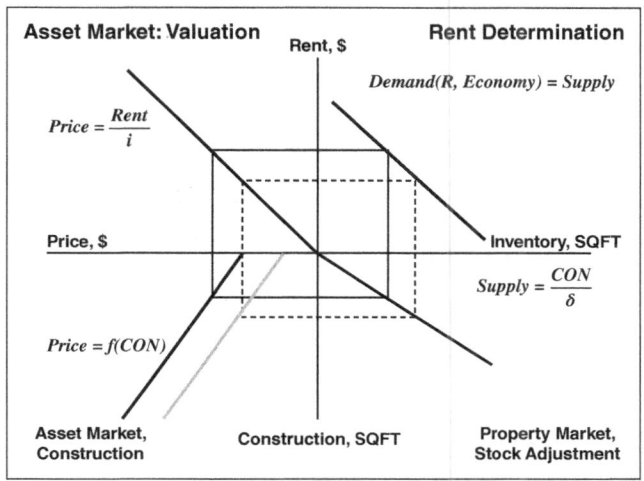

Source: DiPasquale and Wheaton

Conclusions and Investment Implications

- Investors, rather than extrapolating the present, should consider the effect of macroeconomic dynamics on real estate performance. General equilibrium macro models can provide an internally consistent framework that suggests the right questions and reveals important relationships.
- The distributions of the property space inventory and population across and within MSAs are similar.
- Property return correlations across MSAs are very high, which may undercut the value of geographic diversification. Even if the correlations are high and variable (risky) over time, then geographic diversification may be of much less value.
- The measured MSA return volatilities of property are unrealistically low due to serial correlation.
- Unlike returns, the underlying fundamentals of MSAs are sufficiently different to justify their own risk metrics, a topic which investors have often ignored.
- Property performance is a function of quality, among other factors.
- Property returns vary less across property quality ratings than do fundamentals.

Q&A: Interview with Owen Thomas, Chairman and CEO, BXP, Inc.

An Office REIT with Flexibility During Good and Bad Times

How did you choose real estate for a profession?

I was exposed to real estate early. I grew up on a farm in Virginia; ours was a multigenerational farm family. My father started a real estate business in which he was a broker to other farmers. When I was in high school, I worked for him and learned real estate.

I studied mechanical engineering at the University of Virginia. I worked as an engineer and then attended Harvard Business School, which rekindled my interest in real estate. I worked at Morgan Stanley for 24 years. In 2013 I joined BXP (Boston Properties) as CEO.

Tell us about BXP?

BXP is the largest publicly traded developer, owner, and manager of premier workplaces in the nation, is in the S&P 500, and is BBB rated. The firm owns 181 properties across six regions and is an active developer and at times acquiror of assets. Though the strategy is generally long-term hold, we do sell less strategic assets each year. BXP competes for industry leading clients in the premier workplace segment of the office industry, representing the top 10% of buildings in each market where vacancy is 30% lower and asking rents 50% higher than the broader office market.

Does being a public REIT give you advantages, especially during tough times?

Yes. Being a public REIT gives us significant advantages. We have access to both the public and private debt and equity markets, allowing us to raise capital at all points in the cycle and optimize execution. Our current cost of borrowing in the IG bond markets is around 140 bps over the 10-year UST, which is very attractive vs. the private mortgage market. Sponsorship and stability are increasingly important to our clients as they make leasing decisions allowing BXP to gain leasing market share in tougher times.

Can you comment on risk analysis?

More risk analytics would be helpful in real estate. Monte Carlo could be useful in our work. AI will have a role to play.

What advice would you give young professionals?

Start at a winning larger firm with significant deal volume, great mentors, smart clients, and superb colleagues. Learn. It is always easier to move from big firm to small.

CHAPTER 8

Office Property: COVID-19, Obsolescence, Work From Home (WFH), and Conversions

COVID-19 has dramatically challenged the nature of work and the viability of the office sector.

Pandemics are not new to mankind. Great authors have written eloquently about pestilence. A good example is this quote from **The Plague**,[1] written by the existential novelist, Albert Camus:

They fancied themselves free, and no one will ever be free so long as there are pestilences.

Anne Applebaum, author of **Twilight of Democracy: The Seductive Lure of Authoritarianism**,[2] wrote:

Throughout history, pandemics have led to an expansion of the power of the state. At times when people fear death, they go along with measures that they believe, rightly or wrongly, will save them—even if that means a loss of freedom.

Along with the authoritarian state, I include zealous religious authorities and proto-totalitarians who harbor anti-democratic goals. During the early years of the global COVID-19 pandemic, tribalism, dogma, and conspiracies challenged scientific truth and caused hundreds of thousands of excess deaths according to public health research. I embrace evidence-based thinking.

Some readers may protest that these considerations do not affect property because real estate is somehow hermetically sealed from politics. Nothing could be further from the truth. Any town meeting regarding zoning or development approvals should convince those readers to the contrary. The exercise of power influences just about every aspect of what it means to be a citizen, a tenant, and a landlord. I explore the risks associated with land use controls in Chapter 18.

Why write about disease in a book about commercial real estate investing? After all, most people's interest in epidemiology is limited. Disease, even the specter of disease, transforms how we think about society, collective action, and the built environment.

Pandemics stoke fear, disrupt the functioning of global societies, change trade patterns, destroy wealth, aid the ascent of authoritarian politicians, distort ethical and social norms, divide society, and even change the shape and dynamics of cities. Pandemics are a collective, systemic risk, a known unknown that spills across national boundaries and socioeconomic classes. Investors should think more deeply about disease as another collective risk and challenge to investment performance. Pandemics are a shock that can reveal much about property markets through induced market reverberations.

What does the COVID-19 shock tell us about the office sector pre- and post-COVID-19, across MSAs and within MSAs, and by quality? The long-term impact of COVID-19 on the office sector differs from its short-term effect. In the short-run, immediately following the surge in COVID-19 cases and deaths, fear-induced WFH evolved as the government took measures to ease the caseload on medical facilities, promote social distancing, and keep people at home, while supporting the economy through massive transfers pending the development of a vaccine. Workers vacated many office buildings even though most tenants continued paying rent.

COVID-19 savaged the A-Class, larger properties (over 250,000 square feet) of recent vintage (since 1990) in the largest MSAs, such as New York. Lower quality properties, according to CoStar data, performed relatively better as a group. A suburban exodus strengthened outlying office markets while CBD office performance languished.

The spread between NCREIF appraisal- and transactions-based cap rates widened. Owners were slow to recognize losses, and appraisers were characteristically accommodating.

The long-term impact of COVID-19—accelerated obsolescence—is more insidious but just as real as the prompt impact. Older, smaller, and less functional office properties are at risk of capital erosion, conversion, or demolition. Relative performance by quality will eventually flip as the inventory reprices.

The flow of capital adjusts property prices to equate risk-adjusted returns across assets, asset classes, and even MSAs. Next comes changes in vacancy rates, absorption, and rental growth rates. Labor migration is next in line. Then comes adjustment to the inventory itself, but increases in the inventory proceed at a glacial rate. Since buildings are very durable, downward inventory adjustment is even slower than changes in leasing velocity. Reactions are lagged and complex.

Cities change largely by accretion much as do coral reefs. Sprawl, which I discuss in Chapter 17, is a response to growth, property durability, and price changes.

Office Property

Office market performance deteriorated following COVID-19 but in unexpected ways. From 2019 to 2023 the average office vacancy rate by MSA size increased while space per worker declined. The spread between the transactions cap rate and cash flow returns increased significantly.

Exhibits 8.1 and 8.2 show that the cash flow return is about 2.5% less than the appraisal-based cap rate and almost 5% less than the transactions cap rate. The appraisal cap rate consistently is less than the transactions cap rate.

Importantly, the maximum cap rate spread occurred not at the end of the COVID-19 recession but almost four years later. As NOI weakened, office cap rates rose. Substantial, difficult-to-predict, lags contributed incremental risk. See Exhibit 8.3.

Vacancy rates and space per worker (adjusting for the vacancy rate) rose in all MSAs. The changes were most dramatic for the largest MSAs, as shown in Exhibit 8.4.

CBDs performed worse than the suburbs, as shown in Exhibit 8.5.

The vacancy rate spread—CBD minus suburban vacancy rate—increased almost 600 bps since the end of the COVID-19 recession. The one-standard-deviation confidence interval, defined as plus or minus one standard deviation, also increased, as shown in Exhibit 8.5.

During 2020–2021, many CBDs lost workers as WFH spread. See Exhibits 8.6 and 8.7. The spread between New York CBD and suburban value per square foot increased significantly after the GFC, but that spread narrowed following COVID-19, as shown in Exhibit 8.6. Noteworthy is the relatively tight spread

CHAPTER 8 Office Property: COVID-19, Obsolescence, Work From Home (WFH)

EXHIBIT 8.1   Appraisal cap rates are slow to adjust upward.

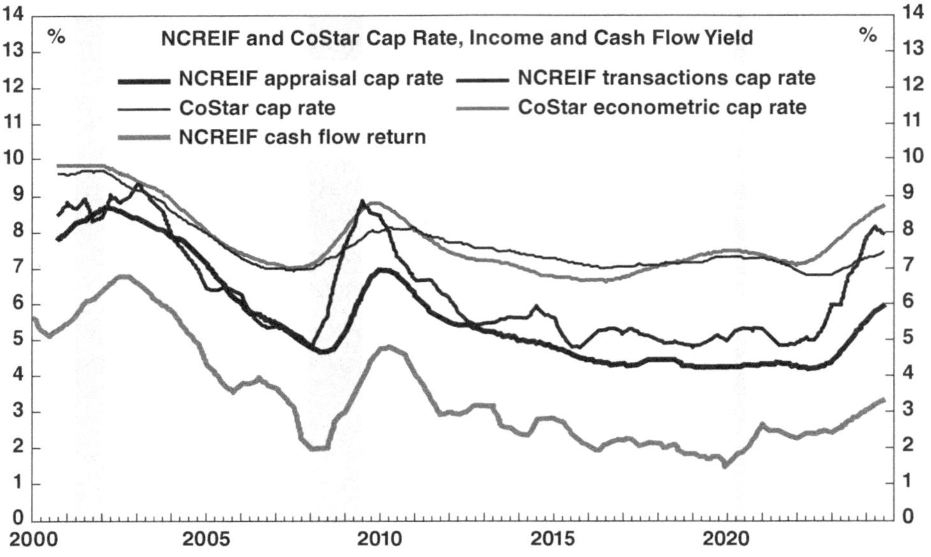

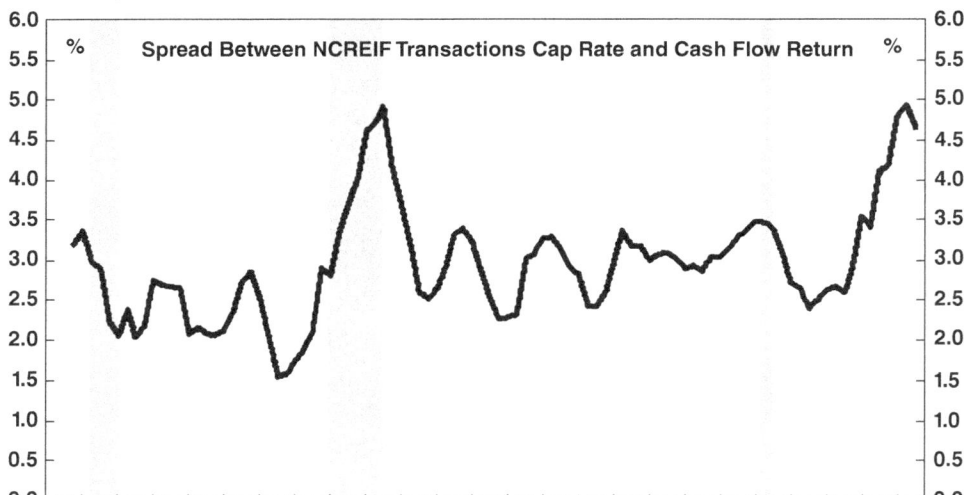

Source: ZCA using CoStar and NCREIF data

EXHIBIT 8.2   The spread between transactions cap rates and cash flow returns is increasing.

Source: ZCA using CoStar data

EXHIBIT 8.3 NOI growth has weakened and cap rates have been rising since 2022.

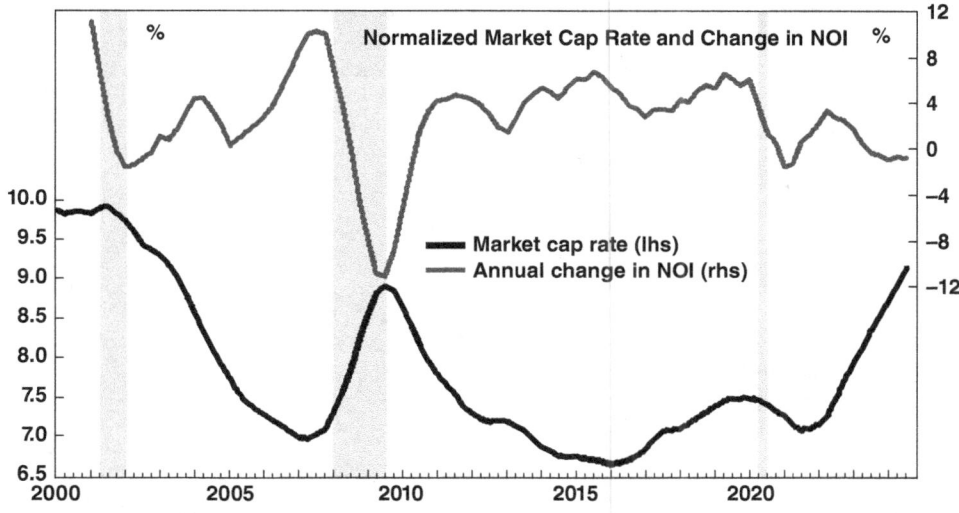

Source: ZCA using CoStar data

EXHIBIT 8.4 Econometrically fitted 2023 and 2019 vacancy rates increase as a function of the size of the office inventory.

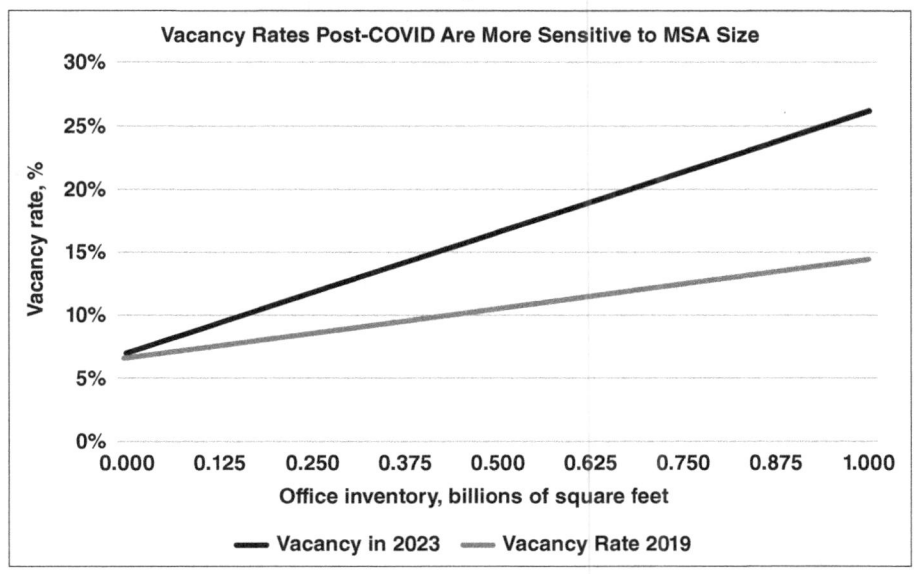

Source: ZCA estimation using CoStar data

EXHIBIT 8.5 The spread between CBD and suburban vacancy rates is rising, indicating an increase in CBD weakness relative to the suburbs.

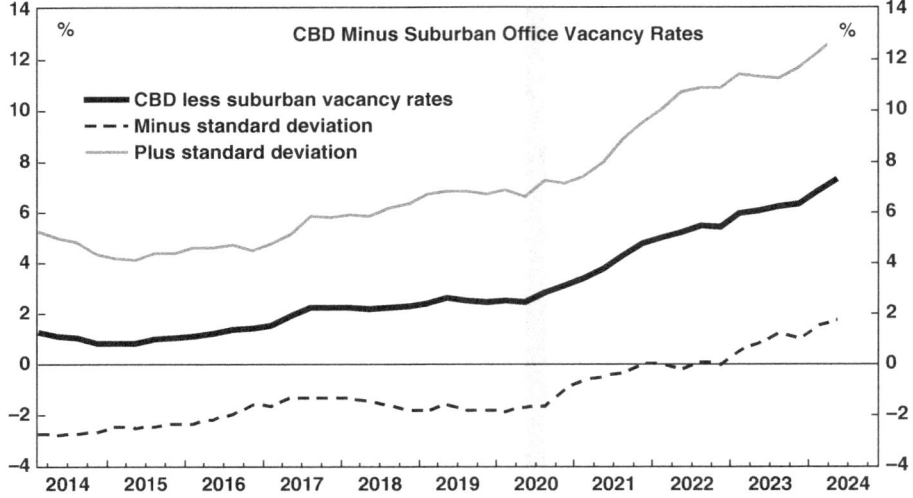

Source: ZCA estimation using CoStar data

EXHIBIT 8.6 New York CBD office values per square foot have fallen more than suburban office values. The CBD drop has been dramatic, rivaling the GFC.

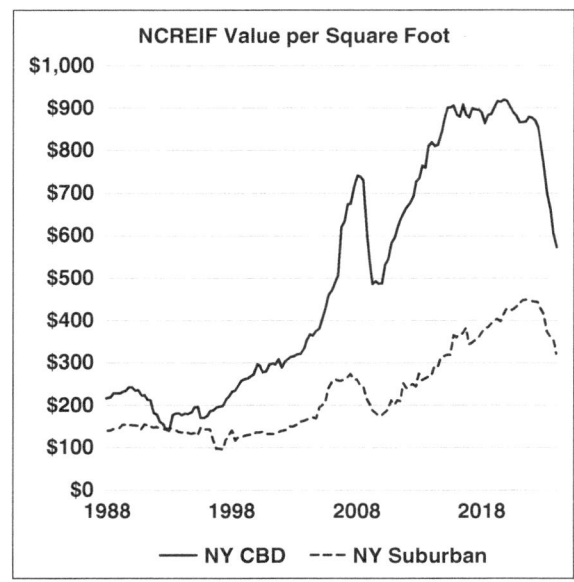

Source: ZCA using NCREIF data

EXHIBIT 8.7 New York and suburban office returns fell to similar extents, indicating a tendency for markets to equilibrate risk-adjusted returns.

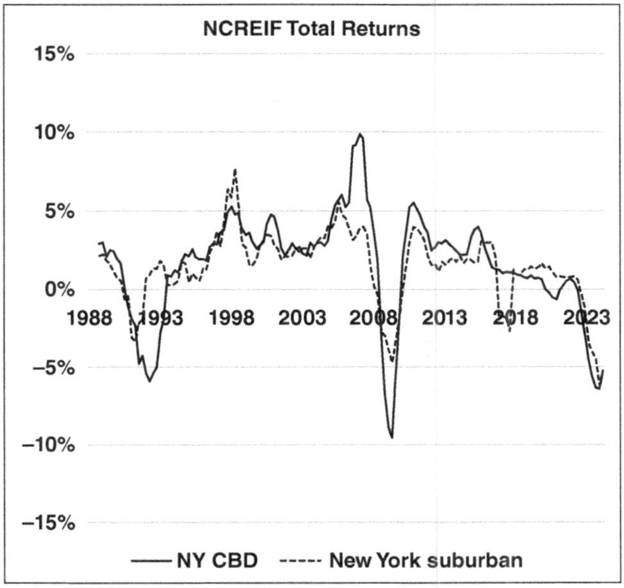

Source: ZCA using NCREIF data

between CBD and suburban total returns. This finding is important. Total return variance within MSAs is not significant. Exhibit 8.7 shows New York CBD and suburban returns.

CBD values declined more than CBD prices. (See Exhibit 8.8.) The largest CBD-suburban performance disparities occur in the largest, densest MSAs. Capital flows to adjust risk-adjusted returns by adjusting property prices. See Exhibit 8.9.

Class A remains in the dumps as of 2025. CoStar assigns quality ratings to office properties. Exhibits 8.10 and 8.11 compare and contrast Class A with Class C performance according to normalized absorption rates, vacancy rates, and total returns.

Exhibit 8.10 shows that absorption was stronger post COVID-19 in the Class C office inventory. Class A vacancy rates, which have been less than Class C vacancy rates since 2000, increased after COVID-19 as shown in Exhibit 8.11. The vacancy rate spread increased from 100 bps in 2020 to over 350 bps in late 2024. The larger MSAs accounted for much of this spread-widening.

Exhibit 8.12 and its magnified duplicate, Exhibit 8.13, show that returns are similar across quality classes.

162   CHAPTER 8   Office Property: COVID-19, Obsolescence, Work From Home (WFH)

EXHIBIT 8.8   The narrowing gap between CBD and suburban values.

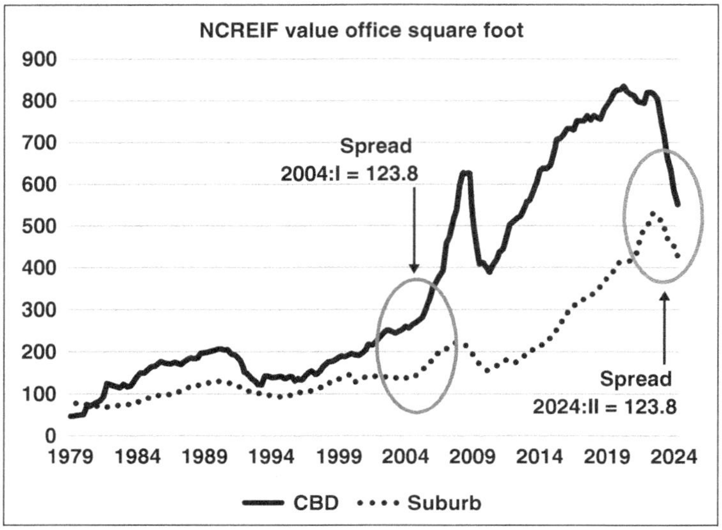

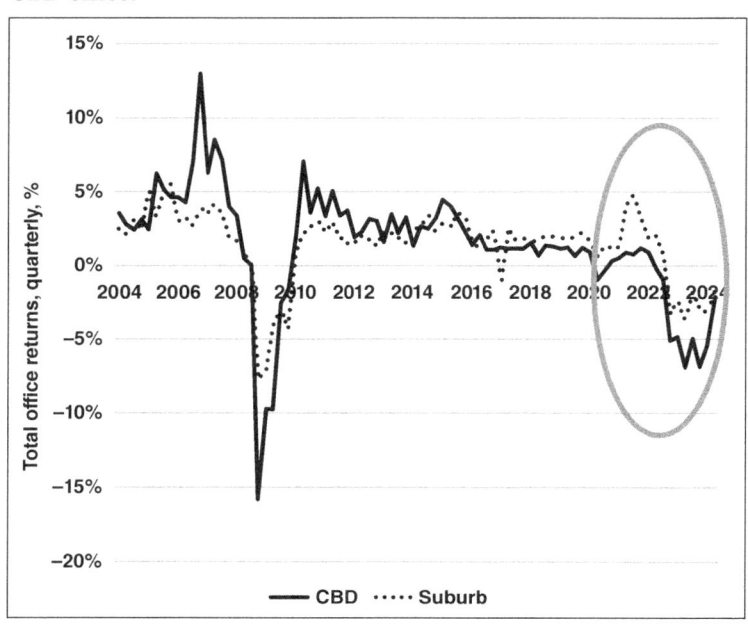

Source: ZCA using NCREIF data

EXHIBIT 8.9   Suburban returns since 2020 have outperformed CBD office.

Source: ZCA using NCREIF data

EXHIBIT 8.10 Normalized absorption rate by class; absorption during COVID-19 was greatest in Class C.

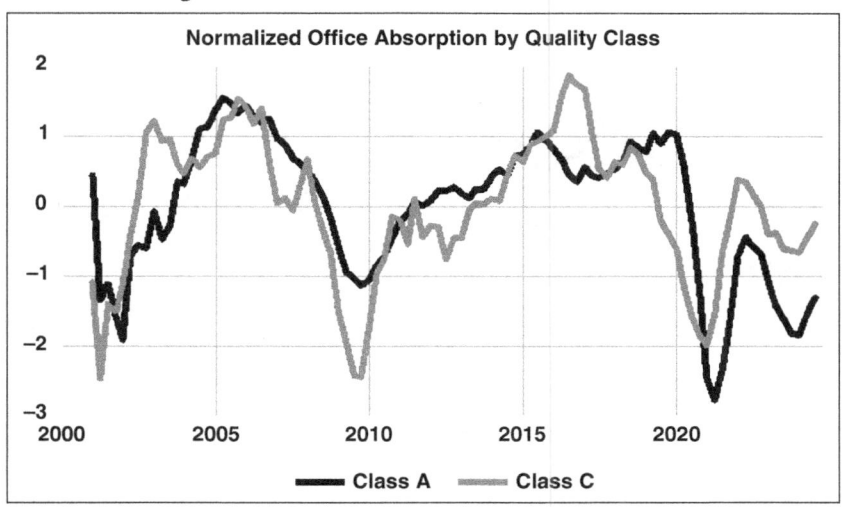

Source: ZCA using CoStar data

EXHIBIT 8.11 Normalized vacancy rate by class; vacancy rates approach equilibrium slowly.

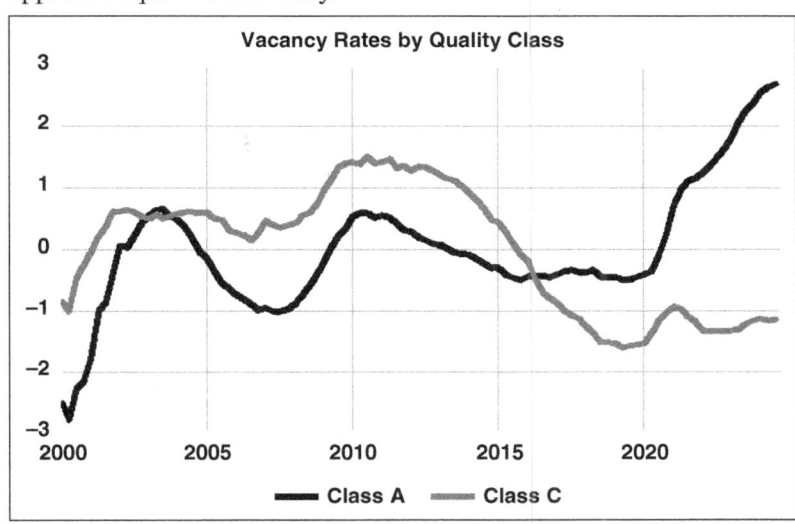

Source: ZCA using CoStar data

164 CHAPTER 8 Office Property: COVID-19, Obsolescence, Work From Home (WFH)

EXHIBIT 8.12 Total returns are similar across classes as capital promptly adjusts prices.

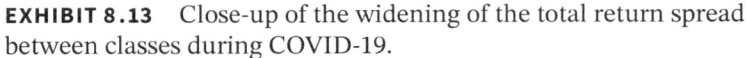

Source: ZCA using CoStar data

EXHIBIT 8.13 Close-up of the widening of the total return spread between classes during COVID-19.

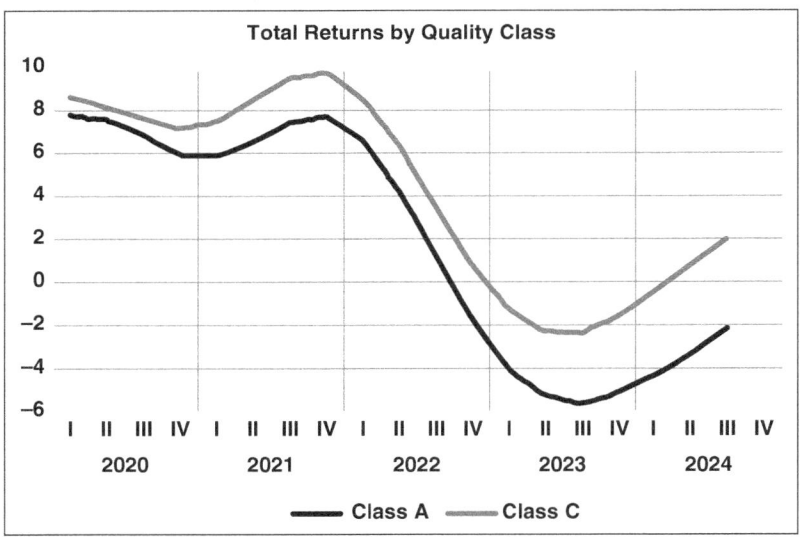

Source: ZCA using CoStar data

The total return quality spread favors the lesser quality properties. CoStar publishes a companion quality index, wherein a "1" is "poor" quality and a "5" is top quality. Exhibits 8.14 and 8.15 show the spread calculated using CoStar's other quality index wherein four and five quality represents the best office buildings.

Why some MSA rental growth rates are more volatile. Why are some MSAs more volatile than others? The MSA elasticities of supply with respect to price and construction costs affect the volatility of MSA performance. An elasticity of minus one means that a 1% increase in price is associated with a 1% decline in new supply. If the elasticity is inelastic, the supply response is less than 1%; if the elasticity is perfectly inelastic, then the response is zero.

Supply elasticities vary across MSAs, largely due to different physical factors and approval processes. If the supply elasticity is very small, then rental growth rates, for example, are more volatile. MSAs, such as Houston with relatively permissive zoning, typically have higher supply elasticities and more of the adjustment occurs through the vacancy rate. If the supply curve is very inelastic, or even perfectly inelastic, as it is in New York, most of the adjustment occurs through rental

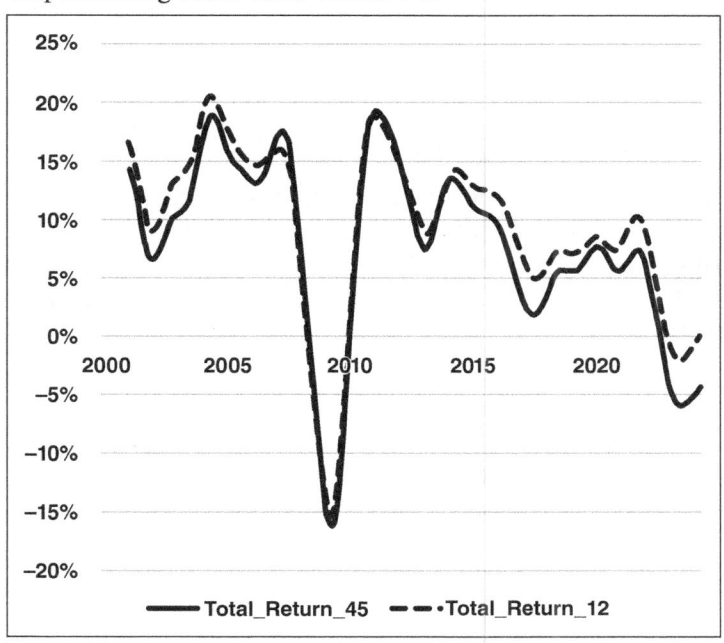

EXHIBIT 8.14 Lesser quality office properties are outperforming better ones: CoStar 4-5.

Source: ZCA using CoStar data

EXHIBIT 8.15 The spread favors lesser quality properties.

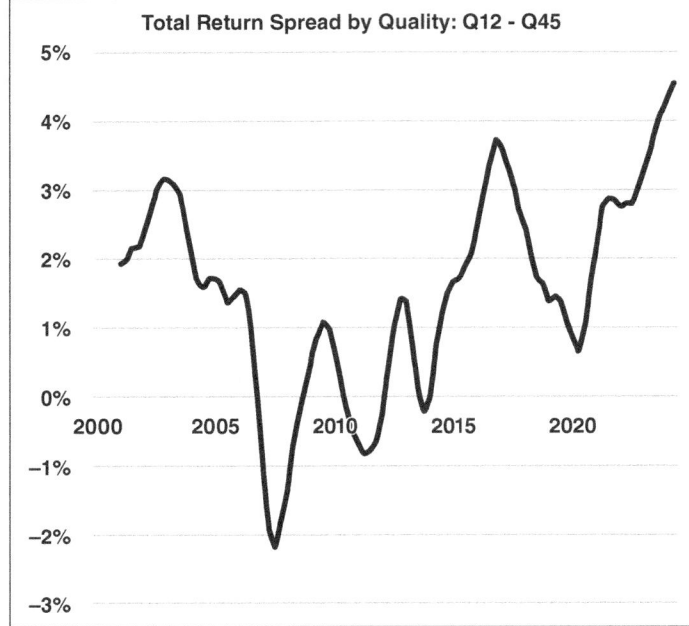

Source: ZCA using CoStar data

rate changes. Hence, as the demand fluctuates against an inelastic supply curve, the more volatile are rents, NOI, and total returns.

Few investors realize that returns, rental growth rates, and prices are riskier in New York than they are in Houston. This finding should not be a concern if pricing reflects this risk. Exhibits 8.16 and 8.17 each show an equal rightward shift in the demand against inelastic and elastic supplies, respectively. Rents rise more when the supply curve is perfectly inelastic, or vertical.

Large MSA vacancy rates are much less volatile than vacancy rates spanning the bottom 75% of the inventory. The volatility of rental growth rates, prices, and returns reflect these elasticities. Clearly, the supply elasticity is critical in determining an MSA's response to random shocks. See Exhibit 8.18.

What is the natural vacancy rate (NVR)? No single office equilibrium vacancy rate fits all MSAs or even CBDs and suburbs within MSAs. When is a vacancy rate too high or too low? This question confounds many investors.

EXHIBIT 8.16 An outward shift in demand results in larger rent swings in larger MSAs with low elasticities.

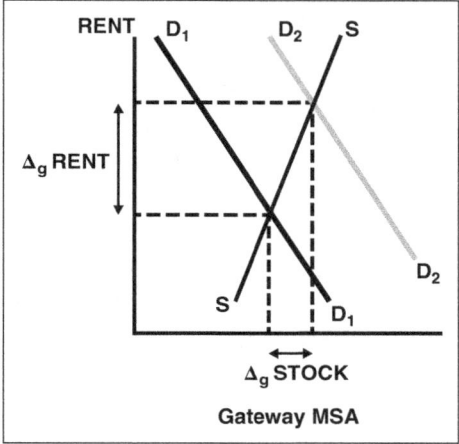

EXHIBIT 8.17 An outward shift in demand results in greater vacancy rate volatility in MSAs with high elasticities.

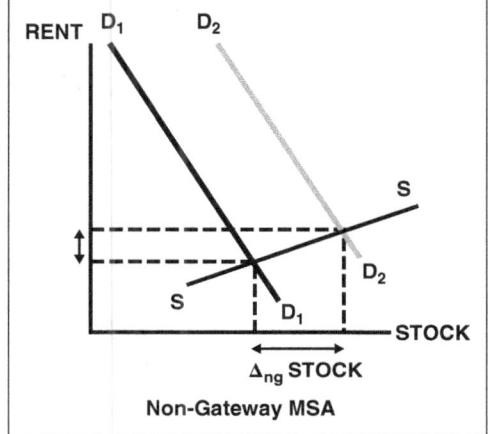

EXHIBIT 8.18 Vacancy rate in the top 25% of the inventory is the least volatile.

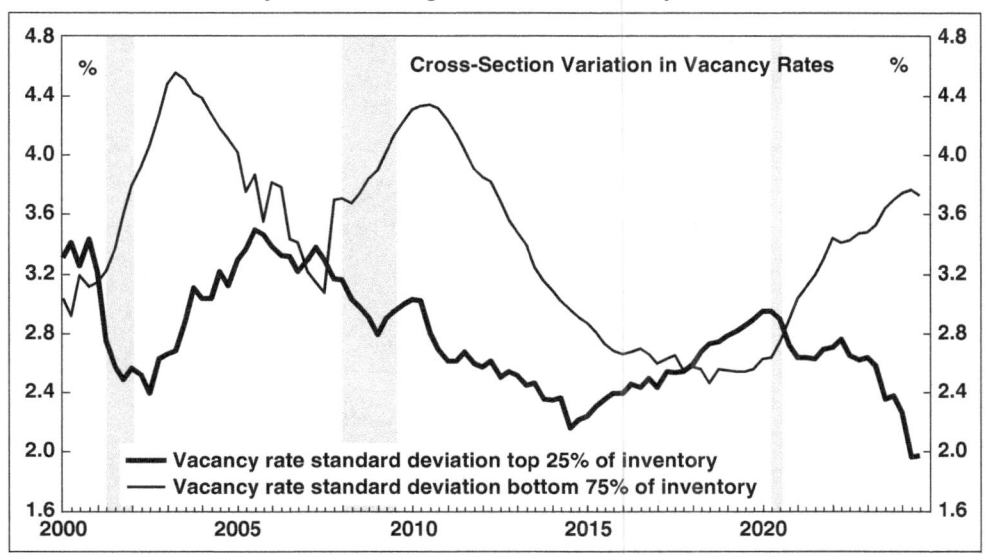

Source: ZCA estimation using CoStar data

The NVR is that rate at which rental rates are neither rising nor falling. The natural vacancy rate in MSA B is low with respect to Market C but high compared to Market A. New York City's vacancy rate of 7% might indicate a loose market in New York City, whereas in a rapidly growing MSA, such as Dallas, that rate would indicate a hot market with rising rents, as shown in Exhibit 8.19.

Exhibit 8.20 shows rental growth versus vacancy rates for New York City, San Francisco, and Phoenix using MSA versions of the US NVR model, Equation (8.1). The intersection with the vacancy rate axis is the NVR, which varies by MSA. The NVR is a function of the size and rate of growth of the inventory.

The derivative of the US NVR with respect to the office inventory is as follows, where RENTGDSD is the standard deviation of rental growth: 0.091 − 1.183 * RENTGDSD. The greater is the volatility, the lower is the NVR. The derivative with respect to rental growth volatility is −1.183, indicating greater rental growth volatility for lower NVRs.

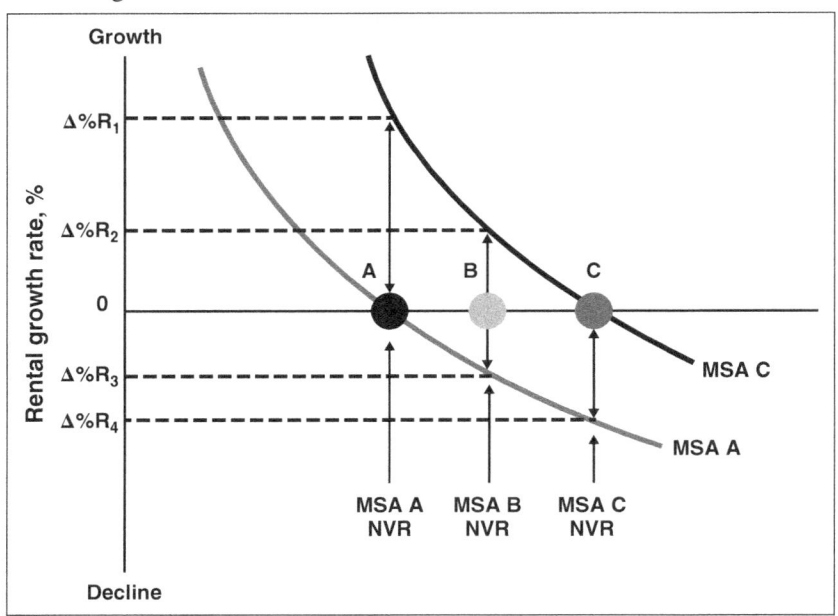

EXHIBIT 8.19 The vacancy rate in MSA B would indicate weakness in A and strength in C.

Source: ZCA using CoStar data

EXHIBIT 8.20 NVRs of New York, San Francisco, and Phoenix.

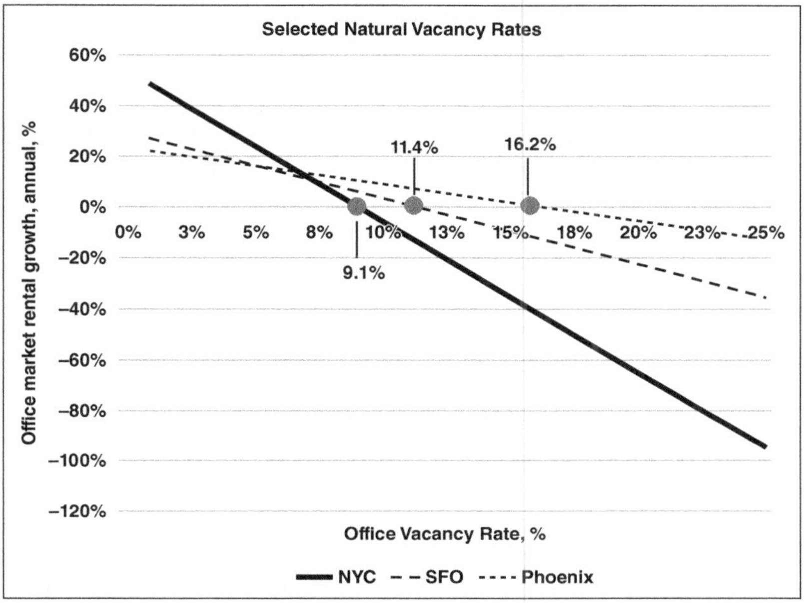

Source: ZCA using CoStar data

Equation (8.1) is statistically significant and the signs of the coefficients are consistent with theory.

$$NVR_i = 0.100 + 0.068 * INVENTORYGR_i + 0.091 * OFFINVENTORY_i$$
$$(10.881)\ \ (2.643) \qquad\qquad\qquad (2.900)$$

$$-\ 1.183 * RENTGRSD * OFFINVENTORY_i$$
$$(-2.883) \tag{8.1}$$

R-squared = 0.374

Adjusted R-squared = 0.299

Standard error of the regression = 0.017

Mean dependent variable = 0.124

F-statistic = 4.975

Higher NVRs are associated with higher growth rates, indicative of a speculative or liquidity-induced demand for vacancies. A 1% increase in the inventory growth rate is associated with a 0.539% increase in NVR, as shown by the coefficient for INVENTORYGR in Equation (8.2).

$$\mathbf{LOG\,(NVR_i) = -2.295 + 0.539 * INVENTORYGR_i + 0.750 * OFFINVENTORY_i}$$
$$(-28.300)\ (2.370) \qquad\qquad (2.688)$$

$$\mathbf{-9.901 * RENTGRSD * OFFINVENTORY_i}$$
$$(-2.721) \tag{8.2}$$

R-squared = 0.367

Adjusted R-squared = 0.257

Standard error of the regression = 0.149

Mean dependent variable = −2.105

F-statistic = 4.232

The greater is the MSA population growth rate, the higher is the percentage change in the office inventory; the office inventory grows at a slow rate in large cities. Rental growth volatility is associated with greater office inventory change, as shown in Equation (8.3).

$$\mathbf{LOG\,(OFFINVENTORY_i) = -1.974 + 2.325 * POPGR_i - 0.074 * POPULATION_i}$$
$$(-9.280)\ (5.859) \qquad\qquad (-3.256)$$

$$\mathbf{+5.081 * RENTGRSD_i}$$
$$(-1.863) \tag{8.3}$$

R-squared = 0.646

Adjusted R-squared = 0.603

Standard error of the regression = 0.017

Mean dependent variable = 0.124

F-statistic = 4.975

San Francisco's rental growth rate is over two times as volatile as Phoenix's.

Linking absorption across office quality classes. Quality matters. Even though institutional investors reflexively prefer Class A properties, Class C is an important indicator of A-class sector health. Recently, it has performed better than Class A office. Similar economic factors drive Class C and Class A performance because the two classes are linked at the margin by tenants closely weighing Class A versus Class C occupancies. See Equations (8.4) and (8.5).

Lagged Class C absorption and contemporaneous Class C vacancy rates have a high and statistically significant relationship with Class A absorption. The pre-COVID-19 sensitivity was 0.722 but, during COVID-19, the sensitivity rose to 2.380, over three times the pre-COVID-19 estimate. During COVID-19, an increase of one million square feet of Class C office space across the US lagged by two quarters was associated with a 2.4 million increase in Class A absorption.

Current vacancy rates before COVID-19 had a negative coefficient, which became eight times more sensitive during COVID-19. Vacancy rates rose during COVID-19 for both classes, but the increase was far greater for A-Class offices. During the period 2020–2024, a 1% increase in the Class C vacancy rate was associated with an 84.8 million decrease in Class A absorption. Pre-COVID-19, the decrease was 10.6 million, as indicated in Equation (8.4).

Pre-COVID-19 Period Absorption:

$$CLASSA_t = 109.6 + 0.722 * CLASSC_{t-1} - 1064.5 * VAC_t$$
$$\quad\quad\quad (2.963)\,(2.284)\quad\quad\quad\quad\quad (-2.089)$$

$$- 1.313 * CLASSVOLGR_{t-2} + 0.927^* AR(1) + 49.964 * SIGMASQ$$
$$(-1.313)\quad\quad\quad\quad\quad\quad (21.988)\quad\quad (8.073)\quad\quad\quad\quad (8.4)$$

R-squared = 0.904

Adjusted R-squared = 0.897

Standard error of the regression = 7.374

Mean dependent variable = 36.896

F-statistic = 127.993

Probability (F-statistic) = 0.000

Durbin Watson statistic = 1.726

2020–2024 Period:

$$CLASSA_t = 442.0 + 2.380 * CLASSC_{t-1} - 8{,}476.6 * VAC_t$$
$$(3.445)\ (2.385) \quad\quad\quad (-3.163)$$

$$+ 1.313 * CLASSVOLGR_{t-2} + 0.894 * AR(1) + 58.064 * SIGMASQ$$
$$(0.243) \quad\quad\quad\quad (7.470) \quad\quad (2.048) \quad\quad\quad (8.5)$$

R-squared = 0.928
Adjusted R-squared = 0.901
Standard error of the regression = 9.212
Mean dependent variable = −7.280
F-statistic = 33.737
Probability (F-statistic) = 0.000
Durbin Watson statistic = 1.171

During the period, 2020–2024, Class A absorption was more sensitive to Class C absorption lagged by one quarter. Absorption sensitivity to past vacancy rates increased. This finding underscores the importance of Class C property performance even if the investor's focus is exclusively Class A.

Relationship between COVID-19 cases and property performance. The rental growth rate is negatively correlated with the vacancy rate and deaths per capita, but positively related to MSA size. The higher death rate in larger MSAs suppressed rental growth rates and encouraged suburban flight. Equation (8.6) underscores the interaction between office performance and COVID-19 cases and deaths.

$$RENTGR2023_i = 0.075 + 0.005 * MSAPOP2021_i - 0.555 * VAC2023_i$$
$$(5.216)\ (2.786) \quad\quad\quad (-4.354)$$

$$-0.0002 * DEATHPERCAP2020_i$$
$$(-2.493) \quad\quad\quad\quad\quad\quad\quad\quad\quad (8.6)$$

R-squared = 0.534
Adjusted R-squared = 0.488
Standard error of the regression = 0.124
Mean dependent variable = 0.124
F-statistic = 11.482
Probability (F-statistic) = 0.000

The changing CBD-suburban equilibrium. The short- and long-term impacts of COVID-19 differ in many ways. The prompt impact is WFH, which has devastated A-class office properties in the larger, denser MSAs. The long-term threat is obsolescence. COVID-19 did not cause obsolescence, but COVID-19 has been an accelerant.

Exhibit 8.21 shows supply and demand curves for the CBD and suburbs. CBD demand is less elastic than suburban elasticities, so rental growth rates will likely be more volatile in the CBD relative to the suburbs. R_{CBD} is the CBD rent; R_{SUB} is the suburban rent. COVID-19 affected the CBD—suburban spread. The spread is a function of the opportunity cost of commuting between the CBD and suburbs, among other factors.

Exhibit 8.21 includes the office rental spread between the two adjoining markets. Exhibit 8.22 shows in this hypothetical example what happens when demand shifts to the left in the CBD (demand declines at current prices) and shifts to the right in the suburbs. The proportional impact of the shift is greater in the suburbs than in the CBD, because the suburban inventory is less than the CBD's. The shift lowers rents in the CBD and increases rents in the suburbs, thus narrowing the CBR-suburban rental spread.

WFH and the value of time. WFH is a natural response to COVID-19. Exhibits 8.23 and 8.24 show how workers determine their work–leisure time trade-off. Assume that the risk (and fear) of disease reduces the effective wage rate, which equals the pre-disease wage rate minus the COVID-19 discount. The slope of the budget constraint, which shifts from AE to BE, is the effective wage rate, W^{eff}. The COVID-19 discount reduces the slope of the budget line. The worker maximizes utility subject to budget and time constraints.

The shift produces an income and substitution effect. Households vary in their preference for leisure, income, and location, represented by U. In Exhibit 8.23, a fall

EXHIBIT 8.21 The CBD office supply exceeds the suburban supply and CBD demand is less elastic.

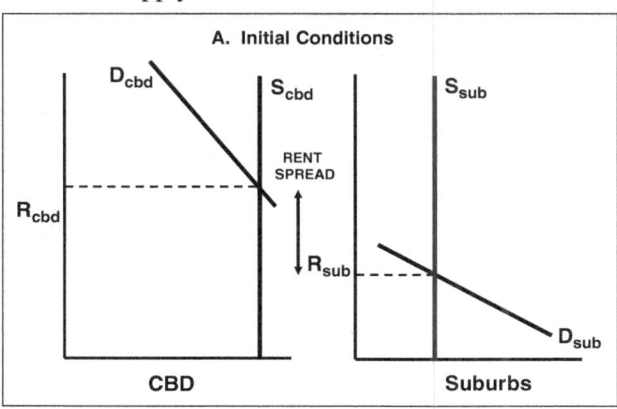

Source: ZCA

EXHIBIT 8.22 Demand contraction in CBD and expansion in the suburbs narrows the rent spread.

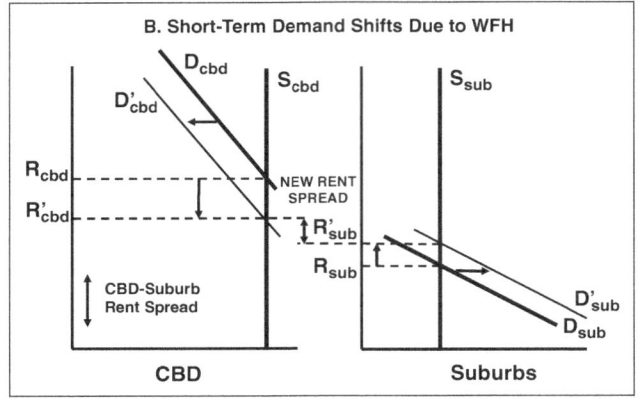

Source: ZCA

EXHIBIT 8.23 Induced work.

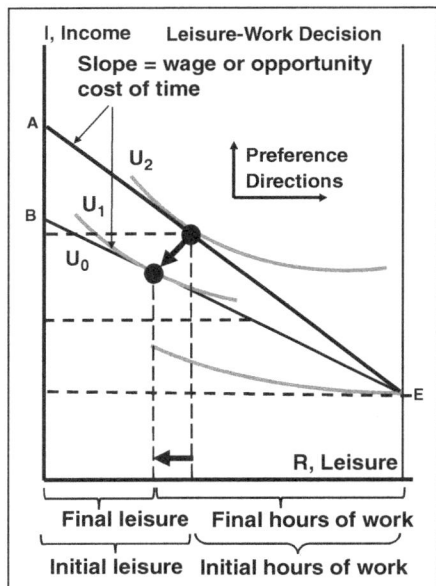

Source: ZCA

EXHIBIT 8.24 Induced leisure.

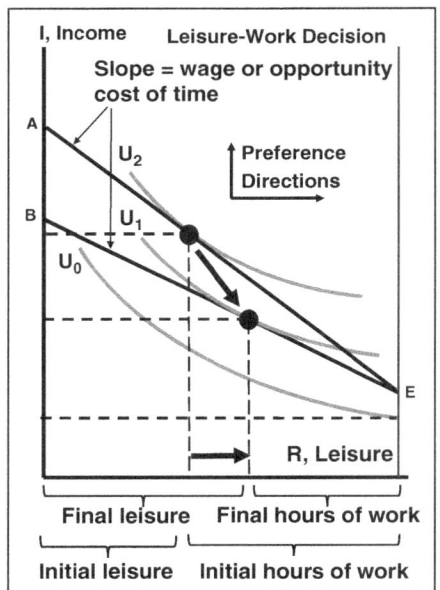

Source: ZCA

in the effective wage rate *decreases* the supply of working hours and increases the amount of leisure, as long as income and leisure are normal goods. The substitution effect, which increases leisure while the income effect decreases leisure, outweighs the income effect in this example, but under certain circumstances, it need not.

Depending on workers' preferences, the income effect can swamp the substitution effect, thus *increasing* the supply of labor (e.g., essential or lower skilled, lower income workers). Under most circumstances, a fall in the effective wage rate *decreases* the supply of working hours and increases the amount of leisure, as long as income and leisure are normal goods. The substitution effect increases leisure while the income effect decreases leisure.

In Exhibit 8.24, worker hours decrease; hence the labor supply response is ambiguous. A tradeoff exists between space per worker (including all of the support) and days worked at home.

Exhibit 8.25 shows the estimated optimum of WFH days, which reflects recent surveys. Skilled workers have a non-zero optimum of days spent at home.

A trade-off exists between space per worker (including all of the support) and days worked at home. See Exhibit 8.26. Exhibits 8.25 and 8.26, which derive from the analysis in Exhibits 8.23 and 8.24, suggest that there is a non-zero optimum for WFH, at least for the more skilled or more mobile workers.

EXHIBIT 8.25 It is optimal for more skilled workers to work from home. Surveys confirm this preference.

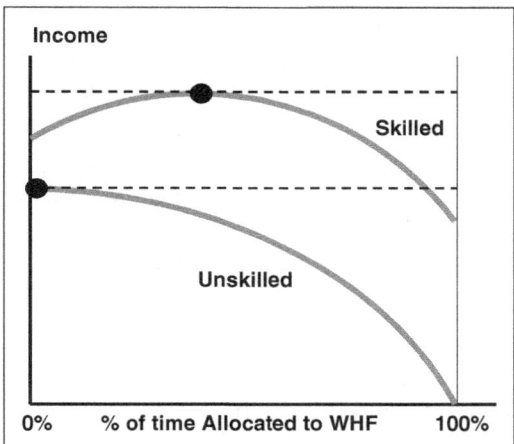

Source: ZCA

EXHIBIT 8.26 The optimal trade-off between days worked at home and space per worker.

Source: ZCA

Performance pre-COVID-19 and during COVID-19. COVID-19 increased the performance divergence between gateway and non-gateway MSAs in 2020. Gateway return volatility exceeded non-gateway volatility. Despite a fall in total office returns, return volatility across MSAs remained high. Before COVID-19, average rental growth across MSAs was lower, but growth was more differentiated. During and following COVID-19, rental growth volatility had declined and cross-MSA performance was more correlated, indicating that cities were miserable in the same way, to paraphrase the Russian novelist Tolstoy's reference to families.

Total returns are negatively correlated with MSA size. The relationship was more negative during COVID-19 as the larger MSAs with higher commuting costs and greater density suffered the most. Return volatility rises gradually with MSA size.

Cap rates are typically lower in larger MSAs and the negative relationship between cap rate and MSA size is no different pre- or post-COVID-19. Higher cap rates are associated with greater cap rate volatility post-COVID-19. Pre-COVID-19 cap rates are an excellent predictor of post-COVID-19 cap rates.

Larger cities suffered most during and following COVID-19. Gateway cities had higher return volatility pre- and post-COVID-19, holding MSA size constant. Rental growth was lower in post-COVID-19 gateway and larger MSAs.

Growth is inversely correlated with MSA size. Faster growing cities show greater volatility with regard to vacancy rates, cap rates, NOI, and returns. Investors, especially those prone to risk illusion, seem to prefer growth, even if faster growing MSAs have more volatile returns, and maybe lower risk-adjusted returns.

The performance of the C-quality inventory is much less volatile. This finding implies that investors should not reflexively assign a higher cost of capital to C-quality properties without carefully considering relative risks. Quality matters when thinking about risk.

Returns and vacancy rates associated with A-quality property performances for New York, in particular, are more volatile. For the US, New York, and DC, A-quality vacancy rates were significantly higher compared to C-quality vacancy rates during COVID-19, whereas C-quality vacancy rates have recently declined. The recent rise in A-quality vacancy rates is stunning.

Transactional sales volume. Low or falling transactions volume is a sign of credit rationing and asymmetric information in the debt markets. During such times, the market becomes in effect a used car market in which Mercedes receive Chevy pricing. Owners who must transact during a downturn sell the most liquid assets first. This behavior biases indexes upward.

The long-term impact of COVID-19: Obsolescence and the repricing of the inventory. Obsolescence is insidious and unpredictable; its pace in not uniform. COVID-19 has been an accelerant, not a primary cause, of obsolescence.

As a rough proxy for energy efficient and healthy buildings, I adopt buildings whose vintage is 21 years or less and size is greater than 250,000 square feet. This subset constitutes less than 6.1% of the national inventory. (I have confirmed the choice of this metric with professional academics who study this topic.)

Using CoStar data on the age and size of office properties by MSA and for the US, I estimated that 70% of the existing office stock will suffer from accelerating obsolescence. Buildings of recent vintage generally have less incurable obsolescence and larger buildings provide economies of scale and greater flexibility.

Total obsolescence in the older MSAs could be substantial. For example, assuming that the 2020 value of the New York MSA office inventory was about $500 billion, I estimated total obsolescence to be in the range of $123 to $190 billion of inventory value, which is not an estimate of the cost to cure.

New York MSA's total obsolescence is 14.1% of total US obsolescence even though the New York MSA's inventory is 7.8% of the US inventory. The New York City office inventory is relatively older. The prices of older and smaller office buildings could eventually decline on average by at least 25% over the next three year to five years, which would wipe out all or most of the investors' equity. This predicament, of course, presents a buying and conversion opportunity of historical proportions for well-capitalized and nimble investors.

Conversion of office to apartments. Use-conversion to reduce the "office" inventory is one way to address the obsolescence problem, but the net effect will not likely reduce the actual size of the office inventory sufficiently to restore market balance. However, persistent disequilibrium for the foreseeable future will support excess returns associated with conversions.

I estimate CBD–suburban performance spreads for rental growth rates, vacancy rates, and NOI change. These spreads strongly favor conversions, especially in larger MSAs. Exhibit 8.27 compares the 12-month moving average of office and apartment rental growth rates. During the post-COVID period apartment rental growth rates exceeded office rental growth rates, a departure since 2000.

Rental, NOI growth, and occupancy rates have been higher in the suburbs. The rental rate spread increases in MSAs with higher office inventory growth, as shown in Equation (8.7). The coefficients are significant even though the model explains only 25% of the variation in rental growth spreads.

EXHIBIT 8.27 Apartment rental growth exceeds office rental growth.

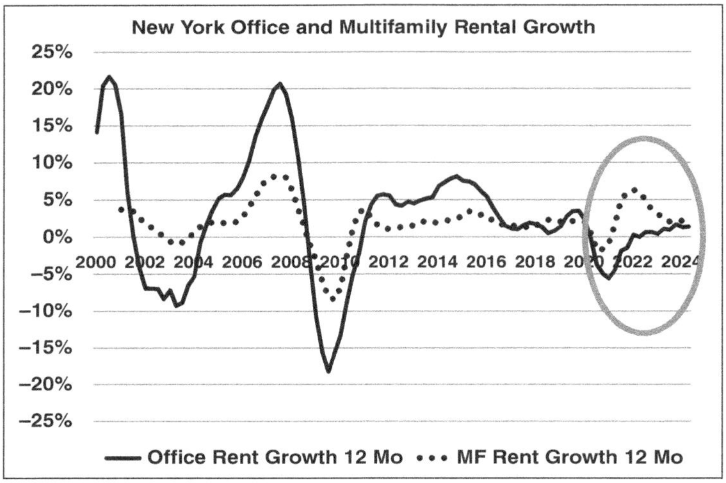

Source: ZCA using CoStar data

$$SPREADASKINGRENT_i = 0.903 + 1.291 * OFFINVENTORY_i$$
$$(11.460) \quad (2.111)$$

$$- 1.195 * OFFINVENTORY_i^2$$
$$(-1.504)$$

$$- 0.039 * SPREADMFMINUSOFFINVENTORYGROWTH_i$$
$$(-4.853)$$

$$+ 0.031 * INVENTORYGR_i$$
$$(1.751) \tag{8.7}$$

R-squared = 0.254

Adjusted R-squared = 0.222

Standard error of the regression = 0.854

Mean dependent variable = 0.800

F-statistic = 11.482

Equation (8.7) is a quadratic; the derivative of the asking rental rate variable with respect to the office inventory, Equation (8.8), produces the inventory size that maximizes the spread or the attractiveness of conversion, 0.540 billion square feet. This model confirms that the optimum office inventory size for conversion to office includes the largest MSAs.

$$\frac{\partial\ SPREAD}{\partial\ INVENTORY_i} = 1.291 - 2.390 * INVENTORY_i = 0 \rightarrow \text{Optimum}$$

$$= 0.540 \text{ billion square feet} \tag{8.8}$$

The occupancy spread equation, Equation (8.9), produces a similar result.

$$SPREADOCCUPANCY_i = 1.479 + 24.238 * OFFINVENTORY_i$$
$$(3.213) \quad (6.780)$$

$$- 17.666 * OFFINVENTORY_i^2$$
$$(-3.807)$$

$$- 0.102 * SPREADMFMINUSOFFINVENTORYGROWTH_i$$
$$(-2.161)$$

$$- 0.127 * OFFINVENTORYGROWTH_i. \tag{8.9}$$
$$(-1.248)$$

R-squared = 0.487

Adjusted R-squared = 0.465

Standard error of the regression = 2.056

Mean dependent variable = 2.732

F-statistic = 22.531

$$\frac{\partial\ SPREAD}{\partial\ INVENTORY_i} = 1.479 - 16.666 * INVENTORY_i = 0 \rightarrow \text{Optimum}$$

$$= 0.686 \text{ billion square feet} \tag{8.10}$$

The optimum conversion favors larger MSAs. See Exhibits 8.28 and 8.29.

Exhibit 8.28 plots asking rental spreads, with and without New York City. Exhibit 8.29 shows the plots of spreads for asking rental growth and occupancy rates. These plots exhibit maximums for the larger MSAs, which indicates that the big cities offer the best conversion opportunities. This result is a reassuring confirmation of what we observe in the property markets in 2025.

Age and size profile of the office inventory: A study in US and New York vulnerability. People normally associate cities with tall buildings and conclude incorrectly that the largest buildings account for most of the office inventory. See Exhibits 8.30 through 8.33.

180   CHAPTER 8   Office Property: COVID-19, Obsolescence, Work From Home (WFH)

EXHIBIT 8.28   The asking rental growth spread during COVID-19 was greatest in the larger MSAs.

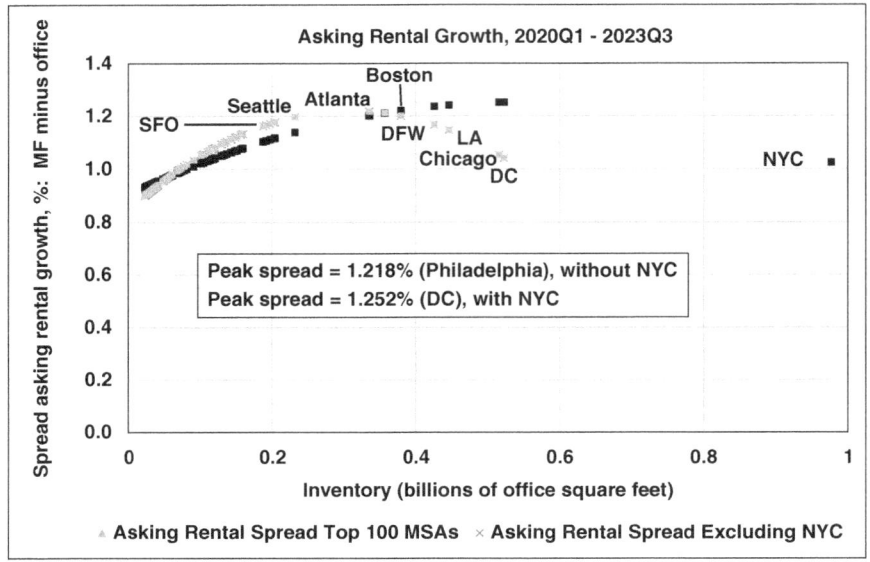

Source: ZCA estimation using CoStar data

EXHIBIT 8.29   Fitted occupancy and rental growth spreads are greatest for larger MSAs such as New York.

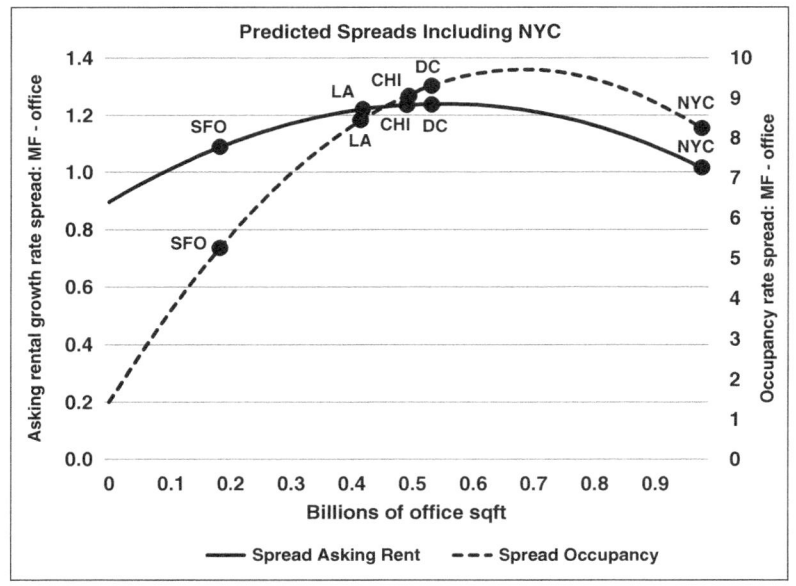

Source: ZCA estimation using CoStar data

EXHIBIT 8.30 Buildings under 250,000 square feet account for 74% of the US space inventory.

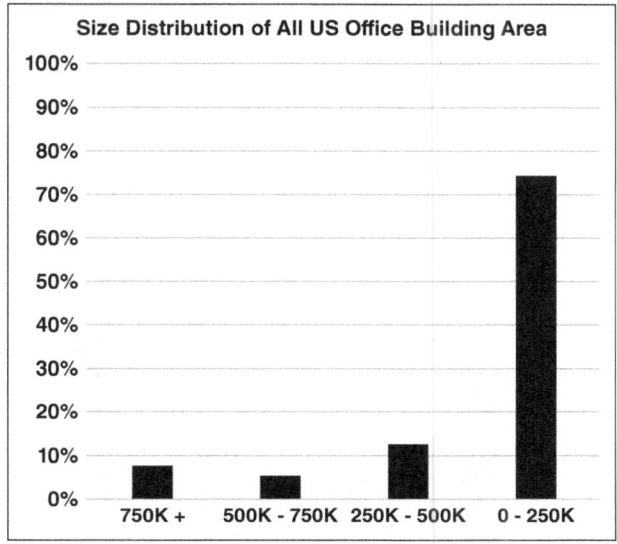

Source: ZCA using CoStar data

EXHIBIT 8.31 Small office buildings by count comprise 99% of total US buildings.

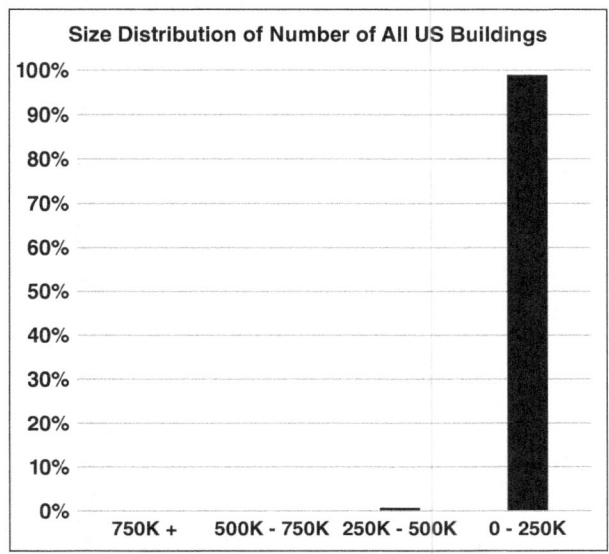

Source: ZCA using CoStar data

EXHIBIT 8.32 Buildings under 250,000 square feet comprise 41.6% of the space inventory.

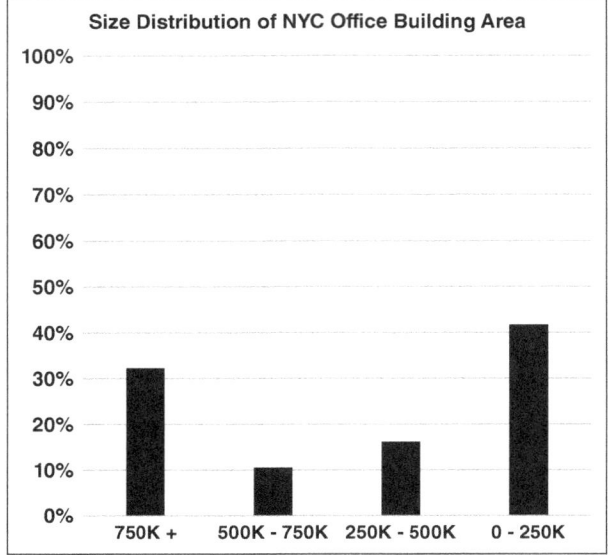

Source: ZCA using CoStar data

EXHIBIT 8.33 Small New York office buildings by count comprise 96% of total buildings.

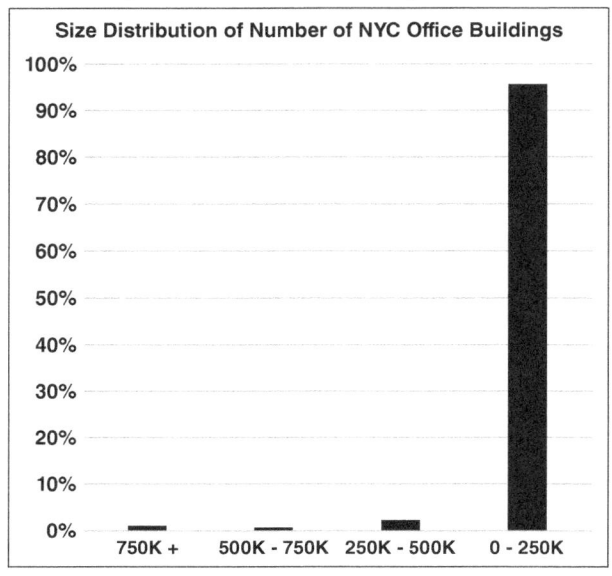

Source: ZCA using CoStar data

Space in buildings under 250,000 square feet accounts for about 74% of all US space and about 1% of all US buildings. New York City differs. About 42% of New York City's office space occurs in buildings with less than 250,000 square feet. Small buildings account for 96% of all New York City buildings. Not surprisingly, most of the obsolescence is found in the smaller and older buildings.

Office building obsolescence and the repricing of the inventory, not WFH, are the long-run challenges. Obsolescence is insidious and unpredictable, but COVID-19 accelerated in-process changes.

In 2025 investors can in many cases acquire certain office buildings at considerable discounts and convert them to apartments or other uses. Not all office buildings are suitable for conversion. However, this opportunity may be one of the greatest since the RTC period of the 1990s.

Conclusions and Investment Implications

- Office valuations have declined significantly in many MSAs but particularly in the largest ones.
- The CBD-suburban dichotomy is stark; the vacancy rate spread has widened, especially in larger MSAs.
- Values-per-square-foot during the period 2024 through 2025 plummeted to levels as low as 25% to 30% of acquisition price. As loans come due, losses will accumulate.
- Prices and rents are more volatile in large cities with very low supply elasticities.
- The natural vacancy rate (NVR), the rate at which rents are neither rising nor falling, is greater in MSAs with higher growth rates and greater volatility.
- The impact of COVID-19 on office buildings was greatest in the largest MSAs. High deaths per capita in those cities suppressed market rental growth.
- The short- and long-run impacts of COVID-19 differ. The A-quality inventory has been hit hard relative to Class C properties, but in the longer-run, a significant repricing of the total inventory will occur.

- Conversion from office to apartments, which is now a very attractive investment strategy, is one way to address the obsolescence problem but the net effect will not likely reduce the size of the CBD office inventory sufficiently to eliminate excess supply at current prices, given demand in 2025.
- Without significant reductions in the CBD office inventory in the largest cities through conversion or, to a much lesser extent, demolitions, a significant repricing of the older office property will occur.
- COVID-19 has accelerated in-process changes that may improve office productivity in the long run due to creative destruction imposed by nature, society, and technology.

Q&A: Interview with John Sischo, Managing Principal, Coretrust Capital Partners, LLC

The best office buying opportunity since the RTC

Given the chaos in the office sector, what is on your mind now?

The office market is at a turning point, shaped by cyclical and structural changes. While the full impact is still unfolding, one trend is clear: Office users prioritize well-located, highly amenitized, thoughtfully designed spaces to attract employees and enhance productivity.

Companies are shrinking office footprints but paying higher rents per square foot for Trophy and Class A buildings. This reflects a flight to quality, where businesses optimize space rather than expand.

The A-quality poor performance is a short-term disequilibrium. The A-quality properties will recover faster and the C-quality will decline further.

Yes, I agree. During COVID-19, people were confined to their homes, and remote work significantly impacted Class A, B, and C properties. However, in nearly every market, Trophy and Class A assets are capturing most new leasing activity and outperforming Class B and C buildings.

Where do you see the opportunity?

The office sector remains undervalued. Many properties selling at steep discounts due to distress will, in hindsight, be seen as exceptional investments.

The best strategy now is raising equity to invest in defaulted office debt, offering attractive yields. Buying debt directly from lenders provides an efficient way to secure top-tier properties below replacement value. Success requires rapid capital deployment, especially in competitive bidding.

(continued)

(*continued*)

Who are the most qualified buyers?

Equity sources should partner with creative operators experienced in Class A properties. A discerning buyer must distinguish between well-located, amenity-rich buildings and commodity-like or obsolete ones. Strong leasing and management expertise are essential to maximizing asset value and performance.

What are some challenges?

Some of the most qualified buyers today are also victims of the valuation collapse. Investors should focus on operators with strong current capabilities and proven pre-COVID-19 performance.

What are your views on obsolescence?

Obsolescence is a persistent issue that investors have ignored. Lower-quality office assets in weaker locations will continue declining. COVID-19 did not cause this trend—it accelerated it.

Beyond buildings, entire sections of cities face challenges like homelessness, affecting property values and city services. In some areas, taxpayers are relocating, eroding fiscal resources. Urban risk is now a crucial investment factor.

How do you view the current investment climate?

This is the best buying opportunity since the RTC era. Investors who act decisively can secure high-quality assets at significant discounts, positioning themselves for long-term gains.

CHAPTER 9

Risk Analysis in Practice: Retail, Self-Storage, and Housing

Preliminaries

Retail centers specialize in services and nondurable consumer goods, the demand for which is much less volatile over the business cycle. Services comprise an increasing share of center sales, which confers additional stability to center performance. Malls focus more on durable goods, which are more sensitive to business cycle fluctuations, especially changes in household income. Centers provide greater downside protection than do malls. Center expenditure growth is greater and less volatile than mall expenditure growth.

Centers provide stability, which is reflected in higher total and risk-adjusted returns, moderate expenditure volatility, and lower cap rates (compared to anchored centers lacking grocery stores). Center cap rates in 2020 were lower than non-grocer anchored and unanchored center cap rates. At the time, center cap rates had declined over 100 bps while other retail concepts' cap rates remained stable or increased. Customers during COVID-19 favored centers and avoided malls.

Centers, compared with malls, offer these advantages: Centers are internet insensitive, are more liquid than malls, and are relatively insensitive to interest rate and credit shocks. Risk per unit of cap rate return is lowest for centers. Grocery anchors add another layer of stability.

Some investors correctly observe that most centers' in-line tenants are not traditional credit tenants. The Asian restaurant or family-run dry cleaners may not enjoy easy access to global capital markets, but it is usually creditworthy. These inline stores are the billboards for many family-owned businesses. If these subtenants' leases were publicly traded bonds, they would likely receive an investment grade rating just based on their low delinquency and default rates.

Centers are replete with options: the option to refocus the tenant mix, resize the tenants, convert all or part of the site to a different use, to select tenants who provide services or consumer nondurables, and adjust lease maturities and renewal options.

The grocery sector, which is relatively concentrated, has scale economies to innovate, especially through capital-intensive automation. Institutions own most of the mall inventory, whereas a fragmented and under-capitalized non-institutional sector still dominates grocery-anchored centers.

The price elasticities of demand for center retail sales are much more inelastic than the demand for mall retail sales, e.g., center sales are less sensitive to price volatility. This finding is consistent with centers' focus on necessities and services. The mall income elasticity is very elastic, which explains why mall sales are more volatile than centers' sales over the business cycle. Centers' income elasticity is highly inelastic, which explains why centers are less sensitive to the business cycle. The demand for services provided at centers are more like necessities; their income elasticity of demand is less than one. By contrast, the income elasticity of demand for consumer durables, which are common to malls, is more income elastic (1.309) than the demand for nondurables at centers, (0.484). (See Exhibits 9.1 and 9.2.) Hence, mall sales have been more volatile over the cycle compared with center service sales.

EXHIBIT 9.1 The income elasticity of demand for consumer durables (malls) is more elastic (1.309) than the demand for nondurables (Centers) (0.484). (T-statistics are in parentheses.)

	Pre-tax disposable income	After-tax disposable income
Consumer nondurables (Centers)	0.484 (14.286)	0.534 (11.568)
Consumer durables (Malls)	1.309 (14.267)	1.393 (11.070))

Source: ZCA

EXHIBIT 9.2 The price elasticity of demand for consumer nondurables is much less than for neighborhood centers; tenant service and nondurable prices for centers are less variable. (T-statistics are in parentheses.)

	Pre-tax disposable income	After-tax disposable income
Consumer nondurables (Centers)	−0.025 (−0.859)	0.054 (1.706)
Consumer durables (Malls)	−0.892 (−4.361)	−0.824 (−3.713)

Source: ZCA

The ratio of nondurable goods and labor and service providers to center area is inelastic, suggesting that if the customer demand for goods and services remains inelastic and household expenditures grow, the demand for space, existing and new, will grow dependably and with relatively little fluctuation over the longer-term. See Exhibit 9.3.

Service categories, such as beauty, health, food and beverage, and fitness will be among the most resistant to shocks. Bricks and mortar will remain critical points of sale for services. After all, while customers can reserve a place in line using the internet, the internet cannot cut hair, as yet.

Self-Storage Leases as Bonds: Using Alternative Approaches When Long Return Series Are Lacking

Self-storage has been important throughout history. While storage in some capacity is not new, the proliferation of buildings dedicated to self-storage is new. The invention of the self-storage building, much like the data center, awaited rising real incomes, technological innovation, and the growth of the population. (Years ago, data storage was consigned to a dark corner of the basement.)

EXHIBIT 9.3 Comparison of service retail and mall elasticities and investment performance.

Centers	Malls
Price elasticity: −0.025 (inelastic, statistically zero)	**Price elasticity:** −0.892 (almost unitary elasticity)
Income elasticity: 0.484 (inelastic, "necessities")	**Income elasticity:** 1.309 ("luxuries")
Price behavior: Long-term increase in the price of services over time; services will comprise a growing share of the household budget.	**Price behavior:** Long-term price per unit will decline due to technological progress and import substitution.
Sold: Mostly services and some nondurables	**Sold:** Mostly consumer durables
Investment implications: • Sales are relatively insensitive to income fluctuations. • Overall service retail sales growth is not negative during downturns. • Services, such as health services, dining, cleaning, and accounting, are typically not storable. • If household income falls by 10.0%, demand falls 4.8%. • Demand is relatively insensitive to price. • If price rises 10.0%, quantity demanded falls by only 0.25%. • The secular increase is important given the price-inelastic demand for services because an increase in price will increase total revenue.	**Investment implications:** • Sales are very sensitive to income fluctuations, which increases risk. • Mall expenditure growth is more volatile than service retail expenditures and it is even negative during downturns. • Durable goods are storable, so households can defer purchases, thus making durable sales more volatile than either consumer services or nondurables. • If household income falls by 10%, demand falls 13.1%. • If price rises by 10%, demand falls by 10%, because the price elasticity is close to −1.0.

Source: ZCA

Self-storage—the building type—is a physical extension of the home. As long as people buy consumer durables, or "stuff," and seek cost-effective ways to store the stuff, then the demand for self-storage should grow faster than real personal income. The increasing dominance of on-line sales will only accelerate this trend.

Self-storage is ubiquitous. Unlike office property or industrial warehouse parks, self-storage is distributed spatially much like the population. Wherever there is housing, there is a need for storage. Still, there are important variations in this distribution. For example, lower-income, growing states, especially in the higher growth southern states, have more self-storage per capita.

The demand for self-storage is a function of income, wealth, available space, and consumer durables. Real personal consumption of durables, which is highly correlated with the self-storage inventory, is growing faster than real household wealth, real disposable personal income, and total housing units.

Income, high or low, is no barrier to the demand for self-storage. The higher is the ratio of stuff-to-housing area, the greater is the need for self-storage. Higher income is a proxy for the ability to buy bigger homes and apartments with more space for storage; with rising income, households tend to buy even more stuff. These households rent self-storage. However, lower-income households cannot afford as much on-site storage and therefore are more likely to rent self-storage. Holding state population growth constant econometrically, a 1% increase in personal income is associated with a 0.69% reduction in the growth rate of an MSA's self-storage area, which means that the elasticity of growth with respect to income is inelastic.

Population growth is a significant demand driver: A 1% increase in population is associated with 1% more self-storage. Per-capita self-storage is greater in fast growing states. The demand for self-storage with respect to household income is 0.7, which indicates that self-storage is a necessity, not a luxury. Consequently, the demand for self-storage is less volatile, or less risky, over the business cycle, compared to the demand for durables. (Note that space dedicated to the storage of durables is not the same as the consumption of durables, nor are they perfectly correlated in the short-run.)

What makes self-storage special? Self-storage leases, which have short maturities, are like short-duration corporate bonds with a return kicker. The landlord can raise rents monthly in all markets; hence self-storage leases are like variable rate bonds. Self-storage rent constitutes a relatively small percentage of the household budget and tenants regard the retention of stuff as an option, much like waiting for a rainy day or a special event. Half of the tenants stay at least for a year, according to industry statistics.

Self-storage facilities have very low loss rates, so low that these facilities, were they corporate bonds, would justify an investment-grade rating. Loss rates, assuming a 4% to 5% cap rate, are in the range of 0.06% and 0.20%. These rates qualify for investment-grade status.

Is the weighted average cost of capital (WACC) too low? Yes, probably! Should self-storage receive a higher valuation and a larger allocation within institutional portfolios? Yes!

Since self-storage is an investment-grade bond equivalent, self-storage cap rates and the associated cost of capital should be lower and asset allocations should be higher. The true loss is the net loss after a lien sale, which occurs after 60 days. Bond loss rates equal the ratio of the loss divided by the bond principal. By analogy, the self-storage facility loss rate equals the true loss divided by the value of the facility. Determining facility value is more difficult and uncertain than simply recording bond principal. Therefore, I estimated facility values using actual losses for three years—2019, 2020, and 2021—and used three cap rates: 4%, 5%, and 6%.

Exhibit 9.4 shows loss rates for these years using three cap rates, 4%, 5%, and 6%. The greater is the facility's value, the lower is the loss rate. Loss rates are between 0.08% and 0.24% and a reasonable cap rate range is between 4% and 5%, given the risk. The more refined loss rate would be between 0.06% and 0.20%.

EXHIBIT 9.4 Self-storage loss rates (2019–2021) calculated under various cap rate assumptions.

	Median Loss Rate Estimated Using Log Logistic Function		
	Cap Rate = 4%	Cap Rate = 5%	Cap Rate = 6%
2019	0.16%	0.20%	0.24%
2020	0.12%	0.15%	0.19%
2021	0.06%	0.07%	0.08%

Source: ZCA

Actual corporate bond default rates increase as the holding period lengthens. I overlay in Exhibit 9.5 the lower and upper self-storage loss rates. Self-storage clearly merits an investment-grade rating for all holding periods.

Self-storage fundamentals are not fleeting; the need is enduring and likely to strengthen. The capital markets still misprice self-storage. As institutional capital consolidates this still highly fragmented sector, new owners will realize greater operating efficiencies; prices will rise and cap rates will fall.

Self-storage is equivalent to core- or core-plus property, and, as such, deserves an allocation within an institutional-grade portfolio.

EXHIBIT 9.5 Cumulative bond default and self-storage defaults.

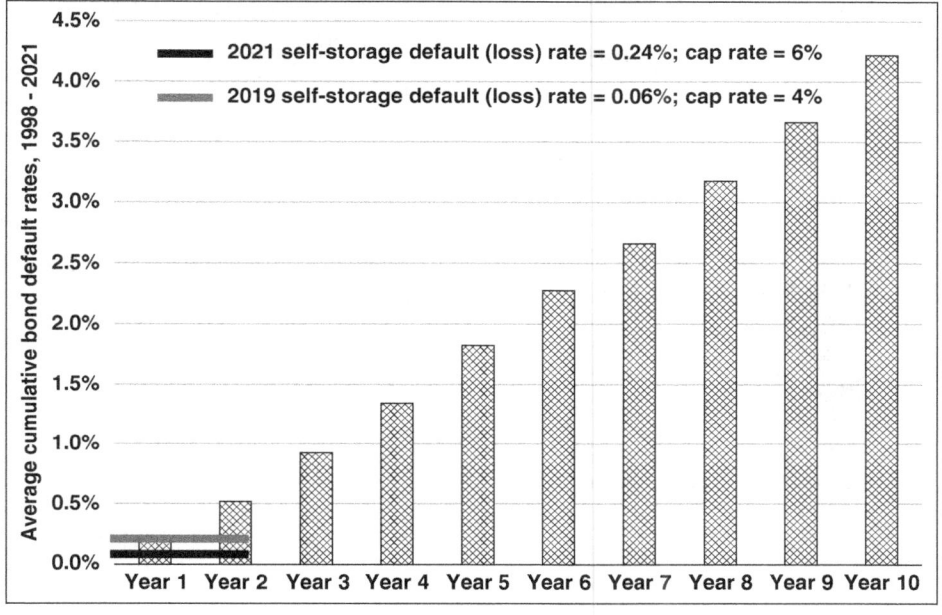

Source: ZCA and Moody's, 2019

Apartment and Single-Family Housing Are Near Substitutes

Pricing in the single-family sector affects pricing in the apartment sector; risk diffuses from one sector to the other.

Factor substitution is the process by which the ratio of inputs changes in response to changes in relative prices. Big cities, which are no exception, are apartment intensive because land prices are higher in relation to physical capital. Their average floor-to-area (FAR) ratios are larger.

For example, when lemon prices increase relative to the price of limes, holding income constant, consumers increase their consumption of limes. This is an example of substitution. The rapid rise in the ratio of total apartment units to households, beginning in 2012 following the GFC, reflects rising income insecurity. Apartment developers responded by building more apartments and reducing the size of apartment units. Many more households, after contemplating their housing tenure choices, choose apartments. (See Exhibits 9.6–9.8.)

EXHIBIT 9.6 The average ratio of units to households increases along with US population.

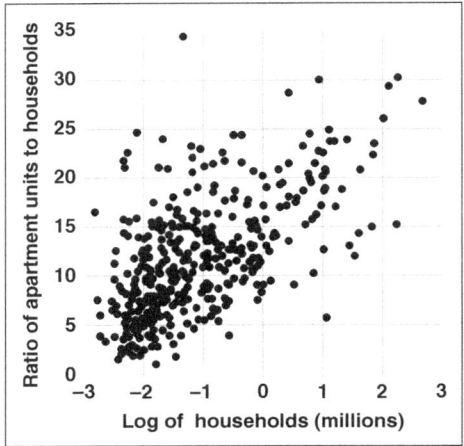

Source: ZCA using Federal Reserve data

EXHIBIT 9.7 The logarithm of ratio of units to households is a function of the log of households.

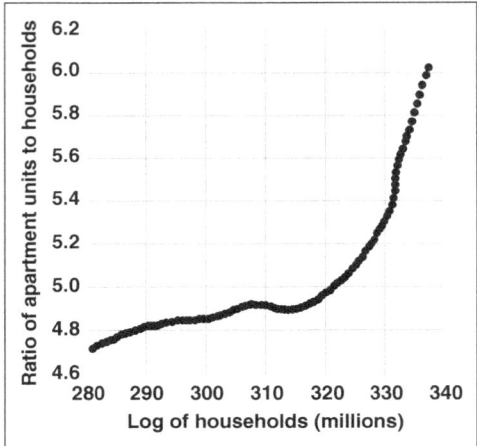

Source: ZCA using Federal Reserve data

EXHIBIT 9.8 Since 2011, the change in the ratio of apartment units to households is increasing, indicating an accelerating shift to a high ratio of apartment units to single family homes.

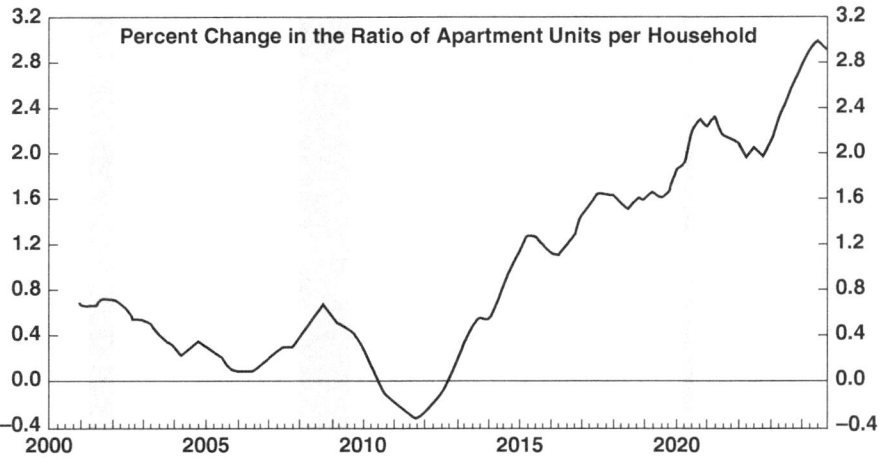

Source: ZCA using CoStar data

The ratio of apartment units to households, RATIO, is greater in faster growing MSAs (%CH_HOUSEHOLD) and in large MSAs. Growing MSAs have a higher transactional demand for apartments, but some families who migrate to growing MSAs do not immediately qualify for mortgages. Hence, people delay household formation (e.g., marriages) and remain longer with parents or roommates.

The impact of rent on RATIO is a function of the number of apartment units in an MSA, as shown in Equation (9.1). The first derivative of RATIO with respect to RENT is .018–0.118 * $INVENTORY_i$. The derivative is negative for MSAs with more than 152,542 units, which implies that as RENT increases in larger MSAs, the RATIO declines.

$$RATIO_i = 0.072 - 0.061 * HOUSEHOLD_i + 0.099 * \%CH\_HOUSEHOLD_i$$
$$(9.121)\ (-3.299) \qquad\qquad (3.636)$$

$$+ 0.769 * INVENTORY_i + 0.018 * RENTSQFT_i$$
$$(7.623) \qquad\qquad (3.534)$$

$$- 0.118 * RENTSQFT_i * INVENTORY_i$$
$$(-6.014) \tag{9.1}$$

$R^2 = 0.386$

Adjusted $R^2 = 0.378$

Mean dependent variable $= 0.118$

S.D. dependent var $= 0.060$

S.E. of regression $= 0.047$

Observations $= 389$ MSAs

According to Equation 9.2, a 10% increase in MSA size is associated with a 6.34% increase in RATIO. This finding confirms intuition that larger cities are more apartment-intensive as are faster growing MSAs. A 10% increase in the rate of MSA population growth is associated with a 1.3% higher RATIO. The greater is population variation across MSAs, as shown in Exhibit 9.9, the less is the ratio of units to households.

RATIO is less in MSAs with uncertain growth. Migration requires a large emotional and financial commitment, often by a family and not by one individual, and the transactions costs are significant. Hence, population volatility, as measured by the 12-quarter moving average of the standard deviation of MSA population, has a negative coefficient. An increase of 10% in the 12-month moving average of population growth volatility reduces RATIO by 0.121%.

EXHIBIT 9.9 Post-COVID-19, the volatility of housing and apartment appreciation has been similar.

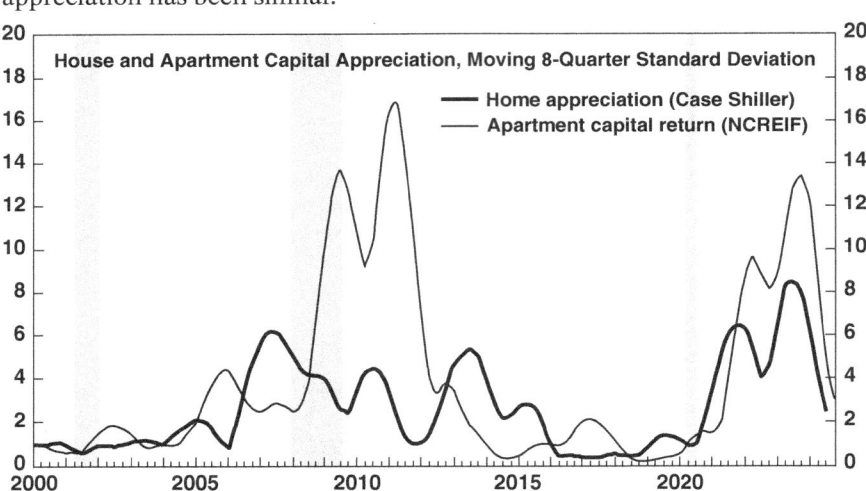

Source: ZCA using CoStar data

The greater is volatility, DMOV12POPULATION, as shown in Equation (9.2), the less is the ratio of units to households. RATIO is higher in larger MSAs and in faster growing MSAs.

$$LOG(RATIO_i) = -4.870 + 0.634 * LOG(POPULATION_i)$$
$$(-8.618) \quad (7.992)$$

$$+0.013 * LOG(\%POPULATION_i)$$
$$(1.196)$$

$$-0.121 * LOG(SDMOV12POPULATION_i)$$
$$(-7.981) \tag{9.2}$$

$R^2 = 0.863$

Adjusted $R^2 = 0.858$

Mean dependent variable $= -2.973$

S.D. dependent var $= 0.064$

S.E. of regression $= 0.024$

S.E. of regression $= 0.024$

Housing price appreciation has led apartment appreciation since COVID-19; appreciation in both sectors declined precipitously as mortgage rates rose after 2021. (See Exhibit 9.10.)

Apartment capital appreciation increases if single-family appreciation is more volatile or risky. The uncertainty in the housing sector diffuses to apartments. Greater volatility increases the value of the call option to defer the purchase of a house.

Housing appreciation leads apartment appreciation by one quarter. Increased disposable income volatility reduces apartment appreciation, as shown in Equation (9.3). A 10% increase in capital appreciation in single family houses in the previous quarter is reflected in a 0.634% increase in the capital return to apartments. A rise of 10% in the standard deviation or volatility of disposable income reduces the apartment capital return by 0.319%.

The model explains 97% of the variation in apartment returns and all of the t-statistics are large, indicating that the coefficients are estimated with precision. The high Durbin Watson indicates this model does not suffer from serial correlation and omitted variables (the standard deviations for disposable income and house appreciation are 8-quarter moving averages).

EXHIBIT 9.10 House price appreciation leads apartment appreciation by one quarter.

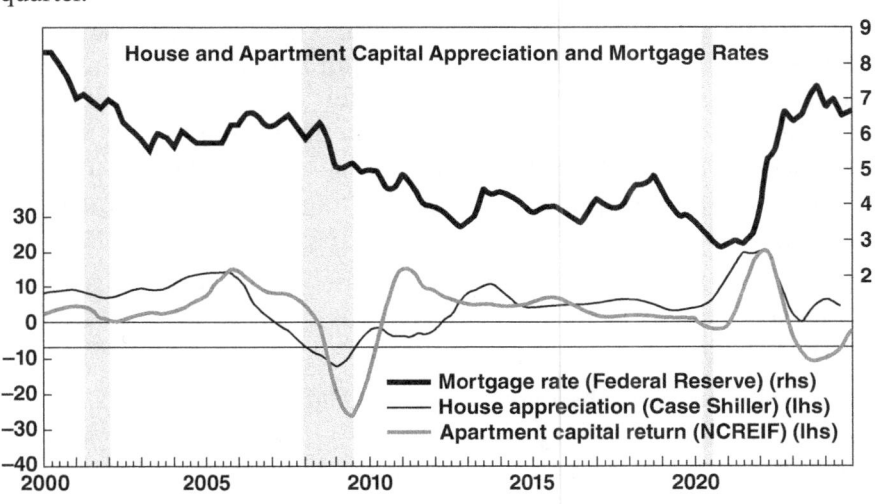

Source: ZCA using Federal Reserve and NCREIF data

$$APTCAP_t = 0.138 + 0.634 * HOUSECAP_{t-1} + 1.670 * APTCAP_{t-1}$$
$$(0.527)\ (3.419) \qquad\qquad (33.628)$$

$$- 0.861 * APTCAP_{t-2} - 0.319 * SDDISP_t +$$
$$(-18.203) \qquad\qquad (-2.534)$$

$$+ 0.197 * SDHOUSECAP_t$$
$$(2.119) \tag{9.3}$$

$R^2 = 0.974$

Adjusted $R^2 = 0.972$

Mean dependent variable = 2.858

S.D. dependent var = 8.394

S.E. of regression = 1.397

Durbin Watson statistic = 1.651

Conclusions and Investment Implications

- The finance sector is linked to property in complex ways that affect pricing, risk, and capital flows.
- Investors often insist on reviewing long return series when considering any new investment idea. If plentiful data are a requirement, investors should either shun new investment ideas and remain safely consigned to the major property "food" groups, or they should devise alternative metrics for underwriting non-traditional asset classes. Leases as bond substitutes serve that purpose.
- Do not ignore the substitutability between different sector and subsector asset classes, such as housing—single family and apartments—and self-storage.
- Analysts should not paint a highly differentiated asset class, such as retail, with too wide a brush.
- Centers are physically and financially different from malls.
- Investors should treat self-storage as they would other core assets.
- The apartment and single-family housing markets are linked. In addition to price and rents, risk, as measured by the standard deviation of cap rates, diffuses from apartments to single-family homes and from single-family back to apartments.

Q&A: Interview with Benjamin Shibe Macfarland III, CEO, SROACapital.com, LLC

Real Estate and Self-Storage

How did you get started in real estate?

I started converting old industrial buildings to self-storage in 2006. They were cheap per square foot compared to self-storage. We also picked up a lot of properties from failed owners that had over-leveraged themselves and lacked an operations platform. I adopted a buy-and-hold strategy. We now own 31 million square feet and manage >$2.5bn of equity from a diverse institutional investor base.

How did your investor base evolve?

Initially, it was 100% high net worth. The majority were single-family offices focused on tax efficiency and recession resistant cashflow. Today, we have about fifty separate institutions, including public and private pensions, Taft Hartley Plans, foundations, insurance companies, and global asset managers. We have our own capital placement team and have run a targeted fundraising process.

What is special about self-storage?

Self-storage has held up in good and bad times. We have lowest CAPEX and highest NOI margins of any multi-tenant property type. Tenants are on month-to-month leases, which means we can raise rates and outpace inflation.

And, the industry is highly fragmented (the top 100 owners own less than 30% of the market)—lots of opportunity for consolidation and adding value with institutional-quality management.

How much leverage?

We use moderate leverage and as the firm stands today we are ~47% LTV across our portfolio. If there is a big recession, higher leverage is a problem. I love to buy good deals from over-leveraged owners.

(continued)

(*continued*)

Do you have a fund?

Yes, we raise the majority of our capital through closed-end private equity vehicles, but we also have a few separate accounts with large public pensions.

Would you become a public REIT?

The private sector gives you the flexibility to be more contrarian. The broader market during downturns can harm public self-storage REITs even if their cash flow is strong. We bought some properties from public REITs. Remaining private has been helpful.

PART III
Performance Analysis, Risk, and Popular Myths

CHAPTER 10

Asset Allocation, with and without Liabilities, and Shortfall Constraints

Preliminaries

Markets are linked. No asset "is an island, Entire of itself," to paraphrase my favorite 16th–17th-century English poet, John Donne. Investors often evaluate investment risk on a stand-alone basis, when, in fact, the asset is part of a larger portfolio of assets, the performance of which determines shareholder value, mortgage losses, and bonuses. Assets fund liabilities, so the nature of the liabilities matters in judging the merits of an acquisition. The asset's marginal contribution to overall portfolio performance may be more meaningful than its IRR.

Diversification attracts many supporters. Warren Buffett, who famously embraces a long-term investment horizon, once said, "Wide Diversification is only required when investors do not understand what they are doing." The benefits of diversification may be greatest in the short to intermediate term.

The renowned biologist, Ernst Mayr, wrote, "As a consequence, geneticists described evolution simply as a change in gene frequencies in populations, totally ignoring the fact that evolution consists of the two simultaneous but quite separate phenomena of adaptation and diversification." How good are investors at adapting? Not very, I have observed.

Harry Markowitz, the father of modern portfolio theory, said, "Diversification is the only free lunch in investing." Since diversification, in practice, is not free,

I regard diversification as the equivalent of a cheap but very tasty lunch, but during a market decline, when needed the most, the benefits of diversification are conspicuously absent.

My former Princeton faculty colleague, Burt Malkiel, once said, "Diversify, diversify, diversify—and do it with low-cost index funds." Malkiel's wisdom is unassailable and still timely; it is certainly applicable to real estate: Embrace low-fee, transparent, relatively liquid strategies that provide true, not naïve, diversification.

Diversification Principles and Asset Allocation Applied to Real Estate

What is diversification? Modern portfolio theory (MPT) is a well-received and widely used technique for managing investment portfolios and just about all portfolio managers use it; some even use it correctly.

Diversification seeks to blend asset classes to achieve the highest long-run return for any given level of portfolio risk by finding assets or asset classes whose returns have low correlations.

Investors can reduce overall portfolio risk without sacrificing return or can increase return without incurring additional portfolio risk. (See Exhibit 10.1.) The suboptimal portfolio resides below the efficient frontier. By readjusting the

EXHIBIT 10.1 Improving sub-optimal performance requires moving to the efficient frontier between A and B by adjusting asset mix.

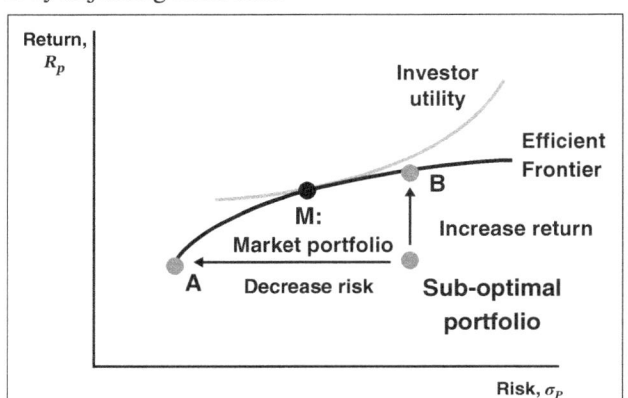

Source: ZCA

portfolio's asset allocation, we can improve performance. The optimal portfolio resides to the northwest of the sub-optimal portfolio. Once on the efficient frontier, we can only increase return by incurring additional risk.

Investors often want to minimize shortfalls or tail risks. Even if a portfolio is well-diversified, what is the likelihood of its incurring a loss of principal? What is the likelihood of losing over 10% of investor capital over a five-year horizon?

The most appropriate definition of an asset's risk is its contribution to overall portfolio risk. Most investors evaluate an asset's stand-alone real estate risk without considering its marginal contribution to overall portfolio risk. This practice is likely wealth-reducing.

A diversifiable risk is a risk that specifically affects a single asset or small group of assets. This type of risk, sometimes known as unique or nonsystematic risk, can be partially hedged by the selection of another asset whose return is not highly correlated.

The market does not reward investors for assuming risks that are diversifiable or those that can be shed using the capital markets. Incurring diversifiable risk is equivalent to bearing needless, uncompensated risk. An example of a diversifiable real estate risk is the unexpected default of one of a thousand tenants or the CEO's contracting a lethal disease. The market rewards investors only for bearing systematic risks, not diversifiable risks. US interest rate risks are an example of a systematic or non-diversifiable risk for a domestic portfolio; such is not the case for an international portfolio.

The number of investments within a portfolio is an important consideration, especially since diversification is not free. When there are too few assets, then too much diversifiable, and hence needless and uncompensated, risk remains. Portfolio risk, in practice, drops as the investor adds additional assets. However, the risk does not drop to zero. What remains is non-diversifiable risk. In theory, if there were no transactions or management costs, one might argue that there is never enough diversification. In practice, how many external managers or assets can an investor (or his advisor) prudently monitor and evaluate?

What are the limits of diversification? How many assets are required to eliminate 84% of diversifiable risk, for example? Edwin Elton and others in *Modern Portfolio Theory and Investment Analysis*[1] calculate the relationship between the number of assets and the extent to which diversification reduces diversifiable risk. The variance of the portfolio is shown as follows:

$$\sigma_p^2 = \frac{1}{N} * \sigma \cdot AVG_j^2 + \frac{N-1}{N} \sigma \cdot AVG_{jk} \qquad (10.1)$$

The contribution by the individual securities to the portfolio variance approaches zero geometrically as the number of securities increases. The contribution of the covariance terms approaches the average covariance, $\sigma \cdot AVG_{jk}$ as N increases. While increasing N decreases diversifiable risk, $\sigma \cdot AVG_j^2$, what remains is risk that is not diversifiable. In the case of stocks that trade on the New York Stock Exchange, by adding securities, the variance of the portfolio approaches average portfolio variance. A single security in their example has an expected portfolio variance of 46.7, two securities have an overall variance of 26.8, 10 securities have a variance 11.0, 100 with 7.5, and 1,000 with 7.1. The marginal gross benefit of diversification declines rapidly with the addition of assets. Ten assets eliminate 55% of the variance and 100 assets eliminate 84%. Hence, the benefits of diversification decline rapidly depending on the average covariance between the assets. I am not saying that diversification does not matter. Instead, I am arguing that the managers of large portfolios with over 100 assets cannot credibly claim that doubling the number of assets confers significant additional diversification benefits. Note, however, I do not claim that managers should not increase AUM beyond 100 assets.

What is the value of diversification, and to whom? If real estate constitutes a small percentage of the pension fund's overall portfolio, the incremental benefits of diversification by a single manager among many within the investor's real estate portfolio are small.

However, there is an additional consideration. The investor benefits from the stability of a manager's firm. Creating new manager relationships is not free. To the extent that the manager is well-diversified, the likelihood of a business failure is less. This benefit may not be available during a crash when most assets phase lock and their return correlations approach one. Diversification, like liquidity, is seldom available when needed the most. Just after the GFC, many managers launched new funds because the promotes associated with existing funds were no longer in the money; they had evaporated and launching a new fund was necessary to retain key employees and secure the viability of the company.

Exhibit 10.2 shows the impact of leverage without considering the burden that imprudent leverage exacts at higher LTVs. Once on the efficient frontier, new opportunities emerge due to the availability of leverage. Let's assume the investor can invest at the risk-free rate. The tangency of a ray with the efficient frontier is the market portfolio, M. Position C is equivalent to holding the market portfolio and lending. Portfolio R consists of the market portfolio and borrowing. Note that any

EXHIBIT 10.2 Optimal portfolio with a risk-free-asset permits removing risk through lending or assuming greater risk through borrowing.

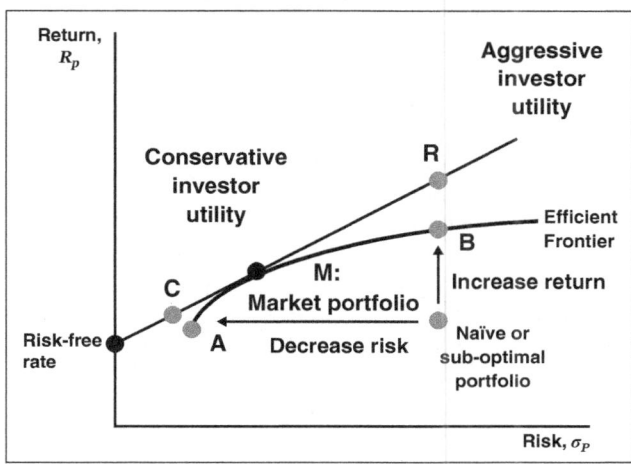

Source: ZCA

point on this ray has the same risk-adjusted return irrespective of the amount or borrowing or lending. (I am assuming that borrowing and lending occur at the same rate, which in practice is not the case, especially at higher LTVs. Otherwise, the slope of the ray would change at M.)

Even if there is a single market portfolio, investors differ in their appetites for risk and return. For example, Exhibit 10.3 shows utility curves for investors C and R. Through borrowing and lending the investor can achieve different outcomes, but leverage does not increase risk-adjusted returns.

Moving along the efficient frontier from the left to the right, return as well as risk increase. As risk increases, the probability distribution of returns widens significantly. Exhibit 10.4 shows the probability distributions at the far left and far right of the efficient frontier.

The far right is the riskiest; the returns, while centered at a higher expected return, are spread out more widely. Even though the efficient frontier rises, and with that the expected return, the likelihood of downside loss increases rapidly. At the far right of the frontier, the likelihood of a loss is 34%; at the far left, the probability is 0.6%. Many sophisticated investors do not appreciate this point.

208 CHAPTER 10 Asset Allocation, with and without Liabilities, and Shortfall Constraints

EXHIBIT 10.3 One risk-free asset, the market portfolio, M, and two investors, each with different preferences (or utility curves).

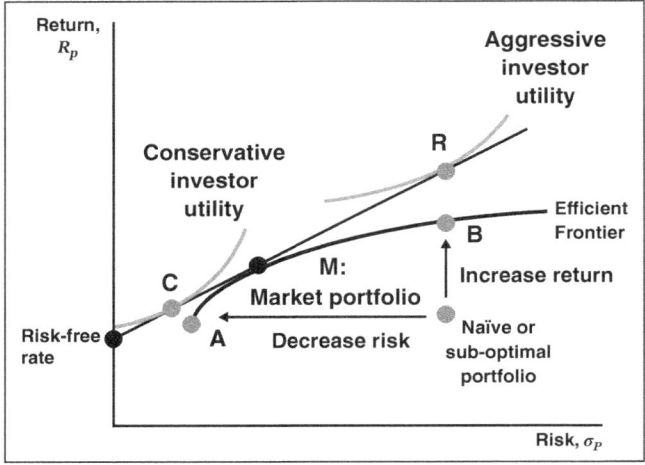

Source: ZCA

EXHIBIT 10.4 The riskiest *efficient* portfolio has the highest standard deviation and greatest downside risk.

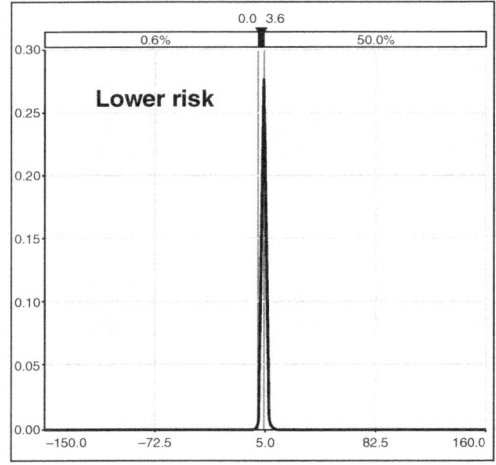
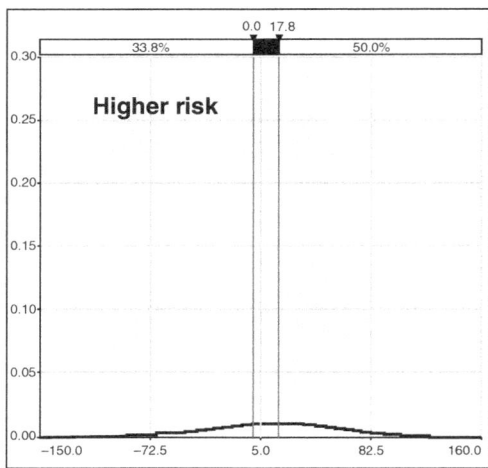

Source: ZCA

Evaluating Risk in Isolation or as Part of a Portfolio

Investors often use deterministic tools, such as the arithmetic mean or single-variable sensitivity analysis, to evaluate risk. Either approach incorrectly values embedded options. Of even greater concern is investors' tendency to assess deal risk in isolation of a portfolio. This makes little sense since all assets fund liabilities. A mediocre deal in isolation may be a terrific deal if it enhances overall portfolio performance at the margin either by increasing expected return without incurring additional risk or by reducing risk without sacrificing return.

Let's say we have three assets—A, B, and C—and we want to determine the optimal asset allocation using the estimated means, standard deviations, and correlation coefficients. Portfolio optimization determines the efficient frontier, along which investors can only increase return by assuming more risk. Exhibit 10.5 shows the three-property efficient frontier and Exhibit 10.6 presents the changing asset allocation along the efficient frontier, from low- to high-risk.

What happens when we add a fourth asset? I set the expected mean return and the standard deviation equal to that of Property A. However, the correlation coefficients between New Property and the other legacy assets are all negative 0.5. The results are dramatically different, as shown in Exhibit 10.7.

EXHIBIT 10.5 Three-property efficient frontier.

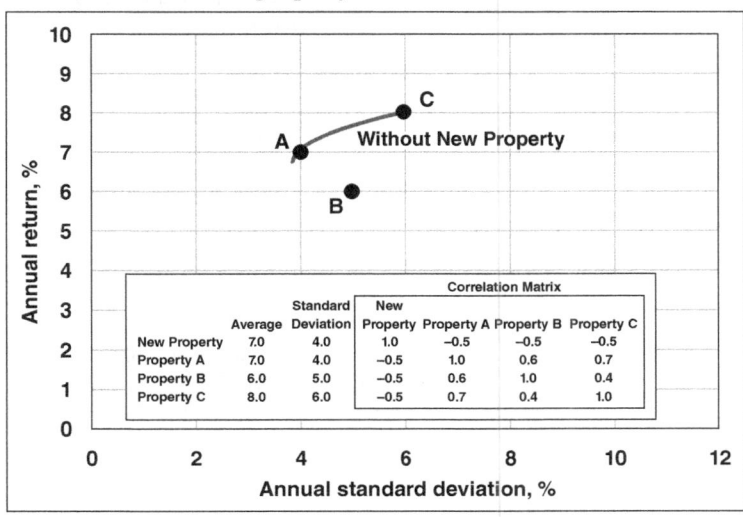

Source: ZCA

210 CHAPTER 10 Asset Allocation, with and without Liabilities, and Shortfall Constraints

EXHIBIT 10.6 Asset allocation along the frontier.

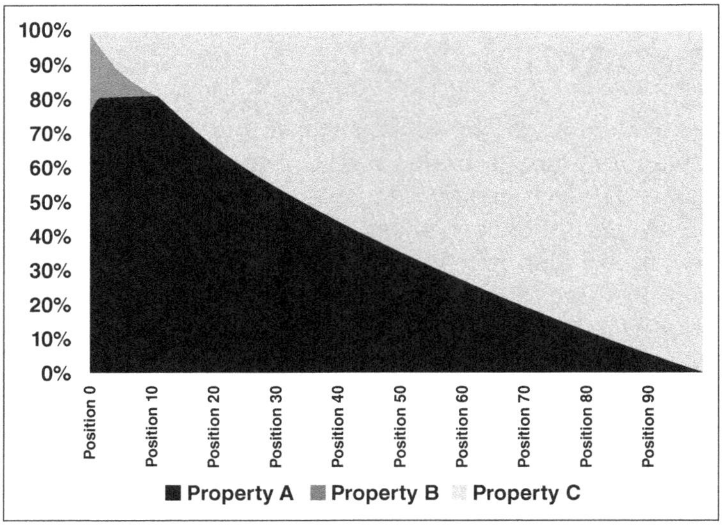

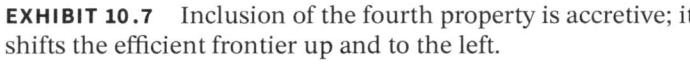

Source: ZCA

EXHIBIT 10.7 Inclusion of the fourth property is accretive; it shifts the efficient frontier up and to the left.

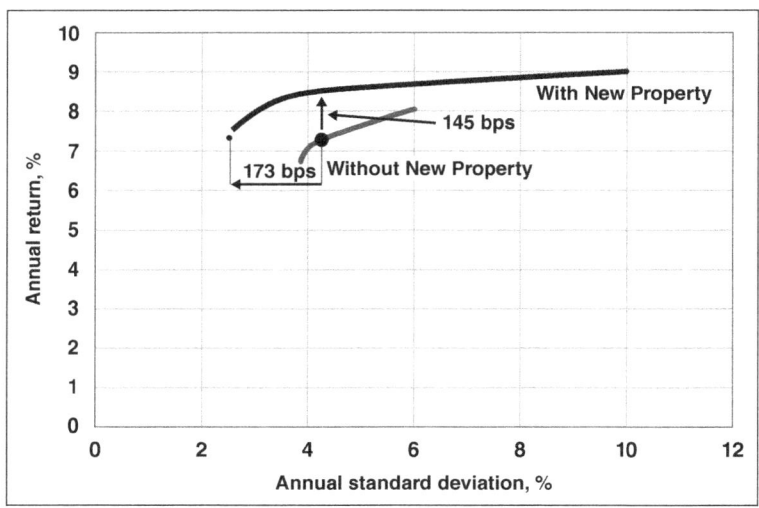

Source: ZCA

The left side of the efficient frontier shifts 173 bps to the left and shifts upward by 145 bps. The marginal portfolio benefits of having included the asset can be significant. Exhibit 10.8 shows that the included property, NEW PROPERTY, has reduced the allocation to Property A and consigned Property A to the most conservative region of the efficient frontier. Investors should not disregard this result. As we move to the right along the frontier, NEW PROPERTY's allocation supplants Property C. Not only does the expected mean and standard deviation matter, but the correlation is critical.

The results of adding another asset to a portfolio can be even more dramatic if we optimize the surplus—assets minus liabilities. Depending on the duration and convexity of the liabilities, a riskless asset, like cash, can become the high-risk asset if the liabilities are long-duration bonds. The liabilities interact with the assets to determine the marginal contribution of an additional asset to overall portfolio performance.

Correlations can be low or even slightly negative if properties are located within MSAs, the performances of which are nearly countercyclical. Location is just one dimension that investors should exploit. Other examples include the tenant's credit worthiness and its business model; is the business countercyclical with regard to the general economic health of the MSA and its submarket?

EXHIBIT 10.8 Inclusion of the fourth property dramatically alters the asset allocation along the efficient frontier.

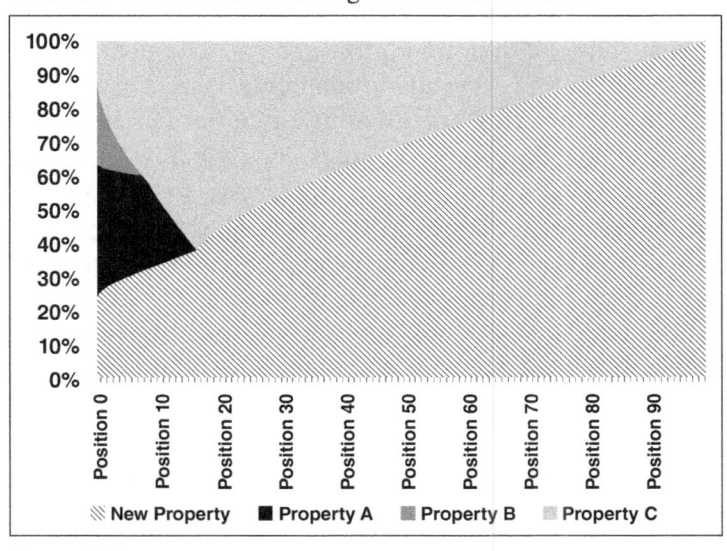

Source: ZCA

Brokers and advisors are fond of claiming that a building's tenancy or the employment base of an MSA is well diversified because no one employment sector by employment seems to be dominant. Just because these sectors look distinct on a pie chart does not mean that the sectors are not highly correlated. Consider Houston. What is the likelihood that law firms that lease space in the same building with energy companies are not linked intimately with the energy sector? Investors should beware of false claims of diversification. Moreover, "not putting all your eggs in one basket" does not address the concern that all of the baskets may be highly correlated.

Shortfall Constraints and Threshold Targets: The Downside of Real Estate Performance

Return and risk are measured by the average return, or mean, μ, and the standard deviation, σ, which is one measure of risk, but by no means the only one (see Chapter 2). Most analyses assume a special probability distribution, the normal distribution (or bell curve), to describe returns. Why choose the normal distribution and not one of the many other extant probability distributions, such as the logistic or log normal distribution? The normal curve is actually easier to manipulate because the mean, μ, and the standard deviation, σ, uniquely describe the entire distribution; it is symmetric and not skewed to the right or left. Many assets, such as REITs, have distributions that are almost normal. The distributions of illiquid assets, such as property, and real estate fundamentals, such as rental growth rates and the size distribution of cities, are not normal; they are highly skewed.

The normal curve, among others, is called a "probability distribution" because the area under the curve is equal to one, or 100%. (See Exhibit 10.9.) We can take any normal distribution, no matter the mean or standard deviation, and convert the return series to a distribution wherein the mean (or z-score) is zero and the standard deviation is one just by subtracting the mean from the series and dividing by its standard deviation, which produces a z-score. This practice is called distribution normalization, which is a good tool for comparing distributions.

One hundred percent is important as the probability distribution explains the relative frequencies of all events, which must add up to 100%, by definition. This exhibit shows a normal curve wherein the mean is 0% and the standard deviation is 1%. One standard deviation ("1 SD") above or below the mean is −1% and 1%,

EXHIBIT 10.9 A higher level of certainty requires a wider confidence interval.

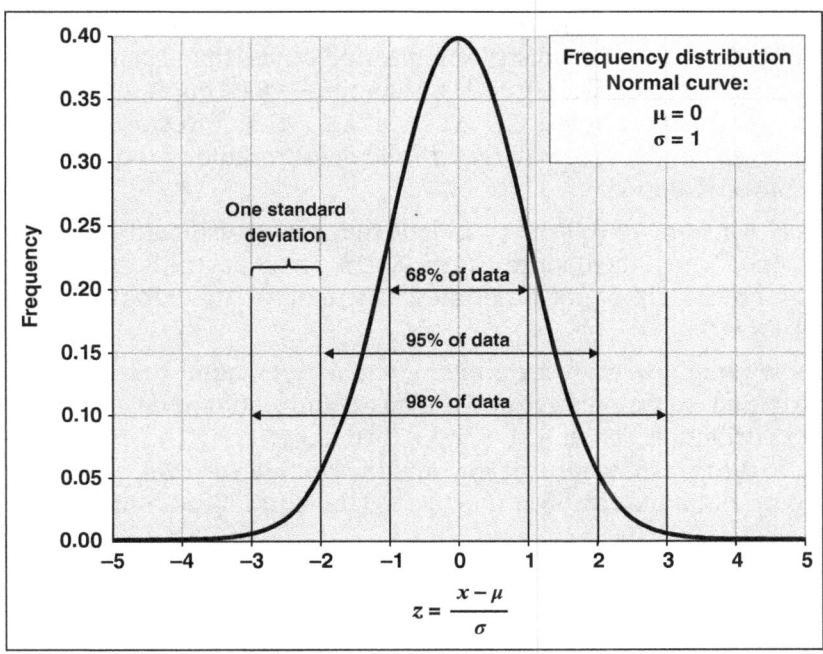

Source: ZCA

respectively. The area under the curve, but within 1 SD on either side of the mean, is 68.3%. In other words, there is a 68.3% chance that the return will be some return between −1% and 1%. Two standard deviations bracket 95.5% of the distribution; 2.25% of the distribution lies either below −12% or above 28%. When I speak of left tail events or downside risk in the case of returns, I am speaking of low probability events to the left of the mean. For example, the likelihood of a return less than minus 2% is 2.3%. Similarly, the chance of a negative return is the area under the curve to the left of zero, or 50.0%. The downside measure of risk, a 2.3% chance of losing some principal, should be more meaningful to risk-averse investors than the standard deviation.

Martin Leibowitz[2], the legendary Director of Research and Managing Director at Salomon Brothers, provided in his many writings an intuitive way to think about downside risk. This section applies his pathbreaking research to real estate portfolios.

I specify a minimum return threshold which the investor would exceed with some probability, say, 90%. Let's assume a security with a mean of 8% and a standard deviation of 10%. (If the normal distribution had a mean of zero and a standard deviation of 1, then 10% of the distribution would be less than 1.28.) By implication, the investor will experience a return less than the −4.82% minimum threshold 10% of the time. (Eight percent less 12.82% is −4.82%.) The investor can increase the confidence level, but doing so will require a lower threshold or return floor. Greater certainty comes at a price.

Let's say we want to be 95% confident that the investment performance will exceed the floor. Then, the floor must be −8.45%. In other words, to be five percentage points more certain of not penetrating the floor, we must lower the floor from −4.82 % to −8.45%.

Let's now generalize these ideas mathematically. I assume that the return is normally distributed, so we only require the mean and standard deviation to describe the entire distribution. There is a simple formula relating the expected portfolio return, R_p, to the threshold return, R_{TH}, and the confidence level, which is the product of the portfolio standard deviation, σ_P, and the normalized confidence level, CL:

$$R_p \geq R_{TH} + CL * \sigma_P \tag{10.2}$$

For example, if the confidence level is 90%, which implies a 10% chance of piercing the floor, then CL equals 1.282 and the threshold, R_{TH}, is −4.82%. (We determine the threshold by plugging in the mean and standard deviation of the distribution, 8% and 10%, respectively.) Thus,

$$R_p \geq -4.82 + 1.282 * \sigma_P \tag{10.3}$$

Substituting an equal sign for an inequality sign, we see that the equation is linear and its slope, 1.282, is positive. This constraint says that any given level of portfolio risk, σ_P, R_P must exceed a minimum. For any return, the higher is the portfolio's volatility, the lower will be the threshold return.

The more confident we want to be, say, 95% rather than 90%, the higher we must set CL. The shortfall constraint becomes steeper as we dial the confidence level higher, as shown in Exhibit 10.10. When I apply this concept to actual portfolios, the implications become clear: The likelihood of exceeding the threshold declines as well.

Let's superimpose the shortfall constraint on the efficient frontier. See Exhibit 10.11. Recall that the portfolio return must exceed the threshold plus CL times σ_P. By restricting returns, I restrict the feasible portfolio of the efficient frontier. See Exhibit 10.11.

EXHIBIT 10.10 The tradeoff between confidence and minimum threshold effect: Increasing the level of confidence of exceeding the threshold from 90% to 95% lowers the threshold.

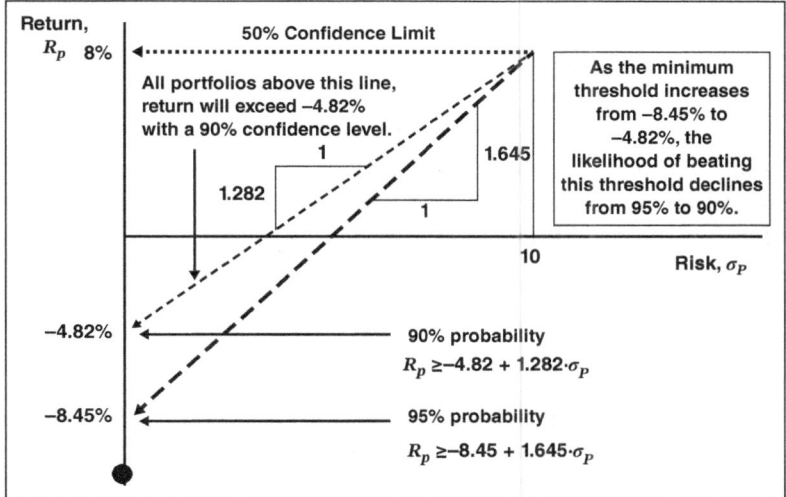

Source: ZCA and Leibowitz

EXHIBIT 10.11 Linking the confidence level, threshold return, portfolio return, and feasible efficient investment choices; the shortfall constraint with negative threshold limits the choices to the left of A along the efficient frontier.

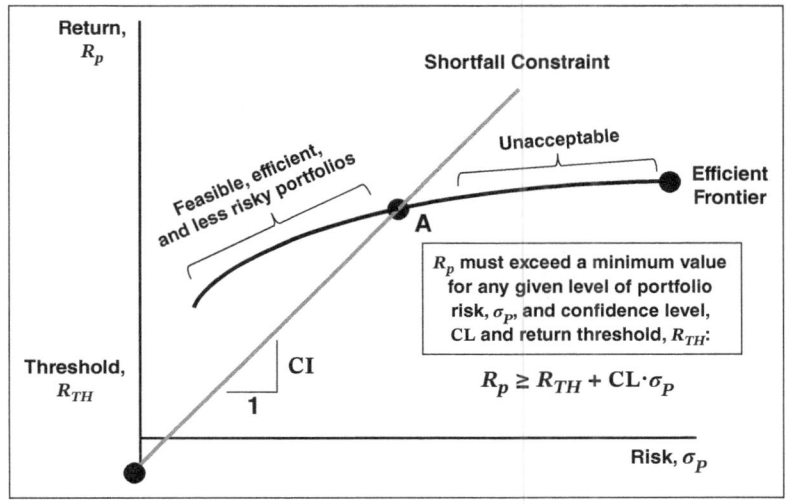

Source: ZCA; Martin Leibowitz

If we want to increase the probability of beating the threshold by adopting a more stringent shortfall probability, then we increase CL, which rotates the shortfall constraint counterclockwise and reduces the feasible portfolios along the efficient frontier. See Exhibit 10.12.

If we reduce the confidence level, we rotate the shortfall constraint clockwise and increase the maximum return along the efficient frontier, but the probability of beating the threshold declines. See Exhibit 10.13.

Increasing the threshold while holding CL constant, reduces choices along the efficient frontier. The maximum expected return along the shortened feasible region of the frontier decreases as shown in Exhibit 10.14.

If we want to assume greater portfolio risk, increasing the standard deviation from 7.8 to 10.0%, while maintaining the confidence level, then we lower the threshold, as shown in Exhibit 10.15.

A parallel upward shift in the shortfall constraint is consistent with an increase in the expected return and an increase in the minimum return threshold, as shown in Exhibit 10.16. This shift means we do not change the confidence level. If we increase the expected return by 400 basis points, the threshold increases from −8.45 to −4.45.

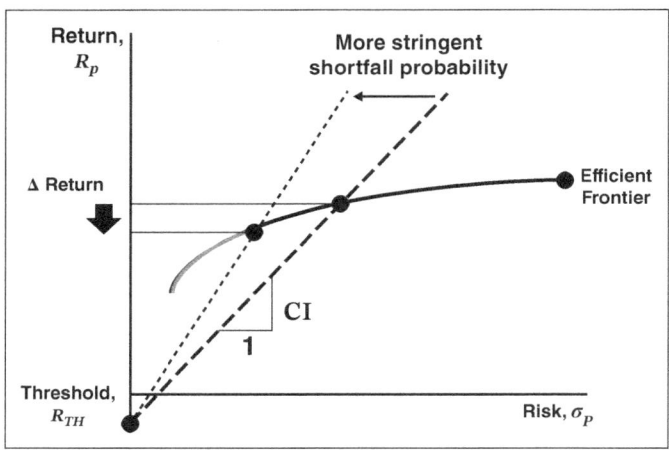

EXHIBIT 10.12 The investor lowers the chance of a shortfall by eliminating riskier portfolios and reducing expected return.

Source: ZCA; Martin Leibowitz

EXHIBIT 10.13 Moving from point A to point D, the probability of beating the zero-threshold constraint decreases. Point D presents higher returns but much greater downside risk.

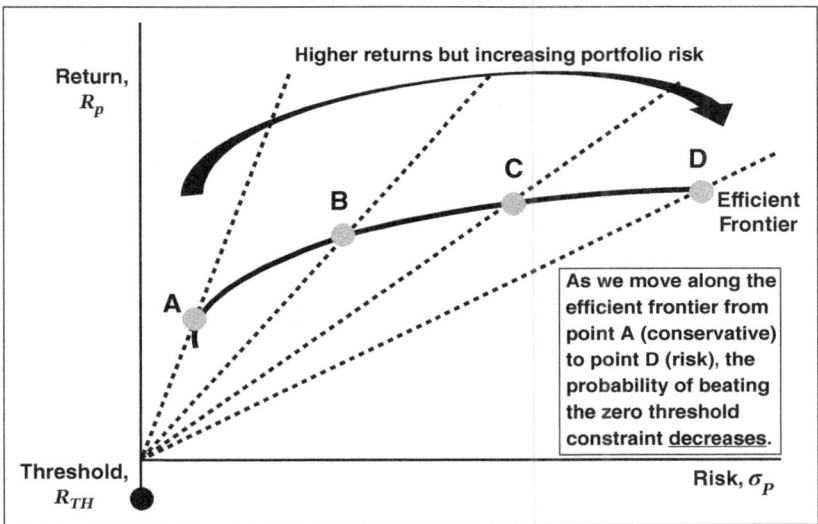

Source: ZCA; Martin Leibowitz

EXHIBIT 10.14 Increasing the threshold, while holding the probability of a shortfall constant, reduces the choice of feasible investments along the efficient frontier but increases the likelihood of preserving capital.

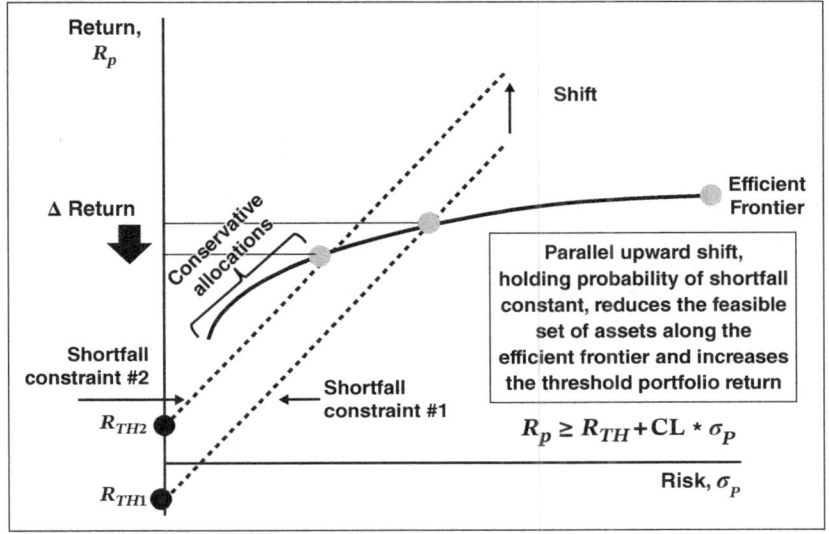

Source: ZCA; Martin Leibowitz

EXHIBIT 10.15 Increasing the portfolio risk and maintaining the same confidence level lowers the threshold from −4.82 to −8.45%.

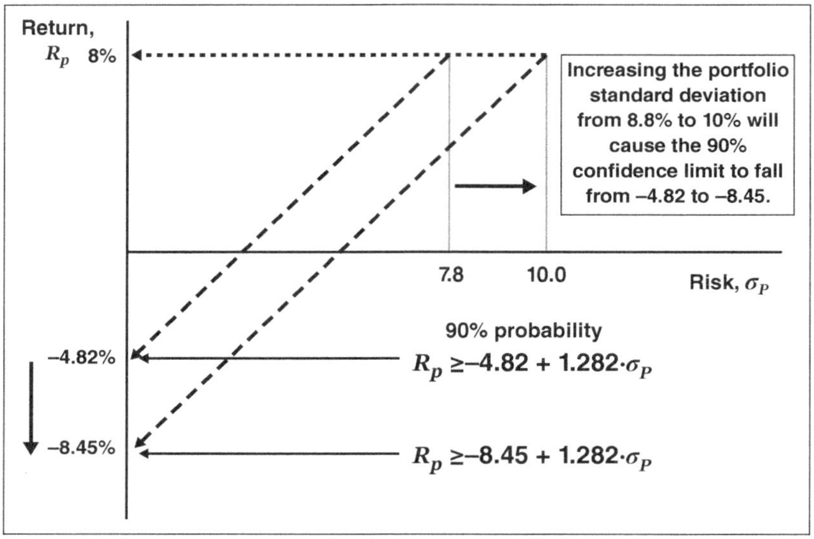

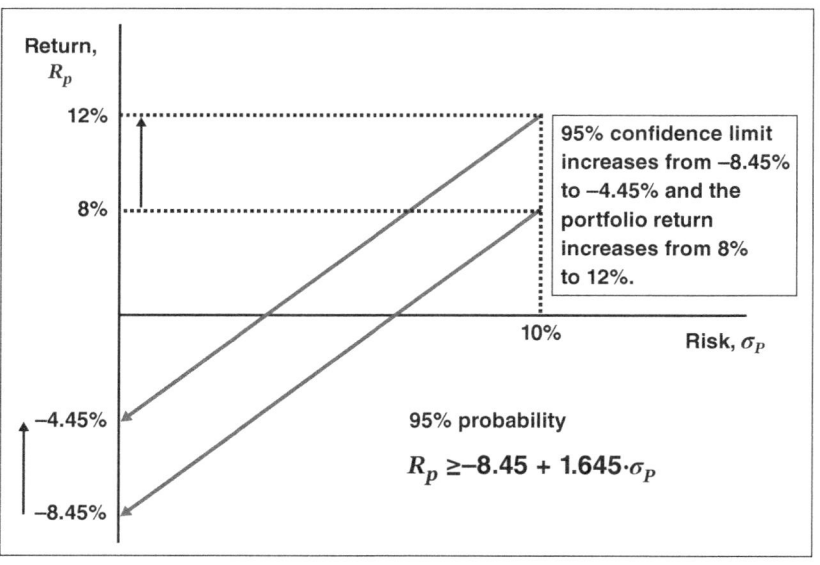

Source: ZCA; Martin Leibowitz

EXHIBIT 10.16 An increase in expected return increases the threshold return from 8.45 to 4.45% without altering the confidence level.

Source: ZCA; Martin Leibowitz

Real Estate Surplus Analysis

The purpose of assets is to finance current and future liabilities. Surplus analysis determines the optimal way to pick these assets so as to maximize the value of the surplus, which equals assets minus liabilities.

For illustrative purposes, I rely upon historical return data to derive means, standard deviations, and correlations for purposes of illustrating certain essential concepts. Our data series start in the fourth quarter of 1978 and extend through 2024. These series cannot possibly replicate the many economic shocks that have rocked the capital markets during the last 150 years. When data are insufficient, users often estimate these critical parameters through other means, including surveys and rules of thumb. Another approach is contingent forecasting, in which the analysis probes the implications of certain user-defined contingencies.

Exhibit 10.17 shows the expected returns and standard deviations for a collection of assets that include T-bills, stocks, bonds, and REITs.

Exhibit 10.18 is the return correlations between these assets.

I assume that liability performance tracks long-term US government bond returns. The asset mix is sensitive to the liabilities. I consider two cases: (1) underfunding (initial funding ratio of assets to liabilities is 0.95 and the surplus is −0.05); and (2) overfunding (initial funding ratio is 1.05 and the surplus is 0.05).

Exhibit 10.19 shows the surplus ratio for the underfunded pension fund. For lower risk portfolios, the surplus is negative. Clearly, the pension fund has an incentive to pursue risk alternatives that include opportunistic real estate funds.

EXHIBIT 10.17 Mean, standard deviation, and correlation inputs to produce pure asset allocation and surplus analyses.

Asset Class	Arithmetic Mean	Standard Deviation
S&P 500	12.560	18.230
Small stocks	17.780	42.581
LT Government	5.594	10.103
LT Corporate	6.302	8.939
T-Bill	3.286	1.530
Equity REITs	12.991	19.614

Source: ZCA using Federal Reserve data

EXHIBIT 10.18 The correlation matrix for a multi-asset analysis.

	S&P 500	Small Stocks	LT Government	LT Corporate	T-Bill	Equity REITs
S&P 500	1.000	0.899	−0.532	−0.053	−0.118	0.778
Small Stocks	0.899	1.000	−0.616	−0.161	−0.196	0.746
LT Government	−0.532	−0.616	1.000	0.762	0.088	−0.257
LT Corporate	−0.053	−0.161	0.762	1.000	−0.026	0,087
T-Bill	−0.118	−0.196	0.088	−0.026	1.000	−0.107
Equity REITs	0.778	0.746	−0.257	0.087	−0.107	1.000

Source: ZCA using Federal Reserve data

EXHIBIT 10.19 Liabilities exceed assets for underfunded pension funds and create strong incentives to invest in higher risk assets.

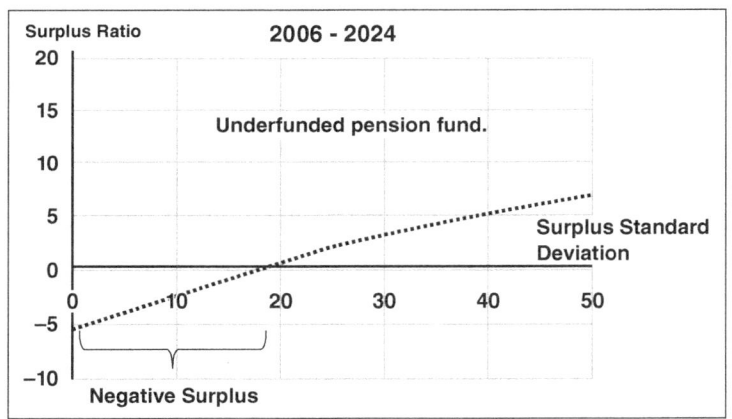

Source: ZCA

The surplus for the overfunded pension fund is positive along the complete efficient frontier, as shown in Exhibit 10.20.

The surplus spread between the under- and overfunded liabilities is about 1,000 bps and relatively constant across low- and high-risk portfolios as shown in Exhibit 10.21.

EXHIBIT 10.20 The surplus is positive along the full length of the efficient frontier. The period 2006–2024 captures the Great Financial Crisis as well as COVID-19.

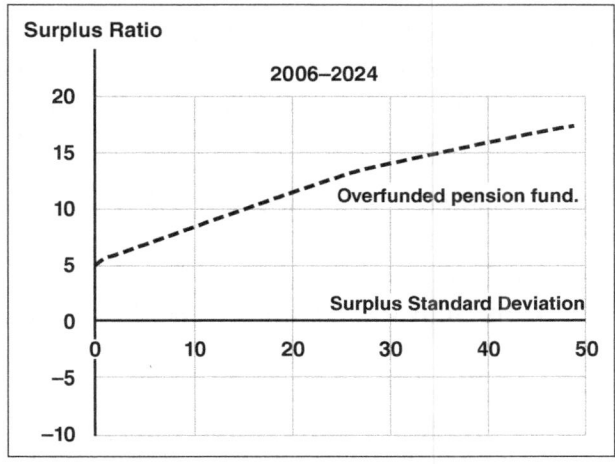

Source: ZCA

EXHIBIT 10.21 The spread between the expected surplus ratios for the overfunded and underfunded pension plan is approximately constant over a wide range of risk.

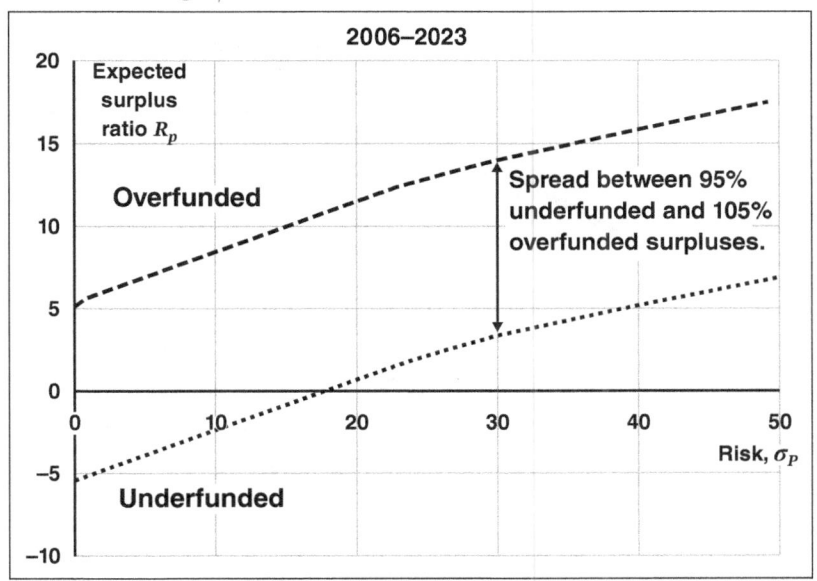

Source: ZCA

Multi-Asset Allocation with REITs and Senior Mortgages: Two Examples of Asset Allocation

Using data from 1978 through 2024 I show that REITs deserve an allocation within a well-diversified all-asset portfolio as well as within a portfolio of assets and liabilities. In this example, REITs have a significant allocation for the mid- to higher-risk portions of the efficient frontier. The optimal asset mix can change depending on the liabilities. REITs, which are interest rate sensitive, play an important role when the liabilities are very bond-like and the pension fund is underfunded. The addition of REITs to a multi-asset portfolio increases mid-frontier performance by up to 32 bps, as shown in Exhibit 10.22.

Exhibit 10.23 shows the spread along the efficient frontier between portfolios with and without REITs.

Senior mortgages. I use a proprietary commercial mortgage database, the Giliberto-Levy (G-L) Commercial Mortgage Index from 1978 through 2020, to determine the optimal allocation of senior mortgages and leveraged property equity. (The use of the NCREIF leveraged index is important since I want to evaluate debt and equity.) The index includes total returns for on-balance-sheet,

EXHIBIT 10.22 Adding REITs to a multi-asset domestic portfolio improves overall mid-frontier performance by up to 32 bps.

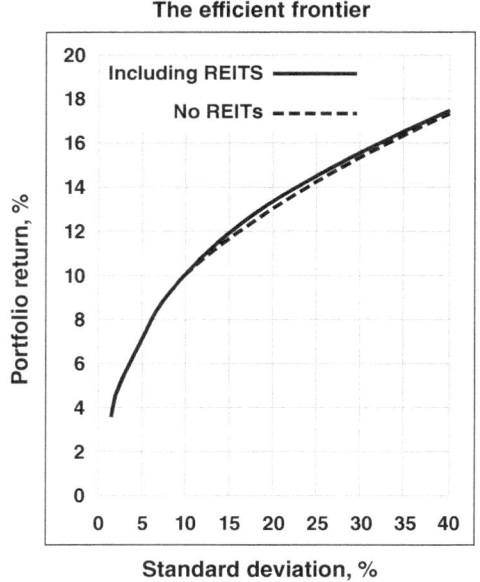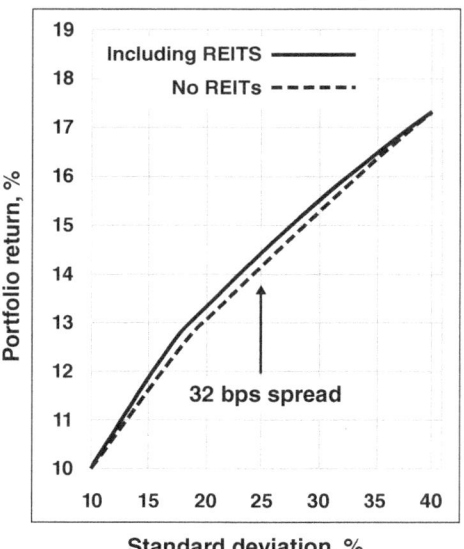

Source: ZCA

EXHIBIT 10.23 Incremental return due to adding REITs to a multi-asset domestic portfolio.

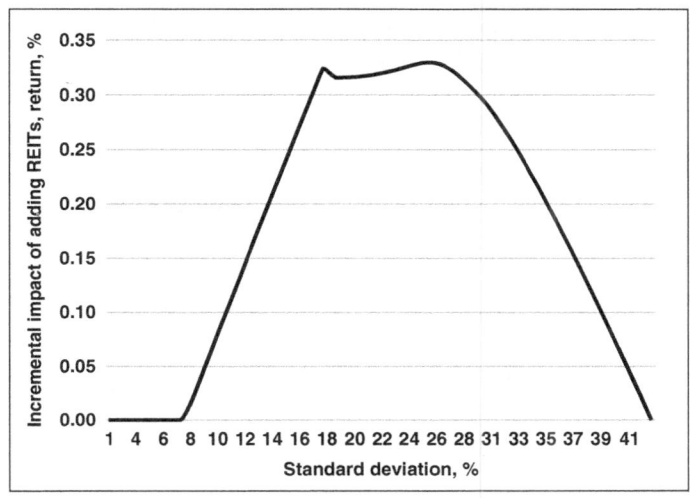

Source: ZCA

fixed-rate mortgages issued by US institutional investors, such as insurance companies and pension funds.

I regard the Giliberto-Levy as the gold standard of mortgage performance measurement and I use the NCREIF leveraged total return property equity index (leveraged NPI) for real estate (property) equity. Senior mortgages confer strong diversification benefits within an all-US pure property portfolio as well as within an international multi-asset portfolio. Senior mortgages within a pure US real estate portfolio of leveraged equity and mortgages merit a significant asset allocation, as high as 61% at the most conservative (left side) portion of the efficient frontier. The funding status of a US multi-asset portfolio has little impact on the senior mortgage allocation; mortgages are a robust diversifier for funds with varying funding conditions.

Exhibit 10.24 shows the mean return, its standard deviation, and correlation matrix for senior mortgage as well as leveraged and unleveraged NCREIF property returns. Note that the property returns exhibit approximately a zero correlation with mortgage returns.

Exhibits 10.25 and 10.26 show the efficient frontier and asset allocations for mortgages and property, leveraged as well as non-leveraged.

EXHIBIT 10.24 Inputs into asset allocation, mortgages, and leveraged equity.

	Senior Mortgages	NCREIF unleveraged	NCREIF leveraged
Mean (annual)	7.8	8.1	11.0
Standard deviation	5.9	7.3	13.9
	Correlation Matrix		
Senior mortgages	1.00		
NCREIF unleveraged	0.03	1.00	
NCREIF leveraged	−0.16	0.62	1.00

Source: ZCA using G-L data, 1978–2020

EXHIBIT 10.25 The efficient frontier with leveraged and unleveraged property and senior mortgages, but no liabilities.

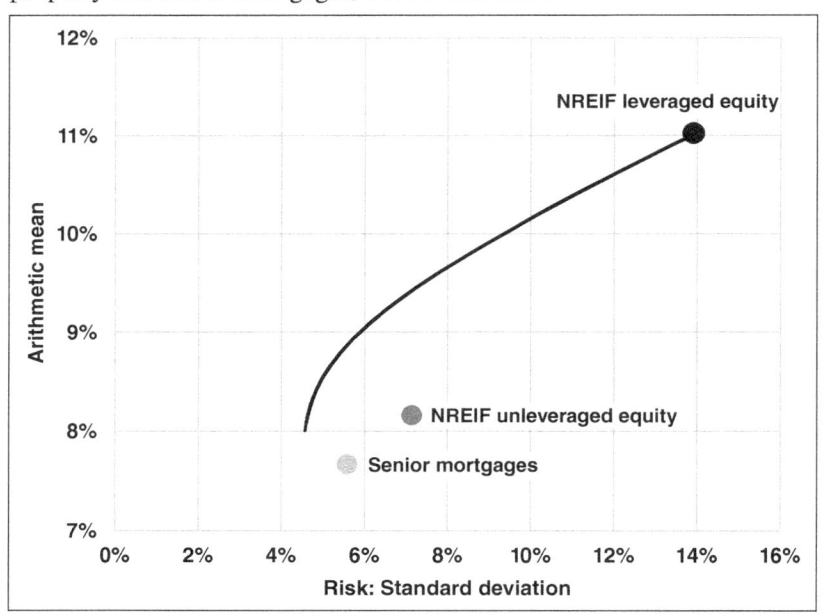

Source: ZCA

EXHIBIT 10.26 Asset allocation with no liabilities.

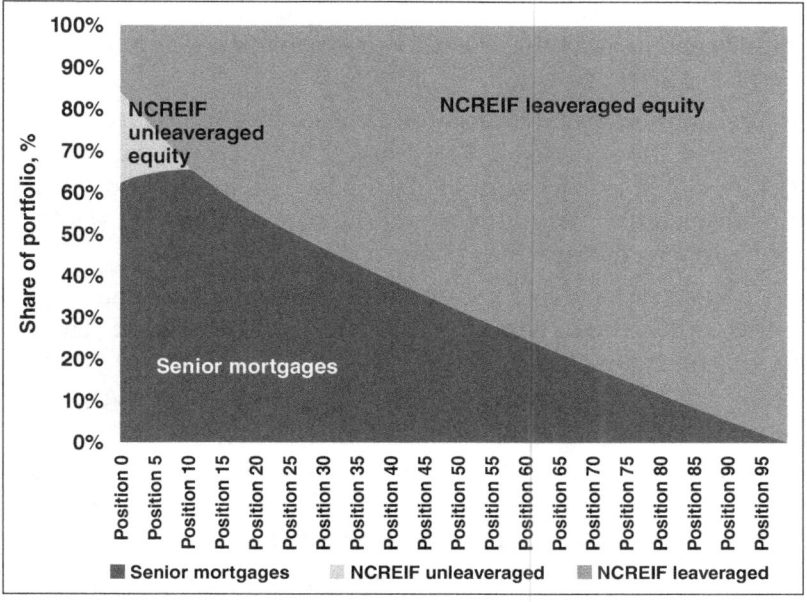

Source: ZCA

The NCREIF leveraged index is appropriate for equity in a private property asset allocation. Portfolios along the efficient frontier for portfolios including leveraged property are more volatile than portfolios that include only unleveraged property.

The risk-adjusted return, or Sharpe Ratio, is greatest along that portion of the efficient frontier that includes senior mortgages. Value at risk (VAR) is greatest at the riskiest, far-right portion of the efficient frontier. VAR is a statistic that measures the level of financial risk within a firm, portfolio, or financial position over a specific time frame.

A portfolio lacking senior mortgages has greater downside risk and lower risk-adjusted return even though the portfolio may produce a greater return. Skewness is greatest for a portfolio without senior mortgages. Greater skewness and excess kurtosis indicate that pure property portfolios are subject to more extreme, low-probability events.

Risk increases at a faster rate per marginal unit of total return in a portfolio with leveraged NCREIF property. The slope of the efficient frontier and the Sharpe Ratio are greater.

The primary objective of asset allocation given the liabilities is the optimization of the surplus performance; the surplus is equal to assets minus liabilities. The assets fund current and future liability payments. The composition of liabilities affects the optimal asset allocation.

When the liabilities resemble long-term corporate bond risks and returns, then cash is no longer the riskless asset. The risk-free asset is now the immunized fund instead of cash, which now becomes a risky asset. Funding status also affects the relationship between the risk and return of the portfolio surplus. (Note, in the US, most public pension funds are underfunded.)

In the surplus framework, long-duration bond components have a much more powerful diversifying impact than in the assets-only framework. The duration of a representative portfolio of senior mortgages is 5.2 years, which is comparable to the duration of many corporate bonds. Hence, the senior mortgage allocation is relatively insensitive to funding status.

Funding status. I establish a set of assets that include senior mortgages, leveraged property, large stocks, long-term corporate bonds, and long-term government bonds. The input parameters are as shown in Exhibit 10.27.

Mortgages have a relatively high correlation with long-term corporate debt but a slightly negative correlation with leveraged property.

EXHIBIT 10.27 Asset allocation assumptions.

	Senior mortgages	NCREIF leveraged	Large stock	Long-term corporate bond	Long-term government bond
Mean, 2001–2021, annual	7.8	11.0	12.8	9.7	9.8
Standard deviation	5.9	13.9	16.5	8.9	11.8
Correlation Matrix					
Senior mortgages	1.00				
NCREIF leveraged	−0.16	1.00			
Large stocks	0.32	−0.15	1.00		
Long-term corporate	0.68	−0.02	0.21	1.00	
Long-term government	0.49	0.18	−0.05	0.87	1.00

Source: ZCA

Exhibit 10.28 shows the simulation assumptions pertaining to the liabilities. The ratio of liabilities to assets for the under-funded pension fund is 1.2, which implies an initial surplus of −0.2. The over-funded system has a ratio of liabilities to assets of 0.8 and an initial surplus of 0.2.

The nature of the liabilities and the funding status affect the shape and position of the efficient surplus frontier. The optimal allocation to senior mortgages is not sensitive to the funding status. The over-funded pension fund has a positive surplus along the entire efficient surplus frontier. Normally, the allocation to property or mortgages for under-, fully-, or over-funded portfolios depends on the liabilities. Investors who want to preserve principal will favor inclusion of senior mortgages. An investor who wants to minimize the likelihood of a negative return will embrace inclusion of senior mortgages as well. Leveraged property increases the risk-adjusted return of a pure senior mortgage portfolio.

Exhibit 10.29 shows three surplus frontiers. Only the riskiest portion of the fully funded pension plan is positive, which implies that even a fully funded pension plan may have a strong incentive to invest in high-risk strategies, such as opportunistic open-end funds.

The goal of investing should be attaining the most efficient funding of liabilities. Therefore, in evaluating the acquisition or disposition of a single asset, the investor should not evaluate the deal on a stand-alone basis, but rather its impact on the surplus. The impact will vary depending on the funding status and the factor risks

EXHIBIT 10.28 Funding status and simulation assumptions.

		Under-funded	Fully funded	Over-funded
Assets	Senior mortgages			
	Leveraged property			
Liabilities	Large stocks	10%	10%	10%
	Long-term corporate bonds	55%	45%	35%
	Long-term government bonds	55%	45%	35%
Initial liability		1.20	1.00	0.80
Initial funding ratio		0.83	1.00	1.25
Initial surplus ratio		−0.20	0.00	0.20
Initial surplus		−0.20	0.00	0.20

Source: ZCA

EXHIBIT 10.29 Surplus frontiers for the over-, fully, and under-funded pension funds.

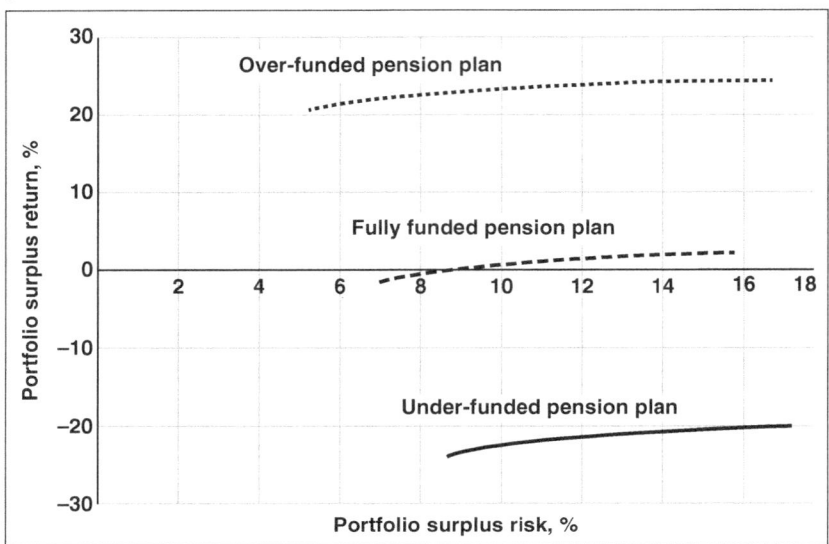

Source: ZCA

associated with the deal and the various liabilities. Cash, which is widely considered to be a riskless asset, may be a high-risk asset in the context of long duration liabilities.

Pure and Hybrid Regional and Property Asset Allocations

Most analysts look at asset allocation either across regions or across property types, but not both at the same time. Doing so can make a difference, so I present a hybrid approach.

Derived optimal asset allocations are not always stable over time. Consider the optimal allocation of regions and property before and during COVID-19. During the period 1978 to 2019, retail and industrial property dominated the optimal allocation, but during COVID-19 apartments played a major role, especially along the medium-risk portion of the frontier. A pure regional portfolio indicates that the riskier portion of the frontier includes the West, South, and the East. The Midwest and the South dominate more conservative portfolios. See Exhibits 10.30–10.32.

EXHIBIT 10.30 Pure property asset allocation along the frontier for the period 1978–2019.

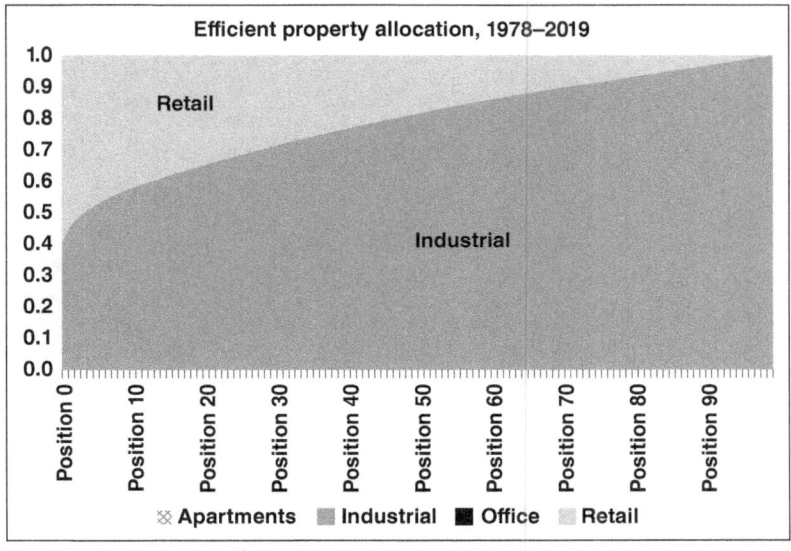

Source: ZCA

EXHIBIT 10.31 During COVID-19, industrial and apartments dominated.

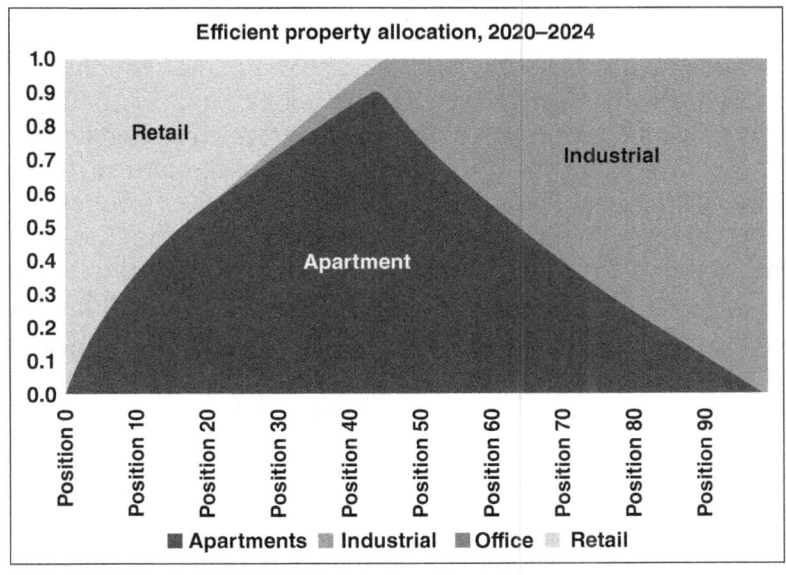

Source: ZCA

EXHIBIT 10.32 Regional asset allocation along the frontier from 2020–2024. The West and the South dominate.

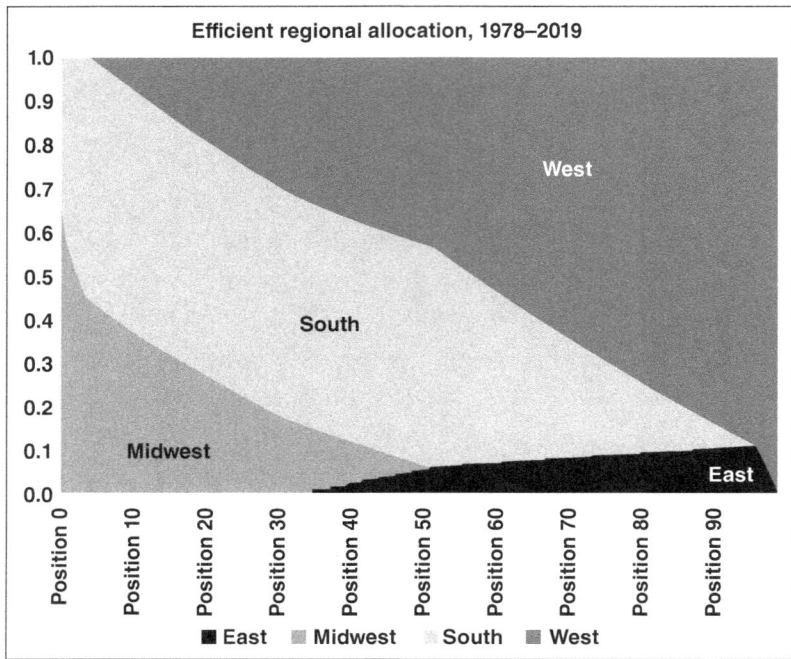

Source: ZCA

What is wrong with this analysis? The problem is that regions and property types are not statistically independent. Each region is composed of different mixes of property types and each property type has different characteristics. In order to address this problem, using NCREIF data for each of the four regions and property types, I created 16 variables and generated an efficient frontier, as shown in Exhibit 10.33. There are many regional-property combinations that are well below the efficient frontier. Office in all regions is a conspicuous example. Industrial in the East is among the nearest to the efficient frontier. See also Exhibit 10.34.

We could divide the data using a finer mesh, but insufficient degrees of freedom would limit analytic precision. Exhibits 10.35 and 10.36 show the asset allocations according to property type and region pre- and post-COVID-19. Retail and industrial in the West dominate the higher risk portion of the efficient frontier. See Exhibits 10.35 and 10.36.

EXHIBIT 10.33 Efficient property allocation (no liabilities) for combinations of regions and property types.

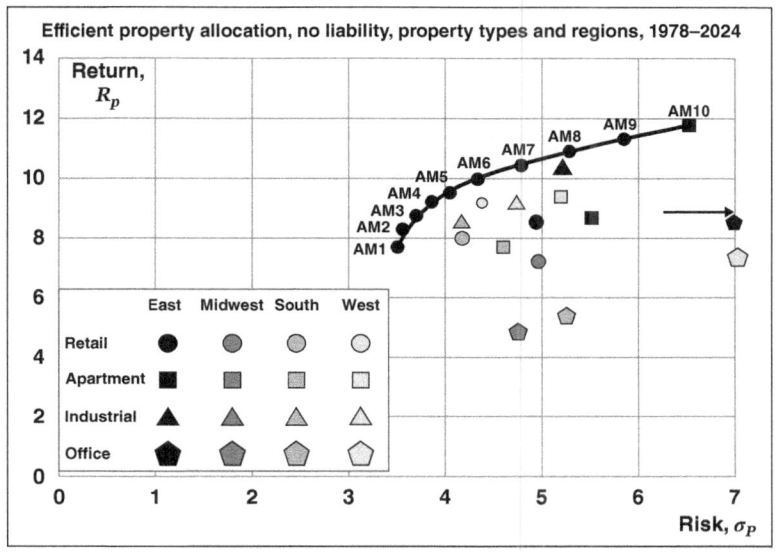

Source: ZCA

EXHIBIT 10.34 By optimally recombining regions and property type, we obtain a significant allocation to industrial.

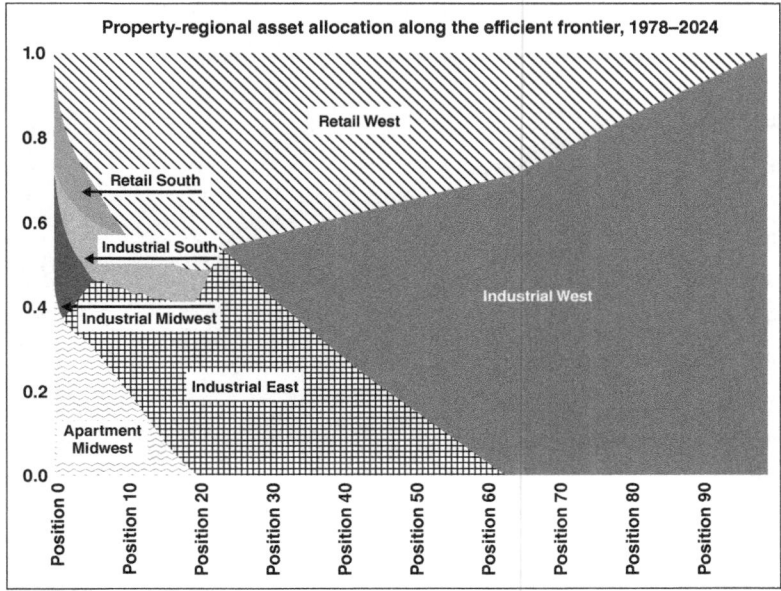

Source: ZCA

232 CHAPTER 10 Asset Allocation, with and without Liabilities, and Shortfall Constraints

EXHIBIT 10.35 During the pre-COVID-19 period, retail and industrial in the West and industrial in the East were dominant.

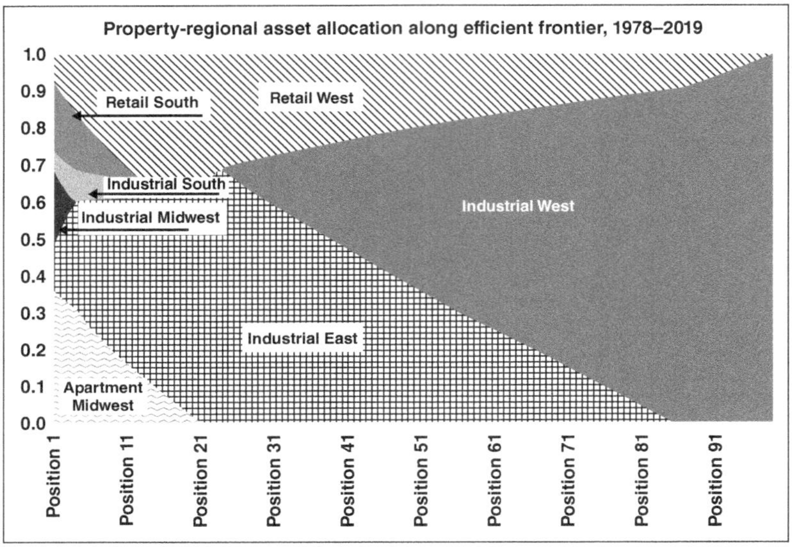

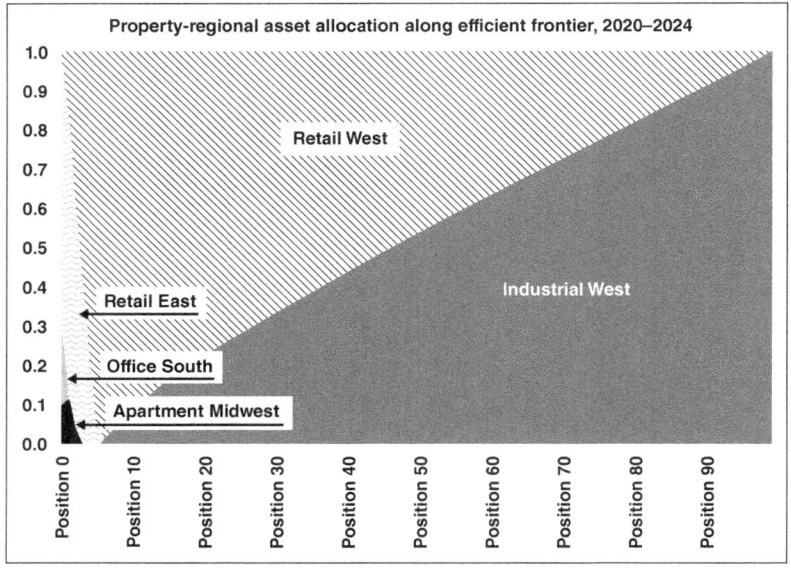

Source: ZCA

EXHIBIT 10.36 During COVID-19, western retail dominates the lower risk portion of the efficient frontier and western industrial is dominant along the riskier portion of the efficient frontier.

Source: ZCA

Shifting Efficient Frontiers and Allocations Pre-COVID-19 and During COVID-19

How did the efficient frontiers compare during the pre-COVID-19 and COVID-19 periods? I used the 16 regional-property pairs discussed in the previous section and derived a comparison as shown in Exhibit 10.37.

Judging from the elongated efficient frontier, COVID-19 was clearly a period of great volatility, and the price of additional return in terms of incremental risk was very steep. De-risking was the trend during COVID-19 as it was during the GFC.

EXHIBIT 10.37 Property-regional efficient frontiers, during and before COVID-19. A slight increase in expected return during COVID-19 was associated with significantly increased risk.

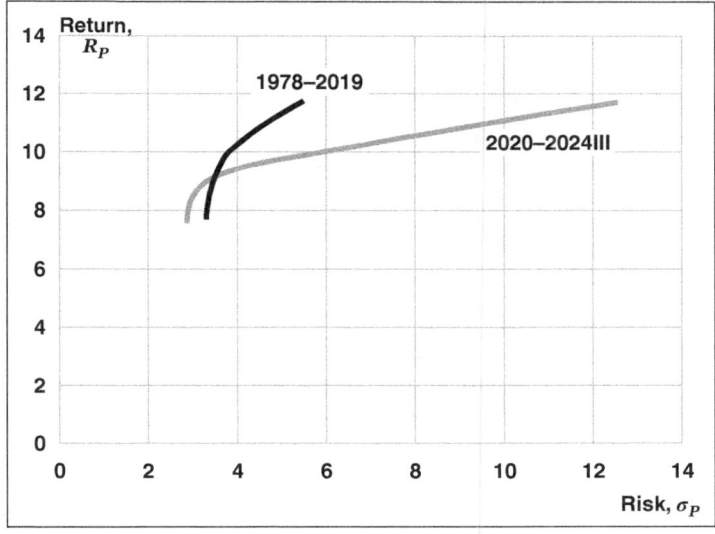

Source: ZCA

Comparison of Smoothed and Unsmoothed Property Returns and an Application to Publicly Traded Equity REITs

REITs constitute one of the real estate quadrants. I showed in Chapter 6 that REITs are not a close substitute for property despite their sharing certain fundamentals. The two asset classes are different. One trades in a continuous auction market and is very liquid, whereas property is the opposite. Serial correlation in property returns indicate lack of liquidity.

The elimination of property return autocorrelation is essential before we can conduct asset allocation modeling that includes REITs, stocks, bonds, and property returns. Too many managers and financial advisors ignore this warning. Consequently, they recommend excessive allocations to property because the smoothed property returns look too good to be true. (This fallacious finding, of course, pleases the capital placement team.)

The analytics of de-smoothing. Fortunately, removing smoothing only affects risk, not returns or correlations in any meaningful way. I show that corrected property volatility is comparable to the volatility of publicly traded REIT volatility. Smoothing occurs due to the backward-looking appraisal process as well as the reluctance of managers to mark real estate assets to market. Opportunistic fund managers are too slow to reflect current losses and very fast to report gains. Fund management in down markets often estimates returns using questionable mark-to-model methods. This practice leads to large queues of investors seeking to redeem their investments.

This procedure is straightforward and not too painful. It is a good example of how a little math can go a long way. There are several approaches to de-smoothing. The late professor Stephen A. Ross and I wrote a paper, which appeared in *Real Estate Finance and Economics*.[3] David Geltner published a similar approach. In this section, I use a hybrid approach, the Geltner-Ross-Zisler de-smoothing process, as reported in Andrew Ang's book, *Asset Management—A Systematic Approach to Factor Investing*.

Observable returns and autocorrelation parameter, ψ, are modeled as a first-order autocorrelated process. Current property returns, according to Equation (10.4), are a function of property returns in the previous period, $NCREIF_{t-1}$. If smoothing exists, then ψ should be statistically different from zero. I use the t-statistic to determine the statistical significance of c, the constant terms, and ψ. The error term, ε_t, is the difference between the actual and fitted value of

NCREIF$_t$. If the estimated equation does not suffer from omitted variables or other pathologies, the error term should be a random walk.

$$NCREIF_t^* = c + \psi \cdot NCREIF_{t-1}^* + \varepsilon_t \tag{10.4}$$

For the period 1978 through 2024, $\psi = 0.796$. The important finding is that current property returns on average equal a constant, c, plus 0.796 of the return from the prior period.

A bit of algebra produces the following result, which de-smooths the observed returns, thus removing the autocorrelation.

$$NCREIF_t = c + \frac{1}{(1-\psi)} \cdot NCREIF_t^* + \frac{\psi}{(1-\psi)} NCREIF_{t-1}^* + \varepsilon_t \tag{10.5}$$

The following shows that the variance (or standard deviation squared) of the true returns exceeds or is equal to the variance of the observed returns. (In the case of stocks, the true and observed variance are equal because $\psi = 0.0$.)

$$VAR(NCREIF_t) = \frac{1+\psi^2}{(1-\psi^2)} \cdot VAR(NCREIF_t^*) \geq VAR(NCREIF_t^*) \tag{10.6}$$

The smoothed return is a weighted average of the unsmoothed true return and the lagged unsmoothed return lagged one period.

$$NCREIF_t^* = (1-\psi) NCREIF_t + \psi \cdot NCREIF_{t-1}^* \tag{10.7}$$

Empirical results. I add a fourth-quarter seasonal dummy coefficient, which reflects in part the return impact of the pension fund appraisal bias; the estimated coefficient has a statistically significant value of 1.8% for the period 1978 through 1988, as shown in Equation (10.8).

$$NCREIF_t = 1.026 + 0.525 * NCREIF_{t-1} + 1.819 * 4QTRDUMMY$$
$$(2.861)\ \ (4.903) \phantom{* NCREIF_{t-1} +\ } (5.801) \tag{10.8}$$

$R^2 = 0.552$

Adjusted $R^2 = 0.531$

Standard error of the regression $= 0.884$

Mean dependent variable $= 3.138$

F-statistic $= 24.770$

Probability (F-statistic) $= 0.000$

236 CHAPTER 10 Asset Allocation, with and without Liabilities, and Shortfall Constraints

The fourth-quarter dummy variable, 4QTRDUMMY, reflects the practice of many institutions' hiring appraisers in the fourth quarter of every year, especially during the early years of institutional real estate investing beginning around the late 1970s. From 1978 to 1988, appraisals in the fourth quarter added 1.8% to total returns, which implies a corrective reduction in property values in the fourth quarter, as shown above. This finding helps account for some of the smoothing in the early NCREIF data.

The associated coefficient is significant through 1991, after which the 1990s real estate crash, RTC, and other improved professional standards helped reduce the significance of the fourth-quarter appraisal dummy. Since 1993, the fourth-quarter effect has largely disappeared; the low t-statistic, (-1.355), indicates low significance, as shown in Equation (10.9).

$$NCREIF_t = 0.445 + 0.525 * NCREIF_{t-1} - 0.339 * 4QTRDUMMY_t$$
$$(2.917)\,(17.350) \qquad\qquad (-1.355) \tag{10.9}$$

$R^2 = 0.708$

Adjusted $R^2 = 0.704$

Standard error of the regression $= 1.209$

Mean dependent variable $= 1.975$

F-statistic $= 150.653$

Probability (F-statistic) $= 0.000$

For the period 1978 to 1988, the lag coefficient, ψ, equals 0.828, which is greater than the lag for the period 1993 to 1994, 0.525.

The de-smoothed standard deviation for the period 1993 through 2024 is 9.6%, compared with REITs, 9.7%. Although the mean quarterly returns differ significantly, 1.975 and 2.917, the standard deviations of property and REITs, respectively, are equivalent. This is a critical insight. Both have the same standard deviation, but their returns differ.

The de-smoothed property returns, whatever the lag, have no power to explain property cap rates. However, the smoothed return lagging four quarters is highly significant.

This model explains only 15% of the variation in the cap rate. Why is this the case? The cap rate is subject to the same autocorrelation as the smoothed property return. Many investors buy property based on cap rates, but they should remember the relationship between cap rates and de-smoothed total returns is tenuous at best. See Exhibits 10.38 and 10.39.

EXHIBIT 10.38 The de-smoothed NCREIF return has no relationship to cap rates, 1989–2024.

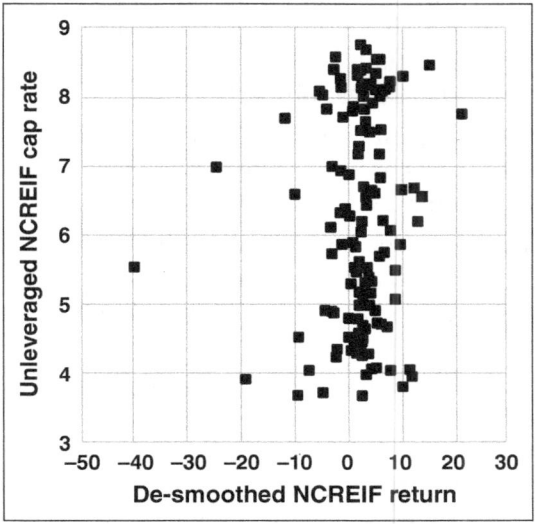

Source: ZCA using NCREIF data

EXHIBIT 10.39 The uncorrected NCREIF return has no ability to predict NCREIF cap rates.

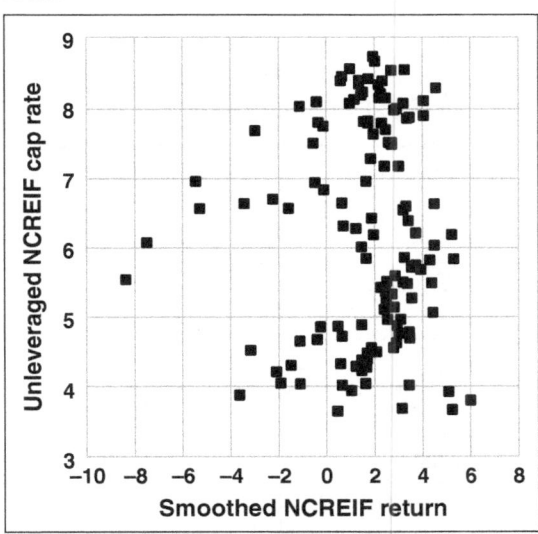

Source: ZCA using NCREIF data

Illiquid—informationally inefficient—markets tend to exhibit smoothing, or autocorrelation. Property is not alone; hedge fund returns are smoothed as well.

This return adjustment is significant and necessary. The volatility of de-smoothed returns, which is four times the volatility of smoothed NCREIF property, is approximately equal to REIT volatility. This difference causes an unwarranted additional allocation to property.

Exhibit 10.40 presents descriptive statistics for NAREIT, NCREIF-de-smoothed, and NCREIF-smoothed. De-smoothing dramatically increases the standard deviation of NCREIT returns, comparable to REITs.

Exhibit 10.41 indicates that de-smoothed property returns have a slightly higher correlation with REIT returns, but even the corrected return correlation is less than 30%. The correlation of the de-smoothed and smoother NCREIF is about 60%. See shaded boxes.

Graphs visually underscore the difference in volatilities of REIT returns and de-smoothed and smoothed property returns. (See Exhibits 10.42 through 10.44.) The de-smoothed property and REIT returns share certain similarities, especially during downturns, but important differences remain. In other chapters, I have explored how REIT returns lead property returns; lag structure is one important difference.

True property risk places this asset class closer to the security market line. Note in Exhibit 10.45 that the shift from "smoothed" (solid black box) to "de-smoothed"

EXHIBIT 10.40 Estimated volatilities for smoothed and de-smoothed property returns compared with traded equity REITs, 1978–2025. Standard deviations of de-smoothed property is approximately similar to REITs during this period.

	NCREIF de-smoothed	NCREIF smoothed	NAREIT
Mean	2.029	2.074	3.210
Median	2.242	2.375	3.167
Maximum	20.650	6.190	33.275
Minimum	−39.974	−8.290	−38.804
Std. Dev.	6.435	2.168	8.918
Skewness	−1.887	−1.636	−0.690
Kurtosis	13.798	7.897	6.742

Source: ZCA using NCREIF and Federal Reserve data

EXHIBIT 10.41 De-smoothed property returns are more correlated with REITs than smoothed property returns, but the correlations are approximately similar.

	NCREIF de-smoothed	NCREIF smoothed	NAREIT
NCREIF de-smoothed	1.000	0.606	0.292
NCREIF smoothed	0.606	1.000	0.125
NAREIT	0.292	0.125	1.000

Source: ZCA using NCREIF and NAREIT data

EXHIBIT 10.42 De-smoothed property returns are much more volatile than observed or smoothed returns.

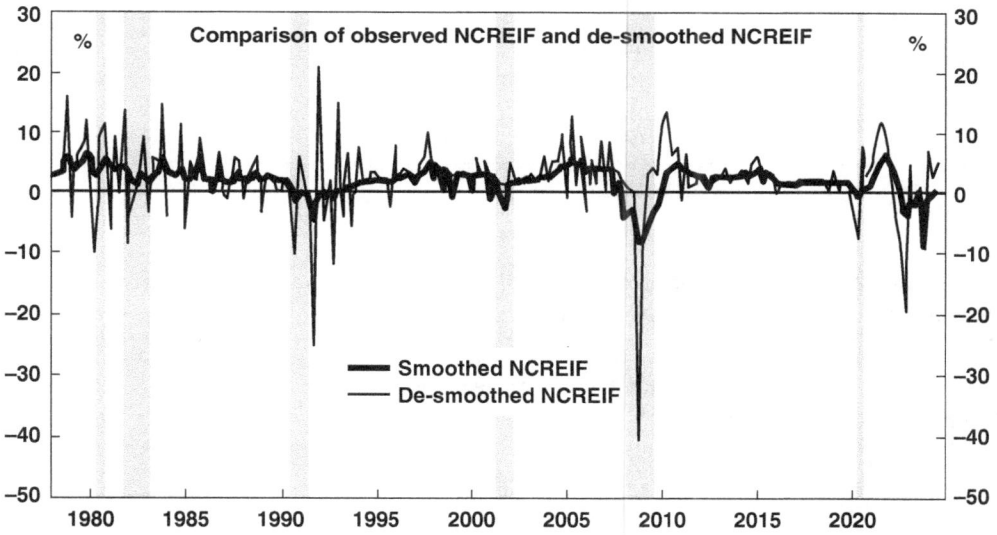

Source: ZCA using NCREIF data

(black bordered square). Exhibit 10.46 shows the impact of de-smoothing of property returns on asset allocation.

What are the implications of de-smoothing for shortfall analysis? Property using de-smoothed returns receives a lower allocation toward the conservative end of the frontier.

If I increase the confidence level of not breaching the threshold, the restriction on the feasible set of portfolios along the frontier is somewhat greater using the de-smoothed data. The same observation applies to an increase in the threshold. However, given our assumptions, this effect does not appear significant. Other data sets could tell a different story, however. See Exhibits 10.47 and 10.48.

EXHIBIT 10.43 Smoothed property returns are much less volatile than REIT returns.

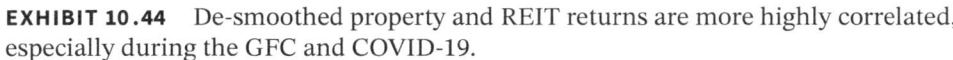

Source: ZCA using NCREIF and NAREIT data

EXHIBIT 10.44 De-smoothed property and REIT returns are more highly correlated, especially during the GFC and COVID-19.

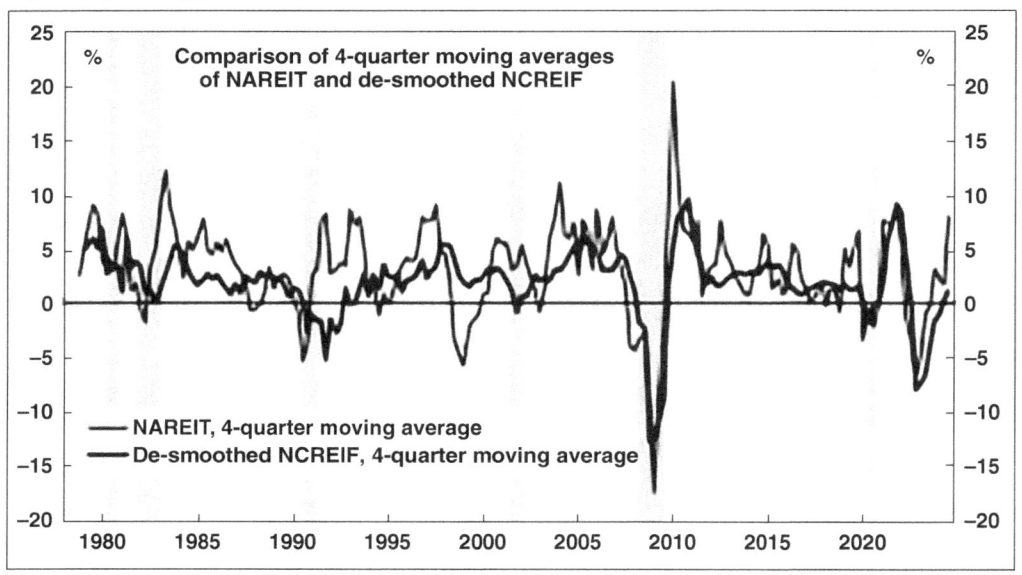

Source: ZCA using NCREIF and NAREIT data

EXHIBIT 10.45 Illiquid property's observed risk is less than the true (de-smoothed) risk. Unless corrected, smoothed returns distort asset allocation.

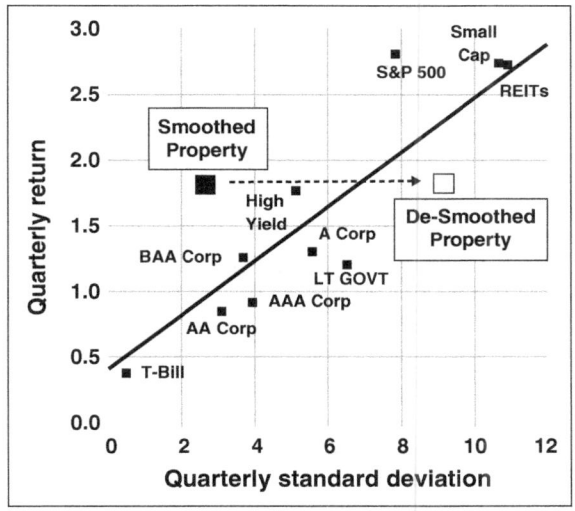

Source: ZCA using NCREIF and Federal Reserve data

EXHIBIT 10.46 After removing property autocorrelation (de-smoothing), the allocation to property drops substantially.

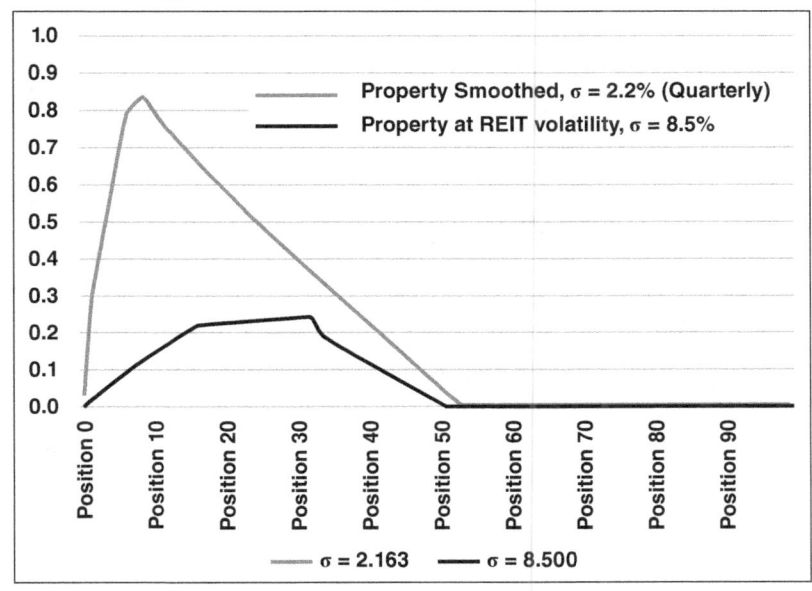

Source: ZCA

EXHIBIT 10.47 A higher confidence level reduces the set of feasible assets whether or not property is de-smoothed.

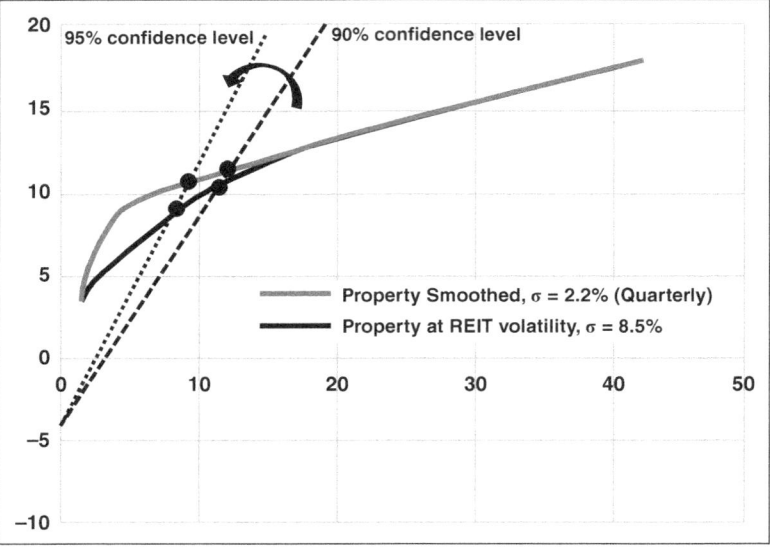

Source: ZCA

EXHIBIT 10.48 Increasing the threshold from negative to zero increases safety and reduces the set of feasible assets more when property is not autocorrelated.

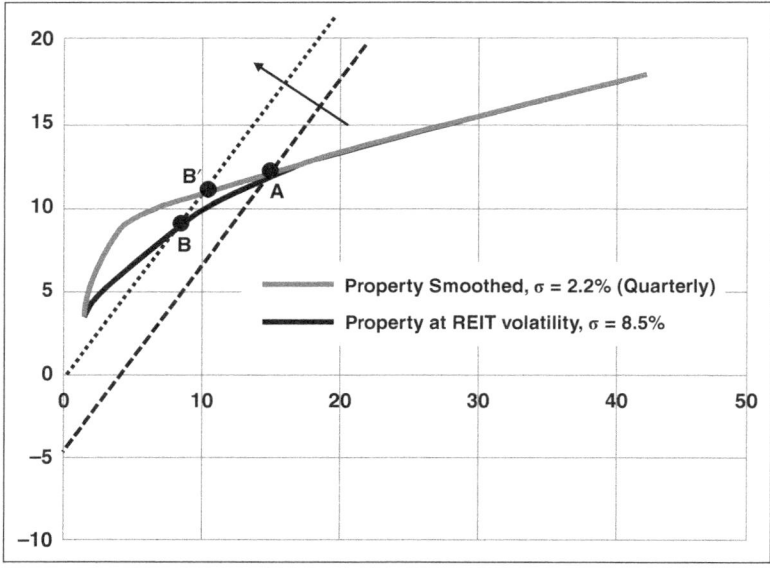

Source: ZCA

Application of Shortfall Analysis to Benchmarks

People have different preferences regarding risk. One manager (or investor) might focus on absolute loss, whereas others might emphasize the probability of a shortfall below some benchmark return. The standard deviation as a risk metric may get us only so far.

Benchmarks provide an excellent application of shortfall analysis. The benchmark should reflect the manager's investment style. A typical benchmark might specify that the manager will not underperform the benchmark by more than four percentage points. If the benchmark is zero, the investor wants 95% confidence that the manager's performance will not be less than -2% in any one year. A minimum threshold is just like a performance benchmark with no volatility. Of course, benchmarks are usually uncertain or stochastic; they fluctuate randomly. Therefore, the spread between the benchmark and the portfolio is stochastic and subject to change; benchmark risk is highly relevant, although often ignored.

The manager should estimate the joint volatility of the portfolio and benchmark as well as the correlation between the two. The correlation will vary depending on which portfolio along the efficient frontier the investor selects. Assume for the moment that the benchmark and the portfolio are perfectly correlated; then the required portfolio return (subject to a shortfall constraint) will increase linearly the greater is the difference between the standard deviation of the benchmark and the portfolio. As the correlation declines, for the same standard deviation, the manager must increase the target return to offset the increased dispersion in the expected spread between the portfolio and the benchmark.

Shortfall Analysis and the Misuse of Leverage

If the pension fund wants to leverage the real estate portfolio, why not overlay recourse debt collateralized by the pension fund's assets or simply use the state's bond-raising capability? The state's debt is cheaper, transparent for all to see. By contrast, property level debt is buried in the deal and not transparent.

Shortfall analysis shows that leverage increases the probability of higher losses even though the overall expected (beta) return increases. The manager must work even harder to avoid the "third rail" of loss of principal and eventually clients.

Leverage does not improve risk-adjusted returns, but it does increase fees and the likelihood of loss, distort incentives, and encourage style drift in the direction of higher risk assets. The balance sheet of the pension fund, which consists of assets and liabilities, does not care whether the liability is on the balance sheet of the property or the pension fund. The pension fund effectively consolidates all of the properties. Leverage at the property level, which encumbers the property, is a liability and offsets to varying degrees the influence of any fixed income assets. In effect, the fixed income portfolio deleverages the leveraged real estate portfolio, synthetically converting the leveraged asset into an all-cash transaction.

For example, the manager leverages the property with a CMBS loan while the fund's fixed income manager, unbeknownst to the CIO, buys an offsetting CMBS bond. Does this make financial sense?

Meanwhile, property leverage changes incentives and promotes misalignment of interests; it also boosts gross assets under management, which in turn can increase the compensation of senior managers at the pension fund. After the offset, what remains are additional fees paid to the CMBS broker and to the manager since she was able to increase gross assets under management. Just as bad, the higher leverage exacerbates existing principal–agent problems.

The pension fund essentially cedes asset allocation to third-party real estate managers. Real estate money managers have neither the perspective, nor the incentive, nor the mandate to act in the interests of the entire pension fund.

Leverage, especially extreme leverage, dramatically increases downside risk without increasing risk-adjusted return even in a normal market. During the credit meltdown, diversification failed to deliver the goods as most markets became systemic: Correlation coefficients approached one and phase-locked. Even had the pension fund (or its managers) selected assets in markets whose expected correlations were somewhat low—few if any are negative—phase locking or synchronization would cause the five properties to act as one, like a $500 million single asset bet with 80% leverage. Many of the properties defaulted.

How Should Pension Funds Use Debt?

Sometimes traders make directional bets. Other times, they may pursue convergence bets. Leverage increases the payoff as well as the loss.

If a manager has unusual property or stock picking abilities, so-called active skills, then maybe the pension fund might authorize the use of leverage for the purpose of making directional bets, but the performance benchmark should be much higher.

How many managers are able to consistently anticipate market movements? Which managers shorted FNMA or bought credit default swaps in June 2007?

To what extent is the manager able to earn excess (after-fee) risk-adjusted returns? This is a tough test that most managers cannot pass. I do believe in theory that a few managers (somewhere ... or somehow) are gifted and have true active management skills. I introduced Bayes Theorem in Chapter 2, which illustrated the difficulty of avoiding false positives in manager (and consultant) selection, especially if superior performing money managers and consultants are rare.

Separating the lucky ones from the gifted is not easy. For example, let's say I invite 131,072 of my most intimate friends to Dewey Cheatum Stadium—seating capacity is exactly 131,072—and give each guest a penny. Let's assume that these guests are stand-ins for busy acquisitive investment managers. Let's also assume that asset prices are a random walk: Returns on any day have an equal chance of increasing or decreasing. I then invite each guest to flip their own penny as I flip my own, which is my way of simulating the market. Those who match, leave the stadium. I repeat the process. Eventually, after seventeen flips, one person remains and *Institutional Investor* magazine features this stand-in's employer on the cover of its next issue and extols her stock-picking ability. The stand-in is now in high demand on the speaking circuit and generously compensated; investors listen with rapt attention and line up to probe her secrets.

It is a mathematical requirement that a single person remains at the end of the coin flips, but should we ascribe any selection skill to that person? Obviously not. But what must we conclude if she wins ten games in a row? Now that result might be statistically significant, but would it indicate skill? So, on what basis do pension plans select (and fire) managers? Does this process recognize the role of chance?

The performance rankings of managers, MSAs, and real estate strategies are not stable over time, so, if investment committees do not want to fly blind, they need a lot of performance data that simply do not exist. So, other than a couple of mega managers, who are the successful managers?

The successful managers are not necessarily the largest management firms. Finding those managers is a big challenge. Can fund-of-fund managers demonstrate their putative ability to find that proverbial needle in the haystack? If not, then why pay double fees? Determining whether a real estate manager has consistent active management skills or is simply lucky is a statistical challenge that even the purveyors of fund-of-fund managers cannot likely pass.

Should pension funds avoid real estate debt entirely? An important consideration is how pension funds use debt, not if they use it. If they want to leverage assets, assigning that task to money managers whose interests are not well aligned with the pension fund's is ill-advised. Instead, the pension fund should make the use of leverage explicit for all to see and borrow at the jurisdiction's borrowing rate. Why leverage at all is another issue. Does it increase risk-adjusted returns? No, it does not. Does it worsen LP-GP conflicts? Yes.

Are there other uses of debt? Instead of *issuing* debt—leveraging properties through their third-party managers—pension funds should *invest* in debt. The best relative value may be found not in leveraged equity but elsewhere in the capital stack. The duration of mortgages closely matches the duration of pension fund liabilities.

Leverage and Diversification

Many prominent, well-seasoned CIOs point to diversification as a justification for additional leverage. With more leverage, so goes the argument, the pension fund is able to buy more assets and uses these assets to further diversify the portfolio. This justification for leverage is simply wrong. There is no increase in the risk-adjusted return due to leverage.

Leverage increases the riskiness of the equity return but also produces a diversification benefit by increasing the number of assets. Is the diversification benefit sufficient to offset the risks due to additional leverage? According to Professor Joseph Pagliari, Jr. of the University of Chicago Booth Business School, the answer is "No."

Here is his reasoning: Assume that the debt is fixed rate and bankruptcy risk is zero. Then the volatility of the debt and the correlation of the debt and asset returns are both zero. The volatility of the equity increases at an increasing rate as the LTV increases:

$$\sigma_E = \frac{\sigma_A}{1 - LTV} \qquad (10.10)$$

The increase in the volatility of the leveraged portfolio relative to the unleveraged portfolio is as follows:

$$\sigma_E - \sigma_A = \sigma_A \frac{LTV}{1 - LTV} \qquad (10.11)$$

When does the diversification effect offset the leverage effect? At this point, the reduction in portfolio volatility due to diversification equals the increase in volatility due to leverage. For small portfolios of three or more assets, there is no correlation between −1 and +1 when this occurs and, for a two-asset portfolio, it only occurs when the asset's returns are perfectly negatively correlated—a virtual impossibility with regard to long-run real estate returns. The volatility of the equity due to leverage increases geometrically as a function of N, the number of assets, but the diversification benefit increases only as a function of the square root of N. The leverage effect quickly swamps the diversification benefit—even more so for large portfolios. See Exhibit 10.49.

For a large portfolio, the marginal diversification benefits are minuscule because increasing the size of the portfolio beyond a certain point produces little incremental diversification benefit, as I have discussed. See Equation (10.11). To the extent that the manager is able to create a larger and more diversified portfolio, the manager is no longer focused, which many consultants and investors believe is important.

So why should public pension funds allow managers to leverage their properties, especially since the public pension funds can borrow more cheaply than the managers? If a money manager puts leverage on a portfolio, the leverage itself introduces serious principal–agent problems, especially at high LTVs. For example, leverage increases the manager's base fees. The expected value of the contingent interest increases due to the interaction of the promote with higher leverage. Leverage creates high beta but no incremental alpha, but investors pay managers to create alpha, not beta. LPs suffer because their returns are diluted and they do not increase

EXHIBIT 10.49 The benefits of diversification due to leverage are swamped by increasing volatility due to the leverage.

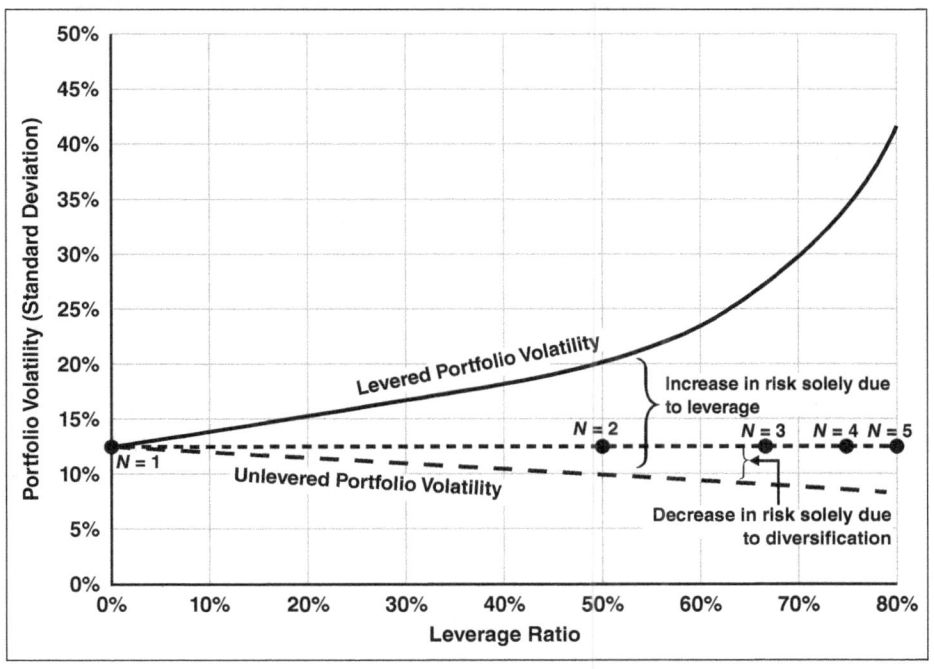

Source: A Technical Note: When Are the Risks of Leverage Offset by Diversification? Almost Never, 2023 / with permission of Joseph L. Pagliari.

their risk-adjusted returns. In fact, due to agency costs and higher leverage-induced fees, investors receive lower risk-adjusted returns.

Conclusions and Investment Implications

- What happens to the IRR or equity multiple if interest rates increase by 1%? Sensitivity analysis can be helpful, but as I stress in this book, perturbing separately each parameter, such as rental growth, the exit cap, or even interest rates, is neither a sufficient nor an accurate approach to risk analytics. At the deal level, these parameters are stochastic, and they should be modeled not as constant terms but as probability distributions linked by correlations. Monte Carlo is the correct simulation tool and it produces useful information.
- During a market downturn correlation coefficients tend toward unity, which vitiates the benefits of diversification when needed the most.
- Importantly, how does a particular deal fit within a portfolio and help fund future liabilities? A deal might seem too risky in isolation, but maybe the deal reduces portfolio risk without sacrificing return or increases return without incurring more risk. This could boost the deal's expected performance.
- High return deals positioned to the far right of the efficient frontier have a much higher risk of loss because even though the average expected return is high, the expected standard deviation, or risk of shortfall, is much higher.
- Investors intuitively understand downside risk; their marginal disutility of loss usually exceeds their marginal utility of gain. While other asset class disciplines, such as fixed income, have created useful downside risk measures, real estate has been slow to adapt.
- Property returns are serially correlated, but stocks and similar instruments that trade in continuous auction markets are not. Without correcting for property return smoothing, or serial correlation, property's asset allocation is excessive.
- The corrected standard deviation for property is comparable to that of REITs.
- Adding property with corrected variance to a naïve equally weighted portfolio of stocks, bonds, and equity moves the portfolio further toward the efficient frontier, thereby increasing overall portfolio return without incurring additional risk or decreasing risk without sacrificing return.
- The addition of property to a balanced portfolio while holding portfolio volatility constant increases the probability of achieving long-term wealth goals.
- REITs within a multi-asset portfolio receive an allocation along the mid-risk portion of efficient frontier.

- The expected return for portfolios at the far-right end of the efficient frontier, which is the domain of opportunity funds, has a much higher standard deviation (risk) and greater likelihood of loss than portfolios at the extreme left.
- As portfolio volatility increases, the chances of breaching the minimum return threshold and incurring losses increase.
- Increasing the threshold reduces investment choices or simply shortens the feasible efficient frontier; property's allocation declines.
- Reducing the probability of breaching the minimum return threshold increases the slope of the constraint and also reduces the allocation to property.
- Value-added and opportunistic deals can reduce portfolio risk without sacrificing average return (before fees), but there is substantial risk of breaching the shortfall constraint and increasing loss.
- A low-risk asset, such as T-Bills, in an asset-only framework, is a conservative asset, but it may be a high-risk asset in the context of long duration liabilities.
- Reducing the probability of breaching the minimum return threshold reduces the allocation to property. Value-added and opportunistic deals present substantial risk of breaching the shortfall constraint and incurring a substantial loss.
- Investors have different liability structures. These differences affect asset allocation, surplus performance, and the likelihood of shortfalls.
- The marginal benefits of diversification decline rapidly with the addition of just ten assets.

Q&A: Interview with Sonny Kalsi, Co-CEO, BGO

Taking Risks and Working the Opportunities

Why did you decide to work in real estate?

I attended Georgetown where I majored in accounting and finance. I interned for E. F. Hutton and then worked for Paine Webber. In 1991 I was offered a position in the real estate group at Morgan Stanley. I thought I would eventually go to business school but I stayed at the firm.

I have often been in the right place at the right time. I was assigned to two big projects as an analyst. The first was helping to raise a private equity fund, MSREF, after the RTC crisis. I also worked on the Taubman IPO, which was the first UPREIT. Then, I thought about business school, but Morgan Stanley assigned me to another successful deal. The first CMBS deal came out of this. We bought non-performing loans for 30 cents on the dollar.

The firm promoted me. I turned down Harvard Business School and worked in London and Stockholm. I returned to New York in 1996 and moved to Asia in 1997, staying more than 10 years. That supercharged my career when others might not have taken the risk. In Asia I met my wife of 26 years. I moved back to New York in 2007 to help take over the global business.

The GFC hit our business hard. I was out of a job by 2009 after 18 years. Some of my former colleagues and I launched Green Oak in 2010, anticipating a lot of opportunity. The first three years were challenging, but with a combination of luck, grit, and hard work, we succeeded. In 2017, we merged with Bentall Kennedy and Sun Life.

Was there one deal that was transformative?

A Japanese firm, Shuwa, was a big US property buyer during the 1990s and the firm encountered trouble. We did an $8 billion restructuring in 2004–2005, earning an 8× multiple.

What are your views about risk analytics?

Investors sometimes pick bad structures, embrace the wrong strategies, and assess risk poorly. Good risk analytics are urgently needed.

What are you doing now at BGO?

Two thirds of our AUM is core and credit; 50% is industrial and 25% is apartment. I learned an important lesson: Buy the highest quality real estate you can.

How would you advise young professionals?

Do not be afraid to take some risk, especially early in your career. Patience is important.

CHAPTER 11

Optimal Development: Linkage, the Internal Cost of Capital, and Risk

Preliminaries

How do we determine the best, and not a "just okay," development solution? Short of divine inspiration, traditional tools are often inadequate for calculating the best outcome either in deterministic or in stochastic settings. Investors and developers suffer from risk illusion and limited bandwidth; they do not deal analytically and effectively with myriad constraints and interdependencies, nor do they integrate risk analysis in the search for optimal development configurations. Instead, they try to decouple the development problem and rely on rules of thumb.

Development is complex and requires the adept phasing of interdependent uses while meeting capital, FAR, and other constraints in the face of uncertainty. Interdependence, or what I call linkage, can be spatial or temporal.

I demonstrate the effects of binding and slack constraints and show how to calculate internal costs, or shadow prices, which express the marginal impact of a constraint on the value of the objective function. If a resource constraint is not binding, then its shadow, or internal price, is zero; if it is binding, then its shadow price is non-zero. We can either maximize the objective function (e.g., maximize NPV) or minimize the objective function (e.g., seek the lowest volatility).

This chapter presents an approach to finding the optimal or best solution where there are substantial interdependencies and complexities. I have personally applied this method to the valuation of the land under an Atlantic City casino and to raising capital for developers' projects.. Stochastic constrained optimization can increase the project©s efficiency and result in a successful capital raise that otherwise would not be possible.

The parameter values used in the constraints and the objective function determine which constraints are binding. By identifying binding constraints and determining their shadow prices, a negotiator is better equipped to make demands or give concessions.

Stochastic Development Optimization

I reject the internal rate of return ("IRR") rule despite its widespread use. The IRR is not a good metric for discriminating among deals or strategies; it is neither a true return nor is it additive like the NPV. This rule has many problems, including the assumption that future cash flows are reinvested at the same rate of return. A more obscure, but real, problem is the chance of multiple IRRs, which is easy to show using Descarte's Rule of Signs: A polynomial function whose terms are arranged in the descending order of the powers of a variable cannot have more positive real roots than the number of sign changes in it. In other words, if the sign of the cash flows flip more than once, multiple IRRs are possible. So, which is the correct IRR?

The NPV is superior, but only under certain conditions. The NPV rule tells investors to rank projects by NPV and chose successive projects starting with the highest NPV project, but the projects must be independent. The NPV rule often fails when we introduce budget constraints, which violates independence. I demonstrate how to deal with this problem.

I like to differentiate these two metrics in the following way: You raise more AUM with higher IRRs but you feed your family with larger NPVs. The IRR is a percent, whereas we express the NPV in a currency. Admittedly, to use the NPV, you must pick a discount rate and doing so requires some knowledge of risk.

Constrained optimization is the process of optimizing an objective function, say total value, with respect to constraints. When the capital constraint is a binding constraint, the internal cost of capital (or shadow price of capital), which is the incremental NPV given a one dollar increase in the budget, can exceed the external market cost of capital. A constrained optimization model can simultaneously calculate the cost of capital along with the optimal allocation and phasing of uses over space. Properly adapted, it can generate risk metrics and distributions. Linkages are mathematical constraints that describe interdependencies. Budgets link activities to operating expenses and capital, for example.

I use mixed integer programming, which consists of integer (or binary, one-zero) numbers and fractional numbers; hence the term "mixed." Integer variables are good "switches" to turn on otherwise dormant constraints in path-dependent optimization problems. Mixed integer optimization can include inequality constraints, which is important.

Consider this application: Turn on the municipal bond constraint only if the optimal solution involves building a school, which in turn leads to the uncertain receipt of a permit to develop 1,500 apartment units. The model sets the binary variable associated with this constraint to either "1" or "0," depending on which value increases the overall NPV.

Surprising outcomes. The value maximizing solution using myriad constraints can be counterintuitive. Linkages (or dependencies) between projects can confound optimal solutions; they impart subtle and difficult-to-predict effects. For example, if we have two projects and fractional projects are not allowed—X, a choice variable, is either zero or one (binary)—then a constraint, such as $X_1 - X_2 = 0$, says that if we pick the first or the second project, we must then select the other project as well, but if we do not select one of the projects, we need not select the other. In other words, X_1 and X_2 are complements. However, if we rewrite the constraint as $X_1 - X_2 \leq 0$, them if we select X_1, we must select X_1. However, if we select X_2, then we have the choice of picking X_1, or not.

A project's capital requirements may be uncertain and initially difficult to determine with precision; the budget over time is always changing. For example, the likelihood of meeting loan covenants may be uncertain. The availability of future building area or FAR may be subject to difficult-to-predict local political factors.

Projects that, in a world of certainty, have the highest NPVs may be less desirable if their projected resource requirements, interdependencies, or availabilities are themselves highly uncertain. A project with a high NPV might have an unacceptably high standard deviation, which causes the model to reject the project. Management seeks resource buffers, such as excess land or acquisition lines, to facilitate better management of balance sheets and other options in the face of uncertainty. What is the optimal risk-adjusted buffer, especially given the brittleness of certain supply chains? Minimizing volatility subject to a minimum total NPV is an alternative goal. An efficient allocation in a deterministic world may be inefficient in a stochastic world if it does not provide sufficient redundancy or flexibility. Stochastic optimization is a tool that developers (and even managers of supply chains) can use with impressive results.

Marginal analysis of capital availability and the shadow price. Determining the incremental change in the objective function, the total project's value, given a unit change in the value of a specific constraint, is useful. If we maximize NPV and if capital is rationed (i.e., the capital constraint is binding), a dollar increase in the available capital will increase the NPV by, let's say, forty cents, or 40%. This incremental NPV is the internal shadow price of capital, or 40%. Since the shadow price, 40%, exceeds the market price of capital, say 14%, the value-maximizing firm should increase its capital raising efforts.

A linear programming example is maximizing the NPV of a project consisting of office and retail property areas, OFFICE and RETAIL, as shown in Exhibit 11.1. (Note that the constraints and the objective function are linear; the variables are real or fractional numbers.) Land per square foot of gross space, L_O and L_R, is the inverse of FAR, the floor–area ratio. The local planners set a maximum space capacity for each use. Total land use cannot exceed the size of the site, LAND. Exhibit 11.1 shows these three constraints, which define the feasible region (gray). Note that there are two provisional objective functions: AA' (dash) assigns a greater *relative* NPV value to office space; the opposite applies to BB' (dot). As we increase OFFICE and RETAIL, the objective function moves upward and out in parallel shifts. Due to the differences in the ratios of the NPV of OFFICE to RETAIL, respectively, AA' and BB' have different slopes. As a result, the optimum for AA' is O_2 while the maximizing solution for BB' is O_3.

The shadow price for retail space (divided by the retail FAR) is the internal or imputed value of land, or the change in the NPV given a unit change in the retail space constraint.

EXHIBIT 11.1 Land use constrained optimization example: What is the optimal combination of office and retail space?

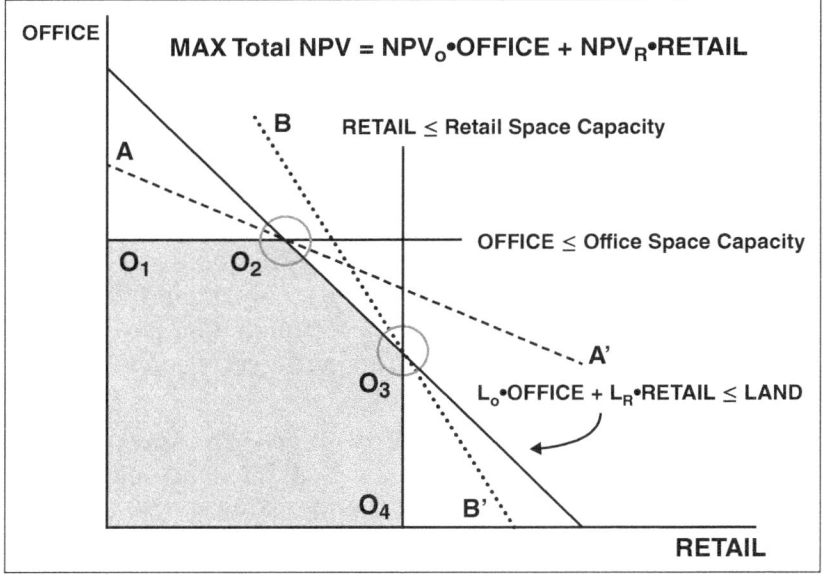

Source: ZCA

The OFFICE and RETAIL allocations associated with AA' and BB' differ significantly. Let's say we want to persuade the planners to increase retail space capacity. If we increase the retail space capacity by 10%, as long as the retail space constraint is binding, which is the case only for BB', then total NPV increases. This increase is the shadow price of retail space.

If the shadow price of land exceeds the market price of adjoining land, then the developer should buy more land because it is accretive. If not, the developer should sell the land to a third party and reinvest the proceeds in a more accretive project. A disposition is accretive in the sense that it increases net worth or NPV.

Shadow prices are often a better indicator of internal value than broad market-based parameters, especially if there is resource rationing. Comparing the shadow price with the market price can then indicate whether the owner should be a buyer or a seller.

Some simple linear programming rules include the following: When the internal accounting cost of selecting a project is greater than zero, the optimal solution excludes that project. If the constraint is binding, then the opportunity cost of the resources associated with that constraint is greater than zero, but if the constraint is not binding, then the interval value of the resource is zero.

Fuzzy constraints. Sometimes constraints are "fuzzy," "soft," uncertain, or not "hard" constraints. For example, let's say that the constraints must be met at least 95% of the time. Exceeding a constraint within those limits may also entail a penalty, which the model determines internally. Exhibit 11.2 illustrates the concept of a fuzzy constraint and shows how its stochastic nature can affect the optimal outcome. As the constraint shifts, so does the feasible region.

The B-B constraint is stochastic and can move according to a distribution the standard deviation of which is σ. As it shifts, it intersects the land use constraint at positions 1 and 3. Assuming an objective function in which the optimum occurs at one of these two vertices, the allocation to office can be in the 68% ranges of O_3 and O_1 for office or R_1 and R_3 for retail. Constraint uncertainty can generate big swings in the optimum solution and specifically in the return distribution.

Constraint uncertainty may pertain to whether or not the constraint is switched on due to other sources of variation. Once we introduce interdependencies with uncertainty, we enter a new world.

Examples of side constraints. I focus on the choice of all-or-nothing (binary) projects subject to density, capital, and other kinds of constraints. Exhibit 11.3 outlines the basic features of the problem. Equation (11.1) says that the maximum NPV is a weighting of the projects. The weights are the NPVs associated with each project.

EXHIBIT 11.2 Fuzzy constraints and an uncertain feasible region.

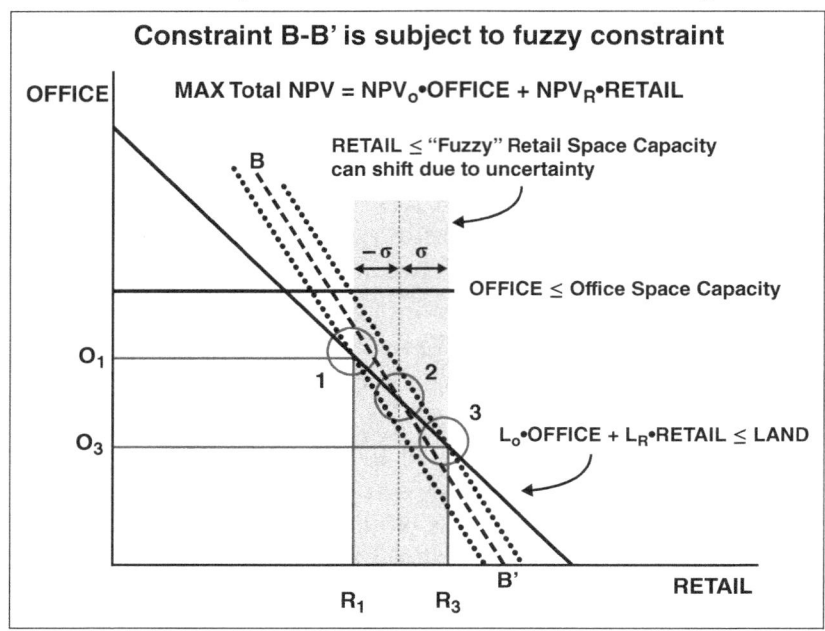

Source: ZCA

EXHIBIT 11.3 The equations of constrained optimization. Numbers to the right are equation numbers.

Objective function. The optimization procedure maximizes NPV by selecting projects subject to various constraints. $\sum$ is the summation function.	$MAXIMIZE\ NPV =$ $\sum_{j=1}^{10} X_j NPV_j$	(11.1)
Projects. There are no fractional projects. The choice is yes (X = 1) or no (X = 0) for each of ten possible projects.	$X_j = \begin{cases} 0 \\ 1 \end{cases}$	(11.2)
Project NPV. The NPV of each project is the sum of the discounted cash flows, CF, which include the acquisitions price, the interim cash flows, and the disposition price. The discount rate is d_i.	$NPV_j =$ $\sum_{i=0}^{3} \dfrac{CF_{ij}}{(1+d_i)^j}$	(11.3)
Capital constraints. There are four capital constraints. Each constraint specifies the available capital for acquisitions over subsequent periods.	$\sum_{i=1}^{4} \sum_{j=1}^{10}$ $CF_{ij} X_j \le C_i$	(11.4)
Density constraint. TOTALFAR is the maximum floor–area ratio ("FAR") that the government allows. Each potential project is assigned a maximum FAR determined by zoning boards.	$TOTALFAR =$ $\sum_{j=1}^{10} X_j FAR_j$	(11.5)

Source: ZCA

Equation (11.2) says that the choice is binary; a project is either selected ($X_j = 1$) or not selected ($X_j = 0$). The NPV of each project is a function of four cash flows. Each project has a unique discount rate, d_i, which represents differential risk. (See Equation (11.3).) In each year there is a capital constraint, as shown in Equation (11.4). The total FAR constraint, Equation (11.5), limits the total buildable area. I show the impact of the capital and FAR constraints on project rankings and compare the constrained ranking with the unconstrained IRR and NPV rankings.

While holding the FAR constraint constant, if I increase each period's capital availability by 10%, we increase the NPV by 8.5%. If we only increase the capital availability for the initial purchase period and the next period by $12 each, then the NPV increases by 33%. Now, if we hold the capital constraint constant and increase the available FAR by 10%, NPV rises by 5.1%.

If we increase all capacities by 10%, then the NPV increases from $62 to $71, as shown in Exhibit 11.4.

The optimal set of accepted projects varies depending on the constraints and the objective function. For example, with only capital constraints, the optimal set of projects consists of projects 1, 3, 4, and 5. If we increase capital availability, the model excludes project 1.

EXHIBIT 11.4 What is the value of relaxing resource constraints? What is the effect on the total NPV of a 10% increase in either capital or FAR availability, or both?

Binding constraints	Base Line		Increase all capacities by 10%		% Change in NPV	Comment
	NPV	Projects	NPV	Projects		
Capital only	$75	3, 4, 5, 6	$77	1, 3, 4, 5	8.5%	Increase all capital capacities by 10% or $24
			$83	3, 4, 7	33.3%	Increase capital availability only for period one and two, each by $12
Spatial (FAR) only	$79	1, 4, 7	$83	6, 7	5.1%	Increase available FAR by 10%
Capital and spatial	$62	3, 5	$71	1, 4, 5, 6		Increase all capital and FAR capacities by 10$

Source: ZCA

Next, we have only an FAR constraint. The optimal set consists of projects 6 and 7. Combining capital and FAR constraints produces an optimal project mix consisting of projects 1, 4, 5, and 6.

Optimal projects, given both the capital and FAR constraints, have NPVs and IRRs that are inconsistent. For example, the NPV criterion ranks in descending order the top four projects as 7, 5, 10, and 3. If we hold capital availability constant and gradually increase the maximum FAR capacity, the NPV increases rather steeply but starts to level off, reaching a ceiling of $75, an example of a diminishing marginal product attributed to FAR. At this point, the FAR constraint is no longer binding. Hence, additional FAR has no value. Maybe we can sell excess FAR through transfer of development rights (TDR).

In New York City, developers use TDRs to sell or transfer unused development rights to other developers for use on their sites. The optimization program can calculate the internal price of the TRD; if the internal value is less than market value, then the owner of the rights should sell the excess. Eventually, the capital constraint is no longer binding when the NPV is $80. At this point, the internal value of additional capital is zero. It's now time to lend instead of borrow.

Linkages. Consider ten constraints according to which the optimization algorithm selects optimal projects. Fractional projects are not allowed. Projects are lumpy. (See Exhibit 11.5.)

Binary variables are also switches that turn on certain constraints or add more capacity. Such a binary variable might trigger a stochastic variable that represents the likelihood of receiving additional development rights from the township or defaulting on a construction loan.

In the example, the capital constraint is binding but the land-use constraint is not. There are 40 excess acres, which implies that the internal or shadow price of land is zero in a certain or deterministic world. Adding uncertainty often changes this result because there is a finite probability that the constraint is binding. If the shadow price of the land is zero, provided that the market price is greater than zero, the developer should sell the land.

What is the significance of a constraint that is binding? Any binding constraint reduces the value of the objective function, in this case, NPV. Hence, the developer should bargain with government to relax those binding constraints in exchange either for constraints that are less binding or for non-binding constraints that are highly valued by the government but which are of little concern to the developer.

EXHIBIT 11.5 Examples of linkage constraints, some of which appear in the base case solution; X_i is a binary choice variable: $1 =$ build the project; $0 =$ do not build the project. Numbers to the right are equation numbers.

Linkage constraint 1. *You can build either project #1 or #2, but not both.* (Example: If we build project #1, then $X_1 = 1$, satisfying the constraint.) Application: You own an urban site and can install surface parking or you can exercise your option to build an office building. Doing the latter extinguishes your option to defer construction and continue operating the parking lot.	$X_1 + X_2 = 1$	(11.6)
Linkage constraint 2. You need not build project #1 or #4. However, if you build one, then you must also build the other. (Note that if you build project #4, you will be forced to build project #1, but, according to linkage constraint 1, if you build #1, you cannot build project #2. Thus, building #4 indirectly forces exclusion of #2.) Application: If you build the apartment complex, you must build a school; conversely, you would not build a school without building apartments.	$X_1 - X_4 = 0$	(11.7)
Linkage constraint 3. You need not build any of projects #1, #2, or #3, but if you decide to build any, you are limited to two or less.	$X_6 + X_7 + X_8 \leq 2$	(11.8)
Linkage constraint 4. You need not build any of projects #3, #5, #9, or #10. You can build any project or group of projects. However, if you elect to build projects #3, #5, #9 and #10, then you must build project #10. If you only select two projects from the set of #3, #5 and #9, then you have the option to build #10.	$X_3 + X_5 + X_9 - X_{10} \leq 2$	(11.9)
Linkage constraint 5. You need not build projects #2, #4, #6 and #8. However, if you build one, you must build another project selected in a special way. For example, if you build project #2, you must build either #6 or #8. If you build project #4 and #2, you must build both #6 and #8. An application might be modeling the relationship between office or retail space and infrastructure.	$X_2 + X_4 - X_6 - X_8 = 0$	(11.10)

(continued)

EXHIBIT 11.5 (*continued*)

Linkage constraint 6. You need not build #5, #7 or #9. However, if you build #5 or #7, then you must build #9. If you build #9, you are not required to build either #5 or #7. Project #9 might be a garage that charges parking fees or an addition to an already crowded garage.	$X_5 + X_7 - X_9 \leq 0$	(11.11)
Linkage constraint 7. You must build at least #2 or #3, or both. "No projects" is not an option.	$X_2 + X_3 \geq 1$	(11.12)
Linkage constraint 8. *Capital bonus.* This is not an ordinary budget constraint. If X_1 is selected, it receives a bonus of λ_1. *If we include constraint (6), a higher λ_1 increases the likelihood of excluding X_2.*	$\beta_1 \cdot X_1 + \beta_2 \cdot X_2 \leq 300 + \lambda_1 \cdot X_1$ or, $(\beta_1 - \lambda_1)X_1 + \beta_2 \cdot X_2 \leq 300$	(11.13)
Linkage constraint 9. If the developer selects X_2 ($X_2 = 1$), then the developer can select X_1 or X_3, but not both; if X_2 is not selected ($X_2 = 0$), then the developer can select up to X_1 and X_3.	$X_2 \cdot (X_1 + X_3) + X_2 \leq 2$	(11.14)
Linkage constraint 10. Total space built over three time periods cannot exceed available land area. The developer builds X_{it} over three time periods and selects from four possible uses.	$\sum_{i=1}^{4} \sum_{t=1}^{3} X_{it} \leq$ LANDAREA	(11.15)

Source: ZCA

A good constrained optimization model can be a powerful aid in negotiating development rights. The model determines the internal price or opportunity cost of a constraint, but only the developer is privy to this information; other parties must rely more on rules of thumb. Relaxing a non-binding constraint does not hurt the developer, but the other side of the negotiation, who does not realize that the constraint is non-binding, may consider the "concession" to be a huge win. Sometimes optics win the day.

Depending on which constraints we relax or add, results will vary. The constrained optimization model provides essential information pertaining to the merits of a capital infusion while simultaneously satisfying a complex set of constraints. The results are not always intuitively obvious, but they are immensely valuable.

Linkage constraints make a difference. For example, the spread in the NPV with and without certain constraints can be substantial. Some of the sources of uncertainty include the expected (risk-adjusted) NPV of each project, capital availability, capital requirements, land availability, human capital resources, complex interdependencies, and phasing.

Stochastic optimization. The standard deterministic analysis, no matter how simple or complex, does not usually produce the same optimal solution calculated using stochastic optimization. Stochastic simulation deals with uncertainty, specifically with random numbers defined by probability distributions and the correlations between those distributions. A typical objective is maximizing project NPV given the standard deviation of each project. Minimizing the value-at-risk (VAR) subject to constraints, for example, is relevant to investors who seek preservation of capital with less risk.

Stochastic constrained optimization produces rich results otherwise unavailable through the use of deterministic methods. Consider ten projects, each with a mean and standard deviation (SD). Assume normal distributions for ease of computation, but there are many other distributions that are not symmetric like the normal distribution. See Exhibit 11.6.

Capital usage must be less than $120 million. See Exhibit 11.7. 150 acres is the maximum allowable land. See Exhibit 11.8.

EXHIBIT 11.6 NPV of potential projects to select; we include standard deviations for each project.

	1	2	3	4	5	6	7	8	9	10
Mean	65	80	100	75	35	20	35	50	47	85
S.D.	20	30	25	60	15	15	10	30	25	15

Source: ZCA

EXHIBIT 11.7 Capital required by project with standard deviations to model the uncertainty of capital availability.

	1	2	3	4	5	6	7	8	9	10
Mean	25	30	60	20	12	5	10	20	10	30
S.D.	5	6	20	5	7	3	4	12	2	5

Source: ZCA

EXHIBIT 11.8 Land required by project with standard deviations to model the uncertainty of land availability.

	1	2	3	4	5	6	7	8	9	10
Mean	10	20	30	25	10	5	10	20	40	20
S.D.	3	6	20	5	2	3	2	4	25	11

Source: ZCA

I include a third constraint that illustrates interdependency. Since the variables are 0 – 1 binary variables, the optimization model can reject both projects 1 and 2, but if it selects one project, it must include the other as well: $X_1 - X_2 = 0$.

Deterministic model. The optimum NPVs of the deterministic version are $372 million with all three constraints and $376 million with just two. These three constraints comprise land and capital availability as well as the linkage constraint, namely, if I build the first project, then I must build project two. Of course, the developer may choose to build neither project. See Exhibit 11.9.

If the linkage were an inequality, $X_1 - X_2 \leq 0$, then the constraint would say, I can build just project two but I cannot *just* build project one. I can still elect to build neither project one nor two. The linkage constraint changes the optimal allocation.

Stochastic model. Let's now introduce risk. What happens if the developer does not obtain enough capital to begin phase two or obtain a zoning variance that permits additional FAR?

The three-constraint model generates an NPV of $386 million and the two-constraint model produces an NPV of $421. The introduction of uncertainty increases the NPV. When adding more binding constraints, expect the value of the objective function to decline further. Stochastic, when compared with deterministic, optimization typically produces different outcomes, as shown in Exhibit 11.10.

The three-constraint deterministic solution is $372 million. The differences reflect constraints as well as embedded options, the correct value of which only stochastic optimization can determine.

EXHIBIT 11.9 Project selection based on deterministic NPV; "1" means "selected."

	1	2	3	4	5	6	7	8	9	10
3 constraints	1	1	0	1	0	1	1	1	1	0
2 constraints	1	0	0	1	0	1	1	1	1	1

Source: ZCA

EXHIBIT 11.10 Project selection based on stochastic NPV; "1" means "selected."

	1	2	3	4	5	6	7	8	9	10
3 constraints	1	1	0	1	1	0	0	0	1	1
2 constraints	1	1	0	1	0	1	0	1	1	1

Source: ZCA

Dominance. Stochastic inputs include means and the standard deviations, which represents risk. For a moment, let's ignore the constraints. In general, investors should always favor higher NPVs unless doing so incurs additional risk.

Exhibit 11.11 is a plot of the expected NPV and risk for each project. Investors should prefer less risk without sacrificing NPV. (Of course, there is the gray area in which an investor might prefer greater NPV and assume more risk, but the trade-off depends on other factors.) Using this logic, investors should prefer project 3 over project 9, project 2 over project 8, or project 10 over either projects 5 or 6. The stochastic solution violates the dominance principle in the case of constraint three. Project 3 dominates project 9, but the solution omits project 3 and accepts project 9. (Such is also the case in the deterministic model.)

EXHIBIT 11.11 NPV expected average and risk (standard deviation).

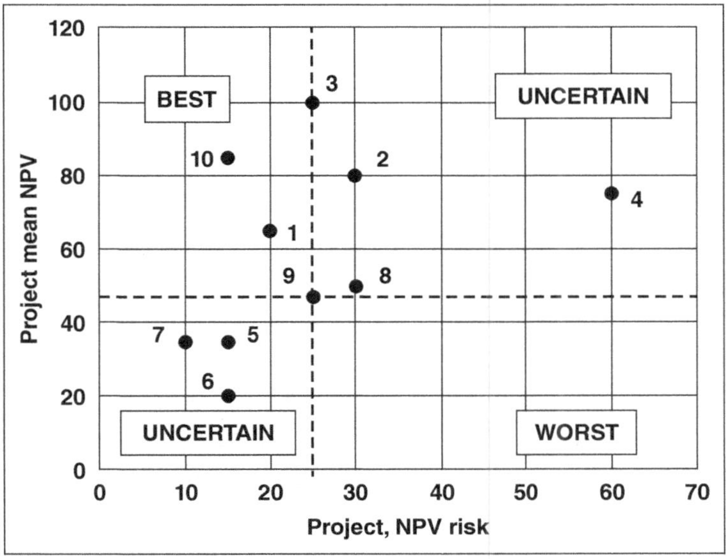

Source: ZCA

A graphic analysis. This section provides distributions of the outputs and inputs to our stochastic optimization example. Exhibits 11.12–11.15 show the NPVs with and without the linkage and with land-capital resource correlations of either −1 or +1. Eliminating the binding linkage constraint changes the combination of selected projects, which increases the total NPV from $386 to $421, a 9% increase. Capital and land availability are negatively correlated. A plausible scenario is that when capital is plentiful and land prices are increasing, land owners may exercise their option to delay, the value of which is a function of volatility. (See Exhibit 11.12.)

Exhibit 11.13 summarizes the complete stochastic model and includes the correlation matrix, expected means and standard deviations, choices, resource constraints, and a linkage equation. The correlation between capital and land availability is −1, which is consistent with ample capital, rising prices, increased volatility, and landowners exercising their options to defer a sale. Deferrals reduce land availability.

EXHIBIT 11.12 Negative correlation between capital and land availability reduces NPV. The maximum NPV is 362 assuming that land and capital are perfectly negatively correlated. If the model accepts project 1, then project 2 must be accepted, as shown in the linkage line.

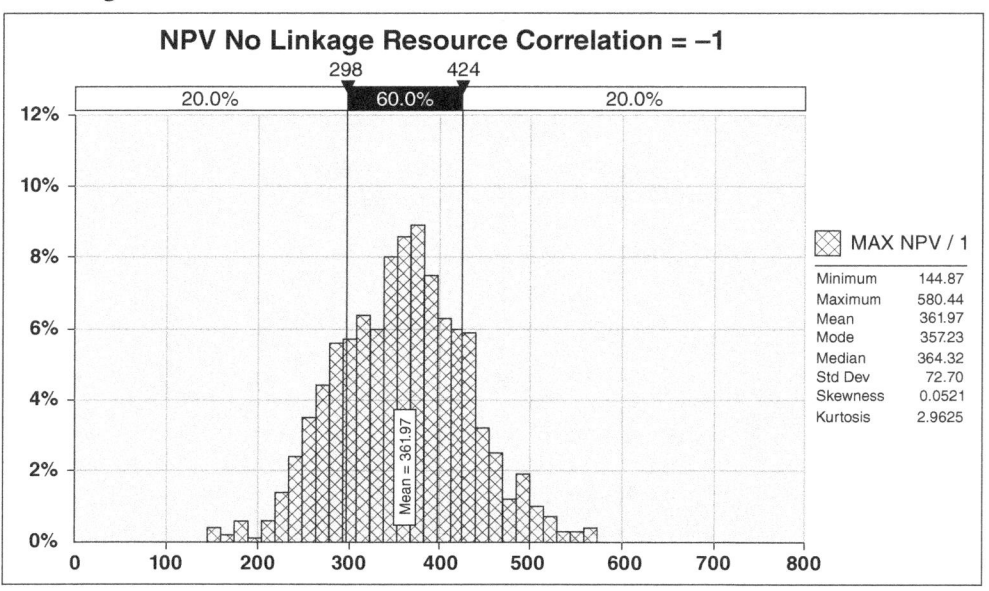

Source: ZCA

EXHIBIT 11.13 Inputs to the stochastic optimization model.

Project	1	2	3	4	5	6	7	8	9	10
Mean	65	80	100	75	35	20	35	50	47	85
SD	20	30	25	60	15	15	10	30	25	15
NPV	65	80	100	75	35	20	35	50	47	85
Choice	1	0	0	1	1	1	1	0	1	1
MAX NPV	362									
					Constraints					
Mean	25	30	60	20	12	5	10	20	10	30
SD	5	6	20	5	7	3	4	12	2	5
Required Capital	25	30	60	20	12	5	10	20	10	30
Mean	10	20	30	25	10	5	10	20	40	20
SD	3	6	20	5	2	3	2	4	25	11
Required Land	10	20	30	25	10	5	10	20	40	20
Linkage	1	−1	0	0	0	0	0	0	0	0

				Mean	SD	Correlation Matrix		
							Capital	Land
Capital	112	<=	120	120	20	Capital	1.000	
Land	120	<=	150	150	10	Land	−1.000	1.000
Linkage (NONE)	1	EQ	0					

Source: ZCA

Exhibits 11.14 and 11.15 show the distributions for land and capital availabilities, which are distinct from land and capital utilizations.

A constraint that is binding in a deterministic approach may not be binding in a stochastic model because in a stochastic model we are dealing with distributions and not means or single numbers, See Chapter 2. In Exhibit 11.15, mean capital utilized is 112, whereas mean capital available is 120. Similarly, available land is 150, as shown in Exhibit 11.16, but mean land used is 120, as shown in Exhibit 11.17.

The NPV is 362 in the stochastic model with linkage and a capital and land availability correlation of −1.

EXHIBIT 11.14 Capital availability is defined by a normal curve. The coefficient of variation (CV) is 0.167.

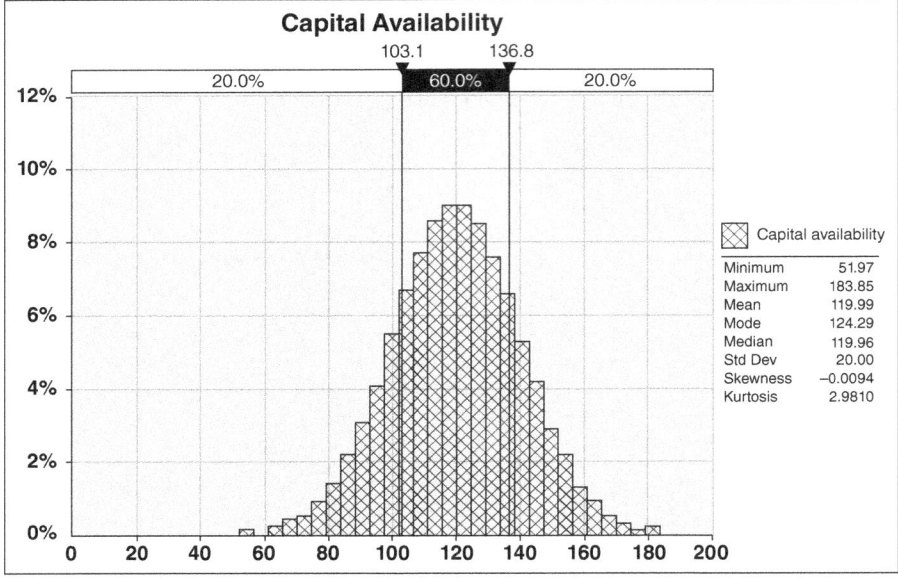

Source: ZCA

EXHIBIT 11.15 Capital that is utilized is roughly symmetric but the tails are thicker than a normal distribution. The CV is 0.112, which is smaller than the CV associated with capital availability.

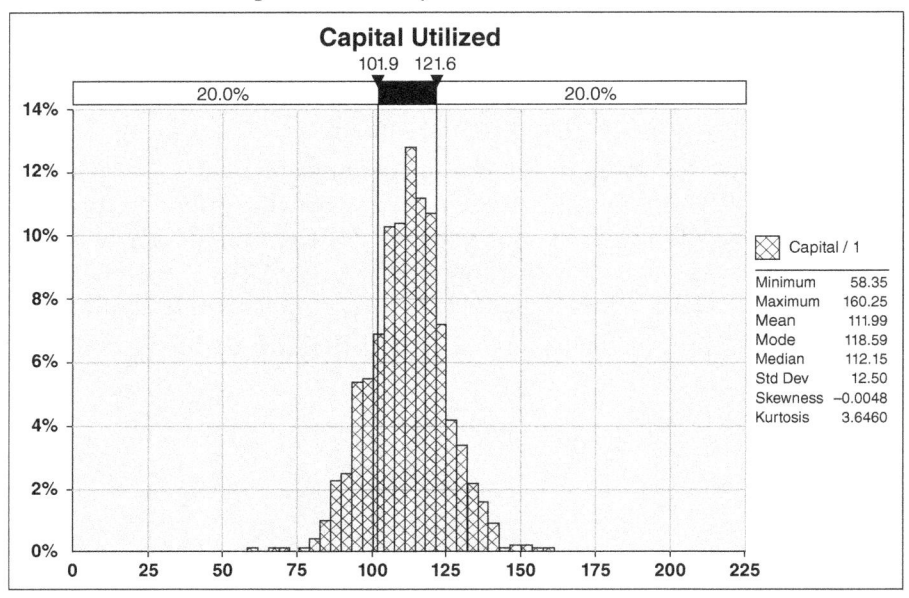

Source: ZCA

EXHIBIT 11.16 Land availability is symmetric with a CV of 0.067.

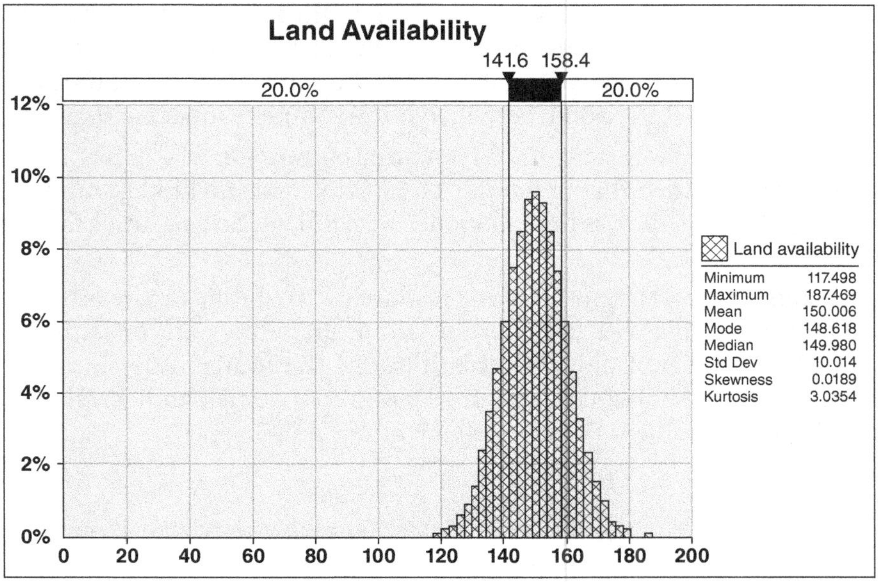

Land Availability
141.6
158.4
20.0%
20.0%
12%
10%
8%
6%
4%
2%
0%
0
20
40
60
80
100
120
140
160
180
200
Land availability
Minimum 117.498
Maximum 187.469
Mean 150.006
Mode 148.618
Median 149.980
Std Dev 10.014
Skewness 0.0189
Kurtosis 3.0354

Source: ZCA

EXHIBIT 11.17 Land utilization is slightly skewed to the left and the tails are thinner than the normal distribution. The CV is 0.236, which indicates that land utilization is riskier in relation to land availability.

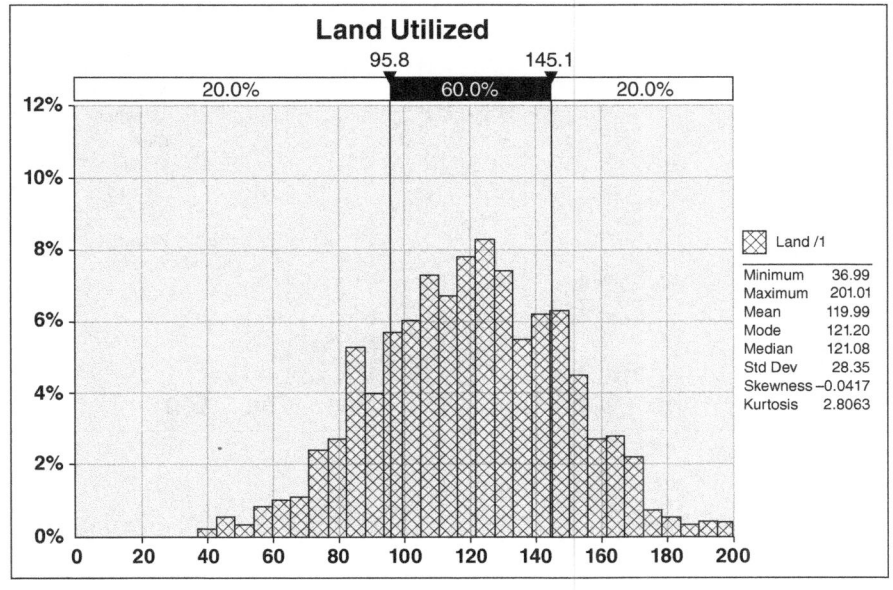

Land Utilized
95.8
145.1
20.0%
60.0%
20.0%
12%
10%
8%
6%
4%
2%
0%
0
20
40
60
80
100
120
140
160
180
200
Land /1
Minimum 36.99
Maximum 201.01
Mean 119.99
Mode 121.20
Median 121.08
Std Dev 28.35
Skewness -0.0417
Kurtosis 2.8063

Source: ZCA

Capital utilized is more certain than available capital in the sense that the standard deviation of the former is lower in relation to the mean. The reverse is true for land in this example. The demand for land (utilized) is much more volatile than the supply (availability). If there is no linkage and the correlation is +1, the NPV rises to 460. (See Exhibits 11.18 and 11.19, which is the complete model with no linkage.)

The NPV distribution with linkages and a correlation of −1 has a standard deviation that is less than that of Exhibit 11.18, which has no linkage but has a correlation of +1. Exhibit 11.20 is the full model with linkage and negative land-capital correlation.

Increasing the correlation between resource availabilities increases the NPV. When the correlation is −1, by contrast, the availabilities are offsetting, which reduces NPV. Hence, not only the volatilities of the availabilities but also their correlation matter. We discover that, once we introduce risk and correlations, the optimal allocation changes. See Exhibits 11.21 and 11.22.

EXHIBIT 11.18 If there is no linkage and the land-capital correlation is one, then the NPV is 456.98 and the distribution is almost normally distributed.

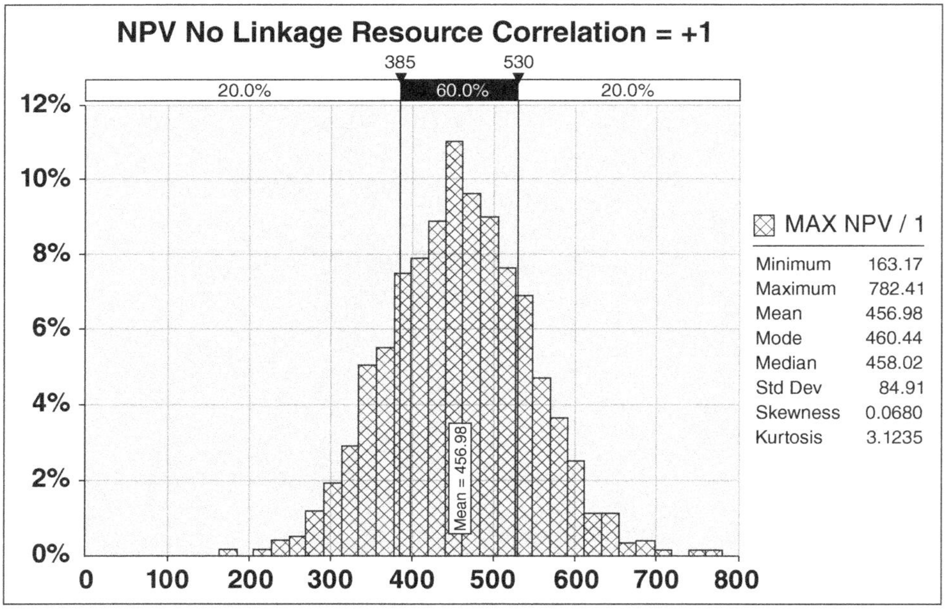

Source: ZCA

EXHIBIT 11.19 Model with no linkage and a land-capital correlation of 1.

Project	1	2	3	4	5	6	7	8	9	10
Mean	65	80	100	75	35	20	35	50	47	85
SD	20	30	25	60	15	15	10	30	25	15
NPV	65	80	100	75	35	20	35	50	47	85
Choice	1	1	0	1	1	1	0	1	1	1
MAX NPV	457									

						Constraints				
Mean	25	30	60	20	12	5	10	20	10	30
SD	5	6	20	5	7	3	4	12	2	5
Required Capital	25	30	60	20	12	5	10	20	10	30
Mean	10	20	30	25	10	5	10	20	40	20
SD	3	6	20	5	2	3	2	4	25	11
Required Land	10	20	30	25	10	5	10	20	40	20
Linkage	1	−1	0	0	0	0	0	0	0	0

				Mean	SD	Correlation Matrix		
Capital	152	<=	120	120	20		Capital	Land
Land	150	<=	150	150	10	Capital	1.000	
Linkage (NONE)	0	EQ	0			Land	1.000	1.000

Source: ZCA

Sensitivity analysis. What is the marginal change in NPV if we increase capital availability by 10%? We begin with the base case in which capital availability is 120. The NPV is $372. Included is the linkage constraint. See Exhibit 11.23.

A 10% boost in capital availability increases the NPV by 9.4%. With the additional capital, I include projects 5, 7, and 8 but drop project 10. Due to the lumpiness of the projects—only binary solutions are accepted. The land is not binding. See Exhibit 11.24.

EXHIBIT 11.20 Model with linkage and negative land-capital correlation; capital constraint is binding.

Project	1	2	3	4	5	6	7	8	9	10
Mean	65	80	100	75	35	20	35	50	47	85
SD	20	30	25	60	15	15	10	30	25	15
NPV	65	80	100	75	35	20	35	50	47	85
Choice	1	1	0	0	1	1	1	0	1	1
MAX NPV	367									
					Constraints					
Mean	25	30	60	20	12	5	10	20	10	30
SD	5	6	20	5	7	3	4	12	2	5
Required Capital	25	30	60	20	12	5	10	20	10	30
Mean	10	20	30	25	10	5	10	20	40	20
SD	3	6	20	5	2	3	2	4	25	11
Required Land	10	20	30	25	10	5	10	20	40	20
Linkage	1	−1	0	0	0	0	0	0	0	0

				Mean	SD	Correlation Matrix		
							Capital	Land
Capital	122	<=	120	120	20	Capital	1.000	
Land	115	<=	150	150	10	Land	−1.000	1.000
Linkage	0	EQ	0					

Source: ZCA

EXHIBIT 11.21 NPV with linkage and land-capital correlation = +1.

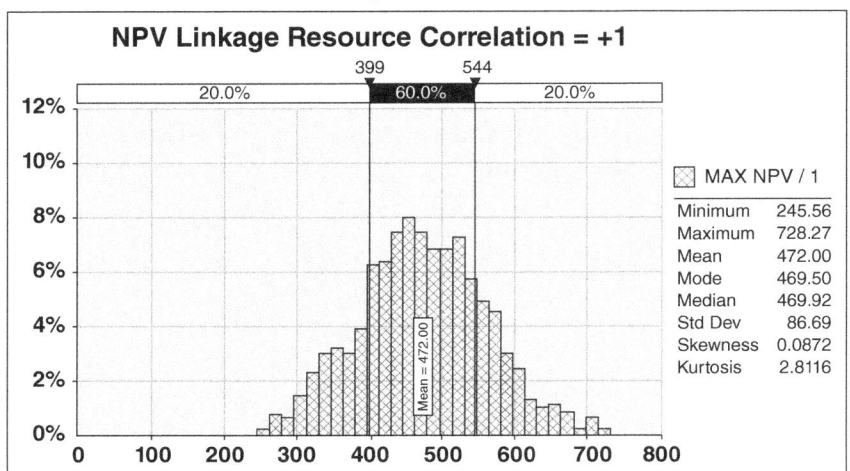

Source: ZCA

EXHIBIT 11.22 Model with linkage and positive land-capital correlation.

Project	1	2	3	4	5	6	7	8	9	10
Mean	65	80	**100**	75	35	20	35	50	47	**85**
SD	20	30	**25**	60	15	15	10	30	25	**15**
NPV	65	80	**100**	75	35	20	35	50	47	**85**
Choice	1	1	**0**	1	1	0	1	1	1	**1**
MAX NPV	472									
					Constraints					
Mean	25	30	60	20	12	5	10	20	10	30
SD	5	6	20	5	7	3	4	12	2	5
Required Capital	25	30	60	20	12	5	10	20	10	30
Mean	10	20	30	25	10	5	10	20	40	20
SD	3	6	20	5	2	3	2	4	25	11
Required Land	10	20	30	25	10	5	10	20	40	20
Linkage	1	−1	0	0	0	0	0	0	0	0

			Mean	SD	Correlation Matrix		
Capital	157	<=	120	120	20		Capital	Land
Land	155	<=	150	150	10	Capital	1.000	
Linkage	0	EQ	0			Land	1.000	1.000

Source: ZCA

EXHIBIT 11.23 Base case: Capital is binding at 120; NPV is 372.

Project	1	2	3	4	5	6	7	8	9	10
NPV	65	80	**100**	75	35	20	35	50	47	**85**
Choice	1	1	**0**	1	0	1	0	0	1	**1**
MAX NPV	372.00									
					Constraints					
Required Capital	25	30	60	20	12	5	10	20	10	30
Required Land	10	20	30	25	10	5	10	20	40	20
Linkage	1	−1	0	0	0	0	0	0	0	0
Capital	120	<=	120							
Land	120	<=	150							
Linkage	0	EQ	0							

Source: ZCA

EXHIBIT 11.24 Increasing capital availability by 10% increases the NPV 9.4%. Note that the capital constraint is still binding.

Project	1	2	3	4	5	6	7	8	9	10
NPV	65	80	100	75	35	20	35	50	47	85
Choice	1	1	0	1	1	1	1	1	1	0
MAX NPV	407.00									
					Constraints					
Required Capital	25	30	60	20	12	5	10	20	10	30
Required Land	10	20	30	25	10	5	10	20	40	20
Linkage	1	−1	0	0	0	0	0	0	0	0
Capital	132	<=	132							
Land	140	<=	150							
Linkage	0	EQ	0							

Source: ZCA

Conclusions and Investment Implications

- Analysts typically do not systematically search for the best outcome; they satisfice. If their goal is finding the best, then their tools may not be up to the task.
- I explore constrained optimization in two contexts, certainty and uncertainty.
- The objective function, total NPV, represents the criterion we want to maximize or minimize. In a stochastic optimization, we might want to minimize the variance of the NPV if minimizing risk is paramount.
- Deterministic constrained optimization can produce initially counterintuitive results, but stochastic programming can produce even stranger results, which can offer deep insights.
- Stochastic optimization helps us better manage uncertainty and provides a deeper appreciation of the interdependencies and risks that permeate complex developments.
- Risk analytics, in particular stochastic optimization, are important tools for evaluating optimal development, which has often been a "seat of the pants" business: all intuition and little analysis.

- The NPV rule is usually superior to the IRR, which is not a true return. Depending on the alternation in the signs of the cash flows, the IRR may not be unique; there may be multiple IRRs. Furthermore, unlike the NPV, the IRR is not additive and it is easier to manipulate with the intent of deceiving the investor. In the presence of side constraints, such as capital rationing, exclusivity and inclusivity constraints, phasing, zoning, height, and density constraints, the NPV criterion usually fails in its simple form and requires modification. For example, the most preferred project may not be the one with the highest NPV.
- Introduction of interdependency constraints often produces counterintuitive results.
- Uncertainty complicates the search for optimal development but the use of constrained stochastic optimization can deliver powerful and valuable results, especially in a negotiation.
- A constraint's shadow price is the marginal impact on the objective function given a unit increase in the value of the constraint. In the case of the budget constraint, the shadow price is the internal cost of capital and reflects the interaction of other constraints within the model. The shadow price of the land constraint is the imputed price of land. If the imputed price of land is greater than the market price, then the owner should buy more land. If it is less, then the owner should sell excess land.

Q&A: Interview with Steve Wechsler, President and CEO of National Association of Real Estate Investment Trusts

Witness to the Growth of the REIT Industry

Describe your early years in the real estate business.

I worked as a lawyer representing real estate clients.

Then, I became General Counsel to The Real Estate Roundtable, becoming its CEO in 1990.

The 1990 recession was an action-forcing event. To raise capital to repay debt to banks, many of my members converted to REIT status, in tandem with listing themselves on the stock exchange.

The public market recapitalized these companies, creating the critical mass we know today as the REIT industry.

That's what led me to NAREIT in 1997.

Comment on the evolution of securitization.

Attempts to securitize real estate were tried many times in the past, but were never truly successful until the late 20th century.

REITs are an innovation which permit investors from all walks of life to easily, effectively, efficiently, and collectively share in the tangible benefits of owning commercial real estate.

The total US REIT equity market capitalization is now $1.5 trillion; public and private REITs together own about $4 trillion in real estate assets.

The public invests in REITs today directly or through ETFs, index funds, mutual funds, retirement funds, and more.

The rest of world is following the lead of the US, with REIT regimes established in over 40 nations. Most real estate companies listed on stock exchanges in the developed world now operate as REITs.

What were the early REITs like?

Early REITs were generally mortgage REITs. They were highly leveraged. It didn't work out.

Describe the modern REIT.

The modern REIT is a real estate company focused on its ability to generate cash flow and appreciation over time.

REITs are taxed as a corporation; but achieve pass-through, single-level tax status through the dividends paid deduction provided to REITs for their taxable income.

Three key policy adjustments made the modern REIT possible: internalization of management, adoption of the UPREIT, and use of taxable subsidiaries.

Should pension funds invest in just REITs?

Why not? REITs bring with them accountability, liquidity, low leverage, transparency, and a focus on total return, income, and appreciation.

Most importantly, the REIT approach to real estate investment disciplines management.

What advice would you give young professionals?

Real estate intersects with most activities, so think broadly about where you might enter the space.

Pay attention to everyone. Through my interactions with others, I've learned as much about what *not* to do as I have learned about what *to do*.

CHAPTER 12

Cap Rates and Hidden Information: Avoiding Traps with Caps

Preliminaries

I dedicate this chapter to all those who are convinced they understand cap rates.

What is the cap rate? The cap rate is the ratio of the net operating income (NOI) divided by the sales price or estimated value. Exhibit 12.1 is a one-year cash flow statement of revenues and expenses. A simplified behavioral definition is as follows: The cap rate is equal to the risk-free rate plus the credit spread minus expected NOI growth. Net operating income (NOI) is line B subtracted from line A: total operating income minus total operating expenses. The cap rate, which is the ratio of line C (NOI) over line E (property value), is 7.1%. Capital and leasing expenses (capital items) are typically not included in NOI, but they affect overall building performance, specifically cash flow. The ratio of line D (cash flow) to line E (property value) is 6.7%.

Why are cap rates less volatile than returns? The cap rate is distinct from returns, as shown in Exhibit 12.2, but why is the volatility of the cap rate so much less than fluctuations in the total return? The cap rate is the ratio of NOI (in the numerator) to price (in the denominator) and both are positively correlated. Their correlation is 0.454 for the period 2000 through 2024Q2. See Exhibit 12.3. Were they negatively correlated, then cap rate volatility would be greater than the volatility of its components. Cap rates are an insensitive market indicator compared with total returns and other variables. See also Exhibit 12.3.

EXHIBIT 12.1 Dewey Cheatum & Howe Building Cash Flow.

	OPERATING INCOME	
	Rental income:	
	Gross potential rental revenue	$ 5,000,000
	Vacancy	$ (35,000)
	Net rental revenue	$ 4,965,000
	Percentage rents	$ 50,000
	Total rental income	$ 5,015,000
	Expense reimbursements	
	Common area maintenance	$ 550,000
	Property tax	$ 350,000
	Other income	$ 35,000
	Gross income	$ 5,950,000
	Loss due to bad debts	$ 80,300
A	**Total operating income**	$ 5,869,700
	OPERATING EXPENSES	
	Reimbursable expenses	
	Common area maintenance	$ 550,000
	Property tax	$ 350,000
	Non-reimbursable expenses	
	Utilities	$ 130,000
	Insurance	$ 65,000
	Management	$ 90,000
B	**Total operating expenses**	$ 1,185,000
C	**Net operating income (NOI)**	**$ 4,684,700**
	CAPITAL AND LEASING COSTS	
	Tenant improvements	$ 50,000
	Leasing commissions	$ 25,000
	Capital expenditures	$ 200,000
D	**Cash flow before leverage**	$ 4,409,700
E	**Market value of property**	**$ 66,000,000**
F	**Cap rate ("C" divided by "E")**	**$ 7.1%**

Source: ZCA

EXHIBIT 12.2 Cap rates and total returns have a weak correlation; cap rates are less volatile.

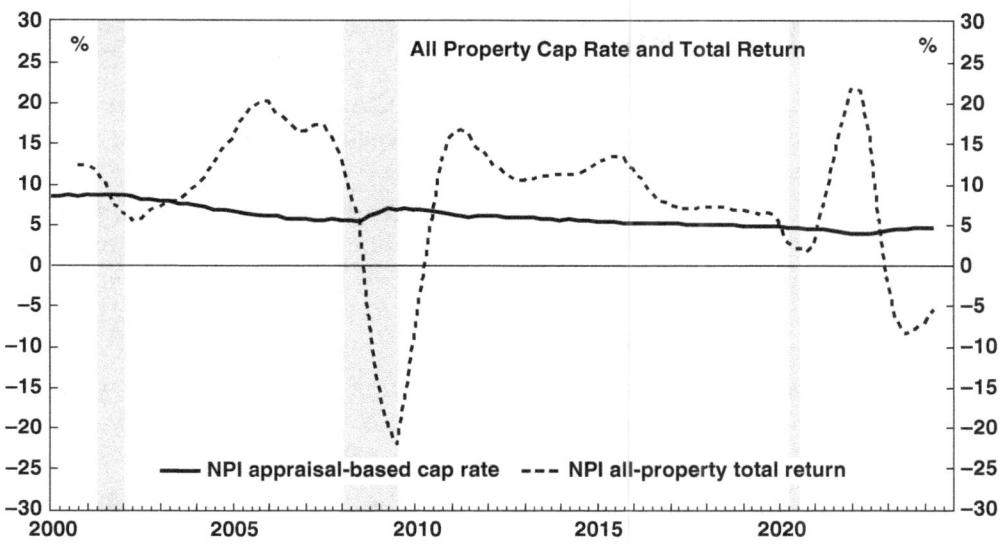

Source: ZCA using NCREIF data

EXHIBIT 12.3 NOI and price growth rates are positively correlated.

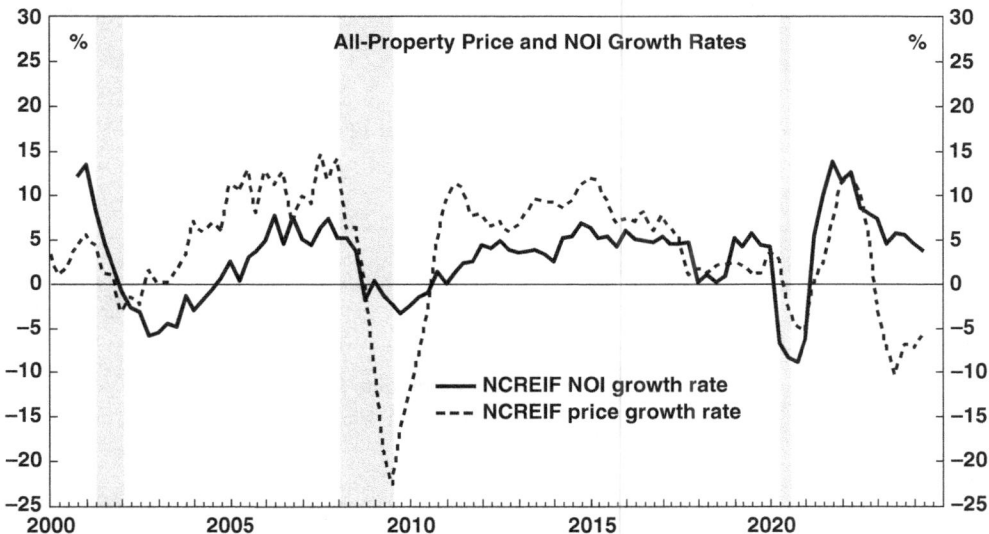

Source: ZCA using NCREIF data

The Tower of Babel: Too Many Seemingly Incompatible Cap Rates?

Primary cap rate vendors include NCREIF and CoStar. Each uses different collection methodologies; both have changed how we measure and analyze real estate in the most fundamental ways.

While their approaches differ, clever econometrics can adjust for these differences. Cap rate values exceed Baa-rated corporate bond yields, which is important in explaining property total return performance. See Exhibit 12.4. Appraisal- and transactions-based cap rates, respectively, are 4.646% and 5.244% greater than the Baa-rated bond yield from 2000 through 2024Q2.

Bond yields and cap rates. The NCREIF income return is statistically similar to the cap rate. The cap rate is much less volatile than the total return, which has a larger interquartile range; the outliers are more extreme.

The NCREIF appraisal-based cap rates are determined by appraisers, often in the fourth quarter for smaller properties and in every quarter for the larger properties. The transactions cap rate since the GFC has significantly exceeded the appraisal-based cap rate and it has been more volatile. See Exhibit 12.5. I do not want to criticize our appraisal friends unfairly because similar

EXHIBIT 12.4 Cap rates and the Baa rated bond yield.

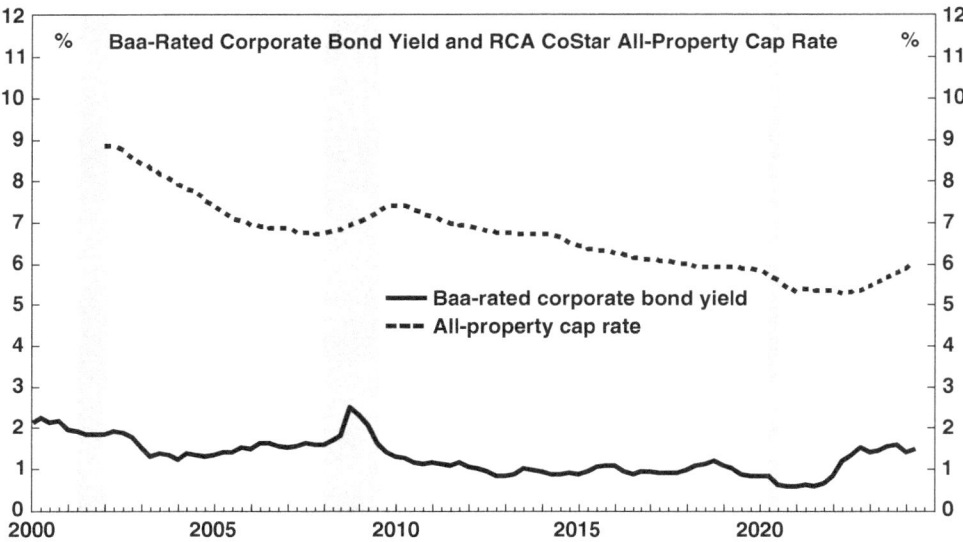

Source: ZCA using NCREIF data

EXHIBIT 12.5 The NCREIF transactions-based cap rate has exceeded the appraisal-based cap rate since the beginning of the GFC.

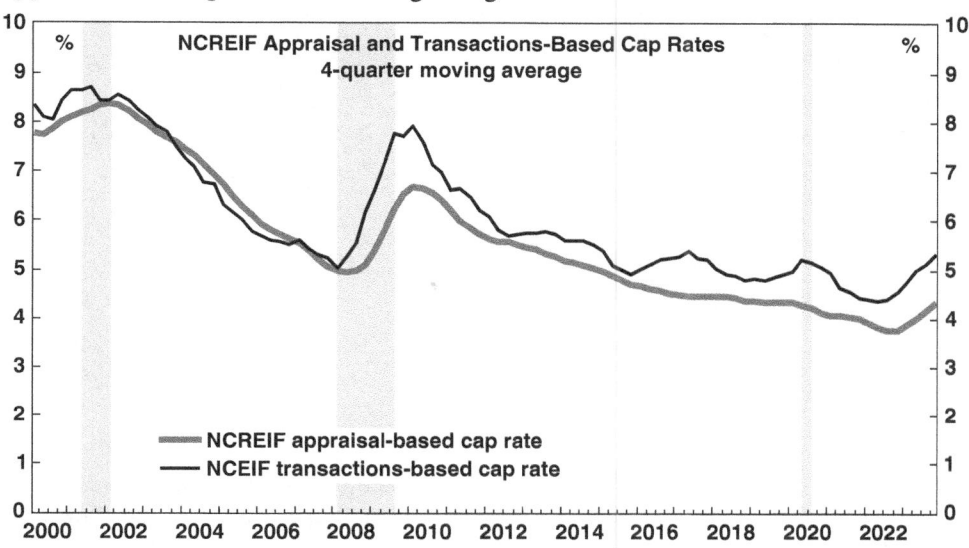

Source: ZCA using NCREIF data

approaches—mark-to-model or modified mark-to-market—are practiced in the hedge fund, private equity, and even the thinly traded corporate bond sectors.

Stock prices fluctuate as if they follow a random walk because stocks immediately impound in the price any news. Hence, investors cannot predict the next period's stock price. Cap rates and returns, by contrast, do not follow a random walk. They are serially correlated. This means that investors can use yesterday's cap rate to predict today's cap rate, but they likely cannot beat the market after fees and transactions costs.

Exhibit 12.6 is a box whisker plot that compares cap rates with leveraged as well as unleveraged NCREIF returns. The dispersion of the leveraged cap rate is significantly greater than the appraisal-based cap rate. The income rate of return has a narrow spread and a lower mean than either cap rate. The transactions cap rate has a greater spread and a wider IQR than the appraisal-based cap rate.

Exhibit 12.7 shows the box plots for the NCREIF all-property appraisal-based cap rate and the change in its components, NOI growth and property value, as estimated by an appraiser or advisor. Property asset classes have similar mean income returns but the variances are different. The REIT income return is comparable but its distribution is more compact. The cap rate is much less volatile than either of its components as shown by the much shorter IQR and distance between the lower

EXHIBIT 12.6 Cap rates are less volatile than their components.

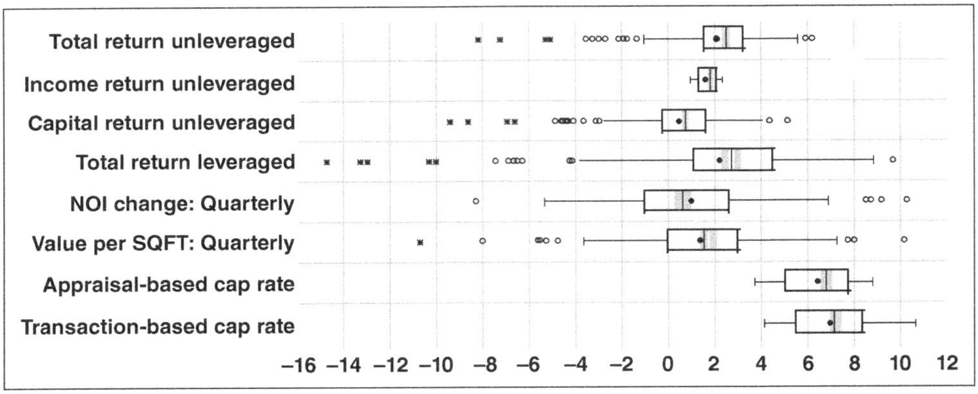

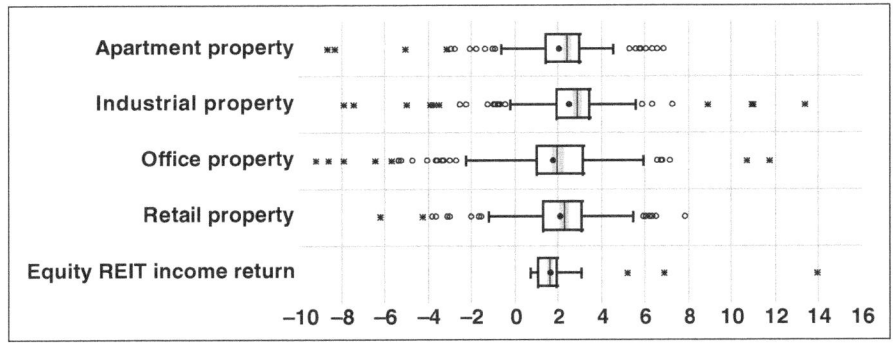

Source: ZCA using NCREIF data

EXHIBIT 12.7 Bonds and all-property cap rate comparison. The appraisal cap rate is less than the transactions cap rate; both are much greater than the bond yields.

Source: ZCA using NAREIT and NCREIF data

and upper whisker of the cap rates. Note that both components are skewed to the left—the mean is less than the median.

Exhibit 12.8 shows bond yields with cap rates. Cap rate levels and volatilities exceed that of bonds.

EXHIBIT 12.8 Average bond yields are less than cap rates by 500 to 600 bps.

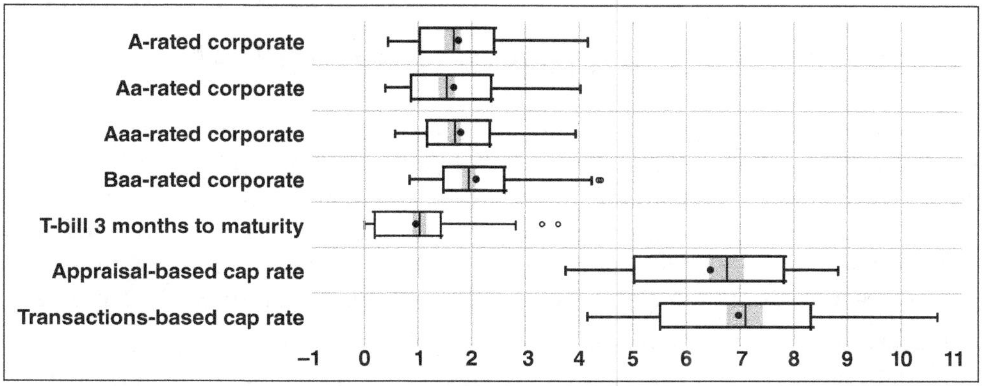

[Box plot showing ranges for:
- A-rated corporate: ~1-4, median ~2
- Aa-rated corporate: ~1-4, median ~2
- Aaa-rated corporate: ~1-4, median ~2
- Baa-rated corporate: ~1-4, median ~2
- T-bill 3 months to maturity: ~0-2, median ~1
- Appraisal-based cap rate: ~5-9, median ~7
- Transactions-based cap rate: ~5-9, median ~7
X-axis: -1 to 11]

Source: ZCA using NAREIT, NCREIF, and Federal Reserve data

The NCREIF appraisal-based cap rate, which represents a smaller institutional sample, is more than 200 bps less than the CoStar cap rate. Even though the transactions cap rate exceeds the appraisal cap rate, they are both highly correlated, as shown in Exhibit 12.9.

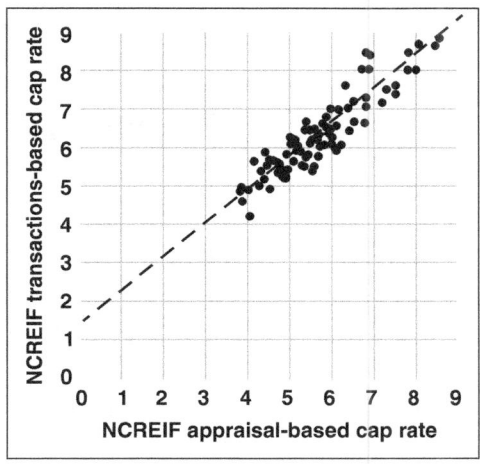

EXHIBIT 12.9 The correlation between the transactions and the appraisal-based cap rates is strong.

Source: ZCA using NCREIF data

A Cap Rate Myth: An Increase in Interest Rates Will Necessarily Increase the Cap Rate

An increase in interest rates does not <u>necessarily</u> increase cap rates. The bivariate correlation of these rates is low, as Exhibits 12.10 and 12.11 show, but the cap rate–interest rate relationship is often swamped by other factors. Hence, the bivariate relationship between cap rates and interest rates fails to reveal the true relationship. The 16-quarter moving correlations between AAA- and BAA-rated bond yields and cap rates are not stable over time, as shown in Exhibits 12.12 and 12.13.

I estimate a multiple regression model that controls for other sources of variation and find that cap rates increase if the Baa/T-bill spread increases; it decreases if either the overall economy's debt-to-GDP ratio or expected real (inflation-adjusted) NOI increases. See Exhibits 12.10 through 12.13.

Even though the AAA-rated bond yield and the BAA yield play roles in determining value, cap rates, and discount rates, the rolling correlations of these yields with cap rates is not consistently positive; they fluctuate, indicating that there are other factors at work.

EXHIBIT 12.10 The T-bill and appraisal-based cap rate is 0.149.

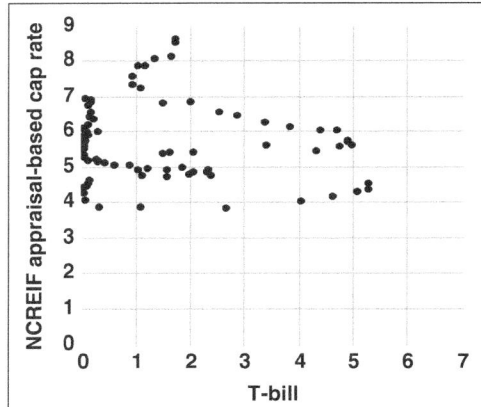

Source: ZCA using NCREIF data

EXHIBIT 12.11 The T-bill and appraisal-based cap rate is 0.185.

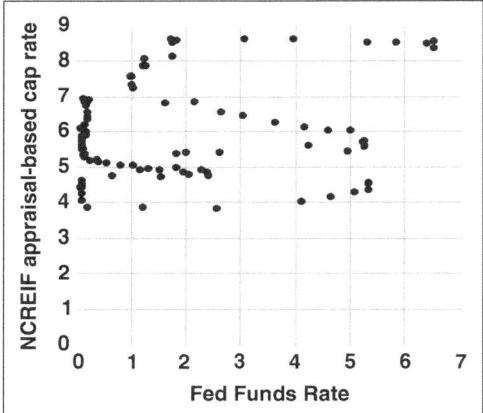

Source: ZCA using NCREIF and Federal Reserve data

EXHIBIT 12.12 Moving correlation of the BAA bond yield and cap rates is not constant.

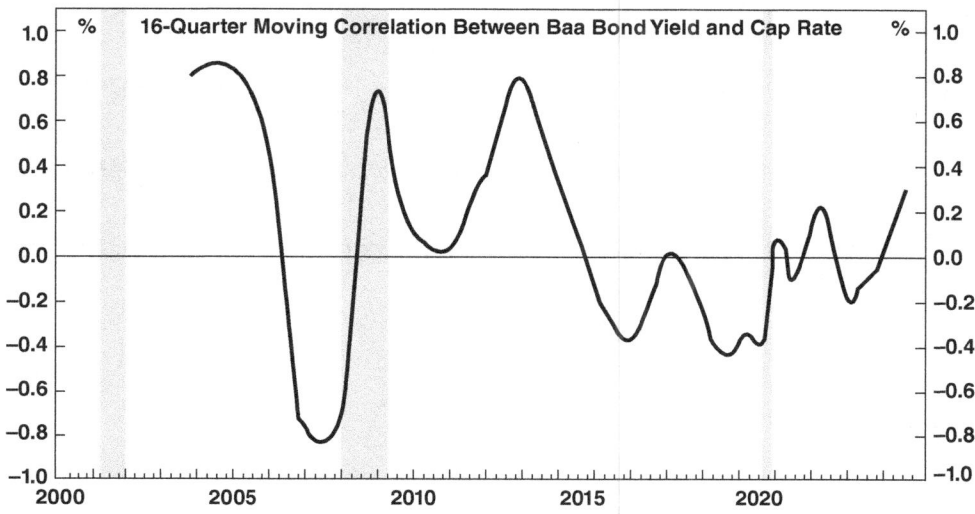

Source: ZCA using NCREIF and Federal Reserve data

EXHIBIT 12.13 Moving correlation of the AAA bond yield and cap rates is not constant.

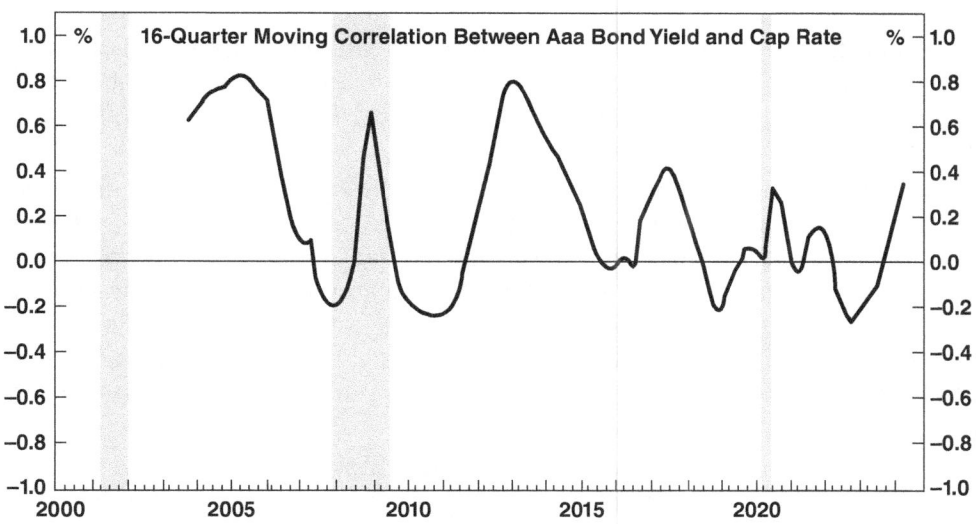

Source: ZCA using NCREIF and Federal Reserve data

Equation (12.1) explains the relationship between the NCREIF appraisal-based cap rate and other explanatory variables, including the ratio of economy-wide debt to GDP.

$$LOG(CAPAPP_t) = \underset{(-4.379)}{-0.301} + \underset{(14.095)}{1.371 * LOG(CAPAPP_{t-1})} - \underset{(-5.214)}{0.488 * LOG(CAPAPP_{t-2})}$$

$$+ \underset{(2.409)}{0.485 *[BAABOND_t - TBILL_t]} + \underset{(2.132)}{0.020 * \Delta DEBTGDPRATIO_t * REALNOIGR_t}$$

$$- \underset{(-2.658)}{0.058 * DEBTGDPRATIO_t} - \underset{(-2.482)}{0.258 * REALNOIGR_t} + \underset{(5.424)}{0.031 * DUMMY2QTR_t}$$

$$+ \underset{(6.275)}{0.038 * DUMMY4QTR_t} \quad (12.1)$$

R-squared = 0.987

Adjusted R-squared = 0.986

Standard error of the regression = 0.021

Mean dependent variable = −2.899

F-statistic = 726.352

Probability (F-statistic) = 0.000

Durbin Watson statistic = 0.858

Debt availability helps determine transactions volume; it also drives cap rates.[1] The greater is the amount of economy-wide debt, or the higher the debt ratio, the greater are liquidity and upward pressure on prices. Accordingly, cap rates fall as prices rise.

The higher is the Baa-bond spread over T-bills, the greater is the cap rate. If real NOI growth increases by one percentage point, the percentage decline in the cap rate is −2.5 plus 0.020 times the increase in the debt-to-GDP ratio. Cap rates are higher in the second and fourth quarters by 3.1% and 3.8% of the mean cap rate, respectively. The estimates of the quarterly dummy variables, while significant in a narrow statistical sense, are not material in their values. (Each of these seasonal dummy variables assume a "0" or a "1" depending on the quarter with which an observation is associated.)

All of the estimated coefficients are statistically significant and have the right signs. The model explains 99% of the variation in the NCREIF appraisal-based cap rate. Lagged cap rates predict current cap rates. A 10% increase in last quarter's cap rate is associated with a 14% *increase* in the current cap rate; the same increase in the cap rate lagged two quarters yields a 4.9% *decrease* in the current cap rate.

Cap Rate Variation by Quality and Across Cities

Cap rates vary according to MSA size and quality. Exhibit 12.14 indicates that for the top 25% of the office inventory, the spread between cap rates for high- (CoStar 4 and 5) and low-quality (CoStar 1 and 2) buildings is relatively constant. Rental growth rate spreads fluctuate, as shown in Exhibit 12.15. Since COVID-19, vacancy rates in the best office buildings have increased significantly.

The flow of capital across MSAs has adjusted building prices to roughly equate risk-adjusted returns with a spread since 2012, as shown in Exhibit 12.16. The vacancy rate spread has expanded significantly due to higher vacancy rates in better quality buildings. (See Exhibit 12.17.)

EXHIBIT 12.14 Lower quality office buildings in the top 25% of the inventory have higher cap rates.

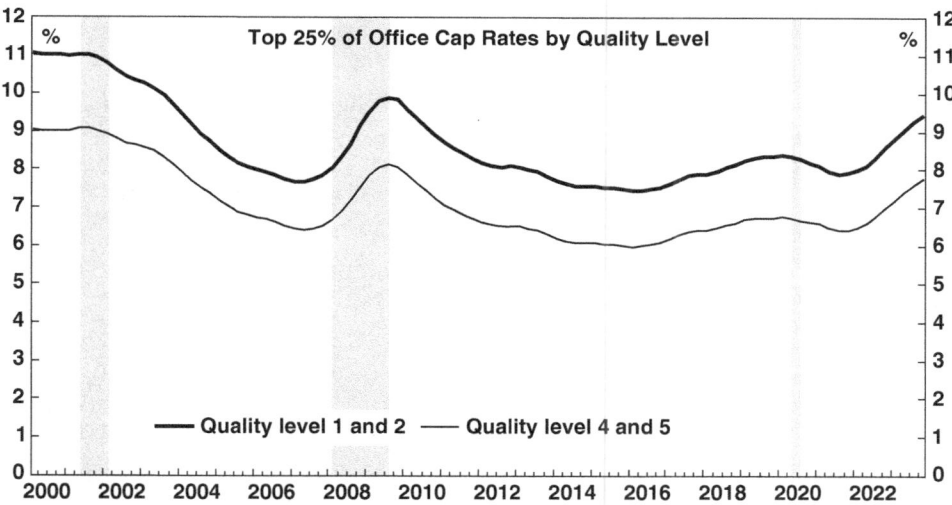

Source: ZCA using CoStar data

EXHIBIT 12.15 Lower quality buildings now have higher cap rates, but that was not always the case.

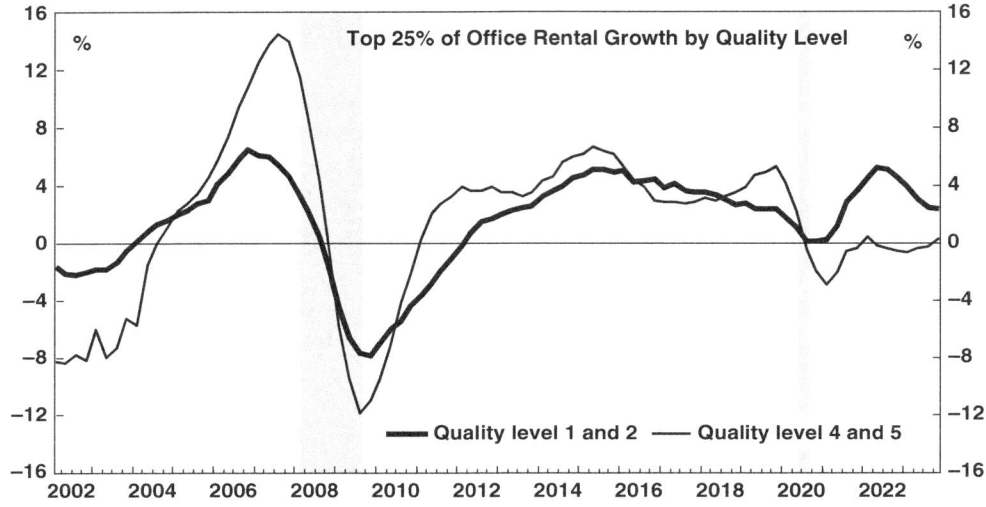

Source: ZCA using CoStar data

EXHIBIT 12.16 Lower quality office buildings have slightly higher total returns possibly as compensation for perceived greater risk.

Source: ZCA using CoStar data

EXHIBIT 12.17 The highest quality portion of the top-25% office inventory exhibits higher and more volatile vacancy rates.

Source: ZCA using CoStar data

Cap Rates Over the Cycle: Single Tenant Property Bidding

Using 21 years of transactions data, I combine 21 *collapsed, rotated* annual histograms in Exhibit 12.18, such as the cap rate distribution for 2007, shown in Exhibit 12.19. During 2007 to 2010, the distributions shifted to the right from A to B; the mean increased from 6.5% to 7.8%. Importantly, the positive skewness—long tail to the right—increased from 0.4 to 1.1, indicating a deterioration in office performance and an increase in the risk of worse performance. See Exhibits 12.20 and 12.21.

The height of each column and the positions of the left and right tail vary as well. During hot markets, the left tail, which includes low cap rates, lengthens as buyers stretch on price. When the property market is in decline, the column and the left tail shorten. The left tail contracts more than the right tail.

The left tail—low cap rates—represents the most desired assets. Unfortunately for investors, this is the riskiest position in the entire distribution. Exhibit 12.22 shows the variation in mean cap rates over the property cycle. I calculate cap rates for the mean as well as the 25th and 75th percentile. See also Exhibit 12.23.

292 CHAPTER 12 Cap Rates and Hidden Information: Avoiding Traps with Caps

EXHIBIT 12.18 The changing cap rate distribution.

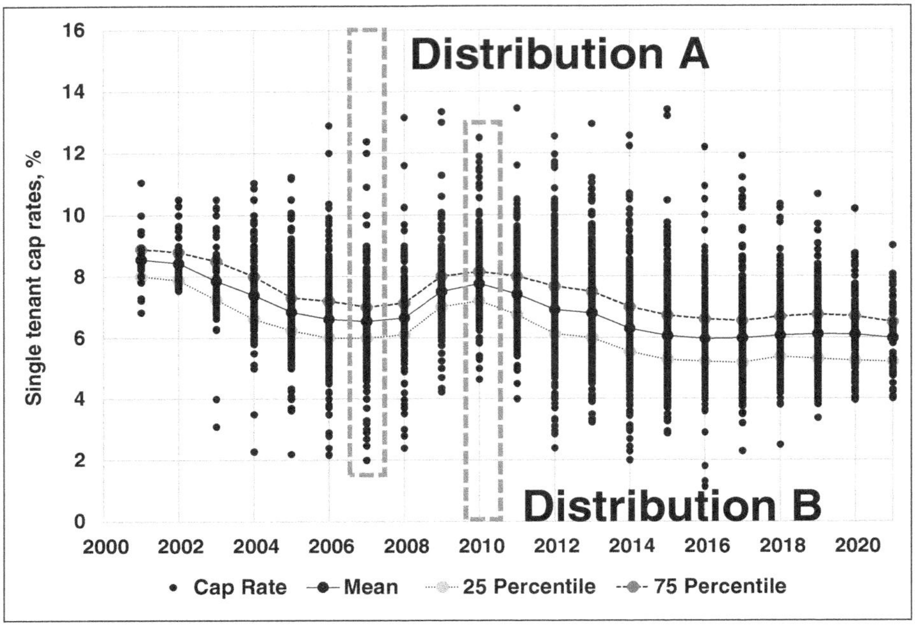

Source: ZCA using proprietary data

EXHIBIT 12.19 Distribution A: 2007.

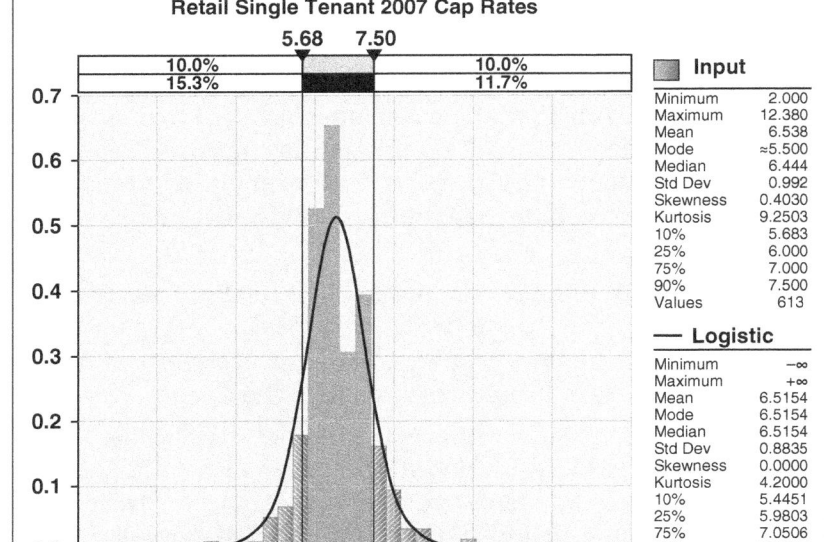

Source: ZCA using proprietary data

EXHIBIT 12.20 Shifting distributions and changing shapes over time.

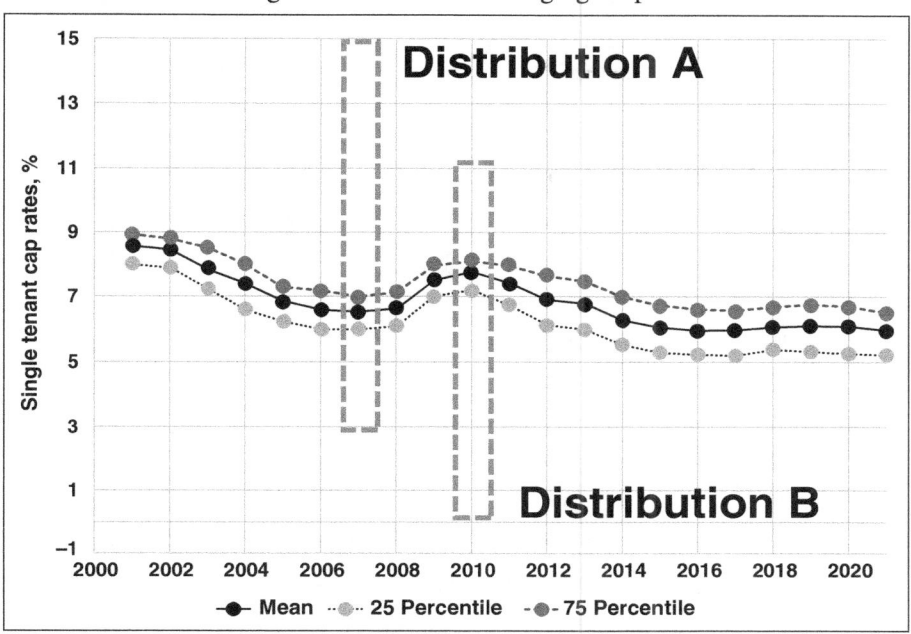

Source: ZCA using proprietary data

EXHIBIT 12.21 Distribution B (2010) is skewed to the right and the tail is fat.

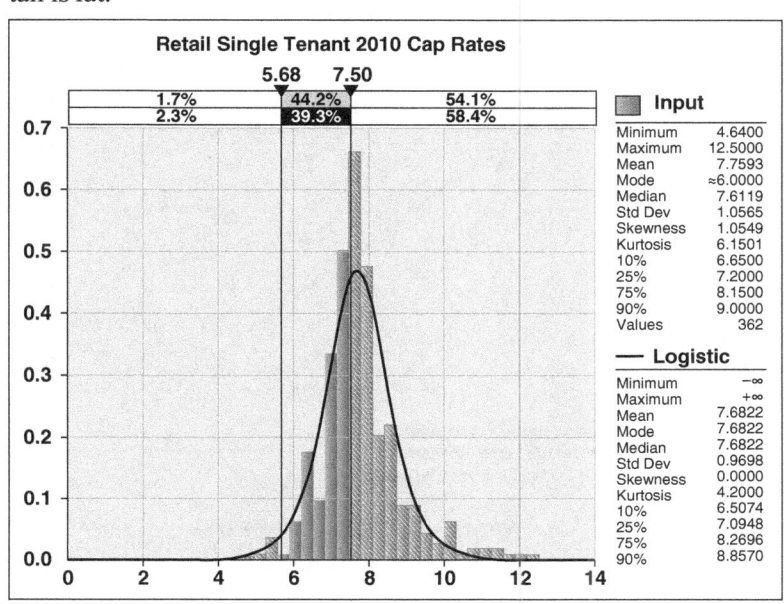

Source: ZCA using proprietary data

294 CHAPTER 12 Cap Rates and Hidden Information: Avoiding Traps with Caps

EXHIBIT 12.22 As the single tenant cap rate rises, the spread narrows.

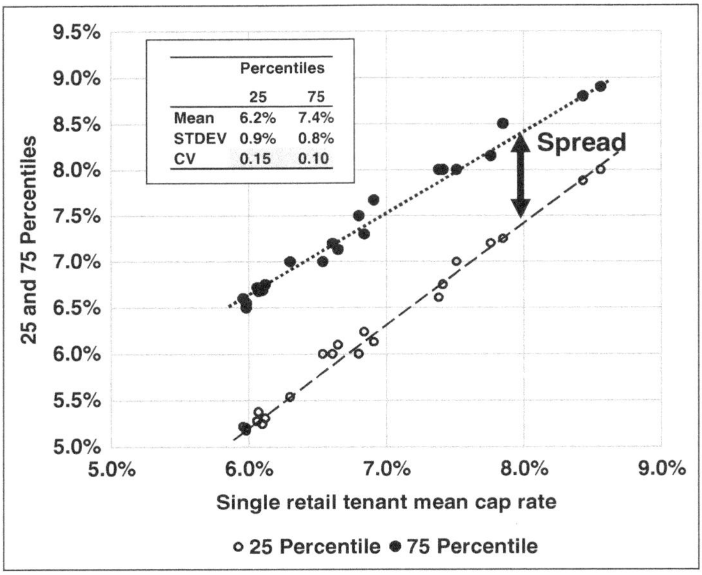

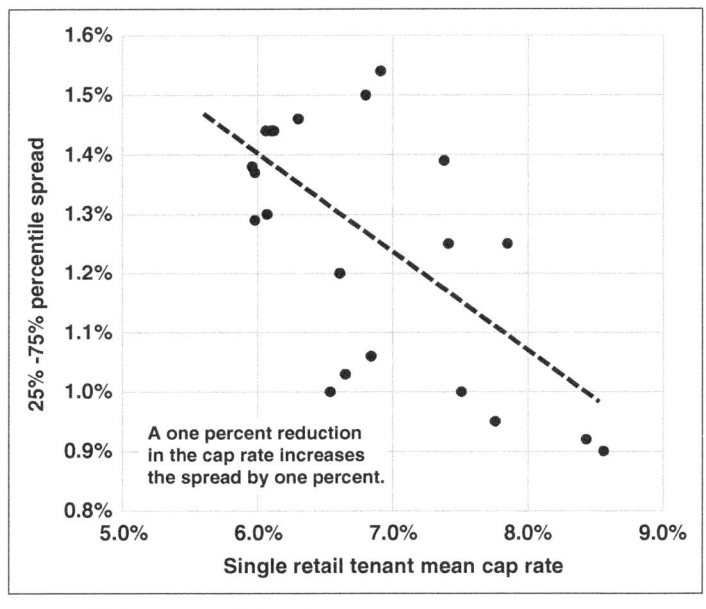

Source: ZCA using proprietary data

EXHIBIT 12.23 This figure illustrates spread narrowing as a function of cap rates.

Source: ZCA using proprietary data

The spread between the 25th and 75th percentile narrows as cap rates increase. The spread is the lowest when cap rates are highest. The overall pattern of cap rate behavior over time and across space provides important, albeit neglected, information which some investors can exploit successfully.

A Multivariate Analysis of Cap Rates Over Time and Space Using a Large Data Set

Exhibit 12.24 is a more comprehensive cross-sectional model that includes dummy variables for various property types, years from 2000 through 2021, and regions. With this model and its very large proprietary data set, an investor can estimate the true cap rate based on a number of observable attributes. The model includes regional and annual dummy variables.

Dummy variables, which act like switches that either take the value of zero or one. If I observe an apartment sale in the Northeast in 2020 located in the CBD but not in a gateway city, some of the variables would take the following values:

APARTMENT =	1	**CBD =**	1	2009 =	0	2018 =	0
INDUSTRIAL =	0	**GATEWAY =**	0	2010 =	0	2019 =	0
OFFICE =	0		2002 =	0	2011 =	0	**2020 =**	1
RETAIL =	0		2003 =	0	2012 =	0	2021 =	0
SINGLE =	0		2004 =	0	2013 =	0		
MIDATLANTIC =	0		2005 =	0	2014 =	0		
MIDWEST =	0		2006 =	0	2015 =	0		
NORTHEAST =	1		2007 =	0	2016 =	0		
SOUTHEAST =	0		2008 =	0	2017 =	0		

EXHIBIT 12.24 Results of cross-sectional cap rate regression over 23 years.

Dependent Variable : CAPRATE * 100				(12.2)
Method: Least Squares				
Date: 09/11/24 Time: 10:14				
Sample (adjusted): 1465926				
Included observations: 70107 after adjustments				
Variable	Coefficient	Standard Error	t-Statistic	Probability
Constant term	15.005	0.454	33.021	0.000
1 APARTMENT	−2.206	0.030	−73.637	0.000
2 INDUSTRIAL	−0.998	0.033	−30.165	0.000
3 OFFICE	−1.018	0.031	−32.591	0.000
4 RETAIL	−1.362	0.031	−44.309	0.000
5 SINGLE	−0.320	0.015	−21.816	0.000
6 AREA	−0.576	0.027	−21.579	0.000
7 MIDATLANTIC	0.900	0.021	41.864	0.000
8 MIDWEST	1.333	0.018	75.915	0.000
9 NORTHEAST	0.721	0.026	27.445	0.000
10 SOUTHEAST	0.809	0.016	52.152	0.000
11 SOUTHWEST	0.785	0.017	45.835	0.000
12 CBD*GATEWAY	−0.673	0.037	−18.211	0.000
13 GATEWAY	−0.391	0.021	−18.351	0.000
14 CBD	−0.579	0.026	−22.542	0.000
15 POPULATION	−0.072	0.006	−12.292	0.000
16 (POP/1000000)^2	0.005	0.000	10.736	0.000
17 YEARBLT	−0.002	0.000	−9.881	0.000
18 Y2002	−0.372	0.053	−7.008	0.000
19 Y2003	−0.953	0.051	−18.576	0.000
20 Y2004	−1.639	0.049	−33.554	0.000
21 Y2005	−2.318	0.045	−51.495	0.000
22 Y2006	−2.599	0.045	−58.310	0.000
23 Y2007	−2.705	0.045	−60.455	0.000
24 Y2008	−2.303	0.049	−47.338	0.000
25 Y2009	−1.479	0.055	−26.657	0.000
26 Y2010	−1.544	0.052	−29.708	0.000
27 Y2011	−1.900	0.049	−39.175	0.000
28 Y2012	−2.162	0.047	−46.173	0.000
29 Y2013	−2.389	0.047	−50.633	0.000
30 Y2014	−2.697	0.046	−58.674	0.000
31 Y2015	−2.898	0.045	−64.164	0.000
32 Y2016	−3.003	0.046	−65.952	0.000
33 Y2017	−3.019	0.046	−66.344	0.000
34 Y2018	−3.116	0.046	−67.739	0.000
35 Y2019	−3.176	0.046	−69.272	0.000
36 Y2020	−3.264	0.057	−56.773	0.000
37 Y2021	−3.442	0.061	−56.642	0.000
38 NORTHEAST*(COVID) [Note that COVID=Y2021 + Y2022]	0.160	0.080	2.000	0.046
39 MIDWEST*(COVID) [Note that COVID=Y2021+ Y2022]	−0.182	0.076	−2.404	0.016
40 SOUTHEAST*(COVID) [Note that COVID=Y2021+ Y2022]	−0.364	0.055	−6.569	0.000
41 SOUTHWEST*(COVID) [Note that COVID=Y2021+ Y2022]	−0.460	0.057	−8.068	0.000
R-squared	0.422	Mean dependent variable		6.547
Adjusted R-squared	0.421	Standard deviation dependent variable		1.677
Standard error of regression	1.276	Sum squared residual		114084
F-statistic	1245			
Prob(F-statistic)	0.000			

Source: ZCA using a confidential database

The model includes a multiplicative variable, the product of CBD and GATEWAY. This construction allows the sensitivity (derivative) of the cap rate with respect to CBD status to equal a constant term and the GATEWAY dummy. In Exhibit 12.24, I calculate the joint impact of the CBD and the GATEWAY dummies. If either variable is zero, the product term is zero.

In my apartment example, the cap rate impact of CBD without GATEWAY status is −0.581. GATEWAY without CBD is −0.072. The model explains 42% of the variation in cap rates and all of the coefficients are highly significant and have the right sign.

Is there a COVID-19 impact on cap rates? The multiplicative variables, NORTHEAST*COVID, MIDWEST*COVID, SOUTHEAST*COVID, SOUTHWEST*COVID, where COVID takes the value of one if the year is either 2020 or 2021, explain the impact of the COVID-19 years on cap rates. The incremental impact of the COVID-19 years by region is 0.160 (Northeast), −0.182 (Midwest), −0.364 (Southeast), and −0.460 Southwest. Whereas the incremental impact on the Northeast during these years was 0.160 in cap rate movement, the marginal impact on the Southwest was −0.460 relative to the WEST. Cap rates rose by 2.4% in the Northeast but fell 7.0% in the Southwest; hence, despite COVID-19, markets tightened in the Southwest relative to the West and the Northeast. The impact of COVID-19 on cap rates was not uniform. See Exhibit 12.25.

Exhibit 12.26 shows the value of the yearly dummy variables relative to 2001. The dummy variable for 2020 is about −3.5, which means that the *incremental* cap rate is −3.5. Exhibits 12.27 and 12.28 show the partial impacts on cap rates of property types relative to hotels and regions relative to the West.

Exhibits 12.29–12.31 are scatter graphs that illustrate the bivariate relationship of multifamily cap rates with other variables, including volatility. These bivariate relationships are consistent with more complex multiple regressions.

EXHIBIT 12.25 Impact of CBD (0 or 1) and GATEWAY (0 or 1) status.

Equation		No CBD	No Gateway	Gateway	
$\dfrac{\partial CAP}{\partial GATEWAY}$ = $-0.072 - 0.393 \cdot CBD$		−0.072	−0.465		(12.3)
$\dfrac{\partial CAP}{\partial CBD}$ = $-0.581 - 0.393 \cdot GATEWAY$			−0.581	−0.974	(12.4)

Source: ZCA

298 CHAPTER 12 Cap Rates and Hidden Information: Avoiding Traps with Caps

EXHIBIT 12.26 Cap rate adjustments by year relative to 2001.

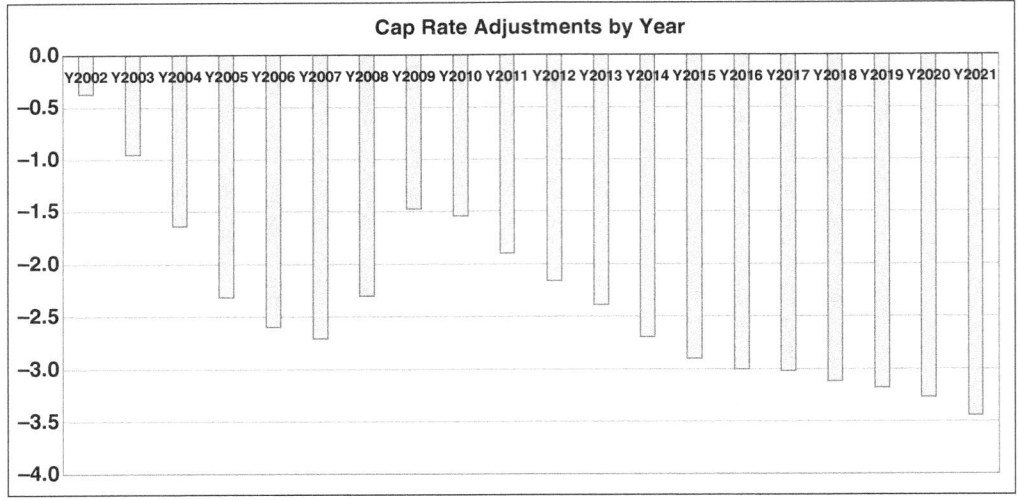

Source: ZCA

EXHIBIT 12.27 Impact of property types relative to hotels.

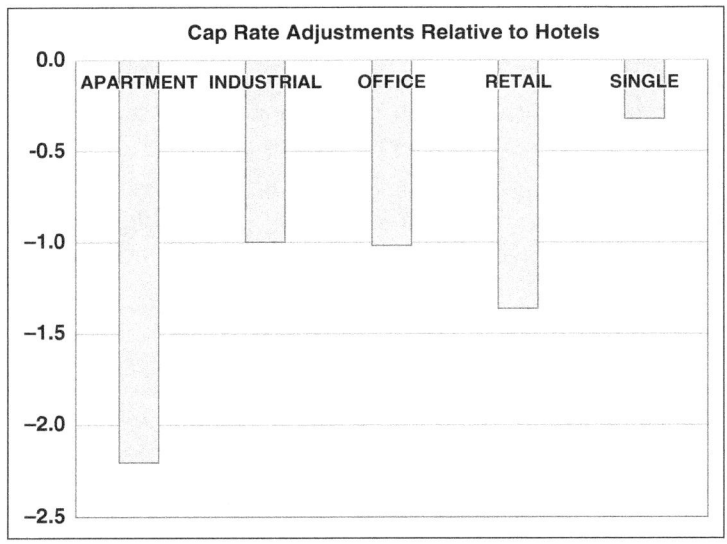

Source: ZCA

EXHIBIT 12.28 Impact of region relative to the West.

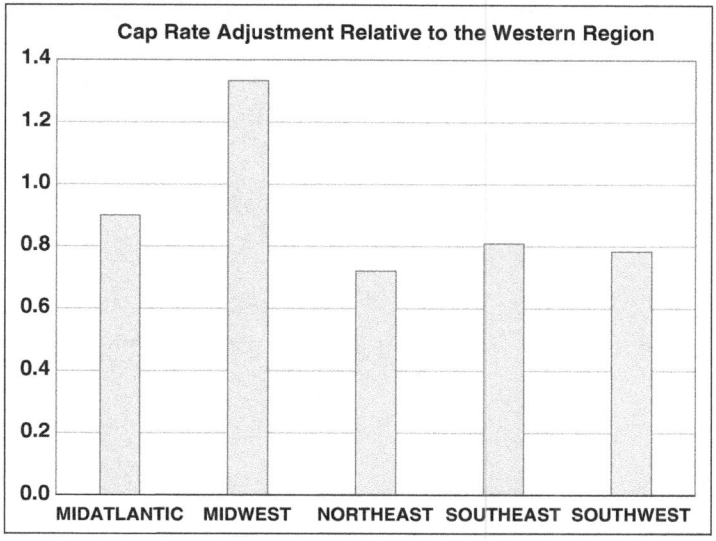

Source: ZCA

EXHIBIT 12.29 Cap rates are inversely related to MF rental growth.

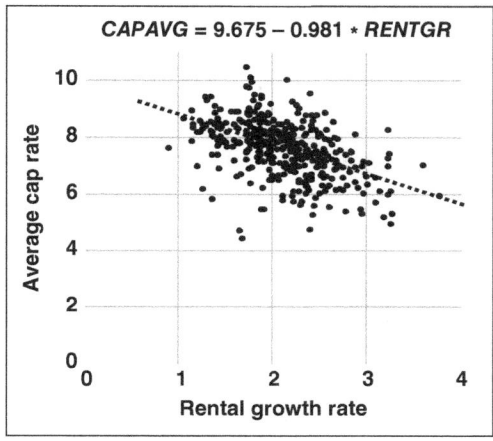

Source: ZCA using CoStar data

EXHIBIT 12.30 Rental growth volatility versus higher rental growth rates.

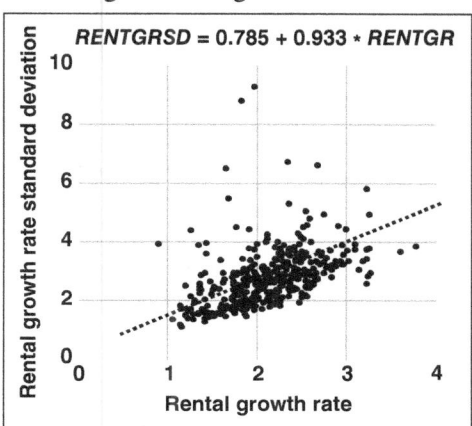

Source: ZCA using CoStar data

The higher is the rental growth rate, the lower is the cap rate. The estimated cap rate for zero rental growth is 9.7%. Rental growth rate volatility increases with the rental growth rate, so cities with more rapid rental growth are riskier. Cities with very low elasticities tend to have greater rental growth volatility. (See Exhibits 12.31–12.33.) Larger cities have lower cap rates and higher cap rates are associated with greater cap rate volatility.

EXHIBIT 12.31 The lower the supply elasticity, the greater is rent volatility.

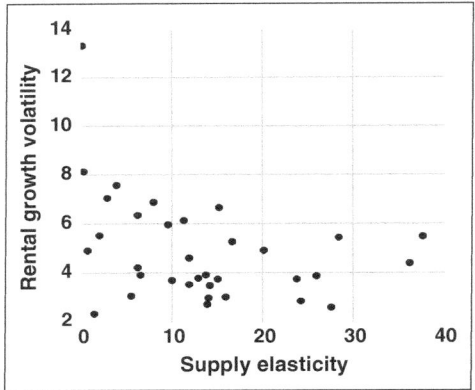

Source: ZCA using CoStar data

EXHIBIT 12.32 Simulated cap rate is negatively sloped relative to city size.

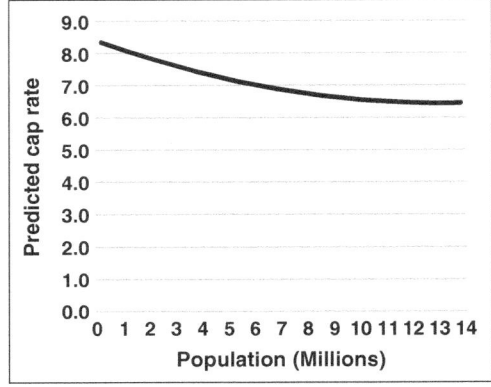

Source: ZCA simulation using CoStar data

EXHIBIT 12.33 Cap rate volatility is higher for cities with larger cap rates.

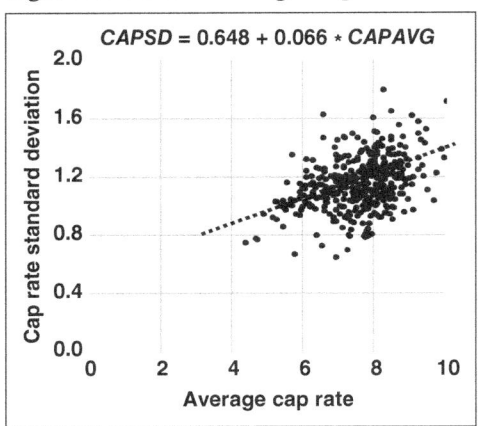

Source: ZCA simulation using CoStar data

Cap Rates, Property Fundamentals, and City Size: Office Buildings

I divide the US office inventory into four tiers. The top tier accounts for 25% of the office inventory. The next tiers account for 25–50% and 50–70% of the inventory, respectively. Lower tiers have more buildings than the top tier.

Cap rates for three inventory size tiers fluctuate over the cycle but the relative ranking of average cap rates is relatively stable. Such is not the case for rental growth rates, cap rate volatility, office rental volatility, and the office vacancy rate. Capital diffuses across all regions and MSAs in order to equate the supply of and demand for capital, which, in turn, equilibrates risk-adjusted returns.

Exhibit 12.34 shows little variation in the relative ranking of the cap rate across the three inventory tiers. By contrast, office rental growth rates are more volatile. Cap rate and rental volatilities are not constant, as shown in Exhibits 12.35, 12.36 and 12.37.

EXHIBIT 12.34 Office cap rate.

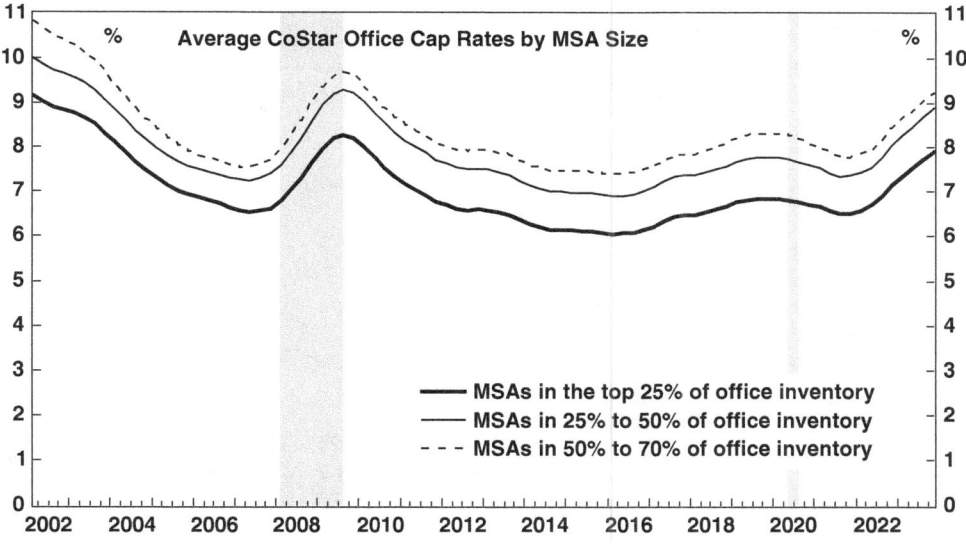

Source: ZCA using CoStar data

EXHIBIT 12.35 Office rental growth rate.

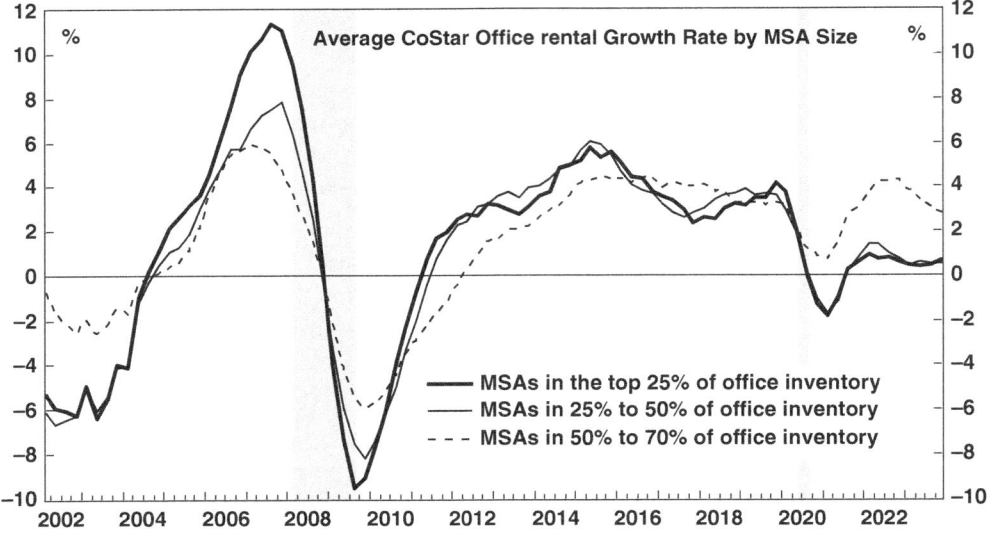

Source: ZCA using CoStar data

EXHIBIT 12.36 Office cap rate volatility.

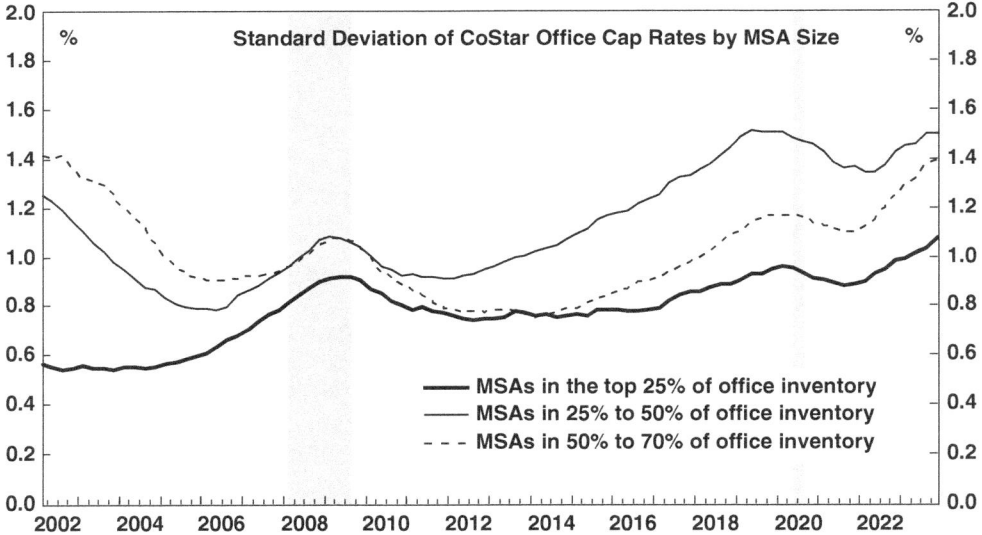

Source: ZCA using CoStar data

EXHIBIT 12.37 Office rental volatility.

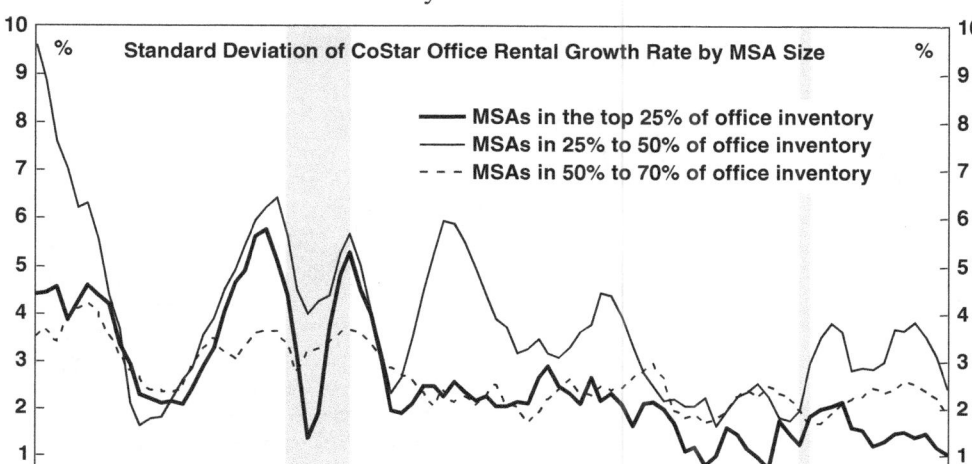

Source: ZCA using CoStar data

Institutions direct most of their investment capital to the ten largest MSAs, which drives down cap rates; other factors held constant, investment capital flows favor faster growing MSAs, which are generally not the largest MSAs. Cap rates are slightly lower and riskier in the faster growing MSAs. See Exhibits 12.38 and 12.39.

The volatility of total return and vacancy rate by MSA size varies over time, as shown in Exhibits 12.40 and 12.41. MSA cap rates tend to move together as shown in Exhibit 12.42. However, there is greater rental growth rate volatility with the larger MSAs. See Exhibit 12.43.

The appraisal-based cap rate is highly correlated with lagged cap rates; hence, cap rate volatility, unlike stock return volatility, is highly smoothed. As a result, unadjusted, cap rate volatility may not be the most appropriate measure of risk. See Exhibits 12.42–12.45. For selected MSAs office vacancy rates are much more volatile than total returns. This finding is consistent with the view that prices adjust more rapidly due to capital flows than do vacancy rates.

EXHIBIT 12.38 Office total return.

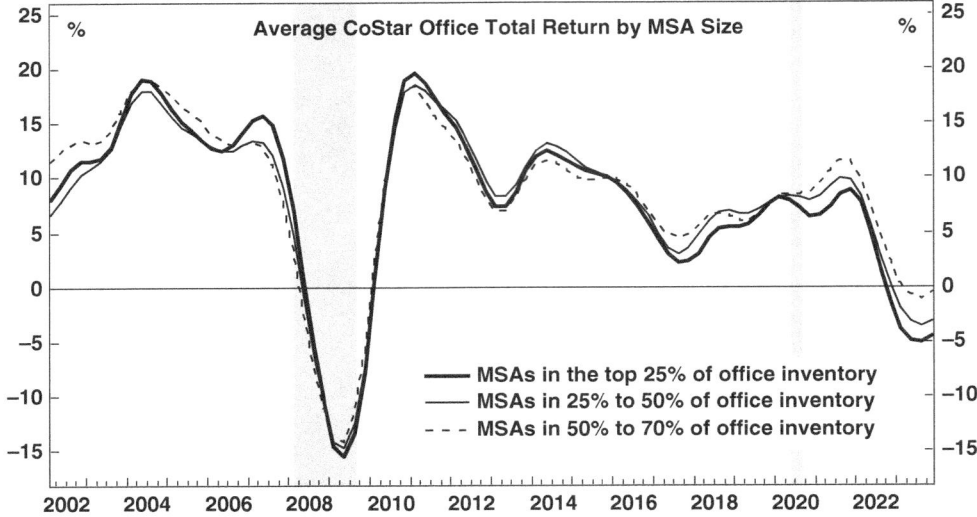

Source: ZCA using CoStar data

EXHIBIT 12.39 Office vacancy rate.

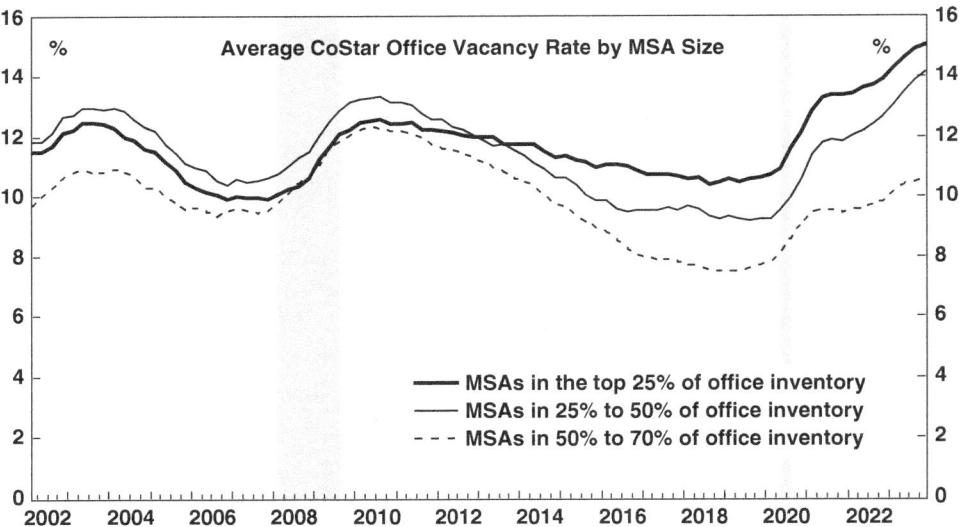

Source: ZCA using CoStar data

EXHIBIT 12.40 Office total returns standard deviation.

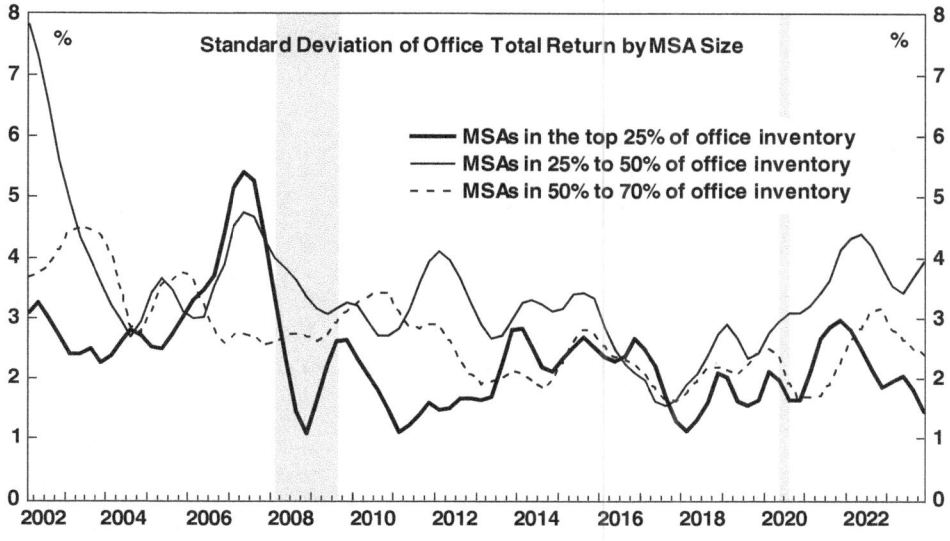

Source: ZCA using CoStar data

EXHIBIT 12.41 Office vacancy rate standard deviation.

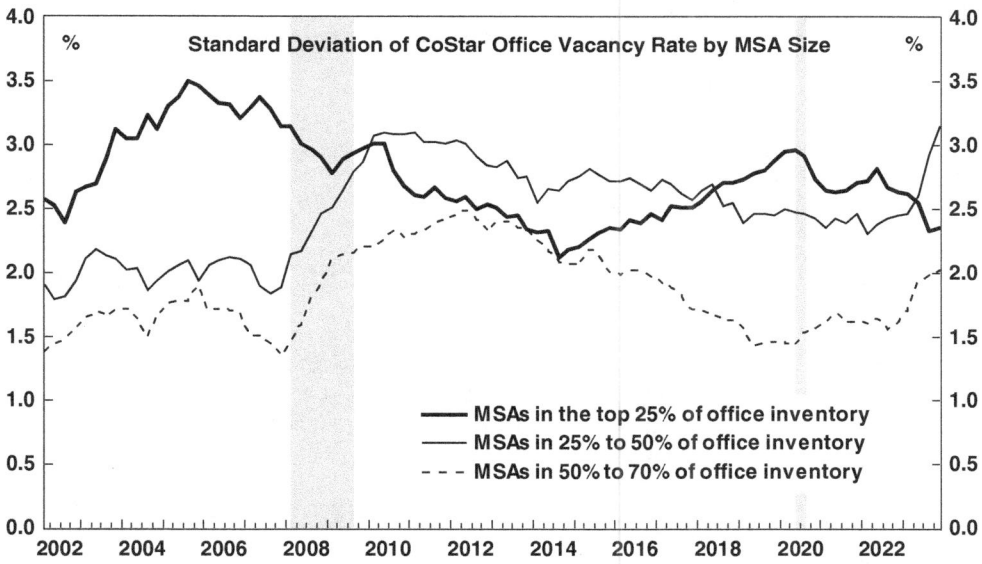

Source: ZCA using CoStar data

EXHIBIT 12.42 Office cap rates in MSAs in the 25%-tier.

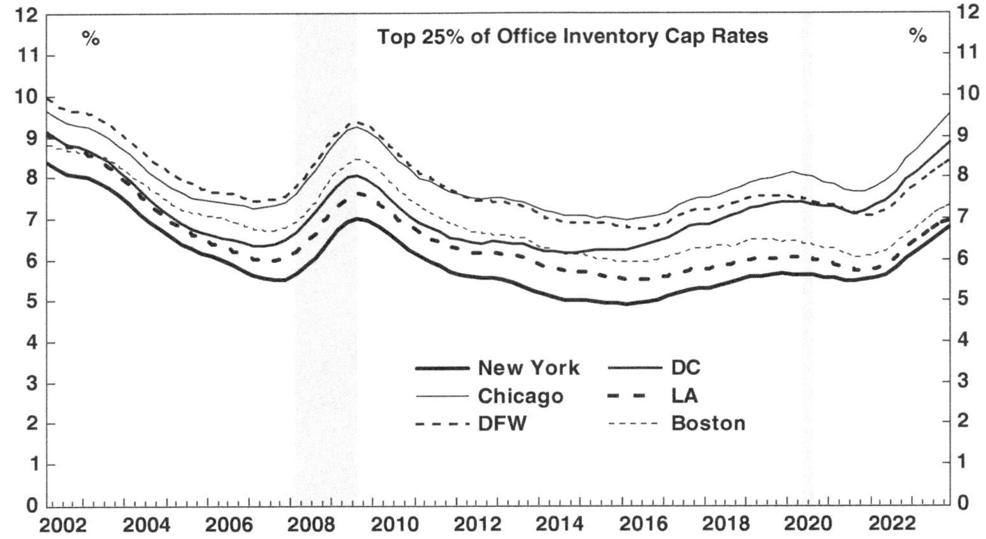

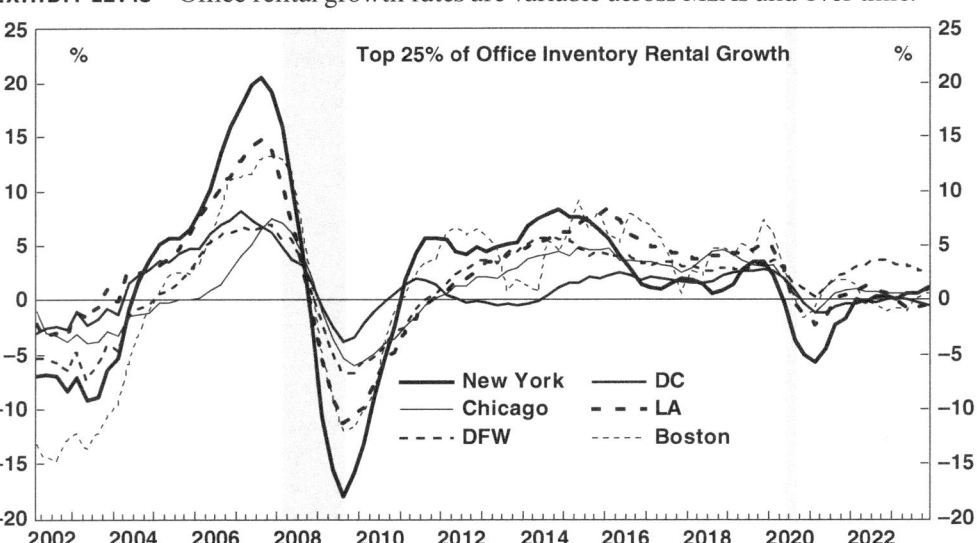

Source: ZCA using CoStar data

EXHIBIT 12.43 Office rental growth rates are variable across MSAs and over time.

Source: ZCA using CoStar data

Cap Rates, Property Fundamentals, and City Size: Office Buildings 307

EXHIBIT 12.44 Total returns for MSAs across the 25%-tier is highly variable.

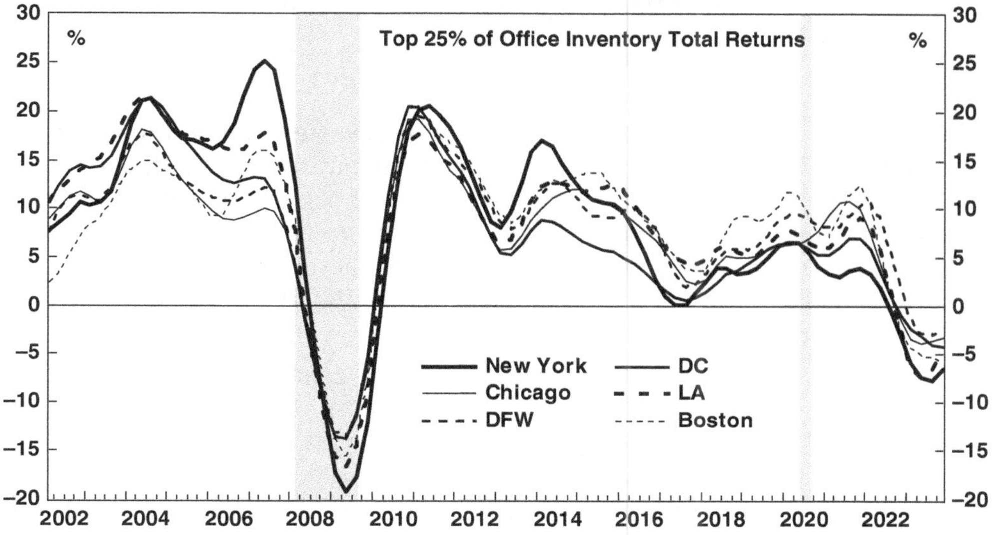

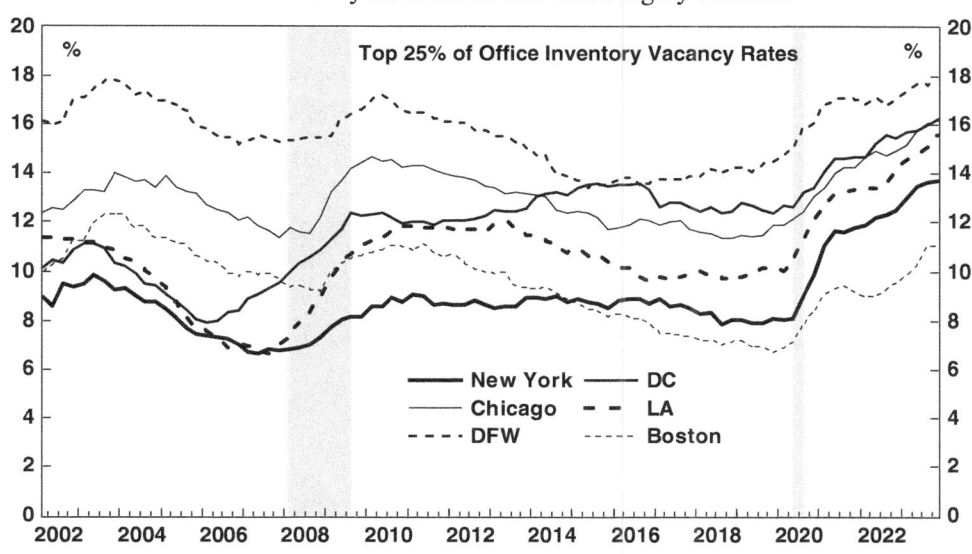

Source: ZCA using CoStar data

EXHIBIT 12.45 Office vacancy rates across MSAs are highly variable.

Source: ZCA using CoStar data

Cap Rates and Supply Elasticities:[2] The Case of Office

No one cap rate fits all cities; cities are varied in how they respond to economic shocks. Like carillon bells, they each have their own natural frequency, and, therefore, risk characteristics vary across all 393 MSAs. Shock any single MSA with a GFC-type downturn, it will react one way while the response of a another MSA, even one in close proximity, may be quite different. These differences reflect many factors, such as the nature of the economic base, regulatory factors, the ease with which development occurs, to name just a few.

What is elasticity and how does it affect cap rates? Elasticity is a measure of the responsiveness of the inventory to the rental rate. Most MSA supply and demand elasticities are inelastic. Exhibit 12.46 shows elastic demand and supply curves. If the supply curve is very inelastic, or even perfectly inelastic, most of the adjustment occurs through rental rate changes. Exhibit 12.47 shows the same rightward shift in the demand curve, but demand now is also highly inelastic, as it would be for New York. There is little change in the quantity of space demanded and more of the adjustment occurs through office rent. The lower is the supply elasticity, the greater is cap rate volatility. Greater volatility increases the value of embedded options,

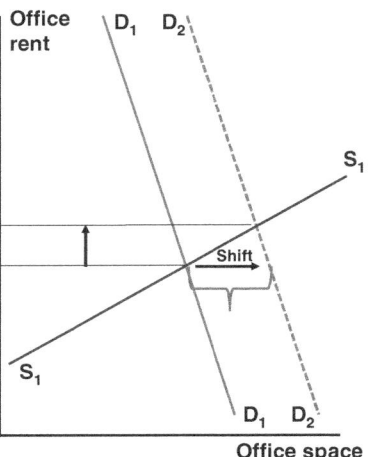

EXHIBIT 12.46 Effect of demand shift when supply is elastic.

Source: ZCA

EXHIBIT 12.47 Effect of demand shift when supply is inelastic.

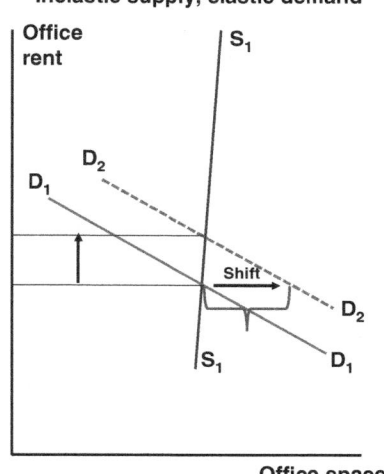
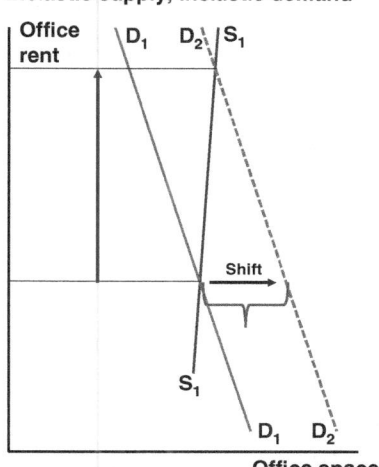

Source: ZCA

which favors the GP position in a leveraged deal with a waterfall. An important factor causing a low supply elasticity is the high durability of office buildings, urban density and physical complexity.

Office leases are complex, long-term contracts. Hence, landlords maintain vacant space in anticipation of achieving rents that exceed their reservation lease rate. The landlord, who does not want to prematurely lease the space at too low a rate, holds an option to lease, the value of which increases with market volatility. The greater the volatility, the greater is the likelihood of signing a tenant who will pay a higher rent. In high-growth MSAs with higher rental volatility and very inelastic supplies, landlords tend to hold space off the market for a longer time. In those MSAs, especially the faster growing MSAs, the precautionary or speculative demand for vacant space is higher.

In Equation (12.5), the supply elasticity coefficient has the right sign according to theory but the t-statistic indicates that the estimate is not statistically different from zero. Assuming we accept the coefficient as the best point estimate, then the higher is the elasticity, the higher is the cap rate, holding constant other variables such as rental growth, rental growth volatility, and inventory size. Of course,

310   CHAPTER 12   Cap Rates and Hidden Information: Avoiding Traps with Caps

this relationship could be swamped by other factors. Cap rates are lower if rental growth rates, rental growth rate volatility, and MSA size are greater.

$$CAPAPP_i = 9.358 + 1.327 * INVENTORY_i - 0.276 * RENTGR_i$$
$$(17.307)(-2.157) \qquad\qquad (-0.951)$$

$$- 0.199 * RENTSTDEV_i + 1.214 * SUPPLYELAST_i$$
$$(-3.130) \qquad\qquad\qquad (0.671) \qquad\qquad\qquad (12.5)$$

R-squared = 0.673
Adjusted R-squared = 0.616
Standard error of the regression = 0.601
Mean dependent variable = 7.861
F-statistic = 11.833
Probability (F-statistic) = 0.000
Durbin Watson statistic = 2.549

Equation (12.6) is an econometric model of the office cap rate volatility as a function of the supply elasticity, the rental growth rate, and rental growth rate volatility. The higher is the supply elasticity, the lower is cap rate volatility. The supply elasticities of MSAs such as San Francisco and New York are close to zero, which implies that cap rate volatility is higher for these kinds of cities, as confirmed by Equation (12.6).

$$CAPAPPVOLATILITY_i = 1.135 - 0.766 * SUPPLYELAST_i$$
$$(24.046)(-2.209) \qquad\qquad\qquad (12.6)$$

R-squared = 0.158
Adjusted R-squared = 0.126
Standard error of the regression = 0.001
Mean dependent variable = 1.050
F-statistic = 4.879
Probability (F-statistic) = 0.036

MSAs such as New York and San Francisco have near-zero supply elasticities, which implies a volatility of 5.9%. By comparison, Houston's elasticity is about 0.363, which is still inelastic, implying average rental volatility of 1.6%. The investor can reduce rental growth risk through the careful choice of MSA. When bidding, investors should take into consideration cap rate volatility. (See Chapter 19, which presents a Monte Carlo simulation of the winner's curse.)

When NOI is growing most rapidly, cap rate volatility is highest. Inventory size does not explain NOI volatility, but average rental growth does. In those markets where rental growth is highest, NOI volatility is elevated.

Markets with higher rental growth and greater population growth exhibit greater risk. MSAs with highly inelastic supply and smaller movements in demand can generate outsized swings in market rental growth and, to a lesser extent, NOI growth and NOI volatility. Growth is not necessarily an unalloyed good.

Conclusions and Investment Implications

- Even though cap rates play a prominent role in real estate, cap rates are still a mystery to many and misused by most.
- Expected exit cap rates are volatile and this expected volatility increases with the holding period of a value-add or opportunistic deal. (See Chapter 15.)
- What is the difference between a cap rate and total return? Cap rates are much less volatile than total returns because the cap rate's numerator and denominator are positively correlated.
- Since the GFC, NCREIF transactions-based cap rates have exceeded appraisal-based cap rates. Both exhibit serial correlation, or smoothing, which requires a statistical correction for asset allocation and multi-asset performance comparison purposes.[3]
- The greater is the volatility of the office inventory or of office worker employment growth, the lower is the cap rate. Faster growing MSAs exhibit greater cap rate volatility, which is inversely related to cap rate levels.
- The higher is the inventory's supply elasticity with respect to construction price—a measure of the ease of adding new space to the existing MSA inventory—the greater is the cap rate. San Francisco and New York, whose elasticities are near zero, have low and riskier cap rates.
- Changes in capital availability, credit spreads, and expected NOI growth (supply–demand imbalances) mask the true relationship between interest rates and cap rates.

- Cap rates are lower for better quality buildings even though the rental growth and vacancy rates of better buildings are more volatile.
- Institutional investors have two biases: an edifice complex and gateway illusion. Cap rates are higher in the non-gateway cities even though the total returns show little variation across MSAs by size tiers.
- MSAs' responses to shocks vary according to MSA characteristics. Some MSAs adjust to shocks through the vacancy rate while others adjust primarily through rental rates.
- Landlords have a speculative or buffer demand for vacant space. The value of this call option increases with market volatility and contributes to sticky vacancy rates.
- The greater is the elasticity, the larger is the cap rate. Cap rates are lower if rental growth rates, rental growth rate volatility, and MSA size are greater. Larger and higher growth MSAs have greater rental volatility.

Q&A: Interview with Steve Rosenberg, Founder and CEO, Greystone

The Role of Creative Improvisation

Steve, tell us about your career odyssey.

I was a terrible student who lacked much self-esteem. However, I eventually got on the right track; one small success led to a bigger success.

My father passed when I was 18 and we were destitute. I did not know what to do. Fortunately, University of Pennsylvania Dental School admitted me and while in dental school, I discovered that I could simultaneously attend Wharton and earn an MBA at no additional cost. Failure was not an option; I had nothing to fall back on. I never took life too seriously but I was always driven and open to opportunity. Out of graduate school with two graduate degrees from Penn, I explored a Wall Street career but I could only get one interview out of 300 attempts.

In 1988 I founded Greystone; we first invested in defaulted HUD insured loans. A little-known regulation said that, if a loan is in default for 90 days, I had the unilateral right as loan servicer to pay off the investor even though the loan was locked out. I obtained a line of credit from a Japanese bank without putting up any equity and created a huge business. That was just the beginning.

Today, Greystone is a private commercial real estate finance and investment company with unmatched experience in debt, equity, investment sales and loan servicing solutions. Our firm is the number-one overall HUD multifamily and healthcare lender by firm commitments, and a top 10 Fannie Mae and Freddie Mac multifamily real estate lender.

These days we want to be at the frontier. Greystone does not hire anyone without an AI mindset and the instinct to question everything. For example, we started a not-for-profit to invest in affordable properties—we already own 15,000 rented apartment units—and are very focused on rent stabilized and regulated housing.

(continued)

(continued)

What advice would you give young professionals?

I discovered that there is lots of opportunity where people do not look; there is gold in the garbage. We ask, how is the world thinking about something? Is that the only way to think about it? My aspiration was creating solutions or products that no one had created and knowing how to explain it simply.

CHAPTER 13

Liquidity: Turnover, MSA Liquidity, and Investment Horizon

Preliminaries

Benjamin Franklin once said, "When the well is dry, we know the worth of water." Like air or other human cravings, unless it is absent, we do not give it any thought. Liquidity (and diversification) are often absent, when needed the most.

Liquidity is the ability to sell or buy large quantities of an asset promptly with little, if any, price impact. Trading an illiquid asset is difficult, costly and time consuming. Due to commonality across seemingly unrelated capital market sectors, property types, and MSAs, liquidity crises spread and even spiral.

Liquidity pressures affect performance volatility. During liquidity crises, a flight to quality occurs wherein the most transparent and least complex properties transact with lower price impact. The "best" need not be photogenic trophy properties, however.

The greater are transactions costs and short-term volatility, the longer is the ideal holding period since investors with long duration liabilities have a comparative advantage in bearing illiquidity risk.

The Many Faces of Liquidity[1]

Two types of liquidity bear consideration:

- Funding and market (or trading) liquidity. Funding liquidity typically refers to the liability side of the balance sheet: the ease with which investors can obtain funding. When liquidity is tight, funding constraints are binding and lenders resort to non-price rationing. The marginal value of funds rises significantly.
- Market or trading liquidity. Traders—sellers and buyers—provide market liquidity. Their funding requirements—LTV and other terms—depend on the asset's liquidity. Funding and market liquidity are mutually reinforcing. Positive feedback can lead to liquidity spirals or cascades.

Flight to quality, greater volatility, and sudden stops or transaction crashes are characteristics of a liquidity crisis. These events spill across sectors, MSAs, and nations. The risk premium should reflect illiquidity since property is an illiquid asset.

Liquidity has the following characteristics:

- Low cost of trading in small amounts. Round trip costs include commissions, exchange fees, bid-ask spreads, market impact costs, and taxes. Investing in an office building involves a round-trip fee of 3% on the sale- and 2% on the buy-side, or 5%. By comparison, round trip costs for stocks need not be much greater than 1%.
- Depth or the capacity to sell or buy without causing a price impact.
- Resilience or the speed at which the marginal price impact increases as trading increases.
- Breadth or the overall size of a traded deal.
- Immediacy, the cost (discount or premium) to be applied when selling or buying quickly.

The demand and supply of liquidity are shown in bold lines in Exhibit 13.1. If there were no illiquidity, the demand and supply curves would be horizontal—see dotted lines. Price would be constant irrespective of the size or frequency of the trade. There would be no bid-ask spread.

The buyer must buy at the ask price, which is above the fundamental price for a perfectly liquid asset. The seller must accept a discount. The sum of the premium and discount is the bid-ask spread. Usually when the buyer elects to acquire or sell, there is little price impact, but in real estate, as in the case of most other private

EXHIBIT 13.1 The elements of liquidity: Tightness (or spread), depth, resilience, breadth.[2]

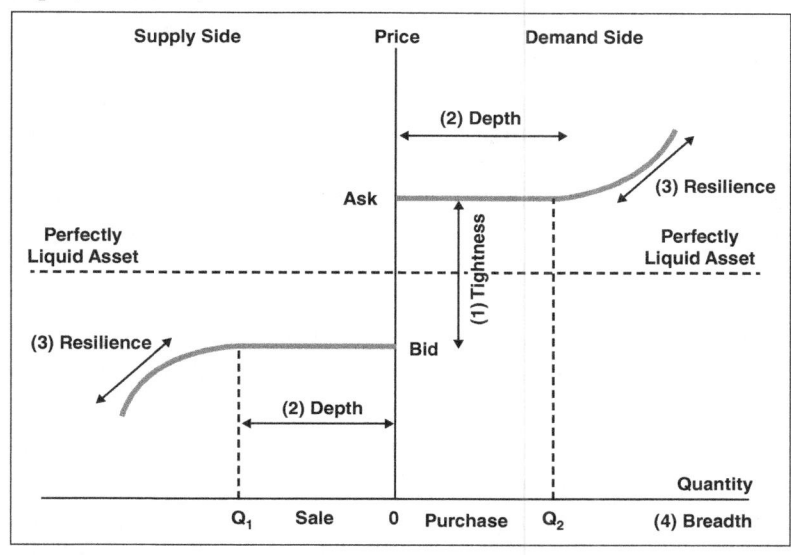

Source: Adapted from Ametefe, Devaney, and Marcato

asset classes, transactions, especially the larger ones, can move price, especially in certain submarkets.

If the buyer decides to increase the size of the purchase to include a portfolio of properties located in close proximity, the initial marginal impact is zero and the length of the initial horizontal section of the demand curve defines the market depth; the longer is the line, the deeper is the market. However, if the buyer's actions stimulate buyers' frenzy, then the marginal impact of trading increases; the rate of increase is a measure of market resilience. The same logic applies to the seller.

Liquid markets are information-rich. Properties with the same cash flows should have nearly identical valuations if there are no transaction fees or hidden information (asymmetry), but markets are imperfect and these imperfections lead to different prices for similar assets.

Some of these market imperfections include the following:

- The absence of a secondary market. Agents who wish to enter the market incur a cost so they are only willing to invest if they receive a liquidity premium. As market liquidity declines, sellers who must transact are more likely to suffer losses.

- Transactions costs. Transaction costs vary by asset. The higher the transactions cost, the lower is the price relative to equilibrium in a perfect market. Buyers with long investment horizons, such as pension funds and insurance companies, have a comparative advantage in bearing illiquidity.
- Asymmetric information. Asymmetric information occurs when buyers and sellers do not share the same information set. The liquidity premium reflects this asymmetry. During the GFC, counterparties often could not judge solvency of other agents. Liquidity premiums rose substantially, and in some cases, parties withdrew from the market. Spillover effects, cascades, and liquidity spirals affected all property types and MSAs. These effects were extreme, widespread, and destructive. Owners struggled to deleverage, a painful process.
- Imperfect competition. Not all players have the same market impact. Information flows to some players faster than it does to others, which confers market power.
- Hidden information and funding constraints. The more asymmetric is information, the less liquid is the market.
- Credit rationing is more severe in the absence of liquidity: (a) Among prospective borrowers who appear to be identical, some receive a loan and others do not, and the rejected applicants would not receive a loan even if they offered to pay a much higher interest rate; or (b) there are identifiable borrowers who, with a given supply of credit, are unable to obtain loans at any interest rate, even though with a larger supply of credit, they would. At the rationed interest rate, demand exceeds supply so banks use non-price rationing.
- Search costs. Real estate markets are fragmented and decentralized. Traditionally information remains Balkanized, but large data vendors, such as NCREIF and CoStar, promote information transparency and capital immediacy.
- Buyers arrive sequentially. Linking buyers and sellers entails costly search, which is a characteristic of real estate, primarily property and even mortgages, but less so with publicly traded REITs or senior CMBS bonds. Sellers must decide whether to transact or wait for the arrival of another buyer. The greater is the volatility of offers, the greater is the likelihood that a better offer will arrive. Hence, the option to wait, a call option, has greater value in liquid markets. (See Chapter 20.)
- Unreliable returns. Measured illiquid asset returns are typically too high and the risks are too low due to infrequent sampling (transactions volume is low), survivorship bias (not the full performance universe due to failed investments or manager reluctance to submit performance), and selection bias (observed in markets in which returns and transaction volume are high).

These characteristics affect liquidity, which, in turn, affect total returns and volatility, especially in thin markets.

Liquidity Measures

The most prevalent liquidity measures include the following:

- Transactions costs. A million-square-foot A-quality office property with AAA-rated tenants and located on Park Avenue would incur lower transactions costs as a percentage of value than a 20,000-square-foot building consigned to the suburbs in Biloxi. However, the highest quality NYC office building had no buyers for months following the Lehman bankruptcy on September 15, 2008.
- Volume measures. Volume measures are useful in assessing the breadth and depth of the market. I introduce an absolute property transactions measure as well as transactions as a percent of the space inventory and show that these metrics are good, predictive liquidity measures that are highly correlated with lagged total returns, cap rates, and prices. Turnover is negatively correlated with transactions costs. When transactions are low, uncertainty increases, which pushes some agents off to the side of the market. The higher is the turnover, the greater is the liquidity. Notably, stocks have a higher turnover than property.
- Size of transaction. Liquidity should increase when there are many bids and lots of counterparties from which to choose. I have collected the actual bids for properties and observed that the spread between the winning bid and the second bid always increases during hot markets and contracts when markets declined.
- Serial correlation. The greater is the serial correlation (or autocorrelation) of returns or cap rates, the less liquid is the asset. At the market level, higher serial correlation implies lower market liquidity.
- Other measures include price impact and time on the market. Illiquidity is important when buying or selling opaque assets, such as complicated open-end opportunity funds or hedge funds.

Total Returns Lead Liquidity

Just as funding and market liquidity are interdependent, there is clearly two-way causality between total returns and office liquidity. Returns lead liquidity by about two quarters, which is about the time required to sell a building under normal circumstances. Exhibit 13.2 shows total returns and liquidity dipping during the GFC with returns taking the lead, which is confirmed by Equation (13.1).

During COVID-19 returns were not as volatile as was liquidity. Many office building owners were reluctant to sell given the uncertainty surrounding COVID-19

EXHIBIT 13.2 Total office returns (quarterly) lead office liquidity.

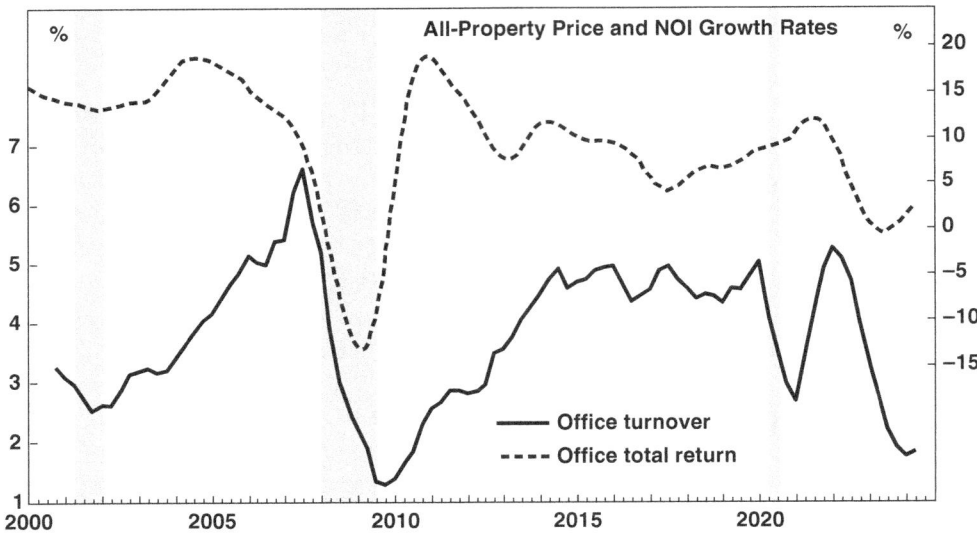

Source: ZCA using CoStar data

and WFH, so lesser properties were withheld from the market, and the decline in total returns did not fully reveal the latent deterioration in the value of the entire unsold inventory.

Investors require a greater liquidity premium. Illiquid markets are riskier and required returns should be less in highly liquid markets. This is true at the level of the individual asset, but it may not be always true at the macro level if markets are in extreme disequilibrium. Equation (13.1) shows that 10% increase in total return lagged two quarters is associated with a 0.7% increase in liquidity or turnover.

$$TURNOVER_t = 2.885 + 0.070 * TR_{t-2} + 0.844 * AR(1) + 0.109 * SIGMASQ$$
$$(4.060) \quad (4.023) \quad\quad (24.605) \quad\quad (6.914) \quad\quad\quad (13.1)$$

R-squared = 0.923

Adjusted R-squared = 0.918

Standard error of the regression = 0.337

Mean dependent variable = 3.752

F-statistic = 353.709

Probability (F-statistic) = 0.000

Durbin Watson statistic = 0.858

EXHIBIT 13.3 The price per square foot of office property descended faster than CoStar total returns.

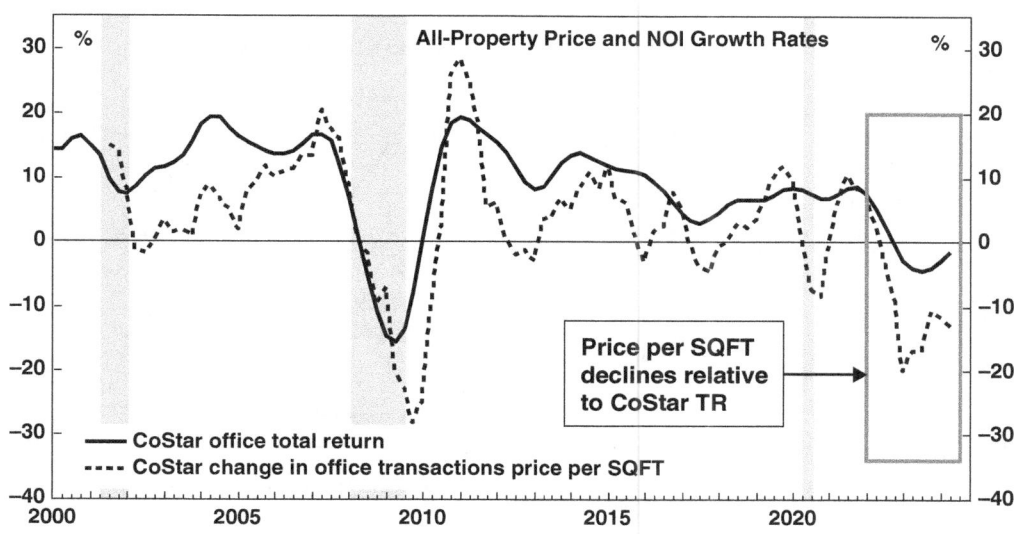

Source: ZCA using CoStar data

Exhibit 13.3 shows CoStar total office returns and the change in the transactions price of office buildings. Note that after COVID-19, the price per square foot and CoStar's total return metric diverged. Perhaps appraisers or transactors in the CoStar universe, unlike NCREIF contributors, were slower to write down properties.

Exhibit 13.4 compares the NCREIF and CoStar total returns. Institutional office properties, as measured by the NCREIF Index, performed worse than CoStar properties. Was this due to something inherent in institutionally owned properties or was this a reporting fluke reflective of two databases with different characteristics and methodologies? I believe it to be the latter.

Exhibit 13.5 shows the tight post-COVID-19 correlation of NCREIF total return and change in the CoStar price per square foot.

EXHIBIT 13.4 NCREIF data indicate that institutional investors marked their properties down more than did many contributors to CoStar.

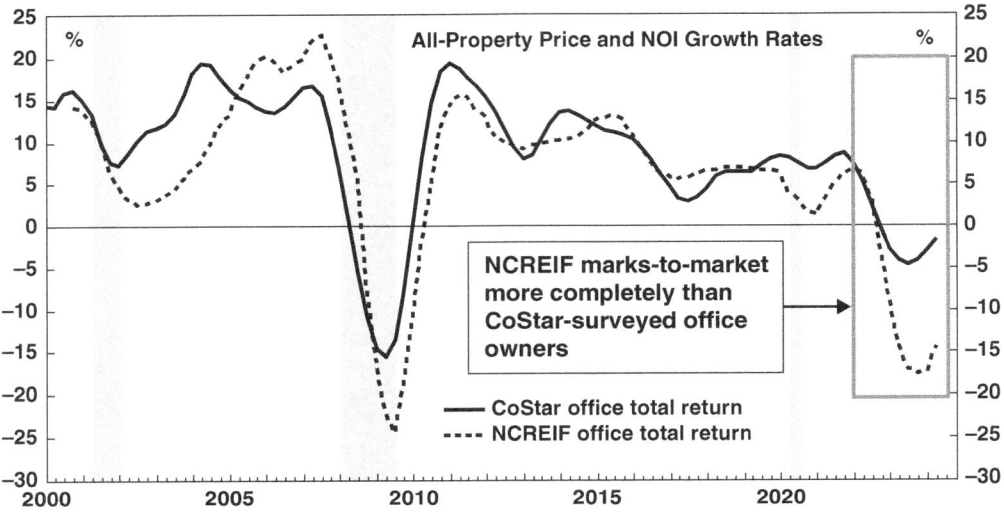

Source: ZCA using CoStar data

EXHIBIT 13.5 NCREIF total returns and the COVID-19 transactions change in price per square foot are highly correlated.

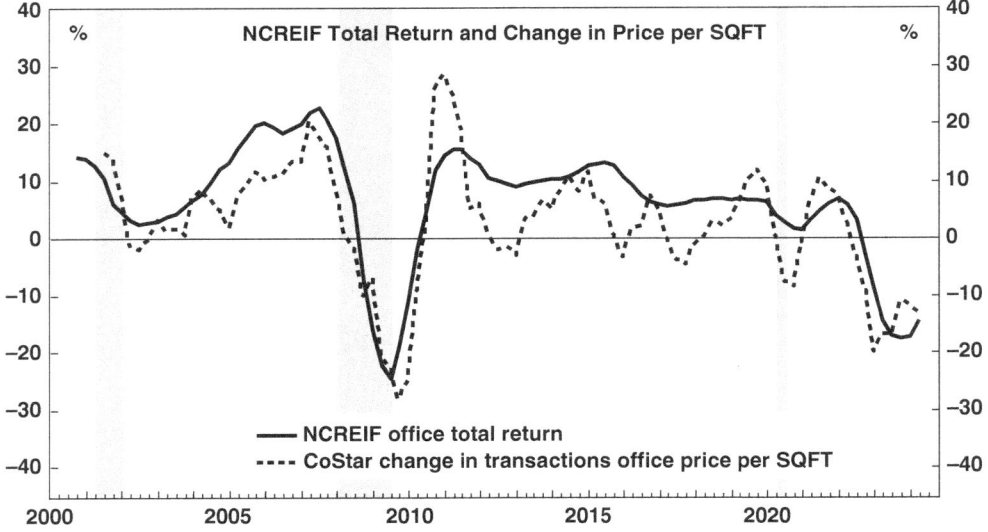

Source: ZCA using CoStar data

Office Liquidity: A Turnover Approach

The turnover measure is the annualized sale of office buildings expressed in square feet divided by the office inventory. While the inventory, net minor demolitions, is always increasing due to new construction, the greatest source of volatility is sales.

Liquidity varies significantly across MSAs. During extreme downturns, liquidity across all MSAs approaches zero and the correlation of liquidities across MSAs approaches one. Essentially there is no diversification benefit, either for liquidity or total returns, when it is needed the most.

Predicting MSA liquidity based on prior liquidity is challenging because the ranking of MSAs by liquidity, much like the performance of money managers, is not stable over time. See Exhibit 13.6.

Exhibit 13.7 extracts descriptive statistics from Exhibit 13.6. For each quarter I construct a histogram or turnover distribution across all MSAs. For each quarter, I derive the 25th and the 75th percentiles. Note that the maximum liquidity is much more volatile than the 75th percentile. The gap between the 25th and 75th percentiles is the narrowest during downturns, which is consistent with Exhibit 13.6.

Total returns across MSAs follow a similar pattern (see Exhibit 13.8). The return dispersion is typically wide, as shown in Exhibit 13.8. The return correlation across MSAs increases during downturns, or phase locks, thus vitiating the putative benefits of geographic diversification when they are needed the most.

EXHIBIT 13.6 Office property market liquidity (or turnover) is variable over the business cycle and across cities; liquidity drained from the system during the GFC and recently.

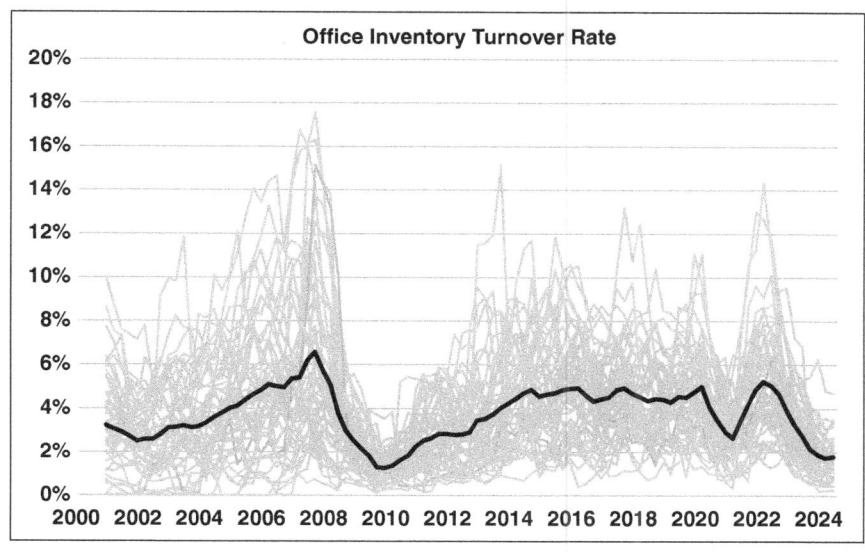

Source: ZCA using CoStar data

324 CHAPTER 13 Liquidity: Turnover, MSA Liquidity, and Investment Horizon

EXHIBIT 13.7 Average, min-max and percentile of office property liquidity cycles.

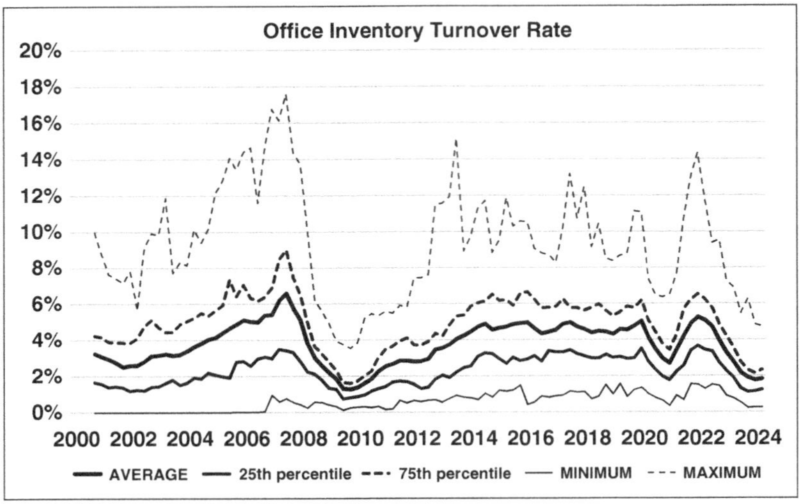

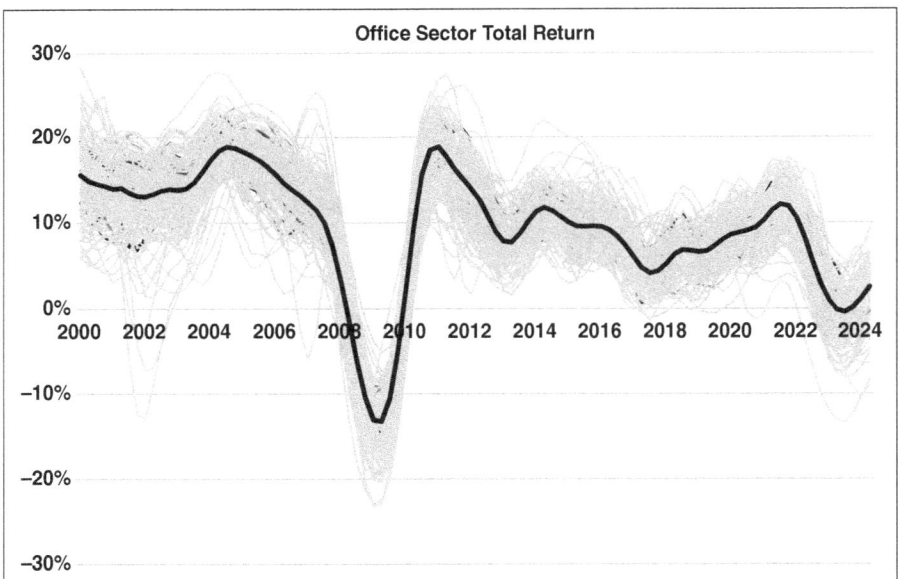

Source: ZCA using CoStar data

EXHIBIT 13.8 Total office returns over 390 MSAs.

Source: ZCA using CoStar data

The return correlation across MSAs increases during downturns (see Exhibits 13.9 and 13.10). MSA liquidity and liquidity risk are positively correlated. The cap rate is inversely correlated with market liquidity: The greater the liquidity, the lower is the cap rate. (See Exhibit 13.10.)

Liquidity increases with higher vacancy rates. Growing cities are those with a natural vacancy rate (NVR), which is the rate at which the rental growth rate is neither rising nor falling. (See Chapter 8.) The NVR varies across MSAs.

An NVR of 7% might indicate oversupply in some MSAs but undersupply in others. In growing cities, there is a greater precautionary demand for vacancies by landlords who are exercising their option to wait and not accept the first eager tenant. This embedded optionality in markets, especially as it pertains to both new construction and leasing, is very important in MSA performance and liquidity.

Exhibit 13.11 indicates that as the vacancy rate rises, so does MSA liquidity, volatility, and the option value of waiting to transact. Exhibit 13.12 shows that MSA liquidity increases with rental growth variation across MSAs.

EXHIBIT 13.9 A 1% increase in MSA liquidity is associated with a 0.57% increase in volatility.

EXHIBIT 13.10 MSA office cap rates are inversely related to liquidity; the greater is the liquidity, the lower is the cap rate.

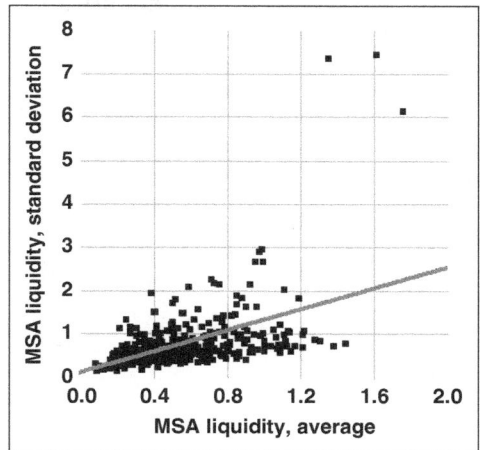

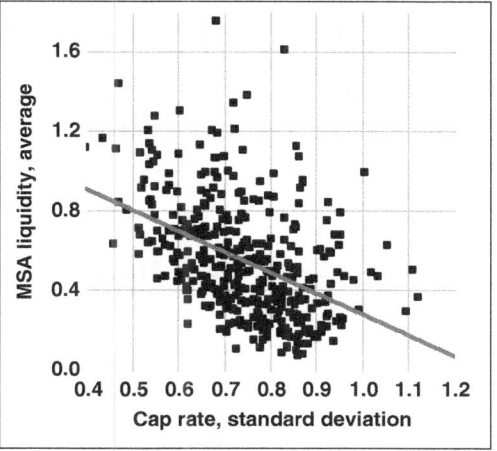

Source: ZCA using CoStar data

Source: ZCA using CoStar data

EXHIBIT 13.11 MSA office liquidity increases with a higher average vacancy rate.

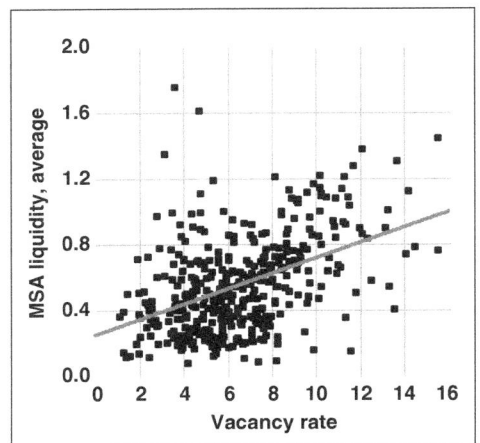

Source: ZCA using CoStar data

EXHIBIT 13.12 With greater rental growth volatility comes greater MSA office liquidity.

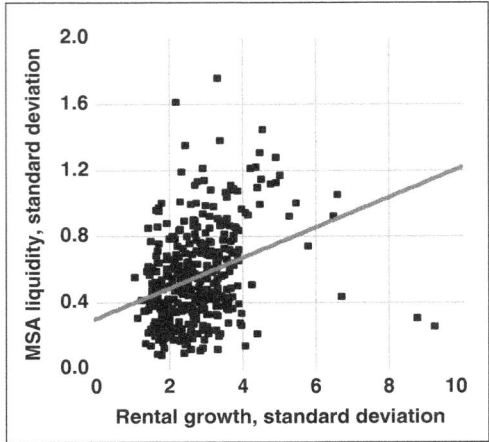

Source: ZCA using CoStar data

Equation (13.2) predicts liquidity across 390 MSAs. For a cross-section model, the explanatory power is excellent—71%. All of the coefficients are significantly different from zero and have signs consistent with theory.

$$TURNOVER_i = 0.336 + 0.371 * INVENTORY_i + 0.232 * TURNOVERSD_i$$
$$(3.791)\ \ (3.201)\ (19.801)$$

$$-0.699 * CAPSD_i + 0.249 * NOIGR_i$$
$$(-9.809)\ \ \ \ \ \ \ \ \ \ \ \ \ \ (3.085)$$

$$+0.143 * NOIGRSD_i - 4.652 * VACSD_i$$
$$(3.590)\ \ \ \ \ \ \ \ \ \ \ \ \ \ \ (-4.844)$$

$$+4.424 * VAC_i + 0.029 * RENTGR_i \tag{13.2}$$
$$(11.614)\ \ \ \ \ \ \ \ \ (3.168)$$

R-squared = 0.706

Adjusted R-squared = 0.700

Standard error of the regression = 0.158

Mean dependent variable = 0.550

F-statistic = 114.367

Probability (F-statistic) = 0.000

The model indicates that greater liquidity is positively related to an increase in the city office inventory, the volatility of liquidity, NOI growth, the volatility of NOI, the vacancy rate, and the volatility of rental growth. Negatively associated with liquidity are increases in the volatilities of cap rates (CAPSD) and the vacancy rate (VACSD). Volatility or risk play important roles in affecting liquidity. Liquidity increases with higher liquidity variability across MSAs. Since these explanatory factors are not perfectly correlated, changing rates can affect the relative rankings of MSA with respect to liquidity.

The Small MSA Liquidity Myth: Are Smaller MSAs Less Liquid?

Small MSAs are not materially less liquid; some smaller MSAs may be *more* liquid! Larger MSAs are only slightly more liquid than smaller MSAs and if we exclude New York, which is an outlier, then there is no MSA size effect, as shown in Exhibit 13.13. Some investors may prefer larger MSAs because the larger cities have bigger buildings that can absorb larger amounts of capital more quickly. While the basis for that preference is likely true, what is not true is that smaller MSAs are materially less liquid and, by implication, off limits to larger, sophisticated institutional investors.

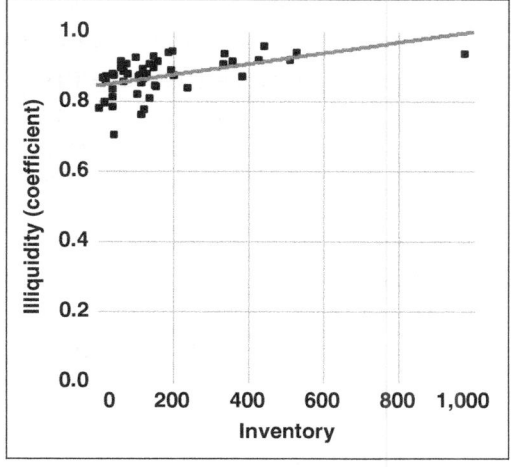

EXHIBIT 13.13 Liquidity increases with MSA size but the increase is not significant; there is no significant small-MSA liquidity issue.

Source: ZCA using CoStar data

While there may be some small increase in liquidity by MSA size, the increase does not justify investors' redlining smaller cities, which has been their traditional practice. Why do smaller MSAs offer similar liquidity? The reason is that building sizes are smaller in less populated MSAs. They are not only less lumpy but, as a group, they are scaled to the size of their respective MSAs.

Equation (13.3) is an econometric model of the relationship between MSA size and average office building size; the findings are consistent with casual empiricism. The greater is the office inventory, or MSA population, the larger is the average office building size. A 10% increase in inventory is associated with a 2.7% increase in average building size.

$$LOG(BUILDINGSIZE_t) = 0.305 + 0.268 * LOG(INVENTORY_t)$$
$$(2.106)\ (17.826) \tag{13.3}$$

R-squared = 0.450

Adjusted R-squared = 0.449

Standard error of the regression = 0.442

Mean dependent variable = 2.853

F-statistic = 317.762

Probability (F-statistic) = 0.000

Larger buildings may grace the skylines of our largest cities, but as we show elsewhere, larger buildings do not account for most of the area or the number of buildings. Whatever the size of the MSA, there are plenty of properly scaled buildings to suit just about every investor and size preference. There is virtually no difference in the liquidity of larger and smaller MSAs. See Exhibits 13.13 and 13.14.

Calculating serial correlation, a measure of illiquidity. Serial correlation, whether it is serial correlation of returns or cap rates, is an indication of illiquidity. For each of over 50 MSAs I generated a time series of inventory sales as a percentage of the inventory. We then estimated for each MSA the coefficients, a_0 and a_1, for the following equation:

$$TURNOVER_t = a_0 + a_1 * TURNOVER_{t-1} \tag{13.4}$$

The coefficient, a_1, is a measure of serial correlation, which is the sensitivity of current TURNOVER or liquidity in the previous period. The greater is the value of this coefficient, the greater is *illiquidity*. In a highly liquid market, stock prices,

EXHIBIT 13.14 Area per office building is less in smaller MSAs, which promotes small-MSA liquidity.

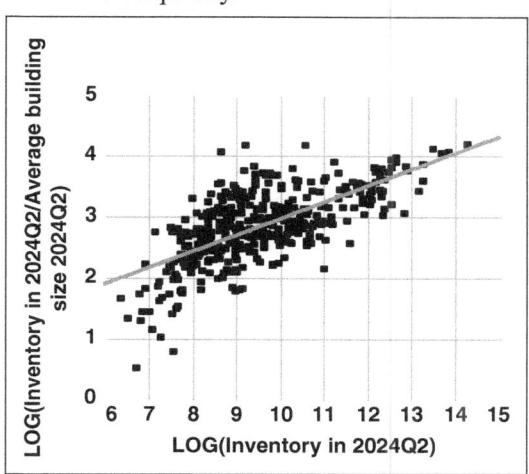

Source: ZCA using CoStar data

for example, have no serial correlation and this coefficient would be statistically zero. MSAs with higher return serial correlation are less liquid.

Exhibit 13.15 indicates that the coefficients associated with returns lagged one period range from the very small or statistically insignificant to relatively large. The NCREIF property index (NPI) is highly serially correlated, and the underlying properties are illiquid compared with the S&P 500. Assets highlighted in grey are very illiquid.

I estimated the serial correlation for 50 MSAs selected for data availability and other considerations.

Liquidity in one financial sector is related to liquidity in other sectors, including real estate. Liquidity is correlated to varying degrees across MSAs.

Exhibit 13.16 shows the relationship between stock and office property turnover.

Exhibit 13.17 is a scatter plot of the logarithm of office liquidity, or turnover, versus the logarithm of the stock market lagged one year. The fit is good.

Equation (13.5) shows the relationship between stock liquidity and office liquidity. A 1% increase in stock turnover lagged three quarters is associated with a reduction of 0.91% turnover in office. The two are negatively correlated even though stocks are much more liquid. One possible explanation for the negative coefficient

EXHIBIT 13.15 Serial correlation smooths performance and reduces measured volatility; assets highlighted in gray exhibit high serial correlation.

	Constant	T-Statistic	Coefficient(−1)	T-Statistic	Adjusted R^2	Serial Correlation (DW)
Equity REIT	2.704	2.469	0.074	0.728	−0.005	1.967
Mortgage REIT	2.654	2.069	−0.085	−0.828	−0.003	1.956
S&P 500	2.099	2.376	0.037	0.360	−0.009	2.000
Small stocks	2.914	2.424	−0.061	−0.605	−0.007	1.961
AAA corporate bond	1.138	2.867	−0.066	−0.647	−0.006	2.002
BBB corporate bond	1.156	3.064	0.149	1.467	0.012	1.997
Corporate high yield	1.317	2.470	0.251	2.538	0.054	1.898
T-bills	0.051	0.819	0.969	40.114	0.944	0.595
NPI cap rate	0.001	1.124	0.978	70.835	0.981	1.555
NPI apartment	0.003	1.605	0.839	14.937	0.698	1.474
NPI industrial	0.004	1.809	0.836	14.679	0.691	1.657
NPI office	0.001	0.751	0.882	17.570	0.762	1.824
NPI retail	0.004	2.112	0.788	12.432	0.615	2.343

Source: ZCA using NCREIF, NAREIT, and Federal Reserve data

is that a booming stock market, or the growing fear of a possible bubble, leads to tightening by the Fed and a slowdown in office transactions.

$$LOG(TURNOVER_t) = 6.066 - 0.907 * LOG(STOCKTURNOVER_{t-1})$$
$$(6.087)(-4.973)$$

$$+ 0.555 * AR(1) + 0.037 * SIGMASQ$$
$$(2.134) \qquad (2.394) \tag{13.5}$$

R-squared = 0.744

Adjusted R-squared = 0.693

Standard error of the regression = 0.218

Mean dependent variable = 1.445

F-statistic = 14.535

Probability (F-statistic) = 0.000

Durbin Watson statistic = 1.976

EXHIBIT 13.16 Stock turnover was high during the GFC in 2008.

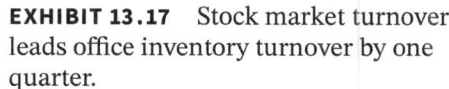

Source: ZCA using data from World Bank Group and CoStar

EXHIBIT 13.17 Stock market turnover leads office inventory turnover by one quarter.

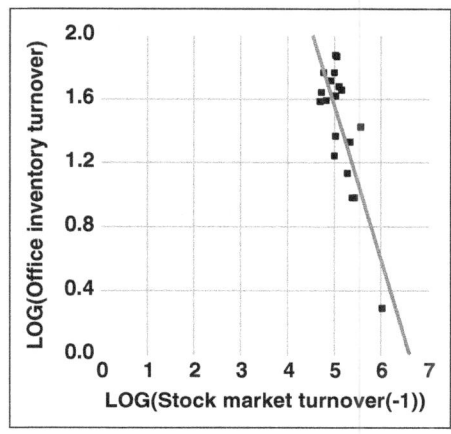

Source: ZCA using CoStar and Federal Reserve data

The life of many private equity funds is about ten years and secondary trades, which are infrequent, occur at substantial discounts, which are indicative of extreme illiquidity. The average annual turnover of all US stocks since 2000 is 172%; the stock market turns over almost twice each year. By contrast, the average turnover of the office property inventory is 4.3%. The municipal bond market turns over 10% per year. Turnovers of the office inventory and stock market, although different in magnitude, have a correlation of −0.45.

Another predictor of liquidity. Real transactions price per office square foot leads liquidity by one quarter as shown in Exhibit 13.18 and models in Equation (13.6).

When building prices fell during the GFC and following COVID-19, liquidity plummeted. The price per office square foot lagged by one quarter is a good predictor of liquidity movements.

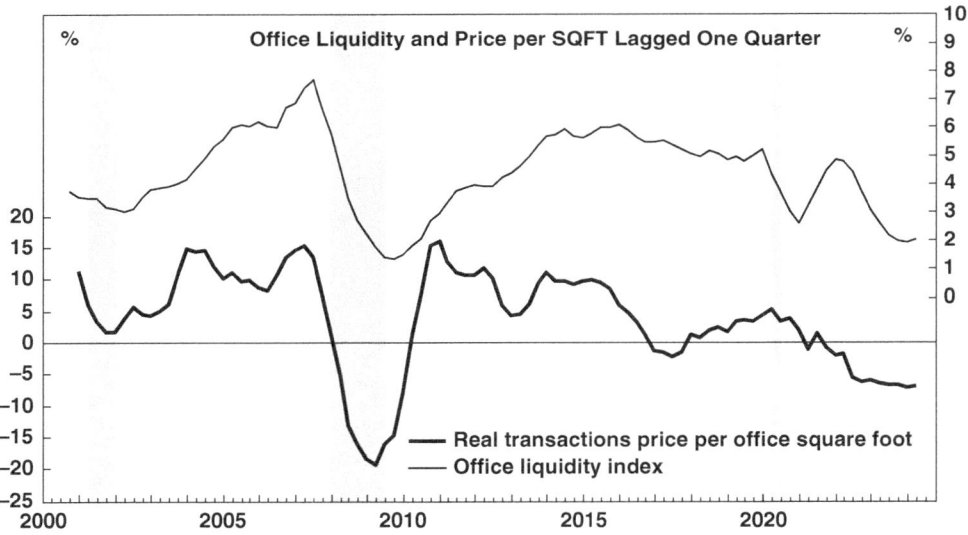

EXHIBIT 13.18 Office prices per square foot lead liquidity by one quarter.

Source: ZCA using CoStar data

$$LOG(TURNOVER_t) = 3.596 + 0.068 * PRICE_{t-1} + 0.959 * AR(1)$$
$$\phantom{LOG(TURNOVER_t) = {}}(4.052)\ (5.566)\phantom{+ 0.068 * PRICE_{t-1}}\ (29.374)$$

$$+ 0.037 * SIGMASQ$$
$$(2.394) \hspace{6cm} (13.6)$$

R-squared = 0.943
Adjusted R-squared = 0.941
Standard error of the regression = 0.355
Mean dependent variable = 4.362
F-statistic = 490.736
Probability (F-statistic) = 0.000

Flight to Quality

During the GFC, liquidity drained from the system. Information was so asymmetric that the only well-performing asset was US Treasuries, which in 2008 delivered a 26% return. The market retreated to safety. Other asset classes suffered. See Exhibit 13.19.

EXHIBIT 13.19 Investors fled to the safest asset during the GFC, long-term US Treasury bonds, which in 2008 had a 26% total return; in 2009 the return was −15%.

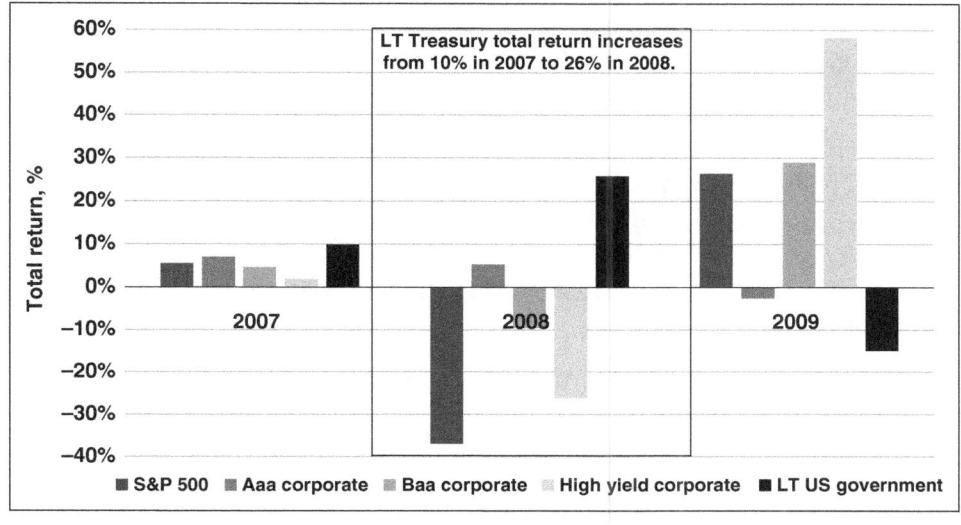

Source: ZCA using Federal Reserve data

In order to de-leverage and convert assets into cash, many property owners sold their more liquid properties with more creditworthy tenants. Even though cap rates were rising, sold properties did not represent the accumulating hidden loss of wealth in the remaining unsold office inventory. Had these owners elected to sell their legacy assets, recorded sales prices would have been lower. Hence, return indexes were biased upward.

Cap Rates, Serial Correlation, and Liquidity

Cap rates reflect office liquidity, which, lagged three quarters, is associated with higher cap rates, as shown in Equation (13.7). High liquidity leads to higher cap rates nine months later.

An increase in cap rates implies a decrease in NOI, which is generally associated with a falling market. A 1% increase in office liquidity lagged three quarters reduces the appraisal-based NCREIF cap rates by 1.37%.

$$CAP_t = -0.301 + 1.371 * TURNOVER_{t-3} - 0.488 * AR(1)$$
$$(-4.379)\;(14.095) \qquad\qquad\qquad (-5.214)$$

$$+0.485 * SIGMASQ$$
$$(2.409) \qquad\qquad\qquad\qquad\qquad\qquad\qquad (13.7)$$

R-squared = 0.961

Adjusted R-squared = 0.959

Standard error of the regression = 0.268

Mean dependent variable = 5.513

F-statistic = 715.227

Probability (F-statistic) = 0.000

Durbin Watson statistic = 1.976

Exhibits 13.20–13.23 show the strong negative correlation between liquidity and cap rates for four property types.

EXHIBIT 13.20 Retail liquidity and cap rates.

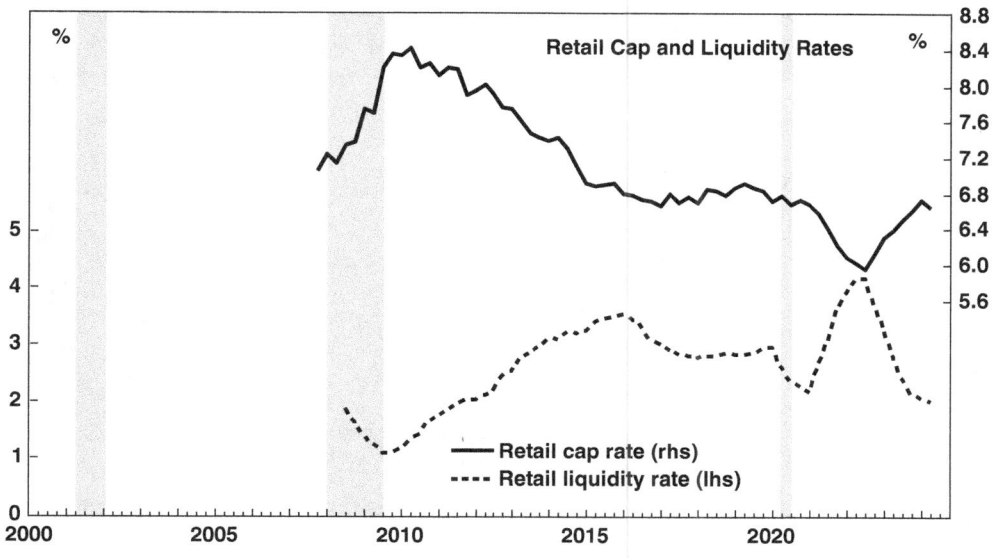

Source: ZCA using CoStar data

EXHIBIT 13.21 Office liquidity and cap rates.

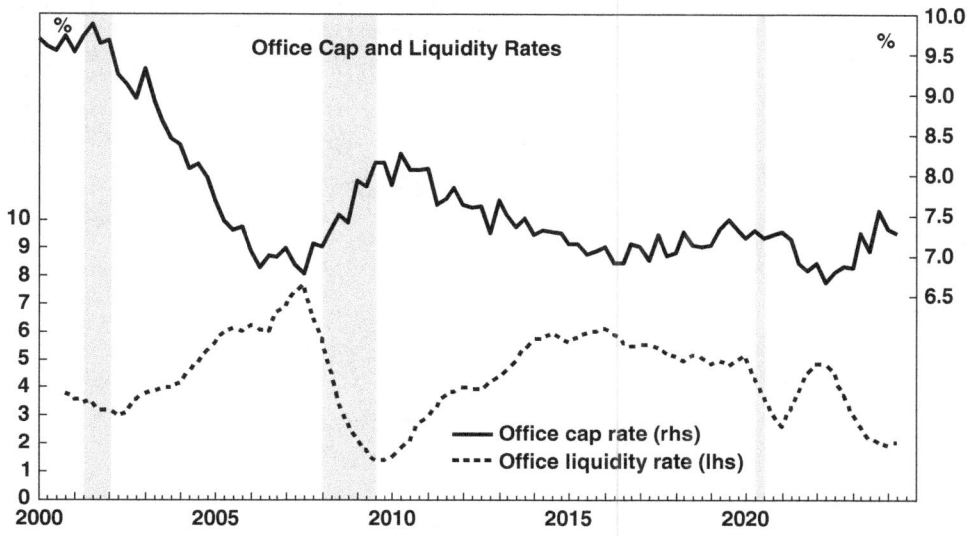

Source: ZCA using CoStar data

EXHIBIT 13.22   Multifamily liquidity and cap rates.

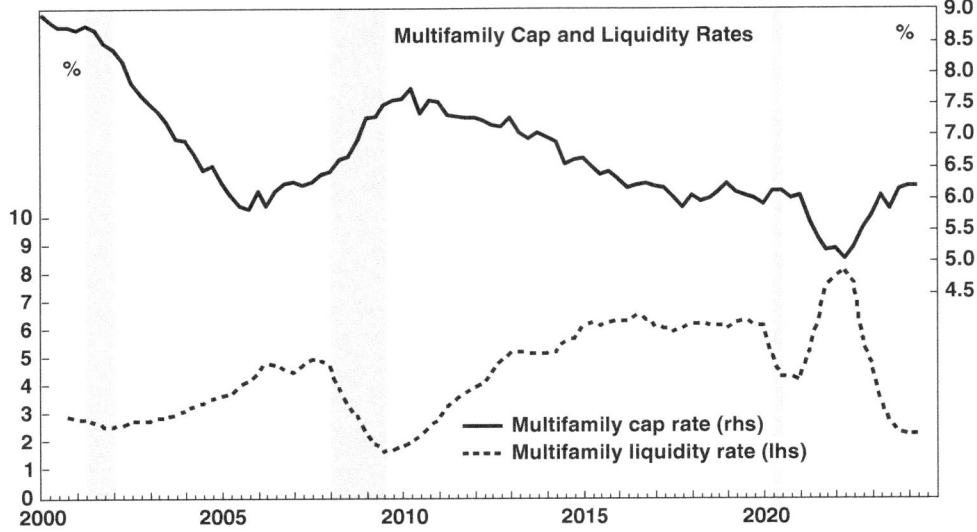

Source: CoStar and Zisler Capital Associates

EXHIBIT 13.23   Industrial liquidity and cap rates.

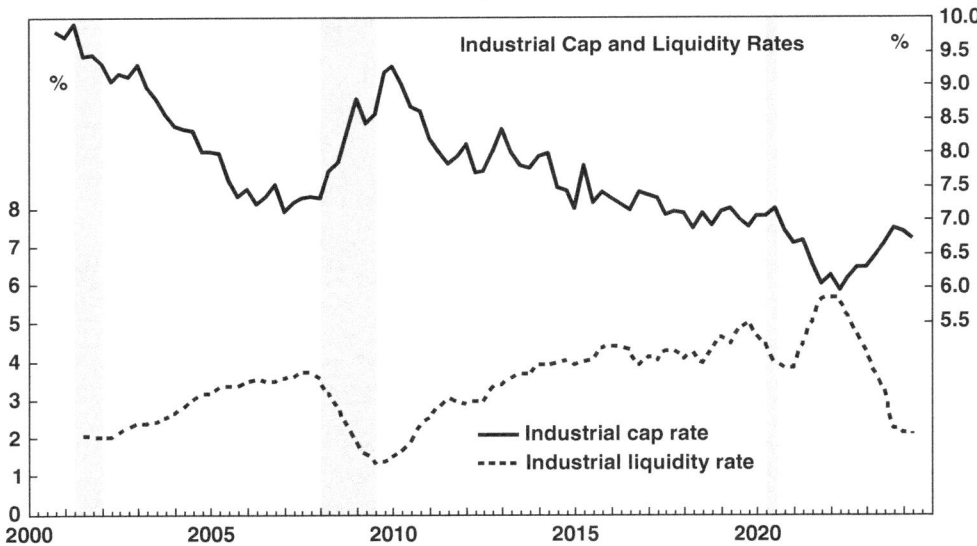

Source: CoStar and Zisler Capital Associates

Quality and Liquidity During Economic Downturns

Most investors like "quality" assets, or so they say. Does quality reside only in the physical characteristics of an asset or in a more elusive, but very real, form, such as liquidity? I measure quality using the CoStar system.

During the GFC, transactions volume cratered and the market was very discriminating. Quality mattered but in ways that seemed surprising. One might have expected that the highest quality-ranked properties would have assumed an increasingly dominant share of those properties that actually did transact, but such was not the case.

As shown in Exhibit 13.24, four- and five-ranked quality properties declined as a share and one- and two-ranked properties. I suspect that the better properties were larger and lumpier, possibly burdened with vacancies; the rent rolls of these so-called lesser properties might have been more stable.

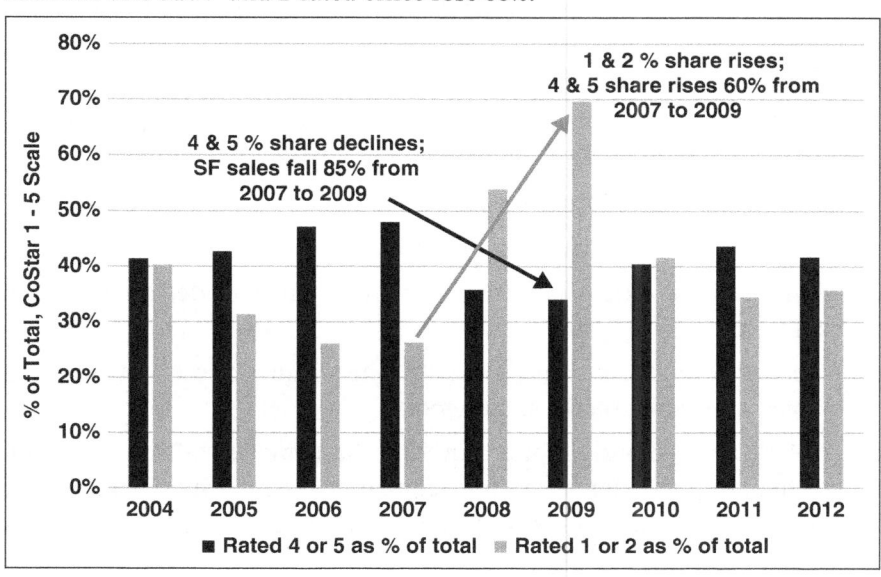

EXHIBIT 13.24 The relative share of 4- to 5-rated CoStar office from 2007 to 2009 fell 85% but 1- and 2-rated office rose 60%.

Source: ZCA using CoStar data

Conclusions and Investment Implications

- A liquid asset is one in which investors can buy in large quantities with no impact on prices. Liquidity risk is the uncertainty that an asset will be more illiquid when it is time to sell and a liquidity crisis is a period when many assets become illiquid at the same time.
- I have linked liquidity to the property sector and to the general capital markets.
- Even though illiquidity seems as elusive as risk, reasonable proxies, such as inventory turnover, exist.
- Both time series and cross-section analyses support my conclusions: Liquidity, often ignored by investors, is important at the deal, MSA, and overall macroeconomic levels.
- To ignore liquidity is to leave value on the table and incur needless risk.
- The time required to consummate a sale reflects, among other factors, prevailing liquidity.
- Investors should add a quality-driven liquidity premium to transactions.
- There are two kinds of liquidity: funding liquidity and market (or trading) liquidity. *Trading liquidity*, which reflects market frictions, is the ease with which investors can trade an asset without a price impact. *Funding liquidity* is the ease with which investors can obtain funding.
- Liquidity is always changing. Liquidity varies over time, across asset classes, property types, MSAs, and property quality.
- There is no perfect illiquidity measure.
- Serial correlation[3] of returns is a good proxy for illiquidity.
- Bid-ask spreads are widely used in measuring publicly traded asset liquidity but not real estate.
- In the absence of bid-ask spreads, I adopt the volume of property sales relative to the inventory expressed in square feet.
- Larger MSAs have slightly higher liquidity than smaller MSAs but not enough to merit avoiding smaller MSAs for acquisitions. Investors have long believed that smaller MSAs are significantly less liquid than the largest MSAs, but this is a myth.
- Prices and total returns tend to fall when liquidity evaporates. At the national and MSA levels, liquidity drains from the entire system during a severe downturn, such as the GFC and the COVID-19 recession.

- The benefits of diversification are dependent on liquidity. During bad liquidity downturns, asset returns are phase-locked: Their return correlations approach one and the benefits of diversification vanish.
- Flight to quality follows liquidity shocks and spirals. Liquidity varies by quality level and is higher in Class-A properties, but so is liquidity risk.
- Some fund structures include redemption features that supposedly protect investors during market weakness. Managers too often do not honor these provisions during extreme downturns and managers fail to honor redemption requests. During these times, secondary limited partnership shares sell at steep discounts
- Liquidity risk is greater in low-liquidity MSAs. Not all smaller MSAs are low-liquidity MSAs, however. Trading is greater and price discovery is enhanced in liquid MSAs, so these MSAs have a higher precautionary demand for vacancy and higher vacancy rate volatility.
- MSAs with greater liquidity have lower total returns, which implies that markets require a higher liquidity premium in low-liquidity markets.
- Investors with long investment horizons have a comparative advantage bearing liquidity risk. Their exit strategy is less time-sensitive.

Q&A: Interview with Ron Havner, Chairman of Public Storage and Chairman Emeritus of Shurgard

Securitizing Self-Storage

How did you enter the real estate business?

I joined Public Storage in 1986, held various management positions, and was CEO from 2002 to 2018.

Along the way, what were some of the challenges and opportunities?

During the early 1990s, we bought back our partnership interests at 50 cents on the dollar and received a 14% return. Many institutional investors at the time sold because they preferred office buildings since self-storage was not considered "institutional grade." Now self-storage is main stream. We went public in 1995 and received an investment grade rating; institutions woke up. Now we are an A-credit; our loss ratio is lower than comparable CMBS bonds.

Talk about the economics of self-storage.

There are about 20 million units in the US. At the company we have between 2.2 and 2.5 million leases. The economics of the business is compelling: 60–70% profit margin, low CAPEX, no brokerage fees or TIs. Public Storage is a household space substitute. With work-from-home, people cleaned out their house to make room and rented self-storage. Churn is a big part of the business. We must balance our rental rate increases with a tenant's propensity to move out. The top four players own less than 20%; this is a fragmented business. There is great consolidation potential: 30% is the breakeven occupancy with no leverage. In a hotel, your EBITDA can go away in six months; this is not the case with self-storage.

What is the future of demand for self-storage?

Apartments are getting smaller and more expensive; people accumulate more stuff and Amazon has really helped because shopping is easier.

More stuff means increased demand for storage. There are markets where there is 25 square feet of self-storage per capita, e.g., Carson City, Nevada, and where there is no great population or income growth, but vacancies are low despite there being few barriers to entry.

When you look at MSAs, which ones do you pursue?

We emphasize the Southeast and Texas. We look at growers as well as slow-growth cities. In the Mid-West, cap rates are higher, but the total returns are good. It took us a while to get past our obsession with growth. Higher growth markets often have higher volatility.

What advice would you give young professionals?

Focus on good mentorship and great colleagues.

CHAPTER 14

Is Real Estate an Effective Inflation Hedge? Only in the Long Run[1]

Preliminaries

Advisors and brokers have long promoted real estate, especially property, as an effective short- to intermediate-term hedge against unexpected and expected inflation. This is a self-serving myth.

Inflation is an increase in the economy's overall price index and represents a loss of purchasing power. The rate of inflation is calculated as the percentage price increase of a basket of goods and services.

Inflation does not affect everyone equally. For instance, inflation can help debtors. A deflation, which is a drop in prices and an increase in purchasing power, helps borrowers.

A Stylized Model of the Economy, Inflation, and Inflation Risk Premiums

Interest rates and inflation may rise either in an expanding or contracting economy irrespective of the behavior of the leasing market. Stagflation, which occurred in the late 1970s, is the combination of a recession and inflation.

Interest rates and GDP are a function of the interaction of two curves, the LM curve and the IS curve. LM pertains to the monetary sector and IS—investment savings—captures the relationship between GDP and consumption, investment, government spending, and net exports.

The real money supply equals the sum of the speculative demand for money and the transactional demand for money. The speculative demand is a function of interest rates. As rates rise, the opportunity cost of holding money increases. The transactional demand for money is a function of GDP. In a hot economy, the transactional demand for cash increases.

Holding the IS curve constant, if the Fed decreases the growth rate of the money supply, the LM curve shifts to the left; interest rates rise by ΔI and GDP falls by ΔGDP. (Δ means change.) See Exhibit 14.1 for Case A and Exhibit 14.2 for Case B.

Cases A and B indicate that an interest rate increase can have different impacts on property value depending on whether or not the interest rate increase is associated with a stimulation of the leasing market and an improvement in tenant credit, or a contraction in output that adversely affects tenant quality.[2]

Combining the LM and IS curves produces the demand curve for the overall economy. Exhibit 14.3 shows the upward-sloping supply curve and the negatively sloped demand curve.

A rightward shift in demand due to increased spending increases GDP and prices; the steeper is the demand curve, the greater is inflation volatility. If demand shifts to the right, prices rise (or inflation increases) along with output, GDP. If

EXHIBIT 14.1 Case A. Contraction of the money supply shifts the LM (demand for money) curve left, which increases interest rates and reduces GDP.

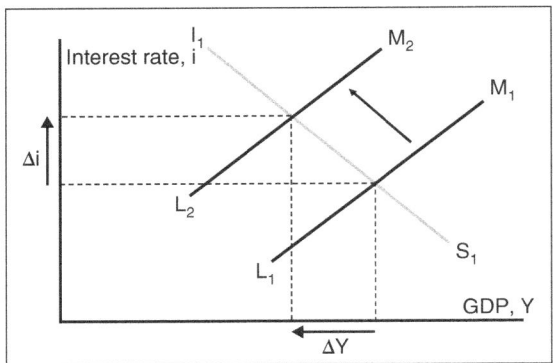

Source: ZCA

EXHIBIT 14.2 Case B: Expansion of government spending or tax reduction shifts the IS (investment-saving) curve rightward, increasing GDP and interest rates.

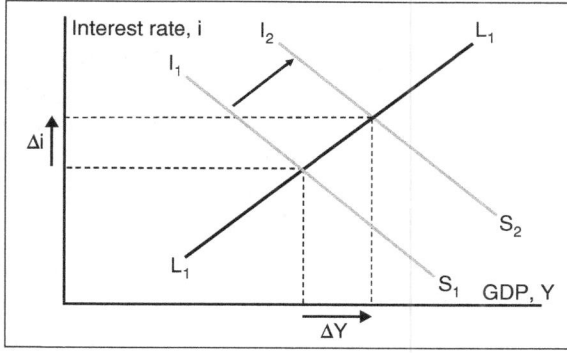

Source: ZCA

EXHIBIT 14.3 Demand curve for the macroeconomy.

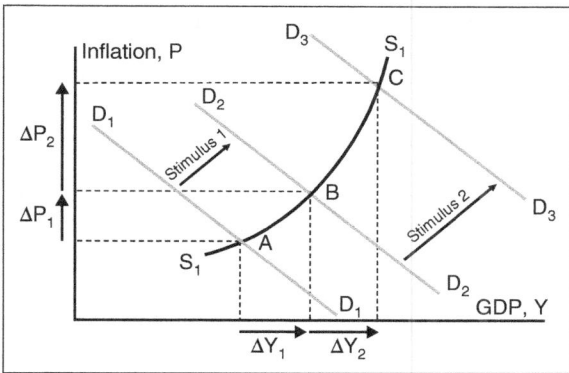

Source: ZCA

monetary policy is restrictive, money growth declines, interest rates rise, and the economy-wide demand curve shifts to the left, reducing interest rates and output.

A rightward shift in demand due to increased spending increases GDP and prices; the steeper is the demand curve, the greater is inflation volatility. If demand shifts to the right, prices rise (or inflation increases) along with output, GDP. If monetary policy is restrictive, money growth declines, interest rates rise, and the economy-wide demand curve shifts to the left, reducing interest rates and output.

The 10-year Treasury bond reacts to changes in inflation with a lag. The spread between inflation and the Treasury bond is not constant. There is no single determinant of inflation. Bivariate scatters of inflation, on the one hand, and Treasury bond yields and total returns on the other, as shown in Exhibits 14.4 and 14.5, indicate that there is no unique rate of inflation for government bond yields or returns.

An increase in the inflation risk premium can either increase or decrease value when net operating income (NOI) is declining, stable, or growing. The values of the leases and the equity need not move together over time. In a declining real estate market, interest rates and inflation may either increase or decrease during this period. Equity values may be negatively correlated with the value of the leases, thus suppressing the volatility of total real estate returns.

Total unleveraged property returns are less volatile when interest rates and rents (and tenant credit quality) move in the same direction. Property prices tend to move rapidly up or down when the leases and the equity are all pulling in the same direction. The net effect of changes in the present value of the leases and of the equity depends on the magnitude of each of these changes. (See Chapter 3, which discusses the influence of four risk factors on value.)

A reduction in the tenant risk premium and an increase in cash flow can offset or even swamp an increase in inflation. Hence, investors and their advisors should consider the impact of inflation in a general equilibrium context that controls for other sources of variation.

EXHIBIT 14.4 There is no unique bond yield for any given inflation rate.

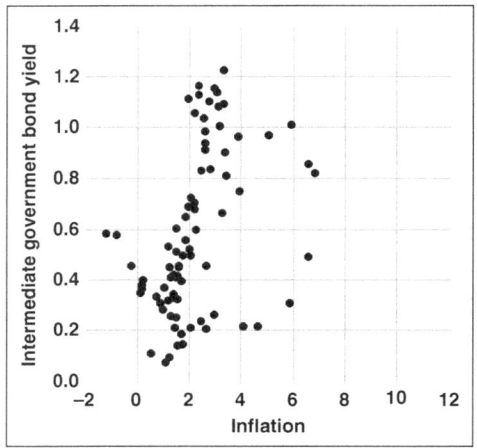

Source: ZCA using Federal Reserve data

EXHIBIT 14.5 Inflation and bond total returns.

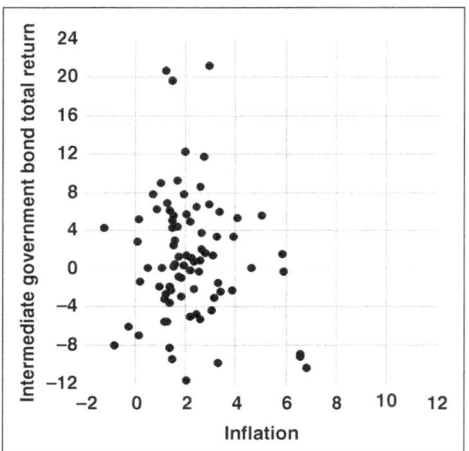

Source: ZCA using Federal Reserve data

EXHIBIT 14.6 Local market NOI volatility usually obscures the effect of inflation on property performance.

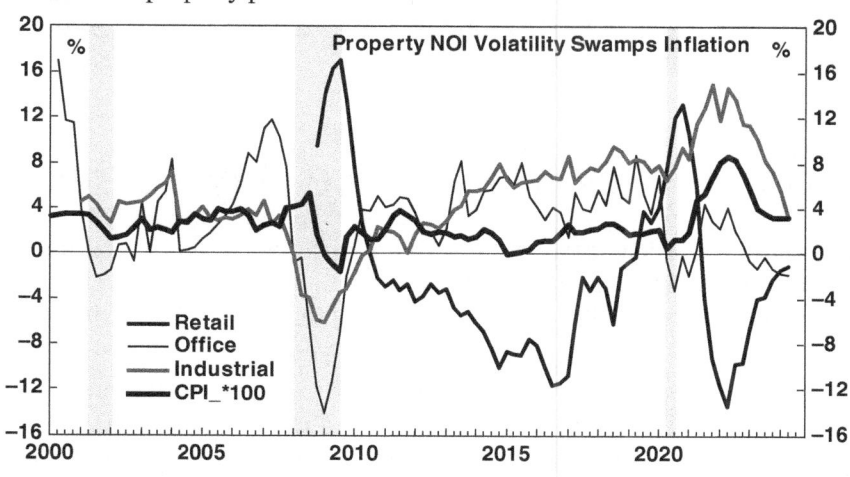

Source: ZCA using CoStar data

I show that apartments are not good inflation hedges. Contrary to some managers' long-held beliefs, short lease terms do not increase the inflation hedging power of apartments. Whatever their inflation hedging strength, constant supply–demand shocks mute and even offset the effect. Office buildings, hotels, and even self-storage (which has very short-term leases) are not the inflation hedges that many people believe.

Exhibit 14.6 shows that property NOI for each of the four major property types is far more volatile than CPI volatility.

Why Should Real Estate Investors Care About Inflation?

In-place and future leases have bond-like characteristics; hence, inflation through its association with interest rates can hurt real estate performance. Not all leases pass through inflationary shocks to tenants, and those that do may do so only imperfectly and with a lag. Inflation increases the opportunity cost of holding money. Higher nominal rates induce people to go to the bank more often to avoid holding money balances, which often pay no interest.

Inflation distorts relative prices and expectations, thereby increasing uncertainty. Inflation helps debtors and harms creditors. Lower-than-expected inflation helps retirees; higher than expected inflation hurts them. The burdens of inflation are inequitably shared.

Inflation Indexes: The Choice May Matter

Indexes vary by statistical construction. Knowing which to use really matters. CORE CPI excludes used cars, public transportation, and lodging (including apartments), all three of which were affected following COVID-19. See Exhibit 14.7 and Exhibit 14.8.

During COVID-19 there was a wide disparity in the performance of CPI subcomponents. The volatility of these three CPI components exceeds the CPI's overall volatility, and their most extreme values are deflationary. During this period, apartment rental inflation was much less volatile than the other two components.

In contrast to the CPI, the PPI focuses on prices received by producers. This index is very broad, as it includes goods and services from across a chain of production, including raw materials, intermediary manufacturing, and retail sales. The CPI targets prices paid by consumers for a fixed basket of goods and services. Both

EXHIBIT 14.7 Apartment rental inflation has been absolutely less volatile than energy and used cars.

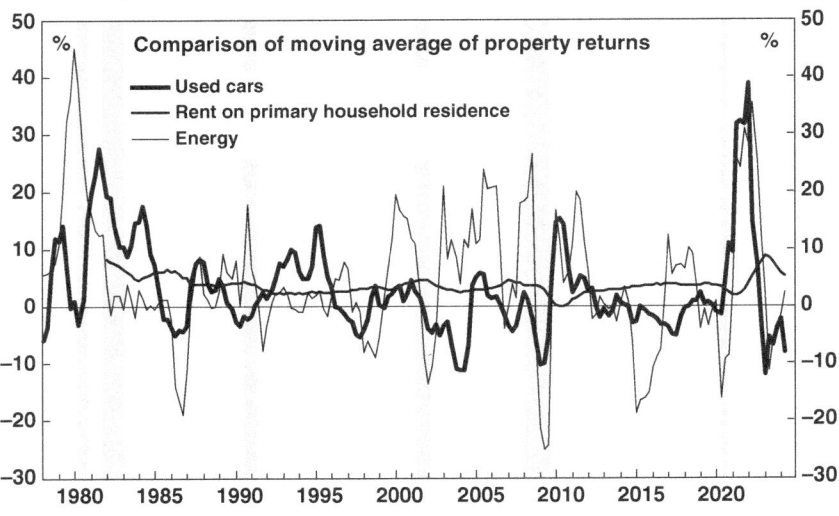

Source: ZCA using CoStar data

EXHIBIT 14.8 Normalizing these data reveals the deleterious role played by rental and used car inflation following COVID-19.

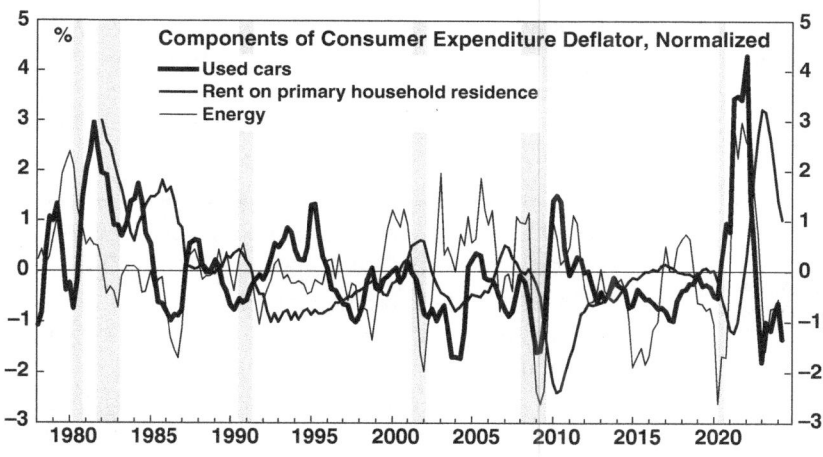

Source: ZCA using CoStar data

indexes are fixed-weight indexes, which measure only price changes, uninfluenced by technological change or shifts in consumer preferences. The personal consumption index (PCE) is not a fixed-weight index. After 2022, the PPI and the CPI significantly diverged.

The CPI, PPI, and Supply Chain-Induced Inflation

An efficient supply chain results in lower costs and faster production. There are many ways to evaluate supply chains. An important consideration is the optimal level of supply chain redundancy. Redundancy does not mean waste any more than cash reserves suggest corporate profligacy. If there is inadequate redundancy built into a supply chain, then the chain is brittle, and disruptions, such as COVID-19, can create cascading havoc globally.

Global supply chain problems following the COVID-19 recession have been an important factor explaining inflation during the 2021–2023 period. Global price competition caused myopic behavior on the part of buyers and supplies. The supply chain disruption did not affect all property classes equally. Industrial property performed better than all other major property types.

Since 2022 the CPI rose relative to the PPP final demand services. Upstream goods prices increased relative to the purchasing managers' index but downstream prices declined with a lag as upstream goods moved along the pipeline.

Immediately following the COVID-19 recession, the PPI index for upstream goods increased relative to purchasing managers (ISM) price index, a downstream index. Downstream prices declined with a lag as upstream goods moved along the pipeline.

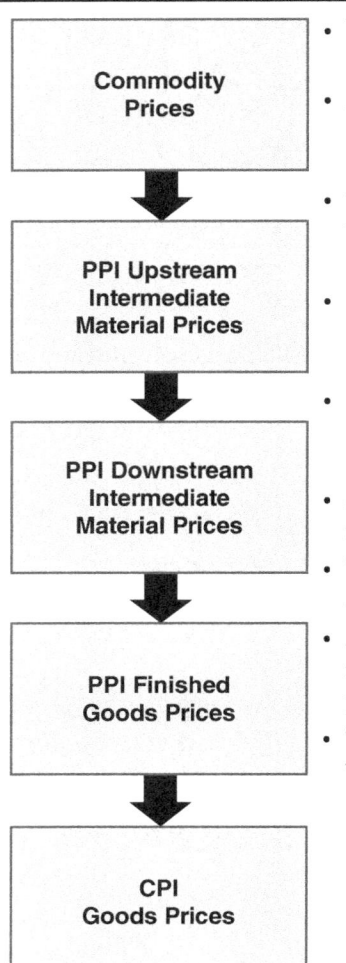

- What is the supply chain and how does it affect the economy and property specifically?
- A supply chain is a network of companies and people that manage the production and delivery of a product or service.
- The components of supply chain include producers, vendors, warehouses, transportation companies, distribution centers, and retailers, not services.
- Changes in production and transportation costs, materials availability, and consumers' buying power can exacerbate inflation in supply chains.
- Global supply chain disruptions following the onset of the COVID-19 pandemic contributed to the rapid rise in US inflation from 2021 through 2024.
- Supply chain pressures began easing substantially in mid-2022, contributing to the slowdown in inflation.
- The correlation between the Producer Price Index (PPI) and the Fed's supply chain index (GSCPI) is about 0.53.
- A one standard deviation shock to the GSCPI leads to an increase in headline PCE inflation of about 0.5 percentage points at the peak.
- The effects are relatively short-lived, statistically vanishing about a year after the impact.

Do Not Confuse a Change in Relative Prices with a Change in the Overall Price Level

Exhibit 14.9 shows the isoquant and budget constraint for two goods, Good 1 and Good 2. Consumers derive the same satisfaction with any combination of goods along the isoquant, U_0. See Exhibit 14.10. Inflation reduces household purchasing power much as a tax would. This income effect shifts the budget constraint to the left. Even though inflation affects the price of all goods and services equally, due to the shape of the isoquant, consumers may change the ratio of one good (or service) to another. Inflation distorts choices even if the initial inflation shock affects all prices equally. Inflation is not neutral.

What happens if inflation changes just the relative price of goods, e.g., oranges become more expensive relative to apples? Inflation, as in Exhibit 14.11, causes real income to decline as purchasing power deteriorates. Given a pure substitution effect with no income effect, relative prices change. (See Exhibit 14.12.) Good 2 becomes cheaper relative to Good 1, and, as a result, households consume more of the second good in relation to the first. The new equilibrium shifts from A to B. Distinguishing between a change in relative prices and inflation is not easy in practice.

EXHIBIT 14.9 The basic analytics of consumer choice.

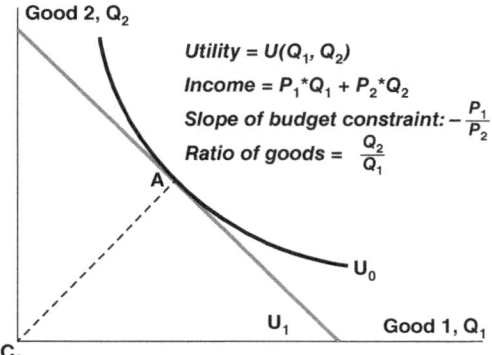

Source: ZCA

EXHIBIT 14.10 A pure income effect due to inflation affecting all prices the same.

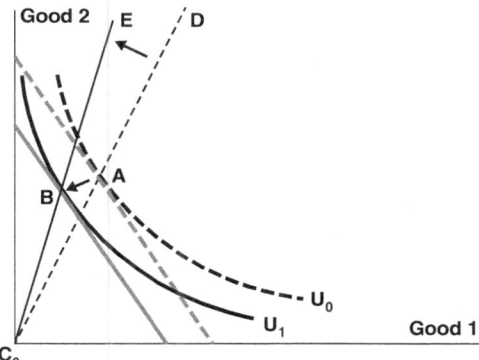

Source: ZCA

EXHIBIT 14.11 The effect of an inflation that changes relative prices.

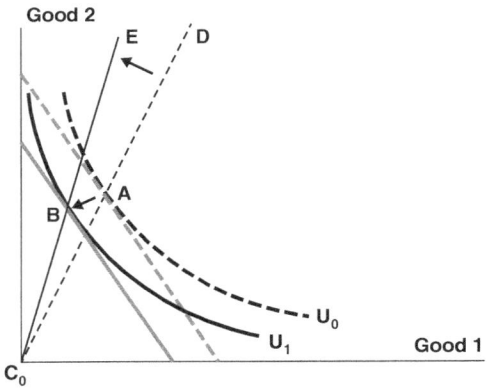

Source: ZCA

EXHIBIT 14.12 Pure substitution due to a change in relative prices holdings utility constant.

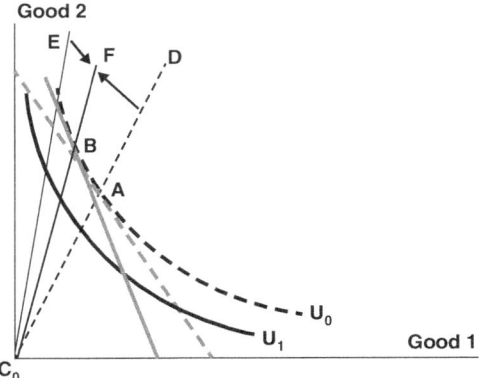

Source: ZCA

Real estate investors often confuse a reduction in the rate of inflation with a reduction in the price level. Deflationary months have been few in number. Since 1948, the monthly change in the CPI has been negative for only 40 months, which is 4.4% of 918 months.

History of US Inflation and Real Estate

Commercial real estate performance data series, which appear in 1978, are too short to accurately measure the long-term relationship between inflation and real estate performance. There have been only four policy regimes since 1950. See Exhibit 14.13.

Role of the Federal Reserve and enhanced monetary stability during the post-WW II period. Since the Great Depression, macroeconomic stability has improved and recessions are fewer in number due in part to the elimination of the on- and off-again deflationary effects of the gold standard.

Exhibit 14.14 shows that gold performed well as a very long-term inflation, but it increased macroeconomic instability.

EXHIBIT 14.13 Only four monetary policy experiments and four inflation regimes since the 1950s.

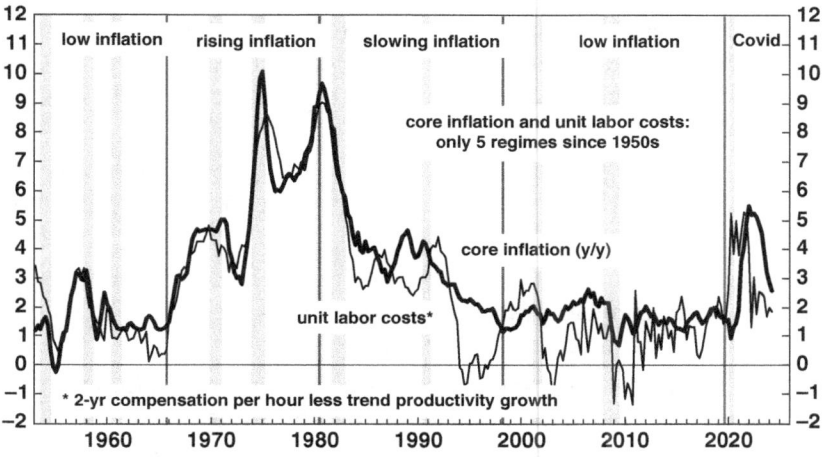

Source: ZCA using Federal Reserve data

EXHIBIT 14.14 Gold, an inflation hedge over the very long term, has significantly outpaced the CPI since the end of the gold standard.

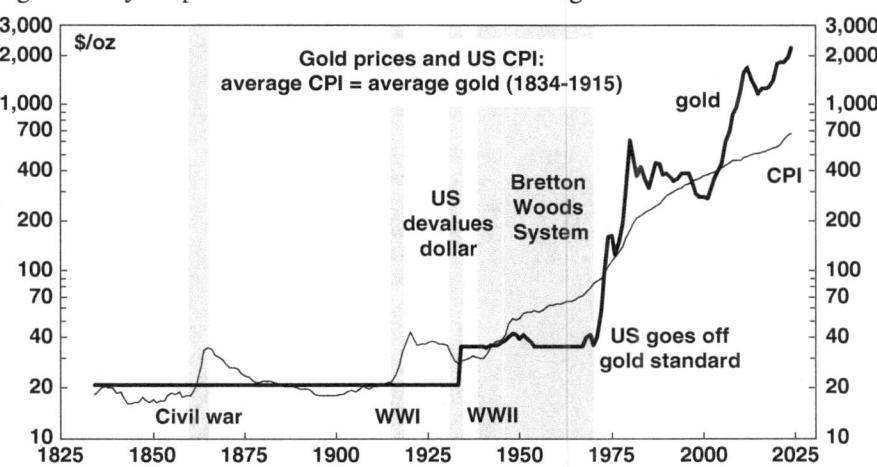

Source: ZCA using Federal Reserve data

Hedging

A perfect inflation hedge eliminates all the effects of inflation. Real estate is not a good hedge, but it need not be an inflation hedge in order to justify a portfolio allocation. Stocks and bonds play prominent portfolio roles but these assets are poor inflation hedges.

Real estate is a good diversifier, as I show in Chapter 10. Inflation affects not only the assets but also the liabilities, both of which should be part of any asset allocation analysis.

The relative importance of the income rate of return compared to the total can indicate the extent to which an asset is either debt- or equity-like. The income intensive assets should be more sensitive to inflation.

Exhibits 14.15 and 14.16 show the relationship between inflation, on the one hand, and property cap rates, the S&P 500, and bond yields.

The S&P 500 capital return accounts for most of the S&P 500's total return, whereas the opposite is true for property. This finding is consistent with the assertion that property has debt- as well as equity-like characteristics. See Exhibit 14.17 and Exhibit 14.18.

EXHIBIT 14.15 Inflation drives the long-term trend of yield on stock. The highs and lows of earnings yield in the S&P 500 are closely related to the average level of long-run inflation.

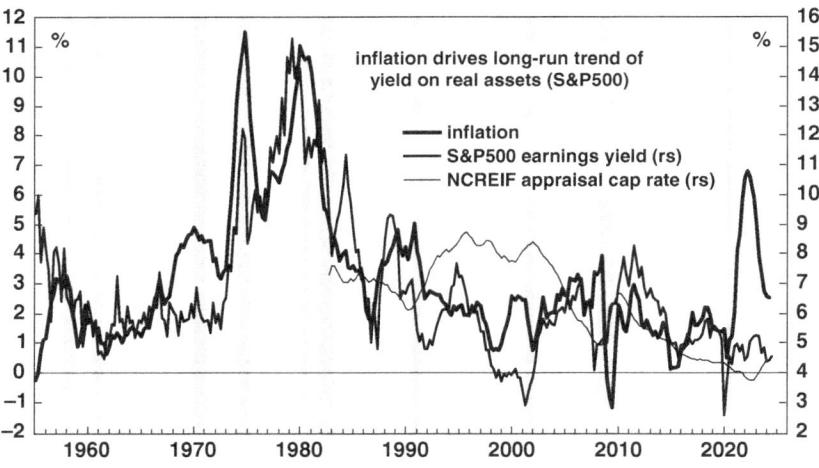

Source: ZCA using Federal Reserve data

EXHIBIT 14.16 The response to declining inflation of long-term (Treasury and corporate) interest rates since 1980 has been gradual.

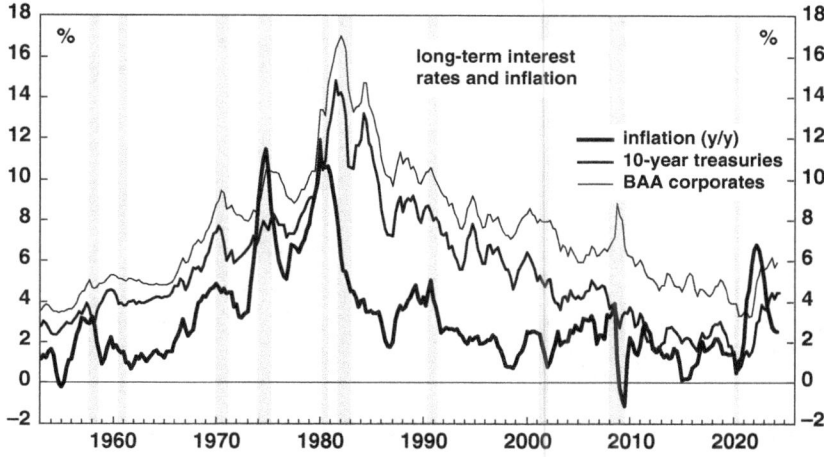

Source: ZCA using Federal Reserve data

EXHIBIT 14.17 Stock price appreciation represents 80% of total returns for the S&P 500.

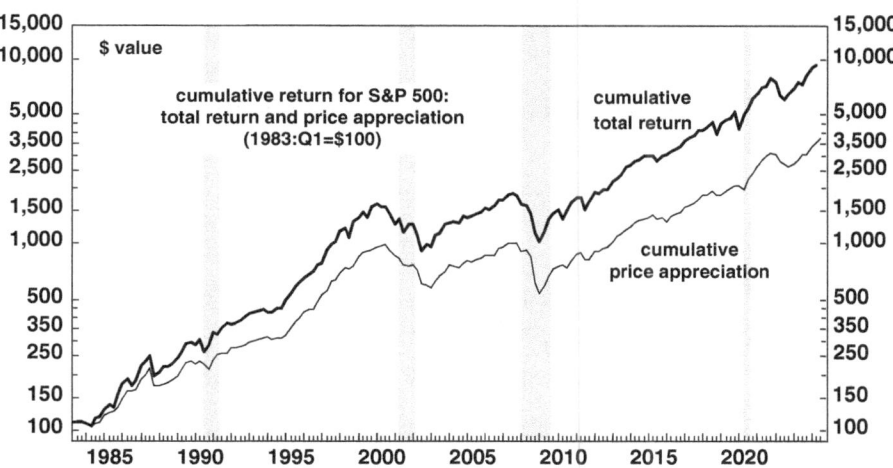

Source: ZCA using Federal Reserve data

EXHIBIT 14.18 Capital appreciation for property is a relatively smaller percentage of total returns.

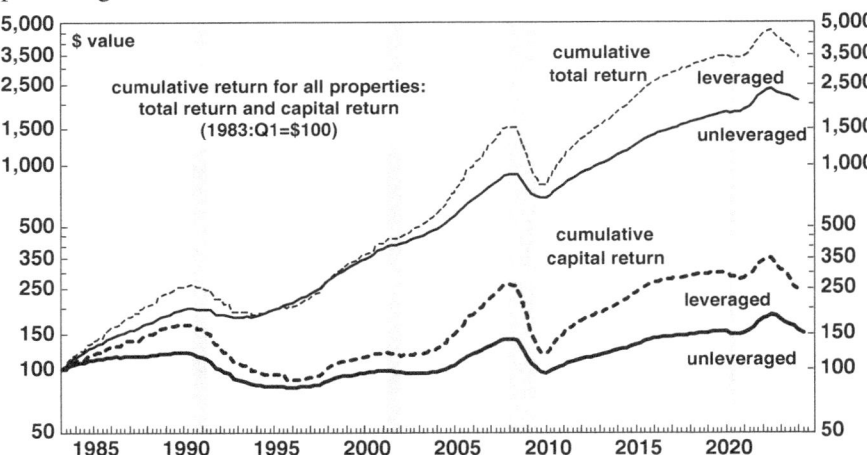

Source: ZCA using Federal Reserve data

Is Real Estate a Good Inflation Hedge?

The following are the attributes of a good inflation hedge:

- An effective hedge should have a strong and consistently positive correlation with inflation.
- A hedge should be a long-term store of value.
- Volatility along trend should be low.

An asset whose correlation with inflation oscillates from negative to positive is inconsistent and unreliable. See Exhibits 14.19 and 14.20.

Long-term store of value. Exhibit 14.21 shows the accumulated value of various assets from 1978.

Exhibits 14.22 and 14.23 show that property outperforms inflation as a very long-run store of value. Especially noteworthy is that the five property types are closely grouped. Apartments perform better than office long-term but not as well as industrial property. Inflation-adjusted performance shown in Exhibit 14.23 confirms this finding.

EXHIBIT 14.19 Five-month rolling return volatility.

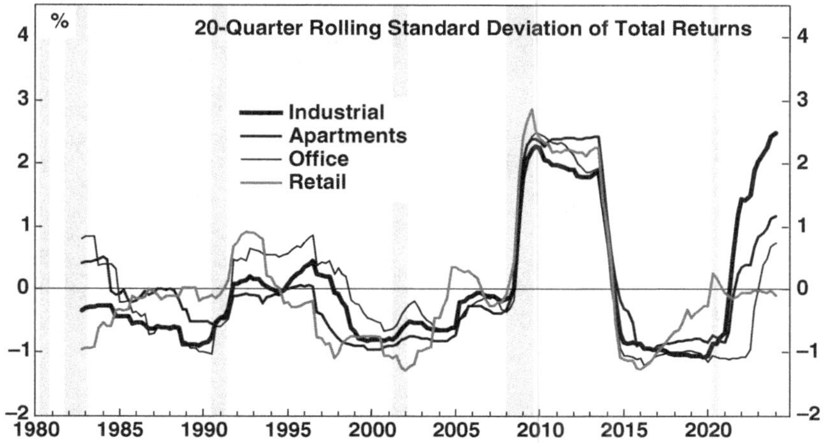

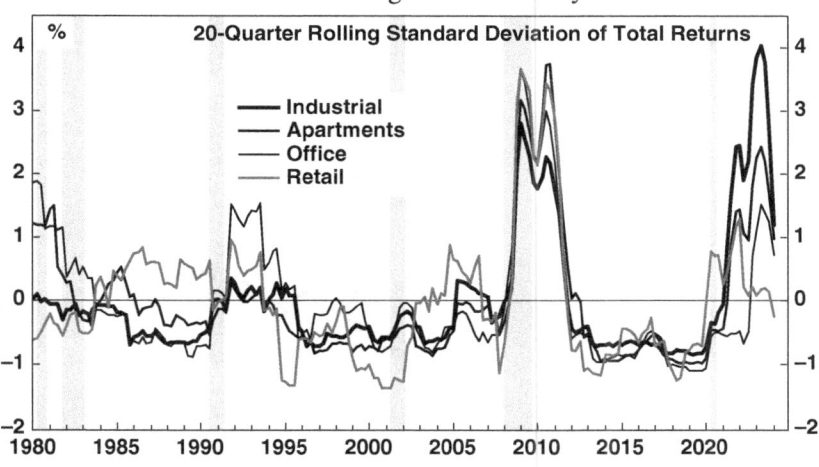

Source: ZCA using NCREIF data

EXHIBIT 14.20 Two-month rolling return volatility.

Source: ZCA using NCREIF data

Most institutional investors, especially those who pursue opportunistic investments, have relatively short holding periods, 5- to 7-years. They should not expect an inflation bailout.[3]

Correlation test. The correlation test is the most important leg of the inflation-hedging test, illustrated in Exhibit 14.24. The moving average of correlations for 2-, 10-, and 20-years fluctuate. NCREIF is not a good inflation hedge according to our first criterion.

EXHIBIT 14.21 Accumulated value by asset class.

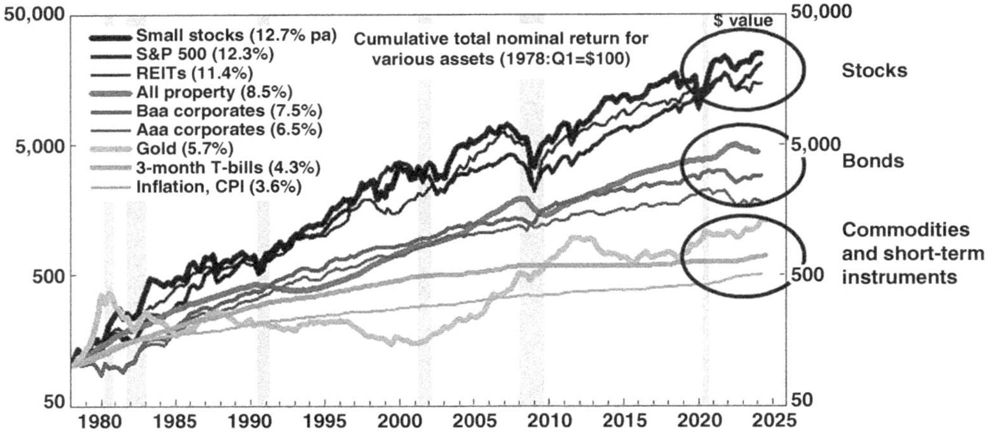

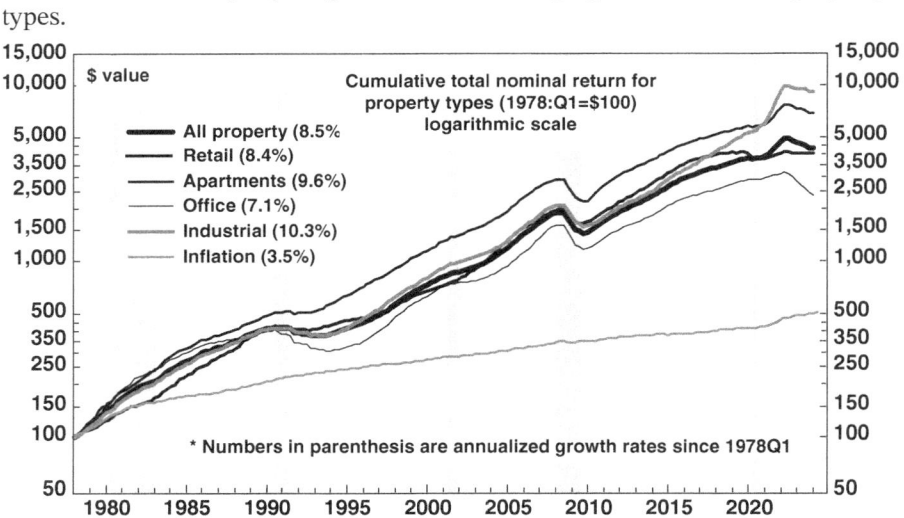

Source: ZCA using NCREIF, NAREIT, and Federal Reserve data

EXHIBIT 14.22 Property long-term nominal hedging is similar across property types.

Source: ZCA using NCREIF, NAREIT, and Federal Reserve data

EXHIBIT 14.23 Apartments' inflation-adjusted accumulated value since 1978 has been strong.

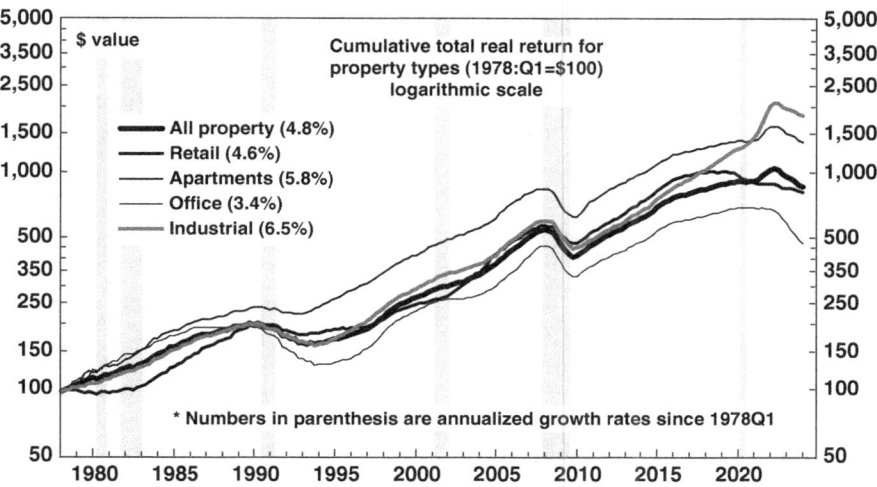

Source: ZCA using NCREIF, NAREIT, and Federal Reserve data

EXHIBIT 14.24 All-property total return correlations oscillate in the short and longer term.

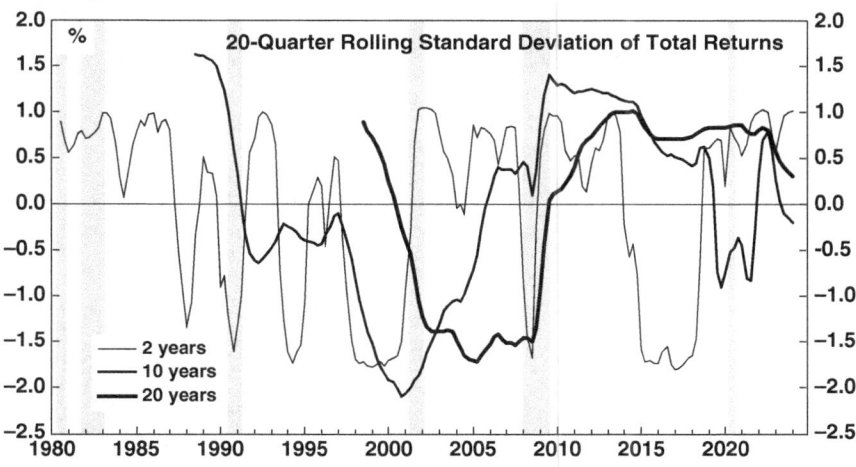

Source: ZCA using NCREIF data

A strong inflation hedge should have a large and consistently positive correlation, whereas a poor hedge would exhibit a negative or wildly fluctuating correlation from positive to negative.

The long-term—20-year rolling window—income return is mostly negative or weakly positive, a sign of property's debt-like features, as shown in Exhibit 14.25. The long-term capital return is much more equity-like: The 20-year rolling correlation is mostly positive but unreliable. See Exhibit 14.26.

EXHIBIT 14.25 All-property NCREIF intermediate and long-term income returns are debt-like.

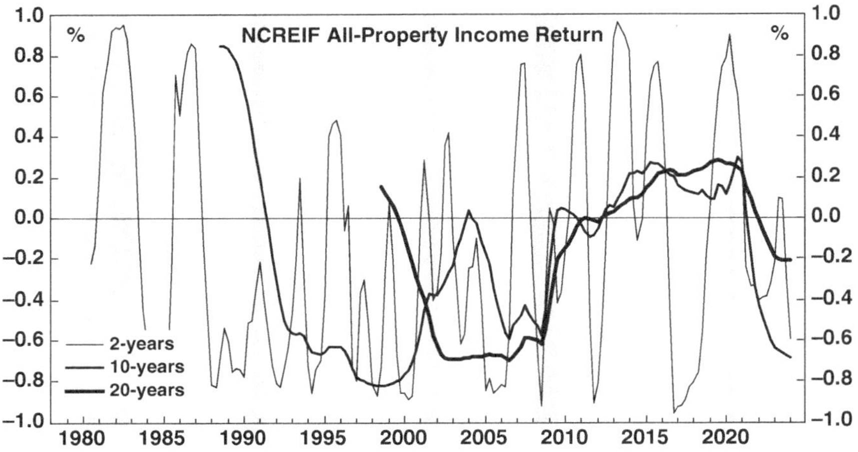

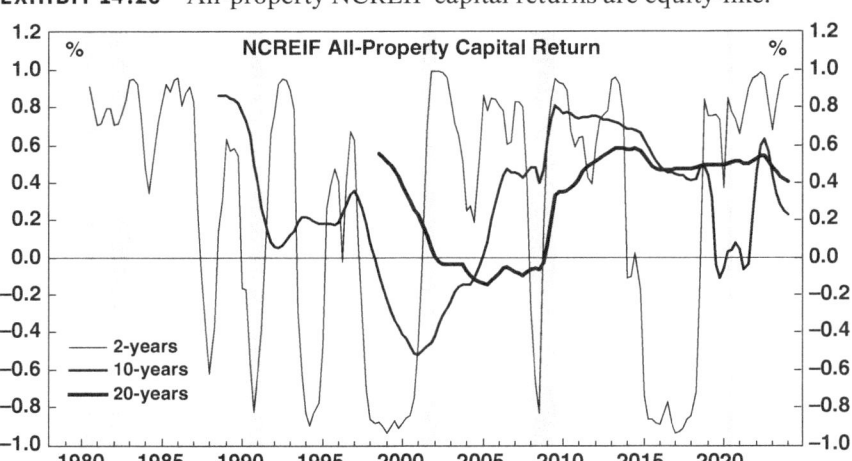

Source: ZCA using NCREIF data

EXHIBIT 14.26 All-property NCREIF capital returns are equity-like.

Source: ZCA using NCREIF data

Exhibit 14.27 shows the rolling correlations of the Giliberto-Levy (G-L) all-mortgage index with inflation. The 10- and 20-year correlations are mostly negative, as we would expect for a debt instrument.

Exhibits 14.28 and 14.29 compare and contrast apartment total returns and apartment mortgage returns. The latter is clearly debt-like since the moving correlations are largely, but inconsistently, negative.

EXHIBIT 14.27 G-L credit-adjusted retail mortgage total return.

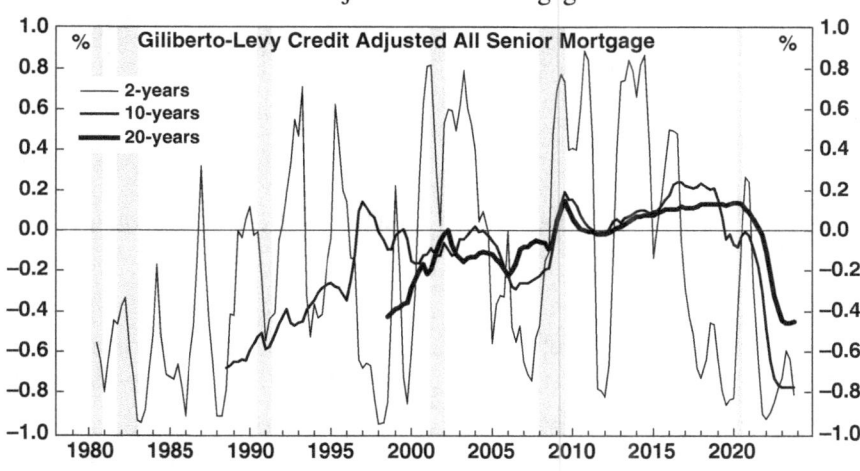

Source: ZCA using NCREIF data

EXHIBIT 14.28 Apartment property total return.

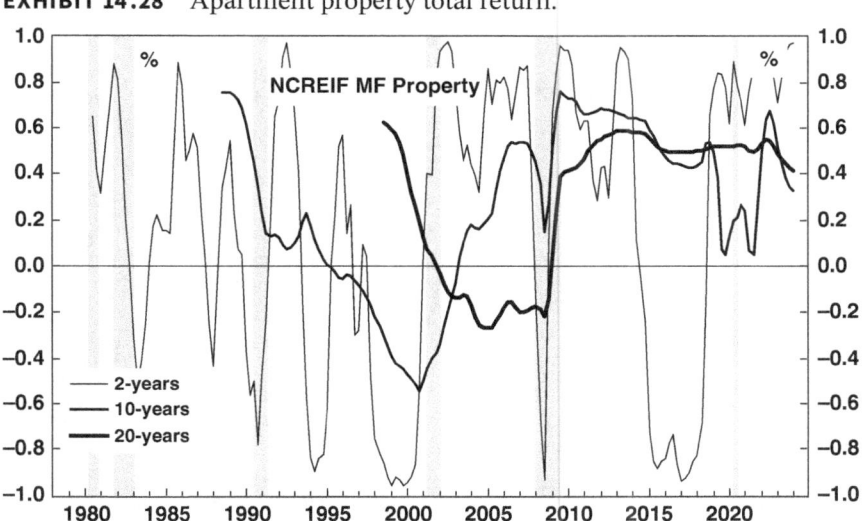

Source: ZCA using NCREIF data

EXHIBIT 14.29 Apartment mortgage total return.

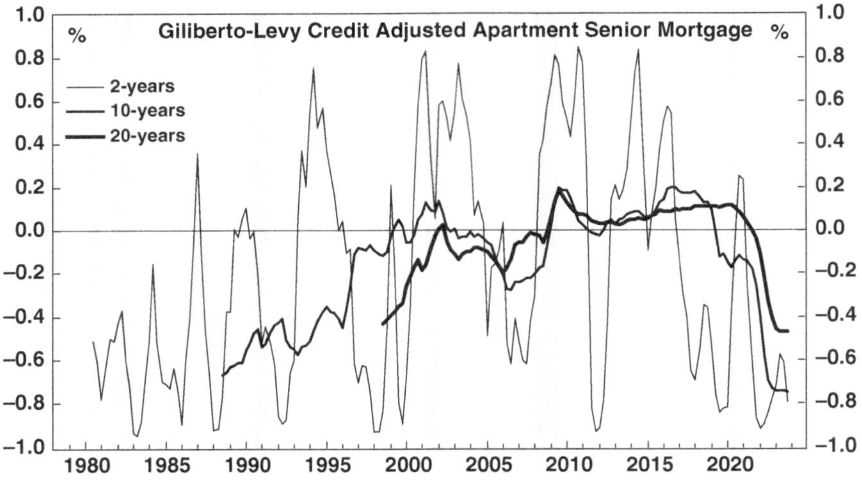

Source: ZCA using NCREIF data

The data do not support claims that apartments with their shorter lease terms are better inflation hedges. Apartment supply–demand imbalances swamp any significant inflation hedging potential.

Exhibit 14.30 shows that the rolling correlation of property total returns and inflation is not stable over time. Mortgages' rolling correlation is more consistently negative than property returns, as one might expect. See Exhibit 14.31.

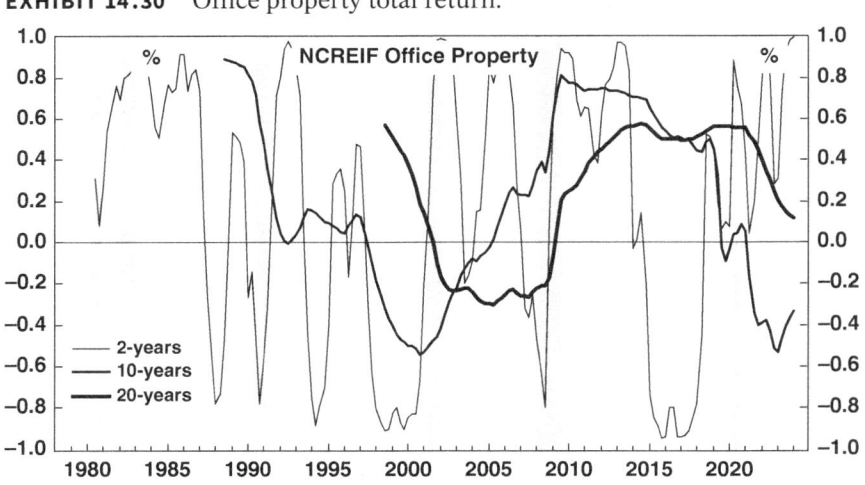

EXHIBIT 14.30 Office property total return.

Source: ZCA using NCREIF data

EXHIBIT 14.31 Office mortgage total return.

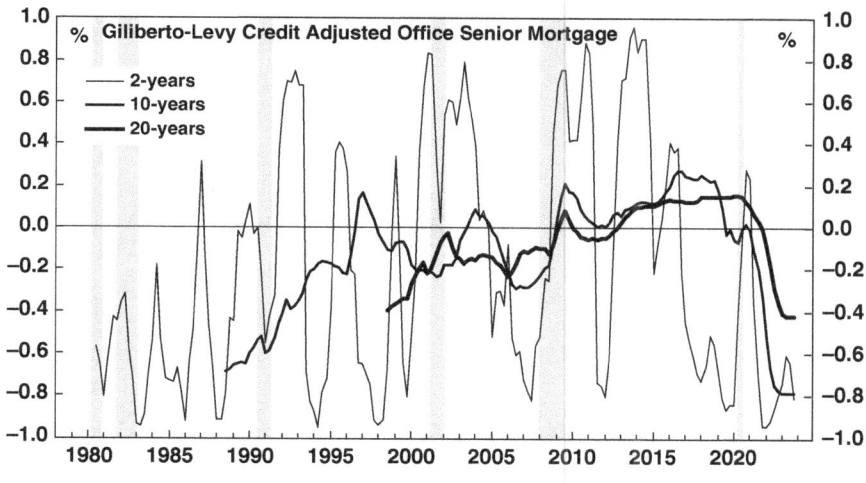

Source: ZCA using NCREIF data

Office mortgage returns oscillate significantly in the short run but the moving correlation is essentially zero for the 20-year rolling window.

Exhibits 14.32 through 14.35 compare retail and industrial property sector pairs of NCREIF returns with G-L mortgage returns. The 20-year moving correlations of the mortgage returns are more consistently negative than the NCREIF total return correlations are consistently positive.

EXHIBIT 14.32 Retail property total returns.

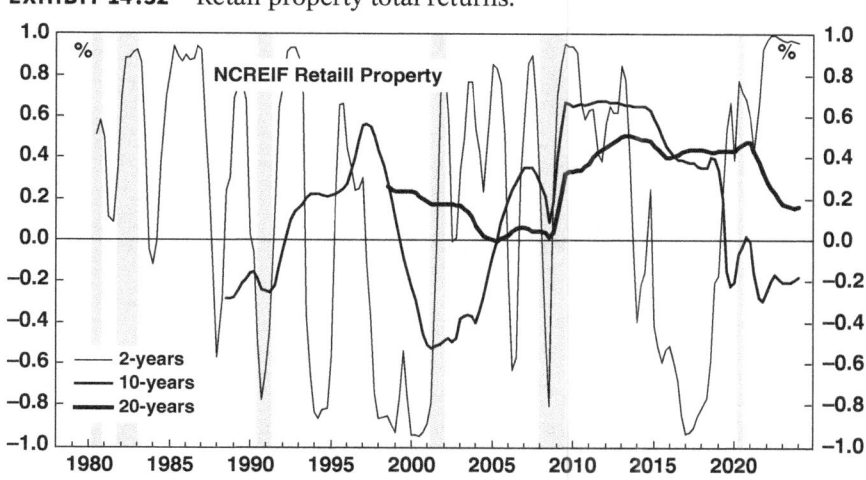

Source: ZCA using NCREIF data

EXHIBIT 14.33 Retail mortgage total return.

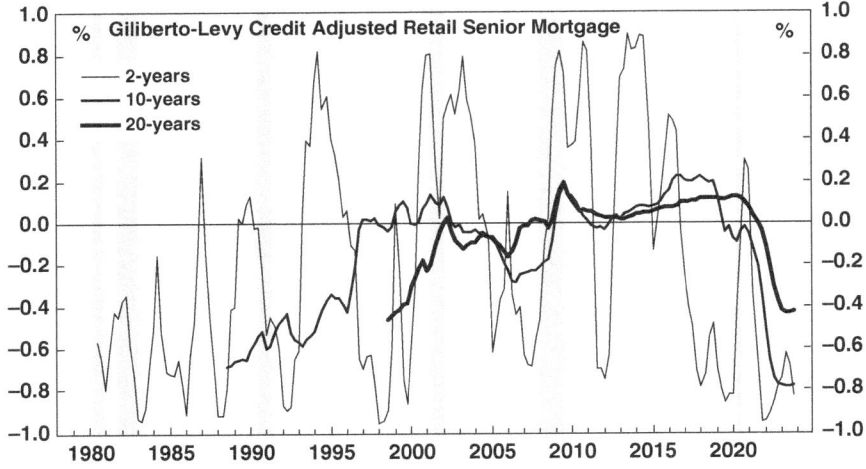

Source: ZCA using NCREIF data

EXHIBIT 14.34 Industrial property total returns.

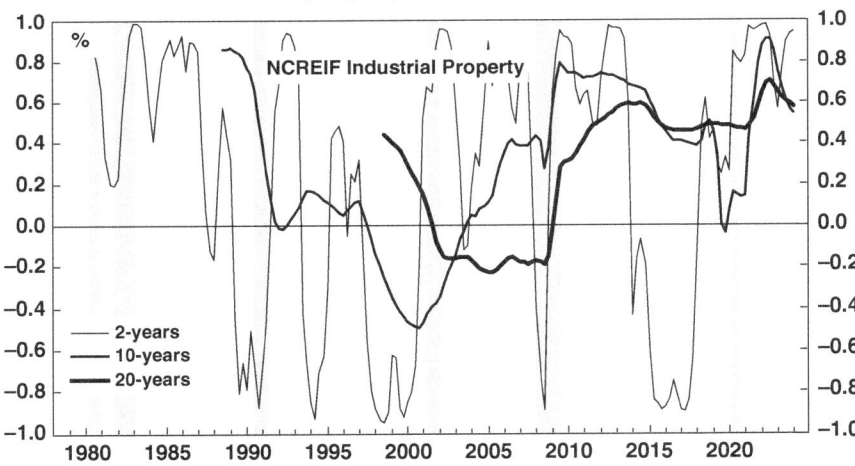

Source: ZCA using NCREIF data

Hotels, which have some of the shortest lease terms, are not good hedges. (See Exhibit 14.36.) Hotels cannot match T-bills as an inflation hedge. (See Exhibit 14.37.) However, T-bills introduce reinvestment risk. REITs are weak inflation hedges as shown in Exhibit 14.37.

EXHIBIT 14.35 Industrial mortgage total return.

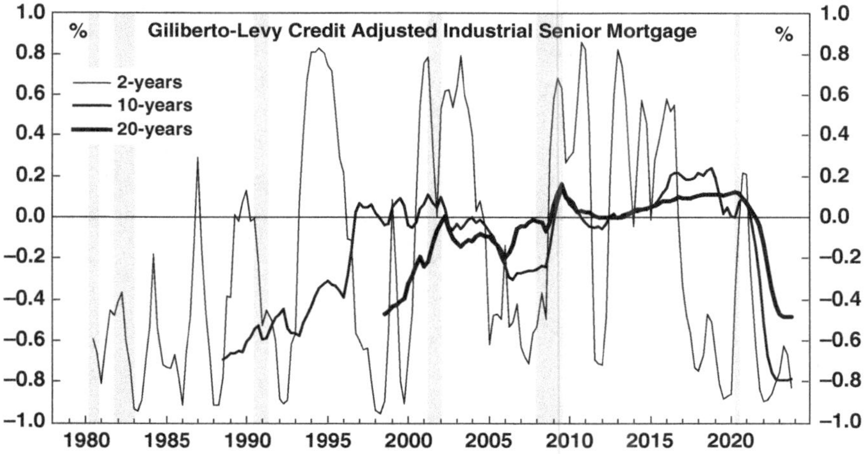

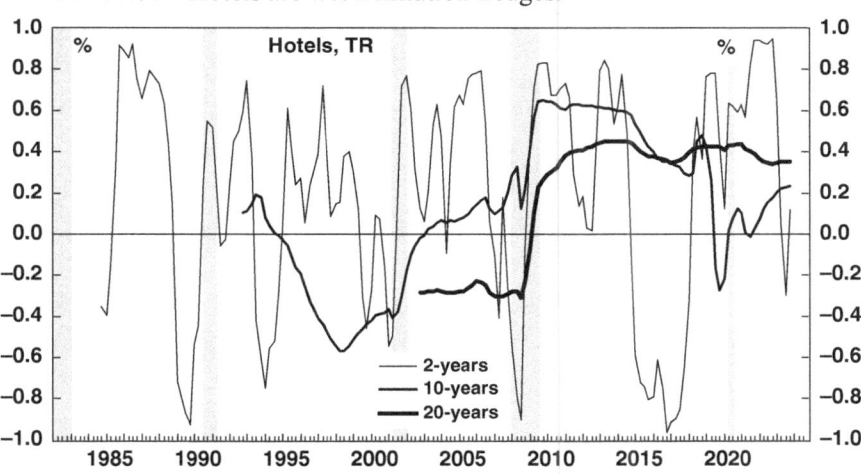

Source: ZCA using NCREIF data

EXHIBIT 14.36 Hotels are weak inflation hedges.

Source: ZCA using NCREIF data

Exhibit 14.38 and Exhibit 14.39 show that 30-day T-bills and stocks (S&P 500), are not good inflation hedges; the 20-year rolling correlation is approximately zero and when it is not, it is negative. AAA- and Baa-rated corporate bonds exhibit negative longer-run rolling correlations with inflation, as shown in Exhibits 14.40 and 14.41.

EXHIBIT 14.37 Equity REITs are weak hedges.

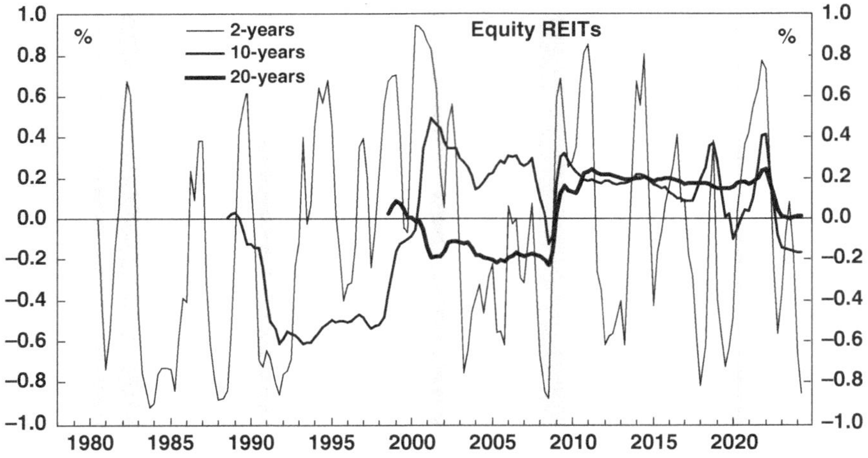

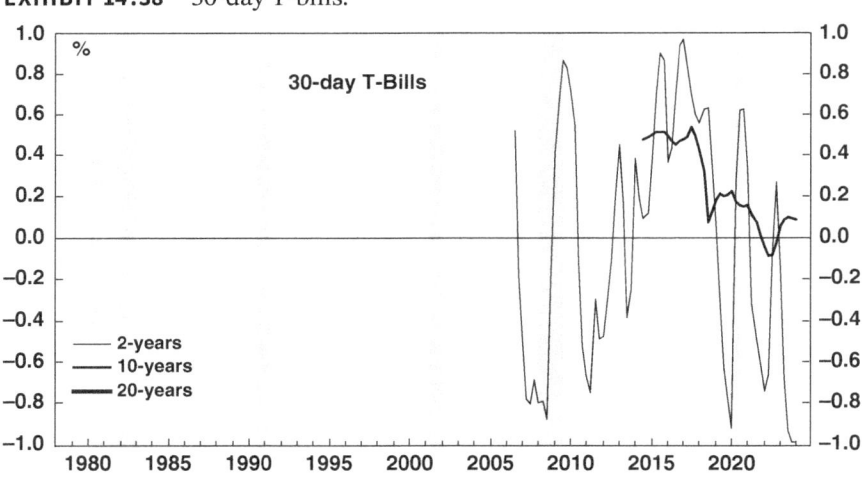

Source: ZCA using NCREIF data

EXHIBIT 14.38 30-day T-bills.

Source: ZCA using Federal Reserve data

How effective is a lease's pass-through provision? Real estate's debt-like features contribute to real estate's weak inflation hedging characteristics. The majority of property total returns are bond-like due to the underlying lease structure. By contrast, growth is a larger component of stock returns. Still, stocks are not a good inflation hedge, either. Even if there is some inflation protection

EXHIBIT 14.39 S&P 500.

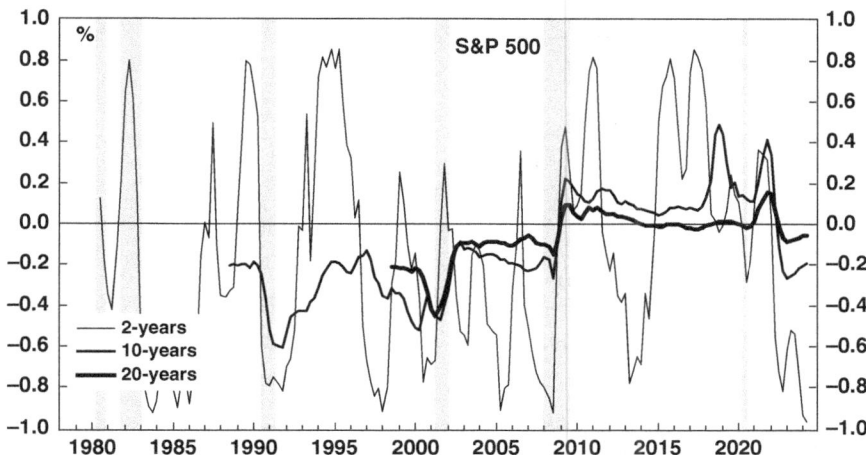

Source: ZCA using Federal Reserve data

EXHIBIT 14.40 AAA-rated corporate bond.

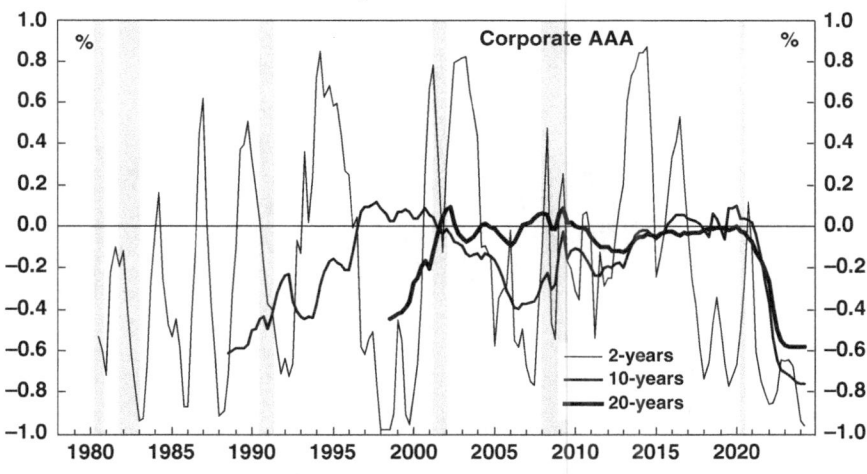

Source: ZCA using Federal Reserve data

within leases, the inflation pass-through is imperfect at best, usually lagged, and swamped by local demand–supply pressures.

Real estate is a poor and inconsistent inflation hedge, especially in the short to intermediate run. The inconsistency is evident with shorter moving correlation

EXHIBIT 14.41 BAA-rated corporate bond.

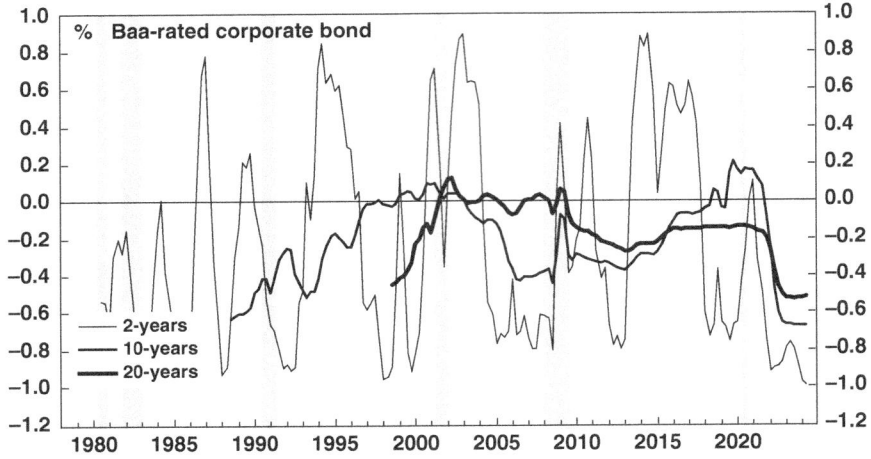

Source: ZCA using Federal Reserve data

EXHIBIT 14.42 The two-year rolling total return correlations for all property types are similar.

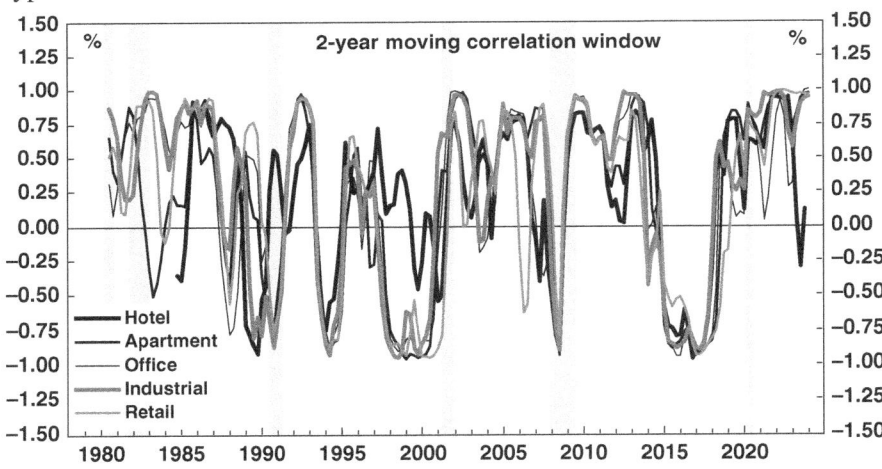

Source: ZCA using CoStar data

windows. (See Exhibit 14.42.) This exhibit may at first glance appear confusing, but it shows the high-frequency oscillation of correlations between positive and negative.

Exhibits 14.43 and 14.44 show that the greatest and most consistent period of inflation hedging was between the GFC and the short COVID-19 recession.

EXHIBIT 14.43 Property is a better, but inconsistent, mid-term hedge.

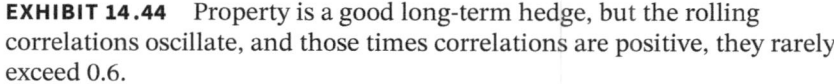

Source: ZCA using CoStar data

EXHIBIT 14.44 Property is a good long-term hedge, but the rolling correlations oscillate, and those times correlations are positive, they rarely exceed 0.6.

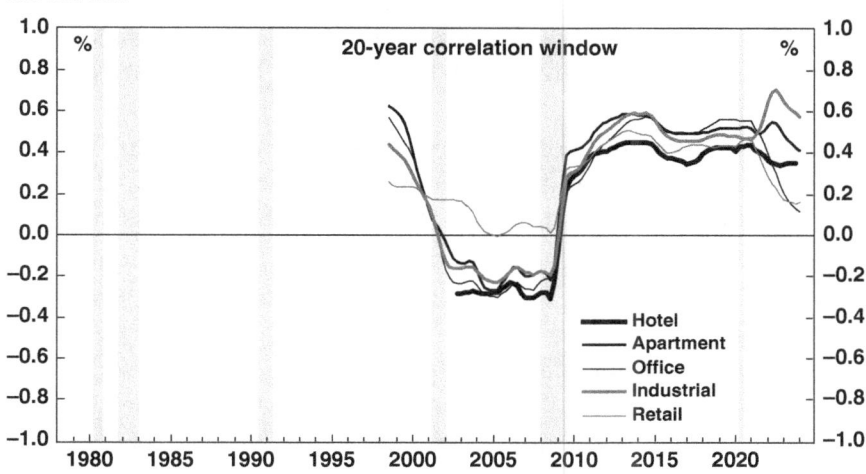

Source: ZCA using CoStar data

370 CHAPTER 14   Is Real Estate an Effective Inflation Hedge? Only in the Long Run

Since COVID-19, apartments exhibit the greater hedging power and office the least. Retail generally excelled from the early 1990s through the dot-com recession.

The 20-year rolling correlation indicates that from the GFC through the COVID-19 recession, property had its greatest period of inflation hedging, but the average rolling correlation was not much greater than 0.5.

Real estate, while an acceptable-to-good long-term hedge, is at best a weak and inconsistent short- to intermediate-term hedge.

Conclusions and Investment Implications

- Inflation is the rate by which the overall price index increases.
- Investors have trouble differentiating a change in relative prices from inflation.
- Do not expect a runaway Weimar-type hyperinflation, which has never occurred in the US.
- Apartments, office, retail, and industrial properties are poor short- and mid-term inflation hedges.
- During and immediately following COVID-19, supply and demand pressures accounted for most of the inflation pickup.
- Inflation, in addition to eroding households' purchasing power, does not affect all goods, services, and contracts equally, not does it harm all property types the same.
- Criteria for assessing inflation's hedging potential include whether (1) the asset is a long-term store of value, and (2) the asset's total returns are highly correlated with inflation, and (3) asset returns have low volatility around trend.
- Stocks and property are poor short-term hedges but are good inflation-adjusted long-term stores of value. T-bills, which are a much better hedge, pose significant reinvestment risk.
- Bonds and senior commercial mortgages are poor hedges.
- All major property types, no matter how short their lease maturities, are poor short- to intermediate-term inflation hedges.
- Even if real estate is not a good short- or intermediate-term inflation hedge, diversification remains the most important reason to invest in real estate.

Q&A: Interview with Jason Benderly, President, Benderly Economics and former Chief Economist of Goldman Sachs

Dealing with Messy Data on Wall Street

Jason, how did you become a Wall Street economist?

Serendipity. My wife worked with a group of analysts who were starting a new company selling Washington policy research to Wall Street. They needed an economist and there I was. But instead of doing policy research, I was able to spend a decade developing economic models.

When did you work on Wall Street?

The company ended up being bought by Prudential Insurance and the new COO hired me in 1982 to replace their Chief Economist, who was retiring. I was then hired by Kidder Peabody, a private investment bank, to be their Chief Economist. From there I was recruited by Goldman Sachs to be their Chief Economist. I left in 1989 to start Benderly Economics so I could focus more on research (and move to Colorado) and less on the extensive travel and marketing that GS required.

You have been an advocate of careful work with data.

I have focused on combining creative top-down modeling with careful bottoms-up analysis of data, which has been referred to as "statistical pointillism" or finding patterns and relationships where none seem to exist. From the top down, broad theory does not provide specific guidance, and seeking simplicity and intuition has always worked best for me. From the bottom up, there are data issues in measuring every aspect of economic behavior and phenomena.

Our joint project on real estate and inflation featured messy data which required clever technique. The consequences of the supply chain issues caused by COVID-19 could be neatly quantified by carefully parsing the price data through the supply pipeline.

(continued)

(*continued*)

How do you use statistics to make investment decisions?

There is no way to make unconditional forecasts of financial asset prices in the short and intermediate term. Cause and effect in the financial markets occur too quickly for that, which is why the most success comes from investing for the very long term. What statistical relationships can do is provide a baseline for direction, buying the dips or selling the rallies.

Describe a good relationship between economists and investors.

I have been dealing with investment managers from my own company for 35 years. By dealing with a manageable number of clients, I can provide feedback that gives them direction and ideas.

CHAPTER 15

A Monte Carlo Model of GP and LP Interests in a Structured Joint Venture

Preliminaries

We live stochastically, but think deterministically. The challenge of crossing a busy street, street map in hand, should underscore this point. What could possibly go wrong?

This chapter evaluates a simple structured model that includes leverage, a promote structure, and the interests of the LPs and the GPs. There are multiple sources of risk; some are internal to the transaction itself and others are externally imposed.

Monte Carlo Applications

Monte Carlo is a tool that many industries routinely use; real estate is an obvious application but a conspicuous exception, which makes real estate risk analysis ripe for change. Many industries routinely use Monte Carlo tools; they include pharmaceuticals, aeronautics, finance, energy, insurance, defense, manufacturing, new product development, and hedging, for instance.

Complex projects, especially capital-intensive ones, are good examples, but there are many others, such as the assessment of federal tax policy, the impact of crime on property values, supply chain management, optimal flexibility, corporate performance and risk, optimal working capital, budgeting, the valuation of a start-up company and its eventual disposition, the impact of climate change on property values along the coast, the valuation of penalty clauses and damages, the optimal corporate tax structure, and the valuation of new customers.

What do these applications have in common? They all involve risk and, in most cases, irreversibility, durability, complex phasing, and embedded real options, the values of which are a function of volatility. Real estate risk is poorly understood and the standard methods for estimating the effects of risk are flawed and wealth-reducing. Embedded options are valuable and they are just as real as bricks and mortar. Consequently, investors should include in a discounted cash flow analysis the opportunity cost of exercising (or extinguishing) these options.

Tax policy risk is usually ignored at the deal level. Tax changes are uncertain and affect investment performance and asset pricing, even for tax-exempt institutions such as pension funds that compete with taxable investors. Monte Carlo can help evaluate changes in the following tax provisions: capital gains and ordinary income tax rates, inflation adjustments to these rates, estate and gift taxes, treatment of interest rate expense, tax credits and subsidies, the carried interest provision, and the tax treatment of pass-through businesses. Changes can be temporary or "permanent."

Tax policy simulations at the macroeconomic level almost exclusively use deterministic tools that do not properly model embedded options and volatility. Many of the models used by tax policy advocates ignore the uncertain, lagged shifting of the tax burden and its effect on relative prices and income. As a result, estimates of the prompt and long-run impacts of a proposed tax change are often different and biased. Markets, like most systems, adjust prices to minimize the impact of a shock.[1] The expected impact and burden of the tax may not be the actual burden.

Public sector risk, which I discuss in Chapter 20, is a good application of Monte Carlo. For example, the underfunding of public pension funds will have a very large impact on state and local property taxes and the delivery of services, but the size, timing, and burden of the impact are uncertain. Investors should be aware of these tax-related risks.

Other applications of Monte Carlo modeling. Projects in which timing and irreversibility are important are good candidates for Monte Carlo analysis. Timing can include expansion and modification (switching) options, multi-period development, abandonment, and delay. Options to speed up a project or slow it down without penalties can be valuable.

Monte Carlo can estimate the variance of a project's performance, which helps determine performance confidence intervals and downside risk. Sequencing can follow linear or complex patterns that include switching between simultaneous and consecutive execution. The value of some options, especially those found in multistage projects, can be path-dependent.

In Chapter 11, I discuss how to apply stochastic optimization in search of the "best" development solution. The analyst can maximize NPV subject to various constraints, such as uncertain budgets or building permit issuance, or the analyst can minimize overall project variance subject to a minimum NPV. These are objectives that deterministic methods address poorly, if at all.

Monte Carlo Analysis of a Deal

Using a hypothetical Monte Carlo model of an apartment acquisition, I explore the relationship between structure and performance. Monte Carlo is an effective tool to help investors understand risk. Monte Carlo focuses on probability distributions (the face of uncertainty) and not averages. It captures interdependences, reflects correlations between distributions, renders risk explicit, and establishes probability distributions for stochastic variables based on empirical analysis and theory.

I establish probability distributions for each uncertain variable based either on empirical analysis or on theory. The stochastic variables, in the following hypothetical structured joint venture, include the exit cap rate (in years five through seven) and the annual rental growth rate. The two variables interact because the disposition price is a function of both the exit cap rate and the expected change in NOI, which I proxy for illustrative purposes using the rental growth rate.

The correlation is important because cap rates tend not to increase when NOI increases. By establishing the correlation between the two distributions, we exclude meaningless scenarios. Rising cap rates means falling prices. For purposes of illustration, the correlation between the two distributions is minus one; they are inversely correlated.

Exhibit 15.1 shows the negative correlation between rental growth rates and cap rates for the entire period, 2001 through 2024. I use market rental growth rates as a proxy for NOI growth rates in this exercise. The actual correlations across MSAs are between −0.25 and −0.50, as shown in Exhibit 15.1.

Average correlation coefficients do not tell the entire story. I introduced in Chapter 14 moving correlations, which are correlations calculated using a moving window of quarters.

Exhibits 15.2 and 15.3 show for six MSAs cap rates and market rental growth rates. Dallas is a rapidly growing MSA, whereas NYC is not. Cap rates are volatile over the long run but they are much less so compared to market rental growth rates.

EXHIBIT 15.1 Correlations of rental growth rates and cap rates for selected MSAs.

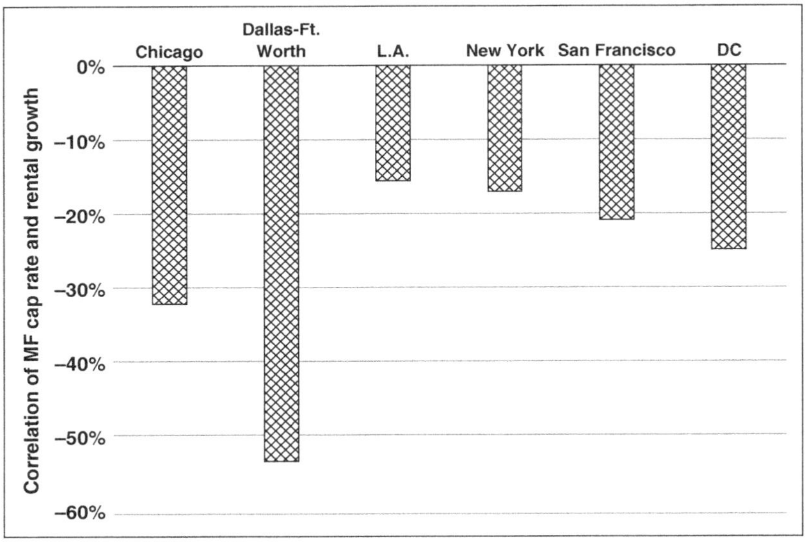

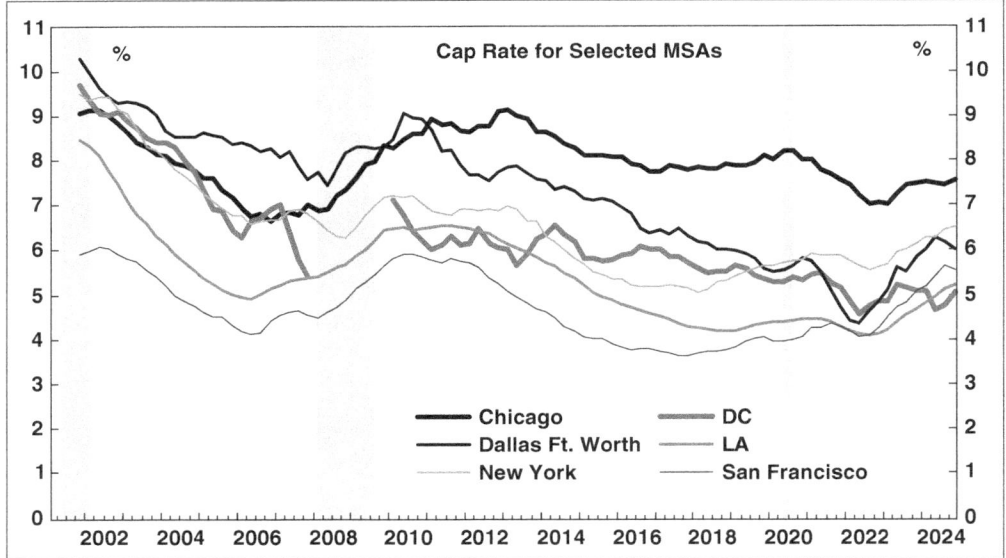

Source: ZCA using CoStar data

EXHIBIT 15.2 Apartment cap rates for six large MSAs.

Source: ZCA using CoStar data

EXHIBIT 15.3 Apartment market rental growth rates for six large MSAs.

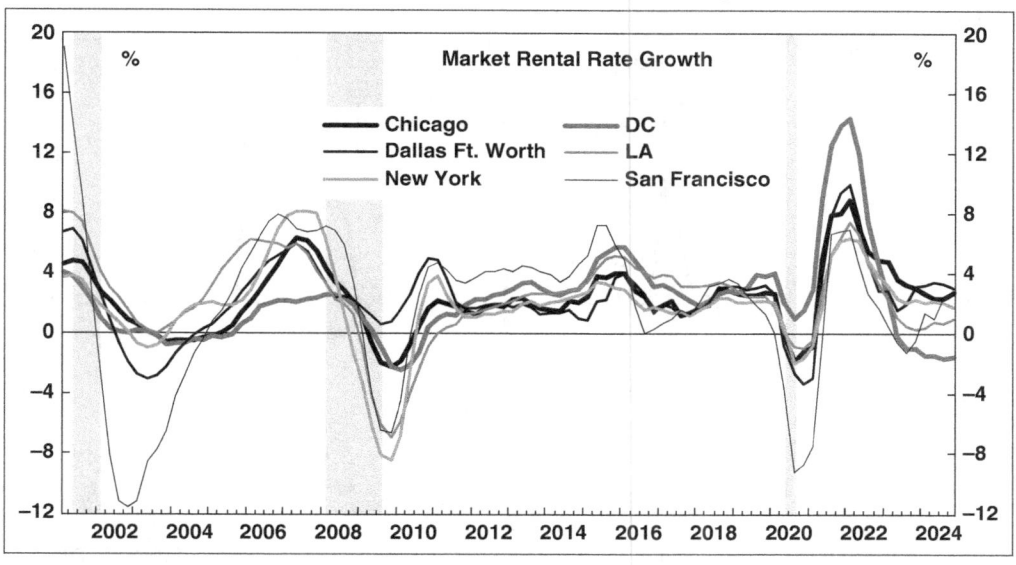

Source: ZCA using CoStar data

The ranking of cities by market rental growth rates is not stable over time. Selecting MSAs based on ranks may be counterproductive.

The values of the correlations can make a significant difference in the estimate of downside risk and other outputs. A simple question, such as "What is the likelihood of an IRR within 15% and 20%," depends crucially on the values of the correlation coefficients as well as the shapes of the distributions.

Exhibits 15.4 through 15.7 illustrate the instability of the moving correlations between MSA cap rates and market rental growth rate. Not only are the correlations unstable, but they vary by MSA. No one assumption fits all MSAs.

The model's assumptions are as shown in Exhibit 15.8.

Leverage increases the return on equity as well as its volatility at the overall deal level and for the LP and GP positions. As leverage increases, volatility rises at an increasing rate. In general, doubling the leverage from 25% to 50% quadruples the volatility. The GP's return increases rapidly due to leverage and the embedded options. The GP has strong incentives to increase risk. See Exhibits 15.9 and 15.10.

Exhibits 15.11 and 15.12 show the input distributions of rental growth rates and exit cap rates. Both are inputs. The former is symmetrically distributed while cap rates are skewed to the right. The output is sensitive to the shape of the distribution.

EXHIBIT 15.4 12-month moving correlation of New York cap rates and market rental growth rates.

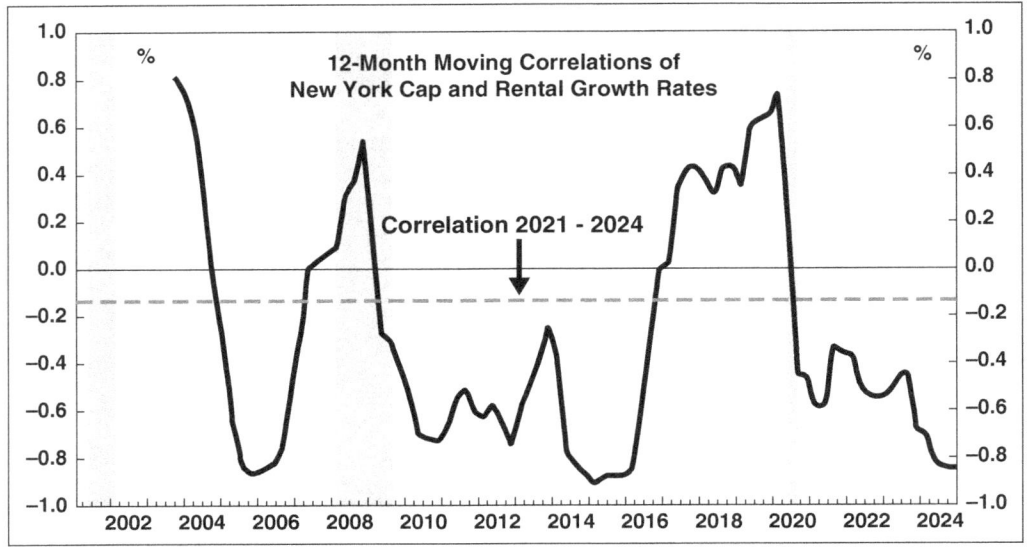

Source: ZCA using CoStar data

EXHIBIT 15.5 20-month moving correlation of New York cap rates and market rental growth rates.

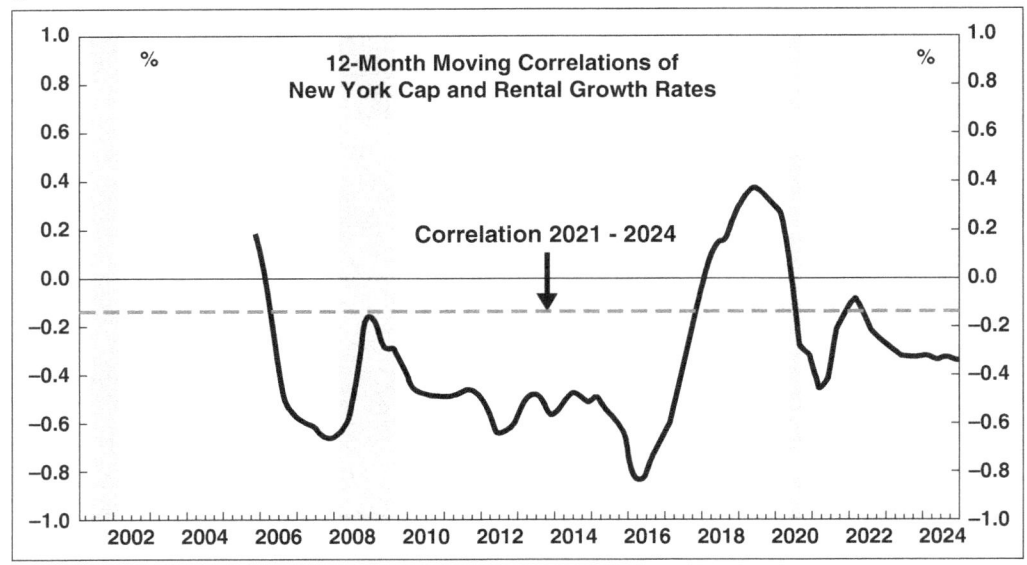

Source: ZCA using CoStar data

EXHIBIT 15.6 20-month moving correlation of Chicago cap rates and market rental growth rates.

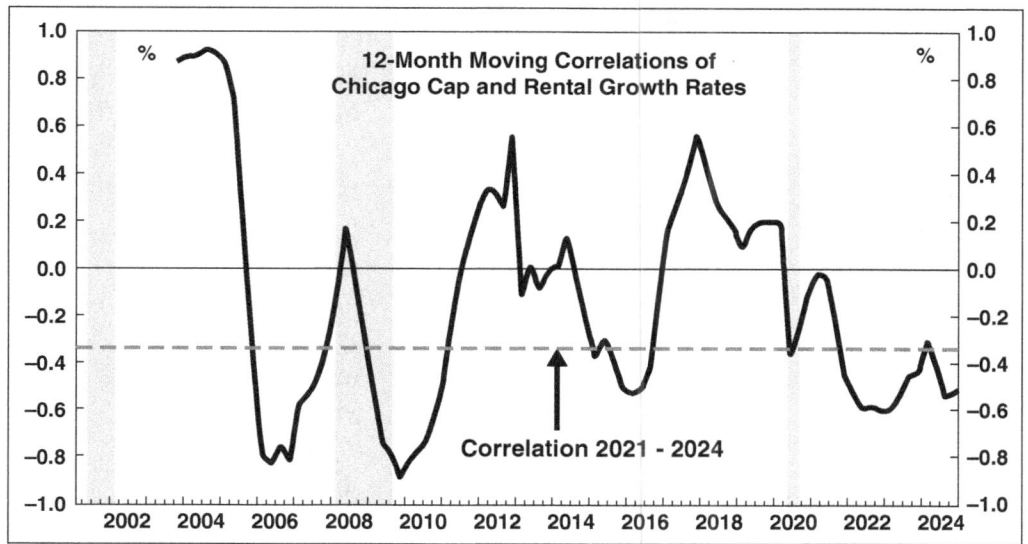

Source: ZCA using CoStar data

EXHIBIT 15.7 20-month moving correlations of Dallas-Ft. Worth cap rates and market rental growth rates.

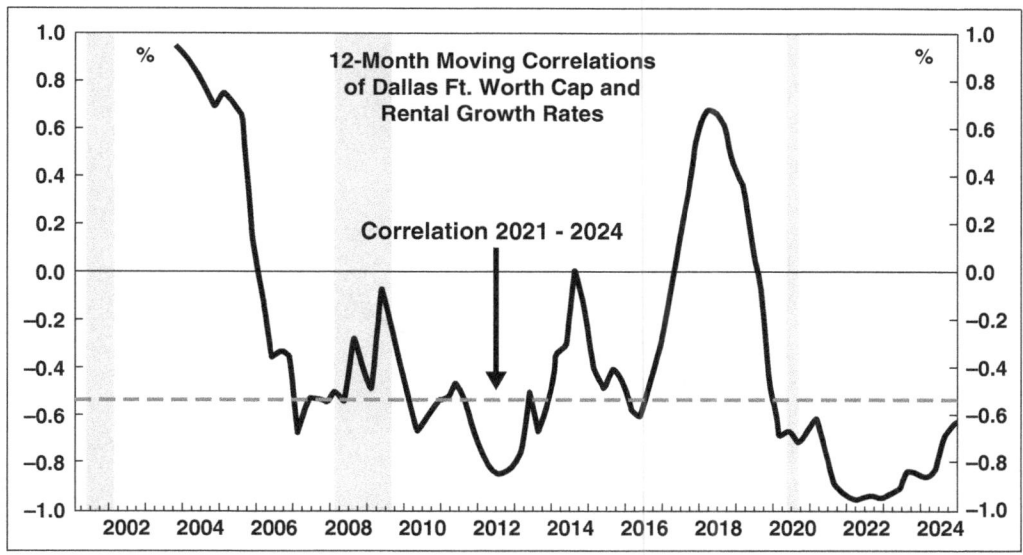

Source: ZCA using CoStar data

EXHIBIT 15.8 Monte Carlo model inputs.

Property types	Apartment
Purchase price	$10,000,000
Expense ratio	40%
Number of units	100
Going in cap rate	6.66%
Equity required	25%
Coupon	5.5%
Preferred return	10%
Promoted return	50% over the preferred return
LP investment	90%
GP investment	10%
Selling costs	2%
Holding period	5 years
Amortization period	30 years
Monte Carlo Inputs	
Exit cap rate	Mean = 6.6%; SD = 3.0%
Rental growth rate	Mean = 2.0%; 0.50%
Correlation of exit cap and NOI growth rates	−1.0

Source: ZCA

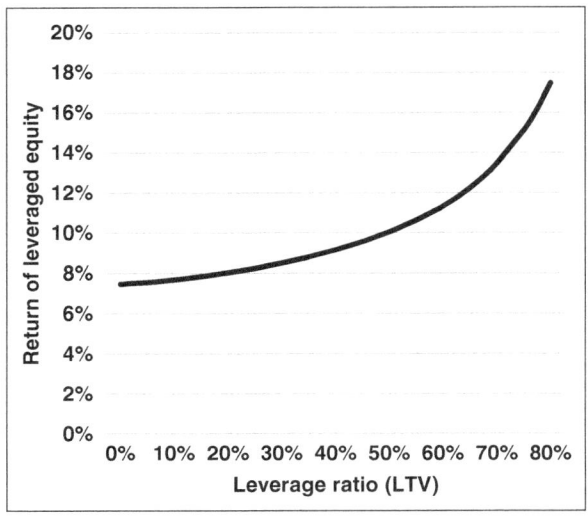

EXHIBIT 15.9 Leveraged equity returns increase with additional leverage.

Source: ZCA

EXHIBIT 15.10 The volatility of equity returns increases rapidly with leverage. The ratio of volatility to return more than doubles as LTV increases from 0% to 80%.

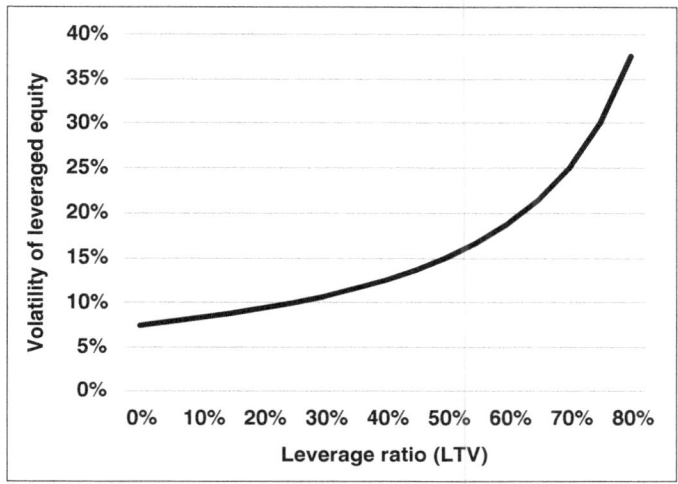

Source: ZCA

EXHIBIT 15.11 Rental growth rate distribution.

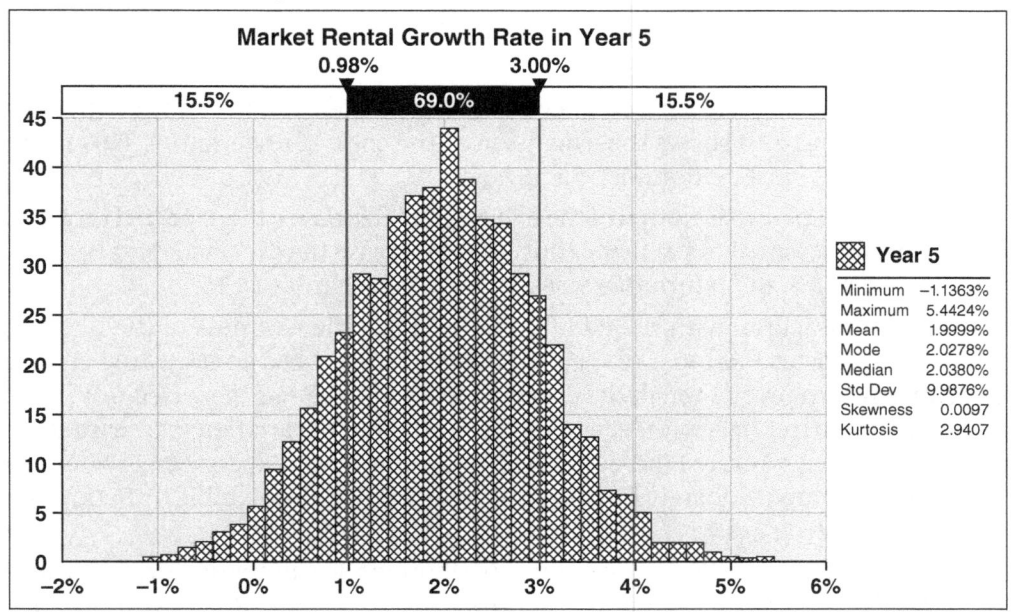

Source: ZCA

EXHIBIT 15.12 The exit cap rate distribution.

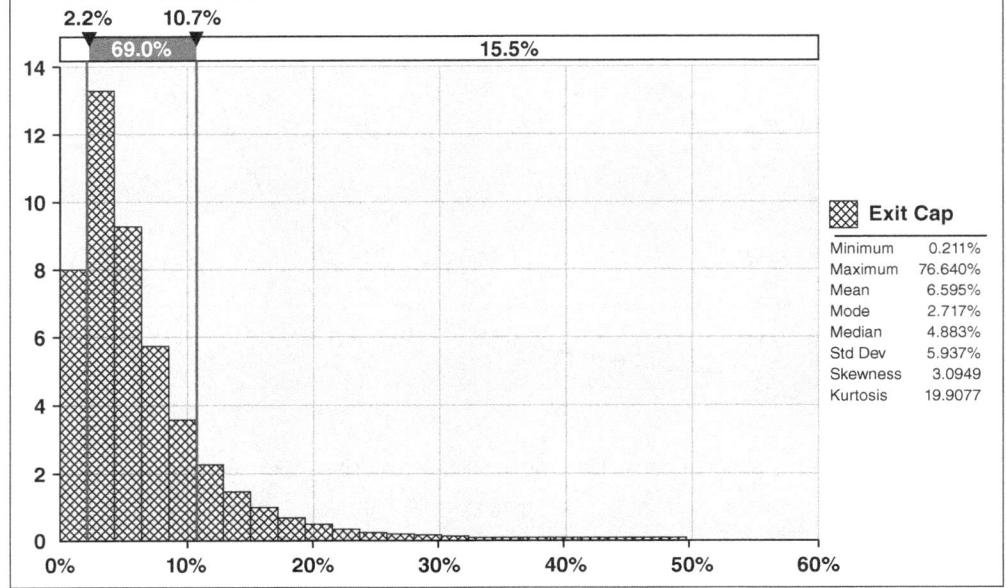

Source: ZCA

Exhibit 15.13 tracks 5,000 samples. Each point is a simulation. Note the general negative correlation.

As the deal horizon extends, the 95% confidence interval for rental growth rates expands. Exhibit 15.14 shows the expansion of the cone of uncertainty. This result is not found in typical deterministic analysis.

When the standard deviation of the exit cap rate increases, the expected property level return increases along with volatility. If we increase the expected rental growth rate from 1% to 2%, the return increases, as shown in Exhibit 15.15.

In this transaction, with the addition of leverage, the riskiness of the LP position increases faster than that of the GP position. The LP has an increased chance of negative returns even though the expected IRR to the LP has increased from 9.6% with no leverage to 17.8% with leverage. The coefficient of variation (standard deviation divided mean return) increases by 29% for the LP but decreases 11% for the GP. Risks shift proportionately from the GP to the LP. See also Exhibit 15.16 through Exhibit 15.18.

Exhibits 15.16 and 15.17 show the distributions for property level IRR and equity multiple. Note that Exhibit 15.16, the property level IRR, shows a negative IRR with a 9.8% probability.

EXHIBIT 15.13 Monte Carlo samples both distributions; the average correlation is −1.0.

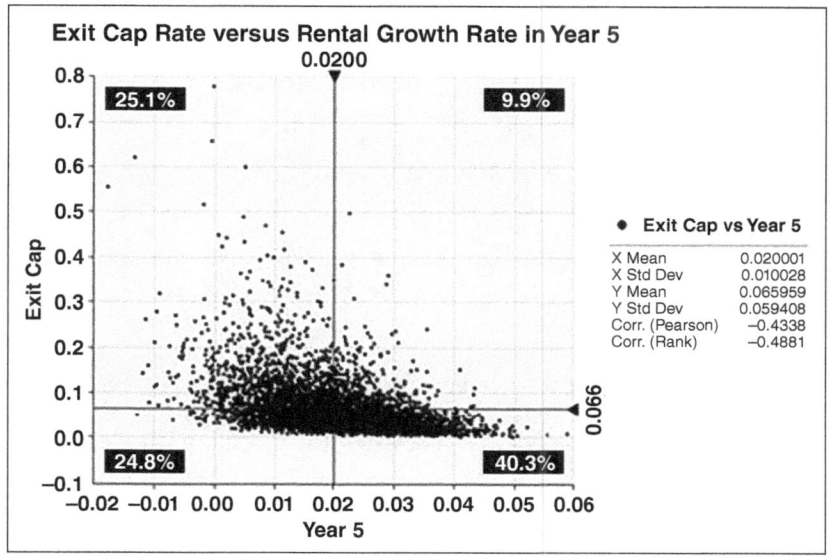

Source: ZCA

EXHIBIT 15.14 With time the volatility of the rental growth rate increases.

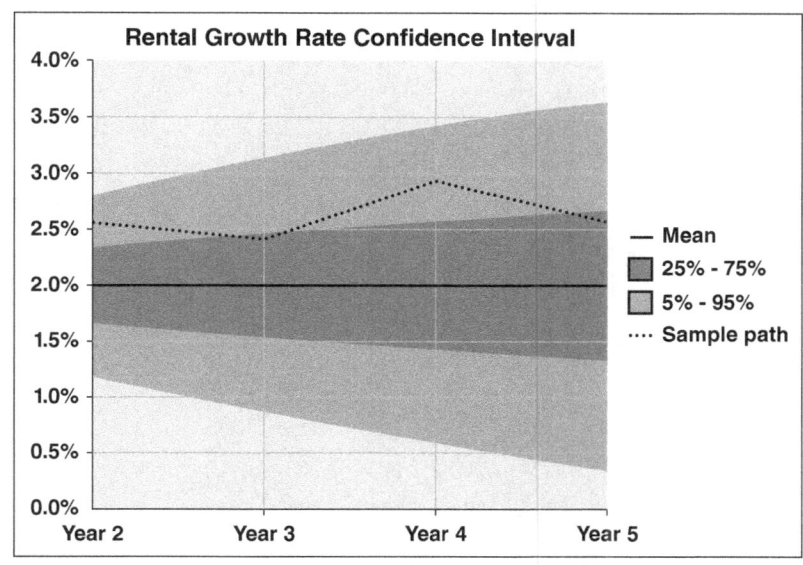

Source: ZCA

EXHIBIT 15.15 Return and risk increase as exit cap rate volatility increases.

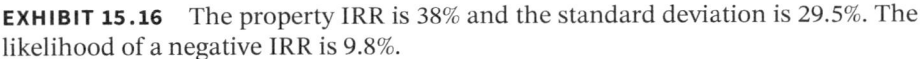

Source: ZCA

EXHIBIT 15.16 The property IRR is 38% and the standard deviation is 29.5%. The likelihood of a negative IRR is 9.8%.

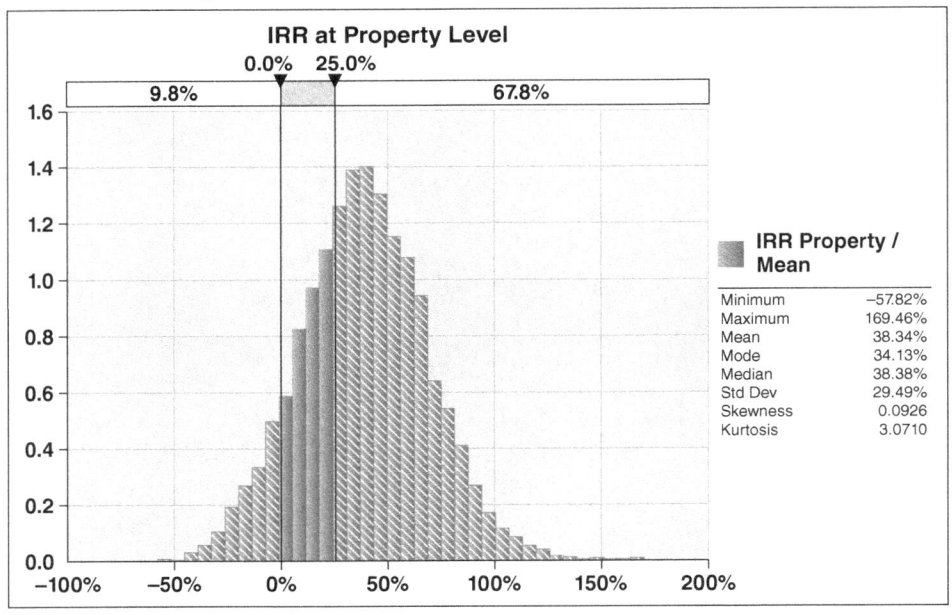

Source: ZCA

EXHIBIT 15.17 The equity multiple, which is highly skewed to the right. The chance of a multiple in excess of 3 is 55%.

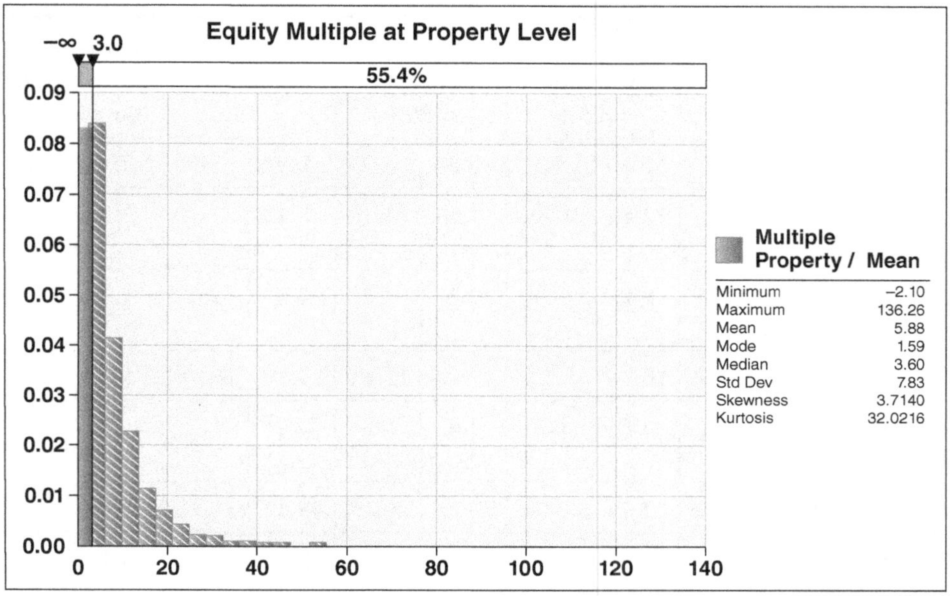

Equity Multiple at Property Level
−∞ 3.0
55.4%
0.09
0.08
0.07
0.06
0.05
0.04
0.03
0.02
0.01
0.00
0
20
40
60
80
100
120
140
Multiple Property / Mean
Minimum −2.10
Maximum 136.26
Mean 5.88
Mode 1.59
Median 3.60
Std Dev 7.83
Skewness 3.7140
Kurtosis 32.0216

Source: ZCA

Exhibits 15.18 and 15.19 show that the GP benefits from leverage; the greater the leverage, the greater is the volatility. With more volatility comes higher IRRs and equity multiples to the GP. Leverage increases the IRR and also the fees that the GP receives through the promote. Should the manager be rewarded for assuming excessive leverage or beta?

The likelihood of a greater equity multiple with additional leverage increases for the LP, but much faster for the GP. The distribution of the GP multiple is highly skewed to the right, and this skewness increases with greater leverage. Additional volatility benefits the GP at the price of greater likelihood of greater downside.

Exhibits 15.19 and 15.20 juxtapose the LP and GP return and multiple distributions for the cases where the standard deviation is one and six. The GP distributions are highly skewed to the right and this skewness increases with volatility. By contrast, the LP distribution has a much lower mean IRR and the standard deviation is less as well.

EXHIBIT 15.18 Leverage and performance: The GP's multiple increases faster than the LP multiple with increasing leverage.

	Leverage = 0%		Leverage = 25%		Leverage = 50%		Leverage = 75%		Multiple 75% leverage versus none	
	Mean	SD	Mean	SD	Mean	SD	**Mean**	SD	Mean	SD
IRR property	11.2%	8.5%	12.4%	10.8%	14.6%	15.0%	23.4%	20.6%	2.1	2.4
Multiple property	1.7	0.7	1.86	0.9	2.2	1.3	3.0	2.6	1.8	4.0
IRR LP	9.6%	6.6%	10.3%	8.5%	11.4%	12.1%	17.8%	16.3%	1.8	2.5
Multiple LP	1.6	0.4	1.6	0.6	1.8	0.8	2.2	1.6	1.4	3.7
IRR GP	20.1%	19.0%	23.9%	23.0%	30.1%	29.3%	48.4%	38.3%	2.4	2.0
Multiple GP	3.0	2.8	3.8	3.8	5.4	5.8	10.3	11.9	3.4	4.3

Source: ZCA

EXHIBIT 15.19 The GP's IRR increases more rapidly than the LP's position with greater volatility.

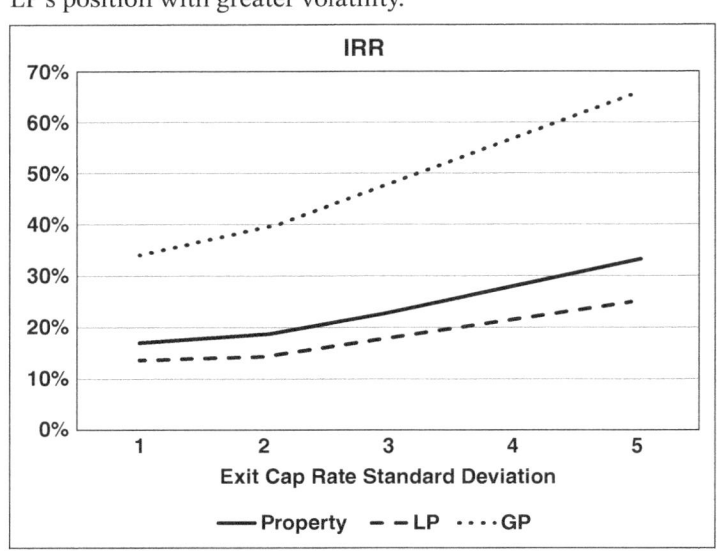

Source: ZCA

EXHIBIT 15.20 The LP's equity multiple rises more slowly than the property multiple. The GP's position rises rapidly.

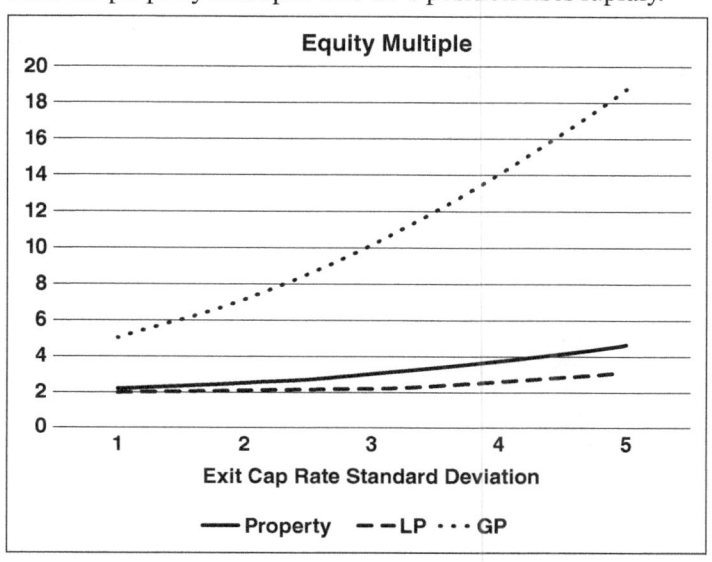

Source: ZCA

Exhibits 15.21 and 15.22 juxtapose the LP and GP return and multiple distributions for the cases where the standard deviation is one and six. The GP distributions are highly skewed to the right, and this skewness increases with volatility. By contrast, the LP distribution has a much lower mean IRR and the standard deviation is less as well.

Increasing volatility increases the likelihood of negative IRRs for both the LP and GP from 6.1% to 10.5%, a 72% increase in downside risk. Knowing the source of risk, the degree of risk, and how risk affects promotes and GP performance is critical.

The distributions for the LP's and GP's equity multiples show that the GP's multiple expands substantially with additional leverage. See Exhibits 15.23 and 15.24.

EXHIBIT 15.21 The likelihood of an IRR to the LP in excess of 25% if the exit cap rate volatility is 1%; the GP's probability is 66%. The likelihood of a loss to the LP and GP is 6%.

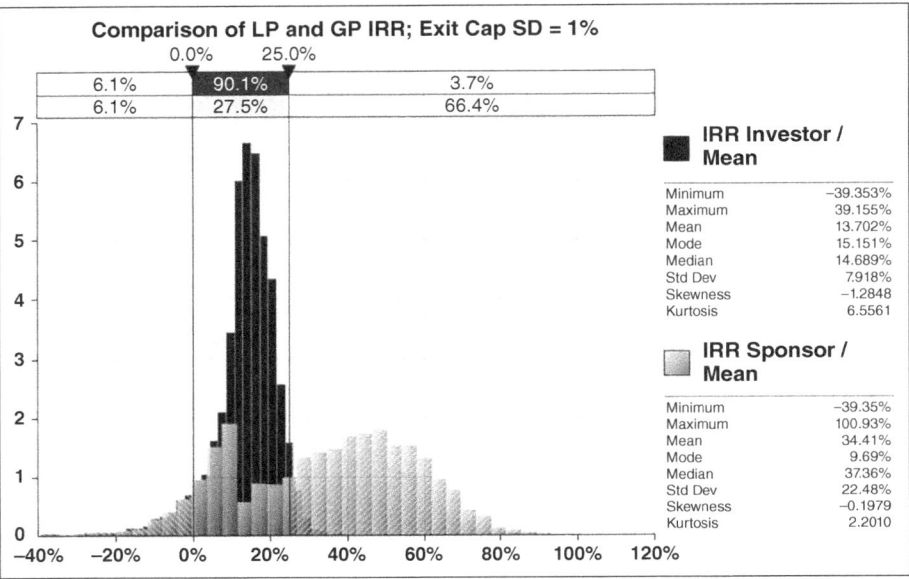

Source: ZCA

EXHIBIT 15.22 Increasing the exit cap rate standard deviation from 1% to 6% dramatically increases the likelihood of the LP's IRR in excess of 25% but increases the GP's probability as well, but not by as much. The likelihood of a loss is 10.5%.

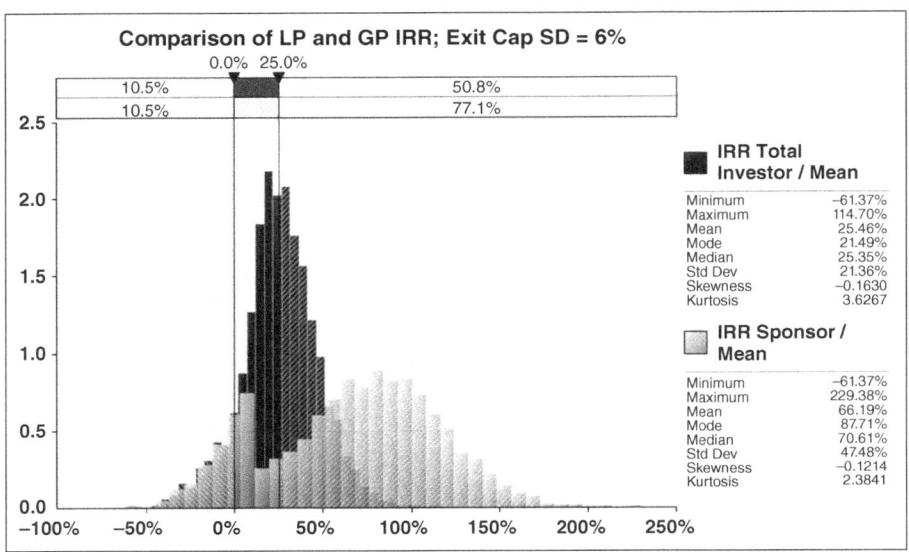

Source: ZCA

EXHIBIT 15.23 With exit cap rate volatility of 1%, the likelihood of a multiple in excess of 3 for the LP is about 2%; for the GP it is 65%.

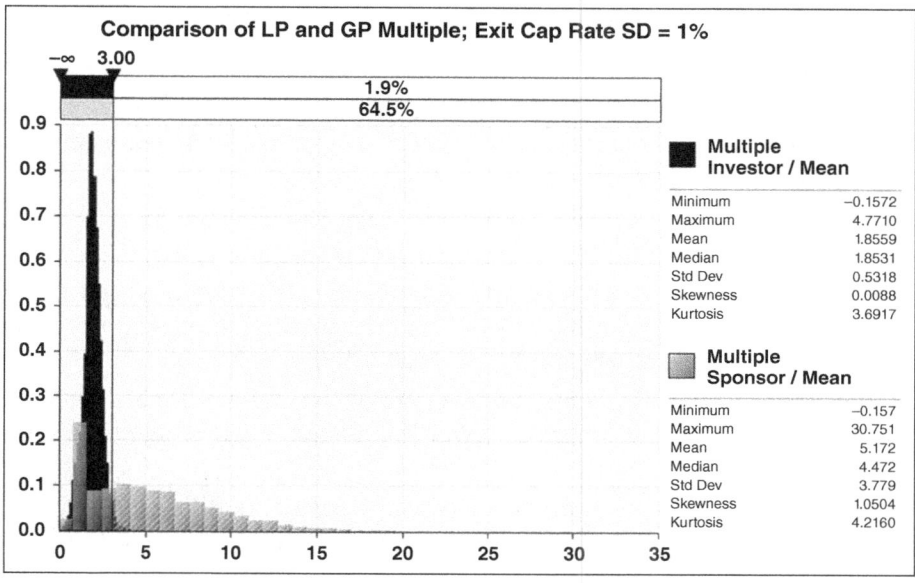

Source: ZCA

EXHIBIT 15.24 By increasing the exit cap rate standard deviation from 1% to 6%, the likelihood of a multiple greater than 3 increases to 47% for the LP and 67% for the GP.

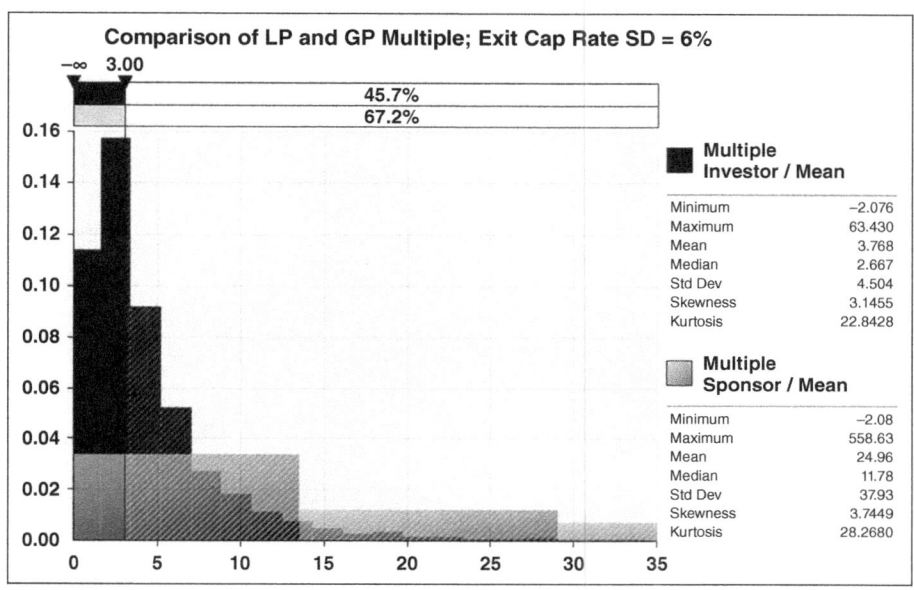

Source: ZCA

Conclusions and Investment Implications

- Monte Carlo is a powerful tool for evaluating risk within highly structured deals as well as leases, mortgages, portfolios, and even markets.
- Greater leverage brings higher equity returns as well as greater equity return volatility. At high leverage levels, the probability of loss increases even though expected returns have increased.
- I have shown in Chapter 4 that if one increases the leverage from 25% to 50%, still a seemingly low amount of leverage, volatility quadruples.
- The promote interacts with leverage and increases the promoted return, much of which is beta and not alpha. The promoted return consumes proportionately more of the total return as volatility increases.
- GP fees increase with incremental leverage. If leverage and manager skill are not related, why should investors reward managers for leveraged incremental returns?
- The value of the GP's position increases with greater volatility.
- Due to the many embedded real options, including the promote, the GP benefits disproportionately.

Q&A: Interview with Ralph Rosenberg, Chairman of Real Assets, KKR

Nimble Navigator of Cycles and Sectors

When did you join Goldman Sachs?

I graduated from Brown University in 1986 and accepted an offer from Goldman Sachs. I was a real estate analyst from 1986 to 1988 and then attended Stanford Graduate School of Business. In 1990, I returned to Goldman to join the new real estate principal investment group. The growth of principal investing in the 1990s was meteoric. I was promoted to help run the business and became a partner in 1998. In 2003, Hank Paulson, Chairman and CEO of Goldman, asked me to move into the fixed income division. I co-founded the special situations group and from 2003 to 2006 co-headed Goldman's business focused on proprietary investing in principal finance, high-yield bonds, and public and private bank loans. Goldman had already gone public so I had access to a large balance sheet. I left Goldman because I wanted to try something new.

When you left Goldman, you did something very unusual.

I set up a $500 million fund in late 2006; the investors included Goldman partners and LPs. By the summer of 2007 market conditions had worsened and there were signs of unusual activity. Ten months after I had raised the capital, I gave the money back and released everyone from their fund commitments because I did not feel our strategy could be deployed responsibly. All of Goldman's partners who had invested applauded the decision, but the LPs thought we lacked nerve.

I took my team and merged with Eton Park, which had the right strategy to short the excesses in the market. Real estate was a notable area of opportunity. For example, we shorted German banks who, at the time, originated the 85% to 95% LTV piece of mortgage loans at 6%. That was just crazy. We were fortunate and did well for our clients during this period.

(continued)

(*continued*)

Why did you join KKR?

By the end of 2010, most of the major players, other than Blackstone, Starwood, and Lonestar, had left the real estate business. KKR saw this as an opportunity to build a leading real estate platform, and leverage their global platform and LP relationships. I had led the acquisition of Rockefeller Center in the early 1990s, serving on the board with Jerry Speyer of Tishman Speyer, a good friend of Henry Kravis. Jerry recommended me to lead the effort and I joined KKR in March 2011.

PART IV
The Public Sector and Collective Risk

CHAPTER 16

Public-Sector Risk: Introduction to Sprawl and Rent Control

Preliminaries. An Introduction to Public Finance for Real Estate Professionals

Local government consists of fragmented jurisdictions that often compete rather than cooperate; they impose uncompensated costs and risks on other jurisdictions. Private investors and local governments should reconsider how they evaluate risks. Public sector-induced volatility is part of urban life, but private investors do not always recognize much less quantify these risks.

Economic life is full of externalities. When the activity of one entity—a firm or household—directly affects the welfare of another without its being reflected in the cost of goods or services involved, such as pollution, then that is an externality. Market prices do not price externalities properly, which distorts prices and affects investors' ability to evaluate joint risks in a public-private real estate partnership.

Public goods. A public good, which is distinct from a private good, is a good that is nonrival and nonexcludable. Nonrival means that the marginal cost of another person's consuming the good is zero, and nonexcludable means that there is no practical way to prevent an entity's consuming it. Air, clear or dirty, is a good example of a good that is nonrival and nonexcludable. A private good, such as oranges, is rival and excludable. Individuals have no incentive to reveal their true public goods preference. They are free riders, so efficient taxing of public goods is a problem.

The property tax is the preserve of local government. The tax is visible to households because they pay the tax directly or through their monthly mortgage payment.

Many goods and services, such as the services of a spouse's or partner's tending to small children, do not go through the GDP accounts and are not priced in the market. Taxes and externalities distort many prices, so these prices do not represent true marginal social costs. This disparity complicates discounted cash flow analysis of public-private projects. How should investors account for risk in the presence of these distortions? How should they value non-traded or public goods?

Competitive jurisdictions. How to handle public goods provision efficiently is a challenge. One model states that the ability of households to move among local jurisdictions—voting with their feet—produces a market-like solution to the public goods problem and minimizes or eliminates the free rider problem.

A household searches for a most preferred bundle of public goods, housing, and property taxes. The model assumes no externalities or spillover effects, households are perfectly mobile, people have perfect information with respect to a jurisdiction's services and cost of admission, the cost per unit of public service is constant, and there are enough communities to satisfy the preferences of each household. The CBD is not homogeneous, which contradicts an important assumption of our public finance model.

Local governments are financed by a property tax, and communities approve exclusionary zoning laws, specifically laws that promote homogeneity. If the demand for public services is a function of income, then this system promotes spatial inequality. Low-income people clearly have an incentive to move into high-income, high-amenity communities, but they often lack the means to do so. The lack of affordable housing and sufficient income is a serious and chronic problem.

Some people regard the poor as undeserving free riders. As more poor families move into a high-income community, average tax revenue per family falls, which affects tax rates and the provision of goods and services by government. The rich can either vote with their feet, which erodes the tax base, or they can lobby to exclude so-called undesirable people, which they often do.

Local governments therefore take actions to control externalities, minimize the free rider problem, promote homogeneity of tastes, and maximize the property values of current, not future, taxpayers. Zoning is an example. Excess demand for housing in desirable communities causes rising home prices and rents and strains affordability. The clamoring for relief becomes palpable. By excluding certain uses and users, firms and households leapfrog to other jurisdictions. Simple in concept, the process is fraught with risk and complexities, which investors should understand.

Rent control, instituted in New York City following WWII and the return of soldiers, was an attempt to redistribute income to lower income families through the use of rent ceilings. Some jurisdictions, such as New York City in recent decades, have modified first-generation rent control and adopted rent stabilization—not hard ceilings—to balance redistribution so that higher income families do not vote with their feet. (Note that income redistribution is more self-defeating in smaller jurisdictions where moving by the higher income families may be less costly or inconvenient.)

The government meets the capital markets: The value of a life and the welfare of future generations. Real estate of all kinds is subject to governmental regulations. Development, which requires permits, must comply with all kinds of use and code restrictions.

Local governments also partner with private investors in multi-generational, highly durable projects that generate long-term private and public goods benefits. A conflict—how to value risk—arises. Business and government evaluate investments in different ways. For instance, the objectives of government are more expansive and government may use a different discount rate reflecting a view of risk that is different from that of private investors.

Firms rely on market prices and interest rates. However, market prices do not exist for some goods and services that do not trade in markets. (See Chapter 2 on the analysis of non-traded attributes that do not trade separately.) In addition, market prices may not represent the true marginal social cost or benefits, especially if there is market failure due to externalities or economies of scale. If capital markets falter, the government may reject a market rate of interest when discounting future net benefits. Such is clearly the case when public pension funds choose a high discount rate to value their pension liabilities, as I discuss in Chapter 20.

Valuing non-market services, goods, and lives. The market fails to price many social benefits, such as the value of social networking in public spaces, clean air, health and safety, etc. Conspicuous is the failure to value correctly a human life or time wasted in traffic.

Not all lives are valued in the same way. Placing a price on a life is controversial, but local governments implicitly price statistical lives all the time when they make budgetary decisions. How should we balance lives saved from installing new traffic lights with the benefits of building a new high school football stadium?

How should we value a life? One approach is to calculate remaining income forgone, but consider the implications for the value of seniors' lives. Another approach is to consider the additional income required for a person to assume greater risk on the job, such as high voltage line maintenance or the raising of venomous reptiles. No one method is politically acceptable to all.

I discussed in Chapter 11 the calculation of shadow prices using constrained optimization. The shadow or implicit internal price is the increase in the objective function—the sum of all project NPVs—given an additional budgetary dollar. Sometimes we can infer the implicit price of some governmental services or constraints using this approach.

Discounting lives and risk. Discounting facilitates the comparison of future with current net benefits. A dollar today is worth more than a dollar tomorrow. The investment horizon and the discount rate make a big difference. If the discount rate is zero, then the length of the horizon matters if we assume no risk. If the rate is higher, then governments have a strong incentive to ignore the welfare of future generations. Exhibit 16.1 shows the present value of $1,000 received next year, as well as 10, 100, and 250 years later.

Some people say, "Ignore future generations; technology will save the day so let them pay-as-they-go." Societies implicitly make intergeneration tradeoffs—future generations and nonresidents are conspicuously absent from the deliberations—but current market discount rates may be too high. Even very low discount rates can make a big difference in the economic viability of highly durable, very long-lived assets such as the Brooklyn Bridge.

EXHIBIT 16.1 The impact of discount rates and investment horizon.

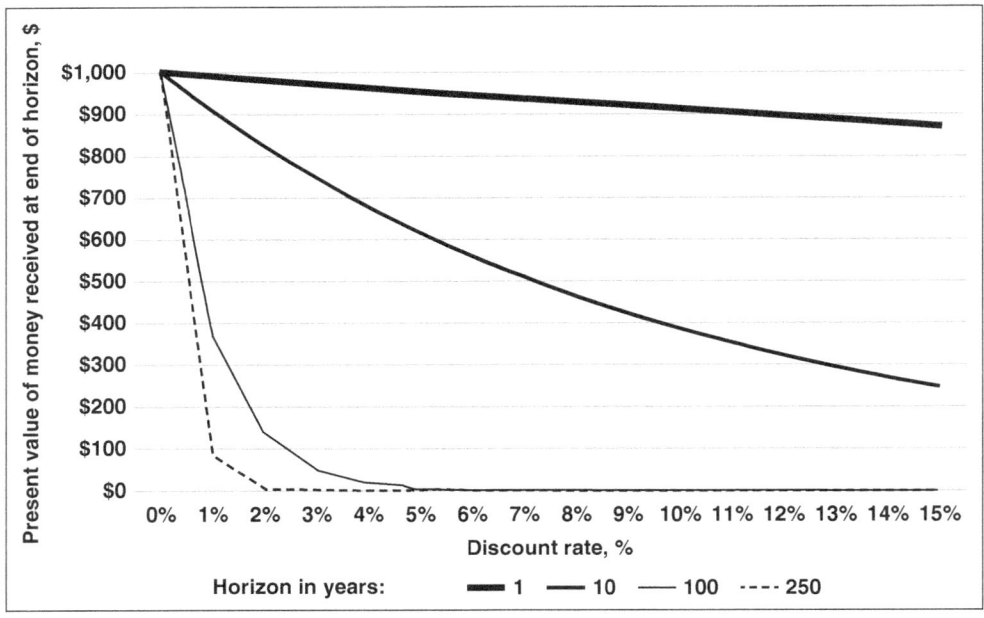

Source: ZCA

I once valued a portfolio of office building ground leases located near Grosvenor Square in London; some had 950 years left on their 1,000-year leases. Now, that is dynastic discounting!

In business, the discount rates used to value a bond-like investment are less than the rate used to value highly leveraged opportunistic deals. Increasing the discount rate reduces the present value of risk-related costs.

What rate should the government use? This rate is sometimes called the social discount rate. If capital markets functioned perfectly, the opportunity cost of capital would likely match the social discount rate. What is the relationship between this rate and the rate facing businesses and households?

A deal that works at a 3% rate may be infeasible at 10%. It is not clear what rate to use. Should it be the rate at which the jurisdiction can borrow? In Chapter 20 I argue that public pension funds should value their liabilities at the rate at which the jurisdiction can borrow in public markets. There seems to be no consensus among economists.

To evaluate risks in public projects, some economists use the concept of certainty equivalent, or the risk-adjusted probabilistic expectation of net benefits in each year. To evaluate the project, simply take the present discounted value of the certainty equivalents. Alternatively, we can adjust the discount rate to reflect incremental risk. However, risk-adjusting both the numerator and denominator is wrong. Choose one or the other but be consistent.

The risk-adjustment can be complex. For instance, governments can diversify risks across the population, which reduces non-systematic risk and the risk premium. If a project's net benefits have a low or negative correlation with macroeconomic income, then the discount rate should be lower.

Private and governmental approaches to valuation may diverge, which adds another layer of uncertainty with which investors must contend, especially in private-public partnerships. Before managers pitch public-private sector opportunities, they should be prepared to discuss these matters.

Conclusions and Investment Implications

- Local government consists of fragmented jurisdictions that often compete rather than cooperate.
- Externalities cause mispricing and reduce market efficiency.
- A public good, which is distinct from a private good, is a good that is nonrival and nonexcludable.

- Education and social services are mostly locally provided and financed, which affects incentives. Local governments can affect income, wealth, and inequality from their expenditure decisions, such as the provision of public transportation linking lower income housing with jobs, access to education, and delivery of social services.
- As more poor families move into higher-income communities, average tax revenue per family falls.
- The rich can either vote with their feet or exclude undesirable uses or households.
- How the public sector evaluates the value of a life often conflicts with business valuation, which is a risk that investors should recognize.

Q&A: Interview with Matthew Zisler, Senior Managing Director, Greystone

Starting a Career During Times of Volatility

Describe your real estate journey.

After Boston College, my first job was at Goldman Sachs in equity derivatives trading. I learned about risk and how institutional investors hedge and leverage their portfolios. I left to work in private equity acquisitions at Heitman, a real estate investment manager in Chicago. It was my first exposure to private equity and real estate investments. I eventually moved with my wife to the West Coast and worked for Buchanon Street Partners. Just before the GFC in August 2006, Randy Zisler, my father, and I formed Zisler Capital. We placed equity and debt capital for developers and owners around the country. During the GFC we redirected our efforts to workouts, consulting assignments, and advising on distressed asset acquisitions. While still with ZCA, we moved to Denver after the GFC to start our family. Later I led commercial acquisitions for a family office during COVID-19.

While in Denver, I joined New York–based Greystone, one of the nation's largest multifamily lenders and servicing companies. The firm needed help with equity and mezzanine debt solutions. I established an equity services group for the company.

What was your most challenging professional experience?

My first day after training at Goldman was 9/11 and it was a shock that provoked a lot of soul-searching. I decided to eventually return to my roots, which was real estate.

At Goldman, I learned a great deal about risk, how markets price assets, and ways in which markets fail, especially during periods of low transactions volume. Downturns teach you a great deal about cycles, pricing, and the functioning of the capital stack. I discovered that first movers often do well, but to be a successful first mover, you need capital, which is precisely what most people lack at the bottom of a cycle.

(continued)

(*continued*)

At ZCA, we saw signs of the impending GFC quite early. By mid-2007, cracks appeared in the debt markets but many borrowers ignored the signs. All of a sudden transactions volume crashed. Underwriting was impossibly difficult in 2008.

How would you advise young professionals contemplating a career in real estate?

Investment professionals need a basic understanding of accounting, finance, and a penchant for networking. Find a firm that executes a lot of transactions. Seek great mentors and colleagues and work really hard. Tenacity and curiosity matter.

CHAPTER 17

Sprawl: An Options Perspective

Preliminaries

Why write about sprawl in a book about investment risk?

Sprawl creates risks. Sprawl usually means excessive suburbanization, which is distinct from leapfrogging. Leapfrogging may or may not be a collateral benefit, or cost, of suburbanization. Sprawl lowers density, extends the urban-rural boundary, and promotes suburbanization.

Sprawl can occur without growth. The urban-rural boundary will expand more rapidly if local land use controls are onerous. Characteristics of sprawl include leapfrog development, low density residential and commercial development, no centralized or interjurisdictionally coordinated planning, fiscal disparities among localities, and segregation of land uses into different zones, just to name a few.

Risk and Fragmented Government

Local governments are a significant source of risk, especially for developers.

Development plans are like putty; they are initially malleable like wet clay, but once the concrete and steel bars are in place, putty hardens. Adjustment costs thereafter rise. The inventory adjusts to shocks not by removing the clay but rather by decreasing the intensity of land use by households and firms. Since buildings are fixed in place and durable, rather than move the buildings from Detroit to Dallas, we move the people instead. In declining, hollowed-out cities, left behind are the husks of abandoned or underutilized buildings, as well as families and businesses which, for various reasons, cannot move; they are often dependent on social services largely supplied by government, especially in central cities.

In California, more than one half of housing price appreciation is a result of growth controls, supposedly intended only to preserve the environment. Most incumbent voters who own housing are not in favor of easing growth controls. Doing so would increase supply, which, some voters fear, would depress home prices and thereby redistribute wealth. These transfers accelerate the migration of people whom local governments have traditionally excluded socially and economically; those seeking housing and access to employment and some of the most attractive state-owned amenities are effectively barred, further increasing economic and social segregation.

Most planning is not comprehensive; it is incremental, which is to a great degree dictated by economic and political uncertainty. Sprawl and leapfrogging are rational short-term responses by individuals, firms, and jurisdictions, but these responses are collectively irrational or inefficient. The public decries leapfrogging and sprawl, often on aesthetic grounds, but the criticism is directed at the symptoms, not the causes, which are economic, political, and sociological. The public deplores the degradation of the urban landscape but fails to appreciate the complexity of the land use succession process, the causes of this degradation, and its uncertainty.

Leapfrogging entails landowners' holding back land that has a current agricultural or a lower density use such that new development must leapfrog over the site and occur at more remote locations, thus creating gaps in the urban fabric and increasing commutation and other costs. The risks are at once individual and collective and in most cases the structure of local government is not up to the task of efficiently and equitably guiding this process.

How Does Population Growth Affect the Shape of a Hypothetical Single-Center City?

Population growth increases the distance to the edge of the city and the price of CBD land. The higher opportunity cost of urban land, in turn, makes the city more compact or denser, i.e., increases the physical capital-to-land ratio

Rising income increases housing demand and expands the geographical extent of the city, whereas higher commuting costs per mile due to congestion and greater commuting distances lowers disposable income at all locations, which reduces housing demand and the size of the city. The marginal costs of a mile of additional travel balances the marginal decrease in housing costs, thus determining optimal location and land rents as a function of distance from the city and the cost of transportation. Urban development extends to the point where urban uses at the urban-rural boundary cannot outbid agricultural uses.

Some voters want to curtail growth because they incorrectly believe that the costs of growth outweigh the benefits for society at large, if not for them alone. With growth comes density, including congestion, but cities are about more than traffic congestion. Despite advances in digital networking, cities also offer a special kind of congestion, namely the density of ideas, human capital, innovation, and social networking in which physical proximity and propinquity are reinforcing.

Local governments' land use controls are often a response to pressures to curtail growth and exclude minorities, people of lower income, or simply the "other." Given the fragmented nature of government, local governments have little incentive to take into account the impact of these controls on other localities, much less on overall regional economic performance. Regional governments, if they exist as such, usually lack the political and legal teeth to compel local jurisdictions.

Speculation and Leapfrogging: A Different Point of View

Speculation should not be an ugly word. Everyone—households, firms, investors—speculates. Speculation is nothing more than the attempt to buy at a low price and sell later at a higher price. Without speculation, markets would be less efficient. Speculators take the opposite side of the trade. Grain storage, time honored since antiquity, is an example of speculation and intertemporal redistribution. Lacking speculation, decentralized urban markets function less efficiently.

Owners that hold land off the market help to increase the intertemporal efficiency of land utilization over time. These owners take risks, for which they expect just compensation. Land speculators, just as the grain elevator operator, bear costs for waiting.

Holding back land means that development must occur at more remote locations. Offsetting the benefits of speculation, these gaps increase the cost of infrastructure and personal travel. However, a benefit of speculation is that, if there is an ample inventory of underutilized sites, a buyer is more likely to find the most appropriate site when that site is needed the most.

Speculation is a way of taking land off the market with the intention of realizing even greater future profits. Even if there were no urban growth or extension of the urban-rural boundary, speculation would occur, leapfrogging being just one result. Leapfrogging is a product of speculation and optimal management by individuals, if not by society. Leapfrogging is not restricted to the suburbs. It occurs even in our urban cores: For example, an owner of a CBD parking lot owns a call option, the strike price of which is the cost of building a tall office building.

When the owner converts the lot to a building, the owner extinguishes an option, the value of which should be included as a cost in the discounted cash flow analysis. The option to defer is as valuable and as real as bricks and mortar. Thus, the developer should include not only the traditional hard and soft costs of development but also the opportunity cost of extinguishing the many embedded call options that precede development and even those that include the actions of governments. The greater is the uncertainty, the greater is the option's value and the more likely that the land owner (and government) will delay development. As uncertainty declines, three things happen: The value of the option to delay decreases, cap rates fall, and transactions volume increases.

Urban land markets are not efficient in the short run; they adjust at a glacial pace compared to public securities markets. A key ingredient is market uncertainty and the costs associated with the durability of property. Land prices are slow to impound new information, so prices may not be locally efficient, especially in the short-run, and may convey false signals. This is a major source of risk. This observation does not contradict the previous paragraph, which deals with the relative speeds of leasing and capital markets.

What Should Governments Do?

Political markets tend to rely on command-control resource allocations, whereas private markets are largely decentralized pricing systems, albeit flawed. The decentralized market is great at generating pricing signals but political markets are not, at least in the same way.

The problem is not speculation *per se*. Local governments, which are often responsible for poorly conceived land use controls, encourage leapfrogging through their many sins of commission and omission. Markets are slow to adjust because the future is unknown, but this is not the only reason. Governments and private individuals withhold information. Hidden information and information asymmetry are important characteristics of private real estate, but they also lurk at the interface of private markets and governments.

Part of the problem is the misapplication of command-control to decentralized systems. The public deliberative process too often sidesteps the most basic cost-benefit analysis and ignores the many ways in which private market reactions can defeat well-meaning planning decisions. Voters reveal their preferences differently through the political process than they do through private markets.

Governments should focus more on the inefficiency (and the inequity) of controls; they should better appreciate the role of embedded optionality. Many of the proponents of tougher land use controls seek to exclude lower- and middle-income workers, especially those who prefer rental apartments, have large families, and are dependent on local social services such as schools and health services. These renters, especially the poor who cannot afford cars, must leapfrog to the CBD or less appealing outlying locations, thus increasing economic and political segregation and the cost of access to good jobs and services.

A related concern is that most line-haul rapid transit systems are radial, which accommodates middle to upper income, but not lower income, commuting demands. What is often lacking is circumferential rapid transit that serves the needs of lower income workers. Where is the constituency that will support investment in transit systems that best serve the poor and the lower working class? Fragmented government does little to promote broad interjurisdictional coalition building and equity, despite its putative efficiency.

Local governments' use of land use controls often increases market uncertainty, which can itself increase the option value of deferred development and promote leapfrogging. Of course, even if we had optimal land use controls, uncertainty and intertemporal efficiency would require speculation, which in turn would lead to leapfrogging, given the durability and cost of property development.

Some policies, while seemingly inefficient in a static world, may be dynamically efficient in a stochastic world. However, these policies may be difficult to design much less sell to the voters and other constituencies.

Local governments respond to local, highly focused political interests; they have an incentive to preserve excessive amounts of land if they can indiscriminately use the police power. By contrast, the poor are less well organized politically; they are dispersed geographically. Their influence is relatively weak and their power is diffuse.

Local governments promote excessive suburbanization through land use controls that limit the density of residential and commercial uses. Voters have a pecuniary interest in land use controls that limit the supply of new housing and increase the wealth of incumbent property owners, especially those who bought homes before the imposition of more restrictive land use controls.

The price of auto transportation including congestion is significantly underpriced. When we commute each morning, we weigh average costs and not the marginal costs we impose on other drivers. If we value commuting time at one half the wage rate, for example, then there is a significant resource misallocation due to the inefficiencies of land use policy. The higher is the wage rate, the greater is the opportunity cost of congestion.

All levels of government over-subsidize auto transportation by underpricing the opportunity cost of land for roads, depreciation, and congestion. Drivers over-consume transportation capacity, especially during rush hours, because governments are largely still resistant to congestion pricing, a good example of decentralized pricing. Congestion pricing helps equate supply with demand. Cheap transportation increases sprawl and flattens the city's rent gradient.

This chapter has focused on a special kind of risk that lurks at the boundary of economic and political markets. Investors must make intelligent risk-assessments. Much of the complexity is not always evident. Leapfrogging is a source of uncertainty, but so are local land use controls that encourage leapfrogging. Knowing the source of uncertainty is important. Calculating its opportunity cost is another matter.

Many studies have shown that the politics of grievance and inequality often lead to authoritarian governments and greater concentration of wealth and power. The wealthiest, most mobile, and best educated 10% can float above the social and political chaos seething below, while the aggrieved must contend with indignities and inequities, some of which are exacerbated by poor land use planning and bad political leadership.

Cultural memes in the end will not satisfy the most essential needs of these disadvantaged groups. The integrity of society and the functioning of democracy itself may be at risk, seemingly too remote and complex to command the thoughtful attention of the media, government, brokers, and the rest of the voters.

Conclusions and Investment Implications

- The imposition of new land use controls and building codes is stochastic.
- The availability and timing of development permits are often as uncertain as the availability of capital, which lenders often ration using non-price means, e.g., redlining.

- Governments perform many functions that private markets fail to do well.
- Fragmented local government is an important risk factor. Uncertainty causes officials to exercise their option to delay, the value of which increases with risk.
- Sprawl and leapfrogging are rational responses to uncertainty.
- Unresponsive local governments must contend with voters who vote with their feet.
- Uncertainty causes officials to exercise their option to delay, the value of which increases with risk.
- The source of this uncertainty is not a single local government but a matrix of many local governments and private firms or households, each interacting in ways that are largely uncoordinated, individually rational and self-serving, but collectively irrational.
- Investors and developers should recognize the risk of working with governments and quantitatively incorporate these risks in their investment analysis.
- Governments perform many functions that private markets fail to do well, such as provide clean air, water, and income security, an observation that all taxpayers should consider.

Q&A: Interview with Daniel Cummings, Managing Director, Bain Capital

A Strategic Builder of Investment Opportunities

How did you get into real estate?

I attended Dartmouth. In 1979 I started my career in real estate after attending the University of Chicago business school. LaSalle Partners recruited me. My first assignment was working out six land investment partnerships that were syndicated to HNW individuals. Understanding land and workouts is excellent preparation. LaSalle at that time was raising a fund. We grew the business during the early years of real estate institutionalization. In the early 1990s, I took over client relations and workouts. In the mid-1990s, I became co-CEO and joined the board. I then joined Carlyle and helped grow its international business just before the Tech Bust. Around 2007 we had backers to start a data center business but it was not the right time to start a new platform.

Tell us about your work at the Harvard Endowment.

In June 2009, Harvard Endowment recruited me to manage real estate. Over the following seven to eight years, we restructured our approach to indirect investing and closed-end funds. Harvard had only been investing in closed-end funds and had recently expanded the fund. The values declined significantly and there were outstanding future commitments. The portfolio was out of balance. The first year, we developed a new approach to value-add; we managed secondary sales and made buyers identify line-item bids for various funds. We generated significant liquidity. The first trades in 2010 had a discount of 10% or less, substantially better than average market experience. We obtained capital and flexibility to rebalance the fund's portfolio for value add. When I joined there was a high expected correlation across a number of opportunistic deals which we reduced. Our program was the top performing strategy at Harvard. We were growing our portfolio faster than anticipated, which raised our target allocation levels to 16%.

By 2017, we became very capital constrained. Our options included downsizing the portfolio or spinning out. We spun out with Harvard's support and capital and moved to Bain Capital. We sold down some of their exposure and launched other funds.

Do you have any advice for young professionals?

Work for a firm with a great reputation, access to enough capital to stay busy, and great colleagues and mentors. Seek out people you admire with good personal values.

CHAPTER 18

Rent Control Redux: Prediction, Assessment, and Opportunity

Preliminaries

What is rent control? Rent control, which means rent regulation, not just hard rent ceilings, is a system of laws and procedures that includes price controls, rent stabilization, eviction controls, maintenance restrictions, landlord obligations, and oversight by government.

Rent control, which historically has been a counterproductive response to the problems of income insecurity, is pernicious, and those intended beneficiaries, not the well-placed lucky ones who find a controlled unit, suffer the most.

Rent control is capricious. Rather than rent control, solutions should include more, not less, housing construction, as well as income support for the less fortunate. Land use controls artificially restrict the supply of new housing, which I discuss in Chapters 16 and 17. Rent control, even the specter of rent control, restricts new supply and encourages a change in the tenure choice between rental and ownership.

The rise of inequality, the worsening not-so-silent crisis of affordability and rental insecurity, and decades of stagnant real wages for much of the working middle class have reignited calls for rent control, especially in those cities with rapid rental growth.

What are the deleterious effects of rent control, and are these effects sufficient to undermine institutional investors' commitment to apartments? Who is helped by rent control? Who suffers? Does the market eventually defeat the intended purpose of rent control over time by not producing enough rental housing? If local governments seek to redistribute income without inducing the flight of high-income residents, is rent control the best tool, or even a second-best tool?

Types of Rent Control

Rent control with hard ceilings covers very few markets. Those with more rapid rental growth and policies restricting the addition of new dwelling units are more likely to adopt rent regulation, which comes in many forms, some less harmful than others. The basic types of rent control are ceilings or limitations on rent increases.

New York City's rent control immediately following WW II, a true rent ceiling, is an example of a first-generation rent control that severely damaged the quantity and quality of the apartment inventory. An alternative is rent stabilization, or second-generation rent control. Rent control allows for tenant-landlord negotiation but imposes a limit on the amount of the rent increase.

Rent Control as a Price Ceiling

Economists are practically unanimous in their opposition to rent control as a hard ceiling. Long-term rent ceilings reduce the quantity and quality of controlled rental units. Since rents are not allowed to clear the market, property deteriorates to the point where the investor's equity receives a competitive return. Exhibit 18.1 shows the apartment demand and supply curves for a local municipality. The equilibrium price is P_0. Imposition of a ceiling sets the price at P_1, which creates excess demand, Q_3-Q_1.

The consumer surplus, as shown in Exhibit 18.1, refers to the difference between what a consumer is willing to pay and the landlord's marginal cost. The producer surplus is the difference between the market price and the lowest price a producer is willing to accept to produce a good. The equilibrium quality-adjusted supply declines from Q_2 to Q_1. At P_1, the price ceiling creates excess demand of Q_3-Q_1.

Consumer surplus increases and producer surplus decreases with the imposition of a price ceiling, but one does not offset the other. There is a deadweight loss, which is a loss to society. The increase in consumer surplus is a transfer from producers.

EXHIBIT 18.1 Analysis of rent control showing the shift of producer's surplus to the tenants.

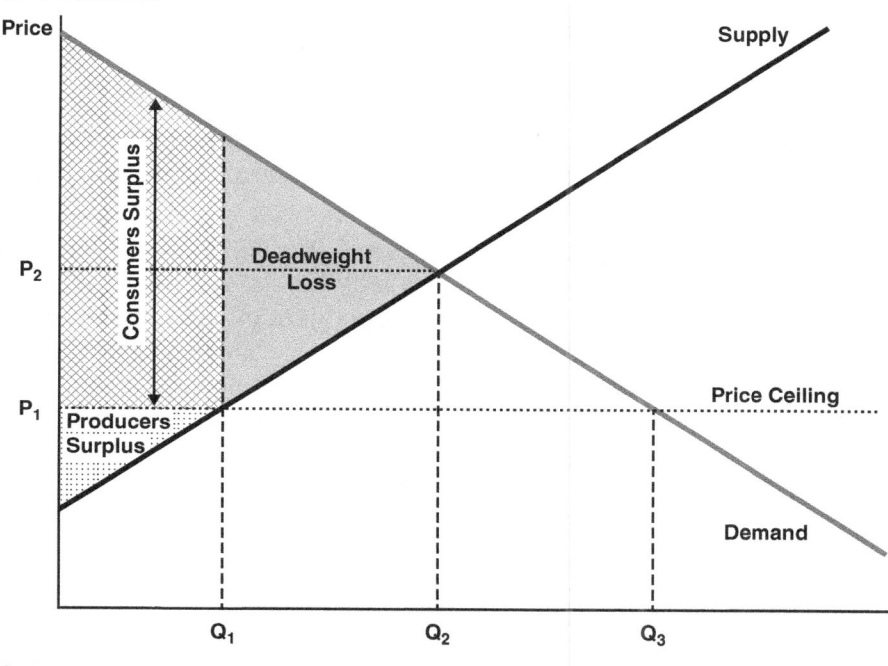

Source: ZCA

Apartments are highly durable, so the inventory in the short run does not shrink. Instead, the quality-adjusted inventory declines while the number of units in the *short-run* remains constant. In the short-run, even though rent control inhibits increases in rent per dwelling unit, quality-adjusted attributes can decline sufficiently due to under-maintenance so that the price per quality-adjusted attribute unit actually increases. I write elsewhere that quality-adjusted poor housing is not necessarily cheap housing even if the rent per dwelling unit is lower than other dwelling units in the housing stock. In the long-run, if investor equity vanishes, then the investor may have a strong incentive to abandon the property, which, in itself, can generate negative externalities and contribute to the deterioration of an entire neighborhood.

The targeted beneficiaries may not be the ones who secure a rent-controlled unit. Housing access becomes a lottery and often the well-connected, the better educated, and the wealthier win.

Rent control distorts labor and property market decisions. The price system fails to direct resources to those who are willing the pay the most. Rent control through its implicit subsidy discourages tenant mobility and increases tenant commutation and tenant search costs. Reduced mobility is inefficient. Tenants settle for second-best employment opportunities that are less threatening to their rent-controlled tenancy.

Rent control increases tenant search costs. Locating a rent-controlled unit is itself an exercise in asymmetric information and an unwarranted imposition on the less well informed. Knowing a relative or a friend who rents a controlled unit can confer generational value.

A market without rent controls, by contrast, continually provides a variety of rental choices in many locations, at various quality levels, and *when needed*, especially in the absence of growth controls. A properly functioning market provides greater choice and generates information that signals developers when it is time to add new units to the inventory. A non-controlled market encourages innovation as well. Rent control blunts market signaling and injects costly distortions.

Rent control tends to transfer units from the rental sector to the ownership sector through conversion, thus reducing the inventory of rental apartments. Landlords, constrained in their ability to establish a market-clearing rent, use non-price rationing, which can include racial discrimination, quality deterioration, reduced maintenance by landlords, bribes, conversions to condominiums and other uses, as well as price increases within the uncontrolled sector. Rent control tends to transfer units from the rental sector to the ownership sector through conversion, thus reducing the inventory of rental apartments. The price of non-controlled units often increases in response. Suppliers of new rental apartments may exit the market and shift their business focus to the construction of condominiums and single-family rental housing. Housing supply in the controlled rental sector typically declines, causing a city-wide rent increase shouldered by non-controlled units.

Rent control in New York City has increased renters' probabilities of staying at their addresses by nearly 20%. While not quite frozen in amber, reduced tenant turnover impairs price and rent discovery. Rental housing supply in the controlled sector has decreased by as much as 15%, causing a 5.1% city-wide rent increase shouldered by non-controlled units.

Anti-growth controls and related restrictions on new construction increase the propensity to regulate rents. Seemingly unrelated controls worsen affordability and inefficient regulatory responses.

Rent control is a very blunt instrument with numerous negative effects that hurt the very constituencies that rent control supposedly serves. It corrupts government.

Advocates of tenant rights propose rent control as a means to address the housing affordability problem. If insufficient income is the problem, then appropriate levels of government, such as the federal or state, should provide housing subsidies in the form of credits or vouchers. Income transfers are politically unpopular because the transfers make the subsidy explicit; the cost affects the public budget while rent control imposes a silent initial burden on owners, which eventually shifts to the population at large. Increasing building permits, while an important solution to lowering the overall cost of housing, creates political controversies of its own.

The Crazy Quilt of Rent Control: A Geographic Perspective with a Focus on New Jersey

The state with the longest history of rent control is New York, where one quarter of the population lives in apartments. In New York City in 2017, 45% of all apartment rentals were rent stabilized and 1% were rent controlled. In DC, 36% of units were rent controlled and in San Francisco, 75% of the units were controlled. Los Angeles as of 2014 controlled 80% of apartment rentals.

New Jersey with 564 municipalities is a good example of a state that has no statewide rent control laws; 117 municipalities with rent control are located in Essex, Hudson, Bergen, and Middlesex Counties, bedroom communities to New York City. These local governments have created a patchwork of rent control regulations that distort regional housing markets. The state has 32 counties, and those counties have 564 municipalities or minor civil divisions. Bergen County alone has 70 municipalities of which 26 have rent control; 70% of the renters in this county live in rent-controlled apartments.

Wealthier, more suburbanized and homogeneous counties have a lower propensity to institute rent control. Each minor civil jurisdiction has its own variant. The probability of a locality's instituting rent control is susceptible to risk-based analysis. My own research has shown that most jurisdictions are not rent control–prone and the likelihood of instituting controls is predictable, using the correct econometric tools.

Parameters Used by Rent Control Legislation

Picking the right rental growth index and formula is important to both landlords and tenants. The CPI has many components, and they each behave differently, as the following scatter of the All-CPI and the Rent-CPI shows in Exhibit 18.2. The change in the CPI-rent index, not surprisingly, is more highly correlated with the Northern New Jersey rental growth rate.

EXHIBIT 18.2 The changes in the CPI indexes and Northern New Jersey rental growth are not highly correlated.

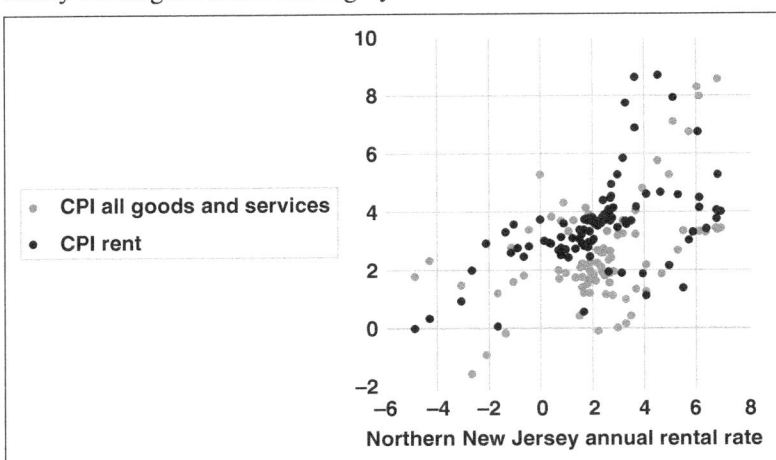

Source: ZCA using Federal Reserve and CoStar data

The indexes, which are stochastic, do not measure the same market dynamics over the cycle, as shown in Exhibit 18.3. The CPI is a measure of the price index including energy, housing, goods, and services. The CPI-rental index and the Northern New Jersey apartment rental index are real estate specific. The differences raise an important question: Should rent escalation provisions be based on a change in the overall price index or on changes in relative prices? Perhaps it does not matter to tenants or landlords, but it should.

Most of the rental increase caps prescribed by municipalities are often not binding, which hurts landlords. Even worse, the caps sometimes ignore inflation, which can be high when market rental increases are not significant. In Northern New Jersey, average rental growth since 2000 according to CoStar is 2.2%. A better choice is the rental component of the CPI, which has averaged 3.5% during this period. Sometimes, the law provides for rent escalation to the degree that the index exceeds a floor, such as 2% or 3%. Since the indexes are stochastic, the right, but not the obligation, to increase rents is a call option, the valuation of which increases with the volatilities of the index and market rents.

Should escalation be based on the actual increase in local rents, on the overall CPI, or rental component of the CPI? The rental-based CPI is more favorable to the landlords, as shown in Exhibit 18.4.

EXHIBIT 18.3 Three seemingly related price indexes.

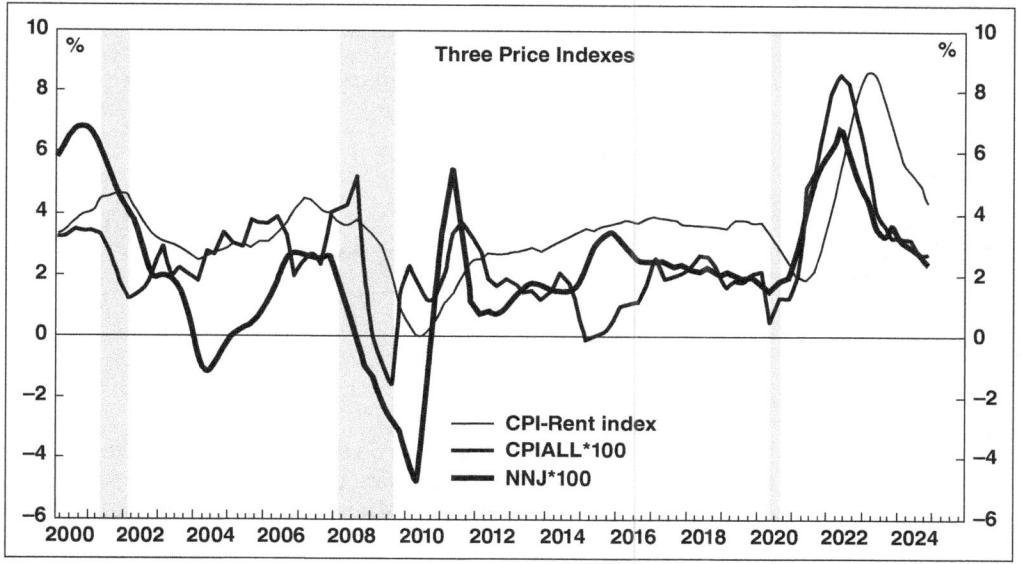

Source: ZCA using Federal Reserve and CoStar data

EXHIBIT 18.4 The lesser of the local apartment index and the rental CPI was negative following the GFC.

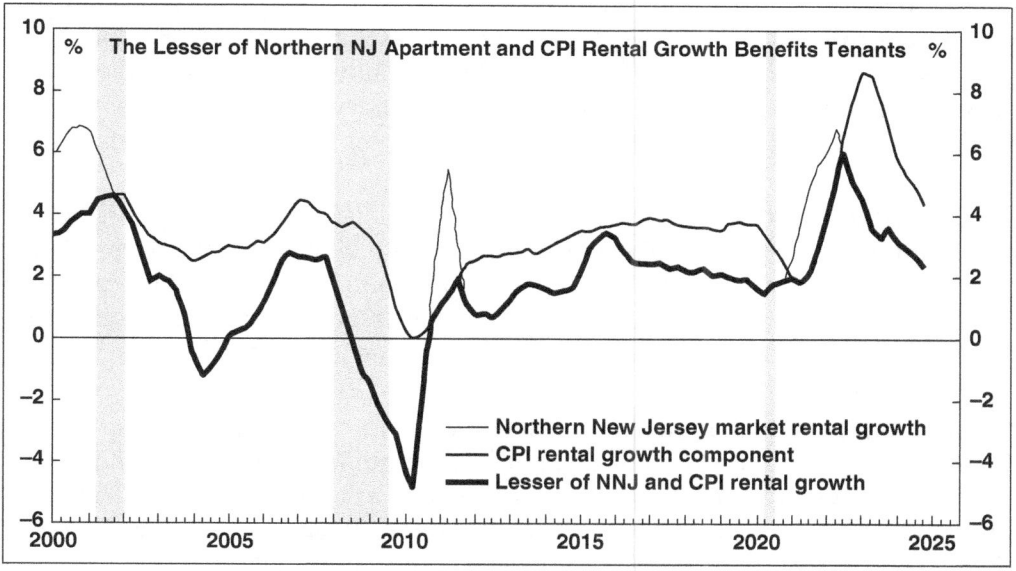

Source: ZCA using Federal Reserve and CoStar data

EXHIBIT 18.5 The greater of the local apartment index and the rental CPI is consistently positive and favors landlords.

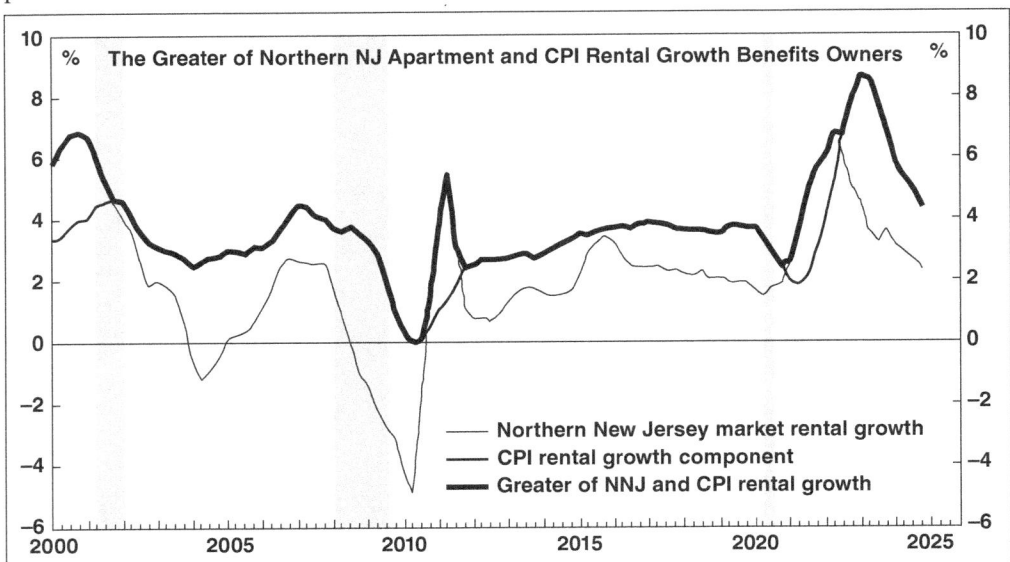

Source: ZCA using Federal Reserve and CoStar data

Read the fine print: "... whichever is less... or greater than." One frequently encounters the phrases, "whichever is less" or "whichever is greater," in rent control regulations. Lurking behind these phrases are embedded options, the value of which increases with volatility. "The percentage of the increase in the CPI or the maximum of 2% increase in market rent, whichever is less," is an example.

Exhibit 18.5 shows the impact of "whichever is less" function. The function was significantly negative following the GFC. "Whichever is greater" produces dramatically different results, as shown in Exhibit 18.6. Given the stochastic nature of the indexes, valuing the option to escalate requires Monte Carlo analysis. This approach is useful when considering the acquisition of well-seasoned, rent-stabilized properties.

Most tenant and landlord advocates, not to mention politicians, do not realize the impact of uncertainty on the valuation of the right to escalate. Even if they did understand, they lack the tools to evaluate the impact of this uncertainty. The landlords' and tenants' options are path-dependent on the tenant's decision to vacate or remain. The difference between the changes in the CPI-rental index and the local market rental rate growth can be significant, as shown in Exhibit 18.6.

EXHIBIT 18.6 The landlord should favor the "greater than" approach, especially following downturns such as the GFC and the COVID-19 recessions.

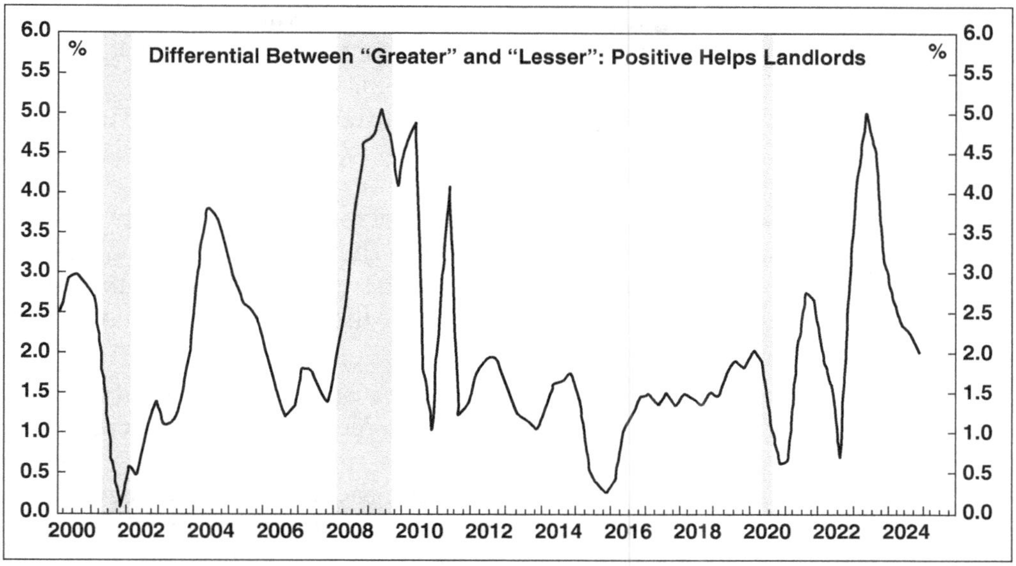

Differential Between "Greater" and "Lesser": Positive Helps Landlords

Source: ZCA using Federal Reserve and CoStar data

What drives the share of renters that are subject to some form of rent control? Two factors are important in predicting which municipalities will adopt and maintain rent control: (1) the number of voters who live in rent-controlled apartments and (2) the degree to which rent payments exceed 35% of median household income within the municipality.

The following model shows the extent to which various factors explain the percentage of renters that live in rent-controlled buildings, or %**RENTRC**.

$$\%RENTRC = -20.022 + 0.053 * APTS\%DU + 0.502 * \#RENTRC$$
$$(-0.661) \quad (0.076) \quad\quad\quad\quad (2.938)$$

$$+\, 0.996 * PAYOVER35$$
$$(1.742) \tag{18.1}$$

Adjusted $R^2 = 0.732$

Observations $= 19$

Mean of dependent variable $= 46.053$

S.D. of dependent variable $= 31.559$

S.E. of regression $= 16.356$

The apartment share of total dwelling units, *APTS%DU*, is not a significant variable since the t-statistic, 0.076, is very low; it should be close to two. However, the sign of the coefficient, 0.053, is consistent with expectations. If there are more renters in a municipality with rent control, *#RENTRC*, rent control will be a more important political issue. This variable represents the number of voters potentially supporting rent control. The percentage of households paying more than 35% of their household income for rent, *PAYOVER35*, is statistically significant. A 1% increase in renters paying more than 35% of their income to cover rent is associated approximately with a 1% increase in the share of renters in the county that live in rent-controlled units. The model explains 73% of the variation in the dependent variable, *%RENTRC*, which is impressive given that it is a cross-sectional model with a small sample size. Investors should conclude that the incidence and risk of rent control is predictable and quantifiable.

Fiscal implications. Rent control inhibits new apartment construction and reduces the value of controlled units, which in turn reduces property tax revenues and impairs the provision of governmental services. A partially offsetting factor is the spillover impact of rent control on rents within the uncontrolled sector. Rents in the non-controlled sector increase along with property values, which, in turn, increase tax revenues from the uncontrolled sector. The uncontrolled sector satisfies some, but not all, of the excess demand; uncontrolled rents rise to market levels. Conversion from controlled apartments to condominiums or coops, or from other uses to apartments, meets some of the excess demand. Rent control's impact on the *overall* housing supply, controlled and uncontrolled, is ambiguous. In some cities, such as New York, investors are raising capital to acquire office buildings for conversion to apartments.

The CPI and effective apartment market rental growth during 2022. The spreads between (1) the change in the CPI-primary residence rental index and (2) the effective market rental growth rate is sufficiently different, especially by city size, that landlords should exercise care when drafting lease escalation clauses. Tenants should also be careful. The largest MSAs, most favored by large institutions, had higher vacancy rates and the greatest spreads.

Inflation in 2022 was 8.0%, the highest since the inflations of 13.5% in 1980 and 11.0% in 1974. During 2022 inflation–apartment rental spreads, defined as either CPI-All minus effective rental growth or CPI-Rent minus effective rental growth, were highest in the larger MSAs, as shown in Exhibit 18.7, and the size of these negative spreads indicates that the rental component of the CPI was significantly less than actual apartment rental growth. Is the CPI-primary residence rental index the best index for owners?

Since 2022, the rental component of the CPI spread index has exhibited more volatility than the broader CPI spread index, reflecting the higher volatility of the

EXHIBIT 18.7   2022 spreads of inflation minus effective apartment rental growth according to MSA size.

	Spread CPI Minus Effective Rental Growth		
	CPI-All	CPI-Rent	Vacancy Rate, %
390 MSAs	−3.0	−1.0	6.3
Top 20 MSAs	−4.6	−2.7	6.6
Top 50 MSAs	−4.0	−2.0	7.1
50 – 100 MSAs	−3.0	−1.0	6.6

Source: ZCA using CoStar data

underlying apartment sector relative to the goods and services sectors. The levels of the spreads since 2000 are −0.36 and −1.33, respectively. Both spreads exhibit significant serial correlation, which means that past spreads, unlike stock returns, are a predictor of current spreads. The previous three quarters explain 95% of the variation in current spreads.

Is It Possible to Invest Successfully in Rent-Controlled Apartments?

Rent control scares investors, but this fear may not be justified. Not all rent controls are alike and most jurisdictions lack rent control. Profiting from rent control depends on the details as well as the timing.

Consider an example: Rent control operates in the presence of asymmetric information. How can landlords exploit this market imperfection? Landlords of rent-controlled apartments prefer to rent to tenants who will remain in their apartment for only a short time because the landlord may have the option to adjust the rent upward sooner if the tenant leaves. However, tenants have little incentive to reveal their expected leasing horizon. The propensity to leave is a stochastic process reflecting life's vicissitudes as well as basic economics. Using Monte Carlo analysis, we can provide better risk and valuation estimates.

Investors realize a higher return if more tenants vacate. This position is comparable to owning a principal-only CMBS bond and hoping that the bond pays off early. The cash flows associated with existing rent-controlled apartment buildings are like bonds with a coupon and a participation that reflects allowable rent increases and tenant turnover. When the owner sells the current rent-controlled property, the price of the property reflects not just the impact of rent control but also the market's assessment of tenant rollover. Discerning buyers who have private information that is not already discounted in the price of the asset may have a significant edge. I have advised clients (in Brooklyn) who have made this very strategy work.

Conclusions and Investment Implications

- Properties that deliver the most attractive risk-adjusted returns may not be the most photogenic, trendy "institutional quality" properties.
- Timing is important; buying after, not before, the imposition of rent control is critical. Having an insider's view of government and an actuarial mindset might help.
- Rent control, which is more than simply controlling the level of rents, includes price controls, eviction controls, maintenance provisions, and independent oversight.
- One form of rent control is a price ceiling, which can create unmet excess demand and suppress new construction, postpone maintenance of controlled units, increase inequality, and encourage the removal of units from the rental pool.
- Rent control erodes the tax base, which impairs the delivery of critical social services.
- Allowable rent-increase formulas may not always protect the landlord or the tenant.

Q&A: Interview with Aly Worthington, Head of Capital Markets, Summit Development

Development Risk and Mental Toughness

Describe your professional path.

I grew up in a real estate family, with my dad, Scott Toombs, working for the renowned developer Jim Rouse. Dad was heavily involved in notable projects like Columbia, Faneuil Hall, and South Street Seaport before starting his own company in the 1980s. I was fortunate to be deeply involved in his business from a very early age—probably middle school! I always knew I would be active in CRE, and started my career at Morgan Stanley. In 2003, my dad and I teamed up to buy a 365-room Princeton conference center, marking the start of our partnership. I'll always cherish that time in my life, and all the wisdom he passed on.

I met your dad when I was at Goldman. He was a visionary; can you give an example?

Dad consistently sought innovative approaches to development, demonstrating foresight in public-private partnerships and lifestyle initiatives long before they gained popularity. One example is Princeton Forestal Village, which opened in 1986, and was about 20 years ahead of its time and featured a blend of office, hotel, and retail spaces.

What are your views on development risk?

The most significant risks that models fail to address. Developments rarely go exactly as planned. Effective developers are not only nimble, but have the ability to evaluate risks objectively. Overlooking or undervaluing crucial embedded optionality and interdependence within the overall economic framework of a project is always a danger. Over the past few years some projects have succeeded due to cap rate compression. The current environment is different.

(continued)

(continued)

Most successful developers cannot articulate why they did not fail; they act as if their success was inevitable. The failed developers are silent. Would you agree?

Yes. Some of the personality attributes that contribute to development success are agility, resilience, persistence, and problem-solving skills. Importantly, humility, effective listening, and lack of hubris make the difference between a successful or failed project.

How do you deal with misogyny?

Success is a powerful motivator that often serves as a response to adversities. It is important to concentrate on constructive relationships and surround yourself with good, constructive people.

Any advice for the young professionals?

I learned a lot in a small firm. However, I recommend a large firm as a first stop to learn basics.

PART V
Behavioral Bias, Investment Risk, and an Investor's Guide

CHAPTER 19

Cognitive Errors, Picking Winners, and the Risk of Overpaying

Preliminaries

Investors, managers, and consultants commit cognitive errors all the time. This chapter discusses how these errors can affect investment performance. I include a simulation of bidding behavior, which helps us understand the precipitous drop in transactions volume, the erosion of total returns, and the decline in prices during downturns. How can investors avoid a bidding frenzy? Stochastic analysis, or Monte Carlo, is the best approach.

What is the role of cognitive errors? Let's begin with some examples.

Cognitive Errors and Real Estate

The compulsion to beat the market in stocks, but also in real estate, is a "loser's game,"[1] especially after adjusting for fees and transactions costs. Even in real estate, a small sector compared to stocks, very smart professionals try to beat the market, but most fail. Institutions play a bigger role in real estate, which makes beating the market harder for nonprofessionals. Property is much more inefficient than stocks but it does not follow that managers can consistently win in an inefficient market after accounting for fees and transaction costs. The market is efficiently inefficient.

The spread between bid and ask finances the real estate transactional infrastructure that includes appraisers, brokers, investment bankers, maintenance firms, to name a few.

Advice to investors: If the investment is opaque, then insist on more liquidity. Typically, when markets crash, open-end property funds that claim to offer redemption, or liquidity, cannot meet investor liquidity needs when needed the most.

Investors do not always make rational decisions even if they have access to good information and risk analytics. They frequently evaluate risk using rules of thumb or heuristics, which are useful because collecting information and evaluating the data are costly, but not all heuristics produce better results.

Here are some examples of behavioral biases in which heuristics often play a role:

- **Framing.** Investors make different decisions depending on how investment options are presented, which is why real estate is the province of stories and little science.
- **Loss aversion.** Losses are avoided more than equivalent gains are sought.
- **Nudge.** A nudge is a non-coercive method to manipulate investors' choices. A manager-sponsored "educational" conference in Bermuda is a good example.
- **Availability heuristic.** Investors rely on easily recalled information, rather than actual data, when evaluating the probability of an outcome.
- **Bounded rationality.** People have limited cognitive ability and do not always make the right choice, especially given limited time and available information.
- **Sunk-cost fallacy.** Investors keep investing in a negative NPV project because they are already heavily invested even if doing so means risking further losses. Career risk is a factor.
- **Satisficing.** There is some minimum search effort required, not necessarily the optimum, and once this minimum is reached, search stops. Many managers, once they hit their targeted performance threshold, engage in style drift and try to lock in returns: They satisfice.
- **Anchoring.** Investors have a mental reference point with which they compare results. Expectations play an important role.
- **Gambler's fallacy.** An event that has occurred often in the past is less likely to occur in the future, despite the probability remaining constant. Example: preferring a manager with three years of wins.
- **Hot hand fallacy.** An event that has occurred often in the past is more likely to occur again in the future such that the streak continues.

- **Narrative fallacy.** Investors use narratives to connect the dots between random events to make sense of arbitrary information. Stories help fill in the gaps where data are unavailable. Clever managers present the right set of dots and investors fill in the rest.
- **Recency bias.** An outcome is more likely because a similar outcome just occurred. The reverse is a CIO avoiding retail today because his firm lost money investing in retail malls five years ago.
- **Confirmation bias.** Investors tend to prefer information consistent with their beliefs even if doing so conflicts with the evidence. Does confirmation bias explain managers' preferences for gateway cities?
- **Status quo basis.** Investors are averse to change and hesitate to change their views even if faced with compelling evidence to the contrary. Their reluctance to change managers, wealth managers, or simply outmoded notions about real estate investing is an example.

Some investment implications. Research professionals make forecasts, usually using naïve and biased methods. Nobody questions the difference between forecast and investing. Investing entails making a bet and remaining committed. Forecasters have little skin in the game.

Most pay-to-play conferences, save for the putative benefits of networking, are not worth the time or money. These conferences parade a stream of gurus promoting the same bromides. A psychologist once said, "The reason that 'guru' is such a popular word is because 'charlatan' is too hard to spell."[2]

Brokers and managers like to make interest rate forecasts, the bolder the better, even though most do not invest in interest rate futures or any other related asset that might demonstrate commitment and skill. They boldly venture outside of their skill set. Achievements in one field usually do not translate well into useful expertise in other fields. That is why most small company developers do not make great CEOs of large companies.

Occasionally, the forecasters get it right but usually only by chance. The note-taking audience ascribes excessive weight to correct outlier calls and places unjustified faith in future outlier calls, which typically disappoint. Just about all the top performing money managers are terrible at economic forecasting, but, alas, they persist and people have short memories. Their track record is poor, and consensus forecasts are hardly much better, as this book demonstrates.

When attending conferences, do not pay attention to articulate incompetents, hard-charging salespeople, perpetual Cassandras, the untutored masses, those who lack conviction, and any invidious, cretinous bores. The more self-confident the forecaster and the manager, the more vulnerable is the investor. Just because someone made a billion dollars by raising buckets of capital and investing other people's money in highly leveraged, questionable real estate does not mean this person possesses any forecasting skill, much less a scintilla of fiduciary commitment to investors.

Investors should adopt long-run plans, the success of which should not hinge on the accuracy of short-term forecasts. For example, diversification is a durable strategy; management through macro forecasting is not. Contingent forecasting, however, can suggest the right questions and provide a useful framework for contemplating risk.

Risk analysis and prediction are different. Prediction is fraught with risks of its own whereas the former, if well executed, reduces risk. Probability simulations using Monte Carlo are good examples.

Do not spend too much time listening to reporters on television or at conferences. If the information were valuable, they would not be sharing it with a large audience. Listening to the so-called "wise heads" that frequent the real estate conference circuit is like proceeding through life while looking through the rear-view mirror. They likely do not know more than the attendees. When managers "talk their book" or advance their self-serving story, it is all about sales and persuasion, not prediction, and it certainly is not news; so, either ignore the chatter or ask tough questions. Do not be bashful.

Managers provide carefully curated research for free, but the research is really not free since, at best, reading and thinking about it takes time and discernment. At worse, it confuses. When research is free, the investor becomes the commodity. Moreover, most research is backward looking; it is an emotional distraction confected by managers who are competing for attention in the crowded capital placement marketplace. Widely understood information is already expressed in prices.

Investors give the media too much credit. The real estate media is largely irrelevant in making investment decisions. They parrot the received wisdom and they are usually late to the game. The media often discuss trends as they peak, and the discussion is advanced by people who lack skills in economics or investing. Often, they just sample money managers' opinions, over-weighting the opinions that emanate from firms with the most AUM. Most media stars lack a thorough understanding of economics, finance, or investments; some even migrate to politics. They ask the wrong questions, fail to thoroughly interrogate or challenge their guests, and dwell on personalities rather than concepts.

We need to rethink our use and understanding of models. Models are important, but good models should explicitly recognize risk. Keep in mind that models are usually wrong, but some models are useful, as the great statistician, George Box, once said. John von Neumann of the Princeton Institute for Advanced Research remarked in 1947 that "truth is much too complicated to allow anything but approximations."[3] I embrace that sentiment.

Models can help us appreciate the limits of our knowledge, suggest the right questions, and leave us with a serviceable framework that feeds our imagination and/or helps us search for deeper insight. They can also teach us about the dysfunctional implications of our most cherished beliefs.

Bonini's paradox warns that as we seek to replicate reality in greater detail, our models become less understandable. Their opacity is a source of risk. So, be forewarned. Just because the manager modeled the deal does not mean the results are useful, much less accurate.

How Good Are Money Managers at Forecasting Market Performance? Not Good!

Picking a winning manager based on return performance alone is fraught with uncertainty. In Chapter 2, I discussed Bayes Theorem with which I calculated the astonishingly high likelihood of false positives in the search for a skilled manager. The exit cap rate is critical in a value-add or opportunistic deal, but cap rates are stochastic; they fluctuate. However, most managers are not good cap rate forecasters and neither is the research community. The same observation applies to the prediction of total returns across MSAs. In order to give the reader a sampling of the issues, I focus on office, although my findings extend to other real estate and capital market sectors.

MSA selection. Manager office performance rankings in real estate and in stocks are unstable over time and are therefore unreliable. Good current performance is not a good predictor of performance five years later. MSAs are no different. Many managers claim that they have special skills in picking markets. Most do not. If they seem skilled, is this skill still apparent after accounting for transactions costs and fees?

MSA selection is challenging in ways that seem similar to stock selection, but there is a crucial difference. Stocks trade in public, continuous auction markets, whereas hidden information is a characteristic of private property markets. Stock transactions costs, compared to property, are extremely low, reflecting higher stock liquidity.

While property total returns fluctuate over time, they do so within a tightly bundled group of MSAs. There are some outliers: San Francisco, New York, and Chicago are examples of MSAs that fluctuate around total US office total return, as shown in Exhibit 19.1.

Cap rates are a different matter; the cross-sectional ranking of cap rates is not stable over time or across MSAs. (See Exhibit 19.2.) Cap rates, which exhibit low volatility compared with total returns, not only fluctuate wildly across MSAs, but the 8-quarter moving correlation of MSA cap rates with the national aggregate cap rate indicates that the correlations, while often positive, can oscillate from negative to positive, as shown in Exhibit 19.3. This exhibit illustrates this point with 12-quarter moving correlations of the US cap rate with the cap rates of New York, San Francisco, and Chicago. The exit cap rate associated with an opportunistic deal with a 5- to 7-year exit can be quite variable, as this exhibit shows.

Managers, try as they may, demonstrate little if any skill in anticipating absolute or relative cap rate changes over time, especially over the long run. See Chapter 15, which shows the critical impact of investment horizon and the volatility of the exit cap rate at the time of sale.

Managers select preferred MSAs, but this selection is seldom informed by the study of market dynamics, cap rate, or total return volatility, cross-MSA correlations, and the ranking of changes in preferences over time. For example, the total return, vacancy rate, and cap rate rankings of MSAs changed dramatically before,

EXHIBIT 19.1 MSA total returns are tightly grouped over the cycle.

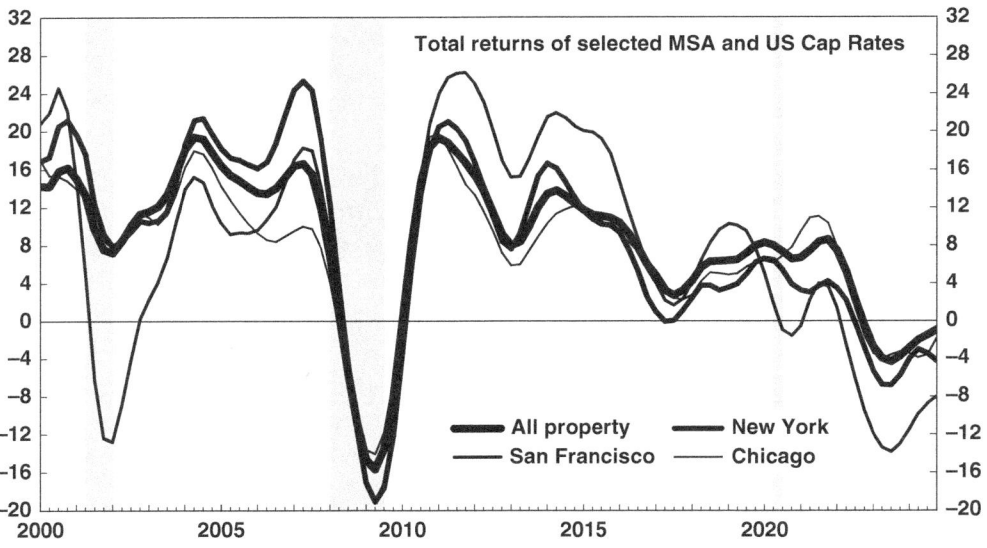

Source: ZCA using CoStar data

EXHIBIT 19.2 Cap rates are relatively volatile and move within a 300- to 400-bps band.

Source: ZCA using CoStar data

EXHIBIT 19.3 Moving correlations of MSA cap rates with the US office cap rate are not stable.

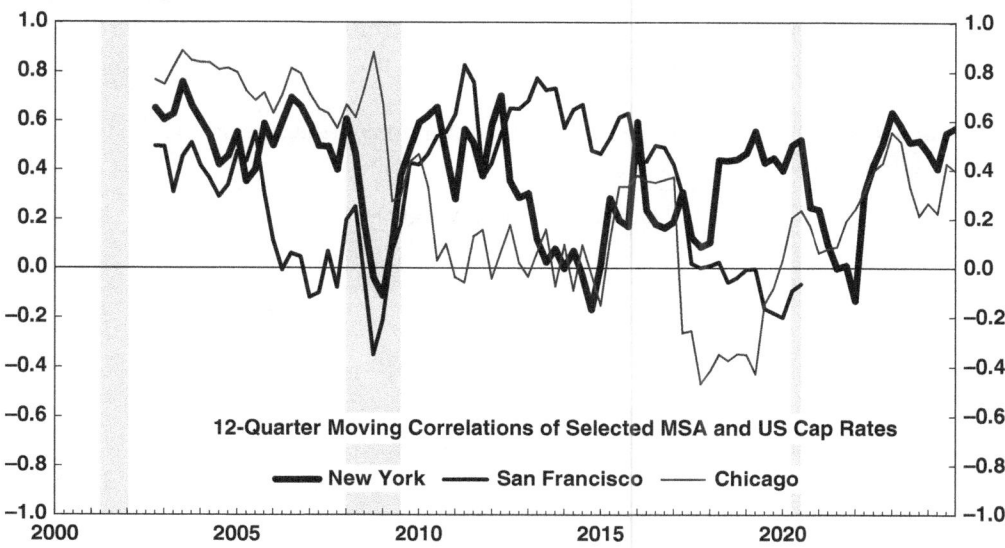

Source: ZCA using CoStar data

during and after COVID-19. Epidemics are difficult to forecast, but the instability of MSA rankings alone introduces significant risks.

Consensus total return forecasts of overall real estate performance. This section reports that managers' and investors' expectations of total return performance are imperfect at best and suggests that return forecasts with horizons greater than a year or two are very unreliable, a finding which is relevant to investors in opportunistic joint ventures with five- to seven-year horizons wherein the exit cap rate is uncertain. If forecasts beyond two years are unreliable, what confidence can we ascribe to a manager's projected exit cap rate? This problem is by no means the exclusive preserve of real estate; consider the disappointing forecasting records of macroeconomists and stock technicians.

The following analysis relies on data from a unique managers' expectations survey conducted by the Pension Real Estate Association.[4] The survey focuses on the current year as well as on one-year, two-year, and five-year periods. Manager performance forecast uncertainty increases rapidly as the forecast horizon increases, as shown in Exhibit 19.4. I calculated 4-quarter moving averages for the variances of actual and expected performance as a function of horizon length. The current year variation is small, but the variance increases rapidly beyond the first year, as shown by the arrow in the exhibit.

The current and actual year's performance closely track each other except before or following the COVID-19 recession, as shown in Exhibit 19.5.

Beyond one year, survey participants' performance expectations deteriorate as the investment horizon increases. The rapid deterioration beyond the current year is surprising. Real estate strategies, such as opportunistic joint ventures, envision

EXHIBIT 19.4 With longer expectations horizons comes greater risk (2010 through 2024).

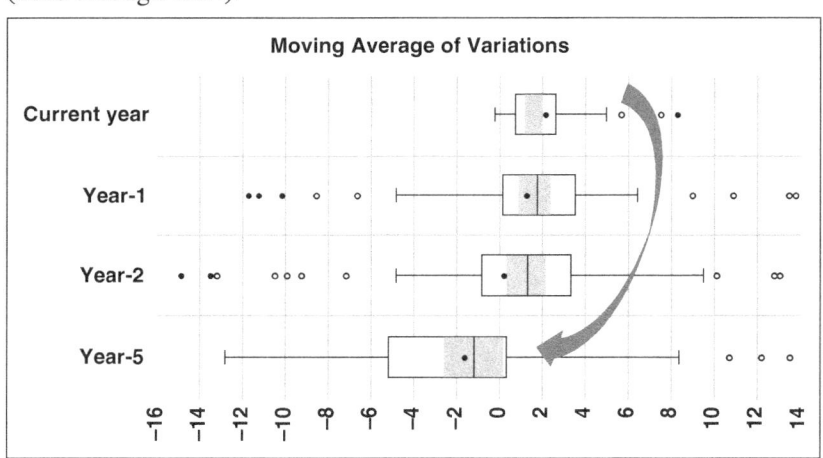

Source: ZCA using PREA survey data

EXHIBIT 19.5 Current year expectations and actual performance.

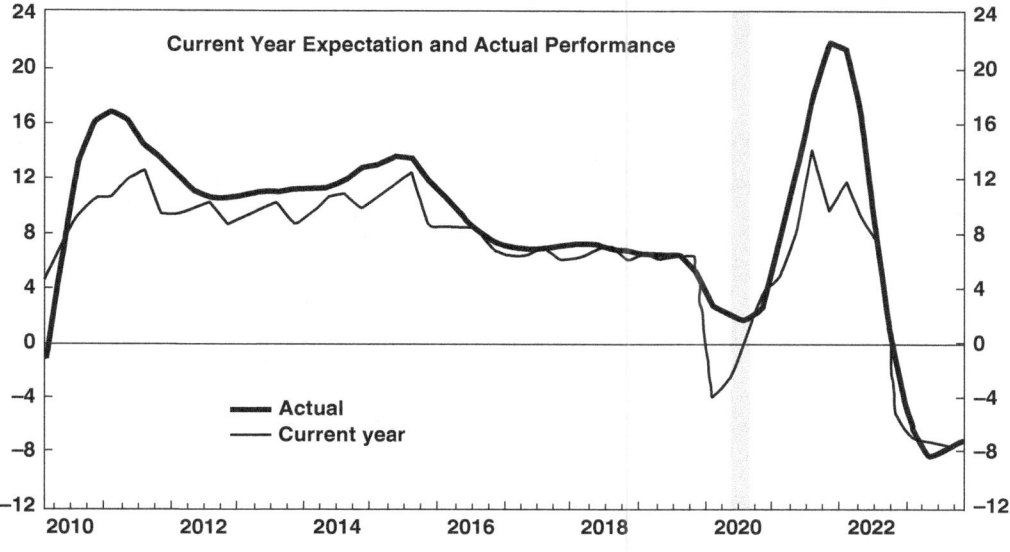

Source: ZCA using PREA survey data

a five- to seven-year holding period during which rental growth and exit cap rates can fluctuate wildly, as I have shown in Chapter 15. Investors should question any claims of omniscience by managers who believe they have superior return forecasting skills. See Exhibits 19.6 and 19.7. The variance of forecasts increases dramatically as the forecasting horizon increases.

Forecasting winning MSAs is difficult. This section presents some preliminary but very provocative findings that readers should consider. If the rapid deterioration of expected performance beyond one year of performance expectations surveyed by the Pension Real Estate Association (PREA) is disheartening, so is the poor correlation of 206 MSA office total return rankings beyond four years.

This is not good news for managers whose investment mandate includes picking the "best" markets. What does "best" mean? Does it mean the fastest growing? Markets with the highest absorption rates and brokerage fees? The highest risk-adjusted returns? Markets that are most likely to book managers' fees? Not only must the manager accurately predict <u>absolute</u> MSA total returns but the manager must predict <u>relative</u> performance as well since in any manager search investors routinely <u>rank</u> managers' return performance. However, the data clearly show that these rankings beyond four years are not stable; rank is not preserved. Whereas predicting total return performance accurately beyond two years is difficult, forecasting MSA rankings is even more challenging.

EXHIBIT 19.6 Performance expectations by horizon.

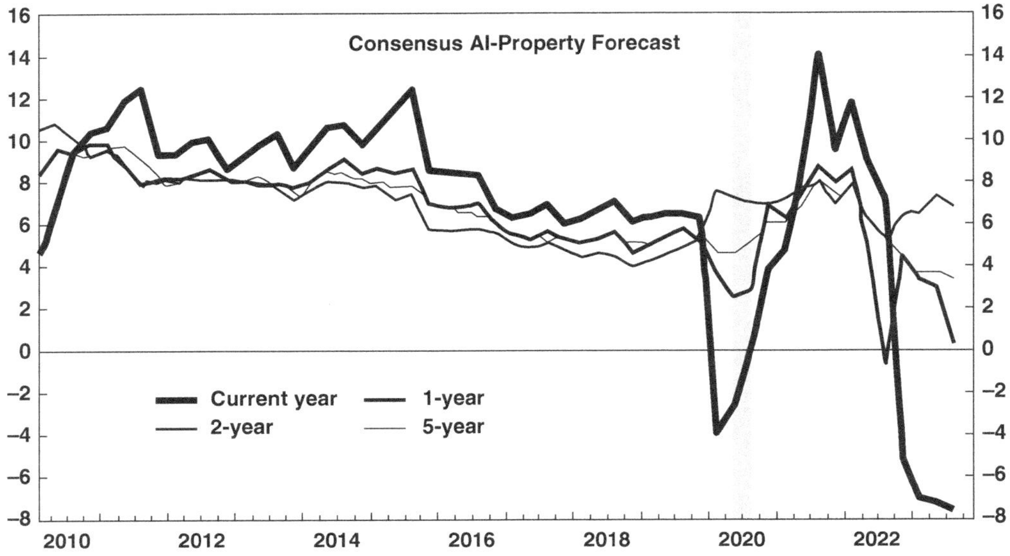

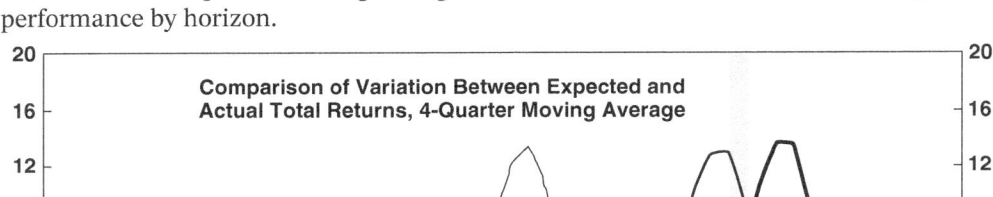

Source: ZCA using PREA survey data

EXHIBIT 19.7 4-quarter moving averages of the difference between actual and expected performance by horizon.

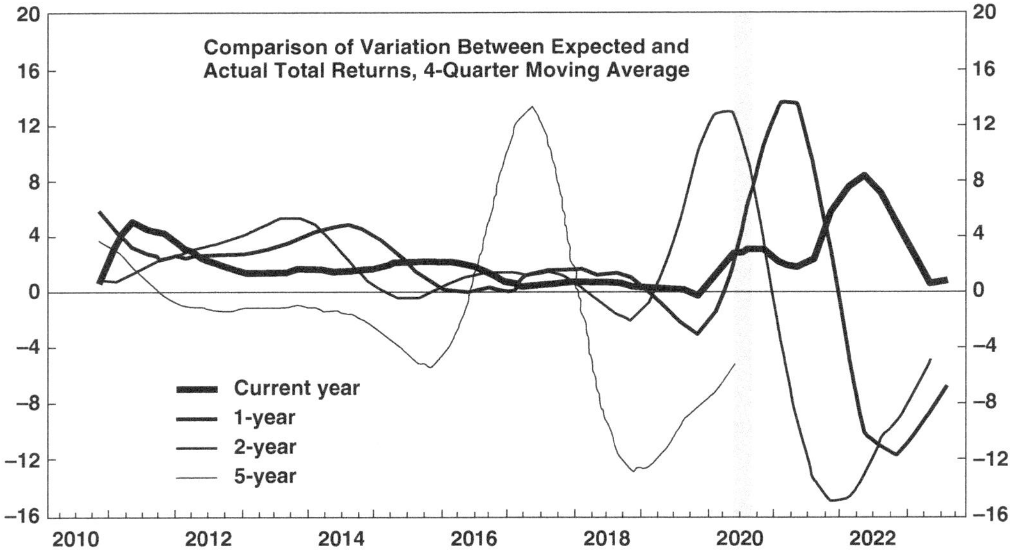

Source: ZCA using PREA data

Using CoStar quarterly office total return data for 206 MSAs, I generated moving correlation windows of varying length between current returns and past returns: 1-, 2-, 3-, 4-, 5-, 7-, and 10-years, as shown in Exhibit 19.8. The correlations oscillate from negative to positive over time. Observe the minimum and maximum correlations in the exhibit. As the correlation window expands past one year, the likelihood of a negative correlation is 52% for the 5-year window.

Predicting relative MSA performance can be challenging. The likelihood that today's hot performing MSA will replicate its rank five or more years ahead is low. Unfortunately, our ability to forecast MSA performance more than two years ahead is imprecise.

Opportunistic and value-add deals typically specify a 5- to 7-year holding period and adopt an exit cap rate that usually reflects the current consensus view, which, I have shown, exhibits systematic biases, but performance is extremely sensitive to the realized exit cap rate.

I acknowledge that exceptionally skilled managers who can consistently pick winning MSAs and generate positive alpha may exist, but I find that identifying those managers in a way that is statistically significant is a daunting task.

Many managers claim special skills in consistently picking markets, but those who make extraordinary claims should provide extraordinary evidence, not just anecdotes or vapid claims.

Institutional real estate research is not much better at predicting events beyond a year than are the managers. Most research, which is designed to persuade, rather than illuminate or educate, is descriptive and anecdotal, not structural or predictive.

EXHIBIT 19.8 Average correlations for seven rolling windows from 2000 to 2025.

Window	Average	Max	Min	Probability of negative correlation, %
1-Year	0.487	0.746	0.178	0.0
2-year	0.343	0.607	−0.144	8.2
3-year	0.222	0.594	−0.153	12.3
4-year	0.101	0.545	−0.181	26.0
5-year	−0.002	0.396	−0.293	52.1
7-year	−0.026	0.463	−0.312	46.6
10-year	−0.016	0.277	−0.281	47.5

Source: ZCA using CoStar data

When and How Do Investors Overpay? Introducing the Winner's Curse

When I directed real estate research on Wall Street, I studied money managers' bidding behavior, specifically the separation of bids for trophy properties. I found that in some cases the spacing of the first relative to the second bid increased dramatically as transactions volume increased. I observed the winning bid for many trophy properties exceeded the second bid by as much as 25% in frothy markets. Clearly, our firm was great at creating excitement in the marketplace. I learned the meaning of the winner's curse. Even the most sophisticated and admired managers at the time and their trophy-obsessed investors suffered as a result.

The winner's curse states that the optimal property bidding strategy entails bidding a substantial amount below your assumed value for the property. The idea is that if you do not bid under your assumed value, your uncertainty about the actual value of the property will often lead you to win property bids for which you lose money after paying your high bid. The winning or highest bidder pays too much.

When transactions volume increases and cap rates decline, investors stretch on price and often overpay. In a recovery, after prices have declined and market uncertainty has dissipated, a bidding frenzy can reemerge as cash-rich buyers see blood in the streets. During the GFC, cap rates rose and transactions fell. Since interest rates rose in 2020, real-time cap rates have risen and transactions volume has declined again. The equity of many investors who bought before interest rates in 2022 rose have lost much if not all of their equity. Many are victims of the winner's curse. How can investors protect themselves in bidding contests?

The incidence of the winner's curse is a direct consequence of the number of auction bidders and asset volatility. This is especially true of value-add and opportunistic investments; their opacity increases uncertainty. Auction participants fail to adapt their bidding strategy to the number of competitors; behavior is suboptimal. Lacking sufficient information, bidders are more susceptible to the winner's curse.

A cognitive illusion causes investors to make systematic errors. Do investors learn from their errors? No! Are bidders repeatedly surprised? Usually, they are. Let's consider an example:

Parable of the lamb and the claw: The essence of this example is a possible bubble preceding a recession, and the venue is sunny Phoenix, land of "perpetual" growth and continued apartment development. Our imaginary firm, *Red in Tooth and Claw, LLC* ("Claw"),[5] is a wealthy manager with fine wood paneling and thick carpets. It claims the ability to consistently buy low and sell high; it wants to determine the profit-maximizing bid for a portfolio. *Innocent Lamb Family Office* ("Lamb") is Claw's client. The family's leader is a hubristic billionaire who believes that whatever he touches turns to success; he is about to learn a harsh lesson. Claw has assured Lamb that real estate is an excellent inflation hedge and prices only go up. Lamb, in an effort to increase AUM aggressively, embraces high leverage and historically has bought properties at historically low cap rates during times of high transactions volume; Lamb, who subscribes to the hot hand fallacy, is heading for a fleecing.

This portfolio, which is owned now by a headstrong GP and his financially traumatized covey of underfunded public employee retirement systems, features a grab bag of properties and land that either lack entitlements or require down-zoning. The exact value of this overleveraged portfolio is uncertain. Market volatility is troubling this highly motivated seller. In anticipation of winning the bid, Claw, acting as GP, has structured a joint venture with Lamb as LP that includes a complex promote, aggressive leverage, and opaque embedded options, all of which are difficult to assess without the right stochastic tools and information.

The bidding will likely be intense, although the number of bidders—no more than seven—is unknown. The value of this portfolio is unknown as well, but it is equally likely to be any value between $10 million and $110 million, admittedly a wide range. Each bidder's (including Claw's) estimate of the value of the portfolio is equally likely to be some number between 50% and 150% of the actual value of the portfolio. Based on past history, Claw believes that each competitor is equally likely to bid between 60% and 80% of their respective value estimates. Given this information, what fraction of Claw's estimate should Claw bid in order to maximize its expected profit?

Although the bidding process will be sealed bid, Claw has retained an advisor, Dantez N. Furnow, LLC, a well-respected capital placement firm. Claw clearly wants to tip the scales in its favor.

The approach. How do uncertainty and volatility affect optimal bidding strategy? The method of choice is stochastic constrained optimization, which combines the power of genetic algorithms and Monte Carlo analysis. Lamb is impressed because this sounds very "high tech."

The objective is to estimate Claw's bid. Claw's base-case analysis assumes that the actual value of the land, a random variable, follows a uniform probability distribution. The lowest and highest bounds are $10 million and $110 million respectively. In market analysis, you never "see" the real value. Claw's bid is "drawn" from a uniform probability distribution of numbers bracketed by 50% and 150% of Claw's estimate of value—Claw's acquisition team may be off as much as 50% either way, but that's the land business! Claw computes its bid as the bid fraction (of the estimate of value) times Claw's bid. The purpose of the analysis is to determine the optimal bid fraction. Each competitor's estimate of value reflects a stochastic or random process similar to Claw's, which is why we call this auction "a common value bidding process." If Claw's bid exceeds all other bids, Claw wins and pockets the actual value minus the bid, or its profit.

Results. The simulation produces important practical insights, which I summarize below.

- The optimal bid is sensitive to the number of competing bidders. The greater the number of bidders, the higher is the optimal bid fraction and risk.
- The average profitability declines exponentially as the number of bidders increases.
- The higher is the volatility or uncertainty of value, the lower are both the optimal bid and bidding profitability.
- Profitability as a function of the number of bidders declines faster in more volatile or more uncertain markets.
- If you must engage in auctions, avoid crowded bidding situations in volatile markets. In order to win, you must increase your bidding fraction, which, in turn, dramatically increases the probability that you will lose money.
- Just because the mean profitability is low, but positive, does not mean that you do not face a substantial likelihood of loss. If you participate in auctions, be sure to avoid volatile markets or markets where you lack a competitive informational edge.
- If you cannot avoid large auctions in volatile markets, especially if you and everyone else shares the same market study and short list of "institutional" investors, then go deeper than the competition. Make it your life's work to be the world's expert in the few markets in which you bid.

Raising discretionary capital so that you can offer capital immediacy and take properties off the market before your competitors notice increases an investor's odds. If the investor buys all cash in a high-interest rate environment, the investor can later deleverage or refinance at a lower rate.

Unfortunately, Claw overbid and Lamb was fleeced. The impetus to herd is so irresistible that investors seem like lambs destined for a shearing. Estimating asset value is more challenging given the widespread volatility in the capital markets. Unfortunately, the industry depends on deterministic analysis, not stochastic risk analysis. Adding to the problem, unbridled hubris may push desperate lambs to the slaughter.

The plot thickens! Psychologists who have studied the winner's curse observe that bidders learn little from their errors; the average bid over a number of repeated trials drifts successively higher. The outcome may be worse if the interests of investors and managers are misaligned, information is asymmetrically shared by LPs and GPs, and projected holding periods are no longer short term.

When a manager overbids, the LPs are generally unaware of the extent of the overbidding. A reputation for overpaying does not help the capital placement effort; it also hurts the disposition process and performance if the manager is carrying the asset at too high a value. The incentive not to sell the asset increases for fear that a capital loss could impair the value of other legacy assets. The incentive to hold the asset long-term is irresistible.

The winner's curse predicts that the *average* bid will be less than the value of a property or portfolio, while the *winning* bid will exceed the value. The winning bid is often much greater than the second-to-the-highest bid, and the dispersion of bids increases with the number of bidders and their uncertainty regarding true value. Since markets are prone to irrational exuberance or fads, certain "hot market" property bids, influenced more by capital flows (momentum or herding) than underlying fundamentals, may produce junk returns. The winner, meanwhile, is cursed by a bid exceeding true value and an acquisition that is less profitable than expected.

The pressure to invest is almost irresistible. Avoiding this problem is not easy, especially when bidders, wracked with conflict, must balance relatively certain asset management fees with uncertain future returns (and promotes). Most potential buyers do not appreciate the need for conservative bidding. However, as bidders increase in number, hope springs eternal. Besides, back at the office, Claw must feed hungry colleagues.

Rational investors should distinguish between the expected property value conditioned only on prior information available and the expected value conditioned on winning the auction. The two are usually quite different. Even if bidders understand this concept, they can still overpay if they underestimate the necessary adjustment to compensate for the presence of other bidders. The greater the number of bidders, the more aggressively one must bid in order to win, so a winning buyer is more likely to overestimate the property value. While the former point suggests that one should be more aggressive, the latter finding implies conservatism. What, then, is the optimal bid?

A seller usually possesses inside information and, therefore, a bidder must calculate the expected property value conditioned on the seller's bid acceptance. This is asymmetric information with a vengeance. A successful bidder will almost certainly lose since she is cursed at the outset. Playing a winning game becomes very difficult, and this is why the ranking of real estate money managers is not stable: Today's darling is often tomorrow's sheared sheep.

Bidders make systematic errors due to market uncertainty, herding, and many competing bidders. The way to avoid the winner's curse is to reduce a bid to some estimated value fraction, the optimal value of which declines with market volatility and the number of bidders. Unfortunately, by reducing a bid, the eager investor, or her manager, decreases the likelihood of winning auctions and maintaining the growth of AUM, thus sacrificing incremental fees. Investors may decide not to bid at all, which is a choice that depresses transactions volume in a weak market. Some wise sellers who need not transact have already retreated to the sidelines. Alternatively, the investor may succeed in exploiting certain informational or first-mover advantages, thereby changing the odds favorably.

Auction participants often fail to adapt their bidding strategy according to competitive models; their behavior is suboptimal. This failure is systematic and repeated, as if there were no learning process. Do market participants have the incentive and ability to adjust their behavior to informational complexities? If pricing is the outcome of a flawed bidding process, what can we conclude from appraisals and comparable sales data, especially when transactions volume is low? Many factors feed the bubble, hubris being just one.

It is clearly an empirical question whether or not the winner's curse dominates, and when. I believe that the winner's curse is a threat once interest rates decline and transactions volume increases, especially in real estate markets whose chief characteristic, besides location, is hidden, asymmetric information. My overly simplified recommendation is, do not be a lamb, unless you crave a fleecing.

Conclusions and Investment Implications

- Bidding is a stochastic process. The winner's curse states that the optimal property bidding strategy entails bidding a substantial amount below your assumed value for the property.
- Bidding behavior could be a factor explaining the precipitous drop during economic downturns in transactions volume, the erosion of total returns, and the decline in prices.
- Whenever there is a period of stress, such as we observed during the GFC and more recently during COVID-19, transactions volume declines. Fewer trades means that investors have less information, which increases market uncertainty. The uncertainty affects the value of embedded options and optimal bidding strategy.

- The left tails of the cap rate distribution—lower cap rates—are the most volatile along trend. The minimum cap rate increased in 2008 and even more dramatically in 2009 as fear seized the market.
- The properties that do transact are typically the most liquid and the least opaque informationally. These properties may transmit limited information regarding the properties that do not sell.
- During a bidding frenzy, the separation between the winning bid and the next bid can be considerable.
- The incidence of the winner's curse is a direct consequence of the number of auction bidders and asset value uncertainty.
- The optimal bid is sensitive to the number of competing bidders. The greater the number of bidders, the higher is the optimal bid fraction. The average profitability declines exponentially as the number of bidders increases.
- The higher is value uncertainty, the lower are both the optimal bid and bidding profitability. Profitability, which is a function of the number of bidders, declines faster in more volatile or more uncertain markets. If one must engage in auctions, avoid crowded bidding situations in volatile markets.
- Thinking you can beat the market consistently after accounting for fees and transactions costs is a loser's game, unless you have some advantage. Some firms are successful at raising AUM rapidly. However, few can beat the market consistently after fees and expenses.

Q&A: Interview with Susan Stupin, Managing Director, Prescott Holdings, LLC; The Prescott Group, LLC

Acquiring and Creating Operating Platforms After Wall Street

Describe your journey in real estate.

Real estate has been a holistic way to use my left and right brain analytic and writing talents to build a challenging and satisfying career. After my Princeton graduation as a liberal arts major, I worked on Wall Street before attending Harvard Business School. I was inspired there by the great professor and entrepreneur Bill Poorvu. After HBS, I started my career at Eastdil Realty then joined Goldman Sachs' real estate department which was growing dramatically and dominating the real estate investment banking landscape in the 1980s and 1990s. I was surrounded by great mentors, impressive colleagues and clients, cutting-edge capital markets work, and opportunities for leadership and teamwork.

When did you start Prescott Holdings?

I left Goldman in the late 1980s to co-found Prescott as a NY-based investment, advisory, and asset management firm. We brought in an outside investor, which accelerated our growth as a principal. We acquire and/or create real estate operating platforms along with our property investments. For example, we acquired a portfolio of outlet centers making us one of the largest US owners in this sector. We branded the centers and formed a management, leasing, and development platform to operate them. The capitalization was Sharia compliant, adding structuring and legal complications.

What were some of your lessons learned?

Leverage is a powerful but dangerous tool. We've found, as an operating partner, there is always an imbalance of power with an institutional partner. They can outgun you in a buy–sell and deal stress will highlight their control provisions. For any operating business, working capital is essential. Having sufficient capital means you can invest with greater conviction and weather financial storms. Finally, once you ink a partnership agreement, the renegotiation is just starting.

Tell us about Prescott.

Prescott is a principal investor in commercial real estate assets and entities and a strategic advisor. We are known for our deep understanding of the global real estate capital markets and our expertise in property financing and operations. As a small firm, we are nimble and creative in devising and executing successful investment and capitalization strategies for our own and our clients' accounts.

What advice would you offer young professionals?

Seek a challenging place to work where you will have a steep learning curve. Developing a body of knowledge is essential.

CHAPTER 20

Underfunded Public Pension Funds, Risk, and Alternatives

Preliminaries

State retirement systems are underfunded and have increased their allocation to alternatives, which includes real estate value-add and opportunity funds. This underfunding is a major source of real estate investor risk, especially in large cities. The average funding ratio for all government systems is about 76% as of 2023, but the funding ratio can be as low as 31%.

These funds on average have underperformed leveraged core investments, risk-adjusted and net of fees. LPs have transferred substantial fees to GPs despite this underperformance.

If the pension fund's leadership, in lieu of raising taxes or reducing plan benefits, wants to take the system to the casino and incur more risk, then is investing through highly leveraged value-add and opportunistic *funds* the best choice? Why not just add leverage to low-volatility core real estate, rather than embrace higher leverage with risky opportunity funds? Is it not odd that core investments with stable cash flows have low leverage but higher risk strategies, such as opportunistic funds, carry much higher leverage? The clue may be the interaction between the promote (fees) and leverage.

Return smoothing and inappropriately low benchmarks make manager performance appear too good to be true. Some investment committees embrace this systematic downward bias because doing so provides short-term political cover, which eventually may prove to be a fragile fig leaf.

Some Stylized Facts About Value-Add and Opportunistic Funds and the Search for Alpha

Alternative assets (including private equity, real estate, and hedge funds) now account for 60% of the assets of large endowments and 30% of those of large public pension funds. Why do public pension funds embrace these strategies? Riddiough, a professor at the University of Wisconsin, writes that the chronic underfunding is the result of aggressive retirement benefit promises and poor investment performance. I agree.

Li and Riddiough report that "RE [real estate] funds perform the worst, with a mean size-weighted IRR of 7.02% and a direct IRR of −4.63%. Even the highest-risk, development-oriented, value-add and opportunistic real estate fund strategies—which represent about 70% of real estate fund capitalization—return only 7.86% and 7.08%, respectively ... real estate fund performance is seen to deteriorate as a function of ... "[1] the pension fund's tilt toward alternative investments.

Investors' hands are not clean, either. The underfunding has created powerful incentives for investment committees to take the fund to the casino. Another problem is the overweighting of local investments, such as infrastructure, especially in states where political self-dealing and corruption are more accepted. No one should be surprised that many of these investments underperform.

Research has also shown that the number of consultants is highly correlated with the number of political appointees on the investment committee. Consultants, who supposedly help manage, inform, and cleanse the investment process, are very accommodating to the parochial political priorities of these appointees and are often too heavily influenced by and dependent on the managers.

Accounting rules distort decisions. The Government Accounting Standards Board (GASB) Statement Number 25 establishes accounting rules for states and local governments and these rules encourage pension funds to shoulder more risk. GASB 25 links the liability discount—inappropriately and perversely in my opinion[2]—to investment returns. The higher is the investment return, the greater is the liability discount rate, which in turn artificially depresses the present value of the liability stream and partially hides the underfunding problem. This approach is tantamount to using the return performance on a household's portfolio of stocks to value a home mortgage.[3] Who said accounting is not creative and fun?

Minimizing the appearance of underfunding through accounting tricks is a deception and it is corrupt. Since the liability stream is not very volatile, the liability discount should be close to the risk-free rate or at least the rate at which states and municipalities borrow. A lower discount rate decreases the funding ratio further.

The 2022 10-year municipal bond yield was 2.85%; by contrast, targeted value-add and opportunistic returns were in the range of 16–18%. The average asset return in 2023 was 6% to 8%. The differences in the values of the liability stream using either the risk-free rate or 7% is huge; liabilities may be undervalued by at least 60%. So, as worrisome as the reported public pension fund underfunding may be, the truth may be truly alarming. Is there any wonder why these retirement systems have tilted toward alternative assets?

Many alternative real estate funds have not served pension funds well. The pension fund pays higher management fees, shoulders hidden, often purposely disguised risk, earns lower risk-adjusted returns, receives negative alpha, pays, but does not receive, a liquidity discount, and, according to Riddiough, enters into a "gamble for resurrection,"[4] all for the privilege of not knowing a true mark-to-market price or return and attending educational money manager events at tropical resorts.

Li and Riddiough conclude that "there are a host of agency problems that contribute to this outcome, including incentives associated with volatility laundering. In the end, public pension funds … seem to be maximizing something other than investment return, which is behind our main finding that private real estate fails to conform to the 'survival of the fittest' private equity paradigm." They add, "There is no significant relation between the IRR on a prior real estate fund and the probability of raising a new fund." The authors report that "real estate fund managers with five or more liquidated funds … underperform less experienced fund managers." Compared to buyout funds and venture capital, real estate fund managers displayed the worst performance and exhibited worsening fund performance as a function of management experience.

If corrected for downward bias, the risks of their private equity investments could be 40% higher. Most private equity investments reduce measured portfolio liquidity and some fund managers, especially those who manage private listed REITs, have reported subjective, mark-to-model, returns that only faintly resemble what is actually happening in the market.

The corrected volatility of conservatively leveraged property is equivalent to the volatility of public REITs.[5] Money managers claim that property volatility is significantly less than public REIT volatility. This conclusion is wrong and self-serving, which I demonstrate in this book.

Private equity fund fees are typically 2% annual management fees and 20% performance fees. By contrast, stock and bond index fund managers charge one tenth of one percent, and the risk-adjusted returns of these index funds are often greater.

Professor Joe Pagliari, Jr. of the University of Chicago and Mitchell Bollinger report that "investors during the period 2000 through 2017 would have been better served by merely leveraging their core investments … value-add funds have on average generated a negative alpha of −3.26%; similarly, opportunistic funds have generated a negative alpha of −2.85% … Had investors in core funds used more leverage (loan-to-value ratios of 55% to 65%), they would have saved approximately $7.5 billion per year in unnecessary investment management fees."[6] I agree. Public pension funds are willing to accept a 3 to 4% discount on their rate of return for the "privilege" of investing through an opportunistic fund, especially ones with highly persuasive capital placement teams.

Benchmarks. Most pension funds adopt benchmarks that are too low given the risks. These benchmarks, which do not adequately reflect high leverage and promotes, are opaque and hypothetical, and they put the active manager in an unjustifiably attractive light.

Some CIOs have a personal financial incentive to lobby for low benchmarks, especially benchmarks that include return hurdles without specifying risk. The pension consultants, whom the CIOs and their investment committees hire, never seem to object.

Benchmarks traditionally consist of weightings of various indexes, assets, or asset classes. Choosing the correct benchmark is critical. What are the characteristics of a good benchmark?

- Unambiguity. The benchmark should be free of ambiguity and it should be verifiable.

- Tradeable. Alpha must be measured against a tradeable benchmark. The choice of benchmark affects the measurement of alpha. Using the capital asset pricing model, beta is the ratio of excess fund returns (relative to the risk-free asset) over the excess market's excess return. The market benchmark might be the S&P 500 or some other index. NCREIF is not tradeable and therefore NCREIF is not a true return index. It is subject to many data biases that include smoothing bias and selection bias. However, all illiquid assets share these biases.

- Replicable. In principle, the manager or investor should be able to replicate the benchmark. If the benchmark is not replicable, then estimating the contribution of the manager is not possible.

- Risk-adjustment. Most benchmarks are not risk-adjusted. There are many risk factors other than equity market risk. Credit and property liquidity are examples.

Factor benchmarks. Investors are often unaware that they are not buying assets but rather bundles of risk factors. The notion of an <u>asset</u> is far too blunt and does not address investors' primary concern, which should be risk management. That is why two properties with seemingly identical physical attributes, but with different non-physical risk factors, can perform differently. Exposure to these factors earns factor risk premiums. Investors should not think of asset performance in isolation of the risk factors associated with the assets and the liabilities.

Customized benchmarks should reflect these risk factors. Usually, they do not. Another idea is to create synthetic benchmarks especially suitable for funds and constituent assets that reflect leverage, waterfalls, and other nonlinearities.[7] While NCREIF is in many cases too easy a bar to clear,[8] NCREIF could be one of several variables used in the mathematical formulation of a synthetic benchmark.

Another approach is to create large, passive investment portfolios with negligible fees. The sovereign fund of Norway is successful in this respect, so what prevents US public pension funds from doing the same?[9]

Underwriting what really counts. If the market rewards investors only for bearing risks that are not diversifiable, then how should we underwrite real estate investments? As I have mentioned elsewhere, when evaluating risk, we should do so relative to a portfolio that includes the liabilities. Then we must pick a benchmark that fits the strategy. The application of appropriate risk analytics, not the usual deterministic sensitivity analysis, is essential. This approach is contrary to widely used, deterministic underwriting procedures.

Some performance measures applied to illiquid assets, such as opportunity funds. Investing has its own jargon. Here is a list of terms with definitions and cautionary notes regarding opportunity funds.

- Alpha. Alpha is a measure of the excess return over a benchmark; it is used as a measure of value added by the manager. Depending on the risk factors comprising the benchmark, the alpha can be either negative or positive.
- Total portfolio risk. Total risk is the sum of systematic and nonsystematic risk. Systematic risk, or market risk, is the tendency of all assets to move together. The market, in principle, compensates the investor for this risk, which is not diversifiable. Unsystematic or idiosyncratic risk, which includes those risks pertaining to a specific asset, is diversifiable; the market does not compensate the investor for bearing risks that the investor can shed.
- Beta. The sensitivity of an asset's excess market returns to market returns over the riskless rate is beta. Beta is essentially a measure of systematic risk. The market index has a beta of one. If the asset's beta is 0.5, then the asset has one half the market's volatility. How do we define the market, especially for illiquid assets such as property? Leverage increases beta (and fees), not alpha.

- Diversification and unsystematic risk. In Chapter 10, I introduced diversification principles. To review, true diversification eliminates unsystematic risk. Few assets are needed to accomplish this objective. Stocks are a good example. Assuming we pick 30 to 35 stocks at random and the betas are all one, then these stocks eliminate a large fraction of the diversifiable risk. This principle applies to illiquid assets as well. An important insight is that not all of an asset's risk is relevant for determining the risk premium. Theory says that expected return should be related to beta.
- Tracking error. Tracking error, which is the standard deviation of excess returns, indicates how closely the manager's performance tracks the benchmark. The choice of benchmark is critical. If the tracking error is risk-adjusted, then the tracking error is idiosyncratic volatility.
- Information ratio. The information ratio is the ratio of alpha divided by the tracking error. This is alpha per unit of risk. An asset with high alpha can have a low information ratio. For example, on average, opportunity funds have a negative alpha of 300 bps. The crude tracking error does not account for return smoothing due to illiquidity and other factors. If we divide the negative alpha by the statistically corrected tracking error, true performance is even worse than measured performance. When the benchmark is the risk-free rate, alpha is the average return over the risk-free rate and the information ratio becomes the Sharpe ratio.

We are all winners. Misuse of performance indexes reminds me of all the children who live in Lake Wobegon, a fictional town, where "all the children are above average." That manager performance usually exceeds the NCREIF Index, a small bar to clear, especially for value-add and opportunistic deals, is no coincidence.

Managers do nothing to correct the benchmark bias and pay-to-play conference organizers seldom, if at all, include this as a panel topic for fear of manager retribution. For example, NCREIF, which I regard as a superbly engineered and well-maintained index, is cynically misused by many managers; it is too easy a bar to clear in its unadjusted form.[10]

Institutional investors should mark-to-market their assets and liabilities, not mark-to-model, especially given the underfunding problem; most do not. Riddiough[11] characterizes this psychological state of mind as "paying for a veil" that intentionally hinders price discovery. How valuable is this veil? Is it worth giving up a 4% to 5% annual return?

Richard Ennis, a well-respected pension and financial consultant, reports that the low volatility of alternative assets is a "creative myth," unsupported by the data once appropriate statistical adjustments are made. Alternative assets are not "volatility dampers" that hide or disguise volatility. Ennis further emphasizes that certain alternative asset returns are highly correlated with US equities, not exactly a powerful diversifier.[12] The average returns of alternative assets underperformed stock and bond portfolios; the underperformance coincidentally matches the fee differential.

Managers, not just public pension funds, disguise risk. Recall that volatility increases the value of options and that the GP position in a structured deal is replete with options. A clever manager's deception is reducing financial leverage and making up for the volatility loss by investing in MSAs with greater volatility. What has changed from the perspective of the LP's return? Little.

A neglected risk factor is MSA risk, which varies across MSAs. Rents are more volatile in some favored cities such as New York and San Francisco. There is clearly a tradeoff between leverage and MSA rental and return volatility. With a promote, the risk to the LP increases. Most institutional investors favor the larger MSAs, especially the gateway cities. Size facilitates the quicker deployment of capital, but doing so incurs greater rental growth volatility.[13] This helps the GP position, the value of which increases with volatility.

Not all MSAs are the same. The natural vacancy rate, which is that rate at which rents are neither rising nor falling, varies by MSA. An 8% vacancy rate may indicate a soft market in one MSA but a tight market in a growing MSA, where there is a higher transactional demand for vacancies. The difference can critically affect underwriting.

Diversification benefits vanish during downturns, but why then do investors participate in opportunistic open-end vehicles offering redemption rights when it is unlikely investors will be able to exercise these rights when these rights are needed the most? What are these investors implicitly paying for these rights?

Fund Performance

Funds that perform better over the long-term are more likely to perform relatively better over the short-term.[14] The 10- and one-year performances of all public funds are highly correlated. State systems' one-year performance is 4.2% less than other public systems' performance.

$$TR.1YR_i = -22.308 + 0.693 * STATE_i * TR.10YR_i + 2.059 * TR.10YR_i$$
$$(-4.124)\ \ (0.861)(3.020)$$

$$ -4.157 * STATE_i$$
$$(-0.642) \tag{20.1}$$

Mean dependent variable: −4.567

Adjusted $R^2 = 0.362$

Observations: 94

The distribution of one-year returns ranges from −13.4% to 9.5%, indicating wide variance. The distribution of 10-year returns exhibits less variance than one-year returns. Publicly traded stock equity returns are highly skewed to the right but, compared with private equity and real estate, are tightly grouped around the mean.

Ninety-five percent of the public funds had negative returns in that year. Publicly traded equity returns have little or no smoothing. Less than 10% of private equity and real estate funds produced returns less than zero in 2022. Publicly traded equities had a highly skewed mean return in 2022 of −14.9% and a standard deviation of 7.7%. Private equity returns had a mean return of 18.2% and a standard deviation of 10.8%, whereas real estate returns in 2022 had a mean return of 22.9% and a standard deviation of 9.5%. From 1978 to the present, 8.6% of the quarterly REIT total returns were less than zero; only 2.1% of property returns were negative. Moreover, *measured* property return volatility was one quarter that of REIT volatility. This smoothing is a statistical artifact that makes no sense. After de-smoothing property returns, the standard deviation of property equals REIT volatility. Many pension fund CIOs and their investment committees deny this inconvenient and indisputable truth, as do their property managers.

State Pension Funding Ratios in 2022

Public funds have tilted their portfolios toward riskier and more opaque alternative assets that include hedge funds, real estate, and private equity. The average pension fund surplus is negative, and the distribution is highly skewed to the left. The funding ratio, which is the ratio of assets to liabilities, is 0.76. The surplus of the sample of 94 pension funds in 2022 was negative. Larger pension funds tend to have slightly higher funding ratios. There is a positive relationship between the funding ratio and pension fund size, holding other factors constant. See Equation 20.2.

$$FUNDING.RATIO_i = 54.573 + 40.874 * ASSETS_i - 5.784 * STATE_i$$
$$(4.962) \quad (1.682) \qquad\qquad (-1.518)$$

$$+2.968 * RED_i + 3.021 * TR10YR_i$$
$$(0.927) \qquad\qquad (2.273)$$

$$-23.482 * TEACH_i * STATE_i + 16.070 * TEACH_i$$
$$(-2.396) \qquad\qquad\qquad\qquad (1.777) \qquad\qquad (20.2)$$

Mean of dependent variable: 6.051
Adjusted $R^2 = 0.129$
Observations: 94

The STATE coefficient is negative and, while only significant at the 13% level, indicates that the funding ratio for state pension funds is almost 5.8% lower than other public pension funds. If the state pension fund is also a teachers' retirement system, the funding ratio is 23.5% lower, evidently because teachers' unions are very effective politically at the state level. If the teachers' retirement system is a municipal fund and not a state-managed system, the funding ratio is 16.1% higher, but still low. Republican Party dominance of many state legislatures, signified by the dummy variable, RED, has no effect on the funding ratio.

National politics can play an important role in asset allocation. Certain RED states in 2025 withdrew their capital from money managers who offered products focused on DEI, which stands for diversity, equity, and Inclusion.

Comparing private and public pension funds. Private pension funds do not exhibit the same degree of underfunding as the public pension funds. ERISA regulatory and accounting standards are some of the reasons why. Lack of public capital market discipline is another. Companies with underfunded pension funds are required to make larger contributions to the pension fund, thus reducing profits and earnings. Underfunding can lead to benefit cuts for participants and a shift of the burden of pension obligations to future shareholders. Wall Street equity and bond analysts scrutinize quarterly corporate filings. Who is studying public pension fund filings? Often state financial reports do not post the degree of underfunding. Lacking the intense scrutiny of Wall Street bond and equity analysts, public pension funds kick the can down the road.

The underfunding problem has grown worse and is becoming a significant risk factor that real estate investors should assess, especially for acquisitions and dispositions in jurisdictions whose retirement systems suffer from extreme underfunding.

Asset Allocation: Shifts to the Alts

Public pension funds have shifted their focus from liquid assets to opportunistic and value-add strategies. These two categories comprised 68% of capital raised between 2018 and 2023. Public pension funds, in contrast to their corporate counterparts, increased their allocation to alternative assets from about 3% in 2000 to over 9% in 2022. Corporate pension funds' allocations to alternative investments declined but public pension funds' allocations increased. What explains this disparity?

State pension retirement systems have allocated more to private equity than have other public pension funds. This behavior is consistent with public pension funds' assuming greater, hidden risks. See Equation 20.3.

$$PR.ALLOCATION_i = -0.153 + 0.060 * FUNDING.RATIO_i - 0.231 * TR.PUBEQ_i$$
$$(-3.006) \quad (1.043) \quad\quad\quad\quad\quad (-2.080)$$

$$+ 0.158 * TR.FIXED_i + 3.124 * TR5YR_i + 0.037 * STATE_i$$
$$(0.957) \quad\quad\quad\quad (6.918) \quad\quad\quad (1.877)$$

$$- 0.014 * RED_i - 0.013 * TEACH_i - 0.0002 * ASSETS_i$$
$$(-0.787) \quad\quad (-0.898) \quad\quad\quad (-1.551) \quad\quad\quad\quad (20.3)$$

Mean of dependent variable: 15.612

Adjusted $R^2 = 0.400$

Observations: 94

The higher is the five-year total fund return, the greater are the allocations to private equity and real estate funds. If publicly traded equity returns are strong, then private equity allocations are lower. Larger pension funds have lower private equity allocations; such is not the case with real estate funds. See Equation 20.4.

$$RE.ALLOCATION_i = 0.032 + 0.054 * FUNDING.RATIO_i + 0.022 * TR.PUBEQ_i$$
$$(1.075) \quad (1.837) \quad\quad\quad\quad\quad (0.316)$$

$$+ 0.022 * TR.FIXED_i + 0.515 * TR5YR_i + 0.009 * STATE_i$$
$$(0.219) \quad\quad\quad\quad (1.880) \quad\quad\quad (0.864)$$

$$- 0.002 * RED_i + 0.009 * TEACH_i$$
$$(-0.291) \quad\quad (-0.959) \quad\quad\quad\quad\quad\quad (20.4)$$

Mean of dependent variable: 0.114

Adjusted $R^2 = 0.056$

Observations: 94

A good predictor of fund private equity and real estate asset allocation is the spread between 10-year and 1-year returns, as shown in Equation 20.5.

$$PR.ALLOCATION_i = 0.245 - 1.002 * (TR10YR_i - TR1YR_i) - 0.254 * TR.PUBEQ_i$$
$$(10.406)(-5.965) \qquad\qquad\qquad (-2.577) \qquad\qquad (20.5)$$

Mean of dependent variable: 0.156
Adjusted $R^2 = 0.273$
Observations: 94

The average real estate allocation is 11%. Only 25% of funds have a real estate allocation over 13.5%.

Conclusions and Investment Implications

- Chronicallly and severely underfunded public pension funds have become a sigificant real estate underwriting risk. From 2018 to 2023, nearly 70% of new investments were either value-add or opportunistic funds, which, as a group, produced negative alpha,[15] an amount equal to fees charged. This tilt will increase the risk, not solve the problem.
- Investors have increased their allocations to funds focusing on value-add and opportunistic investing. These funds have not delivered positive alpha but have collected enormous fees.
- Value-add and opportunity funds—not necessarily opportunistic separate accounts or joint ventures—have underperformed core funds net of fees.
- The portfolio allocation to private equity increased from 3.5% in 2000 to over 9% in 2022. By contrast, the corporate allocation during this period remained relatively flat.
- State pension funds, which have a 5.8% lower funding ratio than other public funds, have a 3.2 percent higher allocation to private equity. Larger pension funds have higher funding ratios.
- Teacher pension funds have higher funding ratios unless they are state-level teacher retirement systems.
- The higher the 10-year return, the greater is the funding ratio. The greater is the performance of publicly listed equities, the lower is the allocation to private equity and to real estate opportunity funds.

Q&A: Interview with Richard F. Burns, Senior Advisor & Trustee, The NHP Foundation

Early Advocate of Institutional Real Estate and Rescuer of Troubled Companies

You have had a long, distinguished career, working with the best. How did you get started in real estate and where did it take you?

After brokerage in Boston, I migrated to the world of real estate debt and equity. John Hancock real estate hired me. We financed powerhouse developers like Mel Simon and Milt Cooper. I was also financing New York office buildings, hotels, and using subordinated land sale leasebacks. It was my early exposure to complex capital stacks. After five years I started the third open-end real estate fund for pension funds. After 10 years at Hancock, I was recruited by Putnam Investment Management to start an institutional real estate fund. My strategy was to produce higher returns by selling tax write-offs to developers who would value those write-offs. Peter Aldrich, Tom Eastman, and Mark Waltch, who were leaving the Boston Company to launch AEW, had a similar strategy and recruited me as a founding partner. In 10 years, we grew AUM to $10 billion. I was then asked by a friend, the CEO of Boston Financial, an affordable housing tax credit syndicator, to start up an institutional fund. Building my own team was appealing. We successfully raised the capital for a series of five private REITs that had strong returns. Morgan Stanley bought the investment business of Boston Financial and, after a two-year stay, I left and successfully invested in a senior living company. Then an affordable housing nonprofit recruited me to be CEO and President. I rescued the company from near-bankruptcy and created a very successful organization.

How did you navigate the internal and external challenges?

Fortunately, I had a high-powered Board that gave me full support. The properties were seriously underperforming, but there was a shortage of affordable apartments. I sold some and began tax credit financed rehabilitation on others. I replaced staff and recruited fresh talent. Next came the repair of damaged lender relationships. We executed a plan that succeeded beyond the Board's expectations.

What advice would you give aspiring real estate professionals?

Research several real estate investment firms to determine their performance ranking. Be willing to start at the bottom and impress everyone. Choose a larger firm and learn everything you can. Seek a great mentor.

CHAPTER 21

Investor's Checklist and Conclusions

My Prescription

I do not avoid risk if I understand it and if the risk premium is appropriate. If the deal is illiquid and opaque, I insist on personally underwriting the deal, including the leases, the market, the promote structure, and any other embedded options. True, not naïve, diversification is essential, certainly at the portfolio level, because the market does not reward investors for shouldering diversifiable risk.

Additionally, I expect the following provisions from any private real estate transaction and so should investors:

- Strong control rights that are appropriate for the position in the deal.
- Careful, transparent, detailed underwriting.
- A reasonable expectation of liquidity when needed the most.
- No excessive leverage that enhances fees without delivering true alpha.
- A compelling explanation of the sources of all risks, the degree of risk and how risk affects promotes and the generation of LP and GP performance.
- Quantitative risk analysis should employ some of the methods I outline in this book.
- No cherry-picking the performance statistics; I want to see everything for all deals and all years, including portfolios that were merged with other funds.
- I want to see only benchmarks that are appropriate for the strategy, the leverage, the promote, and the MSA.

- The manager's skill and the strategy must match.
- Excellent performance reporting that includes risk analytics.
- If I cannot obtain most of the aforementioned, then I prefer publicly traded assets. I like to sleep well and so should the reader.
- If you have no control, have not studied the deal, and lack liquidity, tread carefully or, better still, do not do the deal. If you are willing to sacrifice control and do not care about investment details, then invest in traded stocks (including REITs) through mutual funds or ETFs.
- I lack stock-picking skills, so I favor low-fee index funds. Unless I have an information advantage, I am unlikely to succeed consistently in picking winning stocks, especially since I derive no thrill from gambling. If I did, I would allocate only a small portion of my portfolio to this losing strategy. Remember, attempting to outguess the market consistently is a loser's game.
- If your country club friends invite you to invest in their deals, be careful, especially if they cannot accurately describe the deal in detail or they cannot intelligently discuss the many issues I have raised in this book. If your friend recommends the deal, what is his hidden compensation, if any? How much of his own capital will he commit? Will the investment terms your friend receives be different from the terms you are offered? When your friend recommends a deal and justifies the investment by the "quality" of the investors, beware. For example, if Goldman Sachs Asset Management is an investor, does Goldman have a special arrangement, such as control rights or a priority position that you lack? If these questions irritate your friend, then find a new friend.

Investor's Checklist

- Make sure your investment plan quantitatively addresses risk.
- The implementation plan is just as important as the plan to be implemented. What is your plan if the deal does not meet its objectives and you have redemption rights that the GP will not honor?
- I do not redline investments by style or risk. I focus instead on alignment of interest, liquidity, transparency, expected risk-adjusted returns, information asymmetries, among many other considerations.
- Do not let stock volatility be a reason not to invest in REITs; after statistical correction, property returns are no less risky than REITs.
- Avoid excessive leverage. Remember, deal-level leverage offsets your fixed income performance and encourages higher fees.

- Expected returns increase but with greater risk of loss; the likelihood of loss grows faster than expected returns.
- Your advisor should explain investment risks in precise quantitative terms that you can understand. If she is unable to do so, find another advisor.
- Avoid needless complexity. After adjusting for fees, leverage, and risk, would you be better off investing in a leveraged core real estate fund or a public REIT?
- You should evaluate a deal's merits in the context of the liabilities you seek to fund.
- Market timing does not work in stocks or in real estate, private or public, after deducting fees and expenses. Attempting to beat any market is a loser's game.[1]
- Property markets are inefficient, but do not conclude that you can consistently beat the market after fees and expenses.
- Diversification is not free. Even though it is not a free lunch, it is certainly the cheapest meal in town. The market does not reward investors for assuming diversifiable risks.
- Your advisor should embrace risk analytics. If your manager cannot explain the deal or strategy in clear quantitative terms, find a new manager.
- If you invest in illiquid assets, make sure you can expect an adequate, quantifiable illiquidity premium.
- MSAs have different risk characteristics and these characteristics should affect your underwriting. What determines the manager's property allocation across MSAs?
- Carefully evaluate those MSAs with massive fiscal problems such as underfunded pension plans. In addition to the taxpayers, those who suffer will include the needy, elderly, and disabled as well as owners of real estate.
- Sometimes the lemmings are correct, but they are seldom wise. Be suspicious of the herd. As Warren Buffett said, when the market is greedy, be fearful; when it is fearful, be greedy. When it is time to be greedy, make sure you have free cash available to buy bargains.

Time to emerge from the cave. A new golden age of real estate has emerged, and it will be transformative, yet uncertain, in the path it takes and who benefits or loses.

It is time to emerge from **Plato's Cave**[2] with eyes wide open.

People of the Cave have spent their entire lives chained in front of an inner wall with a view of the empty outer wall of the cave. They observe the shadows projected onto the outer wall by objects carried behind the inner wall by jailers who are invisible to the chained prisoners and who walk along the inner wall with a fire behind them, creating shadows on the inner wall in front of the prisoners. The shadows are the prisoners' distorted reality. Only a few rise to the challenge. The most risk-averse cave dwellers remain, for they know no better life and fear the unknown.

Are investors stuck in Plato's Cave and, if so, is it time to emerge?

Conclusions and Investment Implications

- A single theme unifies this book: Risk is real, but investors ignore, misunderstand, or miscalculate risk, leaving value on the table and shouldering risk for which the market provides no compensation.
- Investors should reconsider how they analyze and manage risk, especially regarding complex, non-public vehicles.
- Real estate, bereft of science, is the preserve of stories and myths, e.g., real estate is a good short- to intermediate-term inflation hedge. It is not!
- Typical deterministic sensitivity analysis is no substitute for stochastic Monte Carlo analysis.
- Asset risk should be considered in the context of the liabilities, not in isolation. A low return asset at the margin can be a high return asset in the context of a portfolio's asset and liabilities.
- Property investors suffer from the consequences of hidden information. Private vehicles do not trade in public stock markets and do not receive daily market pricing and ongoing scrutiny by independent third-party analysts. Many of these vehicles lack the transparency that investors need to evaluate risk properly.
- REITs have strict disclosure requirements. Calculating the performance of a REIT is trivial compared to the performance of a property joint venture or unlisted private opportunistic REIT.
- Private vehicles often have significant leverage even though leverage does not increase risk-adjusted returns; leverage, which increases fees by increasing gross, not net, assets under management and it increases beta but not alpha.
- Private deals seldom compensate investors for bearing illiquidity risks. These risks are substantial, judging by the discounts prevailing in the secondary market for limited partnership units.

- Property returns are serially correlated or smoothed, but this is just an artifact of the valuation process. Measured risk is too low and, as a result, property looks too good to be true.
- Some investors believe that the artificial smoothing of property returns is a benefit, either because they incorrectly believe that property is less risky than REIT share prices, or because the smoothing acts like a fig leaf, hiding multiple sins from investment committees, investors, and trustees.
- Interests in private real estate are usually not well aligned, conflicts are endemic, and fees are high and partially hidden. Modern REITs, by contrast, disclose all fees and own the management company.
- Public pension funds' tilt toward alternative investments, such as opportunistic funds, reflects chronic underfunding. Many investment committees take the pension fund to the casino using illiquid, risky, opaque investments—essentially a "kick the can down the road" strategy.
- Most manager-sponsored real estate research is compromised and biased; it remains the stepchild of the marketing department. One manager recently said, "Research is just about stories that cause investors to write checks."
- Great strides have been taken in the development of risk analytics, factor analysis, derivatives, AI, and portfolio theory for products that trade in public markets. Real estate has been a laggard in the adoption of these innovations.
- Real estate is spatially fixed, durable, and complex. The greater is its complexity, the more investors should worry about asymmetric information, hidden interdependencies, latent risks, and excessive fees.
- MSAs have distinct risk characteristics, which many managers and investors ignore or misunderstand. For example, investors prefer growing cities, but with growth comes volatility. Do growing cities offer superior risk-adjusted returns to LPs? Not necessarily.
- Real estate is replete with options and the value of these options increases with risk. Prevailing analytic techniques are mostly deterministic, not stochastic, and fail to evaluate embedded options correctly. I recommend Monte Carlo as a risk analytic tool.
- Investors focus excessively on total returns and ignore risk. Many CIOs are compensated for exceeding an inappropriately low absolute return benchmark, the incentives are wrong.
- Gifted managers are a rarity. I estimate that the chance of a false positive—recommending an unskilled manager—exceeds 80%.

CHAPTER 21 Investor's Checklist and Conclusions

- Many private equity firms realize that pension funds no longer hold the same allure as they once did, given the declining role of defined benefit plans and the ascendancy of defined contribution plans. Other sources of AUM, such as insurance company premiums, 401Ks, and high net worth capital are investor targets. The goal is to build AUM quickly, charge high and sustainable private real estate fees, exploit the deceptively low measured (but not true) volatility of property, and, in the case of publicly traded private equity firms, boost earnings and stock prices.

- A private equity fund's reported performance typically ignores the performance-dilutive effects of capital call timing, investment duration, and capital deployment speeds. The opportunity cost to the investor of reserving for committed but uncalled capital can be substantial and uncertain; seldom is this cost netted against reported performance.

Q&A: Interview with Russell Platt, Co-Founder and CEO of Forum Partners

Creating Value, Growing Businesses, and Managing Risk

How did you get started in real estate?

I attended Williams College and Harvard Business School. After Williams, I joined Morgan Stanley, rejoining after business school. Working in the real estate group, my focus was real estate operating companies. I launched the REIT investment business and the Firm's special situations fund, targeting venture investments in real estate platforms. My experience underwriting startups led to my leaving to launch Forum Partners in 2002, where I was co-founder and CEO. Forum is a real estate private equity firm that has invested in every property type in over a hundred companies across the world.

Tell us more about real estate operating companies.

Companies, which have their own life cycle, are complex organisms that can change radically over a decade or less in ways that surprise; they require innovation, feeding, and cultivation. Forum provides more than just capital; it plays an active role in these companies, focusing on those that can consistently outperform their competitive set, particularly in opaque private markets, which are less efficient.

Preparing companies for a successful exit is critical. We try to anticipate the changing and often divergent needs of investors and identify ways to facilitate investors' exit through an IPO or M&A without forcing liquidation of the business.

Have you made many mistakes?

We have had many successes; most of our mistakes have been people decisions. Markets are more predictable than people!

(continued)

(continued)

What do you seek in your investments?

We seek growth opportunities at a reasonable price. Stable, slow growers are all about cash flow; you cannot overpay if growth is not there to bail you out.

What are the biggest long-term challenges we face?

Demography. Many countries face dramatic depopulation with a deteriorating dependency ratio. The world's average replacement ratio is 2.1. The population of South Korea, whose replacement ratio is between 0.6 and 0.7, will be 90% less in two generations without immigration, which itself is a cultural challenge for some societies. Depopulation will change valuations, challenge the meaning of work, and change our relationship to the planet.

What is your assessment of the state of risk analytics?

Powerful risk analytics that include Monte Carlo simulation and econometrics are underutilized by the real estate industry to its detriment. Investors should demand better risk analytics.

What advice can you give young professionals contemplating a career in real estate?

We have an insufficient number of generalists schooled in the humanities. I'm much less impressed by a command of current events and much more focused on one's ability to apply critical judgment to the rapidly changing world we inhabit.

Notes

Acknowledgments

1. Timothy Snyder. *On Tyranny*. New York: Crown. 2017.

Preface

1. Nassim Nicholas Taleb. *The Bed of Procrustes—Philosophical and Practical Aphorism*. New York: Penguin Random House, LLC. 2016.
2. Upton Sinclair. *The Jungle*. New York. Doubleday, Page & Co. 1906.
3. Selected quotes from various back copies of Real Estate Americas, provided by Institution Real Estate, Inc.

Chapter 1

1. John Maynard Keynes. *The General Theory of Employment, Interest, and Money*. New York: BN Publishing (reprint edition). Hawthorne, California. 2008.
2. Warren Buffett Speaks: *The Wit and Wisdom of America's Greatest Investor*. Hoboken, New Jersey. 1997.
3. Institutional Real Estate, Inc. IREI.IQ—Real Estate Manager's Guide. May 29, 2025.
4. "Defense.gov News Transcript: DoD News Briefing—Secretary Rumsfeld and Gen. Myers." United States Department of Defense. February 12, 2002. Archived from the original on April 6, 2016.
5. Jennifer R. March. *Dictionary of Classical Mythology* (2nd ed.). Oxford: Oxbow Books. p. 260, 2014.

Chapter 2

1. Pierre-Simon Laplace. *A Philosophical Essay on Probabilities*, translated by F W Truscott and F L Emory. New York: Dover. 1953.
2. Sam L. Savage. *The Flaw of Averages: Why We Underestimate Risk in the Face of Uncertainty*. Hoboken, NJ. 2012.

3. John Kay and Mervyn King. *Radical Uncertainty: Decision-Making Beyond the Numbers.* New York: W. W. Norton.
4. Douglas Hubbard. *The Failure of Risk Management: Why It's Broken and How to Fix It.* Hoboken, NJ: John Wiley & Sons. 2009; *How to Measure Anything: Finding the Value of "Intangibles" in Business.* Hoboken, NJ: John Wiley & Sons. 2014.
5. Fisher Black. "The Trouble with Econometric Models," *Financial Analysts Journal.* March–April, 1982, Vol 38, No. 2, pp. 29–27; Edward E. Leamer. "Let's Get the Con out of Econometrics," *The American Economic Review*, Vol. 73, No. 1, March 1983, pp. 31–43; and R. Carter Hill, William E. Griffiths, Quay C. Lim. *Principles of Econometrics* (4th ed.). Hoboken, NJ: John Wiley & Sons. 2011.

Chapter 3

1. Adam Smith. *The Wealth of Nations.* New York: Modern Library. 1994.
2. This section benefits from Arthur O'Sullivan, *Urban Economics*. New York: McGraw-Hill. 2009, as well as Edwin S. Mills, my Princeton Ph.D. advisor, and Bruce W. Hamilton, *Urban Economics* (5th Edition). Upper Saddle Ridge, New Jersey: Harper Collins, 1994.

Chapter 4

1. Kenneth D. Garbade. *Pricing Corporate Securities as Contingent Claims.* Cambridge, Massachusetts. The MIT Press. 2001.
2. Stephen A. Ross, et al. *Fundamentals of Corporate Finance.* New York: McGraw-Hill. 2022.

Chapter 5

1. This section benefits from Steven R. Grenadier's work on leases, especially "Leasing and Credit Risk." *Journal of Financial Economics* 42 (1996) 333–364 and "Valuing Lease Contracts: A Real Options Approach." *Journal of Financial Economics* 38, 297–331.

Chapter 6

1. One of the best articles written on the Monte Carlo analysis of mortgage risk is David P. Jacob, et al. "An Options Approach to Commercial Mortgages and CMBS Valuation and Risk Analysis" in *Commercial Mortgage-Backed Securities*, edited by F. Fabozzi and D. Jacob, Frank J. Fabozzi Associates, 1997.
2. Andrew W. Lo. *Hedge Funds: An Analytic Perspective.* Princeton: Princeton University Press. 2008.

Chapter 8

1. Albert Camus. *The Plague* (translated by Laura Marris). New York: Vintage. 2022.
2. Anne Applebaum. *Twilight of Democracy: The Seductive Lure of Authoritarianism.* New York: Vintage. 2021.

Chapter 10

1. Edwin J. Elton, Martin J. Gruber, Stephen J. Brown, and William N. Goetzmann. *Modern Portfolio Theory and Investment Analysis.* Hoboken, NJ. 2014.
2. Martin L. Leibowitz. Chapter I-8 "Portfolio Optimization under Shortfall Constraints" and Chapter I-10 "Shortfall Risk and the Asset Allocation Decision," *Investing: The Collected Works of Martin L. Leibowitz.* Edited by Frank J. Fabozzi. Chicago. Probus Publishing. 1992.
3. Stephen A. Ross and Randall Zisler. "Risk and Return in Real Estate." *Journal of Real Estate Finance and Economics*, 4, 175–190.

Chapter 12

1. This section benefits from an important article: Serguei Chervachidze, James Costello, and William Wheaton. "The Secular and Cyclic Determinants of Capitalization Rates: The Role of Property Fundamentals, Macroeconomic Factors, and 'Structural Changes,'" *The Journal of Portfolio Management.* 2009, Vol. 35, no. 5, pp. 50–69.
2. I used MSA office supply elasticities published in Gianluca Marcato and Lok Man Michelle Tong, "Supply Constraints and Search Equilibrium in Office Markets," *The Journal of Real Estate Finance and Economics.* Springer. July 2023. doi: 10.1007/s11146-023-09955-y.
3. See Stephen, Ross and Randall Zisler, "Risk and Return in Real Estate," *Journal of Real Estate Finance and Economics.* 1991, Vol. 4, pp. 175–190. This article shows how to remove the effects of serial correlation.

Chapter 13

1. M. K., Brunnermeier. "Deciphering the Liquidity and Credit Crunch 2007-2008," *Journal of Economic Perspectives.* 2009, Vol. 23, pp. 77–100.
2. Frank, Ametefe, Steven Devaney, and Gianluca Marcato. "Liquidity: A Review of Dimensions, Cause, Measures, and Empirical Applications in Real Estate Markets," *Journal of Real Estate Literature.* 2016, Vol. 24, No. 1, pp. 3–30.

3. Serial correlation, or autocorrelation, is the correlation between a variable and a lagged version of itself over various time intervals. The higher is the serial correlation of returns, the greater is the smoothing, which often masks true risk and distorts risk analytics and asset allocation.

Chapter 14

1. This chapter benefits from joint research prepared over the years with my former colleague and very good friend, Jason Benderly, who was Chief Economist of Goldman Sachs & Co. He is President and CEO of Benderly Economics. Jason is one of the best business economists I know.
2. Junior or subordinate debt is more sensitive to real estate market conditions than senior mortgages.
3. Even high net worth investors in effect sell assets within a 5- to 10-year period. The IRS code helps investors minimize capital gains taxes through 1,031 tax-free exchanges, which actually reduce the investment holding period.

Chapter 15

1. Economists refer to this phenomenon as Le Chatelier's principle: In the long run, the market can adjust other factors to mitigate the effects of the initial change.

Chapter 19

1. I quote Charles D. Ellis from his classic, *Winning the Loser's Game* (5th ed.). New York: McGraw-Hill. 2010.
2. William Bernstein. *The Four Pillars of Investing: Lessons for Building a Winning Portfolio.* (Second Edition.) New York. McGraw-Hill. 2023.
3. George E. P. Box (1976), "Science and Statistics," *Journal of the American Statistical Association*, 71 (356): 791–799.
4. I thank Greg MacKinnon, Research Director of PREA, for his providing raw survey data.
5. Alfred Lord Tennyson's *In Memoriam A. H. H.* (1850) wrote "Tho' nature, red in tooth and claw," underscoring the Darwinian nature of life. A real estate downturn, especially a downturn such as the GFC, is a herd-thinning event. Bidding wars, nasty and brutish, are implements of natural selection, truly a Hobbesian world tailored for real estate.
6. Claw believes that high net worth investors have often outbid the institutions, probably because some wealthy individuals, focusing on capital preservation, ignore the time value of money and overestimate the speed of recovery.

Chapter 20

1. Da Li and Timothy J. Riddiough. "Persistently Poor Performance in Private Equity Real Estate," working paper, May 2023.
2. There is no theoretical link between the liability discount rate and asset returns.
3. Robert Novy-Marx and Joshua D. Rauh. "The Liabilities and Risks of State-Sponsored Pension Plans." *Journal of Economic Perspectives*, 23, 4 (Fall 200): pp 191–210.
4. See Riddiough, "Pension Funds and Private Equity Real Estate: History, Performance, Pathologies, Risks."
5. Stephen Ross and Randall Zisler. "Risk and Return in Real Estate," *Journal of Real Estate Finance and Economics*, 4, 175–190.
6. Mitchell A. Bollinger and Joseph L Pagliari, Jr. "Another Look at Private Real Estate Returns by Strategy." *The Journal of Portfolio Management. Special Real Estate Issue.* 2019.
7. ZCA routinely creates synthetic benchmarks using risk-based analytics.
8. Many of the managers who unjustly criticize the NCREIF Index are the same managers who benefit by using NCREIF as a benchmark.
9. See Richard Ennis, "Excellence Gone Missing," report, May 12, 2023.
10. Many of the managers who unjustly criticize the NCREIF Index are the same managers who benefit by using NCREIF as a benchmark.
11. Timothy Riddiough. "Pension Funds and Private Equity Real Estate: History, Performance, Pathologies, Risks," mimeo.
12. Cambridge Associates used 12 years of data ending June 2020.
13. When I am in a playful mood, I like to tell managers that there is a large correlation between MSA preferences and the number of restaurants with Michelin stars. I conclude that in certain areas, managers are humorless.
14. I modeled 94 public pension fund observations from a database of 183 observations provided by the Center for Retirement Research at Boston College.
15. Alpha, which shows how well (or badly) an investment has performed compared to a benchmark index, is very sensitive to the factors used to construct the benchmark and may not be a good indicator of skill involved in beating the benchmark. A positive alpha under one set of factors can be a negative alpha given a different set of factors.

Chapter 21

1. Charles Ellis. *Winning the Loser's Game*. New York: McGraw-Hill. 2021.
2. Plato. *The Republic*, translated by Desmond Lee. New York: Penguin. 2007.

Index

A

AAA bond yield, cap rates (moving correlation) 287e
AAA-rated corporate bond, inflation hedge
    (weakness) 367e
Absorption, office property 157, 161, 163e, 171–172
Accumulated value, asset class classification 358e
Adjusted R-squared 169–172, 178, 179, 288, 310, 320,
    326, 328, 330, 333, 334
Affordability 396, 413, 416
Agglomeration economies 60–61
Akaike Information Criterion (AIC) 24
All-property NCREIF capital returns, equity-like
    characteristic 360e
All-property NCREIF intermediate/long-term income
    returns, debt-like characteristic 360e
All-property total return correlations, oscillation 359e
Alpha 47, 390, 463
    incremental alpha 247
    positive alpha/negative alpha 74, 75e, 439, 459
    returns 5–6
    stylized facts about value add and opportunistic
        funds and the search for alpha, 450–455
Apartments
    appreciation 196e, 197e
    cap rates, for six large MSAs 376e
    inflation-adjusted accumulated value,
        strength 359e
    market rental growth 377e, 422–423
    mortgage total return 362e
    apartments and single-family rentals are near
        substitutes 193–198
    office conversion to apartments 177–179
    property total return 361e
    rental growth, compared with office, 178e 423e
    rental inflation, volatility (contrast) 348e
    rent-controlled apartments, investing in seasoned
        controlled apartments 423–424

units to households, ratio (change) 194e
units to single family homes, ratio (accelerating
    shift) 194e
Applebaum, Anne, on authoritarianism 155
Appraisal-based cap rate, compared across
    properties 283e
    T-bill, relationship 286e
    Transactions cap rate, correlation 285e
    spread adjustment speed 158e, 284e
Area per office building (reduction), smaller MSAs
    (relationship) 329e
Asking rental growth spread 180e
Asset allocation 203, 222–228
    alteration, property inclusion 211e
    alternative assets, shifts 458–459
    application to real estate 204–208
    assumptions 226e
    efficient frontier 210e
    inputs 224e
    liabilities, absence 225e
    limits of diversification 205
Assets
    liabilities, contrast 220e
    when liabilities exceed asset value, 220
    macroeconomics of markets 148–151, 148e
    improving suboptimal performance, adjustment to
        the mix of assets 204e
    multi-asset analysis, correlation matrix 220e
    prices, demand curve (rightward shift) 149e
    serial correlation in returns 137, 138e
Assets under management 244, 466
Asymmetric information,, transactions volume 176,
    318, 416, 423, 443–444, 467
Attributes 38–45, 54, 72e, 295, 356. *See also* Uncertain
    attributes
Availability 350, 408. *See also* Capital availability;
    Data; Debt; Land availability

Index

Average bond yields, cap rates (contrast) 285e
Average office rental growth 19e, 20e
Average vacancy rate, MSA office liquidity increase (relationship) 326e

B

BAA bond yield, cap rates (moving correlation) 287e
BAA-rated corporate bond, inflation hedge (weakness) 368e
Bayes matrix 32e
Bayes rule 13
   false positive likelihood, calculation 30–32
   investment analysis tool 29–33
Bayes Theorem 29, 30, 245, 433
Behavioral biases, examples 430–431
Benchmarks and volatility 452
   shortfall analysis, application 243
   usage, quality-adjusted benchmarks 45
Benderly, Jason (interview) 371–372
Best-fitting distribution 24
Beta 47, 74–75, 74e, 452–453. *See also* Property
   confusion, beta versus alpha returns 5
   returns 243
   risk 385
Bidding 185, 291, 311, 429, 440–445
Binary choice variable 261e–262e
Binary variable, zero-one variable 255, 260, 264
Binding constraints and shadow price 254, 260, 264
Bivariate office cap rate model 28e
Bivariate regression 15, 27–28, 132, 137
Bivariate time series model 23e
Bonds
   correlation matrix 143e
   default premium 109, 113, 122, 124–127, 137
   property cap rate, comparison 284e
   total returns, inflation (relationship) 346e
   yields 282–285, 346e
Box-whiskers plot 25–27, 26e
Breadth (liquidity element) 317e
Buildings 53
   cash flow 280e
   lower quality, higher cap rates 290e
   small New York office buildings 182e
   type, evolution 54–59
Burns, Richard F. (interview) 460–461
Businesses, growing 468–469

C

Call option, equity (equivalence) 69e
Camus, Albert 155
Capital
   binding 273e
   constraints 272e
   cost, equity/fixed income (relationship) 74–75, 74e
   impact 164e
   land availability, negative correlation 266e
   preservation, likelihood 217e
   requirement 263e
   return 197, 354, 360, 360e
   stack 65–72, 66e, 99–100
   usage 268e
Capital availability, constrained optimization 271, 311
   defining 268e
   increase 259e, 274e
   marginal analysis 255–257
   uncertainty 263e
Capitalism, the division of labor and proliferation of building types 54–59
Capitalization rate (cap rate) 279, 291–295, 301–307
   AAA bond yield, moving correlation 287e
   adjustments 298e
   appraisal cap rates, upward adjustment 158e
   average bond yields, contrast 285e
   BAA bond yield, moving correlation 287e
   bond yields, relationship 282–285
   correlation 147e
   CoStar cap rate 1023
   cross-sectional regression, results 296e
   defining 279
   distribution 38e, 292e
   function, spread narrowing 294e
   incompatibility 282–285
   industrial liquidity, association 336e
   level, appropriateness 101
   MF rental growth, inverse relationship 299e
   MSA correlation 376e
   multifamily liquidity, association 336e
   multivariate analysis 295–300
   myth, increase in interest rates will not necessarily increase cap rates 159e, 286–288
   NOI/Price, equivalence 37
   office liquidity, relationship 334–336, 335e
   retail liquidity, relationship 335e

Index **479**

simulation, city size (relationship) 300e
supply elasticities, relationship 308–311
total return, correlation weakness 281e
transactions cap rates/cash flow returns, spread (increase) 158e
variation, function of quality 289–291
Capitalization rate (cap rate) volatility 302e, 435e
   increase, higher rental growth rate associated with lower cap rates 300e
   level, cap rates less volatile than returns 279, 284e
Capital markets 103
   asset/user markets 148e
   governmental regulations 397
Cap rate distribution 18e
Cash flow 57–59, 280e
Causality versus correlation 20–27
CBD-suburban equilibrium, change 172–173
Central business district (CBD) 55, 166
   apartment sale, observation (hypothetical) 295
   CBD/GATEWAY product 297
   CBD-suburban equilibrium, changes 172–173
   CBD, suburban vacancy rates (spread) 160e
   CBD-suburban performance spreads 177
   demand contraction 174e
   demand contraction/expansion 174e
   homogeneity, absence 396
   impact of CBD and gateway status on cap rates 297e
   the spread between CBD and suburban office vacancy rates has increases 160e
   urban growth and land prices 404
   New York CBD office values 160e
   New York/suburban CBD office returns 161e
   parking lot, call option 406
   CBD-suburban values, gap (narrowing) 162e
   values/suburban values, gap (narrowing) 162e
   weakness, increase 160e
Central business district (CBD) office performance 162e
   CBD challenges pre- and during COVID-19 156, 157
   suburban returns, contrast 162e
   relationship between suburban and CBD supply 173e
   values per square foot, decline 160e
Certainty, higher level (confidence) 213e

Chicago cap rates/market rental growth rates 20-month moving correlation 379e
Cities 53
   capitalization rate 289–291, 300e
   existence, reasons 60
   size 300e, 301–307
Class A office performance challenges 161
Coefficient estimates 28
   Bias and omitted variables 14–15, 25
   imprecision 116–117
   senior management interest 29
Coefficient of variation (CV) 142, 268e
   increase 382
Cognitive errors 429–433
Cold market, improvement 83e
Commercial mortgage backed securities (CMBSs) 62, 110–120
   AAA-rated CMBS 111, 111e, 115e, 117e, 119, 119e
   BBB-AAA spread 113e
   BBB-rated CMBS 109, 111, 112e, 114e, 115e, 117e, 120e, 126–129, 132, 133, 134e
   Birth of CMBS 139
   bonds 116, 340
   deal, appearance 250
   loan, usage 244
   prepayment protection 110
   principal-only CMBS bond, ownership 423
   public debt CMBS 110–120
   senior CMBS bonds 318
   senior/subordinate CMBS tranches, yields 120
   spreads, increase 113e
   structure, priority assignment (presence) 110e
   tranches 119
   yields 114e, 116, 118
Commercial mortgage positive convexity 121e
Competitive and fragmented local jurisdictions, beggar-thy-neighbor 396–397
Composite good, hybrid asset, property (equivalence) 39
Confidence, minimum threshold effect (tradeoff) 215e
Confidence interval 28, 29, 213e, 382
   correlation/volatility, impact 34
   stylized lease structure, volatility and rental growth scenarios 56e
   expansion as function of horizon and volatility 94e
   leasing and lower volatility 93e

480 Index

Confidence interval (*continued*)
  material increase, absence 93e
  measurement parameters for alternative statistical distributions 16
  one-standard deviation confidence interval, defining 157
  rental confidence interval and volatility 93
Confidence level
  impact of high confidence interval on set of feasible assets along frontier 242e
  linking with threshold return, portfolio return and feasible asset choices 215e
  Increasing portfolio risk and maintaining the same confidence interval 218e
Consensus total return forecasts and errors 436–437
Constrained optimization, equations 258e
Construction, asset/user markets 148e
Consultant, skill (absence), likelihood of false positive 33e
Consumer choice, preferences and relative prices, analytics 351e
Consumer durables
  income elasticity of demand 188, 188e
  price elasticity of demand 189e
  elasticities for centers and malls 190
Consumer nondurables
  price elasticity of demand 189e
  income elasticity of demand 188
Consumer Price Index (CPI) 349–350
  apartment market rental growth, relationship 422–423
  changes in CPI and Northern New Jersey apartment rents 418e
  performance, gold performance (contrast) 353e
Consumer surplus 414
Contingent forecasting 29–33, 219, 432
Contingent value, risk and capital stack 69–72
  decline, senior debt and volatility 70e
  equity increases with additional volatility 71e
  reduction/decline, senior debt 67, 70e
Conversions, office to apartment 155
Corporate bonds, compared with CMBS 115
Correlated unleveraged NPI and BBB-rated CMBS TR (relationship) 134e
Correlation, contrast with causality 20–27, 35e–37e
  Circle, no correlation 22e
  Inputs for asset allocation modeling 219e
  random design 22e
  test, inflation hedging 357
CoStar
  contributors 322e
  total returns, compared with office price per square foot change 321e
CoStar cap rate 102e
  NPI office appraisal cap rate, spread (increase) 103
  office, relative share by CoStar quality index 337e
Cost of capital 74–75, 74e
Cost of debt, increase due to incremental risk 75e
COVID-19
  absorption 163e
  asking rental growth spread 180e
  cap rates, correlation 147e
  cases, property performance (relationship) 172
  de-smoothed property/REIT returns, correlation 240e
  efficient frontier/allocation 233
  industrial/apartment dominance 229e
  long-term impact 177
  performance 176
  post-COVID-19, housing/apartment appreciation (volatility) 196e
  post-COVID rental/used car inflation, impacts 349e
  pre-COVID-19, retail/industrial dominance 232e
  recession 155
  residual analysis of model during economic downturns 23e
  total return spread 164e
  transactions, change 322e
  vacancy rates, increase 146e
  western retail, performance pre- and during-COVID-19, dominance 232e
Creative improvisation, role 313–314
Credit adjusted mortgage TR 122e
Credit rationing 176, 318
Credit spread 55–56, 80, 150, 279, 311
  increase 87e, 88
  lease credit spread 57, 82, 86, 86e
Credit support, providing 111
Cross-sectional data 16

Cross-sectional regression of cap rates and attribution, results 296e
Cummings, Daniel (interview) 410–411
Cumulative bond defaults 193e

D

Daedalus, hubris, investor and manager cognitive errors 9
Dallas-Ft. Worth cap rates/market rental growth rates 20-month moving correlation 379e
Data
    distribution, fitting 24e
    exploratory data analysis 15–27
    representation, box-whiskers (usage) 25–27
    set, usage 295–300
Days worked at home, space per worker (optimal trade-off) 175e
Debt
    Attributes of subordinate debt 72e
    Availability and transactions volume 288
    cost, increase due to incremental risk 75e
    usage by pension funds 244–246
Default option held by tenant 90e
Default premium 115e, 125e
    relationship to senior mortgage TR 127
Default trigger 121
    Increase in prepayment 86
    lease value ratio and credit spread 87e, 88
    tenant asset value ratio and required pre-payment 89e
Demand, property macroeconomics 148
    curve, rightward shift (impact) 149e
    income elasticity 188e
    shift, against supply curve, effect 308e, 309e
Depth of market (liquidity), information richness 317e
De-smoothed NCREIF return/cap rates, relationship (absence) 237e
De-smoothed property, standard deviations 238e
De-smoothed property returns
    REIT returns, correlation 239e, 240e
    volatility 239e
De-smoothing, analytics 234–238
Deterministic versus stochastic models 264
Deterministic NPV, basis 264e
Development risk 425–426

Dhaka (Bangladesh), infrastructure/building diversity (absence) 55
Discount rates, impact of discount rates and horizon on PV 398e
Distribution 292e
    fitting 24e
    shift 19e
    shift/shape change 293e
    skew 293e
    uncertainty, shape of risk 15
Diversification 204–207
    benefits, leverage (impact) 247e
    principles, application 204–208
    risk 454
Dominance, risk versus return 265
Donne, John 203
DOT.COM recession, residual analysis 23e
Downside risk 208e, 217e
Dummy variable 236, 288, 295, 297, 457
Durbin Watson statistic 23, 119, 127, 137, 171–172, 197–198, 288, 310, 320, 330, 334

E

Econometric fit 159e
Econometric models, challenges 14–15
Economic downturns, quality/liquidity (connection) 337
Economy, stylized model 343–347
Edifice complex 4, 312
Efficient frontier, leverage and market portfolio 204e
    investment choices, reduction 217e
    leveraged/unleveraged property 224e
    riskiest portion of efficient frontier 232e
    senior mortgages 224e
    shifts 210e, 233
Efficient property allocation 231
Elasticity 165–166, 308–310
Elastic supply, demand shift (effect) 308e
Employment retirement Income Security Act (ERISA) 4, 457
Enhanced monetary stability, post-WWII role 352
Ennis, Richard 455
Equilibrium base rent, decline 90e
Equity 103
    attribute 72e
    call option, equivalence 69e

Equity (*continued*)
  contingent value, increase 71e
  multiple, skewed to the right 385e
  present value, negative correlation 59e
  returns volatility (increase), leverage (impact) 381e
Equity REITs 129e
  inflation hedge 366e
  returns (tracking), small cap stock returns (usage) 131e
Estimated volatilities 238e
Exit cap rate 382e, 384e, 388e, 389e
Expectations horizons, lengthening (impact) 436e
Expected return 216e, 218e
Expected surplus ratios, spread 221e
Externalities 395–397, 415

F

Factor benchmarks 453
False negative 32e
False positive 30–32, 32e, 33e
FAR (floor-area-ratio) availability, increase 259e
Fascitelli, Michael (interview) 62
Favorable and unfavorable investments above and below the efficient frontier 75e
Feasible assets reduction 242
  confidence level, impact 242e
  threshold, impact of increase for different volatility assumptions 242e
Feasible set of alternatives given constraints 239
Federal Reserve
  post-WWII role 352
  stimulation, expansionary monetary policy, impact of change on performance 150e
Firm (value), leverage (impact) 76e
Fitted occupancy spreads 180e
Five-month rolling return volatility 357e
Fixed income 103
Flat rent, lease (equivalence) 96e
Floor-area ratio (FAR) 256
Forward rent, decline 84e
Fragmented government, risk (relationship) 403–404
Funding liquidity 316
Funding ratio 219, 449, 451, 456–457
Funding status, under- and over-funded pension funds 226–228, 227e
Funds, performance 455–456

Future benefits, intergenerational welfare 397
Future returns, past property returns (prediction ability) 106e
Fuzzy constraints, budget and land constraint in optimization in model 257, 258e

G

GATEWAY, impact 297e
General partner (GP) 34
  equity multiple to LP and GP, increase (contrast) 387e
  interests of GP 373
  IRR to LP and GP
    excess level (likelihood) 388e
    increase and volatility (contrast) 386e
  multiple, increase (contrast) 386e
Giliberto-Levy Mortgage Index (G-L) 122
  commercial mortgage loss 124e
  credit-adjusted retail mortgage total return 361e
  mortgage, Baa bond TR (relationship) 124e
Giliberto, Michael (interview) 79
Gold, inflation hedge 353e
Goldilocks market, shorter-term/longer-term leases (performance differences) 85e
Government spending, expansion 345e
Great Financial Crisis (GFC)
  asset, investor flight 333e
  CoStar cap rate/NPI office appraisal cap rate, spread (increase) 103e
  de-smoothed property/REIT returns, correlation 240e
  pre-Great Financial Crisis vacancy rates 21e
  residual analysis 23e
  stock turnover, high level 331e
Gross Domestic Product (GDP), increase 345e
Growth, elasticity 191

H

Havner, Ron (interview) 340–341
Hedging 354–356
Hedonic analysis 39, 44
Hidden information 279
High yield corporate yields 120e
Hotels, inflation hedges (weakness) 365e
Households, of ratio of units-to-households as a function of the log of households 194e

House price appreciation, impact 197e
Housing 187
Houston, office property/risk evaluation/elasticity 165, 166, 212, 310
Hubris, impact 8–9
Hybrid regional asset allocations 228–230

I

Icarus 9
Illiquid assets, performance measures (application) 453–454
Illiquidity, measure 328–332
illiquid property, observed risk 241e
Income elasticity 39, 188
Income return 282, 283, 360, 360e
Incremental return, REIT (adding) 223e
Index problem 44
Induced work/leisure 174e
Industrialization 54–59
Industrial liquidity, cap rates (relationship) 336e
Industrial mortgage total returns 365e
Industrial property total returns 364e
Inelastic supply, demand shift (effect) 309e
Inequality constraint, interdependencies. 255
Inflation
    bond total returns, relationship 346e
    bond yields, relationship 346e
    hedges, weakness 365e–367e
    indexes, selection (importance) 348–349
    real estate investor concern 347–348
    regimes (1950s+) 353e
    risk premiums, stylized model 343–347
    spreads 423e
    stylized model 343–347
    US inflation, history 352–353
Information ratio 454
institutional investors, NCREIF data 322e
Interest rates
    directions 59e
    increase, effect 286–288, 345e
    long-term interest rates, declining inflation (response) 355e
    volatility, impact 56–57
Interests, misalignment 244
Internal cost of capital 253

Inventory 63–64, 141, 149–151, 157, 159e, 161, 166 167e, 188
    distribution 142e
    growth 168, 170
    performance/quality 176, 183
    repricing 177
    size 178–179
    supply shocks 147
    vacancy rate 167e
Investment
    choices, link 215e
    horizon 315, 398e
    opportunities, strategic builder approach 410–411
    performance 190e
Investment analysis tool, Bayes rule usage 29–33
Investment-saving (IS) curve, shift 345e
Investors
    checklist 463–466
    overpayment, timing/process 440–444
    winner's curse 440–444
IS curve 344

K

Kalsi, Sonny (interview) 250–251
Keynes, John Maynard, succeeding conventionally or unconventionally 5
Kurtosis 16, 18, 225

L

Labor, division/segmentation 54
Lack of knowledge distribution 25e
"Lamb and Claw" (parable), bidding and bubbles 440–444
Land
    capital, correlation 270e–272e
    rent 60, 405
    requirement 264e
    use, constrained optimization 256e
    utilization, skew 269e
Land availability
    capital, negative correlation 266e
    symmetry 269e
    uncertainty modeling 264e
Laplace, Marquis de, uncertainty and determinism 13
Leapfrogging, jurisdictional fragmentation, viewpoint (difference) 405–406

Leased asset, value (decline) 88e
Leases 53, 81, 82–91
  credit spread 57, 82, 86, 86e
  escalation 92–97, 92e
  flat rent, equivalence 96e
  pass-through provision, effectiveness 366–368, 370
  portfolio 55–56
  present value, negative correlation 59e
  spreads, term structure 86e
  stylized lease structure 56e
  term, increase 84e
Lessee
  asset value ratio, increase 89e
  business, correlation with market, volatility (increase) 88e
Lesser quality properties, spread 166e
Lessors, credit spread charge 87e
Leverage
  diversification, relationship 246–248
  impact 72, 247e
  increase 73e
  misuse, shortfall analysis (application) 243–244
  taxable investor, benefits 76e
Leveraged equity
  inputs 224e
  return, increase 73e, 380e
Leveraged NPI TR 125e
Leveraged property
  NCREIF loan-to-value ratio 135e
  total returns 133e
Leveraged real estate 59
Liabilities 203, 220e, 224e
Life (lives), value of a life, controversy, implicit valuation, discount rate 397–399
Limited partner (LP) 34
  equity multiple, increase (contrast) 387e
  interests 373
  IRR
    exceeding a minimum (floor) return in a structured deal 388e
    increase in LP and GP (contrast) 386e
  multiple, increase 386e
Linkages and interdependencies 253, 260–263
  absence 270e, 271e
  constraints 261e–262e
  modeling 272e, 273e

Liquidity 315, 334–336
  characteristics 316
  economic downturns, connection 337
  elements 317e
  increase, MSA size (relationship) 327e
  measures 319
  MSA office cap rates, inverse relationship 325e
  MSA office liquidity, rental growth volatility (association) 326e
  office prices per square foot, relationship 332e
  predictor, transactions price per square foot 332–333
  total office returns (quarterly) lead office liquidity 320e
  total returns lead liquidity 319–322
  turnover, relationship 107–108
  types, market and funding liquidity 316
LM, stylized economic model, shift 344e
Local apartment index values 419e, 420e
Local market NOI volatility, impact 347
Lognormal distribution, superimposition 16e
Longer-term leases 85e
Long return series, absence 189–193
Long-run equilibrium, market reversion 84e
Long-term hedge, usefulness 369e
Long-term interest rates, declining inflation (response) 355e
Long-term US Treasury bonds, total return 333e
Loser's game 429, 445, 464, 465
Lyons, Doug (interview) 99

M

Macfarland III, Benjamin Shibe (interview) 199–200
Macroeconomics 148–151
Macroeconomy, demand curve 345e
Malkiel, Burt 204
Mall elasticities, comparison 190e
Manager selection error, contingent likelihood 31e
Marginal analysis 255–257
Market
  crises 62–64
  liquidity 316
  long-run equilibrium reversion 84e
  performance, money manager forecasting ability 433–439
  portfolio 208e

prices, firms reliance 397
public/private market data, comparative analysis (challenges) 103–107
rental growth 56e, 378e
size 54
tenant credit, correlation 87e
volatility 96e
warmth 84e
weakness expectation 83e
Maturity, increase 71e
Mean 15
Mean inputs 219e
Measured volatility, reduction 330e
Median 15
Messy data, handling 371–372
Metropolitan Statistical Area (MSA)
   apartment cap rates 376e
   apartment market rental growth rates 377e
   capitalization rates 376e, 435e
   COVID-29, asking rental growth spread 10e
   elasticities 167e
   fitted occupancy spreads 180e
   forecasting, difficulty 437–439
   inventory distribution 142e
   liquidity 315, 325e
   low elasticities, rent swings (outward demand shift) 167e
   MSA B, vacancy rate (weakness indication) 168e
   office capitalization rates 306e, 325e
   office liquidity 326, 326e
   office rental growth rates, variation 306e
   office vacancy rates, variation 307e
   rental growth rates 165–166, 376e
   space/population, size distribution 141
   total office returns 324e
   total returns 307e, 434e
Mezzanine debt 66–67, 68e, 99, 127, 139, 401
   seniority 68e
MF rental growth, cap rates (inverse relationship) 299e
Mid-efficient frontier performance, improvement 222e
Mid-term hedge, usefulness 369e
Misspecification of models 15, 46
Mode and other measure of central tendency 15
Monetary policy experiments (1950s+) 353e

Money managers, forecasting ability 433–439
Money supply, contraction (impact) 344e
Monte Carlo analysis 13, 34–45, 92–97, 92e, 375–389
Monte Carlo applications 373–374
Monte Carlo model 373, 380e
Monte Carlo modeling 374–375
Monte Carlo samples, average correlation 383e
Mortgage default 65
Mortgage performance 122, 223
Mortgages 120–127
   Default option 65
   inputs 224e
   residential mortgage negative convexity 121e
Mortgage total return (mortgage TR) 125e
Moving correlation 286, 287e, 361, 363, 367, 375, 377, 378e, 379e, 434, 435e, 439
MSA cap rate distribution 27e
Multi-asset allocation, REITs/senior mortgages (inclusion) 222–228
Multi-asset analysis, correlation matrix 220e
Multi-asset domestic portfolio, REITs (adding) 222e, 223e
Multicollinearity 29
Multifamily liquidity, cap rates (relationship) 336e
Multiple regression 27–29, 28e
Multivariate analysis 295–300

N

Natural vacancy rate (NVR), relationship to growth, volatility and rents, 166 168, 169e
NCREIF
   all-property NCREIF capital returns, equity-like characteristic 360e
   all-property NCREIF intermediate/long-term income returns, debt-like characteristic 360e
   appraisal value 102e
   cap rates, prediction (inability) 237e
   data 322e
   loan-to-value ratio 135e
   total returns 322e
   transactions-based cap rate, contrast 283e
NCREIF Property Index total return (NPI TR) 113e, 114e
Negative land-capital correlation 272e
Neidich, Daniel (interview) 10–11

Net asset value (NAV) 6, 48
Net Operating Income (NOI)
    local market NOI volatility, impact 347e
    price growth rates, positive correlation 281e
Net Operating Income (NOI) growth 116, 117e
    leads appreciation 135e
    unleveraged total return, relationship 134e
    weakening 159e
Net present value (NPV) 270e
    estimation 273e
    expected average/risk 265e
    land-capital correlation 272e
    linkage, presence of use, land and budget interdependencies 272e
    reduction 266e
New construction 149e, 151e
New Jersey rent, ren control 413–424
    control, perspective 417
    CPI indexes, changes (correlation) 418e
    "Greater than" and "less than" language in regulations, benefits to landlord 421e
    local apartment index/rental CPI values 419e, 420e
    prices indexes, interrelationship 419e
New York
    cap rates/market rental growth rates 12-month/20-month moving correlation 378e
    fitted occupancy spread 180e
    natural vacancy rate (NVR) 169e
    office returns, decline 161e
    rental growth spreads 180e
    vulnerability, office inventory (age/size profile) 179–183
Non-credit adjusted mortgage TR, comparison 122e
Nondurables, demand/prices 188e, 189e
Non-market services/goods/lives, valuation 397–398
Non-recourse debt 67e, 68e
Non-traded attributes 397
Normal distribution, superimposition 16e
Normalization of data17 212
Normalized absorption rate 163e
Normalized loan/sales volume, correlation 126e
Normalized office market cap/rental growth rate 17e
Normalized vacancy rate 163e
NPI office appraisal cap rate, CoStar cap rate spread (increase) 103e

NPI property TR 129e
Null hypothesis, determination of statistical significance, 15

O

Obsolescence 155, 177
Occupancy rate 177, 179
Office
    capitalization rates 28e, 301e, 302e, 306e
    conversion 10–11, 177–179
    liquidity 323–327, 334–336, 335e
    market rental growth/cap rates, normalization (absence) 17e
    mortgage total return 363e
    prices per square foot, liquidity (relationship) 332e
    quality classes, absorption (link) 171
    REIT, flexibility 152–153
    rental volatility 303e
    space, retail space (optimal combination) 256e
    total return 304e, 305e
    vacancy rate 304e, 305e, 307e
Office buildings 289e, 290e, 301–307
    Conversions to apartments 10–11
Office inventory
    age/size profile 179–183
    size distribution, function 159e
    vacancy rates, volatility 291e
Office property 155, 157
    lesser quality office properties, outperformance 165e
    liquidity cycles, average/min-max/percentile 324e
    market liquidity/turnover 323e
    price per square foot 321e
    total return, inflation correlation test 362e
Office rental growth
    apartment rental growth, contrast 178d
    average 19e, 20e
    rates 302e, 306e
Omitted variables, serial correlation problem, bias of coefficient estimates 43–44
Operating platforms, acquisition/creation 446–447
Opportunistic funds, stylized facts 450–455
Opportunities, working 250–251
Opportunity funds, performance measures (application) 453–454
Optimal development 253

Optimal leverage 65, 76–77
Optimal portfolio, with risk-free asset and leverage 207e
Optimization 77, 209, 226, 254–274, 441
Options, embedded, lease options 81–91
Options value
   increase 94e
   rent function 91
   simulated option values, rents (association) 94e, 95
Outcomes, surprise 255
Overall price level (change), confusion (avoidance) 351–352
Overbidding, problem 442
Overfunded pension plan, expected surplus ratios (spread) 221e
Overpayment risk 429

P

Pagliari, Jr., Professor Joseph L. (interview) 47
Penner, Ethan (interview) 139–140
Pension funds
   comparison 457
   debt usage 244–245
   decisions (distortion), accounting rules (impact) 450–452
   investment committees, managers (recommendation) 30
   real estate debt avoidance (question) 245–246
Pension Real Estate Association (PREA), performance expectations survey 437
Performance
   confidence interval, determination 374–375
   COVID-19 176
   macroeconomics 141
   measures, application 453–454
   pre-COVID-19 176
Performance indexes 44
Phoenix
   natural vacancy rate (NVR) 169e
   office property/rental growth rate 168, 169e, 170
Plague, The (Albert Camus) 155
Platt, Russell (interview) 468–469
Population
   growth, impact 404–405
   size distribution 141

Portfolio
   return, linking 215e
   risk 209–212, 218e
   riskier portfolios, elimination 216e
Positive alpha, presence 75e
Positive land-capital correlation 273e
Pre-COVID-19
   efficient frontier/allocation 233
   performance 176
   retail/industrial dominance 232e
Pre-Great Financial Crisis (GFC) vacancy rates 21e
Present discounted value (PDV) 399
Price growth rates, NOI (positive correlation) 281e
Price index(es) 44, 419e
Principal-only CMBS bond, ownership 423
Private debt 120–127
Private equity property 132–136
Private market data, challenges (comparison) 103–107
Private pension funds, public pension funds (comparison) 457
Producer Price Index (PPI) 349–350
Producer surplus, tenant shift 415e
Project selection 264e, 265e
Property 141
   allocation, decline 241e
   asset allocations 228–230
   autocorrelation, removal 241e
   beta 142
   capital appreciation. contrast 356e
   cap rate, bonds (comparison) 284e
   correlation matrix 143e
   division/segmentation 54
   fundamentals 301–307
   inclusion of additional property in a portfolio, impact on portfolio returns 210e, 211e
   IRR/standard deviation 384e
   leased and unleased property 55–56
   long-term nominal hedging, property types (comparison) 358e
   markets, macroeconomics 148–151
   mid-term hedge/long-term hedge, usefulness 369e
   performance 142–145, 147, 172
   subcategories, means/standard deviations 145e
   supply, short-run elasticity 146
   taxes 374, 396
   turnover, stock market turnover (comparison) 108e

Property (*continued*)
   types, two-year rolling total return correlations (similarity) 368e
   unleased space portfolio 55–56
Property-regional efficient frontiers, pre- and during-COVID-29 233e
Property types
   average correlation 123e
   fundamentals, comparative analysis 146
   impact of cap rate adjustments relative to hotels 298e
   risk metrics 144e
Public debt 110–120
Public equity (REITs) 128–132
Public finance, real estate professional considerations 395, 399
Public goods 395–396
Publicly traded equity REITs, application 234–242
Public market data, comparative analysis (challenges) 103–107
Public pension funds, pathologies/misalignment of interests 47–49
Public-sector risk 395
Pure income effect, inflation (impact) 351e
Pure property asset allocation 219e, 228–230, 229e
Pure substitution effect 352e
Put and call options in the capital stack 68e, 90e

Q

Quadrants. *See* Real estate quadrants
Quality
   economic downturns, connection 337
   flight 333–334
Quality-adjusted index numbers 45e
Quality class, importance 147

R

Rare events 29
Real estate 199
   asset allocation, impact 204–208
   career, initiation 401–402
   cognitive errors 429–433
   current year expectations/actual performance 437e
   debt, avoidance (question) 245–246
   defining 53
   funds, pathologies/misalignments 47–49
   inflation hedge, effectiveness 343, 356–370
   investment climates, valuation 58e
   investors, inflation concern 347–348
   mental toughness 425–426
   mythology 8–9
   professionals, public finance considerations 395–399
   rolling windows, average correlations 439e
   surplus analysis 219–221
   US real estate, history 352–353
Real estate investment trust (REIT) 128–132, 222–228
   adding 222e, 223e
   behaviors 107
   correlation matrix 143e
   industry, growth 276–277
   returns 106e, 128, 240e
   smoothed property returns, correlation 239e
Real estate performance
   actual/expected performance, difference (four-quarter moving averages) 438e
   consensus total return forecasts 436–437
   downside 212–217
   expectations 437e, 438e
   explanation 104e
Real estate quadrants 101
   equations, information flow 109e
   linkages, analysis 109–136
   private debt 120–127
   private equity 132–136
   public debt (quadrant one) 110–120
   public equity 128–132
   total 102e
Redemption queues 5
Region, impact on cap rates and returns 299e
Regional asset allocation 230e
Regions, property type (recombination) 231e
Relative prices, confusion/change 351–352, 352e
Relative value, search 99–100
Renewal option premium (increase), lease term to expiration (correlation) 90e
Rent
   escalation (increase), market volatility (relationship) 96e
   increase 91e, 149e
   simulated option values, association 94e, 95

sublet option value, increase 91e
volatility, supply elasticity (relationship) 300e
Rental change, simple bivariate time series model 23e
Rental CPI, values 419e
Rental growth
    directions, CBD minus suburbs 59e
    spreads and MSA size 180
    standard deviation 94e, 95e
    volatility 93e, 299e
Rental growth rates, relationship within the MSA size distribution 302e
    Distribution in a Monte Carlo analysis of a deal 381e
    rental growth, volatility (contrast) 299e
    variation across MSAs 306e
    volatility, relationship to rental growth 383e
Rental growth rates, MSA correlation 376
Rental inflation, post-COVID impact 349e
Rental pre-payment, decrease 89e
Rent control 395, 413
    analysis 415e
    fiscal implications 422
    geographic perspective 417
    legislation, parameters 417–423
    municipalities adoption, factors 421–422
    price ceiling function 414–417
    types 414
    rent-controlled apartments, investment success (possibility) 423–424
Repricing 177, 183–184
Residential mortgages, negative convexity, compared with commercial mortgages 121e
Residual analysis 23e
Resilience (liquidity element) 317e
Resolution Trust Corporation (RTC) 6, 128, 183
    crash 62, 110
    meltdown 62
    office buying opportunity 185
    opportunities 11
Resource constraints, relaxation (value) 259e
Retail 187
Retail liquidity, cap rates (relationship) 335e
Retail mortgage total returns 364e
Retail property total returns 363e
Return
    correlations 142–145

    increase 73e
    volatility 279
Riddiough, Timothy 450, 451, 454
Risk 69–72, 253, 449
    analysis 187
    assets, investment 220e
    discounting 398–399
    evaluation 209–212
    fragmented government, relationship 403–404
    holistic view 7–8
    increase 207e, 436e
    inflation risk premiums, stylized model 343–347
    macroeconomics 141
    management 468–469
    metrics 144e
    reduction 59e
    sources 57–59
    taking 250–251
    uncertainty, relationship 14
Risk-adjusted returns, equilibration (tendency) 161e
Risk-free asset 207e, 208e
Riskier portfolios, elimination 216e
Riskiest efficient portfolio, standard deviation/downside risk 208e
Rockefeller Center REIT 10–11
Rosenberg, Ralph (interview) 391–392
Rosenberg, Steve (interview) 313–314

S

Sample size, problem 44
San Francisco
    natural vacancy rate (NVR) 169e
    rent control/market, performance 417, 433–434, 455
Scale economies 60, 141, 188
Scatter plot 329
Search costs 318, 416
Sectors, navigation 391–392
Security market line (SML) 74, 74e, 75e
Self-storage 3, 29, 82, 86, 187, 199
    defaults 193e
    leases, bonds function 189–193
    loss rates, calculation (cap rate assumptions) 192e
    securitization 340–341
Senior CMBS bonds 318

Senior debt 70e
Senior mortgages 222–228
Sensitivity analysis 271
Serial correlation 319, 328–332, 330e, 334–336
Service retail, comparison 190e
Shadow price 253–257, 260, 275, 398
Shadow prices 255–257
Sharpe Ratio 225, 454
Shorter-term leases, longer-term leases (differences) 85e
Shortfall
   analysis, application 243–244
   lowering the chance of shortfall by eliminating riskier portfolios 216e
   constraints 203, 212–218, 217e
Side constraints, examples 257–259
Significance 142, 234, 236, 260
Simulated option values, rents (association) 95e
Simulation assumptions 227e
Simultaneity, inherent in all markets 8, 14, 29
Single-center city (shape), population growth (impact) 404–405
Single-family housing, near substitutes 193–198
Single tenant cap rates, increase 294e
Single tenant property bidding 291–295, 292e
Sischo, John (interview) 185–186
Size distribution, population and space 141–142, 212
Small cap stocks 104e, 131e
Small-MSA liquidity
   myth 327–333
   promotion 329e
Small office building (total US building percentage) 181e
Smith, Adam 54
Smoothed property returns
   comparison 234–242, 238e
   REITs, correlation 239e
   volatility, REIT returns volatility (comparison) 240e
Space
   inventory 181e, 182e
   size distribution 141
Speculation, viewpoint (difference) 405–406
Sprawl
   examination 395
   government action, decisions 406–408

options perspective 403
Spread, increase 89e
Standard deviation 263e
   de-smoothed property 238e
   inputs 219e
   office total returns/vacancy rate standard deviation 305e
   one-standard deviation confidence interval, defining 157
   percentage level 97e
   rental growth, standard deviation 94e, 95e
   riskiest efficient portfolio 208e
Standard & Poor's 500 (S&P500)
   earnings yield, long run inflation average level (relationship) 354e
   inflation hedge, weakness 367e
   stocks, small cap stocks (correlation) 104e
Standard & Poor's (S&P) returns (prediction), stock returns (relationship) 106e
State pension funding ratios 456–457
Statistical pathologies, omitted variables, serial correlation, multicollinearity 29
Statistics 13
Stochastic arithmetic 13, 34–45
Stochastic development optimization 254
Stochastic grocer, modeling uncertainty and analyzing attributes 38, 39e, 40e, 42e
Stochastic model 264
Stochastic optimization 263–264, 266, 267e
Stochastic variables, addition/division/subtraction 34–37
Stock market turnover and liquidity 108e, 331e
Stocks
   correlation matrix 143e
   price appreciation, S&P500 total returns (connection) 355e
   turnover, high level 331e
   yield (long-term trend), inflation (impact) 354e
Strike rent, option to sublet and to adjust rents upward, rent function 91e
Structured joint venture, GP/LP interests, Monte Carlo simulation 373
Stupin, Susan (interview) 446–447
Stylized lease structure 56e
Sublet option, value (increase) 91e
Sub-optimal performance, improvement 204e

Index **491**

Subordinate CMBS
  performance sector 118
  property substitute 111
  returns 137
  usefulness 127
Subordinate debt, debt/equity attributes 72e
Subordination 67, 100, 111
Substitution effect 55, 173, 175, 351, 352e
Suburbanization 55, 403, 407
Suburban office returns, decline 161e
Suburban returns, outperformance 162e
Suburban supply, CBD office supply (contrast) 173e
Suburban vacancy rates, CBS (spread) 160e
Suburbs, expansion 174e
Supply chain-induced inflation 349–350
Supply elasticity 300e, 308e, 309e
Surplus
  analyses, production 219e
  frontiers, overfunded/fully funded/underfunded pension funds 228e
  positive length 221e
  funding ratio 219, 221e

T

Tax reduction, impact 345e
T-bills 30-day, inflation hedge (weakness) 366e
Tenant
  asset value to the default trigger ratio, value (change) 89e
  business performance decline, default option 90e
  default, likelihood (increase) 86e
  service 189e
Thomas, Owen (interview) 152–153
Three-property efficient frontier 209e
Threshold 212–218, 215e, 217e, 218e, 242e
Tightness (spread), liquidity element 317e
Time, value 173–175
Time series data 16
Time to maturity, decline 70e
Total mortgage returns 123e
Total NPV, impact 259e
Total office returns
  MSAs 324e
  quarterly (lead office liquidity) 320e
Total portfolio risk 453
Total property returns 123e

transactions volume, relationship 132e
Total returns
  cap rates, correlation weakness 281e
  returns lead liquidity by two quarters 319–322
  similarities 164e
  spread 164e
  volatility, reduction 59e
Tracking error 454
Traded equity REITs, comparison 238e
Trading liquidity 316
Tranches 110–111, 116, 119–120
Transactional sales volume 176
Transactions
  appraisal-based cap rates, correlation 285e
  costs 319
  size 319
Transactions cap rates 158e, 284e
Traps, avoidance 279
Treasury bill (T-bill), appraisal-based cap rate (relationship) 286e
Trend growth 93, 95
Triangular distribution 25
Troubled companies, rescue 460–461
t-statistic 23, 28–29, 41, 43, 107, 116, 127, 142, 145, 188e, 189e, 197, 234, 236, 309, 422
Turnover 315
  liquidity, relationship 107–108
Twilight of Democracy: The Seductive Lure of Authoritarianism (Applebaum) 155
Two-month rolling return volatility 357e

U

Uncertain attributes 13
Uncertain feasible region 258e
Uncertainty
  degrees, variation 42e
  risk, relationship 14
Uncorrected NCREIF return, prediction ability (absence) 237e
Underfunded pension funds, assets/liabilities (contrast) 220e
Underfunded pension plan, expected surplus ratios (spread) 221e
Underfunded public pension funds 449
Underwriting, importance 453
Unfavorable investments 75e

Uniform distribution 24
United States
    inflation/real estate, history 352–353
    office inventory, age/size profile 179–183
    space inventory 181e
Units to households, ratio/average ratio 194e
Unleased space portfolio 55–56
Unleveraged property total returns 133e
Unleveraged total return, NOI growth (relationship) 134e
Unskilled managers, accepting (likelihoods) 32
Unsmoothed property returns, comparison 234–242, 238e
Unsystematic risk 454
Upward-only adjusting leases 81, 92–97
Urbanization 55, 61
Urbanization economies 60
Used car inflation, post-COVID impact 349e
User markets, asset markets (link) 148e
Utility (constancy), relative prices (impact) 352we

V

Vacancy rates
    equilibrium 153e
    increase 21e, 146e, 159e
    simple bivariate time series model 23e
    standard deviation 305e
    volatility 167e, 291e
Value 57–59
    accumulated value, asset class (classification) 358e
    creation 468–469
    long-term store 356–357

Value-add (value add) 410, 433, 440, 449–455
Variables
    box-whisker plots 26e
    omitted variables, problem 43–44
Volatility 142–145
    dampers 455
    decline 70e
    estimated volatilities 238e
    flat rent equivalence 96e
    high volatility, standard deviation/rent probability 97e
    increase 71e, 73e, 87e, 167e, 247e, 325e
    laundering 4, 451
    low volatility, standard deviation/rent probability 97e
Volume measures 319

W

Wechsler, Steve (interview) 276–277
Weighted average cost of capital (WACC) 65, 77e
Winners, the loser's game, selection 429
Winner's curse 440–444
Work from home (WFH) 155, 173–175, 175e
Worthington, Aly (interview) 425–426

Z

Zero-threshold constraint, beating a threshold (probability) 217e
Zisler, Matthew (interview) 401–402